THE COLLECTED SCIENTIFIC WORK OF DAVID CASS
PART B

International Symposia in Economic Theory and Econometrics

Series Editor: ***William A. Barnett***

Volume 14: *Economic Complexity*
Edited by W.A. Barnett, C. Deissenberg & G. Feichtinger

Volume 15: *Modelling Our Future: Population Ageing, Social Security and Taxation*
Edited by Ann Harding & Anil Gupta

Volume 16: *Modelling Our Future: Population Ageing, Health and Aged Care*
Edited by Anil Gupta & Ann Harding

Volume 17: *Topics in Analytical Political Economy*
Edited by Melvin Hinich & William A. Barnett

Volume 18: *Functional Structure Inference*
Edited by William A. Barnett & Apostolos Serletis

Volume 19: *Challenges of the Muslim World: Present, Future and Past*
Edited by William W. Cooper & Piyu Yue

Volume 20: *Nonlinear Modeling of Economic and Financial Time-Series*
Edited by Fredj Jawadi & William A. Barnett

Volume 21A: *The Collected Scientific Works of David Cass – Part A*
Edited by Stephen Spear

International Symposia in Economic Theory and Econometrics
Volume 21B

THE COLLECTED SCIENTIFIC WORK OF DAVID CASS PART B

EDITED BY

STEPHEN SPEAR
Tepper School of Business, Carnegie Mellon University, Pittsburgh, PA, USA

Emerald

United Kingdom – North America – Japan
India – Malaysia – China

Emerald Group Publishing Limited
Howard House, Wagon Lane, Bingley BD16 1WA, UK

First edition 2011

British Library Cataloguing in Publication Data
A catalogue record for this book is available from the British Library

ISBN: 978-0-85724-643-1
ISSN: 1571-0386 (Series)

Contents

List of Contributors

Yves Balasko, (Chs 5, 10, 12)
Lawrence M. Benveniste, (Ch. 8)
David Cass, (Chs 1–15)
Mukul Majumdar, (Ch. 2)
Tapan Mitra, (Ch. 15)
Masahiro Okuno, (Ch. 1)
Herakles M. Polemarchakis, (Ch. 13)
Karl Shell, (Chs 4, 5, 6, 11)
Paolo Siconolfi, (Ch. 12)
Itzhak Zilcha, (Ch. 1)

The Collected Scientific Work of David Cass

David Cass passed away sometime between Friday, April 11 and Tuesday, April 15 of 2008, at the age of 71. He left behind a rich legacy of scientific achievements, not only in the form of publications (which we collect in these volumes), but in his impact on the economics profession through the many graduate students he trained, in his work with Karl Shell to make the *Journal of Economic Theory* a success, and later with Roko Aliprantis in establishing *Economic Theory*. David helped organize and participated in professional meetings that ranged from small workshops on very specific topics to large international conferences covering the full spectrum of economic theory. David started these activities as a young assistant professor at the Cowles foundation at Yale University, continuing through his time at the Graduate School of Industrial Administration at Carnegie Mellon University, and then for his many years in the Economics Department at the University of Pennsylvania.

While a full telling of the professional life of David Cass must await the attention of economic history, our goal here is to provide the full collection of David's 42 published research articles, along with some unpublished material that we felt should be included as well. The introductions to each volume of the series will serve to put David's work in the context of what we feel were his most important contributions to economic theory. Since much of David's thinking about economics evolved in response to his earlier discoveries, it seems logical to organize the work here chronologically. We make no attempt to explicate each of David's many papers, as this would make this introduction the longest entry of the book. Rather, we will briefly discuss the papers that we believe made seminal contributions to economic theory, and comment on the constellation of surrounding work.

Most scientists would be happy to have had one major influential idea over the course of their careers. David Cass had at least three. The first was his seminal work on characterizing optimal growth. The second was his development with Karl Shell of the notion of sunspot equilibria. The third was his work on incomplete markets and what he liked to call General Financial Equilibrium.

In this volume, we catalog David Cass's work from his "middle" years at the University of Pennsylvania, a period that saw his interests in economic dynamics evolve away from the capital model toward the overlapping generations model. This period also saw the development of David's second seminal contribution – the notion of a so-called sunspot equilibrium in dynamic economies that he developed jointly with Karl Shell.

The early impetus for David's interest in this topic stemmed from work he did with Manny Yaari on overlapping generations models, and from his early acquaintance with Bob Lucas at Carnegie Mellon and Lucas's seminal work on rational expectations in dynamic economic models. To quote from the Spear–Wright *Macroeconomic Dynamics* (Spear and Wright, 1998) interview:

> *I wasn't so interested in macro, but what struck me, and this is related to some of my later work, was the assumption that [Lucas] made to solve for equilibrium, that the state variables were obvious. ... Bob and I had some long discussions, and I would say, "Well Bob, why is this the actual state space in this model?" That question came up ... after I came to Penn. At some point Karl [Shell] and I started talking about that and we developed what we called the idea of sunspots.*

The key paper that came out of David's and Karl's discussions was the "Do sunspots matter?" paper published in the *Journal of Political Economy* in 1983. Much of the work leading up to this paper focused on the overlapping generations model:

- "The role of money in supporting the Pareto optimality of competitive equilibrium in consumption-loan type models" (with M. Okuno and I. Zilcha). *Journal of Economic Theory* 20, pp. 41–80 (1979).
- "In defense of a basic approach" (with K. Shell). *Models of Monetary Economies* (J.H. Kareken and N. Wallace, eds.), Federal Reserve Bank of Minneapolis, 1980.
- "Existence of competitive equilibrium in a general overlapping-generations model" (with Y. Balasko and K. Shell). *Journal of Economic Theory* 23, pp. 307–322 (1980).

The first actual model of sunspot equilibrium was produced by Shell in an OLG framework with linear utility functions, which appeared in his "Monnaie et allocation intertemporelle" in 1977, as part of the Malinvaud lecture series in Paris (now published as a vintage paper in *Macroeconomic Dynamics*). David and Karl's *Journal of Political Economy* paper presented a simplified, two-period dynamic model in which one of two sets of agents could trade assets contingent on prices in the second period, while the second set of agents could only trade on the second period spot markets. This captured the friction of restricted participation present in OLG economies, where some agents (the newly entering young) are born into a specific state and cannot insure themselves against outcomes in the birth state.

The paper demonstrated that in static Arrow–Debreu economies with complete markets, extrinsic uncertainty (where no fundamentals of the model are stochastic) cannot matter to equilibrium allocations. They then showed that when some agents were restricted in their trades, so that market completeness was violated, sunspots could matter, that is there could exist rational expectations equilibria in which equilibrium prices depended on the realization of an extrinsic stochastic process. In passing, they made the observation that since the validity of the first welfare theorem implied that there could be no sunspot equilibria, a necessary condition for the existence of such equilibria was a violation of the conditions under which the first welfare theorem holds. This observation took on a life of its own as what Shell called the Philadelphia Pholk theorem: if the first welfare theorem doesn't hold, then you can find an economy where sunspots matter.

In addition to raising troubling questions about what the right state space was for dynamic stochastic economies, the notion of sunspot equilibrium raised a number of deep questions about the overall determinacy of economic equilibria and the role of the welfare theorems in the occurrence or nonoccurrence of sunspot equilibria. These questions spawned a large literature on determinacy in dynamic economies in which the welfare theorems broke down. These include overlapping generations models, growth models with externalities or taxes, and models in which asset markets are incomplete. All were shown to allow the existence of sunspot equilibria. And, in a suitable twist of intellectual fate, macroeconomists have recently begun to explore the question of whether sunspot expectations can provide a more plausible source of fluctuations in dynamic equilibrium models than the conventional aggregate productivity disturbances.

David's third major contribution to economic theory was his work on general equilibrium with incomplete markets, work which grew out of his exploration of the question of existence of sunspot equilibria in models with incomplete asset markets. David's follow-on work on existence and determinacy of general equilibrium in models with incomplete asset markets spawned another large literature that has come to be known simply as GEI. As a historical note, David never really liked this terminology, preferring instead to think of these models as ones of general financial equilibrium (GFE) to emphasize the presence of financial assets and the frictions these introduced.

The earliest work on market incompleteness goes back to Arrow in the 1950s, Diamond in the mid-1960s and a number of related papers in the finance literature between the late 1950s and early 1970s (Geanakoplos (1990) provides an excellent survey of this literature). The canonical GEI model was formulated by Radner in the early 1970s (Radner, 1972) in a paper that also pointed up one of the fundamental puzzles about models with incomplete markets: the possible loss of dimensionality in the span of the asset payoffs as prices vary.

This potential for nonexistence of equilibrium (which was formally developed in Hart's (1975) counterexamples to existence of equilibrium) left the literature in limbo for almost a decade, until David's work on existence in economies with purely financial assets pointed the way out. As Geanakoplos notes:

> *Suddenly in the middle 1980s the pure theory of GEI fell into place. In two provocative and influential papers, Cass (1984), Cass (1985) showed that the existence of equilibrium could be guaranteed if all the assets promise delivery in fiat money, and he gave an example showing that with such financial assets there could be a multiplicity of equilibrium. Almost simultaneously Werner (1985) also gave a proof of existence of equilibrium with financial assets, and Geanakoplos and Polemarchakis (1986) showed the same for economies with real assets that promise delivery in the same consumption good. (Geanakoplos, 1990)*

The first paper that Geanakoplos references above was ultimately published in 1989 as "Sunspots and incomplete financial markets: The leading example" in *The Economics of Imperfect Competition and Employment: Joan Robinson and Beyond* (G. Feiwel, ed.), MacMillan, London. The second paper was left as a 1984 working paper for many years, and was finally published in 2006 ("Musings on the Cass Trick," *Journal of Mathematical Economics* 42, pp. 374–383). As a by-product of the existence results, in these papers David introduced a logical step in the arguments and proofs, which was then used repeatedly by many authors and became known as the "Cass trick," in recognition of David's groundbreaking idea in understanding the structure of these models.

This work was followed very quickly by results showing that the nonexistence problem pointed out by Hart was not generic, and led ultimately to the generic existence results of Duffie and Shafer (1985), and again spawned a new literature looking positively at the welfare implication of market incompleteness, and normatively at issues of asset engineering.

References

Cass, D. (April 1984). Competitive equilibria with incomplete financial markets. CARESS Working Paper, University of Pennsylvania.

Cass, D. (May 1985). On the 'number' of equilibrium allocations with incomplete financial markets. CARESS Working Paper, University of Pennsylvania.

Duffie, D. and Shafer, W. (1985). Equilibrium in incomplete markets, I. *Journal of Mathematical Economics* **14**, 285–300.

Geanakoplos, J. (1990). An introduction to general equilibrium with incomplete asset markets. *Journal of Mathematical Economics* **19**.

Geanakoplos, J. and Polemarchakis, H. (1986). Existence, regularity and constrained suboptimality of competitive equilibrium when markets are incomplete. In Heller, W., Starr, R. and Starrett, D. (Eds), *Essays in Honor of Kenneth Arrow* (Vol. 3). Cambridge, MA: Cambridge University Press.

Hart, O. (1975). On the optimality of equilibrium when the market structure is incomplete. *Journal of Economic Theory* **11** (3), 418–443.
Radner, R. (1972). Existence of equilibrium of plans, prices and price expectations. *Econometrica* **40** (2), 289–303.
Spear, S. and Wright, R. (1998). An interview with David Cass. *Macroeconomic Dynamics* **2**, 533–558.
Werner, J. (1985). Equilibrium in economies with incomplete financial markets. *Journal of Economic Theory* **36**, 110–119.

Stephen E. Spear
Alessandro Citanna
Anna Pavlova

Chapter 1

The Role of Money in Supporting the Pareto Optimality of Competitive Equilibrium in Consumption-Loan Type Models☆, ☆☆

David Cass, Masahiro Okuno[a] and Itzhak Zilcha[b]

[a]*Faculty of Economics, Yokohama National University, Hodogaya-ku, Yokohama, Japan*
[b]*Department of Economics, Tel-Aviv University, Ramat-Aviv, Tel-Aviv, Israel*

1. Introduction and Summary

Perhaps the single most enduring theme in economics is that of the social desirability of the competitive mechanism. In its modern form, this theme occurs as the two basic theorems of welfare economics (see, in particular, Arrow, 1951). Our central concern in this chapter is with the validity of the first of these two theorems – that every competitive equilibrium yields a Pareto optimal allocation – in idealized yet plausible models of intertemporal allocation in a market economy.

What is especially striking about the posture of the "invisible hand" is its apparent widespread reach; all that seems to be required in the well-known standard argument is that there be neither real externalities (in consumption and production) nor local satiation (in consumption). This is very misleading – quite aside from any questions of the existence of competitive equilibrium. One of the most important features of the maintained assumptions in that argument is that they implicitly impose some element of boundedness in order to offset the intrinsic one-directional, open-ended nature of time. In the commonly accepted paradigm, this element is simply imposed by postulating a bounded horizon (see, e.g., Arrow and Hahn, 1971). In another frequently

☆This article was originally published in *Journal of Economic Theory* 20, David Cass, Masahiro Okuno and Itzhak Zilcha, "The Role of Money in Supporting the Pareto Optimality of Competitive Equilibrium in Consumption-Loan Type Models", 41–80, © Elsevier, 1979.
☆☆This chapter was prepared for the Federal Reserve Bank of Minneapolis Conference on Models of Monetary Economies, held December 7–8, 1978.

International Symposia in Economic Theory and Econometrics, Vol. 21B
S. Spear (Editor)

ISSN: 1571-0386/DOI: 10.1108/S1571-0386(2011)000021B004

recurring extension, it is effectively imposed by postulating the alternative – and equally implausible – assumption that there are essentially a finite number of infinitely lived agents (see, e.g., Debreu, 1954). In any case, it is not necessarily true that the "invisible hand" stretches over economies whose evolution extends toward an unbounded horizon – even in the most favorable of circumstances otherwise.

This significant exception was first recognized, at least implicitly, in Malinvaud's classic paper on capital theory (Malinvaud, 1953). However, it only received its first explicit elaboration in Samuelson's equally celebrated seminal contribution (Samuelson, 1958). Samuelson's discussion is the starting point for our own.

Samuelson showed that – in a simple model of a market economy characterized by an unbounded horizon, short-lived, overlapping but essentially identical households and a single, perishable physical commodity – without some extra-market institution, there may be no competitive equilibrium that is Pareto optimal. He also showed that one natural extra-market institution that may set matters aright is fiat money initially owned (i.e., cleverly invented) by the first generation of households, and subsequently purchased with physical commodities (i.e., expressly valued) by each succeeding generation – provided only that money trades for commodities at a sufficiently high (present value) price. A number of others have since refined and extended Samuelson's central argument (see, e.g., Diamond, 1965; Cass and Yaari, 1966; Shell, 1971; Starrett, 1972; Gale, 1973).

Even on his own grounds Samuelson dealt with a special case (boundary endowments) in a special way (stationary allocations). Expanding his analysis – much in the manner of Gale, but in different spirit – it is easy to show that in Samuelson's basic model (with two-period lifetimes) there is the following dichotomy: Without money, the competitive equilibrium is the initial endowment allocation itself, which may be Pareto optimal or not. Furthermore, upon the introduction of money, in the former case nothing is altered. The price of money must be zero and the allocation is again the initial endowments (in this instance, Pareto optimal). In the latter case, however, there now exists a continuum of potential competitive equilibria. Considering just the least complicated possibility, these range from the original autarkic equilibrium – where the price of money turns out to be zero and the allocation is once again the initial endowments (in this instance, not Pareto optimal) – to the "fully" monetized equilibrium – where the price of money is at a maximum and the allocation turns out to be both stationary and Pareto optimal. In the intermediate range – that of the "partly" monetized equilibria – the price of money is positive, but the allocations are neither stationary nor Pareto optimal. In fact, in a "partly" monetized equilibrium, the allocation must be asymptotically the same as in the original autarkic equilibrium.

Thus, a complete analysis of Samuelson's basic model (now including consideration of more complicated possibilities for nonstationary equilibria) leads to several very strong conclusions. These can be summarized, in somewhat general fashion, by the following propositions: Consider the range of potential competitive equilibria with money, and call an equilibrium *barter* if the price of money is zero, *monetary* if it's positive. Then we have

Existence Proposition. *There is a monetary equilibrium if and only if there is no barter equilibrium which is Pareto optimal.*

Optimality Proposition. *If there is a monetary equilibrium, then there is also a monetary equilibrium which is Pareto optimal.*

Note, in particular, that both propositions together imply that there is always some competitive equilibrium (barter or monetary) that is Pareto optimal.

The central issue we address in this chapter is how robust these propositions (and their related implications) are to various generalizations of Samuelson's basic model, and especially to relaxing the assumption that all households are essentially identical (i.e., have the same tastes for and endowments of physical commodities but for date of birth).

It would hardly be surprising if such relaxation required some qualification or modification of the propositions. It is quite surprising, however, that with the introduction of what amounts to fairly routine variety in tastes and endowments – judged by that typically encountered in general equilibrium theory – neither proposition survives in any recognizable form. Specifically, we show that the consumption-loan model with heterogeneous households (and, upon occasion, other extensions) yields the following sorts of counterexamples:

Coexistence Example. There are both barter and monetary equilibria which are Pareto optimal.

Nonoptimality Example. There are both barter and monetary equilibria, but none which is Pareto optimal.

While there is some degree of speciality to our examples, especially those exhibiting "nonoptimality," this seems dictated more by our maintained simplifying assumptions – that there is effectively just a single common good (though perhaps more than one physical commodity) in each period, and that each household survives at most two periods – than by any inherent feature of the issues involved.

The significance of the coexistence examples may not be immediately apparent. But, in fact they do carry an important message. On the one hand, these examples clearly demonstrate that there is no observable criterion for determining whether the existence of fiat money as a store of value is necessary to support the Pareto optimality of competitive equilibrium. On the other hand, much more critically, they graphically illustrate one basic difficulty encountered in assigning a normative role to fiat money – the wide extent of nonuniqueness of monetary equilibrium: Even when the presence of money (trading for commodities at some suitable positive price) can surely guarantee the Pareto optimality of competitive equilibrium, the competitive mechanism by itself offers no assurance whatsoever that it will. *Indeed, our coexistence examples strongly suggest that – in general – something like continuous monitoring of the price level may be an indispensable component of an otherwise neutral monetary (or more accurately, fiscal) policy.*

It is the nonoptimality examples, however, which convey the central message we have to communicate. These examples dramatically highlight a second, even more fundamental difficulty with relying on the mere creation of fiat money to conjure up an effective appeal to the second basic theorem of welfare economics – the limited scope of once-and-for-all augmentation of initial wealth: Just the presence of money (trading for commodities at any conceivable positive price) may possibly not guarantee the Pareto optimality of competitive equilibrium. *Indeed, our nonoptimality examples strongly suggest that – in general – something like continuous redistribution by means of creation (or destruction) of fiat money may be an indispensable lubricant for the efficient operation of an evolving market economy.*

The plan of this chapter is as follows: A partially generalized consumption-loan model is described in Section 2. Section 3 contains a review of the leading special case, Samuelson's basic model. The core examples, exhibiting the coexistence of both barter and monetary equilibria that are Pareto optimal, and the nonexistence of any competitive equilibrium that is Pareto optimal, are presented in Sections 4 and 5, respectively. Finally, the appendix contains some technical results we require involving the construction of offer curves (or equivalently, indifference maps) exhibiting various special properties.

2. The Basic Model

The economy begins operation in period 1, and continues over periods extending indefinitely into the future $t = 1, 2, \ldots$ In each period there are two commodities: one a perishable physical *good* (whose various quantities are subscripted by the period in which it is available) and the other an imperishable fiat *money*. Households or *consumers* (whose various attributes are superscripted by the order in which they are born, say, $h = 0, 1, \ldots$) are either present at the inception of the economy – in which case they live out the balance of their lives during period 1 – or born at the beginning of each period $t \geqq 1$ – in which case they live out the whole of their lives during that and the succeeding period. Thus, in each period there are always just two age groups of consumers: an older *generation* born in the preceding period, say, G_{t-1}, and a younger generation born in the current period G_t. For the most part, we will only be concerned with one or the other of the two simplest conceivable demographic patterns, namely, that either $G_t = \{t\}$ for $t \geqq 0$ – each generation consists of a single consumer – or $G_0 = \{0\}$ and $G_t = \{2t–1, 2t\}$ for $t \geqq 1$ – the oldest generation consists of a single consumer, and each succeeding generation of two consumers.[1]

Each consumer in each generation $h \in G_t$, $t \geqq 0$ (potentially) derives satisfaction or *utility* U^h from consuming goods during his lifetime $c^h = c_1^h$ for $h \in G_0$, and $c^h = (c_t^h, c_{t+1}^h)$ for $h \in G_t$, $t \geqq 1$. This fundamental economic hypothesis is represented by a utility function $U^h = U^h(c^h)$ for $c^h \geqq 0$, herein typically assumed to be at least continuous, quasi-concave (i.e., to exhibit a diminishing marginal rate of substitution) and to have no local maxima (i.e., to exhibit local nonsatiation).[2] Each consumer also has given endowments of the goods available during his lifetime $y^h = y_1^h > 0$ for $h \in G_0$ and $y^h = (y_t^h, y_{t+1}^h) \geqq 0$ for $h \in G_t$, $t \geqq 1$, while each consumer in the oldest generation has a given endowment of money $m^h > 0$ for $h \in G_0$. We assume that the total amount of money in the economy consists of one unit $\sum_{h \in G_0} m^h = 1$ (so that if $G_0 = \{0\}$, then $m^0 = 1$), which amounts to defining the monetary unit. Finally, each consumer can buy and sell (within physical and temporal capabilities) either goods or money on both a spot and a one-period futures

---

[1] Some asymmetry in treating the start of the economy is unavoidable since, for example, consumers in the oldest generation have only themselves to deal with during their first period of life. For this reason, we will typically streamline the various incarnations of our basic model by simply assuming that the oldest generation consists of just a single consumer. It can be easily verified that nothing we have to say depends critically on this particular simplification.

We should also emphasize at the outset that, unlike most of the literature, our specializations of the consumption-loan model will always involve a stationary population (at least after period 1). Once again, nothing depends critically on this particular simplification – and it has the great virtue of completely avoiding the notational clutter inevitably associated with modeling a growing population.

[2] Except in one case (in the second subsection of 5), we always maintain that these properties obtain for the tastes of consumers in the oldest generation. Since the relevant aspect of their lifetime consumption profiles is a single quantity, this simply means that they have utility functions that are continuous and strictly increasing.

Likewise, we will almost invariably assume that, for every good, there is some consumer who has a utility function that is everywhere strictly increasing in that good. The practical import of this hypothesis is that in a competitive equilibrium, every goods price will be positive (see the definition in the next following paragraph, and the subsequent discussion of the characterization of potential competitive equilibria).

market at perfectly foreseen (present value) *prices*, denoted p_t and p_m, respectively.[3]

Given these opportunities, he chooses his lifetime consumption profile rationally, that is, as some optimal solution to the budget-constrained utility maximization problem

$$\begin{array}{ll} \text{maximize} & U^h(c_1^h) \quad \text{for } h \in G_0 \\ \text{subject to} & c_1^h \leqq y_1^h + p_m m^h \\ \text{and} & c_1^h \geqq 0 \end{array} \tag{1}$$

and

$$\begin{array}{ll} \text{maximize} & U^h(c^h) \quad \text{for } h \in G_t, t \geqq 1 \\ \text{subject to} & p_t c_t^h + p_{t+1} c_{t+1}^h \leqq p_t y_t^h + p_{t+1} y_{t+1}^h \\ \text{and} & c^h \geqq 0. \end{array} \tag{2}$$

Aggregate consistency in these choices completes the model: A *competitive equilibrium* is a set of positive goods prices, together with a nonnegative price of money, and optimal lifetime consumption profiles satisfying market clearing

$$\sum_{h \in G_{t-1} \cup G_t} c_t^h = \sum_{h \in G_{t-1} \cup G_t} y_t^h \text{ or } \sum_{h \in G_{t-1}} (c_t^h - y_t^h) = \sum_{h \in G_t} -(c_t^h - y_t^h) \quad \text{for } t \geqq 1. \tag{3}$$

As suggested in the introduction, an important distinction will be that between a *barter equilibrium* – a competitive equilibrium in which $p_m = 0$ – and a *monetary equilibrium* – a competitive equilibrium in which $p_m > 0$. Also, we will occasionally refer to the set of lifetime consumption profiles corresponding to some competitive equilibrium as a *competitive allocation*. In contrast, a *feasible allocation* (explicitly taking the notion of perishable

[3] Generally, we should write the price of money p_{mt}. However, if we expand the budget constraint in Equation (2) below to reflect such opportunities,

$$\begin{cases} p_t c_t^h + p_{t+1} c_{t+1}^h + p_{mt} \Delta m_t^h + p_{mt+1} \Delta m_{t+1}^h \leqq p_t y_t^h + p_{t+1} y_{t+1}^h, \\ \Delta m_t^h \geqq 0 \\ \Delta m_{t+1}^h \geqq -\Delta m_t^h \end{cases}$$

where Δm_s^h represents the purchases (or sales, when negative) of money during period $s = t, t+1$ by consumer h, then an obvious arbitrage argument entails that, in a competitive equilibrium, $p_{mt} = p_m$ for $t \geqq 1$. For this reason, we have chosen simply to adopt this requirement as a postulate – and correspondingly (and legitimately) to ignore transactions on the money markets except insofar as they affect the oldest generation's demand for goods.

physical goods to entail free disposal) is simply a set of nonnegative lifetime consumption profiles satisfying materials balance:

$$\sum_{h\in G_{t-1}\cup G_t} c_t^h \leqq \sum_{h\in G_{t-1}\cup G_t} y_t^h \quad \text{for} \quad t \geqq 1. \tag{4}$$

To complete the list of standard definitions in this context, we define a particular feasible allocation (e.g., some competitive allocation), say, $\{c^{h'}\}$, to be *Pareto optimal* if there is no other feasible allocation $\{c^{h''}\}$ such that

$$U^h(c^{h''}) \geqq U^h(c^{h'}) \quad \text{for all } h \geqq 0$$

and

$$U^h(c^{h''}) > U^h(c^{h'}) \quad \text{for some } h \geqq 0. \tag{5}$$

The foregoing description of an economy generally differs from the canonical consumption-loan model in only one significant respect, namely, in admitting the possibility of heterogeneity in tastes for and endowments of goods both within and across generations. While it is this degree of freedom which plays a dominant role in our analysis, there are several additional, minor variations that we will also call upon for support: (i) *Availability of a second perishable physical commodity*: Formally, such a commodity can be accounted for merely by reinterpreting $\boldsymbol{c}$, $\boldsymbol{y}$, and $\boldsymbol{p}$ as 2-vectors. However, for our particular purposes, it will be less confusing to introduce a more clearly distinct notation for the quantity, endowment, and (present value, i.e., with the first commodity in period 1 as numeraire) price of this second commodity, x, w, and q, respectively. (ii) *Shorter (or longer) lifetimes*: For this extension, we will simply adopt the formality of reinterpreting c^h and y^h – or (c^h, x^h) and (y^h, w^h) – and their aggregate counterparts as needs be. (iii) *Money endowments to consumers in other than the oldest generation*: This extension is easily accomplished by specifying that such endowments occur in the second period of life $m^h = m_{t+1}^h$ for $h \in G_t$, $t \geqq 1$, and including their present value on the right-hand side of the budget constraint in Equation (2). (In particular instances, some of these endowments may be negative, or may correspond to "taxes" rather than "subsidies.")

The virtue – and, as with moral rectitude, limitation – of our basic model is that, because there is only a single good available, and a single-period overlap, the set of potential competitive equilibria can be succinctly characterized. In particular, define (presupposing Equations (1)–(3))

$$z_t = \text{excess demand by generation } t-1 \text{ for the good in their second period of life}$$
$$= \sum_{h \in G_{t-1}} (c_t^h - y_t^h)$$
$$= \sum_{h \in G_t} (c_t^h - y_t^h)$$
$$= \text{excess supply by generation } t \text{ of the good in their first period of life}$$

and

$$g_t = \{(z_t, z_{t+1}) : (z_t, z_{t+1}) = \sum_{h \in G_t} (-(c_t^h - y_t^h), (c_{t+1}^h - y_{t+1}^h)) \text{ such that}$$
$$(c_t^h, c_{t+1}^h) \text{ is an optimal solution to (2) for some } (p_t, p_{t+1}) > 0 \quad \text{for } h \in G_t\}$$
$$= \textit{reflected generational offer curve} \text{ of generation } t$$

for $t \geqq 1$. Now note that (i) $z_1 = \sum_{h \in G_0}(c_1^h - y_1^h) = \sum_{h \in G_0} p_m m^h = p_m$, while (ii) by suitable choice of the units for measuring the good in each period, $\sum_{h \in G_t} y_t^h = y > 0$ for $t \geqq 1$.[4] Then, it is easily seen that the set of potential competitive equilibria is essentially equivalent to the set of solutions to the fundamental dynamical system

$$z_1 \geqq 0$$

and[5]

$$(z_t, z_{t+1}) \in g_t \text{ and } z_t \leqq y \quad \text{for } t \geqq 1. \tag{6}$$

In other words, given the basic data describing population structure G_t for $t \geqq 0$, and individual tastes and endowments U^h and y^h for $h \in G_t$, $t \geqq 0$, the potential evolution of the economy is completely captured, in terms of the "reduced" data describing reflected generational offer curves g_t for $t \geqq 1$

[4] This maneuver presumes that $y_t^h > 0$ for some $h \in G_t$, for all $t \geqq 1$. Otherwise, the upper bound in Equation (6) must be written $\bar{z}_t$, a "0 – y" variable. We will refer to such a polar situation only once in the sequel (see the second example of nonstationarity, that involving only endowments, presented in Section 5 below). In one other case (the third example in the same subsection), we will deliberately choose to streamline the description of a specific model by explicitly employing "natural" units for measuring the good in each period, so that the upper bound in Equation (6) must also be written generally as $\bar{z}_t = \sum_{h \in G_t} y_t^h$.

[5] It should be immediately apparent from the definitions of z_t and g_t that a competitive equilibrium yields a solution to Equation (6). On the other hand, the reverse argument only requires observing that, in the definition of g_t, goods prices can be normalized so that they constitute a consistent sequence – since they are assumed positive, while consumers are assumed rational (so that, among other things, those in each generation $t \geqq 2$ correctly perceive that they are unaffected by equiproportional shifts in the goods prices directly relevant to them (p_t, p_{t+1})).

and aggregate first-period endowment y, by means of the system (6). For future reference, it will be useful to bear in mind that, except possibly for boundary endowments, $0 \in g_t$ for $t \geqq 1$ (so that typically $z_t = 0$ for $t \geqq 0$ is a solution to Equation (6) – which means, of course, that there is some barter equilibrium), while if $(z_t, z_{t+1}) \in g_t$, then

$$z_{t+1} \left\{ \begin{matrix} > \\ = \end{matrix} \right\} 0 \text{ according as } z_t \left\{ \begin{matrix} > \\ = \end{matrix} \right\} 0$$

(so that every solution to Equation (6) is nonnegative – which is, of course, our prime motivation for employing the reflected offer curve rather than the standard offer curve itself). Moreover, perhaps most importantly, points on the reflected generational offer curve that also represent competitive allocations must satisfy the equation[6]

$$\frac{z_{t+1}}{z_t} = \frac{p_t}{p_{t+1}} = 1 + r_t$$
$$= \text{one plus the } \textit{real rate of return} \text{ from period } t \text{ to period } t+1.$$

The core of our analysis involves focusing on a series of special cases, that is, detailed specifications of G_t, U^h, and y^h and hence g_t and y, and answering the following sorts of fundamental questions:

1. What are the solutions to Equation (6), and thus Equations (1)–(3)? In particular (knowing that there is a barter equilibrium), is there a monetary equilibrium? In fact (assuming replication in the basic data), a stationary monetary equilibrium?
2. What properties do these solutions exhibit? In particular, is some barter equilibrium Pareto optimal? If not, is some monetary equilibrium?

Partly as an exercise to gain familiarity with technique, but mostly as a review to provide foundation for comparison, we turn first to utilizing Equation (6) to analyze the competitive equilibria in Samuelson's basic model.

3. Samuelson's Basic Model

Samuelson's central story (and more) can be fully elaborated in terms of the leading special case of our model, where (i) each generation consists of just a single consumer, so that $G_t = \{t\}$ for $t \geqq 0$, and (ii) each consumer but the oldest has the same utility function, so that $U^t(c^t) = U(c^t)$ for $t \geqq 1$ – where $U = U(c_1, c_2)$ for $(c_1, c_2) \geqq 0$ is assumed to be differentiable (but, for

[6] When $z_t = 0$ for $t \geqq 1$, this equation amounts to a definition of 0/0 (and it is obviously necessary to go back to the basic data to uncover the potential paths of the real rate of return r_t for $t \geqq 1$).

simplicity, with $\partial U(0, y)/\partial c_1 = \partial U(x, 0)/\partial c_2 = \infty$ for $(x, y) > 0$), strictly quasi-concave and strictly increasing – as well as the same positive endowments, so that $y^t = (y_1, y_2) > 0$ for $t \geqq 1$.[7] The critical feature of this case is that, besides being stationary, the reflected generational offer curve derives from the rational behavior of the representative consumer, so that

$$g_t = g = \Big\{(z_1, z_2) : (-z_1, z_2) \geqq -(y_1, y_2), \\ \frac{\partial U(-z_1 + y_1, z_2 + y_2)}{\partial c_1} \Big/ \frac{\partial U(-z_1 + y_1, z_2 + y_2)}{\partial c_2} = p_1/p_2, \\ \text{and} - p_1 z_1 + p_2 z_2 = 0 \quad \text{for some } (p_1, p_2) > 0\Big\}$$

for $t \geqq 1$, as illustrated in Figures 1 and 2.

From careful study of these figures, it becomes apparent that this particular feature has two important consequences for the structure of g, the solutions to Equation (6), and thus the nature of competitive equilibrium: First, g intersects the origin just once. In other words, there is a unique (stationary) barter equilibrium, supported by prices $p_1 = 1$, $p_t/p_{t+1} = 1 + r_t = 1 + r$ for $t \geqq 1$ and $p_m = 0$, and yielding the autarkic allocation $c_1^0 = y_1^0$ and $(c_t^t, c_{t+1}^t) = (y_1, y_2)$ for $t \geqq 1$. (Here, as in what follows, we utilize notation that is either formally defined in the text or informally defined in the various accompanying figures.) Second, in addition, g intersects the 45° line in the positive quadrant, just once, if and only if it has slope less than one at the origin. In other words, there will also be a unique stationary monetary equilibrium, supported by prices $p_1 = 1$, $p_t/p_{t+1} = 1 + r_t = 1$ for $t \geqq 1$ and $p_m = p_m^*$, and yielding the trading allocation $c_1^0 = y_1^0 + (y_1 - c_1^*)$and $(c_t^t, c_{t+1}^t) = (c_1^*, c_2^*)$ for $t \geqq 1$ – where $p_m^* = y_1 - c_1^* > 0$ or $c_1^* < y_1$ and $c_2^* > y_2$ – if and only if $1 + r < 1$. In short, the dichotomy emphasized earlier in Section 1 ultimately depends simply on the magnitude of the representative consumer's marginal rate of substitution at his endowments

$$\frac{\partial U(y_1, y_2)}{\partial c_1} \Big/ \frac{\partial U(y_1, y_2)}{\partial c_2} = 1 + r.$$

[7] In this case, as in some others later on, there is no need to distinguish h from t, except insofar as the former appears as a superscript, the latter as a subscript.

It is also worth remarking that consumer 0's tastes and endowments (of goods) can also be assumed the same as any consumer t's, merely by reinterpreting $U^0(c_1^0) = U(y_1, c_1^0)$ and $y_1^0 = y_2$. More generally, in each of the special cases we treat later on in which both tastes and endowments are essentially stationary, we can reinterpret the model so that generation 0 is identical to generation $t \geqq 1$ but for date of birth and absence of ancestors (or, more accurately, ancestors who participate in the market economy). The possibility of such reinterpretation provides the main justification for the assertion made at the end of the first paragraph in Footnote 1.

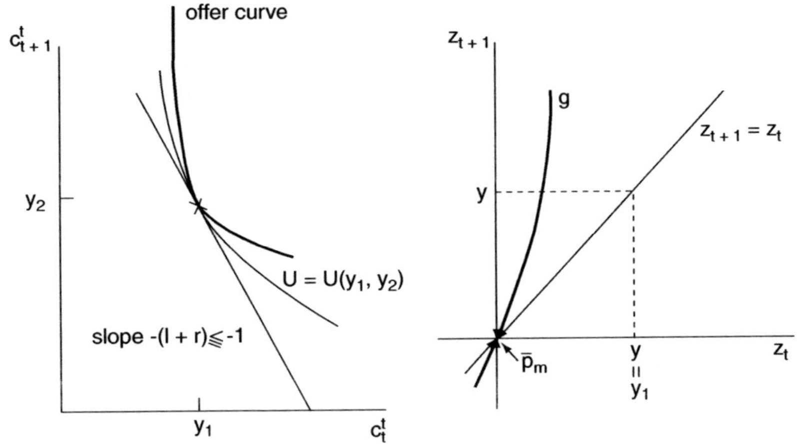

(a) Consumer Behavior (b) Dynamical System

Figure 1: Potential Competitive Equilibria in Samuelson's Basic Model: Just a Single Barter Equilibrium

$$\left(\frac{\partial U(y_1, y_2)}{\partial c_1} \Big/ \frac{\partial U(y_1, y_2)}{\partial c_2} = 1 + r < 1\right).$$

Continuing with an explicit description of that dichotomy – and with heavy reliance on graphical intuition and argument – we notice next that, in fact, there will be a whole range of monetary equilibria, corresponding to prices of money satisfying $0 < p_m \leqq \bar{p}_m$, if and only if there is a stationary monetary equilibrium, that is, once again, $1 + r < 1$.[8] This situation is suggestively exemplified in Figure 3, which contrasts the two possible cases: On the one hand, in the "normal" case (pictured in Figure 3a), we have $\bar{p}_m = p_m^*$, so that (i) if $p_m = \bar{p}_m$, then competitive equilibrium is necessarily the stationary monetary one, while (ii) if $p_m < \bar{p}_m$, then competitive allocation necessarily converges monotonically to the representative consumer's endowments. On the other hand, in the "abnormal" case (shown in Figure 3b), we have $\bar{p}_m > p_m^*$, so that evidently matters are not nearly so transparent. Indeed, in this case, there generally need not be just a single competitive equilibrium corresponding to each (sufficiently large)

[8] A note of warning: Here, as in the sequel, we take for granted that every solution to Equation (6) must satisfy $z_1 \leqq \bar{p}m \leqq y$ – where $\bar{p}_m$ depends on both g_t and y in a way that should be obvious from the diagram representing the relevant dynamical system. That is, otherwise, when $z_1 > \bar{p}_m$, there will be some $\bar{t} < \infty$ such that either $z_{\bar{t}} > y$ or $z_{\bar{t}} \leqq y$ but there is no z such that $(z_{\bar{t}}, z) \in g_{\bar{t}}$, both of which are inconsistent with Equation (6).

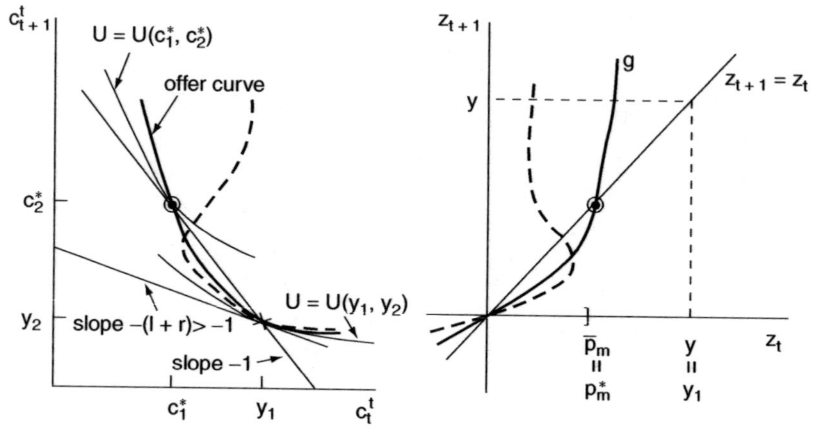

(a) Consumer Behavior (b) Dynamical System

Figure 2: Potential Competitive Equilibria in Samuelson's Basic Model: Also a Continuum of Monetary Equilibria

$$\left(\frac{\partial U(y_1, y_2)}{\partial c_1} \bigg/ \frac{\partial U(y_1, y_2)}{\partial c_2} = 1 + r < 1\right).$$

price of money nor even any recognizable pattern to the asymptotic behavior of competitive allocation – even though we have chosen to depict a competitive equilibrium that replicates cyclically every two periods.[9]

These various cases (i.e., $1+r \geqq 1$ or $1+r<1$ and "normality" or "abnormality") have their counterparts in terms of welfare implications. In particular, using the fact that U is assumed strictly quasi-concave – so that transfers from consumer $t+1$ to consumer t–1 via consumer t, transfers that also (at least) maintain the intermediary consumer's welfare, necessarily involve increasingly unfavorable real terms of trade between good t and good $t+1$ – it can be easily demonstrated that if $1+r \geqq 1$, then the barter

[9] The artistically inclined reader can surely sketch examples with much longer periodicity – once he is reminded that the only significant restrictions on g's behavior in the positive quadrant are that (i) it be continuous, when interpreted as a function of the variable $p_1/p_2 \geqq 1+r$, and (ii) it intersect each sufficiently positively sloped ray through the origin $z_{t+1} = (p_1/p_2)\, z_t$, but just once. (See too the introductory comments in the appendix.) We should also note that our labeling of this second case is not to be taken seriously (paranoically?). The "abnormal" case, which was apparently first mentioned in the literature by Gale, seems just as likely as the "normal" case – even if it is much more bothersome because it so clearly displays the ambiguity inherent in the actual evolution of monetary equilibrium. We shall have more to say about the implications of this characteristic sort of nonuniqueness in the following section.

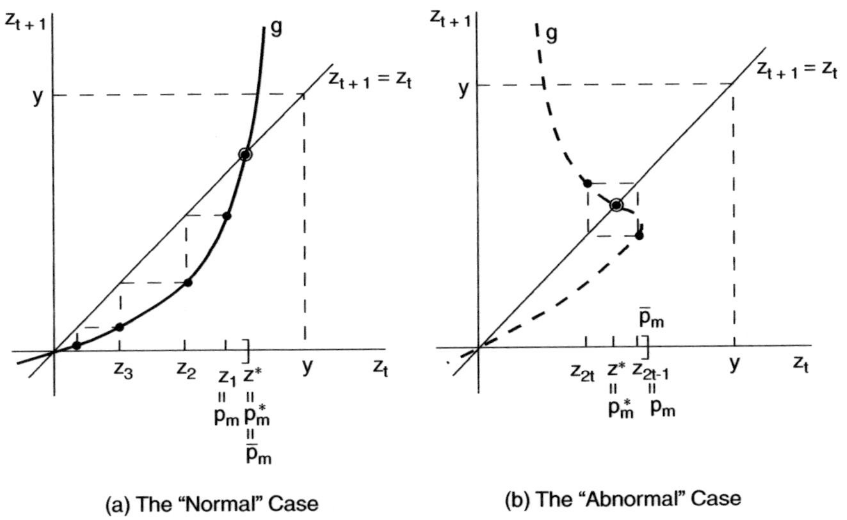

Figure 3: Examples of Both Stationary (◉) and Nonstationary ($\cdots$) Monetary Equilibria in Samuelson's Basic Model.

equilibrium is Pareto optimal, while if $1+r<1$, then the stationary monetary equilibrium is Pareto optimal.[10] In contrast, but again explicitly using the fact that U is assumed strictly quasi-concave – so that $U(c_1, c_2) < U(c_1^*, c_2^*)$ for every $c_1 + c_2 \leqq y_1 + y_2$ such that $(c_1, c_2) \neq (c_1^*, c_2^*)$ – if $1+r<1$, then in the "normal" case, the allocation corresponding to each competitive equilibrium (barter or monetary) except the stationary monetary one is strictly dominated by that corresponding to the latter. In other words, in this case, neither the barter equilibrium nor any nonstationary monetary equilibrium is Pareto optimal.

For the same basic reason, in the "abnormal" case, neither the barter equilibrium nor any nonstationary monetary equilibrium yielding the same (endowments) allocation asymptotically – that is, such that $\lim_{t\to\infty} z_t = 0$ – is Pareto optimal. But in this case, the general welfare status of the nonstationary monetary equilibria is mixed since it can be proven that every competitive equilibrium such that $\limsup_{t\to\infty} z_t > 0$ is in fact Pareto optimal – including, for instance, the specific periodic equilibrium depicted in Figure 3b. (For the sake of brevity we forego justifying this assertion, which is also

[10] These results (and their parallels in the subsequent sections) are so well known that they hardly require documentation; for completeness' sake, however, we refer the skeptically minded reader to Starrett's neat general argument. Note also that such results may be falsified (in case $1+r \leqq 1$) when U is not assumed to be strictly quasi-concave, as in Shell's nice expository piece.

referenced in the following section; the argument is quite straightforward but rather tedious.)

Given our present purposes, the foregoing descriptive analysis of Samuelson's basic model has already been aptly summarized by the two propositions stated in Section 1. We now proceed to the heart of the chapter, to the demonstration that these properties are actually very model bound. Before doing so, however, we might well underline that in each of the following arguments we will utilize essentially the same graphical heuristic utilized here (though bolstered now and then by analytical means). We take this rehearsal as providing license to be somewhat terse in presentation, if not also in interpretation.

4. Coexistence of both Barter and Monetary Equilibria which are Pareto Optimal

The model underlying the two examples presented in this section differs in only one essential respect from Samuelson's basic model, to wit, in that there are two distinct types of consumers in every generation but the oldest. More specifically, suppose now that $G_0 = \{0\}$ and $G_t = \{2t-1, 2t\}$ for $t \geqq 1$, and that the odd-numbered consumers are of α-type, so that $U^h(c^h) = U^\alpha(c^h)$ and $y^h = y^\alpha > 0$ for $h = 2t-1$, $t \geqq 1$, the even numbered of β-type, so that $U^h(c^h) = U^B(c^h)$ and $y^h = y^\beta > 0$ for $h = 2t$, $t \geqq 1$ – where generally $U^\alpha \neq U^\beta$ and $y^\alpha \neq y^\beta$. Even this seemingly minor modification, by permitting greater freedom in specifying the reflected generational offer curves (which are, as before, stationary over time $g_t = g$ for $t \geqq 1$), entails fundamentally contrary consequences for the conclusions outlined in the preceding section. The most important of these, and the one we detail here, is illustrated by the two examples shown in Figures 4 and 5.

The key feature of these counterexamples is that in the first (respectively, second) (i) when the real rate of return is zero, $p_1/p_2 = 1$, the β-type consumer wants to save more (respectively, less) than the α-type consumer wants to dissave during their mutual first period of life, that is, in Figure 4, a<b (respectively, in Figure 5, a>b), while (ii) when the real rate of return is – within an appropriate bound – higher, $1 \leqq p_1/p_2 \leqq \bar{R}$ (respectively, lower, $\underline{R} \leqq p_1/p_2 \leqq 1$), the α-type consumer has a vertical segment on his offer curve, and the β-type a horizontal, that is, c_t^h is constant for $h = 2t-1$, and c_{t+1}^h for $h = 2t$.[11] Thus, in order to simplify their presentation,

[11] The upper bound $\bar{R}$ (respectively, lower bound $\underline{R}$) is chosen so that the length of the vertical and horizontal segments of the respective consumers' offer curves is greater than *b–a* (respectively, *a–b*). This choice guarantees (see directly below) that there are at least two stationary barter equilibria with positive (respectively, negative) real rate of return.

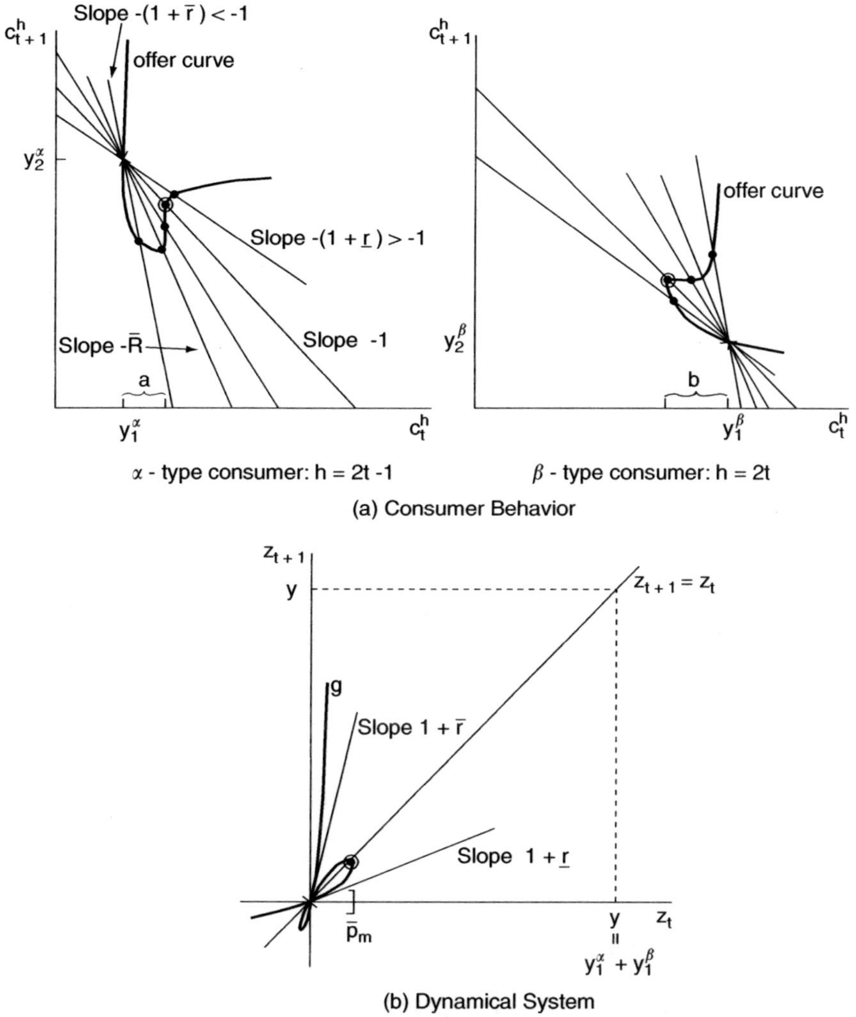

Figure 4: Coexistence with Stationary Monetary Equilibrium ($a<b$).

these specific examples embody somewhat extreme behavior since (partly) vertical or horizontal offer curves implicitly require a region of inferiority for the good whose consumption is unchanged. Verification that this specialization is only a convenient simplification we leave as an exercise; verification that it is also a legitimate simplification we leave to the appendix.

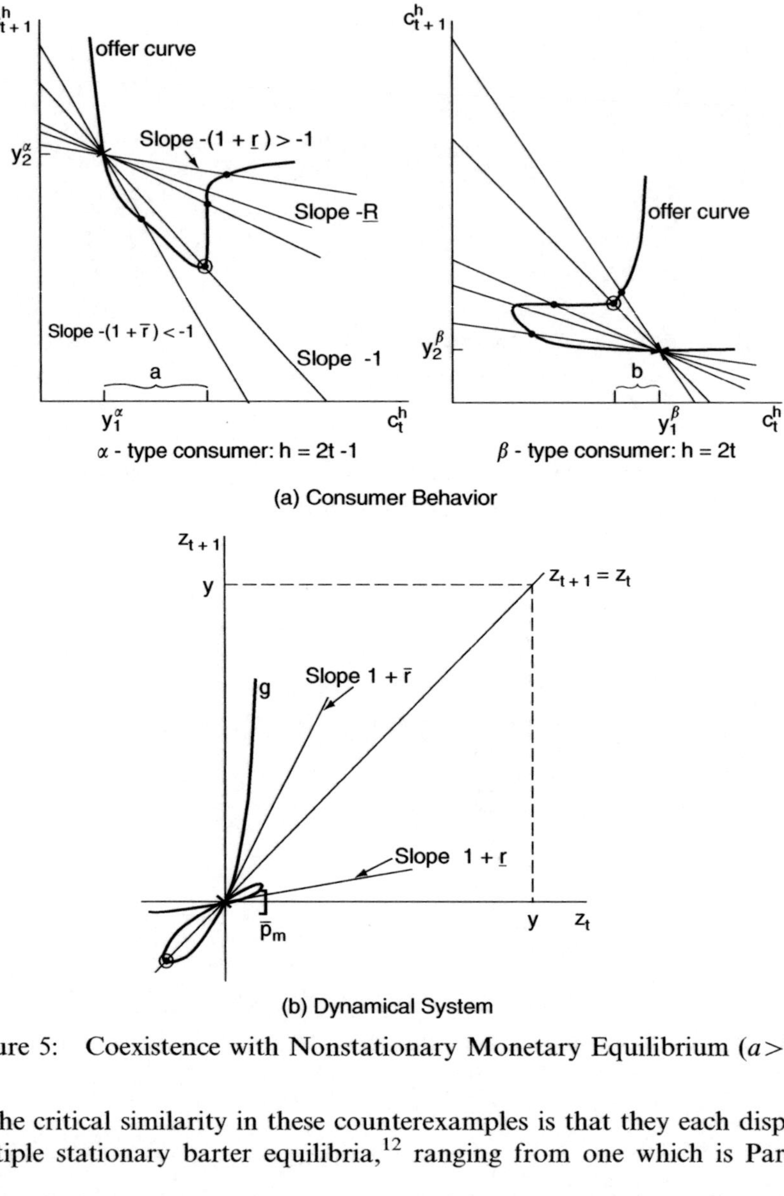

Figure 5: Coexistence with Nonstationary Monetary Equilibrium ($a>b$).

The critical similarity in these counterexamples is that they each display multiple stationary barter equilibria,[12] ranging from one which is Pareto

[12] Since – in consumption-loan type models with only a single-period overlap between generations – barter involves just trade between contemporaries, this also means that barter equilibrium needn't be stationary, nor even periodic (see, however, the closing remark to this section). For instance, there is an "irregular" barter equilibrium corresponding to goods prices that satisfy

$$\frac{p_t}{p_{t+1}} = \begin{cases} 1+\bar{r} & \text{for } t = 2^s, s \geqq 0 \\ 1+\underline{r} & \text{otherwise.} \end{cases}$$

optimal (corresponding to goods prices $p_t = (1+\bar{r})^{-(t-1)}$ for $t \geqq 1$) to one which isn't (corresponding to goods prices $p_t = (1+\underline{r})^{-(t-1)}$ for $t \geqq 1$). Their critical dissimilarity is that the first (in this sense analogous to that shown in Figure 2) also has a single stationary monetary equilibrium – which is, of course (by virtue of its corresponding zero real rate of return), Pareto optimal – while the second (in this sense analogous to that pictured in Figure 1) hasn't. Reflecting on these two considerations, mainly by literally drawing their implications for the solutions to Equation (6) (in diagrams like Figures 4b and 5b), leads to the following important conclusions: On the one hand, in general, there is no direct connection between the level of the price of money and any descriptive or prescriptive properties of competitive equilibrium. On the other hand, in particular, there is no necessary relationship between the potentiality for monetary equilibrium and the optimality of barter equilibrium.

Moreover, the second example suggests an even more striking conclusion. Suppose we ignore the possibility of barter equilibrium (especially the possibility of any that is Pareto optimal) – either on practical grounds (observing that monetary institutions are intrinsic to all but the most primitive societies) or, perhaps better, on theoretical grounds (appealing to the extensions of Samuelson's basic model employed to construct the examples elaborated in the last two parts of the following section). Then, this economy has the property that, though there are competitive equilibria that are Pareto optimal (again, as in the "abnormal" case of Samuelson's basic model, essentially characterized by the condition $\lim\sup_{t\to\infty} z_t > 0$), these may be neither easily discernable nor – on any reasonable grounds – expectedly laissez-faire. In particular, it is straightforward to establish that for large enough values of $\bar{r} > 0$ (or $\underline{r} < 0$), the smallest periodicity of any competitive equilibrium that replicates cyclically and that is also Pareto optimal may be arbitrarily large.[13]

In thus emphasizing the importance of periodicity (of which stationarity is the simplest realization), we are tacitly embracing the widely held professional belief that, in order for perfect foresight (or, more fashionably, rational expectations) to be a reasonable description of individual accommodation to uncertainty, there must be sufficient regularity of aggregate outcomes – so that, for example, correct information about the past provides a sound basis for accurate prediction of the future.

[13] Formally, periodic monetary equilibrium requires that for some finite span of periods, or periodicity $1 \leqq \tau < \infty$, goods prices must exhibit the property that $p_{t+\tau} = p_t$ or $\prod_{\delta=0}^{\tau-1}(p_{t+\delta}/p_{t+\delta+1}) = \prod_{\delta=0}^{\tau-1}(1+r_{t+\delta}) = 1$ for $t \geqq 1$. But in this case, any such periodicity must therefore also satisfy the inequality

$$\min_{1 \leqq \tau' \leqq \tau} (1+\bar{r})^{\tau'}(1+\underline{r})^{\tau-\tau'} = (1+\bar{r})(1+\underline{r})^{\tau-1} < 1,$$

from which the assertion in the text follows immediately.

5. Nonexistence of Any Competitive Equilibrium (Barter or Monetary) which is Pareto Optimal

Merely enlarging on Samuelson's basic model by permitting heterogeneity within each generation does not alter its central welfare implication: In such an economy, there is always some competitive equilibrium that is Pareto optimal, in fact, one which is also stationary (or, alternatively, monetary, provided that such equilibria exist). Here we present a recital of examples denying even the generality of this proposition – counterexamples that depend, in order of their appearance at center stage, on nonstationarity in tastes and endowments (or heterogeneity across succeeding generations), nonmonotonicity in tastes (or satiation from immoderate consumption), and nonconvexity in tastes (or enhancement from unbalanced consumption).

Among these examples, we can distinguish a core (specifically, the subset including only those pictured in Figures 7, 9–11) whose significance extends far beyond their immediate bad tiding. In brief, these particular examples suggest a potentially persuasive argument in favor of continued, conscious government intervention in the competitive, market process – one that doesn't rely on paucity of information, singularity of externalities, or any of the other standard reasons for market failure. Rather, this case rests squarely on their general, fundamental welfare implication: *There may be no once-and-for-all redistribution of wealth between the members of any finite number of generations, which will permit the competitive mechanism unaided to attain a socially desirable allocation.*

The validity of this assertion can be easily established simply by formalizing all such restricted wealth transfers in terms of alternative distributions of money endowments (referring for details to the comment following our description of the basic model in Section 2). Now, each of the core examples, including that which depends on nonstationarity, has a very important characteristic: The particular period during which markets first open (heretofore always taken as period 1) is essentially immaterial to the behavior of the economy in that and each succeeding period – provided that only the then current older generation has a money endowment. Moreover, given any finite distribution of money endowments, there must always come a period after which the creation (or destruction) of money ceases, or equivalently, in which – relative to all later generations – only the then current older generation has a money endowment. A fortiori, the demonstration of nonexistence when only the oldest generation has a money endowment suffices also when – only to some limited extent – other generations have as well.[14]

---

[14] This argument is not quite complete since it implicitly requires that every competitive allocation can be strictly improved upon generation by generation.

Having this point always clearly in mind, we are then well prepared to view the rehearsal of the various types of counterexamples.

5.1. Nonstationarity

The simplest stories involving nonstationarity require only slight perturbations of the most familiar example from Samuelson's basic model, already previously sketched in Figure 2. Explicitly building on that example, suppose now that some maverick consumer $t' \geqq 1$ has either completely inflexible tastes $U^{t'}(c^{t'}) = \min\{c^{t'}_{t'}/y_1, c^{t'}_{t'+1}/y_2\}$ or completely skewed endowments $y^{t'} = (0, y_2)$, while every other consumer is just as before.[15]

Then, the dynamical system characterizing competitive equilibrium is as shown in Figure 6, which has as its only solution $z_t = 0$ for $t \geqq 1$. In other words, under either of these hypotheses the only competitive equilibrium is the barter one, which is obviously not Pareto optimal – since it is possible to improve the welfare of every consumer $t > t'$ (without affecting the welfare of any other consumer $1 \leqq t \leqq t'$) by switching to the alternative allocation

$$c^t = \begin{cases} y^t & \text{for } 1 \leqq t \leqq t' \\ (y_1, y_2 + (y_1 - c_1^*)) & \text{for } t = t' + 1 \\ c^* & \text{otherwise.} \end{cases}$$

Although these examples do illustrate the essential idea underlying the whole argument in this section (namely, to structure tastes and endowments so as to bar any stationary equilibrium that is also Pareto optimal), they have at least two objectionable features. In the first place, the least complicated redistribution schemes that will permit attainment of a socially

---

However, we will, in fact, demonstrate that this stronger form of Pareto superiority is feasible in each of the core examples.

In this context, it is an interesting problem (though not one we will pursue further here) to characterize the simplest wealth transfers that can be (i) achieved, for instance, by assigning just nonnegative money endowments (i.e., ostensibly, by disbursing subsidies rather than collecting taxes) and also (ii) instrumental in supporting the Pareto optimality of competitive equilibrium.

[15] Thanks are due for Charles Hulten of Johns Hopkins for pointing out the relevance of the first of these hypotheses for our present purpose. This hypothesis, of course, already introduces an element of satiation. Note too that, for the second hypothesis to be consistent with the existence of competitive equilibrium, we require the boundary condition

$$\frac{\partial U(0, y_2)}{\partial c_1} \Big/ \frac{\partial U(0, y_2)}{\partial c_2} < \infty.$$

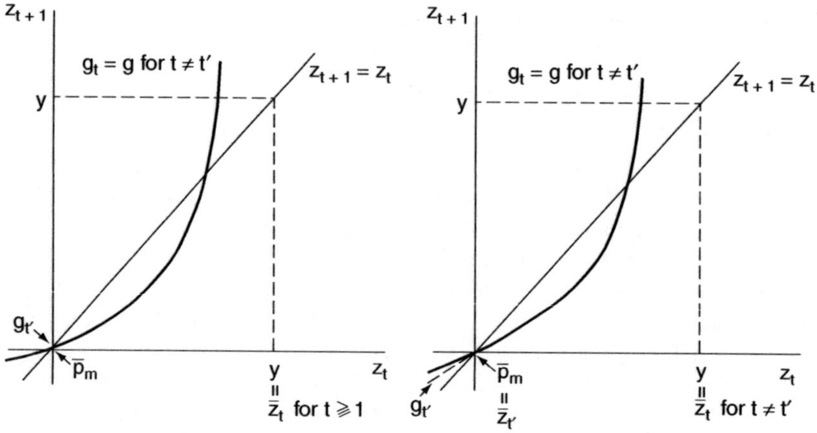

(a) Inflexible Tastes (b) Skewed Endowments

Figure 6: Nonexistence due to Nonstationarity: Two Examples with Singularly Shifting Tastes or Endowments.

desirable allocation are all but indistinguishable from the origination of fiat money itself (albeit at some appropriate later date $t > t'$ in the economy's history). In the second place, there is no room left for the existence of any monetary equilibrium (precisely for the same reason there is no room left for the existence of any Pareto optimal equilibrium). A necessarily more complicated example without either of these limitations – so, in particular, with both barter and monetary equilibria – is depicted in Figure 7. Here again we have $G_t = \{t\}$ for $t \geqq 0$, but now U^t is such that it (i) yields an offer curve that has a vertical segment between (3, 1) and (3, 4) and (ii) satisfies $U^t(2, 2) > U^t(3, 1)$,[16] while $y^t = (3 + 3^{-(t-1)}, 1 - 3^{-t})$ for $t \geqq 1$. Close examination of Figure 7 reveals that, although $\bar{p}_m = 1$, every solution to Equation (6) (with the upper bound y suitably replaced by $\bar{z}_t = y_t^t$) must satisfy

$$\frac{\partial U^t(y^t)}{\partial c_t^t} \bigg/ \frac{\partial U^t(y^t)}{\partial c_{t+1}^t} \leqq \frac{p_t}{p_{t+1}} = \frac{z_{t+1}}{z_t} \leqq \frac{1}{3} \quad \text{for} \quad t \geqq 1,$$

since otherwise, typically, there will be some $\bar{t} < \infty$ such that although $z_{\bar{t}} < \bar{z}_{\bar{t}}$, there is no z such that $(z_{\bar{t}}, z) \in g_{\bar{t}}$, which is inconsistent with Equation (6).

[16] Once again, see the appendix for detailed instructions on how to lay out an indifference map that yields such an offer curve, and yet at the same time satisfies such an additional restriction. In fact, this example doesn't require quite such extreme behavior. The subsequent argument remains true, for instance, provided each offer curve has a segment from (3, 1) to $(\cdot, 4)$ with slope dc_{t+1}^t / dc_t^t (or average $(c_{t+1}^t - 1)/(c_t^t - 3)$) greater than minus one.

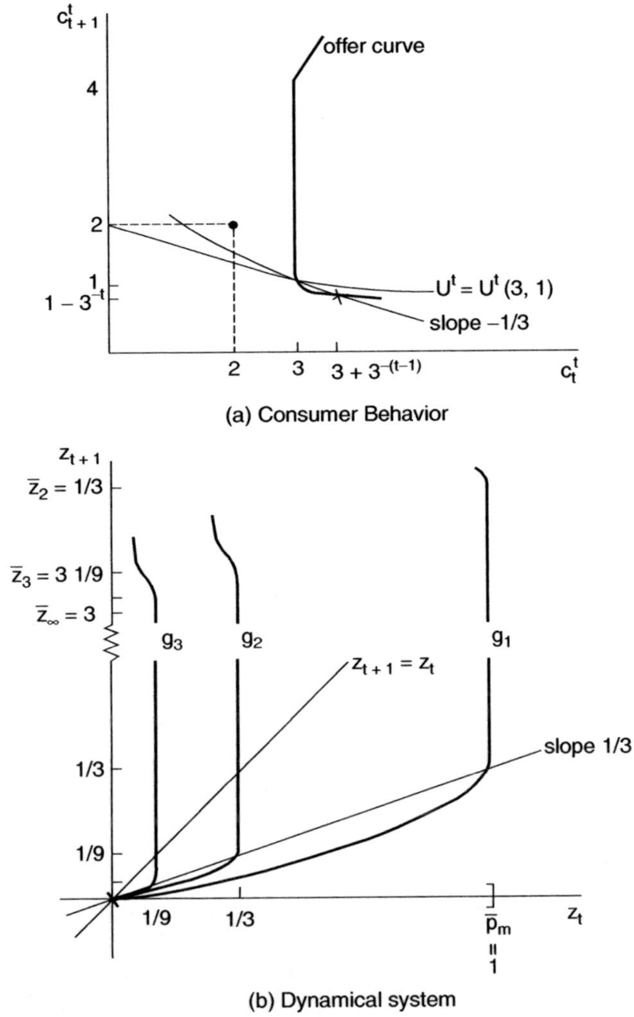

Figure 7: Nonexistence due to Nonstationarity: An Example with Regularly Shifting Tastes and Endowments.

But from this it follows directly that every competitive allocation is strictly dominated by the stationary allocation

$$c^t = \begin{cases} y_1^0 + 2 & \text{for} \quad t = 0 \\ (2, 2) & \text{otherwise,} \end{cases}$$

since $U^0(y_1^0 + 2) > U^0(y_1^0 + \bar{p}_m) \geqq U^0(c_1^0)$ for every $c_1^0 \geqq 0$ such that $c_1^0 \leqq y_1^0 + p_m$, and if

$$\frac{\partial U^t(y^t)}{\partial c_t^t} \Big/ \frac{\partial U^t(y^t)}{\partial c_{t+1}^t} \leqq \frac{p_t}{p_{t+1}} \leqq \frac{1}{3},$$

then

$$U^t(2,2) > U^t(3,1) \geqq U^t(c_1, c_2) \quad \text{for every } (c_1, c_2) \geqq 0$$
$$\text{such that } p_t c_1 + p_{t+1} c_2 \leqq p_t y_t^t + p_{t+1} y_{t+1}^t$$

for $t \geqq 1$ (so that the welfare of every consumer is improved), while $y_1^1 = 4$ and $y_{t+1}^t + y_{t+1}^{t+1} = 4$ for $t \geqq 1$ (so that the allocation is feasible).

5.2. Nonmonotonicity

It is well known that local (and hence global) satiation already raises difficulties for the first basic theorem of welfare economics within the barest standard framework usually employed in expositing the principles of general equilibrium theory. Figure 8 illustrates an example of precisely the same type of difficulty within the present context, an example again patterned after that introduced earlier in Figure 2. Here, because consumer 0 is satiated at the consumption level $\bar{c}_1^0$ – well below $y_2 + (y_1 - c_1^*)$ – every competitive allocation is dominated by one or the other of two alternatives: On the one side, if $p_m \leqq \bar{c}_1^0 - y_2$, then the competitive allocation converges monotonically to the representative consumer's endowments, and is therefore dominated by the stationary allocation (which entails some free disposal of good 1, and hence is itself, for this reason alone, not Pareto optimal)

$$c^t = \begin{cases} \bar{c}_1^0 & \text{for} \quad t = 0 \\ (c_1^*, c_2^*) & \text{otherwise.} \end{cases}$$

On the other side, if $\bar{c}_1^0 - y_2 < p_m \leqq \bar{p}_m$, then – because consumer 0 is "wasting" an amount $p_m - (\bar{c}_1^0 - y_2) > 0$ of good 1 – it is dominated by augmenting the first-period consumption of consumer 1 by some (possibly smaller) amount, everything else remaining the same (a feasible allocation that also may fail to be Pareto optimal).

Since all that this particular argument really requires is that U^0 have a global maximum at a sufficiently low level of consumption, one might sensibly wonder why we've chosen to depict such an apparently unnecessarily complicated example. The sort of intergenerational symmetry consideration remarked in the second paragraph in footnote 7 provides some rationale. A more compelling justification, however, is that the general structure of tastes pictured on the right-hand side of Figure 8a, and reflected in Figure 8b, suggests the possibility of constructing an example in which some lesser degree of satiation naturally puts a damper on the real rate

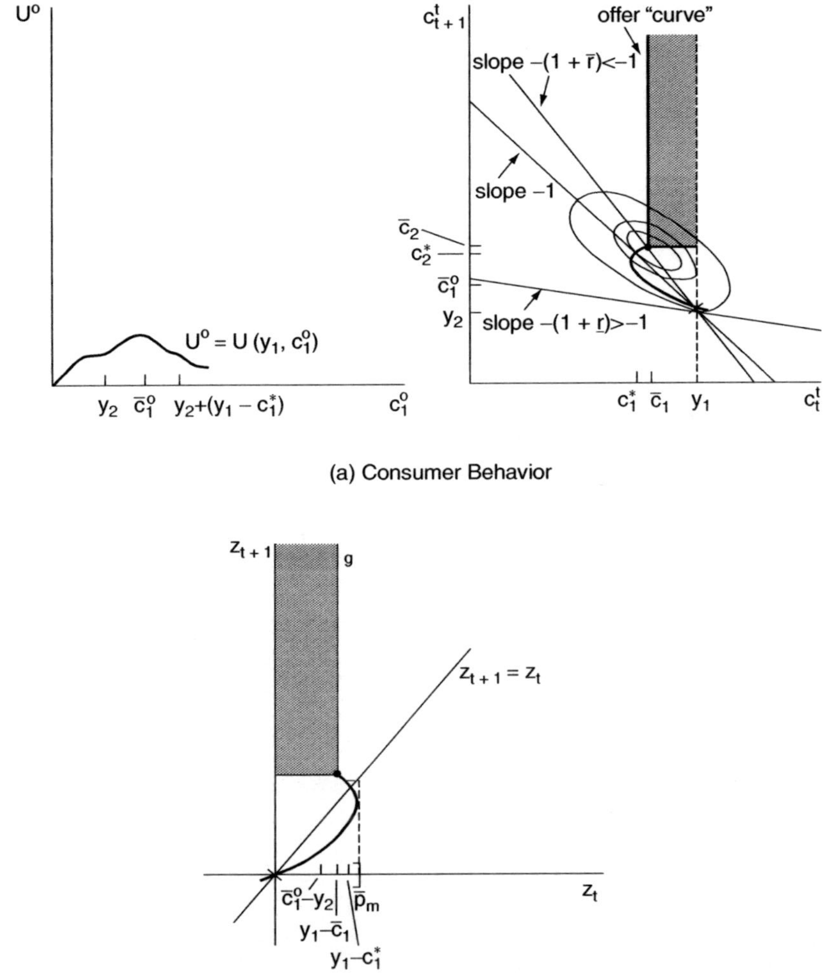

(a) Consumer Behavior

(b) Dynamical System

Figure 8: Nonexistence due to Nonmonotonicity: An Example with Global Satiation, Especially for the Oldest Generation.

return – and hence the efficacy of the mere presence of money as a restorative for Pareto optimality.

In order to follow up this suggestion, we need first to introduce a second perishable physical commodity. So, as outlined previously in Section 2, suppose now that there is another commodity, whose quantity is denoted x, endowment w, and price q. Furthermore, suppose once more that in each generation but the oldest there are two consumers $G_t = (2t-1, 2t\}$ for $t \geqq 1$ whose tastes for and endowments of the two commodities depend only on whether they are odd or even numbered. In particular, odd-numbered consumers $h = 2t-1$ for $t \geqq 1$ are of α-type, and have tastes of the form

$$U^h(c^h, x^h) = U^\alpha(c^h) + V(x_t^h),$$

and endowments of the form

$$(y^h, w^h) = (y_1, y_2, w, 0);$$

U^α is differentiable, strictly quasi-concave and has a global maximum at $(\bar{c}_1^\alpha, \bar{c}_2^\alpha)$, where $\bar{c}_1^\alpha < y_1$, $\bar{c}_2^\alpha > y_2$ and

$$-\frac{\bar{c}_2^\alpha - y_2}{\bar{c}_1^\alpha - y_1} = 1 + \bar{r} < 1,$$

while V is differentiable, concave and strictly increasing, so that

$$\frac{dV(x)}{dx} > 0.$$

In contrast, even-numbered consumers $h = 2t$ for $t \geqq 1$ are of β-type, and have both simpler tastes of the form

$$U^h(c^h, x^h) = U^\beta(c^h)$$

and simpler endowments of the form

$$(y^h, w^h) = (y_1, y_2, 0, 0);$$

U^β is differentiable, strictly quasi-concave and strictly increasing, and also satisfies the condition

$$\frac{\partial U^\beta(y_1, y_2)}{\partial c_1} \bigg/ \frac{\partial U^\beta(y_1, y_2)}{\partial c_2} = \frac{\partial U^\alpha(y_1, y_2)}{\partial c_1} \bigg/ \frac{\partial U^\alpha(y_1, y_2)}{\partial c_2} = 1 + \underline{r} < 1 + \bar{r}.$$

This last assumption merely eases description of the appropriate reflected generational offer curve.

After modifying Equations (2) and (3) in an obvious way to accommodate this second commodity (duly noting that all commodity prices must still be positive in order to be consistent with market clearing), we find that for all practical purposes, this example reduces to a very special case of our basic model, by virtue of the following considerations: Only α-type consumers own and value the second commodity. Hence, in every competitive equilibrium, it must be true that $x_t^{2t-1} = w$ and $q_t > 0$ for $t \geqq 0$. But such market clearing conditions for the second commodity will be a consequence of rational behavior on the part of α-type consumers only if

$$\frac{p_t}{p_{t+1}} < -\frac{\bar{c}_2^\alpha - y_2}{\bar{c}_1^\alpha - y_1} = 1 + \bar{r} < 1$$

and

$$q_t = \left(\frac{dV(w)}{dx_t^{2t-1}} \bigg/ \frac{\partial U^{\alpha}(c^{2t-1})}{\partial c_t^{2t-1}}\right) p_t$$

for $t \geqq 1$.[17] In other words, in this example, the appropriate reflected generational offer curve for the purpose of characterizing the set of potential competitive equilibria is derived from the two representative consumers' offer curves under the hypothesis that the price of the second commodity can and does adjust so as to maintain each α-type consumer's demand equal to his supply for that commodity. This result and its ramifications are pictured in Figure 9.

Two conclusions are immediately deducible from this figure: First, every competitive allocation necessarily converges monotonically to the representative consumer's endowments. Second, and the more significant of the two from our present perspective, every competitive allocation is thus strictly dominated by the stationary allocation

$$c^h = \begin{cases} y_1^0 + (y_1 + \bar{c}_1^{\alpha}) + (y_1 + c_1^{\beta *}) & \text{for} \quad h = 0 \\ (\bar{c}_1^{\alpha}, \bar{c}_2^{\alpha}) & \text{for} \quad h = 2t - 1 \\ (c_1^{\beta *}, c_2^{\beta *} + (y_1 - \bar{c}_1^{\alpha}) + (y_2 - \bar{c}_2^{\alpha})) & \text{otherwise} \end{cases}$$

and

$$x^h = \begin{cases} 0 & \text{for} \quad h = 0 \\ (w, 0) & \text{for} \quad h = 2t - 1 \\ 0 & \text{otherwise} \end{cases}$$

for $t \geqq 1$.[18]

---

[17] The first condition must hold because otherwise, that is, when

$$\frac{p_{t'}}{p_{t'+1}} \geqq -\frac{\bar{c}_2^{\alpha} - y_2}{\bar{c}_1^{\alpha} - y_1} = 1 + \bar{r} \quad \text{for some } t' < \infty,$$

consumer $2t'$–1 would demand $x_{t'}^{2t'-1}$ w – since under these circumstances his budget constraint encompasses the lifetime consumption profile

$$(\bar{c}_1^{\alpha}, \bar{c}_2^{\alpha}, x) \text{ with } x = w + \frac{p_{t'}(y_1 - \bar{c}_1^{\alpha}) + p_{t'+1}(y_2 - \bar{c}_2^{\alpha})}{q_{t'}} \geqq w,$$

while at this particular profile he is completely satiated in both his periods consumption of the first commodity, but not his first-period consumption of the second commodity.

The second condition is then essentially just the first-order requirement for the optimal solution to Equation (2) (suitably expanded) to satisfy $x_{t'}^{2t'-1} = w$ given the first condition.

[18] This assertion implicitly requires that $\bar{p}_m < y_1^0 + (y_1 - c_1^{\alpha}) + (y_1 - c_1^{\beta *})$, a restriction that is easily satisfied, for instance, by specifying the β-consumer's choice of first-period consumption at the real rate of return 0 small enough relative to that same choice at every real rate of return $r \leqq \bar{r} < 0$, everything else unchanged.

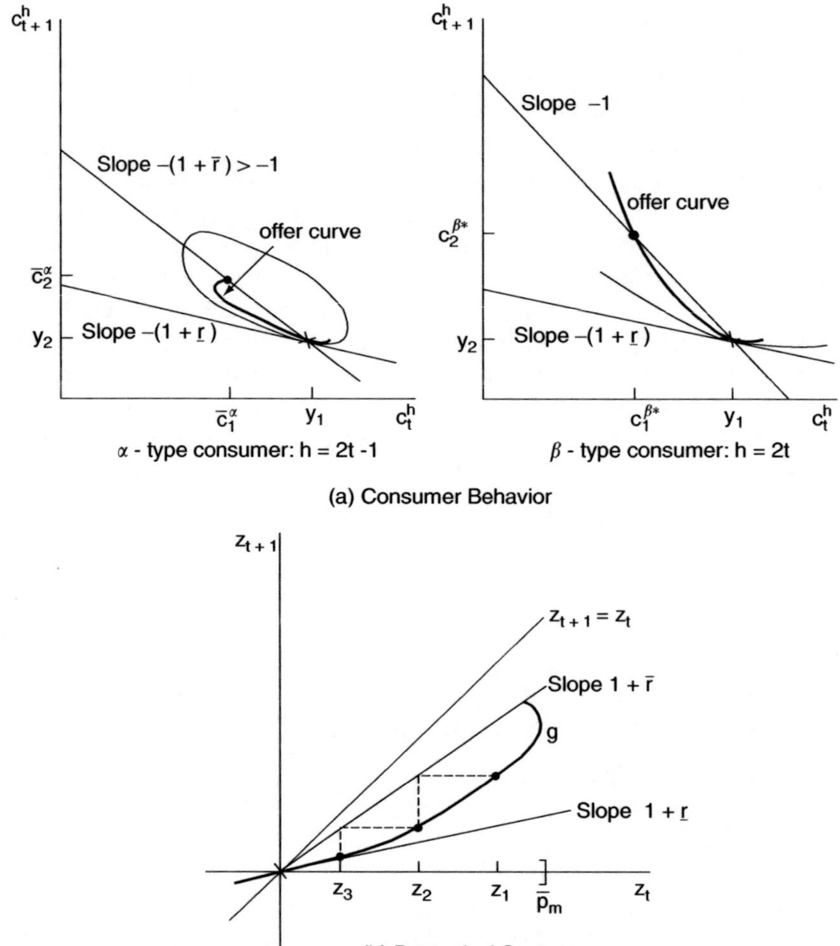

(a) Consumer Behavior

(b) Dynamical System

Figure 9: Nonexistence due to Nonmonotonicity: An Example with Global Satiation in the First of Two Commodities.

Notice especially that this example does in fact presume every consumer being locally nonsatiated, that is, always capable of increasing his utility with some arbitrarily small perturbation in his lifetime consumption profile. Thus, it clearly does not have the common feature of most familiar counterexamples to the first basic theorem of welfare economics. On the other hand, it is also clear that the example depends critically on having just the right combination of some consumption satiation together with some boundary endowments – and, for instance, this special kind of combination is well known to create problems just for the existence of competitive equilibrium within essentially atemporal models of the allocation of consumption goods. Furthermore, since such a concatenation obviously hangs in very delicate balance, it has usually been considered somewhat of an anomaly in that context, so that one could quite rightly ask whether it should also be so viewed in this. While we believe that the speciality of our particular counterexample (and its kin) is dictated more by our technical procedures than by our substantive objectives, this position remains to be satisfactorily buttressed. More to the point, there is a critically important distinction between the two situations being modeled; indeed, it would probably be hard to overemphasize the fact that a large measure of consumption satiation and related endowment sparsity is intrinsic to accurately portraying the essence of the intertemporal allocation of consumption goods – both because individuals are inherently finite-lived, and because their lives are naturally several-staged.[19]

An even more extreme degree of "satiation cum sparsity" can be utilized to model an economy in which, *though there is a stable, stationary monetary equilibrium, there is still no competitive equilibrium that is Pareto optimal.* In outline, this counterexample runs as follows: Suppose now that in each generation but the oldest there are three consumers $G_t = \{3t-2,\ 3t-1,\ 3t\}$ for $t \geqq 1$ whose tastes and endowments are described by

$$U^h(c^h, x^h) = \begin{cases} U^\alpha(c^h_{t+1}, x^h_t) \\ U^\beta(c^h_t, x^h_{t+1}) \\ U^\gamma(x^h_t) \end{cases} \text{and } (y^h, w^h) = \begin{cases} (0, y^\alpha_2, w^\alpha_1, w^\alpha_2) & \text{for} \quad h = 3t-2 \\ (y^\beta_1, y^\beta_2, 0, 0) & \text{for} \quad h = 3t-1 \\ (0, 0, w^\gamma, 0) & \text{otherwise,} \end{cases}$$

where $U^\alpha(c^h_{t+1}, x^h_t) = \min\{c^h_{t+1}, x^h_t\}$ and $(0, y^\alpha_2, w^\alpha_1, w^\alpha_2)$ satisfies $w^\alpha_1 + w^\alpha_2 - y^\alpha_2 > 0$ but ≈ 0,[20] U^β is differentiable, strictly quasi-concave and strictly increasing

[19] In this connection, it is also worth remarking that we have developed variants of the counterexample depicted in Figure 9 that are grounded only on having heterogeneity across generations – but heterogeneity that is repeated regularly (so that, for instance, generations are alternately "thrifty" and "spend-thrifty") – and in which it is inevitable that some consumers possess the only endowments of some goods that they alone value. We have chosen to present the more artificial construct since these alternatives necessarily involve introducing a third stage of the life cycle, and since introducing a specialized second commodity also admits yet another variety of quite interesting counterexample (as we shall now proceed to demonstrate).

[20] The α-type consumers could be assumed to have more flexible tastes; all that is required in the following argument is that their choices of second-period consumption satisfy the lower bound $c^h_{t+1} \geqq y^\alpha_2 + \epsilon$ for $t \geqq 1$, for some fixed positive number $\varepsilon > 0$.

Here and below "≈ 0" means something like "small enough so that Figure 10 is qualitatively accurate."

and also satisfies the condition

$$\frac{\partial U^{\beta}(y_1^{\beta}, y_2^{\beta})}{\partial c_1} \Big/ \frac{\partial U^{\beta}(y_1^{\beta}, y_2^{\beta})}{\partial c_2} = 1 + r^{\beta} \approx 0,$$

and U^{γ} is (like U^0) continuous and strictly increasing, Also, to simplify exposition, suppose that the oldest generation's endowment includes the second commodity in amount w_2^{α} (so that p_m must be reinterpreted as the present value of 1 unit of money together with w_2^{α} units of the second commodity).

For such an economy, after making necessary amendments to Equations (1)–(3), it is easily seen that (i) the γ-type consumers' tastes entail $q_t > 0$ for $t \geqq 1$, while their endowments entail $x_t^h = w^{\gamma}$ for $h = 3t$, $t \geqq 1$, so that (ii) the α-type consumers' tastes and endowments entail both

$$c_{t+1}^h = x_t^h = w_1^{\alpha} + w_2^{\alpha} > y_2^{\alpha}$$

and

$$q_{t+1} = q_t + \frac{w_1^{\alpha} + w_2^{\alpha} - y_2^{\alpha}}{w_2^{\alpha}} p_{t+1} > q_t$$

for $h = 3t-2$, $t \geqq 1$. (All this, of course, based on the provisional supposition that the economy is in competitive equilibrium.) The crucial upshot of these implications is that the appropriate reflected generational offer curve now has a very special form since the representative α-type consumer's offer curve is just a single point – independent of all commodity prices – while the representative β-type consumer's offer curve is just the same as in Samuelson's basic model. Hence, the set of potential competitive equilibria can be represented as shown in Figure 10 (which explicitly assumes the least complicated, but yet still nonempty possibility, that there are only two stationary monetary equilibria). From this figure, it is evident that every solution to Equation (6) must satisfy

$$\frac{z_{t+1} - (w_1^{\alpha} + w_2^{\alpha} - y_2)}{z_t} = p_t / p_{t+1} \leqq 1 + \bar{r}^* < 1,$$

and hence, in fact, that every competitive equilibrium either coincides with the (unstable) stationary monetary equilibrium corresponding to (the first) commodities prices

$$p_t = (1 + \bar{r}^*)^{-(t-1)} \quad \text{for} \quad t \geqq 1,$$

or, typically, converges to the (stable) stationary monetary equilibrium corresponding to (the first) commodities prices

$$p_t = (1 + \underline{r}^*)^{-(t-1)} \quad \text{for} \quad t \geqq 1.$$

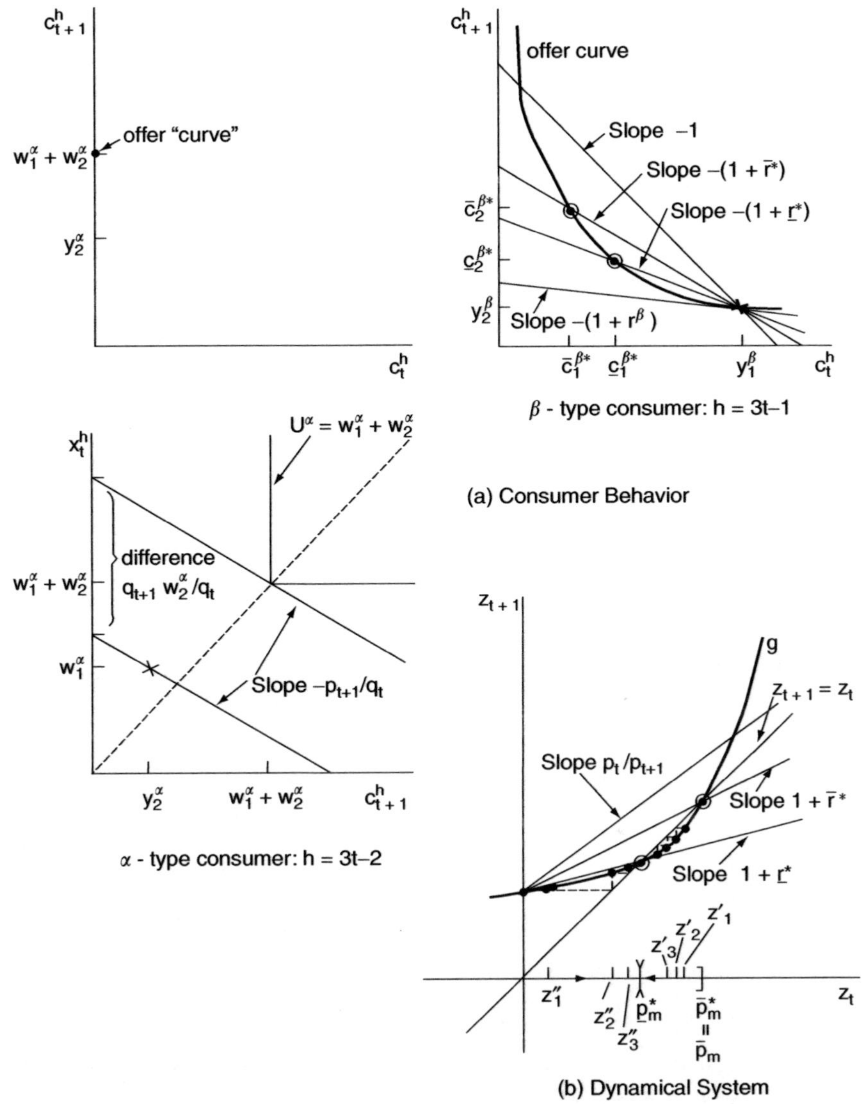

Figure 10: Nonexistence due to Nonmonotonicity: An Example with Local Satiation in the Second of Two Commodities.

Thus, it is also immediately apparent that every competitive allocation is therefore dominated since every sequence of one-for-one forward transfers of the first commodity between only β-type consumers that satisfies the bounds

$$0 < \Delta c_{t+1}^{3t-1} = -\Delta c_{t+1}^{3(t+1)-1} = \Delta c^{\beta} < \bar{c}_1^{\beta *} \quad \text{for} \quad t \geqq 1$$

is both feasible and – from each of their viewpoints (by virtue of the fact that at best they face a uniformly negative real rate of return $(p_t/p_{t+1}) - 1 \leqq \bar{r}^* < 0$ for $t \geqq 1$) – preferable.

5.3. Nonconvexity

This counterexample is nothing more than a straightforward variation of the example presented previously in Figure 5, and beyond simply displaying its

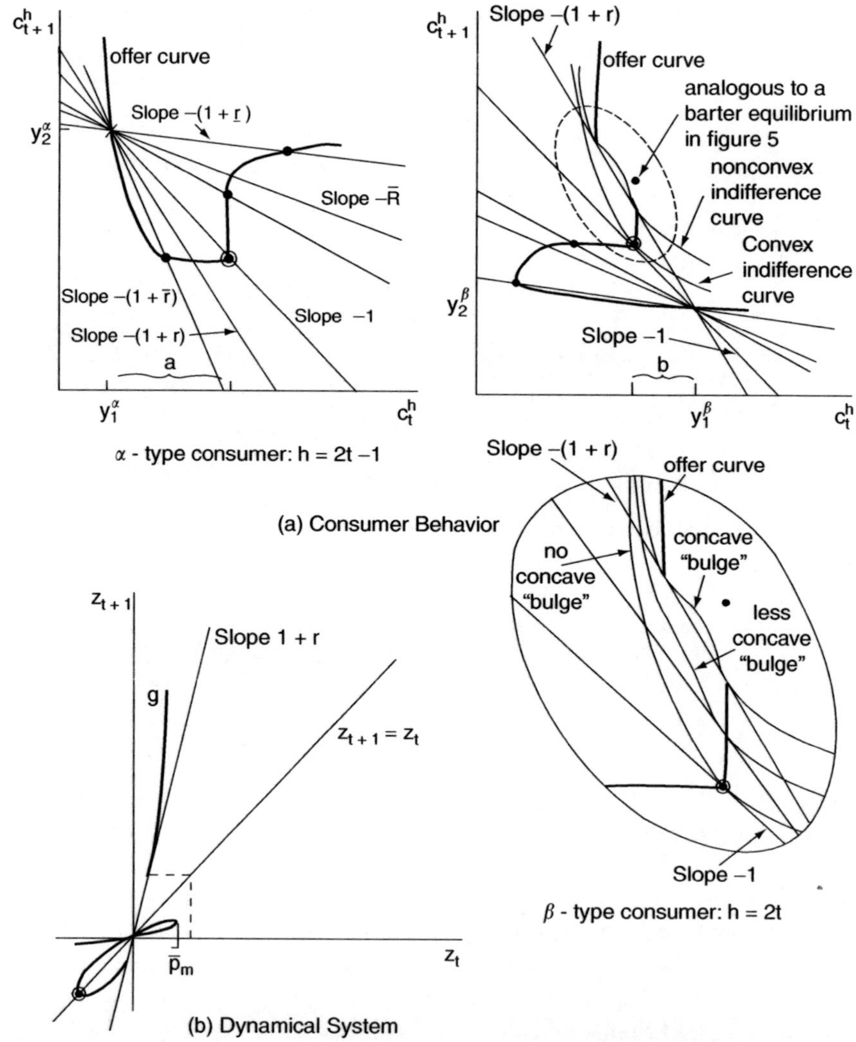

Figure 11: Nonexistence due to Nonconvexity.

structure – as we do in Figure 11 – requires only justifying its construction – as we do in the appendix.

Note, however, that this same device, namely, introducing some nonconvexity into the upper reaches of the β-type consumer's indifference map, can also be employed to provide a solid theoretical foundation for our earlier emphasis on the inherent difficulties attendant on nonuniqueness of monetary equilibrium (at the end of Section 4). The doggedly perservering reader should, by now, be able to follow the dots.

Appendix: Construction of Vertical or Truncated Offer Curves

A1. Introduction and Background

The purpose of this appendix is to substantiate the several claims made in the text (both explicitly and implicitly) regarding the possibility of constructing various types of individual offer curves. In accomplishing this purpose, it essentially amounts to an elementary exercise in demand theory.

The following central result is well known: Consider the typical consumer in our basic model, and suppose that his utility function U^h is continuous, strictly increasing and strictly quasi-concave, while his endowment vector (y_t^h, y_{t+1}^h) is nonnegative and nontrivial. Then, if (c_t^h, c_{t+1}^h) represents the unique optimal solution to his budget-constrained utility maximization problem (2) as depending on (positive, finite) relative prices – or, in common parlance, his *demand* functions – these are (nonnegative and) continuous and satisfy his (relative price) budget constraint

$$\left(\frac{p_t}{p_{t+1}}\right)c_t^h + c_{t+1}^h = \left(\frac{p_t}{p_{t+1}}\right)y_t^h + y_{t+1}^h.$$

Moreover, even if U^h has a strict global maximum, say, at $(\bar{c}_t^h, \bar{c}_{t+1}^h)$ (but is elsewhere strictly increasing or decreasing), the same result remains true provided, in addition, either his endowment vector is weakly dominated, $(y_t^h, y_{t+1}^h) \leqq (\bar{c}_t^h, \bar{c}_{t+1}^h)$, or he is not satiated at his endowment vector, $(y_t^h, y_{t+1}^h) \neq (c_t^h, c_{t+1}^h)$, relative prices are limited in range,

$$\frac{p_t}{p_{t+1}}\left\{\begin{matrix}\leqq\\ \geqq\end{matrix}\right\} - \frac{\bar{c}_{t+1}^h - y_{t+1}^h}{\bar{c}_t^h - y_t^h} \quad \text{according as } \bar{c}_t^h \left\{\begin{matrix}<\\ >\end{matrix}\right\} y_t^h.$$

The converse to these propositions is already falsified by simple examples of the sort pictured in Figures 4 and 5 (assuming their validity, which follows from an argument similar to that presented explicitly in the next section). In particular, under either alternative set of maintained assumptions, the optimal consumption vector will coincide with the endowment vector for at most a single relative price (except in the singular situation where $(y_t^h, y_{t+1}^h) = (\bar{c}_t^h, \bar{c}_{t+1}^h)$, in which case they obviously coincide at every relative price). Hence, it would be accurate to say that the general problem (formulated in terms of specific questions) we are addressing here is: To what extent does the property of representing the demand functions (c_t^h, c_{t+1}^h) – or, equivalently, the *excess* demand functions $(c_t^h - y_t^h, c_{t+1}^h - y_{t+1}^h)$ composing the offer curve, for short, simply the *offer curve* – impose further restrictions beyond just continuity and satisfaction of a budget constraint?

In a very elegant development initiating with Sonnenschein (1972, 1973) and culminating with Mantel (1974) and Debreu (1974), it has recently been established that – under analogous maintained assumptions for $n \geqq 2$ commodities and $m \geqq n$ individuals – aggregate excess demand functions are completely characterized by continuity (in uniformly positive simplicial prices) and Walras' law. While this fundamental result obviously has some indirect bearing on the topic of this essay, especially, on the conclusions exemplified by Figures 4 and 5, even in these examples it is not decisive for our purposes. Indeed, from the main line of argument in the text, it should be clear that both continuity and (the analogue of) Walras' law play crucial roles in delimiting the set of potential competitive equilibria in our basic model. Thus, for instance, the former rules out the possibility that there is no Pareto optimal stationary equilibrium, the latter that there are multiple stationary monetary equilibria in Section 4.

Moreover, it almost goes without saying that the requirement of market clearing is always at center stage in our presentation. This condition is especially important, for instance, in ruling out the possibility that there is some Pareto optimal stationary equilibrium – and, hence, any Pareto optimal competitive equilibrium – in Section 5.

A2. Vertical Offer Curves

We concentrate attention on the details of the nonstationarity example described in Figure 7. Also, in order to simplify the discussion, here we will employ somewhat more conventional notation, namely, (x, y) for the consumption vector (again) U for the utility function and $(\tilde{x}, \tilde{y})$ for the endowment vector. Exactly the same basic principles apply to rationalizing the preference structure underlying the heterogeneity examples described in Figures 4 and 5 – except that, roughly speaking, the roles of x and y become reversed.

What we propose to show, then, is that given (i) $(\underline{x}, \underline{y}) > 0$ such that $\underline{x} < \tilde{x}$ and $\underline{y} > \tilde{y}$ (ii) $\bar{y} > \underline{y}$ and (iii) $(x^*, y^*) > 0$ such that $x^* < \underline{x}$ and $y^* > \underline{y}$, it is possible to construct $U = R_+^2 \to R$ that is continuous, strictly increasing, strictly quasi-concave and such that

1. *The offer curve originating at* $(\tilde{\mathbf{x}}, \tilde{\mathbf{y}})$ *is vertical between* $(\underline{x}, \underline{y})$ *and* $(\bar{x}, \bar{y}) \equiv (\underline{x}, \bar{y})$.[21]
2. *The indifference curve passing through* $(\underline{x}, \underline{y})$ *lies strictly below* (i.e., *to the southwest of*) (x^*, y^*).

The idea of this construction is wholly geometric, and is fully elucidated by Figure A1. An algorithm for the construction proceeds as follows: Pick two functions $\underline{f} : R_+ \to R$ and $\bar{f} : R_+ \to R$ that are differentiable, strictly decreasing and strictly convex, which satisfy $\underline{f}(x) > \bar{f}(x)$ for $x \geqq 0$ and which yield $\underline{f}(x^*) < y^*$, $\underline{f}(\underline{x}) = \underline{y}$, $\underline{f}'(\underline{x}) = (\underline{y} - \tilde{y})/(\underline{x} - \tilde{x})$ and $\bar{f}(\bar{x}) = \bar{y}, \bar{f}'(\bar{x}) = (\bar{y} - \tilde{y})/(\bar{x} - \tilde{x})$, respectively. In particular, this choice entails that the curves $y = \underline{f}(x)$ and $y = \bar{f}(x)$ for $x \geqq 0$ have the following relationships to the budget constraints

$$-\frac{\underline{y} - \tilde{y}}{\underline{x} - \tilde{x}} x + y = -\frac{\underline{y} - \tilde{y}}{\underline{x} - \tilde{x}} \tilde{x} + \tilde{y} \text{ or } y = \frac{\tilde{y}\underline{x} - \underline{y}\tilde{x}}{\underline{x} - \tilde{x}} + \frac{\underline{y} - \tilde{y}}{\underline{x} - \tilde{x}} x$$

and

$$-\frac{\bar{y} - \tilde{y}}{\bar{x} - \tilde{x}} x + y = -\frac{\bar{y} - \tilde{y}}{\bar{x} - \tilde{x}} \tilde{x} + \tilde{y} \text{ or } y = \frac{\tilde{y}\bar{x} - \bar{y}\tilde{x}}{\bar{x} - \tilde{x}} + \frac{\bar{y} - \tilde{y}}{\bar{x} - \tilde{x}} x, \tag{A.1}$$

respectively:

$$\underline{f}(x) \left\{ \begin{matrix} > \\ = \end{matrix} \right\} \frac{\tilde{y}\underline{x} - \underline{y}\tilde{x}}{\underline{x} - \tilde{x}} + \frac{\underline{y} - \tilde{y}}{\underline{x} - \tilde{x}} x \quad \text{according as } x \left\{ \begin{matrix} \neq \\ = \end{matrix} \right\} \underline{x}$$

and

$$\bar{f}(x) \left\{ \begin{matrix} > \\ = \end{matrix} \right\} \frac{\tilde{y}\bar{x} - \bar{y}\tilde{x}}{\bar{x} - \tilde{x}} + \frac{\bar{y} - \tilde{y}}{\bar{x} - \tilde{x}} x \quad \text{according as } x \left\{ \begin{matrix} \neq \\ = \end{matrix} \right\} \bar{x}. \tag{A.2}$$

Generally, such functions $\underline{f}$ and $\bar{f}$ can be found in the parametric class $f(x) = a + be^{\beta x} + ce^{\gamma z}$ with $a + b + c > 0$, $a < 0$, $(b, c) > 0$ and $(\beta, \gamma) < 0$. So, without any loss of generality, assume in addition that $\lim_{x \to \infty} \underline{f}(x) \leqq \lim_{x \to \infty} \bar{f}(x) < 0$, so that, in particular, both functions also intersect the x-axis.

Next, define indifference curves (covering the whole nonnegative quadrant) in terms of the two functions $\underline{f}$ and $\bar{f}$ thus: (i) for $(x', y') \geqq 0$

---

[21] Thus, for the sake of symmetry in various expressions, we will interchangeably use the notation $\bar{x} = \underline{x}$, and later on, $x' = \underline{x}$ as well.

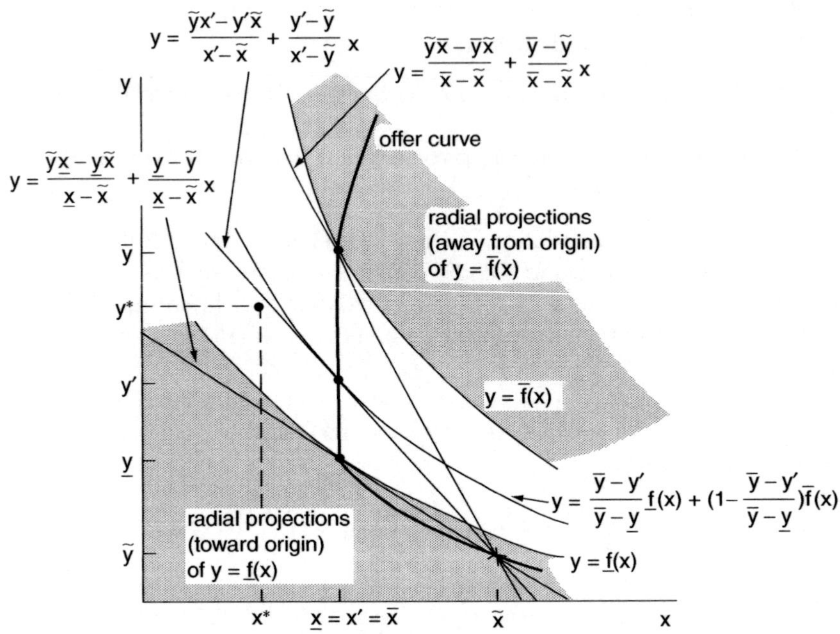

Figure A1: Construction of a Utility Function that Yields a Vertical Segment on the Offer Curve and Satisfies an Additional Dominance Condition.

and $0 \leqq y' \leqq \underline{f}(x')$, the indifference curve is the appropriate segment (i.e., that lying in the nonnegative quadrant) of the radial projections of $(x, \underline{f}(x))$ (i.e., as x varies over the nonnegative half line) toward the origin in proportion

$$\alpha = \begin{cases} 0 & \text{if } x' = y' = 0 \\ y'/\underline{f}(x') & \text{if } x' = 0, y' > 0 \\ x'/x'' & \text{otherwise,} \end{cases} \tag{A.3}$$

where x'' is defined by $\underline{f}(x'')/x'' = y'/x'$ if $x' > 0$; (ii) for $(x', y') \geqq 0$ and $\underline{f}(x') \leqq y' \leqq \bar{f}(x')$, the indifference curve is the appropriate segment of the convex combinations of $(x, \underline{f}(x))$ and $(x, \bar{f}(x))$ using weights

$$\alpha = \frac{\bar{f}(x') - y'}{\bar{f}(x') - \underline{f}(x')} \quad \text{and} \quad 1 - \alpha = 1 - \frac{\bar{f}(x') - y'}{\bar{f}(x') - \underline{f}(x')}, \tag{A.4}$$

respectively; and (iii) for $(x', y') \geqq 0$ and $y' \geqq \bar{f}(x')$, the indifference curve is the appropriate segment of the radial projections of $(x, \bar{f}(x))$ away from the origin in proportion

$$\alpha = \begin{cases} y'/\bar{f}(x') & \text{if } x' = 0, y' > 0 \\ x'/x'' & \text{otherwise,} \end{cases} \tag{A.5}$$

where now x'' is defined by $\bar{f}(x'')/x'' = y'/x'$ if $x' > 0$.

Finally, simply label each indifference curve with the value of its y-intercept.

Establishing that the utility function so constructed has the requisite continuity, monotonicity, and convexity properties is a routine matter. To begin with, observe that, given our particular choice of labeling for the indifference curves, in each of the three regions delineated by $\underline{f}$ and $\bar{f}$ the various definitions of α (Equations (A.3)–(A.5)) can be recast in terms of $U, \underline{f}(0)$, and $\bar{f}(0)$. For instance, Equation (A.4) is equivalent to

$$\alpha = \frac{\bar{f}(0) - U}{\bar{f}(0) - \underline{f}(0)} \text{ and } 1 - \alpha = 1 - \frac{\bar{f}(0) - U}{\bar{f}(0) - \underline{f}(0)}, \tag{A.4$'$}$$

where U is related to (x', y') implicitly by the equation

$$y' = \frac{\bar{f}(0) - U}{\bar{f}(0) - \underline{f}(0)}\underline{f}(x') + \left(1 - \frac{\bar{f}(0) - U}{\bar{f}(0) - \underline{f}(0)}\right)\bar{f}(x'). \tag{A.6}$$

Following this lead through, it is easy to show that, in general, U is defined implicitly in terms of its indifference curves by the formulae

$$y = \begin{cases} (U/\underline{f}(0))\underline{f}(x\underline{f}(0)/U) \text{ for } x \geqq 0, \underline{f}(x\underline{f}(0)/U) \geqq 0 \text{ and } 0 \leqq U \leqq \underline{f}(0) \\ \dfrac{\bar{f}(0) - U}{\bar{f}(0) - \underline{f}(0)}\underline{f}(x) + \left(1 - \dfrac{\bar{f}(0) - U}{\bar{f}(0) - \underline{f}(0)}\right)\bar{f}(x) \text{ for } x \geqq 0, \\ (\bar{f}(0) - U)\underline{f}(x) + (U - \underline{f}(0))\bar{f}(x) \geqq 0 \text{ and } \underline{f}(0) \leqq U \leqq \bar{f}(0) \\ (U/\bar{f}(0))\bar{f}(x\bar{f}(0)/U) \text{ for } x \geqq 0, \bar{f}(x\bar{f}(0)/U) \geqq 0 \text{ and } \bar{f}(0) \leqq U. \end{cases} \tag{A.7}$$

But by virtue of the specification of $\underline{f}$ and $\bar{f}$, each of the functions on the right-hand side of Equation (A.7) is differentiable, strictly decreasing in x, strictly increasing in U, and strictly convex in x on its respective domain. Hence, the desired properties follow directly upon application of well known, elementary results from functional analysis.

Utilizing yet another simple reformulation of Equation (A.4), it is also easy to verify the first additional property motivating this whole exercise – that the offer curve originating at $(\tilde{x}, \tilde{y})$ is vertical between $(\underline{x}, \underline{y})$ and $(\bar{x}, \bar{y})$.

In particular, from Equation (A.6) we see that

$$\frac{\bar{f}(0) - U}{\bar{f}(0) - \underline{f}(0)} = \frac{y' - \bar{f}(x')}{\underline{f}(x') - \bar{f}(x')} = \frac{\bar{f}(x') - y'}{\bar{f}(x') - \underline{f}(x')}.$$

Thus, by fixing $x' = \underline{x} = \bar{x}$ (so that, as in Figure A1, $\underline{f}(x') = \underline{f}(\underline{x}) = \underline{y}$ and $(\bar{f}(x') = \bar{f}(\bar{x}) = \bar{y})$, and considering only the nonnegative region lying between the prespecified curves $y = \underline{f}(x)$ and $y = \bar{f}(x)$ for $x \geqq 0$, the indifference curves described in Equation (A.7) can equally well be described by

$$y = \frac{\bar{y} - y'}{\bar{y} - \underline{y}}\underline{f}(x) + \left(1 - \frac{\bar{y} - y'}{\bar{y} - \underline{y}}\right)\bar{f}(x) \text{ for } x \geqq 0, \underline{y} \leqq y' \leqq \bar{y}. \tag{A.8}$$

Since the budget constraint

$$-\frac{y' - \tilde{y}}{x' - \tilde{y}}x + y = -\frac{y' - \tilde{y}}{x' - \tilde{y}}\tilde{x} + \tilde{y} \text{ or } y = \frac{\tilde{y}x' - y'\tilde{x}}{x' - \tilde{x}} + \frac{y' - \tilde{y}}{x' - \tilde{x}}x$$

is identical to that obtained by taking the same convex combination of the two budget constraints described in Equation (A.1), that is,

$$\begin{aligned} y = &\left(\frac{\bar{y} - y'}{\bar{y} - \underline{y}}\right)\left(\frac{\tilde{y}\underline{x} - \underline{y}\tilde{x}}{\underline{x} - \tilde{x}} + \frac{\underline{y} - \tilde{y}}{\underline{x} - \tilde{x}}x\right) \\ &+ \left(1 - \frac{\bar{y} - y'}{\bar{y} - \underline{y}}\right)\left(\frac{\tilde{y}\bar{x} - \bar{y}\tilde{x}}{\bar{x} - \tilde{x}} + \frac{\bar{y} - \tilde{y}}{\bar{x} - \tilde{x}}x\right) \\ = &\frac{\tilde{y}x' - y'\tilde{x}}{x' - \tilde{x}} + \frac{y' - \tilde{y}}{x' - \tilde{x}}x, \end{aligned}$$

Equation (A.8) together with Equation (A.2) immediately entail

$$\frac{\bar{y} - y'}{\bar{y} - \underline{y}}\underline{f}(x) + \left(1 - \frac{\bar{y} - y'}{\bar{y} - \underline{y}}\right)\bar{f}(x)\begin{Bmatrix} > \\ = \end{Bmatrix}\frac{\tilde{y}x' - y'\tilde{x}}{x' - \tilde{x}} + \frac{y' - \tilde{y}}{x' - \tilde{x}}x$$

accordingly as

$$x\begin{Bmatrix} \neq \\ = \end{Bmatrix}x' = \bar{x} = \underline{x} \text{ for } \underline{y} \leqq y' \leqq \bar{y}, \tag{A.9}$$

which is the precise statement of the desired conclusion, shown in Figure A1.

The second additional property – that the indifference curve passing through $(\underline{x}, \underline{y})$ lies strictly below (x^*, y^*) – was already guaranteed by the value restrictions on $\underline{f}$, specifically, that $\underline{f}(\underline{x}) = \underline{y}$ and $\underline{f}(x^*) < y^*$, also shown in Figure A1.

There are two additional points related to the foregoing construction that merit at least passing comment: (i) The same basic technique can be employed to justify the offer curve originating at $(\tilde{x},\ \tilde{y})$ having a nonvertical linear segment, say,

$$y = a + bx \quad \text{for} \quad 0 < x^1 \leqq x \leqq x^2 < \tilde{x},$$

provided, for instance, that $b < (y^2 - \tilde{y})/(x^2 - \tilde{x}) < 0$. Since the details of such a construction are not especially material to any of our present objectives, we will not elaborate them here.

(ii) The utility function implicitly defined by Equation (A.7) is not differentiable when either $(x, y) = (x,\ \underline{f}(x)) \geq 0$ or $(x, y) = (x,\ \bar{f}(x)) \geq 0$. Wayne Shafer has suggested an alternative procedure for defining a utility function that exhibits all the same properties, but which is also both differentiable and homothetic. The essence of Wayne's clever idea is displayed in Figure A2, and in bare outline (i.e., without any subtleties) goes as follows: Pick a function $f : \{x : x \geqq \underline{x}\} \rightarrow R$, which is differentiable, strictly decreasing and strictly convex, and which yields $f(\underline{x}) = \underline{y}$ and $f'(\underline{x}) = (\underline{y} - \tilde{y})/(\underline{x} - \tilde{x})$. Next, extend this function leftward from $x = \underline{x}$ by solving the ordinary differential equation

$$\frac{dy}{dx} = \frac{(y/x)\,\underline{x} - \tilde{y}}{\underline{x} - \tilde{x}} \quad \text{for} \quad x \leqq \underline{x}$$

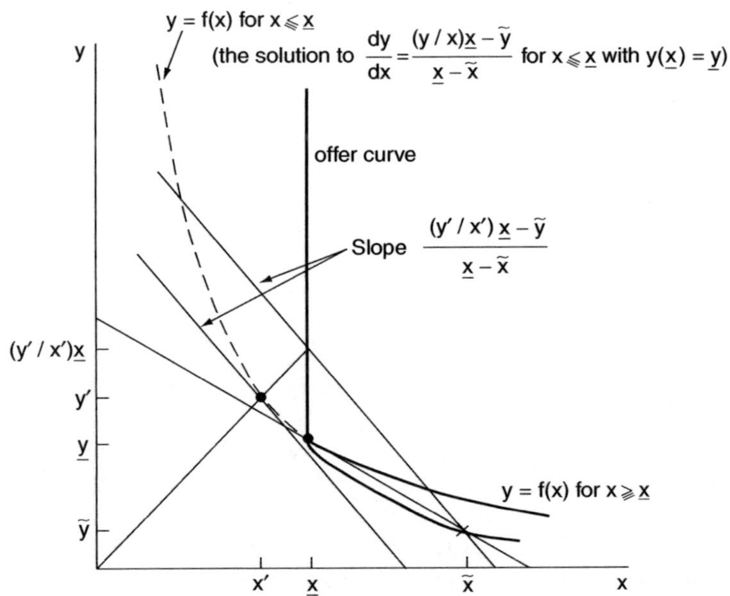

Figure A2: Construction of a Utility Function that Yields an Essentially Vertical Offer Curve and yet is Both Differentiable and Homothetic.

with initial condition $y(\underline{x}) = \underline{y}$; the solution is (no surprise) basically a power function

$$y = f(x) = \frac{\tilde{y}}{\tilde{x}}x + \left(\frac{\underline{y}\,\tilde{x} - \tilde{y}\,\underline{x}}{\tilde{x}}\right)\left(\frac{x}{\underline{x}}\right)^{\underline{x}/(\underline{x}-\tilde{x})} \qquad \text{or} \quad x \leqq \underline{x}.$$

Finally, define the indifference curves as appropriate radial projections of $(x, f(x))$ from 0, and label them in some smooth, monotonic fashion, for instance, according to the y-coordinate of their intersection with the ray $y = (\underline{y} / \underline{x})x$.

Our particular algorithm has two advantages over Wayne's: the first minor and the second not so minor. In the first place, it conveniently enables satisfying the additional dominance condition $U(x^*, y^*) > U(\underline{x}, \underline{y})$ (or, more generally, satisfying various other additional restrictions on the indifference map).

In the second place, and more importantly, it can be used virtually unaltered to construct the sort of indifference map underlying the nonconvexity example described in Figure 11. In fact, the only significant change required is in the choice of $\bar{f}$: Given $(\hat{x}, \hat{y}) > 0$ such that $\hat{x} < \bar{x}$ and $(\hat{y} - \tilde{y})/(\hat{x} - \tilde{x}) = (\bar{y} - \tilde{y})/(\bar{x} - \tilde{x}), \bar{f}$ now needs simply be specified, for instance, to be differentiable and to satisfy

$$\bar{f}(x)\begin{Bmatrix} > \\ = \end{Bmatrix}\frac{\tilde{y}\bar{x} - \bar{y}\tilde{x}}{\bar{x} - \tilde{x}} + \frac{\bar{y} - \tilde{y}}{\bar{x} - \tilde{x}}x \quad \text{according as } x\begin{Bmatrix} \neq \\ = \end{Bmatrix}\bar{x} \text{ or } \hat{x}, \tag{A.10}$$

as shown in Figure A3. (Compare with the second inequality in Equation (A.2), and its representation in Figure A1.) Given such a specification, the earlier argument (where relevant) is identical down to the bottom line (Equation A.9), which only needs to be slightly modified to correspond with Equation (A.10)

$$\cdots x\begin{Bmatrix} \neq \\ = \end{Bmatrix}x' = \bar{x} = \underline{x}\left(x\begin{Bmatrix} \neq \\ = \end{Bmatrix}\bar{x} \text{ or } \hat{x}\right) \text{ for } \underline{y} \leqq y < \bar{y}(y = \bar{y}). \tag{A.9'}$$

In other words, the offer curve must now have the vertical segment with an upper end point discontinuity as depicted in Figure A3. (A separate argument, not spelled out here, establishes that the offer curve in the nonnegative region lying strictly above the prespecified curve $y = \bar{f}(x)$ for $x \geqq 0$ must have the single-valuedness property shown as well, provided that $\bar{f}$ is strictly convex on the interval $[0, \hat{x}]$.)

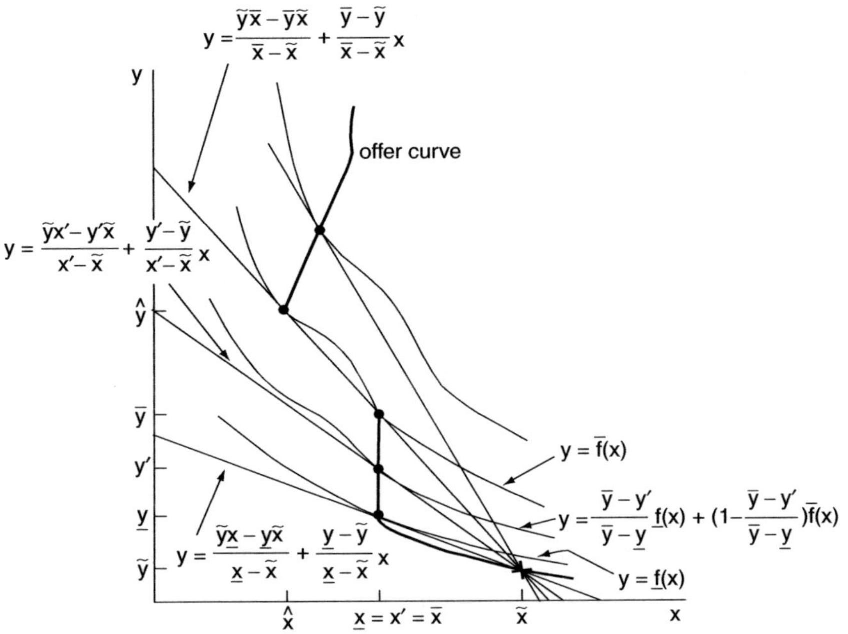

Figure A3: Construction of a Utility Function that Yields a Vertical Segment – with a Discontinuity at Its Upper End Point – on the Offer Curve.

A3. Truncated Offer Curves

It is worth briefly sketching an explicit procedure for obtaining the satiation example described in Figure 9; an obvious elaboration then yields that described in Figure 8. Thus, again employing the neutral notation (x, y), U and $(\tilde{x}, \tilde{y})$, we show here that it is possible to construct a well-behaved utility function that achieves a global maximum at a consumption vector $(\bar{\mathbf{x}}, \bar{\mathbf{y}})$ such that $\bar{x} < \tilde{x}$ and $-1 < (\bar{y} - \tilde{y})/(\bar{x} - \tilde{x}) < 0$. Again, the basic nature of the construction is geometric, and can be completely captured in a diagram, as illustrated by Figure A4. An algorithm for this particular construction runs as follows: Pick an ellipse lying wholly within the positive quadrant, say, $f(x, y) = 0$. Then, let

$$x^{\infty} = \min\{x : f(x, y) = 0 \quad \text{for some } y > 0\}$$

and

$$y^{0} = \min\{y : f(x, y) = 0 \quad \text{for some } x > 0\},$$

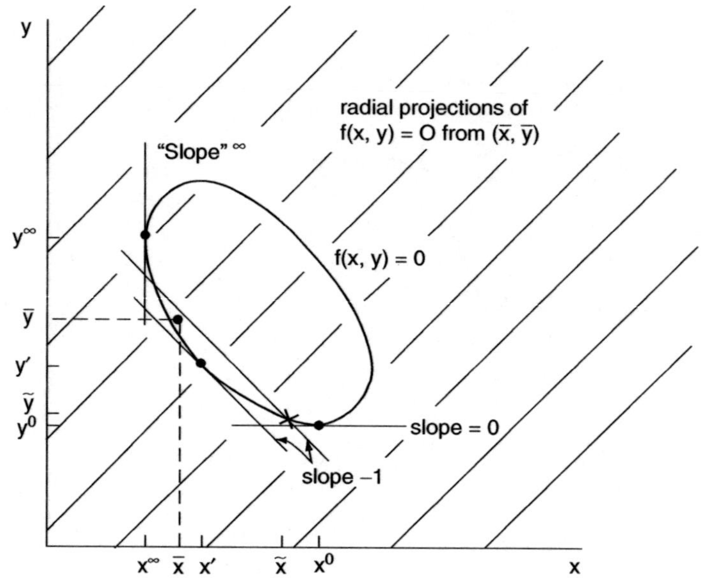

Figure A4: Construction of a Utility Function that Yields a Truncated Offer Curve.

with corresponding abscissa y^∞ and ordinate x^0, respectively, and let (x^1, y^1) be such that $x^\infty < x^1 < x^0$, $y^0 < y^1 < y^\infty$, $f(x^1, y^1) = 0$ and

$$-\frac{\partial f(x^1, y^1)}{\partial x} \bigg/ \frac{\partial f(x^1, y^1)}{\partial y} = -1.$$

(Refer to Figure A4; in this case the picture is surely much more informative than any accompanying algebra!) Next, pick any $(\tilde{x}, \tilde{y})$ such that $x^1 < \tilde{x} < x^0, y^0 < \tilde{y} < y^1$ and $f(\tilde{x}, \tilde{y}) = 0$, so that

$$-1 < -\frac{\partial f(\tilde{x}, \tilde{y})}{\partial x} \bigg/ \frac{\partial f(\tilde{x}, \tilde{y})}{\partial y} < 0,$$

and – given $(\tilde{x}, \tilde{y})$ – any $(\bar{x}, \bar{y})$ lying strictly inside $f(x, y) = 0$ but strictly below $y = (\tilde{y} - \tilde{x}) - x$,, so that also

$$-1 < \frac{\bar{y} - \tilde{y}}{\bar{x} - \tilde{x}} < -\frac{\partial f(\tilde{x}, \tilde{y})}{\partial x} \bigg/ \frac{\partial f(\tilde{x}, \tilde{y})}{\partial x}.$$

Finally, once again define the indifference curves as radial projections, but here of the ellipse $f(x, y) = 0$ from the point $(\bar{x}, \bar{y})$, and label them in some smooth, monotonic fashion, but here so that $(\bar{x}, \bar{y})$ has the highest value, for instance, according to the lower y-coordinate of their intersections with the ray $y = (\bar{y}/\bar{x})x$.

Notice a couple of additional features of the utility function and endowment vector so constructed: (i) The corresponding offer curve will be backward bending (as drawn in Figures 8 and 9) if and only if

$$-\frac{\partial f(x,y)}{\partial x} \Big/ \frac{\partial f(x,y)}{\partial y}\bigg|_{(x,y)=(\bar{x},\min\{y:f(\bar{x},y)=0\})} > \frac{\bar{y}-\tilde{y}}{\bar{x}-\tilde{x}}.$$

(ii) The relationship between particular points on the corresponding offer curve and other strategically chosen points on the indifference map (as drawn, for instance, in Figure 8) can – within limits – be determined by suitably varying f, $(\tilde{x}, \tilde{y})$ and $(\bar{x}, \bar{y})$.

Acknowledgment

Research support from the National Science Foundation is gratefully acknowledged.

References

Arrow, K.J. (1951). An extension of the basic theorems of classical welfare economics. In Neyman, J. (Ed.), *Proceedings of the Second Berkeley Symposium on Mathematical Statistics and Probability*. Berkeley: University of California Press.

Arrow, K.J. and Hahn, F.H. (1971). *General Competitive Analysis*. San Francisco: Holden-Day.

Cass, D. and Yaari, M.E. (1966). A re-examination of the pure consumption loans model. *Journal of Political Economy* **74**, 353–367.

Debreu, G. (1954). Valuation equilibrium and Pareto optimum. *Proceedings of the National Academy of Sciences of the United States of America* **40**, 588–592.

Debreu, G. (1974). Excess demand functions. *Journal of Mathematical Economics* **1**, 15–21.

Diamond, P.A. (1965). National debt in a neoclassical growth model. *American Economic Review* **55**, 1126–1150.

Gale, D. (1973). Pure exchange equilibrium of dynamic economic models. *Journal of Economic Theory* **6**, 12–36.

Malinvaud, E. (1953). Capital accumulation and efficient allocation of resources. *Econometrica* **21**, 233–268.

Mantel, R. (1974). On the characterization of aggregate excess demand. *Journal of Economic Theory* **7**, 348–353.

Samuelson, P.A. (1958). An exact consumption-loan model of interest with or without the social contrivance of money. *Journal of Political Economy* **66**, 467–482.

Shell, K. (1971). Notes on the economics of infinity. *Journal of Political Economy* **79**, 1002–1011.

Sonnenschein, H. (1972). Market excess demand functions. *Econometrica* **40**, 549–563.

Sonnenschein, H. (1973). Do Walras identity and continuity characterize the class of community excess demand functions? *Journal of Economic Theory* **6**, 345–354.

Starrett, D. (1972). On golden rules, the "biological theory of interest," and competitive inefficiency. *Journal of Political Economy* **80**, 276–291.

Chapter 2

Efficient Intertemporal Allocation, Consumption-Value Maximization, and Capital-Value Transversality: A Unified View☆,☆☆

David Cass and Mukul Majumdar[a]

[a]*Department of Economics, Cornell University, Ithaca, NY, USA*

1. Introduction and Summary

In recent years, based on Malinvaud's seminal work Malinvaud (1953), there have been a number of important contributions (McFadden, 1967; Kurz and Starrett, 1970; Cass, 1972; Benveniste and Gale, 1975; Benveniste, 1976a, 1976b; Majumdar et al., 1976; Mitra and Majumdar, 1976; Mitra, 1978; Mitra, forthcoming) toward resolving the following fundamental question: What observable properties characterize[1] some (all) competitive price system(s) associated with an efficient growth path? The natural focus in efforts to answer this question has been on the dynamical behavior of capital value – "natural" in the sense that Malinvaud's theorem establishes that under very general conditions efficient growth is tantamount to the existence of an associated competitive price system with the special property

☆Reprinted from *General Equilibrium, Growth and Trade: Essays in Honor of Lionel McKenzie*, "Efficient Intertemporal Allocation, Consumption-Value Maximisation, and Capital-Value Transversality: A Unified View", 227–273, © Elsevier, 1976.

☆☆This chapter is dedicated, with respect, affection, and admiration, to professor Lionel Mckenzie on the occasion of his 60th birthday Lionel's varied and myriad contributions, in print and otherwise, have all been to the profession's great "value-gain."

[1] In every analysis that aims to characterize efficient allocation as competitive allocation (given generalized diminishing returns), a slight gap appears between the statements of necessary and sufficient conditions, a gap occasioned by the fact that every price need not be positive. For this reason, here and in the balance of the paper, we use "characterize" to mean "are necessary and also sufficient provided appropriate prices are positive." Also, partly for this reason, in characterizing efficient (or optimal) growth paths, we concentrate on establishing necessity of various valuation properties. (A more compelling reason for our emphasis is that establishing sufficiency of these same properties is usually a routine matter; see footnote 9 below.)

International Symposia in Economic Theory and Econometrics, Vol. 21B
S. Spear (Editor)

ISSN: 1571-0386/DOI: 10.1108/S1571-0386(2011)000021B005

that in every period capital value is minimized among all potential growth paths yielding the same stream of consumption goods thereafter. In other words, dealing with the question eventually reduces to looking for a more concrete version of Malinvaud's capital-value minimization condition.

Roughly speaking, reported results have come from two distinct approaches: first, from searching for particular productivity and substitution properties of technology, which necessarily require asymptotically insignificant capital value or *capital-value transversality* (a label suggested by the common reference to the "transversality condition," especially in optimal growth theory) (Kurz and Starrett, 1970; Benveniste, 1976a, 1976b; Majumdar et al., 1976; Mitra and Majumdar, 1976; Mitra, 1978) and second, from searching for weaker regularities in the asymptotic behavior of capital value, which necessarily emerge given particular productivity and substitution properties of technology (Cass, 1972; Benveniste and Gale, 1975; Benveniste, 1976a, 1976b; Mitra, forthcoming). The first approach is undoubtedly more appealing intuitively since – at least when there are no primary factors – capital-value transversality is essentially equivalent to *consumption-value maximization*, that is, the property that among all feasible growth paths, and at its associated consumption goods prices, an efficient growth path maximizes the total value of the whole stream of consumption goods. Unfortunately, this approach encounters great difficulty from the mere presence of primary factors[2] (and the second approach from the mere presence of polyhedral-like technology). Nonetheless, it is basically the approach we adopt here. Thus, one of our purposes in this chapter is to present general conditions on static productivity characteristics and substitution possibilities that verify the property of consumption-value maximization and, incidentally, capital-value transversality as well (in Section 5 and Appendices A and B).

A closely related result appears in recent contributions concerning the problem of how to characterize optimal growth paths (Peleg, 1970a, 1970b, 1971; Peleg and Ryder, 1972; Weitzman, 1973): Suppose that we are given some nonnegative, nontrivial values for the whole stream of consumption goods.[3] If at these given consumption goods values, a

[2] We therefore intentionally defer our discussion of the problems attendant on primary factors until later in the chapter (in Sections 7 and 8). It is worth mentioning now, however, that one promising possibility for surmounting these problems is to give explicit consideration to the limitational role of exhaustible resources. Besides displaying our own efforts in this direction (at the end of Appendix A), we strongly recommend looking at the interesting and original work of Mitra (1978).

[3] It is noteworthy that, generally speaking, in this context the units for measuring consumption goods are interpreted in welfare or utility terms. Such interpretation is immaterial to our analysis, provided that the static technology available for producing utility and investment goods from capital stocks and primary factors

particular feasible growth path yields maximum total value among all feasible growth paths, that is, an optimal growth path, then it has an associated competitive price system with the special properties that (i) consumption goods prices are the same as the given values, and (ii) capital-value transversality obtains. In short, the proposition is simply that consumption-value maximization (at given consumption goods values) implies capital-value transversality (at associated capital goods prices). Another of out purposes in this chapter is to present a simpler proof for this proposition (Section 6).

Perhaps our principal purpose, however, is to display the common structure underlying both consumption-value maximization in efficient growth theory and capital-value transversality in optimal growth theory. The mathematical technique we use to establish this connection is application of variants of the basic support theorem implicitly developed in the Majumdar–Mitra–McFadden proof of consumption-value maximization for the closed, multisector model of growth (Majumdar et al., 1976) (see also its precursors Majumdar, 1974; McFadden, 1967), and this unifying methodology is presented first (in Section 2). (The reader who is primarily interested in our economic applications can skim or skip this section, which is unavoidably technical though quite straightforward.) Then, after describing our general growth model (in Section 3), we turn to characterizing efficient and optimal growth paths (in Sections 4–6) and to elaborating the complications arising from the presence of primary factors (in Sections 7 and 8). In the course of accomplishing our avowed purposes, we also develop two subsidiary results of interest in their own right: First, we present an alternative argument leading to Malinvaud's theorem, one that has the additional virtue of introducing a broader sense in which efficient growth paths yield value maximization and hence also capital-value minimization and consumption-value maximization (in Section 4). (See also the various arguments in Radner, 1967; Kurz and Starrett, 1970; Peleg and Yaari, 1970.) Second, we present a general theorem establishing the existence of special competitive price systems associated with feasible growth paths that are optimal in various weaker senses than that of simple consumption-value maximization (at given consumption goods values; in Section 8). (See also the related theorems in Gale, 1967; Peleg, 1972a, 1974; McKenzie, 1976; Peleg and Zilcha, 1977.)

---

exhibits generalized diminishing returns. However, such interpretation does mean that some care must be taken with the parallel interpretation of the competitive price system associated with an optimal growth path since, again generally speaking, it could not be used for the purposes of decentralization.

2. Fundamental Support Properties

We use $x = (x_0, x_1, \ldots)$ and $\pi = (\pi_0, \pi_1, \ldots)$ to denote sequences (later on x will be interpreted as quantities, π as prices), l_1 to denote the space of all summable sequences with sum norm $||x||_1 = \sum_{t=0}^{\infty}|x_t|$ l_0 the subspace of all finitely many nonzero-element sequences with sum norm $||x_0|| = ||x||_1$, and l_∞ to denote the space of all bounded sequences with sup norm $||x||_\infty = \sup_t|x|$. Also, $\pi \cdot x$ means $\sum_{t=0}^{\infty}\pi_t x_t$, $x' \geqq x''$ means $x'_t \geqq x''_t$ for every t, $x' \geq x''$ means $x'_t \geqq x''_t$ for every t and $x'_t > x''_t$ for some t, and $x' > x''$ means $x'_t > x''_t$ for every t.

SUPPORT THEOREM FOR l_1 (Majumdar–Mitra–McFadden). Suppose $X \subset l_1$ is closed, convex, freely disposable (i.e., if $x \in X, x' \in l_1$ and $x' \leqq x$, then $x' \in X$), and uniformly "productive" (i.e., there exists $\delta > 0$ such that for every $t \geqq 0$ there exists $x^t \in X$ such that $x_s^t \geqq \delta$ for $s = t$ and $x_s^t \geqq 0$ for $s \neq t$). If x^* is a boundary point of X (i.e., $x^* \in X$, but $x^* \notin$ interior X), then there exists $\pi \in l_\infty$ such that $\pi \geq 0$ and

$$\pi x^* \geqq \pi \cdot x \quad \text{for every} \quad x \in X. \tag{1}$$

Proof. Our argument is virtually identical to the original argument in Majumdar et al. (1976), but since that argument is imbedded in a fairly long, model-oriented proof, we detail it here for convenience' sake. We will use two basic results from analysis:

1. (Separation of convex sets by a continuous linear functional) If C^1 and C^2 are nonempty, convex subsets of a topological (e.g., normed) linear space S, interior $C^1 \neq \varnothing$, and interior $C^1 \cap C^2 = \varnothing$, then there exists a nontrivial, continuous linear functional f on S such that

$$f(c^2) \geqq f(c^1) \quad \text{for every} \quad c^1 \in C^1, \quad c^2 \in C^2$$

2. (Representation of continuous linear functionals on l_1) If f is a continuous linear functional on l_1, then there exists $\pi \in l_\infty$ such that

$$f(x) = \pi \cdot x \quad \text{for every} \quad x \in l_1$$

(see, e.g., Kelley and Namioka, 1963, especially Section 14 and exercises).

Given these results, the idea of the proof is quite simple: Verify the hypotheses of the separation theorem when $S = l_1$, $C^1 = X$, and $C^1 = \{x^*\}$, and then apply the representation theorem.

Two of the hypotheses required for applying the separation theorem are easily verified (since X is assumed a nonempty, convex subset of l_1 and x^* a boundary point of X). The remaining hypothesis – that interior $X \neq \varnothing$ – requires a little more work. What we need to show is that for some $x' \in X$

there exists $\varepsilon > 0$ such that if $x \in l_1$ and $||x - x'||_1 < \varepsilon$, then $x \in X$. In fact, we show that $x' = 0$ will do: By free disposal and uniform "productivity" $0 \in X$. Now pick $0 < \varepsilon \leqq \delta$ and suppose, without loss of generality, $x_0 \neq 0$ and $||x - 0||_1 = ||x||_1 = \alpha < \varepsilon$. Then (again by free disposal and uniform "productivity"), for every $t \geqq 0$ such that $x_t \geqq 0$ (respectively < 0) there exists $x^t \in X$ such that $x^t_s = \alpha$ (respectively $-\alpha$) for $s = t$ and $x^t_s = 0$ for $s \neq t$. Let $\lambda^t_s = |x_s| / \sum_{u=0}^{t} |x_u|$ for $0 \leqq s \leqq t$, so that $\lambda^t_s \geqq 0$ and $\sum_{s=0}^{t} \lambda^t_s = 1$, and let $z^t = \sum_{s=0}^{t} \lambda^t_s x^s$ for $t \geqq 0$, so that

$$z^t = \left(\alpha \Big/ \sum_{u=0}^{t} |x_u| \right) \quad (x_0, x_1, \ldots, x_t, 0, \ldots).$$

Then (by convexity) $z^t \in X$ while (by closedness) if $\lim_{t \to \infty} z^t = x$, then $x \in X$. But

$$\begin{aligned}
||z^t - x||_1 &= \sum_{s=0}^{\infty} |z^t_s - x_s| \\
&= \sum_{s=0}^{t} \left| \left(\alpha \Big/ \sum_{u=0}^{t} |x_u| \right) x_s - x_s \right| + \sum_{s=t+1}^{\infty} |x_s| \\
&= \left(\alpha \Big/ \sum_{u=0}^{t} |x_u| - 1 \right) \sum_{s=0}^{t} |x_s| + \sum_{s=t+1}^{\infty} |x_s| \\
&= \left(\sum_{s=0}^{\infty} |x_s| - \sum_{s=0}^{t} |x_s| \right) + \sum_{s=t+1}^{\infty} |x_s| \\
&= 2 \sum_{s=t+1}^{\infty} |x_s|,
\end{aligned}$$

that is, $\lim_{t \to \infty} z^t = x$. Now applying the separation theorem, we know that there exists a nontrivial, continuous linear functional f on l_1 such that $f(x^*) \geqq f(x)$ for every $x \in X$. But applying the representation theorem, we know that there exists $\pi \in l_\infty$ such that $f(x) = \pi x$ for every $x \in l_1$. Since f nontrivial, $\pi \neq 0$, while X is freely disposable, $\pi \geqq 0$. Hence, $\pi \geq 0$, and the proof is complete. ■

The key to the foregoing argument is the fact that the maintained assumptions on X are strong enough to guarantee that X has an interior point. Clearly weaker assumptions (e.g., simply that X has an interior – which obviously does not require that X be closed) will suffice for this purpose. For the particular capital-theoretic applications, we are concerned with such weaker assumptions are hard to verify in terms of the underlying economic model. Moreover, the various technological conditions – we will use to substantiate the maintained assumptions – are fairly conventional (or, at least, easily interpretable). However, if – as in several of our applications – X lies in the subspace l_0, then it is possible both to dispense with closedness and to weaken uniform "productivity."

SUPPORT THEOREM FOR l_0. Suppose $X \subset l_0$ is convex, freely disposable, and "productive" (i.e., for every $t \geqq 0$ there exists $x^t \in X$ such that $x_s^t > 0$ for $s = t$ and $x_s^t \geqq 0$ for $s \neq t$). If $x^* \in X$ but x^* is not on internal point of X (e.g., x^* is a maximal point of X), then there exists π (simply some sequence of real numbers) such that $\pi \geq 0$ and Equation (1) obtains.

Proof. This argument differs from the previous one only in that it concerns internal points rather than interior points, and thus linear functionals rather than continuous linear functionals. Once again it is founded on two basic results from analysis:

1. (Separation of convex sets by a linear functional.) If C^1 and C^2 are nonempty, convex subsets of a topological linear space S $\{x : x \text{ is an internal point of } C^1\} \neq \emptyset$ and $\{x : x \text{ is an internal point of } C^1\} \cap C^2 = \emptyset$, then there exists a nontrivial linear functional f on S such that

$$f(c^2) \geqq f(c^1) \quad \text{for every} \quad c^1 \in C^1, \quad c^2 \in C^2$$

2. (Representation of linear functionals on l_0.) If f is a linear functional on l_0, then there exists π such that

$$f(x) = \pi \cdot x \quad \text{for every} \quad x \in l_0$$

(Again refer to Kelley and Namioka, 1963, especially Section 14 and exercises, noting that Kelley–Namioka use different terminology regarding internal points.)

From here the logic of the argument proceeds exactly as before, except that in this case we need only to employ finite convex combinations to establish that 0 is an internal point of X, that is, $0 \in X$ and if $x \in l_0$, then there exists $\alpha > 0$ such that $\lambda \alpha x \in X$ for $0 \leqq \lambda < 1$. The details of this construction are as follows: By free disposal and "productivity," $0 \in X$. Now suppose $x = 0$ but $\max\{t : t \geqq 0 \text{ and } x_t \neq 0\} = \bar{t} < \infty$. Then (again by free disposal and "productivity"), there exists $\alpha > 0$ such that for every $0 \leqq t \leqq \bar{t}$ such that $x_t \geqq 0$ (respectively < 0), there exists $x^t \in X$ such that $x_s^t = \alpha ||x||_0$ (respectively $-\alpha||x||_0$) for $s = t$ and $x_s^t = 0$ for $s \neq t$. Let $\lambda_t = |x_t|/||x||_0$ for $0 \leqq t \leqq \bar{t}$, so that $\lambda_t \geqq 0$, $\sum_{t=0}^{\bar{t}} \lambda_t = 1$, and $z = \sum_{t=0}^{\bar{t}} \lambda_t x^t$, so that

$$z = \alpha(x_0, x_1, \ldots, x_t, 0, \ldots) = \alpha x.$$

Then (by convexity) $\alpha x \in X$, so that (also by convexity) $(1-\lambda)0 + \lambda \alpha x = \lambda \alpha x \in X$ for $0 \leqq \lambda < 1$. ■

Finally, for most of our applications of these two support theorems, it is important to know that the assumption of uniform "productivity" (respectively "productivity") can be replaced by the following pair of assumptions: Possibility of no production (i.e., $0 \in X$) and uniform productivity (respectively productivity) (i.e., there exist $\delta > 0$ and $t^\delta < \infty$ such that for every $t > t^\delta$ there exists $x^t \in X$ such that $x_s^t \geqq -\delta$ for $0 \leqq s \leqq t^\delta$, $x_s^t \geqq \delta$ (respectively $x_s^t > 0$) for $s = t$ and $x_s^t \geqq 0$ for $t^\delta < s \neq t$). This follows from the easily verified fact that if X satisfies these as well as the remaining maintained assumptions of the support theorems, then

$$X^\delta = X + (\overbrace{\delta, \delta, \ldots, \delta}^{t^\delta}, 0, \ldots)$$

satisfies the full set of maintained assumptions, including uniform "productivity" (respectively "productivity").

3. General Growth Model

Feasible real allocations or *growth paths* in the economy are described by

$$\begin{cases} (c_t, z_t, k_t) \in T \quad \text{and} \quad k_{t+1} = z_t \quad \text{for} \quad t \geqq 0, \\ \qquad\qquad\qquad k_0 = \bar{k} > 0 \end{cases} \tag{2}$$

where $\boldsymbol{c} = (c_1, c_2, \ldots, c_m)$ is an m-vector of consumption goods output, $\boldsymbol{z} = (z_1, z_2, \ldots, z_n)$ is an n-vector of ("gross") capital goods, or better, investment goods output, $\boldsymbol{k} = (k_1, k_2, \ldots, k_n)$ is an n-vector of capital stock inputs, $T = \{(c, z, k)\}$ is the static technology available for producing outputs from capital stock inputs,[4] t is an index representing discrete production periods (so that 0 is the initial period), and $\bar{\boldsymbol{k}} = (\bar{k}_1, \bar{k}_2, \ldots, \bar{k}_n)$ is an n-vector of initial capital stocks. (The assumption that initial capital stocks are positive $\bar{k} > 0$ enters the analysis in a nontrivial way.)

Regarding the technology, we will always assume that T is a nonnegative, closed set exhibiting

T1 GENERALIZED DIMINISHING RETURNS. T is convex.
T2 FREE DISPOSAL. If $(c, z, k) \in T$, $0 \leqq (c', z') \leqq (c, z)$, and $k' \geqq k$, then $(c', z', k') \in T$.
T3 CONSTANT RETURNS TO SCALE. T is a cone.[5]

[4] With minor modification, several of the results elaborated in the sequel will also carry over to a model in which the commodities and techniques available change over time (in a foreseeable manner). We have chosen not to generalize our model to encompass this sort of nonstationarity in order to avoid cluttering up the presentation.

[5] This last maintained assumption is, in fact, quite restrictive. Later on we effectively remove the force of this restriction by explicitly introducing (short-lived) nonproduced inputs or primary factors (e.g., labor) into the model. Note that (potentially long-lived) nonproduced inputs, both exhaustible resources (e.g., coal) and inexhaustible resources (e.g., land), are already implicitly incorporated into the

The whole of our analysis depends critically on how productive inputs are (and also, to a lesser extent, on how substitutable outputs are). For the time being, we only postulate the following productivity characteristics:

T4 NECESSITY OF CAPITAL STOCKS. If $(c, z, k) \in T$ and $k = 0$, then $(c, z) = 0$.

T5 PRODUCTIVITY OF CAPITAL STOCKS. If $(c, z, k) \in T$ and $k' > k$, then there exists $(c', z') > (c, z)$ such that $(c', z', k') \in T$.

T4 is one representation of the idea of scarcity, T5 of the idea of (the productivity of) roundaboutness. Note, in particular, that T5 implies that positive outputs can be produced from positive capital stocks. Later on we systematically enlarge on this fairly unrestrictive specification.

Corresponding to Equation (2), the "feasible" value imputations or *price systems* in the economy are described by

$$\begin{cases} (p_t, q_t, r_t) \in M \quad \text{and} \quad r_t = q_{t-1} \quad \text{for} \quad t \geqq 0, \\ q_{-1} \geqq 0 \end{cases} \tag{3}$$

where $\boldsymbol{p} = (p_1, p_2, \ldots, p_m)$ is an m-vector of consumption goods prices, $\boldsymbol{q} = (q_1, q_2, \ldots, q_n)$ is an n-vector of investment goods prices, $\boldsymbol{r} = (r_1, r_2, \ldots, r_n)$ is an n-vector of ("gross") capital stock rents, and $M = \{(p, q, r)\ (p, q) \geqq 0$ and $p \cdot c + q \cdot z - r \cdot k \leqq 0$ for every $(c, z, k) \in T\}$ is the nonnegative subset of the dual cone to T. Equation (3) describe, among others, all the price systems that might be observed in a perfect foresight competitive equilibrium for the economy and simply represent a convenient way of summarizing the possibilities for price systems (in exactly the same manner that Equation (2) simply represents a convenient way of summarizing the possibilities for growth paths).[6] We will refer to a particular feasible growth path (i.e., a particular solution to Equation (2) denoted, say, by asterisks) as being *competitive* or having an *associated competitive price system*, if there is some nontrivial "feasible" price system (i.e., some nontrivial solution to

---

model: A capital stock, say that of type 1, is an *exhaustible resource* when $(c, z, k) \in T$ implies both $z_1 \leqq k_1$ and $(c, (z_1', z_2, \ldots, z_n), (k_1', k_2, \ldots, k_n)) \in T$ for $z_1' \geqq 0$ and $k_1' - z_1' = k_1 - z_1$, while it is an *inexhaustible resource* when $(c, z, k) \in T$ implies both $z_1 \leqq 0$ and $(c, (z_1', z_2, \ldots, z_n), k) \in T$ for $z_1' = k_1$. As mentioned earlier, we will have a good deal more to say about the implications of the presence of exhaustible resources that are also limitational (in Appendix A).

[6] For a more complete discussion of the properties (and virtues) of this sort of representation, see Cass and Shell (1976). There is no loss of generality (and some gain in interpretability) in assuming nonnegative output prices. This assertion follows from the observation that, in light of T2, having more investment goods – and hence capital stocks – in the present never reduces consumption goods possibilities for the future. (The fact that investment goods prices are non-negative $q \geqq 0$, however, enters the analysis in a nontrivial way.)

Equation (3)) at which the given feasible growth path yields maximum profit of zero among all potential input–output combinations in each period:

$$p_t \cdot c + q_t \cdot z - q_{t-1} \cdot k \leqq p_t \cdot c_t^* + q_t \cdot z_t^* - q_{t-1} k_t^* = 0$$
$$\text{for every } (c, z, k) \in T \text{ and } t \geqq 0 \tag{4}$$

Of course, only some feasible growth paths are competitive, and only some competitive growth paths are efficient (or optimal), which is the underlying raison d'être for this chapter.

Before proceeding with the analysis, we emphasize two implications of Equation (4) that we will use repeatedly: Consider a particular competitive growth path (denoted again by asterisks). Since if $k_0 = \bar{\boldsymbol{k}}$ and $k_{t+1} = z_t$ for $t \geqq 0$, then

$$\begin{aligned}\sum_{t=0}^{t} p_t \cdot c_t &= \sum_{t=0}^{t} (p_t \cdot c_t + q_t \cdot (z_t - k_{t+1})) \\ &= \sum_{t=0}^{t} (p_t \cdot c_t + q_t \cdot z_t - q_{t-1} \cdot k_t) + q_{-1} \cdot \bar{k} - q_t \cdot k_{t+1} \text{ for } t \geqq 0\end{aligned}$$

it follows from Equation (4) that

$$\sum_{t=0}^{t} p_t \cdot c_t \leqq \sum_{t=0}^{t} p_t \cdot c_t + q_t \cdot k_{t+1} \leqq q_{-1} \cdot \bar{k} \quad \text{for} \quad t \geqq 0 \tag{5}$$

for every feasible growth path (2), while

$$\sum_{t=0}^{t} p_t \cdot c_t^* \leqq \sum_{t=0}^{t} p_t \cdot c_t^* + q_t k_{t+1}^* = q_{-1} \cdot \bar{k} \quad \text{for} \quad t \geqq 0. \tag{6}$$

Among other things, Equation (5) tells us immediately that consumption value is uniformly bounded

$$\sum_{t=0}^{\infty} p_t \cdot c_t \leqq q_{-1} \cdot \bar{k}$$

for every feasible growth path Equation (2), so that Equations (5) and (6) together tell us immediately that capital-value transversality implies consumption-value maximization

$$\lim_{t \to \infty} q_t \cdot k_{t+1}^* = 0 \Rightarrow \infty > \sum_{t=0}^{\infty} p_t \cdot c_t^* \geqq \sum_{t=0}^{\infty} p_t \cdot c_t$$

for every feasible growth path Equation (2). (The converse to this latter proposition will be established in Section 6.)

4. Characterization of Efficiency

A particular feasible growth path (denoted once again by asterisks) is *efficient* if there is no other feasible growth path that dominates it in terms of the whole stream of consumption goods, that is, if there is no other solution to Equation (2) such that

$$(c_0, c_1, \ldots) \geqq (c_0^*, c_1^*, \ldots). \tag{7}$$

This concept lies at the very core of (neoclassical) economics since efficient growth paths constitute the subset of feasible growth paths that are indisputably "desirable" or "good."

In order to characterize such paths, we now interpret the quantity sequence x as

$$x = (\overbrace{\bar{k} - k_0}^{(\bar{k} - k_0) - (\bar{k} - k_0^*)}, \quad c_0 \cdot - c_0^*, \quad z_0 - k_1, \ldots, \quad c_t - c_t^*, \overbrace{z_t - k_{t+1}}^{(z_1 - k_{t+1}) - (z_t^* - k_{t+1}^*)}, \ldots), \tag{8}$$

the price sequence π as

$$\pi = (q_{-1}, p_0, q_0, \ldots, p_t, q_t, \ldots), \tag{9}$$

and the set X as

$$X = \{x : x \in l_1, c_t \leqq c_t' \text{ and } (c_t', z_t, k_t) \in T \quad \text{for} \quad t \geqq 0\}. \tag{10}$$

That is, x is taken to be the sequence of net final outputs (i.e., outputs today in excess of inputs tomorrow) over and above those generated by a particular efficient growth path, π the corresponding sequence of value imputations, and X the set of all summable x that could be produced, given unlimited free disposal of consumption goods and unlimited costless availability of capital stocks. (It is basically the latter sort of flexibility that finally gives economic content to our various applications of the support theorems; a particular growth path used to generate a particular sequence of net final outputs need only be feasible in the special sense defined by Equation (10) and not in the usual sense defined earlier by Equation (2).)

Given these interpretations, it is relatively straightforward to verify that $X \subset l_1$ is closed,[7] convex, and freely disposable by virtue of our maintained assumptions on T (exclusive of T5). Furthermore, the quantity sequence

[7] In fact, because T is closed and satisfies T4, X is closed in the topology of pointwise convergence (from an argument similar to that found in McFadden (Cass and Shell, 1976, p. 45). Although Malinvaud's original derivation requited neither closedness nor any such intrinsic notion of scarcity, the loss in generality sustained from these additional assumptions seems more than compensated for by the gain in applicability of our basic separation technique. Moreover – looking ahead to the following discussion of the productivity properties of X when defined as in Equation (10) – it

generated by the efficient growth path itself,

$$x^* = (\bar{k} - k_0^*, c_0^* - c_0^*, z_0^* - k_1^*, \ldots, c_t^* - c_t^*, z_t^* - k_{t+1}^*, \ldots) = 0,$$

must be a boundary point of X: Obviously, x^* is in X. Suppose it were an interior point as well. Then (appealing to the way points in X are defined) it would be possible to increase an arbitrarily chosen consumption good output (e.g., $c_{10} - c_{10}^* > 0$), while at the same time maintaining every other consumption good output ($c_{i0} - c_{i0}^* = 0$ for $i \# 1$ and $c_t - c_t^* = 0$ for $t \neq 0$), as well as feasibility ($\bar{k} - k_0 = 0$, $z_t - k_{t+1} = 0$, and $(c_t, z_t, k_t) \in T$ for $t \geqq 0$). But such a possibility contradicts the fact that we began by postulating an efficient growth path.

From these considerations (together with the final comment at the end of Section 2), it follows that if we could only verify that X is uniformly productive, then we could simply apply the support theorem for l_1 to derive a price characterization for all efficient growth paths. This is indeed the strategy we follow in the subsequent section (but for a simplification in the interpretation of the quantity sequence x). However, this line of attack requires more structure on T than we have thus far imposed (see, e.g., T6 and T7 below). Here we proceed instead by noticing that although X is not necessarily *uniformly* productive, by virtue of T5 it is certainly productive in the following sense: There exists $(x'_0, x'_1, \ldots, x'_{n-1}) < 0$ such that for every $t \geqq n$ there exists $x^t \in X$ such that $x_s^t \geqq x'_s$ for $0 \leqq s < n, x_s^t > 0$ for $s = t$, and $x_s^t \geqq 0$ for $n \leqq s \neq t$. This seemingly complicated statement is nothing more than a formalization of the fact that T5 implies that if there were larger initial capital stocks available, then it would be feasible to produce no smaller net final outputs in every subsequent period, and actually larger net final outputs in any given subsequent period. In particular, the quantity sequences x^t for $t \geqq n$ can be generated by a growth path that utilizes given additional initial capital stocks (so that $x'_{j-1} = \bar{k}_j - k_{j0} < 0$ for $1 \leqq j \leqq n$) to produce more investment goods output during periods 0 through $s-1$, or more capital stock inputs for periods 0 through s, and more of both consumption goods output and investment goods output during period s (so that $n + (n+m)s < t \leqq n + (n+m)(s+1)$).

The observation that X is productive immediately suggests the following trick to tender it uniformly so: Choose new units for measuring net final outputs or quantities, say v_t, for $t \geqq 0$, in such a manner that for some $\delta > 0$ and $t^\delta = n-1$, $v_t x'_t \geqq -\delta$ for $0 \leqq t \leqq t^\delta$ and $v_t x_t^t \geqq \delta$ for $t > t^\delta$.[8] Clearly, such a maneuver enables us to apply the conclusion of the support theorem

---

can easily be shown that Malinvaud's theorem itself follows simply by further restricting X to lie in l_0, and then appealing to the support theorem for l_0.

[8] After changing units, of course, the sequences x and π would have to be appropriately reinterpreted: $x_0 = v_0(\bar{k}_1 - k_{10})$, and $\pi_0 = q_{1-1}/v_0, \ldots$. Notice that, given $t^v < \infty$, we can always choose the new units for measuring net final outputs or quantities so that

for l_1 (Equation (1)), and thereby (referring to the interpretations Equations (8)–(10) to establish a fundamental proposition.[9]

4.1. Price Characterization of Efficient Growth Paths

If a feasible growth path is efficient, then there exist positive units for measuring outputs $(\upsilon_{-1}, u_0, \upsilon_0, \ldots, u_1, \upsilon_t, \ldots) > 0$ and nonnegative, nontrivial prices for evaluating outputs $(q_{-1}, p_0, q_0, \ldots, p_t, q_t, \ldots) \geq 0$ such that

$$0 \geqq q_{-1} \cdot (\bar{k} - k_0) + \sum_{t=0}^{\infty} \left(p_t \cdot (c_t - c_t^*) + q_t \cdot (z_t - k_{t+1})\right) \tag{11}$$

for every growth path $(c_t, z_t, k_t) \in T$ for $t \geqq 0$ such that

$$\sum_{j=1}^{n} \upsilon_{j-1} |\bar{k} - k_{j0}| + \sum_{t=0}^{\infty} \left(\sum_{i=1}^{m} u_{it} |c_{it} - c_{it}^*| + \sum_{j=1}^{n} \upsilon_{jt} |z_{jt} - k_{jt+1}| \right) < \infty.$$

The converse obtains provided that consumption goods prices are positive $p_t > 0$ for $t \geqq 0$.

In this form, our price characterization is neither very transparent nor very usable. Three immediate corollaries go part way toward remedying these defects.

$v_t = 1$ for $0 \leqq t \leqq t^{\delta}$ This is a reflection of the fact that it is only the asymptotic behavior of feasible growth paths that create fundamental difficulties in characterizing efficiency.

[9] The converse assertion or sufficiency follows directly upon specializing Equation (11) to encompass only feasible growth paths

$$0 \geqq \sum_{t=0}^{\infty} p_t (c_t - c_t^*) \tag{*}$$

for every feasible growth path (2) such that

$$\sum_{t=0}^{\infty} \sum_{i=1}^{m} u_{it} |c_{it} - c_{it}^*| < \infty,$$

since (*) is inconsistent with (/) when $p_t > 0$ for $t \geqq 0$. For the corollaries to this proposition, as well as subsequent characterizations, proof of sufficiency is only slightly less direct – involving reference to Equations (5) and (6) (or, when there are primary factors, Equations (5′) and (6′)) in order to establish an analog of (*) since each of these characterizations is couched in terms of an associated competitive price system. Because these arguments are essentially similar and straightforward, we will omit them.

4.2. Value Characterizations of Efficient Growth Paths

If a feasible growth path is efficient, then it has an associated competitive price system (4) at which

1. *Restricted Value Maximization* (Net final output value is maximized):

$$\infty > \sum_{t=0}^{\infty} p_t\, c_t^* - q_{-1}\bar{k} \geqq \sum_{t=0}^{\infty} p_t \cdot c_t - q_{-1} \cdot k \tag{12}$$

2. *Restricted Capital-Value Minimization* (Capital value is minimized):

$$\infty > \sum_{t=0}^{\infty} p_t \cdot c_t \geqq (>) \sum_{t=0}^{\infty} p_t \cdot c_t^* \Rightarrow q_{-1} \cdot \bar{k} \leqq (<) q_{-1} \cdot k \tag{13}$$

3. *Restricted Consumption-Value Maximization* (Consumption value is maximized):

$$k \leqq \bar{k} \Rightarrow (q_{-1} \cdot k \leqq q_{-1} \cdot \bar{k} \Rightarrow) \infty > \sum_{t=0}^{\infty} p_t \cdot c_t^* \geqq \sum_{t=0}^{\infty} p_t \cdot c_t, \tag{14}$$

among all growth paths that (i) are feasible from nonnegative capital stocks that satisfy Equation (2) with $\bar{k} = k \geqq 0$ and (ii) yield sufficiently small deviations in the whole stream of consumption goods or satisfy

$$\sum_{t=0}^{\infty} \sum_{i=1}^{m} u_{it} |c_{it} - c_{it}^*| < \infty$$

for some (fixed) positive units for measuring consumption goods $u_{it} > 0$ for

$$1 \leqq i \leqq m, \quad t \geqq 0.$$

In each case (1–3) the converse obtains provided that consumption goods prices are positive $p_t > 0$ for $t \geqq 0$.

Proof. Equation (4) follows from Equation (11) with $(c_s, z_s, k_s) = (c, z, k) \in T$ for $s = t$ and $(c_s, z_s, k_s) = (c_s^*, z_s^*, k_s^*)$ for $s \neq t$. Then, in view of Equations (5), (12)–(14) follow from Equation (11) when comparison is further limited to growth paths that are feasible from nonnegative capital stocks $k \geqq 0$. ∎

"Restricted" here refers to the fact that among growth paths that are feasible from nonnegative capital stocks, we have further confined comparisons to just those that yield sufficiently small deviations in the whole stream of consumption goods. Note, on the other hand, that we could have expanded such restricted comparisons to the class of growth paths that are identical up to period $t, (c_s, z_s, k_s) = (c_s^*, z_s^*, k_s^*)$ for $0 \leqq s < t$, and then are feasible from nonnegative capital stocks in period $t, k_t = k \geqq 0$, and $(c_s, z_s, k_s) \in T$ and $k_{s+1} = z_s$ for $s \geqq t$, for arbitrary distinguished period $t \geqq 0$. (This expansion would permit a more general interpretation of capital goods prices, as detailed by one of us elsewhere.)

Regarding the various value characterizations themselves: Restricted value maximization is the closest analog of the standard characterization of efficient allocation in a static (or equivalently, dynamic but finite) economy, a parallel is also elaborated at length in Cass. Restricted capital-value minimization is essentially a stronger version of Malinvaud's theorem since (in light of the comments above) our condition involves a broader class of comparisons than does his (though at the cost mentioned in Footnote 7). Finally, restricted consumption-value maximization basically speaks for itself. One of our prime goals is to sharpen this particular implication of Equation (11).

Specifically, one can ask whether there are circumstances under which consumption-value maximization obtains without any restriction except feasibility. Alternatively, one can ask whether there are circumstances under which some more qualified notion of optimality obtains without any restriction except feasibility (as is the case, e.g., in the one-good model analyzed by Cass and Yaari, 1971). It is to the former question we now turn; we will also respond, somewhat indirectly, to the latter question later on (in Sections 7 and 8, and at the end of Appendix B).

Before addressing this question, however, we emphasize at this point that each of our subsequent arguments amounts to a variant of the argument presented in this section: Namely, in each specific case, we interpret x, π, X, and x^* in such a way that direct application of a support theorem plus judicious choice of comparison sequences lead to the desired conclusion.

5. Efficiency and Consumption-Value Maximization

The argument in the preceding section underlines the basic difficulty involved in using the support theorem for l_1 as a tool for characterizing efficient growth paths: The requirements of summability (i.e., $X \subset l_1$) and interiority (i.e., interior $X \neq \emptyset$) generally reflect conflicting aspects of the productive capacities of the underlying technology. Thus, a particular growth model in which feasible growth paths necessarily yield a summable stream of consumption goods will typically be incapable of providing consumption goods at a uniform rate in any given future period, and vice versa. This trade-off is most clearly illustrated by the fact that for the general growth model we are considering, by choosing units for measuring consumption goods outputs that embody a sufficiently high rate of discount, we can guarantee summable consumption possibilities, while by choosing units that embody a sufficiently low rate, we can guarantee uniform consumption possibilities, but usually not both.

There is one class of growth models, however, in which these conflicting aspects just balance each other. This class consists of the growth models where technology exhibits the following, additional productivity characteristics:

T6 IMPOSSIBILITY OF STORAGE WITH SUSTENANCE. There exist $p > 0$ and $q \geqq 0$ such that

$$p \cdot c + q \cdot z - q\, k \leqq 0 \quad \text{for every } (c,\ z,\ k) \in T.$$

T7 POSSIBILITY OF STORAGE AND REGENERATION. There exist $0 \leq \hat{k} \leqq \bar{k}$ and $\bar{z} > 0$ such that both $(0, \hat{k}, \hat{k}) \in T$ and $(0, \hat{z}, \hat{k}) \in T$.

T7 is more or less self-explanatory. It simply states that the economy is capable of replicating some capital stocks from which it is also capable of producing positive investment goods output – or together with T5, positive outputs (of both consumption and investment goods) within at most two periods T7 would be true, for instance, if the economy were capable of replicating positive capital stocks, that is, if there exists $0 < \hat{k} \leqq \bar{k}$ such that $(0, \hat{k}, \hat{k}) \in T$ (taking $\hat{k} = \hat{z} = \hat{k}$ in T7).

T6, however, requires a bit more elaboration. Its label was chosen because it implies (and is implied by) the productivity limitation that the (closure of the) set of timeless potential net outputs

$$N = \{(c, y) : y = z - k \text{ and } (c, z, k) \in T\} \tag{15}$$

does not contain any (c', y') such that both $c' \geq 0$ and $y' \geqq 0$. In other words, roughly speaking, T6 amounts to the assumption that the economy is not capable of replicating some capital stocks while simultaneously producing some consumption goods output. In Appendix A, we establish this equivalency and present two alternative conditions on technology: one involving substitution properties of outputs and the other productivity properties of exhaustible resource inputs – which entail T6 (and which are more interpretable, if more restrictive).

In any case, for the class of growth models where the technology satisfies these two assumptions (as well as our other maintained assumptions), we have a slightly generalized version of what might (from our present perspective) be viewed as the central result in (Majumdar et al., 1976):

CONSUMPTION-VALUE MAXIMIZATION. Suppose T satisfies T6 and T7. If a feasible growth path is efficient, then it has an associated competitive price system (4) at which consumption value is maximized

$$\infty > \sum_{t=0}^{\infty} p_t \cdot c_t^* \geqq \sum_{t=0}^{\infty} p_t \cdot c_t, \tag{16}$$

among all feasible growth paths (Equation (2)). The converse obtains provided consumption goods prices are positive $p_t > 0$ for $t \geqq 0$.

Proof. We now interpret the quantity sequence x as simply net final outputs

$$x = (\bar{k} - k_0, c_0, z_0 - k_1, \ldots, c_t, z_t - k_{t+1}, \ldots), \tag{17}$$

but the price sequence π and set X as before in Equations (9) and (10), respectively. ■

The crucial steps in the proof are first (summability) establishing that by virtue of T6,

$$\sum_{t=0}^{\infty} \sum_{i=1}^{m} c_{it} < \infty \tag{18}$$

for every solution to Equation (2), so that the set X contains every sequence of net final outputs that is generated by a feasible growth path, and second (anteriority) establishing that by virtue of T7, the set X is uniformly "productive." The remainder of the argument then simply consists in applying and interpreting the support theorem for l_1.

To see that Equation (18) follows from T6, we use the stationary feasible price system (p, q) to evaluate the whole stream of consumption goods produced along an arbitrary feasible growth path:

$$\begin{aligned}\sum_{t=0}^{t} \sum_{i=1}^{m} ((\min_{i'}\{p_i\}) c_{it}) &\leqq \sum_{t=0}^{t} p \cdot c_t = \sum_{t=0}^{t} (p \cdot c_t + q\,(z_t - k_{t+1})) \\ &= \sum_{t=0}^{t} (p \cdot c_t + q \cdot z_t - q \cdot k_t) + q \cdot \bar{k} - q \cdot k_{t+1} \\ &\leqq q \cdot \bar{k} \quad \text{for} \quad t \geqq 0\end{aligned}$$

An immediate consequence of this value-bound is

$$\sum_{t=0}^{t} \sum_{i=1}^{m} c_{it} \leqq q\,\bar{k} \Big/ \min_{i}\{p_i\} < \infty \quad \text{for} \quad t \geqq 0,$$

and hence Equation (18).

To see that uniform "productivity" follows from T7 (given our maintained assumptions about initial capital stocks and technology), note first that T5 implies that (i) there exists $(\bar{c}', \bar{z}') > 0$ such that $(\bar{c}', \bar{z}', \bar{k}) \in T$ and (ii) $(\hat{c}', \hat{z}') > 0$ such that $(\hat{c}', \hat{z}', \hat{z}) \in T$. Hence, the following quantity sequences $x \in X$ are generated by the corresponding growth paths $(c_s, z_s, k_s) \in T$ for $s \geqq 0$:

$$
\begin{aligned}
x &= (\bar{k},0,\ldots) && \text{when } (c_s,z_s,k_s) = 0 \quad \text{for } s \geqq 0 \\
&= (0,\bar{c}',\bar{z}',0,\ldots) && = \begin{cases} (\bar{c}',\bar{z}',\bar{k}) & \text{for } s=0 \\ 0 & \text{for } s \geqq 1 \end{cases} \\
&= (k-\hat{k},0,0,\hat{c}',\hat{z}',0,\ldots) && = \begin{cases} (0,\hat{z},\hat{k}) & \text{for } s=0 \\ (\hat{c}',\hat{z}',\hat{z}) & \text{for } s=1 \\ 0 & \text{for } s \geqq 2 \end{cases} \\
&(k-\hat{k},0,\ldots,0,\hat{c}',\hat{z}',0,\ldots) && = \begin{cases} (0,\hat{k},\hat{k}) & \text{for } 0 \leqq s \leqq t-2 \\ (0,\hat{z},\hat{k}) & \text{for } s=t-1 \\ (\hat{c}',\hat{z}',\hat{z}) & \text{for } s=t \\ 0 & \text{for } s \geqq t+1 \end{cases}
\end{aligned}
$$

for $t \geqq 2$. By letting

$$\delta = \min\left\{ \min_j \bar{k}_j, \min_i \bar{c}_i', \min_j \bar{z}_j', \min_i \hat{c}_i', \min_j \hat{z}_j \right\},$$

we see that these, in turn, provide the requisite quantity sequences $x^t \in X$ for $t \geqq 0$.

As in the last section, it is again relatively straightforward to establish that $X \subset l_1$ is closed, convex, and freely disposable. Moreover, again letting the quantity sequence x^* be generated by the efficient growth path under scrutiny, x^* is still a boundary point of X. Hence, the desired conclusion follows directly upon application of the support theorem for l_1 since Equation (1) implies Equation (4) when $(c_s, z_s, k_s) = (c, z, k) \in T$ for $s = t$ and $(c_s, z_s, k_s) = (c_s^*, z_s^*, k_s^*)$ for $s \neq t$, and Equation (16) when $k_0 = \bar{k}$, and $(c_t, z_t, k_t) \in T$ and $k_{t+1} = z_t$ for $t \geqq 0$. □

It is worth emphasizing here, although we establish a stronger result in the next section, that capital-value transversality also follows from the argument just given. That is, by taking the quantity sequence $x \in X$ generated by the trivial growth path $(c_t, z_t, k_t) = 0 \in T$ for $t \geqq 0$, Equation (1) yields

$$\sum_{t=0}^{\infty} p_t \cdot c_t^* \geqq q_{-1} \cdot \bar{k}.$$

Putting this inequality together with Equation (6), we see immediately that it must be true that

$$\lim_{t \to \infty} q_t\, k_{t+1}^* = 0. \tag{19}$$

It is also important to be aware of what the consumption-value maximization theorem does *not* claim: Namely, the theorem only asserts that *some* associated competitive price system exhibits the property of consumption-value maximization. And it is easy to construct examples where a particular efficient growth path also has an associated competitive price system that does not exhibit this property. The extended example presented in Appendix B is designed in part to illustrate this point. (For a more detailed elaboration in the context of closed multisector models, see the examples and results in Mitra and Majumdar, 1976.) That extended example also illustrates another obvious but important point, that without T6 (or, more generally, without summability in "natural" units of measurement), an efficient growth path may or may not have an associated competitive price system exhibiting consumption-value maximization (even though in our general model consumption-value is necessarily bounded).

6. Optimality (or Consumption-Value Maximization) and Capital-Value Transversality

Given nonnegative, nontrivial values for consumption goods

$$(\bar{p}_0, \bar{p}_1, \ldots) \geq 0, \tag{20}$$

a particular feasible growth path (denoted once more by asterisks) is *optimal* if

$$\infty > \sum_{t=0}^{\infty} \bar{p}_t \cdot c_t^* \geqq \sum_{t=0}^{\infty} \bar{p}_t \cdot c_t \tag{21}$$

for every feasible growth path (Equation (2)). In the literature on optimal growth theory, it is usually assumed that consumption goods output consists of a single quantity (i.e., that $m = 1$), which is measured in welfare or utility terms (refer again to Footnote 3), and that consumption good values are constant-rate discount factors (i.e., $\bar{p}_t = (1+\rho)^{-t}$ for $t \geqq 0$ with $\rho \geqq 0$). Neither specialization is fundamental to the price characterization of optimal growth paths (though both have been central to the detailed description of their evolution).

In this section, we use the support theorem for l_0 to develop a short, simple proof of the following important proposition:

CAPITAL-VALUE TRANSVERSALITY (Peleg and Weitzman). If a particular feasible growth path is optimal, then it has an associated competitive price system (Equation (4)) such that

$$p_t = \bar{p}_t \quad \text{for} \quad t \geqq 0 \tag{22}$$

and

$$\lim_{t \to \infty} q_t \cdot k_{t+1}^* = 0. \tag{19}$$

The converse obtains without qualification.

Proof. For the purposes of this argument, we interpret the quantity sequence x as net final outputs of welfare and investment goods

$$x = \left(\sum_{t=0}^{\infty} \bar{p}_t \cdot c_t, \bar{k} - k_0,\ z_0 - k_1, \ldots, z_t - k_{t+1}, \ldots \right), \tag{23}$$

the corresponding price sequence π as

$$\pi = (u, q_{-1}, q_0, \ldots, q_t, \ldots), \tag{24}$$

and the set X as

$$X = \left\{ x : x \in l_1, x_0 \leqq \sum_{t=0}^{\infty} \bar{p}_t\, c'_t \text{ and } \{c'_t, z_t, k_t\} \in T \text{ for } t \geqq 0 \right\}. \tag{25}$$

It is easily checked that the quantity sequence

$$\begin{aligned} x^* &= \left(\sum_{t=0}^{\infty} \bar{p}_t\, c^*_t, \bar{k} - k^*_0, z^*_0 - k^*_1, \ldots, z^*_t - k^*_{t+1}, \ldots \right) \\ &= \left(\sum_{t=0}^{\infty} \bar{p}_t\, c^*_t, 0, 0, \ldots \right) \end{aligned} \tag{26}$$

generated by the optimal growth path is not an internal point of X, since otherwise there would be some quantity sequence $x' \in X$ such that $x'_0 > x^*_0$ and $x'_t = 0$ for $t > 0$ corresponding to a feasible growth path yielding higher welfare. Also, the set X contains every quantity sequence generated by a feasible growth path, since then $0 \leqq x \leqq x^*$. Finally, it is quite straightforward to verify that $X \subset l_0$ is convex, freely disposable, and "productive."[10] Hence, now utilizing the support theorem for l_0 to derive Equation (1), we can infer

1. Nontrivial welfare value, that is, $u > 0$ or, without loss of generality, $u = 1$: Suppose otherwise, that is, $u = 0$. Then $\pi x^* = 0$, while – since $\pi_t > 0$ and $x^t \in X$ for some $t \geqq 0$ – $\pi\ x > 0$ for some $x \in X$, contradicting Equation (1).
2. Intertemporal welfare-profit maximization, that is, Equations (4) and (22): For the quantity sequences generated by the growth paths (c_s, z_s,

[10] The last claim is based on two implications of the maintained assumptions $\bar{k} > 0$ and T5, first (by virtue of the hypothesis $(\bar{p}_0, \bar{p}_1, \ldots) \geq 0$), that $x^0 = x^*$ works, and second, that the economy is capable of producing positive investment goods output in any given period, that is, that x^t for $1 \leqq\ t\ \leqq n$ can be generated by the trivial growth path, while x^t for $t \geqq n+1$ can be generated by a growth path involving only pure capital accumulation up through period t.

$k_s) = (c, z, k) \in T$ for $s = t$ and $(c_s, z_s, k_s) = (c_s^*, z_s^*, k_s^*)$ for $s \neq t$, Equation (1) yields

$$\bar{p}_t \cdot c + q_t \cdot z - q_{t-1} \cdot k_t \leqq \bar{p}_t \cdot c_t^* + q_t \cdot z_t^* - q_{t-1} \cdot k_t^* = 0$$
for every $(c, z, k) \in T$ and $t \geqq 0$;

in light of 1 above.

3. Capital-value transversality, that is, Equation (19): The argument is identical to that presented toward the end of the last section, in light of 2 above. ■

There is an interesting, if hardly surprising, corollary to the capital-value transversality theorem.

DUALITY. If there exists an optimal solution to the problem

$$\text{maximize} \sum_{t=0}^{\infty} \bar{p}_t \cdot c_t \quad \text{subject to Equation (2),} \tag{27}$$

then there exists an optimal solution to the problem

$$\text{minimize } q_{-1} \cdot \bar{k} \quad \text{subject to Equation (3) and} \quad p_t = \bar{p}_t \quad \text{for t} \geq 0, \tag{28}$$

and their optimal values are equal.

Proof. On the one hand, we see from Equation (5) that feasible solutions to Equations (27) and (28) must satisfy

$$\sum_{t=0}^{\infty} \bar{p}_t \cdot c_t \leqq q_{-1} \cdot \bar{k}.$$

On the other hand, appealing to the theorem just proved, we see from Equation (6) that there is a feasible solution to Equation (28) (namely, that associated with the optimal solution to Equation (27)) that satisfies

$$\sum_{t=0}^{\infty} \bar{p}_t c_t^* = q_{-1} \bar{k}.$$

But this is then an optimal solution to Equation (28) exhibiting the asserted duality property. ■

We note in passing that many of the recent results concerning global stability of optimal growth paths have their ultimate basis in the capital-value transversality theorem (in particular, see Cass and Shell, 1976 and related contributions to the same symposium).

7. Complications from Primary Factors

The general growth model introduced in Section 3 has one very unrealistic feature; it implicitly rules out the existence of primary factors. In this section we repair this defect, and in doing so establish that all but one of the foregoing results remain virtually unaffected.

Suppose now that the feasible growth paths in the economy are described by

$$\begin{cases} (c_t, z_t, k_t, l_t) \in T', \quad k_{t+1} = z_t \quad \text{and} \quad l_t = \bar{l}_t = \bar{l} > 0 \quad \text{for} \quad t \geqq 0, \\ k_0 = \bar{k} > 0 \end{cases} \tag{2'}$$

where $\boldsymbol{l} = (l_1, l_2, \ldots, l_h)$ is an h-vector of primary factor inputs, $\bar{\boldsymbol{l}}$ is an h-vector of their exogenous supply, and $T' = \{(c, z, k, l)\}$ is the static technology available for producing outputs from capital stock and primary factor inputs. In fact, there is no real loss of generality in assuming that $h = 1$ and that $\bar{l} = 1$, which we henceforth will.[11] Furthermore, we will assume that T' is again a nonnegative, closed set exhibiting properties analogous to T1–T5:

- T′1 T' is convex
- T′2 If $(c, z, k, l) \in T'$, $0 \leqq (c', z') \leqq (c, z)$, and $(k', l') \geqq (k, l)$, then $(c', z', k', l') \in T'$
- T′3 T' is a cone
- T′4 If $(c, z, k, l) \in T'$ and $(k, l) = 0$, then $(c, z) = 0$
- T′5 If $(c, z, k, l) \in T'$, $l > 0$, and $k' > k$, then there exists $(c', z') > (c, z)$ such that $(c', z', k', l) \in T'$

Notice that now $T'3$ is completely innocuous, since feasible growth paths only involve the projection of a particular cross section of T' (namely, the convex set $\{(c, z, k) : (c, z, k, l) \in T')\}$), and any such convex set can be viewed as the projection of a particular cross section of a convex cone in 1 higher dimension. It is also worth mentioning that T′5 is equivalent – given our other maintained assumptions (especially T′1–T′3) – to a seemingly alternative productivity characteristic quite commonly encountered in the capital theory literature since Malinvaud's corrigendum (Malinvaud, 1953).

[11] The former assertion follows from the observation that the structure of the set $\{(c, z, k) : (c, z, k, \bar{l}) \in T\}$ contains all the information we need to know about the structure of T' itself, and that this set can be equally well viewed as the projection of a cross-section from 1 higher dimension as from h higher dimensions (see also the comment concerning $T'3$ below). The latter assertion follows from the observation that setting $\bar{l} = 1$ amounts to defining the unit for measuring the primary factor.

T′5′ NONTIGHTNESS IN CAPITAL STOCKS. If $(c, z, k, l) \in T'$ and $l > 0$, then there exists $(c'', z'') > (c, z)$, $k'' \geqq 0$, and $0 \leqq l'' < l$ such that $(c'', z'', k'', l'') \in T''$.[12]

(See, e.g., the analysis centered around this and other productivity and substitution properties in Kurz, 1969.)

On the price side of the economy, the description of "feasible" price systems corresponding to Equation (2′) is

$$\begin{cases} (p_t, q_t, r_t, w_t) \in M' \quad \text{and} \quad r_t = q_{t-1} \quad \text{for} \quad t \geqq 0, \\ q_{-1} \geqq 0 \end{cases} \tag{3'}$$

where w is a scalar, say, wage and

$$M' = \{(p, q, r, w) : (p, q) \geqq 0 \text{ and } p \cdot c + q \cdot z - r \cdot k - w \cdot l \leqq 0$$
$$\text{for every } (c, z, k, l) \in T'\}$$

is the nonnegative subset of the dual cone to T'. Hence, an associated competitive price system is now defined as a nontrivial solution to Equation (3′) such that

$$p_t \cdot c + q_t \cdot z - q_{t-1} \cdot k - w_t \cdot l \leqq p_t \cdot c_t^* + q_t \cdot z_t^* - q_{t-1} \cdot k_t^* - w_t = 0 \tag{4'}$$

for every $(c, z, k, l) \in T'$ and $t \geqq 0$.

Given this amendment to our general growth model, by and large the only modifications needed in order to validate our previous analysis involve accounting for wage payments to the primary factor. Two such modifications are essential:

1. In the first place, in order for the conclusion of the support theorems (1) to yield competitive price systems (Equation (4′)), in each previous application we must reinterpret the quantity sequence x to include net final outputs of primary factors $1 - l_t$ for $t \geqq 0$, and the price sequence π to include a corresponding wage imputation w_t for $t \geqq 0$.[13] Thus, for

[12] To go from T′5 to T′5 take

$$(c'', z'', k'', l'') = \alpha(c', z', k, l) \quad \text{for some} \quad 0 < \alpha < 1 \text{ such that } \alpha(c', z') > (c, z),$$
$$\text{and from T}'5 \text{ to T}'5$$
$$(c', z') = (1 - \beta)(c, z) + \beta(c'', z'') \quad \text{for some} \quad 0 < \beta < 1 \text{ such that}$$
$$(1 - \beta)k + \beta k'' \leqq k \text{ [and hence } (1 - \beta)l + \beta l'' < l].$$

[13] An alternative method of achieving the same result is simply to reinterpret the technology $T = \{(c, z, k): (c, z, k, l) \in T'\}$ and define the imputation $w_t = p_t c_t^* - q_t z_t^* - q_{t-1} \cdot k_t^*$. Then Equation (4′) follows from the left-hand inequality in Equation (4) – which is demonstrable without reference to T3 – by virtue of T′2 and T′3. However, while this maneuver does reflect the intrinsic economics of

example, in the argument establishing consumption-value maximization, the quantity sequence (Equation (17)) becomes

$$x = (\bar{k} - k_0, c_0, z_0 - k_1, 1 - l_0, \ldots, c_t, z_t - k_{t+1}, 1 - l_t \ldots), \tag{17'}$$

while the price sequence (Equation (9)) becomes

$$\pi = (q_{-1}, p_0, q_0, w_0, \ldots, p_t, q_t, w_t, \ldots) \tag{9'}$$

and the set (Equation (10)) becomes

$$x = \{x : x \in l_1, c_t \leqq c_t', \quad \text{and} \quad (c_t', z_t, k_t, l_t) \in T' \quad \text{for} \quad t \geqq 0\}. \tag{10'}$$

2. In the second place, in calculating bounds for consumption value, we must include an imputation to the stream of primary factors $\bar{l}_t = 1$ for $t \geqq 0$, as well as initial capital stocks $\bar{k}$. Thus, for example, the upper bounds (Equations (5) and (6)) become, respectively,

$$\sum_{t=0}^{t} p_t \cdot c_t \leqq \sum_{t=0}^{t} p_t \cdot c_t + q_t \cdot k_{t+1} \leqq q_{-1} \cdot \bar{k} + \sum_{t=0}^{t} w_t \quad \text{for} \quad t \geqq 0 \tag{5'}$$

for every feasible growth path (Equation (2')) and[14]

$$\sum_{t=0}^{t} p_t \cdot c_t^* \leqq \sum_{t=0}^{t} p_t \cdot c_t^* + q_t \cdot k_{t+1}^* = q_{-1} \cdot \bar{k} + \sum_{t=0}^{t} w_t \quad \text{for} \quad t \geqq 0. \tag{6'}$$

The fact that, in general, we cannot rule out an unbounded imputation

$$q_{-1} \cdot \bar{k} + \sum_{t=0}^{\infty} w_t = q_{-1} \cdot \bar{k} + \lim_{t \to \infty} \sum_{t=0}^{t} w_t = \infty$$

has several important consequences, both analytical and conceptual:

(a) The corollaries to the price characterization theorem (itself modified to include a term $\sum_{t=0}^{\infty} w_t(1 - l_t)$ on the right-hand side of Equation (11) and a term $\sum_{t=0}^{\infty} |1 - l_t|$ on the left-hand side of the inequality restricting comparison paths) must be restated in terms of deviations in

residual payment to a fixed factor, unlike the argument sketched in the text, it does not yield any additional information about value maximization (see the following discussion).

[14] Similarly, in the duality corollary to the capital-value transversality theorem, the dual problem (28) becomes

$$\text{minimize} \quad q_{-1} \cdot \bar{k} + \sum_{t=0}^{\infty} w_t \quad \text{subject to (3') and} \quad p_t = \bar{p}_t \quad \text{for} \quad t \geqq 0 \tag{28}$$

consumption value $\sum_{t=0}^{\infty}p_t(c_t - c_t^*)$ ($= 0$ when $c_t = c_t^*$ for $t \geqq 0$), rather than in terms of simple consumption value $\sum_{t=0}^{\infty}p_t\, c_t(= \sum_{t=0}^{\infty}p_t \cdot c_t^*$ when $c_t = c_t^*$ for $t \geqq 0$).

(b) The argument at the end of Section 5 establishing capital-value transversality must be altered to accommodate the fact that with the reinterpretation (Equation (17′)), the trivial growth path $(c_t, z_t, k_t, l_t) = 0 \in T$ for $t \geqq 0$ no longer generates a quantity sequence in X (since, by definition, the totality of primary factors is unbounded). This is easily accomplished once we observe that the "almost" trivial growth paths $(c_t, z_t, k_t, l_t) = 0 \in T$ for $0 \leqq t \leqq \ell$ and $(c_t, z_t, k_t, l_t) = (0, 0, 0, 1) \in T'$, for $\ell <$, for $\ell \geqq 0$ do generate quantity sequences in X. Hence, for these growth paths, Equation (1) yields

$$\infty > \sum_{t=0}^{\infty} p_t\, c_t^* \geqq q_{-1} \cdot \bar{k} + \sum_{t=0}^{\ell} w_t \quad \text{for} \quad \ell \geqq 0$$

or

$$\infty > \sum_{t=0}^{\infty} p_t \cdot c_t^* \geqq q_{-1}\bar{k} + \sum_{t=0}^{\infty} w_t.$$

In conjunction with Equation (6′), this inequality immediately entails capital-value transversality Equation (19).

(c) The suitability of consumption-value maximization (at given consumption goods values) as the fundamental notion of optimality must be reappraised since it may simply be overly restrictive (as it is, e.g., in the canonical one-good model, where the golden rule path does not yield maximum consumption value at *any* given consumption goods values).[15] Anything like a complete resolution of this issue is way beyond the scope of our paper – if not beyond the limit of our ability. However, we will

[15] Here, of course, we are implicitly accepting the common convention that a maximum must be finite. This makes good sense in this instance since otherwise consumption-value maximization may be essentially vacuous (as it is, e.g., again in the canonical one-good model, with any given consumption goods values such that $\inf_{s \geqq 0}\bar{p}_{t_s} > 0$ for some subsequence of periods $\{t_s\}$).

The example in Appendix B shows that even without primary factors, the notion of consumption-value maximization may be too limiting. Indeed, generally speaking, in order that the problem (27), or better yet, the problem

$$\text{maximize} \quad \sum_{t=0}^{\infty} \bar{p}_t \quad c_t \quad \text{subject to (2′)} \tag{27′}$$

has a solution, the permissible choice of consumption goods values (Equation (20)) will typically exclude perfectly acceptable growth paths (i.e., some efficient growth paths) from serious consideration. (In this sense, the class of growth models considered in Section 5 appears to be quite special.)

briefly discuss one directly pertinent aspect – the variety of similar but broader alternatives and their respective price characterizations – in the following section.

There is a second point in the foregoing analysis at which the introduction of primary factors raises a serious substantive issue. This is in Section 5, where we employed T6 to guarantee summability of the whole stream of consumption goods. While it is true that an appropriate analog

T′6 There exist $p > 0$ and $q \geqq 0$ such that

$$p \cdot c + q \cdot z - q \cdot k \leqq 0 \quad \text{for every} \quad (c, z, k, l) \in T'$$

also implies

$$\sum_{t=0}^{\infty} \sum_{i=1}^{m} c_{it} < \infty \tag{18'}$$

for every solution to Equation (2′), this sort of productivity characteristic may now appear – at least to one steeped in the tradition of neoclassical growth theory – to be quite restrictive. In particular, since T′6 is easily shown to be equivalent to condition A1 in Appendix A,[16] it automatically excludes the possibility of nontrivial (modified) golden rule paths. But while this may be analytically inconvenient, it is surely not intuitively implausible; the mere availability of primary factors may just not be enough to offset the scarcity of essential exhaustible resources. One precise formulation of this latter intuition is outlined in the last comment in Appendix A.

8. Alternative Notions of Optimality

In order to circumvent the limitations of consumption-value maximization as a procedure for choosing a "best" efficient growth path, a number of related but weaker criteria have been proposed in the literature (von Weizsäcker, 1965; Gale, 1967; Block, 1970; Cass and Yaari, 1971; McKenzie, 1976; Peleg and Zilcha, 1977). For our purposes here it is useful to incorporate these in a more systematic listing of candidates, all of which involve evaluating the whole stream of consumption goods at given values (Equation (20)). In rank order of decreasing strength (i.e., so each entails its

[16] Obviously, after N is redefined to be compatible with T'

$$N = \{(c, y) : y = z - k \text{ and } (c, z, k, l) \in T' \text{ for some } l \geqq 0\} \tag{15'}$$

Then the proof of this equivalency is identical to that of Lemma 1A (Appendix A) but for the substitution of (c^s, z^s, k^s, l^s) for (c^s, z^s, k^s), (c, z, k, l) for (c, z, k), and T' for T'.

successor), one could reasonably judge a particular feasible growth path (denoted, for the last time, by asterisks) to be "optimal" according to whether it exhibits

1. *Consumption-value maximization* $\infty > \sum_{t=0}^{\infty} \bar{p}_t \cdot c_t^* \geqq \sum_{t=0}^{\infty} \bar{p}_t \cdot c_t$ for every feasible growth path Equation (2′);
2. *Deviations in consumption-value maximization (or best deviations in consumption value)* $0 \geqq \lim_{\ell \to \infty} \sum_{t=0}^{\ell} \bar{p}_t \cdot (c_t - c_t^*)$ for every feasible growth path (Equation (2′));
3. *Better deviations in consumption value* $0 \geqq \lim \ \sup_{\ell \to \infty} \sum_{t=0}^{\ell} \bar{p}_t (c_t - c_t^*)$ for every feasible growth path Equation (2′);
4. *Good deviations in consumption value* $0 \geqq \lim \ \inf_{\ell \to \infty} \sum_{t=0}^{\ell} \bar{p}_t (c_t - c_t^*)$ for every feasible growth path (Equation (2′));
5. *Restricted deviations in consumption-value maximization* $0 \geqq \sum_{t=0}^{\infty} \bar{p}_t (c_t - c_t^*)$ for every feasible growth path (Equation (2′)) such that $\sum_{t=0}^{\infty} \sum_{i=1}^{m} u_{it} |c_{it} - c_{it}^*| < \infty$; or (only when $\sum_{t=0}^{\infty} \bar{p}_t \, c_t^* < \infty$); or
6. *Restricted consumption-value maximization* $\infty > \sum_{t=0}^{\infty} \bar{p}_t \, c_t^* \geqq \sum_{t=0}^{\infty} \bar{p}_t \cdot c_t$ for every feasible growth path Equation (2′) such that $\sum_{t=0}^{\infty} \sum_{i=1}^{m} u_{it} |c_{it} - c_{it}^*| < \infty$

where, in criteria 5 and 6, $u_{it} \geqq \bar{p}_{it}$ for $1 \leqq i \leqq m$, $t \geqq 0$ are some (fixed) positive units for measuring consumption goods outputs. Since we know that efficient growth paths are "optimal" in the sense of criterion 5 with primary factors (or in the sense of criterion 6 without, both at associated consumption goods prices), it is quite natural to focus on this criterion in generalizing the capital-value transversality theorem of Section 6; similar results can be obtained in exactly the same manner for criteria 2 and 4, but not for criterion 3 (since the lim sup operation does not preserve convexity).

Before we can derive a specific price characterization, however, we will require one additional assumption concerning the possibility of substituting investment goods output for consumption goods output:

I′8 ACCUMULATION FROM FOREGONE CONSUMPTION. If $(c, z, k, l) \in T'$ and $0 \leqq c' \leqq c$, then there exists $z' > z$ such that $(c', z', k, l) \in T'$.[17]

Thus aimed – and fortified by preceding applications of the support theorems – it is almost routine to establish the following general result:

[17] The specific counterexample detailed at the end of Appendix B clearly shows that for the purpose of characterizing weaker notions of optimality than consumption-value maximization, something like this substitution condition cannot be dispensed with. Presently the assumptions $\bar{k} > 0$, $\bar{l}_t = 1$ for $t \geqq 0$, T′5, and T′8 play (and previously, in Section 6, the assumptions $\bar{k} > 0$ and T5 played) precisely the same role as does Slater's condition (or, more generally, some version of "constraint qualification") in ordinary concave programming.

PRICE CHARACTERIZATION OF "OPTIMAL" GROWTH PATHS. Suppose T' satisfies T′8. If a particular feasible growth path is "optimal" in the sense of criterion 5, then it has an associated competitive price system (Equation (4′)) such that

$$p_t = \bar{p}_t \quad \text{for} \quad t \geqq 0 \tag{22}$$

and

$$0 \geqq \sum_{t=0}^{\infty} \bar{p}_t \cdot (c_t - c_t^*) - q_{-1}(k - \bar{k}) \tag{29}$$

for every growth path that (i) is feasible from nonnegative capital stocks, or satisfies Equation (2′) with $\bar{k} = k \geqq 0$, and (ii) yields sufficiently small deviations in consumption, or satisfies

$$\sum_{t=0}^{\infty} \sum_{i=1}^{m} u_{it} |c_{it} - c_{it}^*| < \infty.$$

The converse obtains without qualification.

Remark. Property (29) is only one way of expressing the fact that the associated capital goods prices reflect their marginal "welfare" value. A more complete catalog, along with a more leisurely discussion, can be found in Cass.

Proof. We will only sketch the essential similarities and differences between this and previous arguments. Here the quantity sequence x is interpreted as net final outputs of "welfare," investment goods, and primary factors

$$x = \left(\sum_{t=0}^{\infty} \bar{p}_t (c_t - c_t^*), \bar{k} - k_0, z_0 - k_1, 1 - l_0, \ldots, z_t - k_{t+1}, 1 - l_t, \ldots \right), \tag{30}$$

the corresponding price sequence π as

$$\pi = (u, q_{-1}, q_0, w_0, \ldots, q_t, w_t, \ldots), \tag{31}$$

and the set X as further constrained by the restriction on permissible deviations in consumption

$$X = \left\{ x : x \in l_0, x_0 \leqq \sum_{t=0}^{\infty} \bar{p}_t (c_t' - c_t^*), \right.$$
$$\left. \sum_{t=0}^{\infty} \sum_{i=1}^{m} u_{it} |c_{it}' - c_{it}^*| < \infty \text{ and } (c_t', z_t, k_t, l_t) \in T' \text{ for } t \geqq 0 \right\}. \tag{32}$$

As with the proof of capital-value transversality, it is quite easily seen that $x^* = 0$ is not an internal point of X, and that $X \subset l_0$ is convex, freely disposable but now – rather than "productive" – productive, in the following sense: There exists $x'_0 \leqq 0$ such that for every $t > 0$ there exists $x^t \in X$ such that $x^t_0 \geqq x'_0$, $x^t_s > 0$ for $s = t$ and $x^t_s \geqq 0$ for $0 < s \neq t$.[18] Thus, we can once more utilize the support theorem for l_0 to deduce Equation (1). Then, the same reasoning employed in Section 6 yields, without loss of generality, $u = 1$, as well as Equations (4) and (22), Finally, Equation (29) simply follows by specializing Equation (1) to comparisons with quantity sequences generated by growth paths satisfying the requisite restrictions. ■

Our interest in investigating this kind of characterization was greatly inspired by the careful and comprehensive work of Peleg (1974) and Peleg and Zilcha (1977) relating to the open, multisector model. It would be nice, if possible, to elaborate the connection between the seemingly different productivity and substitution properties underlying their and our quite similar results.

Acknowledgments

The paper was completed during Cass' tenure as a Sherman Fairchild Distinguished Scholar at Caltech. Also, both of us received grants from the NSF during the course of the research reported on. We are grateful to both institutions for their support and encouragement.

Our ideas themselves have benefited from comments by and conversations with many of our colleague theorists, but particularly the participants – including Lionel himself – in the MSSB seminars on dynamical systems in economics. We would especially like to thank Tapan Mitra, who was, perhaps not coincidentally, Lionel's student. His collaboration with each of us has resulted in deeper understanding of the basic issues raised in the paper (to say nothing of his specific contribution to the insights underlying the extended example worked out at the very end of the paper).

[18] Because of T′5 (given $\bar{k} > 0$ and $\bar{l}_t = 1$ for $t \geqq 0$) and (20) we know that $c^*_t \geq 0$ for some $t \geqq 0$. Suppose that $c^*_s = 0$ for $0 \leqq s < t^* < \infty$ and $c^*_{t*} \geq 0$. Appealing to T′8, pick $0 \leqq c' \leq c^*_{t*}$ and $z' > z^*_{t*}$ such that $(c', z', k^*_{t*}, 1) \in T'$ Then the growth path $(c_s, z_s, k_s, l_s) = \alpha(c^*_s, z^*_s, k^*_s, l^*_s) + (1 - \alpha)(0, 0, 0, 1)$ for $0 \leqq s < t^*$, $(c_s, z_s, k_s, l_s) = \alpha(c', z', k^*_s, 1) + (1 - \alpha)(0, 0, 0, 1)$ for $s = t^*$, $(c_s, z_s, k_s, l_s) = (c^*_s, z^*_s, \alpha z', 1)$ for $s = t^* + 1$, and $(c_s, z_s, k_s, l_s) = (c^*_s, z^*_s, k^*_s, l^*_s)$ for $s > t^* + 1$ is feasible from initial capital stocks $0 \leqq \alpha k^*_0 < \bar{k}$ provided only that $0 < \alpha < 1$ and $\alpha z \geqq z^*_{t*}$. Now appealing to T′5, these "surplus" initial capital stocks $\bar{k} - \alpha k^*_0 > 0$ can be used to generate growth paths that yield excess investment goods output $z_t - k_{t+1} > 0$ or excess primary factor input $1 - l_t > 0$ in any given period t. These paths, in turn, generate the requisite quantity sequences x^t for $t > 0$.

Appendix A.

In this appendix, we establish equivalency between T6 and the productivity condition, defining $\bar{N}$ = closure of N (see Equation (15)),

A1 There is no $(c, y) \in \bar{N}$ such that $c \geq 0$ and $y \geqq 0$, and sufficiency for T6 of either the substitution condition.

A2 UNIFORM SUBSTITUTION BETWEEN OUTPUT OF EACH CONSUMPTION GOOD AND OUTPUT OF ALL INVESTMENT GOODS. For every $1 \leqq i \leqq m$ and $\varepsilon_i > 0$ there is a $\delta_i > 0$ such that if $(c, z, k) \in T$ and $c_i \geqq \varepsilon_i$, then $(c', z', k') \in T$ for $c' = c - (0, \ldots, \varepsilon_i, \ldots, 0)$ and $z' = z + \delta_i(1, 1, \ldots, 1)$,
or the productivity condition, assuming that capital stock of type 1 is an exhaustible resource (see Footnote 5).

A3 STRICT DETERIORATION OF CAPITAL STOCKS WITHOUT EXHAUSTIBLE RESOURCES. If $(c, z, k) \in T$, $z_1 = k_1 = 0$ and $(c, z, k) \neq 0$, then $z_j < k_j$ for some $2 \leqq j \leqq n$.

Lemma 1A. T6 obtains if and only if A1 does.

Proof. Necessity: Given T6, suppose that A1 were false, that is, there is $(c', y') \in \bar{N}$ such that $c' \geq 0$ and $y' \geqq 0$. Then (i) there is a sequence $\{(c^s, y^s)\}$ such that $(c^s, y^s) \in N$ and $\lim_{s\to\infty}(c^s, y^s) = (c', y')$ with a corresponding sequence $\{(c^s, z^s, k^s)\}$ such that $(c^s, z^s\ k^s) \in T$ and $y^s = z^s - k^s$, while (ii) $p \cdot c' + q\ y' \geqq p \cdot c' > 0$ Hence, for sufficiently large s,

$$(c^s, z^s, k^s) \in T \quad \text{but} \quad p \cdot c^s + q \cdot z^s - q \cdot k^s = p \cdot c^s + q \cdot y^s > 0,$$

contradicting T6.

Sufficiency: We will use the easily verified fact that given our maintained assumptions on T, $\bar{N}$ is a closed, convex cone exhibiting free disposal in y (i.e., if $(c, y) \in \bar{N}$ and $y' \leqq y$, then $(c, y') \in \bar{N}$).

Given A1, let $0 \leqq n' \leqq n$ be such that if $1 \leqq j' \leqq n'$ $(n'+1 \leqq j' \leqq n)$, then there is no (some) $(c, y) \in \bar{N}$ such that $c = 0$ and $y_j > 0$ for $j = j'$, $y_j = 0$ for $j \neq j'$. Partitioning $y = (y^1, y^2)$ accordingly, consider the set

$$U = \{(c, y^1) : (c, y) \in \bar{N} \text{ and } y^2 = 0\}.$$

Since $\bar{N}$ is a closed, convex cone, so is U. Moreover, the hypothesis A1 together with the choice of n' implies that there is no $(c, y^1) \in U$ such that $(c, y^1) \geq 0$. Hence, appealing to a duality result characterizing 0 as a maximal point of a closed, convex cone (see Nikaido, 1968, pp. 35–36), we know that there exists $(p, q^1) > 0$ such that

$$(p, q^1)\ (c, y^1) \leqq \quad \text{for every} \quad (c, y^1) \in U. \tag{A.1}$$

Now consider the set

$$V = \{(x, y^2) : x \leqq (p, q^1) \cdot (c, y^1) \text{ and} (c, y) \in \bar{N}\}.$$

Since $\bar{N}$ is a convex cone exhibiting free disposal in y, V is a convex cone exhibiting free disposal (i.e., if $(x, y^2) \in V$ and $(x', y^{2\prime}) \leq (x, y^2)$, then $(x', y^{2\prime}) \in V$). Moreover, in light of A1, 0 must be a boundary point of V. Hence, using a standard support theorem (see again, e.g., Nikaido, 1968, p. 35), we know that there exists $(\lambda, q^2) \geq 0$ such that

$$\lambda x + q^2 \cdot y^2 \leqq 0 \quad \text{for every} \quad (x, y^2) \in V$$

or

$$\lambda(p, q^1)\ (c, y^1) + q^2 \cdot y^2 \leqq 0 \quad \text{for every} \quad (c, y) \in \bar{N}. \tag{A.2}$$

But without loss of generality $\lambda = 1$, since if $\lambda = 0$, then $q^2 \geq 0$ and, again by the choice of n', there is some $(0, (0, y^2)) \in \bar{N}$ such that $q^2 \cdot y^2 > 0$, contradicting A2. Hence, we have established that there exist $p > 0$ and $q = (q^1, q^2) \geqq 0$ such that

$$p \cdot c + q \cdot y \leqq 0 \quad \text{for every} \quad (c, y) \in \bar{N},$$

which implies the desired conclusion

$$p \cdot c + q\, z - q \cdot k \leqq 0 \quad \text{for every} \quad (c, z, k) \in T$$

(since $N \subset \bar{N}$). ■

It is worth mentioning explicitly that T5 requires that $q \geq 0$ in T6 (so that, e.g., our use of T6 in the text makes sense).

Lemma 2A. If A2 obtains, then so does T6.

Proof. For this argument, we require the result that the units for measuring investment goods output can be specified, consistent with our maintained assumptions together with T7, so that the following productivity limitation is satisfied.

A4 IMPOSSIBILITY OF SUSTAINED CAPITAL ACCUMULATION. There is no $(c, y) \in \bar{N}$ such that $c \geqq 0$ and $y > 0$.

Since this result is established in exactly the same fashion as the well-known result that the von Neumann growth rate in the closed, multisector model[19] can be specified equal to zero (see, in particular, the discussion and references in Majumdar et al., 1976), we omit the details of its proof.

[19] The closed multisector model is the specialization of our general model in which $m = n$ and $T = \{(c, z, y)$: $c + z = y$, $(c, z) \geqq 0$, and $(y, k) \in S\}$, where $S = \{(y, k)\}$ is the static technology for producing (undifferentiated) outputs from capital stock inputs.

What we will show explicitly, then, is that A2 and A4 imply A1 or, by virtue of Lemma 1A, T6: Given A2 and A4, suppose that A1 were false, that is, there is some $(c', y') \in \bar{N}$ such that $c' \geq 0$ and $y' \geqq 0$ (for definiteness assume $c'_i \geqq 0$ for $i \neq i'$), and hence, that there is a sequence $\{(c^s, y^s)\}$ such that $(c^s, y^s) \in N$ and $\lim_{s\to\infty}(c^s, y^s) = (c', y')$ with a corresponding sequence $\{(c^s, z^s, k^s)\}$ such that $(c^s, z^s, k^s) \in T$ and $y^s = z^s - k^s$. Then, there must be some $\varepsilon_t > 0$ such that, for sufficiently large $s, c_i^s \geqq \varepsilon_i$, and hence, by virtue of A2, some $\delta > 0$ such that, again for sufficiently large $s, (c^{s'}, z^{s'}, k^s) \in T$ or $(c^{s'}, y^{s'}) \in N$ for

$$c^{s} = c^s - (0, \ldots, \varepsilon_i, \ldots, 0), \quad z^{s} = z^s + \delta_i(1, 1, \ldots, 1),$$

and

$$y^{s'} = y^s + \delta_i(1, 1, \ldots, 1).$$

But this means that $\lim_{s\to\infty}(c^s, y^s) = (c' - (0, \ldots, \varepsilon_i, \ldots, 0), y' + \delta_i(1, 1, \ldots, 1)) \in \bar{N}$, contradicting A4 ■

Lemma 3A. If A3 obtains, then so does T6.

Proof. What we will show here is that when capital stock of type 1 is an exhaustible resource, A3 implies A1, and hence T6: Given A3, once again suppose that A1 were false, that is, that (as in the preceding proof). Because capital stock of type 1 is an exhaustible resource, we can also suppose that $z_1^s = 0$ and $y_1^s = k_1^s$ or $\lim_{s\to\infty} z_1^s = \lim_{s\to\infty} k_1^s = 0$ (since $\lim_{s\to\infty}(z_1^s - k_1^s) = \lim_{s\to\infty} y_1^s = y'_1 \geqq 0$). Now consider the sequence $\{x^s\}$ such that

$$x^s = (c^s, z^s, k^s)/||(c^s, z^s, k^s)|| \in T$$

(since T is homogeneous). By the Bolzano–Weierstrass theorem this sequence must have an accumulation point, say, $x = (c, z, k)$. But then $(c, z, k) \in T$ (since T is closed), $z_1 = k_1 = 0$ (since $\lim_{s\to\infty} z_1^s = \lim_{s\to\infty} k_1^s = 0$ but $\lim_{s\to\infty} c^s = c' \geq 0$), and $(c, z, k) \geq 0$ (since $||x^s|| = 1$), but $z_j \geqq k_j$ for all $2 \leqq j \leqq n$ (since $\lim_{s\to\infty}(z_j^s - k_j^s) = \lim_{s\to\infty} y_j^s = y'_j \geqq 0$), contradicting A3. ■

Several comments are pertinent to the foregoing results:

1. If T is polyhedral, then N is polyhedral, and $\bar{N} = N$ (see, e.g., Rockafellar, 1970, pp. 171 and 175). In this case (or, more generally, whenever $\bar{N} = N$), because we need to only consider single points in N and T rather than sequences of points in N and T, Lemma 1A immediately reveals that T6 is necessary as well as sufficient for summability. Moreover, for the same reason, Lemmas 2A and 3A remain true with some weakening of A2 and A3, respectively.

In particular, we can relax the uniformity requirement in A2 (to read "For every $1 \leqq i \leqq m$ and $\varepsilon_i > 0$ if $(c, z, k) \in T$ and $c_i \geqq \varepsilon_i$, then there is a $\delta_i > 0$ such that $(c', z', k) \in T \ldots$," so that $\ddot{a}_i$ can depend on (c, z, k) rather than just c_i) and the strictness requirement in A3 (to read "… then $c = 0$ or $z_j < k_j$ for some $2 \leqq j \leqq n$," so that $(0, k, k) \in T$ such that $k_j > 0$ for some $2 \leqq j \leqq n$ is permitted; see comment 4 below).

2. We can directly generalize A3 and Lemma 3A when capital stocks of type $1, 2, \ldots, n' \leqq n$ are exhaustible resources (by simply replacing z_1, k_1, and 2 with $z^1 = (z_1, z_2, \ldots, z_n)$, $k^1 = (k_1, k_2, \ldots, k_n)$, and $n'+1$, respectively). This sort of productivity condition seems to us a very natural way of modeling the most pessimistic (as well as most unimaginative) "limits of growth" prospect.
3. Neither A2 nor A3 is necessary for T6. This will be demonstrated shortly, in terms of the example we examine in the following appendix.
4. There are alternative substitution conditions that entail T6 when T7 is strengthened to

T7′ POSSIBILITY OF STORAGE WITHOUT SUSTENANCE. There exists $0 < \hat{k} \leqq \bar{k}$ such that $(0, \hat{k}, \hat{k}) \in T$.

For discussion and analysis of some such conditions in the context of the closed multisector model, we once more refer the interested reader to (Majumdar et al., 1976). Note, however, that while A3 is consistent with T7, it is not consistent with T7′.

5. When there are primary factors in the economy, analogs of neither A2 nor A3 are sufficient for T′6. However, if in addition to

A′3 If $(c, z, k, l) \in T'$, $z_1 = k_1 = 0$, and $k \neq 0$, then $z_j < k_j$ for some $2 \leqq j \leqq n$,

we have (some version of)

A′5 LIMITED PRODUCTIVITY OF PRIMARY FACTORS. If $(c, z, k, l) \in T'$ and $l' \geqq |k|$, then $(c, z, k, l') \in T'$,

then minor changes in the argument establishing Lemma 3A yield

Lemma 3′A. If A′3 and A′5 obtain, then so does T′6.

Proof. What we will show is that, when capital stock of type 1 is an exhaustible resource, A′3 and A′5 imply A1 and hence T′6: Given A′3 and A′5, suppose that A1 were false (i.e., as in the proof of Lemma 3A but with (c^s, z^s, k^s, l^s) and T' substituted for (c^s, z^s, k^s) and T, respectively).

As before we can also suppose that $\lim_{s\to\infty} z_1^s = \lim_{s\to\infty} k_1^s = 0$, while here A′5 enables us to suppose that $l^s = ||k^s||$. Now consider

$$x^s = (c^s, z^s, k^s, l^s)/||(c^s, z^s, k^s, l^s)|| \in T' \quad for \quad s \geqq 0$$

with accumulation point $x = (c, z, k, l)$. Then it must be true that $(c, z, k, l) \in T'$, $z_1 = k_1 = 0$, and $k \neq 0$ (since $||x|| = 1$, while if $k = 0$, then by virtue of A′5 $l = 0$, then by virtue of T′4 $(c, z) = 0$), but $z_j \geqq k_j$ for all $2 \leqq j \leqq n$, contradicting A′3. ■

Note finally that A′3 and A′5 are consistent with the analog of T7:

T′7. There exist $0 \leq \hat{k} \leqq \bar{k}$ and $\hat{z} > 0$ such that both $(0, \hat{k}, \hat{k}, 1) \in T'$ and $(0, \hat{z}, \hat{k}, 1) \in T'$.

Appendix B

In this appendix we elaborate an extended example of our general model, one in which there are only two types of both consumption goods and capital stocks. Capital stock of type 1 is an exhaustible resource, while capital stock of type 2 serves as both an inventory of consumption goods and – in a process using up the exhaustible resource as raw material – an originator of consumption goods. Besides generally illustrating the consumption-value maximization theorem of Section 5, the example specifically demonstrates that

1. neither A2 nor A3 is necessary for T6;
2. the question of whether T6 is necessary for summability (i.e., $\sum_{t=0}^{\infty}\sum_{i=1}^{m} c_{it} < \infty$ for every solution to Equation (2)) is both open and subtle;
3. in fact, summability is not necessary for consumption-value maximization; and
4. even with summability, there may be some associated competitive price system that does not exhibit consumption-value maximization, while without summability, there may be no associated competitive price system that exhibits consumption-value maximization.

B.1. Example

$$m = n = 2$$

$$T = \{(c, z, k) : c_1 \leqq h(k_1 - z_1, k_2), z_1 \leqq k_1, c_2 + z_2 \leqq k_2, \text{ and } (c, z, k) \geqq 0\}$$

where $h(x_1, x_2)$ for $(x_1, x_2) \geqq 0$ is differentiable, nonnegative (strictly positive for $(x_1, x_2) > 0$), increasing (strictly increasing for $(x_1, x_2) > 0$), concave, and linear homogeneous and satisfies $h(0, x_2) = h(x_1, 0) = 0$, and

Case 1. $\lim_{x_1 \to 0^+} h_1(x_1, x_2) < \infty$ for $x_2 \geqq 0$, for example, $h(x_1, x_2) = (1 - e-^{(x_1/x_2)})x_2$

or

Case 2a. $\lim_{x_1 \to 0^+} h_1(x_1, x_2) = \infty$ for every $x_2 > 0$ and for every $0 < x_1' < \infty$, $x_2' > 0$ there is some $0 < \alpha < 1$ such that

$$\frac{h_1(x_1, x_2)x_1}{h(x_1, x_2)} \geqq \alpha \quad \text{for} \quad 0 \geqq x_1 \leqq x_1', \quad x_2 \geqq x_2'$$

for example, $h(x_1, x_2) = x_1^\alpha x_2^{1-\alpha}$ with $0 < \alpha < 1$ or

Case 2b. $\lim_{x_1 \to 0^+} h_1(x_1, x_2) = \infty$ for $x_2 > 0$ and for some $0 < x_1' < \infty$, $x_2' > 0$ there is no $0 < \alpha < 1$ such that

$$\frac{h_1(x_1, x_2)x_1}{h(x_1, x_2)} \geqq \alpha \quad \text{for} \quad 0 \leqq x_1 \leqq x_1', \quad x_2 \geqq x_2'$$

for example,

$$h(x_1, x_2) = \begin{cases} (-\log(x_1/x_2))^{-\beta x_2} & \text{for} \quad 0 \leqq x_1/x_2 \leqq e^{-\beta-1} \\ \tilde{h}(x_1/x_2)x_2 & \text{otherwise} \end{cases}$$

with $\beta > 0$, $\tilde{h}(x)$ for $x \geqq e^{-\beta-1}$ any differentiable, strictly increasing, and concave function such that $\tilde{h}(e^{-\beta-1}) = (\beta + 1)^{-\beta}$ and $\tilde{h}'(e^{-\beta-1}) = (\beta + 1)^{-\beta-1}\beta e^{\beta+1}$.

One can easily verify that this particular technology satisfies all of our maintained assumptions. It also satisfies the strong version of T7 mentioned at the end of the Appendix A, T7′. (Indeed, it is obvious that the largest possible growth rate of both capital stocks – achieved only when there is no consumption goods output – is zero.) Notice finally that this technology does not satisfy either Equation (A.2) (since, e.g., consumption good of type 2 cannot be converted into investment good of type 1) or Equation (A.3) (since capital stock of type 2 can be costlessly stored); shortly we will show that it satisfies T6 only in Case 1.

B.2. Results

The example was chosen in large part because it permits direct characterization of efficiency. This in turn permits full concentration on the property of consumption-value maximization.

B.2.1. Efficient Growth Paths

A feasible growth path is efficient if and only if *outputs are not obviously wasted*, that is, consumption goods outputs are never freely disposed, $c_{1t} = h(k_{1t} - z_{1t}, k_{2t})$ and $c_{2t} = k_{2t} - z_{2t}$ for $t \geqq 0$, and *capital stocks are not superfluously maintained*, that is, resources are eventually exhausted, $\lim_{t\to\infty} k_{1t} = 0$, while (i) if resources are exhausted in finite time, then inventories are eventually depleted, and if there is $\bar{t}_t < \infty$ such that $k_{1t} > 0$ for $0 \leqq t \leqq \bar{t}_1$ and $k_{1t} = 0$ for $\bar{t}_1 < t$, then $\lim_{t\to\infty} k_{2t} = 0$; (ii) if inventories are depleted in finite time, then resources are exhausted by the same time, and if there is a $\bar{t}_2 < \infty$ such that $k_{2t} > 0$ for $0 \leqq t \leqq \bar{t}_2$ and $k_{2t} = 0$ for $\bar{t}_2 < t$, then $k_{1t} = 0$ for $\bar{t}_2 < t$ (or, alternatively, if $k_{1t} > 0$, then $k_{2t} > 0$ for $t \geqq 0$).

Proof. For simplicity, here we will denote the given path without superscript, and various comparison paths with prime superscript.

Necessity:

(i) No obvious waste: Suppose otherwise, that is., $c_{1t} < h(k_{1t} - z_{1t}, k_{2t})$ or $c_{2t} < k_{2t} - z_{2t}$ for some t. Then, $c'_{1t} = h(k_{1t} - z_{1t}, k_{2t}) > c_{1t}$ or $c'_{2t} = k_{2t} - z_{2t} > c_{2t}$ is feasible, ceteris paribus, contradicting the hypothesis.

(ii) No superfluous maintenance: Note first that, since $0 \leqq k_{t+1} \leqq k_t$ for $t \geqq 0$, we know $\lim_{t\to\infty} k_t = k_\infty \geqq 0$. Then, on the one hand, suppose $\lim_{t\to\infty} k_{1t} = k_{1\infty} > 0$. It follows that $c'_{10} = h(k_{10} - z_{10} + k_{1\infty}, k_{20}) > c_{10}, k'_{1t} = k_{1t} - k_{1\infty} \geqq 0$ for $t > 0$ is feasible, ceteris paribus, contradicting the hypothesis. On the other hand, suppose first that $k_{1t} > 0$ for $0 \leqq t \leqq \bar{t}_1 < \infty$, $k_{1t} = 0$ for $\bar{t}_1 < t$, and $\lim_{t\to\infty} k_{2t} = k_{2\infty} > 0$. Then $c'_{2\bar{t}_1} = k_{2\bar{t}_1} - z_{2\bar{t}_1} + k_{2\infty} > c_{2\bar{t}_1}, k'_{2t} = k_{2t} - k_{2\infty} \geqq 0$ for $\bar{t}_1 < t$ is feasible, ceteris paribus, again contradicting the hypothesis. Now, suppose second that $k_{2t} > 0$ for $0 \leqq t \leqq \bar{t}_2 < \infty$, $k_{2t} = 0$ for $\bar{t}_2 < t$, and $k_{1\bar{t}_2+1} > 0$. Then (since $c_{1t} = h(k_{1t} - z_{1t}, 0) = 0$ for $\bar{t}_2 < t$) $c'_{10} = h(k_{10} - z_{10} + k_{1\bar{t}_2+1}, k_{20}) > c_{10}, k'_{1t} = 0$ for $\bar{t}_2 < t$ is feasible, ceteris paribus, also contradicting the hypothesis.

Sufficiency: We begin by noting that when there is no obvious waste, feasible capital stocks obey the dynamical equations

$$k_{1t+1} = k_{10} + \sum_{s=0}^{t} (k_{1s+1} - k_{1s}) = \bar{k}_1 - \sum_{s=0}^{t} (k_{1s} - z_{1s}) \quad \text{for} \quad t \geqq 0 \tag{B.1}$$

and

$$k_{2t+1} = k_{20} + \sum_{s=0}^{r}(k_{2s+1} - k_{2s}) = \bar{k}_2 - \sum_{s=0}^{t}(k_{2s} - z_{2s})$$

$$= \bar{k}_2 - \sum_{s=0}^{t} c_{2s} \quad \text{for} \quad t \geqq 0 \tag{B.2}$$

We then proceed by considering a number of mutually exclusive and completely exhaustive subcases. For each subcase the logic of the argument is the same; namely, we show that the supposition of a dominating (refer to Equation (7)) feasible growth path leads to a contradiction:

(i) Suppose first that $k_{1t} > 0$ for $t \geqq 0$ and $\lim_{t\to\infty} k_{1t} = 0$. (a) If $c'_t \geqq c_t$ for $t \geqq 0$ and there is some $t_2 < \infty$ such that $c'_{2t_2}, > c_{2t_2}$, then from Equation (B.2)

$$k'_{2t+1} = \bar{k}_2 - \sum_{s=0}^{t} c'_{2s} = \bar{k}_2 - \sum_{s=0}^{t} c_{2s} - \sum_{s=0}^{t}(c'_{2s} - c_{2s})$$
$$\leqq \begin{cases} k_{2t+1} & \text{for} \quad 0 \leqq t < t_2, \\ k_{2t+1} - (c'_{2t_2} - c_{2t_2}) < k_{2t+1} & \text{for} \quad t_2 \leqq t. \end{cases}$$

But by the last stated hypothesis of the proposition, we know that $k_{2t} > 0$ for $t \geqq 0$. Hence $c_{1t} > 0$ for some $t > t_2$, or without loss of generality $c_{1t_2+1} > 0$ or

$$k'_{1t} - z'_{1t}\begin{Bmatrix} \geqq \\ > \end{Bmatrix} k_{1t} - z_{1t} \quad \text{as} \quad t\begin{Bmatrix} \neq \\ = \end{Bmatrix} t_2 + 1$$

(since

$$c'_{1t} = h(k'_{1t} - z'_{1t}, k'_{2t})\begin{Bmatrix} \geqq \\ > \end{Bmatrix} h(k_{1t} - z_{1t}, k_{2t}) = c_{1t} \quad \text{as} \quad t\begin{Bmatrix} \neq \\ = \end{Bmatrix} t_2 + 1$$

and h is increasing in x) or from Equation (B.1)

$$k'_{1t+1} = \bar{k}_1 - \sum_{s=0}^{t}(k'_{1s} - z'_{1s})$$
$$= \bar{k}_1 - \sum_{s=0}^{t}(k_{1s} - z_{1s}) - \sum_{s=0}^{t}\left[(k'_{1s} - z'_{1s}) - (k_{1s} - z_{1s})\right]$$
$$\leqq \begin{cases} k_{1t+1} & \text{for} \quad 0 \leqq t \leqq t_2 \\ k_{1t+1} - \left[(k'_{1t_2+1} - z'_{1t_2+1}) - (k_{1t_2+1} - z_{1t_2+1})\right] & \text{for} \quad t_2 < t \end{cases}$$

or

$$\lim_{t\to\infty} k'_{1t} \leqq - \left[(k'_{1t_2+1} - z'_{1t_2+1}) - (k_{1t_2+1} - z_{1t_2+1})\right] < 0,$$

which is infeasible. (b) If (ruling out the subcase already considered) $c'_{1t} \geqq c_{1t}$ and $c'_{2t} = c_{2t}$ for $t \geqq 0$ and there is some $t_1 < \infty$ such that $c'_{1t_1} > c_{1t_1}$, then now from Equation (B.2)

$$k'_{2t+1} = \bar{k}_2 - \sum_{s=0}^{t} c'_{2s} = \bar{k}_2 - \sum_{s=0}^{t} c_{2s} = k_{2t+1} \quad \text{for} \quad t \geqq 0$$

or

$$k'_{1t} - z'_{1t} \left\{ \begin{matrix} \geqq \\ > \end{matrix} \right\} k_{1t} - z_{1t} \quad \text{as} \quad t \left\{ \begin{matrix} \neq \\ = \end{matrix} \right\} t_1$$

(since here

$$c'_{1t} = h(k'_{1t} - z'_{1t}, k'_{2t}) \left\{ \begin{matrix} \geqq \\ > \end{matrix} \right\} h(k_{1t} - z_{1t}, k_{2t}) = c_{1t} \quad \text{as} \quad t \left\{ \begin{matrix} \neq \\ = \end{matrix} \right\} t_1$$

and h is increasing in x) or again from Equation (B.1)

$$\begin{aligned} k'_{1t+1} &= \bar{k}_1 - \sum_{s=0}^{t} (k'_{1s} - z'_{1s}) \\ &= \bar{k}_1 - \sum_{s=0}^{t} (k_{1s} - z_{1s}) - \sum_{s=0}^{t} \left[(k'_{1s} - z'_{1s}) - (k_{1s} - z_{1s}) \right] \\ &\leqq \begin{cases} k_{1t+1} & \text{for} \quad 0 \leqq t < t_1 \\ k_{1t+1} - [(k'_{1t_1} - z'_{1t_1}) - (k_{1t_1} - z_{1t_1})] & \text{for} \quad t_1 \leqq t \end{cases} \end{aligned}$$

or

$$\lim_{t \to \infty} k'_{1t} \leqq -[(k'_{1t_1} - z'_{1t_1}) - (k_{1t_1} - z_{1t_1})] < 0,$$

which is also infeasible.

(ii) Suppose second that $k_{1t} > 0$ for $0 \leqq t \leqq \bar{t}_1 < \infty$, $k_{1t} = 0$ for $\bar{t}_1 < t$ and $\lim_{t \to \infty} k_{2t} = 0$. (a) If $c'_t \geqq c_t$ for $t \geqq 0$ and there is some $t_2 < \infty$ such that $c'_{2t_2} > c_{2t_2}$, then (here and after deleting obvious repetitions of parts of the preceding argument)

$$k'_{2t+1} = \leqq \begin{cases} k_{2t+1} & \text{for} \quad 0 \leqq t < t_2 \\ k_{2t+1} - (c'_{2t_2} - c_{2t_2}) & \text{for} \quad t_2 \leqq t \end{cases}$$

or

$$\lim_{t \to \infty} k'_{2t} \leqq -(c'_{2t_2} - c_{2t_2}) < 0,$$

which is infeasible. (b) If (ruling out the subcase already considered) $c'_{1t} \geqq c_{1t}$ and $c'_{2t} = c_{2t}$ for $t \geqq 0$ and there is some $t_1 < \infty$ such that $c'_{1t_1} < c_{1t_1}$, then from Equation (B.2) $k'_{2t+1} = k_{2t+1}$ for $t \geqq 0$ or

$$k'_{1t} - z'_{1t} \left\{ \begin{matrix} \geqq \\ > \end{matrix} \right\} k_{1t} - z_{1t} \quad \text{as} \quad t \left\{ \begin{matrix} \neq \\ = \end{matrix} \right\} t_1$$

or from Equation (B.1)

$$k'_{1t+1} = \leqq \begin{cases} k_{1t+1} & \text{for} \quad 0 \leqq t < t_1 \\ k_{1t+1} - \left[(k'_{1t_1} - z'_{1t_1}) - (k_{1t_1} - z_{1t_1}) \right] & \text{for} \quad t_1 \leqq t \end{cases}$$

or

$$k'_{1t+1} \leqq -[(k'_{1t_1} - z'_{1t_1}) - (k_{1t_1} - z_{1t_1})] < 0 \quad \text{for} \quad \max\{\bar{t}_1, t_1\} \leqq t,$$

which is, once again, infeasible. ■

B.2.2. Conditions for Summability

Although in all three cases actual capital accumulation is infeasible, and only eventual resource exhaustion is efficient, in Case 1 condition T6 obtains, so that

$$\sum_{t=0}^{\infty} (c_{1t} + c_{2t}) \leqq b(\bar{k}) < \infty \tag{B.3}$$

for every solution to Equation (2), while in Case 2 (i.e., both Cases 2a and 2b) condition T6 does not obtain; in fact

$$\sum_{t=0}^{\infty} (c_{1t} + c_{2t}) = \infty \tag{B.4}$$

for some solution to Equation (2).

Proof Case 1. All that needs establishing is that there is some $p > 0$ and $q \geqq 0$ such that

$$p \cdot c + q\,z - q\,k \leqq 0 \quad \text{for every} \quad (c, z, k) \in T.$$

But any stationary feasible price system of the form

$$p_1 = 1, \quad 0 < h_1(0, 1) \leqq q_1 < \infty, \quad \text{and} \quad p_2 = q_2 > 0 \tag{B.5}$$

will do, since if (p, q) satisfies Equation (B.5) and $(c, z, k) \in T$, then (using various properties of h)

$$
\begin{aligned}
&p\cdot c+q\cdot z-qk.rtri\\
&\quad \leqq h(k_1-z_1,k_2)-q_1(k_1-z_1)-q_2(k_2-z_2-c_2)\\
&\quad =\begin{cases}
-q_1(k_1-z_1)-q_2(k_2-c_2-z_2)\leqq 0 & \text{when } k_2=0\\
\left[h((k_1-z_1)/k_2,1)-q_2((k_1-z_1)/k_2)\right]k_2-q_2(k_2-z_2-c_2)\\
F(h_1(0,1)-q_1)(k_1-z_1)-q_2(k_2-c_2-z_2)\leqq 0 & \text{when } k_2>0.
\end{cases}
\end{aligned}
$$

From the argument detailed earlier in Section 5, we can even calculate a minimum value for the bound in Equation (B.3):

$$
\begin{aligned}
b(\bar{k}) &= h_1(0,1)\bar{k}_1+\bar{k}_2=\min_{0\leqq q_2\leqq 1}(h_1(0,1)/q_2)\bar{k}_1+\bar{k}_2\\
&\leqq (h_1(0,1)\bar{k}_1+q_2\bar{k}_2)/\min\{1,q_2\}\leqq q\cdot\bar{k}/\min\{p_1,p_2\}.
\end{aligned}
$$

It is worth emphasizing once more that in this case the technology satisfies T6 without satisfying either Equation (A.2) or Equation (A.3).

Case 2. All that needs establishing is Equation (B.4) (since we demonstrated earlier that T6 implies Equation (B.3), or equivalently, that Equation (B.4) implies the denial of T6). The argument involves constructing a feasible growth path that yields

$$\sum_{t=0}^{\infty}(c_{1t}+c_{2t})=\sum_{t=0}^{\infty}c_{1t}=\infty. \tag{B.6}$$

In particular, consider the efficient growth path with capital stocks described by

$$k_{1t}=\bar{k}_1-\sum_{t=0}^{t-1}\varepsilon_s \quad\text{and}\quad k_{2t}=\bar{k}_2 \quad\text{for}\quad t\geqq 0,$$

where $\varepsilon_t=k_{1t}-z_{1t}>0$ for $t\geqq 0$ with $\sum_{t=0}^{\infty}\varepsilon_s=\bar{k}_1$ is chosen as follows: Pick constants $0<\alpha<1$ and $\beta>0$ and let the subsequence of periods $\{t_s\}$ be such that

$$t_0=0$$

and

$$t_{s+1}=\min\left\{t:t>t_s \text{ and } h_1\left(\frac{(1-\alpha)\bar{k}_1\alpha^s}{t-t_s},\bar{k}_2\right)(1-\alpha)\bar{k}_1\alpha^s\geqq\beta\right\}\quad\text{for}\quad s\geqq 0$$

(The last is legitimate since Case 2 is characterized by the property that $\lim_{x_1\to 0^+}h(x_1,\bar{k}_2)=\infty$ for $\bar{k}_2>0$.) Finally, define

$$\varepsilon_t=\frac{(1-\alpha)\bar{k}_1\alpha^s}{t_{s+1}-t_s}>0 \quad\text{for}\quad t_s\leqq t<t_{s+1},\quad s\geqq 0,$$

which entails

$$< \sum_{t=0}^{\ell} \varepsilon_t < \sum_{t=0}^{\infty} \varepsilon_t = \sum_{s=0}^{\infty} \sum_{u=t_s}^{t_{s+1}-1} \frac{(1-\alpha)\bar{k}_1 \alpha^s}{t_{s+1}-t_s}$$

$$= (1-\alpha)\bar{k}_1 \sum_{s=0}^{\infty} \alpha^s = \bar{k}_1 \quad \text{for} \quad \ell \geqq 0$$

Along this particular efficient growth path consumption goods are produced at the rates

$$c_{1t} = h(\varepsilon_t, \bar{k}_2) \geqq h_1(\varepsilon_t, \bar{k}_2)\varepsilon_t \quad \text{and} \quad c_{2t} = 0 \quad \text{for} \quad t \geqq 0$$

(since $0 = h(0, \bar{k}_2) \leqq h(\varepsilon, \bar{k}_2) + h_1(\varepsilon, \bar{k}_2)(0 - \varepsilon)$ or $h(\varepsilon, \bar{k}_2) \geqq h_1(\varepsilon, \bar{k}_2)\varepsilon$ for $\varepsilon > 0$ by concavity of h). Hence, it follows that

$$\sum_{t=0}^{t_{s+1}-1} (c_{1t} + c_{2t}) = \sum_{t=0}^{t_{\mathscr{s}+1}-1} c_{1t} \geqq \sum_{t=0}^{t_{\mathscr{s}+1}-1} h_1(\varepsilon_t, \bar{k}_2)\varepsilon_t = \sum_{s=0}^{\mathscr{s}} \sum_{u=t_s}^{t_{s+1}-1} h_1(\varepsilon_t, \bar{k}_2)\varepsilon_{t_s}$$

$$= \sum_{s=0}^{\mathscr{s}} \sum_{u=t_s}^{t_{s+1}-1} h_1\left(\frac{(1-\alpha)\bar{k}_1\alpha^s}{t_{s+1}-t_s}, \bar{k}_2\right)\left(\frac{(1-\alpha)\bar{k}_1\alpha^s}{t_{s+1}-t_s}\right)$$

$$= \sum_{s=0}^{\mathscr{s}} h_1\left(\frac{(1-\alpha)\bar{k}_1\alpha^s}{t_{s+1}-t_s}, \bar{k}_2\right) \sum_{u=t_s}^{t_{s+1}-1} \frac{(1-\alpha)\bar{k}_1\alpha^s}{t_{s+1}-t_s}$$

$$= \sum_{s=0}^{\mathscr{s}} h_1\left(\frac{(1-\alpha)\bar{k}_1\alpha^s}{t_{s+1}-t_s}, \bar{k}_2\right)(1-\alpha)\bar{k}_1\alpha^s$$

$$\geqq \sum_{s=0}^{\mathscr{s}} \beta = (\mathscr{s}+1)\beta \quad \text{for} \quad \mathscr{s} \geqq 0,$$

from which we immediately deduce Equation (B.6). ■

We should mention explicitly that the foregoing analysis has shown that, in this example anyway, T6 is necessary as well as sufficient for summability. We have also observed the same result in other easily calculable examples, for all of which $\bar{N} \neq N$ (see comment 1 at the end of Appendix A). Whether this is just a peculiarity of relatively simple specializations of our general model remains to be seen

B.2.3. Consumption-Value Maximization

(For simplicity, here too we will denote a given efficient growth path without superscript and various comparison growth paths with prime superscript.) Given an efficient growth path, in Cases 1 and 2a (i) there is some associated competitive price system such that

$$\lim_{t\to\infty} q_t \cdot k_{t+1} = 0, \tag{B.7}$$

and hence (referring to the discussion at the end of Section 3)

$$\infty > \sum_{t=0}^{\infty} p_t \cdot c_t \geqq \sum_{t=0}^{\infty} p_t \cdot c'_t \tag{B.8}$$

for every (primed) solution to Equation (2), but (ii) there may also be some associated competitive price system such that neither statement is true, while in Case 2b there may simply be no associated competitive price system such that either statement is true.

Proof. We begin by noting that the "pure inventory" competitive price system

$$p_{1t} = q_{1t-1} = 0 \quad \text{and} \quad p_{2t}\left\{\begin{matrix} \leqq \\ = \end{matrix}\right\}q_{2t-1} = 1 \quad \text{as} \quad c_{2t}\left\{\begin{matrix} = \\ > \end{matrix}\right\}0 \quad \text{for} \quad t \geqq 0 \tag{B.9}$$

is associated with every efficient growth path since if prices satisfy Equation (B.9) and quantities satisfy

$$c_{2t} = k_{2t} - z_{2t} \quad \text{and} \quad (c_{2t}, z_{2t}, k_{2t}) \geqq 0 \quad \text{for} \quad t \geqq 0,$$

then

$$\begin{aligned} p_t \cdot c + q_t \cdot z - q_{t-1} \cdot k &= p_{2t}c_2 + q_{2t}z_2 - q_{2t-1}k_2 \\ &\leqq p_{2t}c_{2t} + q_{2t}z_{2t} - q_{2t-1}k_{2t} \\ &= p_t \cdot c_t + q_t \cdot z_t - q_{t-1} \cdot k_t = 0 \end{aligned}$$

for every $(c, z, k) \in T$ and $t \geqq 0$.

Moreover, with such a competitive price system, if, in addition, $p_{20} = 1$ (e.g., $c_{20} > 0$) while $\lim_{t\to\infty} k_{2t} = k_{2\infty} > 0$ (which we already know from Section B.2.1 is compatible with efficiency provided $k_{1t} > 0$ for $t \geqq 0$), then

$$\infty > \sum_{t=0}^{\infty} p_t \cdot c'_t = c'_{20} = \bar{k}_2 > \bar{k}_2 - k_{2\infty} = \sum_{t=0}^{\infty} c_{2t} = \sum_{t=0}^{\infty} p_t \cdot c_t$$

for the alternative feasible growth path defined by

$$c'_{10} = h(\bar{k}_1, \bar{k}_2) \quad c'_{20} = \bar{k}_2,$$

and

$$c'_{1t} = c'_{2t} = k'_{1t} = k'_{2t} = 0 \quad \text{for} \quad t > 0.$$

This is consistent with (though not entailed by) a second observation about the conjunction of Equation (B.9) with an efficient growth path such that $\lim_{t\to\infty} k_{2t} = k_{2\infty} > 0$, namely, that

$$\lim_{t\to\infty} q_t\, k_{t+1} = \lim_{t\to\infty} k_{2t+1} = k_{2\infty} > 0.$$

That is, in both Cases 1 and 2 of the example, the competitive price system described by Equation (B.9) may exhibit neither capital-value transversality Equation (B.7) nor consumption-value maximization Equation (B.8).

In order to establish the rest of the proposition, we utilize the fact that every competitive price system associated with a particular efficient growth path yields (c_t, z_t, k_t) as an optimal solution to the concave programming problem

$$\begin{aligned} &\text{maximize} \quad p_{1t}h(k_1 - z_1, k_2) + p_{2t}(k_2 - z_2) + q_{1t}z_1 \\ &\qquad\qquad + q_{2t}z_2 - q_{1t-1}k_1 - q_{2t-1}k_2 \quad \text{for} \quad t \geqq 0 \\ &\text{subject to} \quad z_1 \leqq k_1 \quad (\text{with dual variable} \quad \lambda_{1t} \geqq 0) \\ &\qquad\qquad z_2 \leqq k_2 \quad (\text{with dual variable} \quad \lambda_{2t} \geqq 0) \\ &\text{and} \qquad \text{nonnegativity} \end{aligned} \tag{B.10}$$

or satisfies that Kuhn–Tucker conditions for $t \geqq 0$[20]

$$\begin{aligned} z_{1t} &\leqq k_{1t}, && \text{equality if } \lambda_{1t} > 0, \\ z_{2t} &\leqq k_{2t}, && \text{equality if } \lambda_{2t} > 0, \\ -p_{1t}h_1(k_{1t} - z_{1t}, k_{2t}) + q_{1t} &\leqq \lambda_{1t}, && \text{equality if } z_{1t} > 0, \\ -p_{2t} + q_{2t} &\leqq \lambda_{2t}, && \text{equality if } z_{2t} > 0, \\ p_{1t}h_1(k_{1t} - z_{1t}, k_{2t}) - q_{1t-1} &\leqq -\lambda_{1t}, && \text{equality if } k_{1t} > 0, \\ p_{1t}h_2(k_{1t} - z_{1t}, k_{2t}) + p_{2t} - q_{2t-1} &\leqq -\lambda_{2t}, && \text{equality if } k_{2t} > 0 \end{aligned} \tag{B.11}$$

It is convenient to analyze the solutions to Equation (B.11) by distinguishing two possibilities, depending on whether $\lim_{t\to\infty} k_{2t} = 0$ or $\lim_{t\to\infty} k_{2t} = k_{2\infty} > 0$:

(i) Suppose that $\lim_{t\to\infty} k_{2t} = 0$. In this case, we need only notice that the Kuhn–Tucker conditions (Equation (B.11)) entail the inequalities

$$-p_{1t}h_1 + q_{1t} \leqq -p_{1t}h_t + q_{1t-1} \quad \text{or} \quad q_{1t} \leqq q_{1t-1} \leqq \quad \leqq q_{1-1} < \infty$$

and

$$-p_{2t} + q_{2t} \leqq -p_{1t}h_2 - p_{2t} + p_{2t-1} \leqq -p_{2t} + q_{2t-1}$$

[20] Equation (B.10) obviously satisfies Slater's condition (since $(z, k) = (0, 0, 1, 1)$ is a feasible solution). Thus, the conditions (B.11) are both necessary and sufficient. It almost goes without saying that in Case 2 these particular Kuhn–Tucker conditions only make sense provided that

$$p_{1t} = p_{1t}h_1(k_{1t} - z_{1t}, k_{2t}) = p_{1t},\ h_2(k_{1t} - z_{1t}, k_{2t}) = 0$$

whenever $c_{1t} = h(k_{1t} - z_{1t}, k_{2t}) = 0$ and hence $k_u - z_u = 0$.

or

$$q_{2t} \leqq q_{2t-1} \leqq \quad \leqq q_{2-1} < \infty \quad \text{for} \quad t \geqq 0$$

Hence, every competitive price system associated with a particular efficient growth path of this sort satisfies

$$q_t \cdot k_{t+1} \leqq q_{-1} \quad k_{t+1} \quad \text{for} \quad t \geqq 0,$$

and therefore

$$\lim_{t\to\infty} q_t\, k_{t+1} \leqq \lim_{t\to\infty} q_{-1} \cdot k_{t+1} = q_{-1} \cdot \lim_{t\to\infty} k_{t+1} = 0$$

(since by hypothesis $\lim_{t\to\infty} k_{1t} = 0$ while by supposition $\lim_{t\to\infty} k_{2t} = 0$).

(ii) Suppose that $\lim_{t\to\infty} k_{2t} = k_{2\infty} > 0$. In this case, we already know from Section B.2.1 that though $\lim_{t\to\infty} k_{1t} = 0$, $k_{1t} > 0$ for $t \geqq 0$. Using this fact in combination with the Kuhn–Tucker conditions, we will show the following: It is always possible to find some competitive price system associated with a particular efficient growth path of this sort that (a) differs from Equation (B.9) and (b) also satisfies $\lim_{t\to\infty} q_{2t} = 0$ if and only if we have Case 1 or Case 2a of the example. Since the second of the listed properties entails capital-value transversality,

$$\begin{aligned} \lim_{t\to\infty} q_t\, k_{t+1} &= \lim_{t\to\infty} (q_{1-1} k_{1t+1} + q_{2t} k_{2t+1}) \\ &= q_{1,-1} (\lim_{t\to\infty} k_{1t+1}) + (\lim_{t\to\infty} q_{2t})(\lim_{t\to\infty} k_{2t+1}) = 0, \end{aligned}$$

together with the preceding result, this establishes that it is in these cases, and only in these cases, that an efficient growth path necessarily exhibits consumption-value maximization (at some, but referring to the earlier discussion concerning Equation (B.9), perhaps not all associated competitive price systems).

The argument proceeds by closely examining the structure of the solutions to Equation (B.11) in light of the supposition that $k_t > 0$ for $t \geqq 0$: Since generally we know that

$$z_{it} \left\{ \begin{matrix} < \\ = \end{matrix} \right\} k_{it} \quad \text{as} \quad c_{it} \left\{ \begin{matrix} > \\ = \end{matrix} \right\} 0 \quad \text{for} \quad i = 1, 2, \quad t \geqq 0,$$

while specifically we have $k_{it+1} = z_{it} > 0 (k_{i0} = \bar{k}_i > 0)$ for $i = 1, 2$, $t \geqq 0$, after some straightforward logical simplification, the Kuhn–Tucker conditions for $t \geqq 0$ reduce to

$$\begin{aligned} &p_{1t}h_1(k_{1t} - z_{1t}, k_{2t}) \leqq q_{1t}, && \text{equality if} \quad c_{1t} > 0, \\ &p_{2t} \leqq q_{2t}, && \text{equality if} \quad c_{2t} > 0. \\ &q_{1t} = q_{1,-1}, \\ &q_{2t} = q_{2t-1} - p_{1t}h_2(k_{1t} - z_{1t}, k_{2t}). \end{aligned} \tag{B.12}$$

Equation (B.12) tells us immediately that if $q_{1,-1} = 0$, then $q_{1t} = p_{1t} = p_{1t}h_1 = p_{1t}h_2 = 0$, and hence $q_{2t} = q_{2,-1} > 0$ for $t \geqq 0$. Thus, a necessary (and, it turns out, also sufficient) condition for finding some competitive price system that differs from Equation (B.9) and also satisfies $\lim_{t\to\infty} q_{2t} = 0$ is finding one with $q_{1,-1} = 1$ (for simplicity, now letting initial capital of type 1 be the numéraire).

In order to establish that only Cases 1 and 2a of the example are consistent with this requirement, suppose that $q_{1,-1} = 1$ and consider the last equation in Equation (B.12)

$$\begin{aligned} q_{2t} &= q_{2t-1} - p_{1t}h_2(k_{1t} - z_{1t}, k_{2t}) \\ &= q_{2t-1} - p_{1t}(h(k_{1t} - z_{1t}, k_{2t}) \\ &\quad - h_1(k_{1t} - z_{1t}, k_{2t})(k_{1t} - z_{1t})) \quad \text{for} \quad t \geqq 0 \end{aligned} \tag{B.13}$$

(since h is linear homogeneous). If $c_{1t} = 0$, then

$$q_{2t} = q_{2t-1}$$

(since $h = 0$ only if $p_{1t}h_1 = 0$). If $c_{1t} > 0$, then

$$q_{2t} = q_{2t-1} - p_{1t}h_1(k_{1t} - z_{1t}, k_{2t})\left(\frac{h(k_{1t} - z_{1t}, k_{2t})}{h_1(k_{1t} - z_{1t}, k_{2t})} - (k_{1t} - z_{1t})\right)$$

(since $h > 0$ only if $(k_{1t} - z_{1t}, k_{2t}) > 0$ only if $h_1 > 0$)

$$= q_{2t-1} - \left(\frac{h(k_{1t} - z_{1t}, k_{2t})}{h_1(k_{1t} - z_{1t}, k_{2t})(k_{1t} - z_{1t})} - 1\right)(k_{1t} - z_{1t})$$

(since, from the first inequality in Equation (B.12), if $c_{1t} > 0$, then $p_{1t}h_1 = q_{1t} = q_{1-1} = 1$). Hence, defining

$$\alpha_t = \begin{cases} 1 & \text{for} \quad c_{1t} = 0 \quad \text{for } t \geqq 0 \\ \dfrac{h_1(k_{1t} - z_{1t}, k_{2t})(k_{1t} - z_{1t})}{h(k_{1t} - z_{1t}, k_{2t})} & \text{for} \quad c_{1t} > 0, \end{cases}$$

Equation (B.13) can be rewritten compactly as

$$q_{2t} = q_{2,-1} - \sum_{s=0}^{t} \left(\frac{1}{\alpha_s} - 1 \right) (k_{1s} - z_{1s}) \quad \text{for} \quad t \geqq 0. \tag{B.14}$$

In Case 2b, by employing a construction similar to that utilized in establishing the second part of the proposition in Section B.2.2 above, we can find an efficient growth path such that[21]

$$\sum_{s=0}^{\infty} \left(\frac{1}{\alpha_s} - 1 \right) (k_{1s} - z_{1s}) = \infty.$$

Thus, for such an efficient growth path, if $q_{1,-1} = 1$, then $\lim_{t \to \infty} q_{2t} = -\infty$, which is "infeasible"; Case 2b of the example may in fact require a "pure inventory" competitive price system.

In Cases 1 and 2a, on the other hand, by picking $0 < \alpha < 1$ such that

$$\frac{h_1(x_1, x_2)x_1}{h(x_1, x_2)} \geqq \alpha \quad \text{for} \quad 0 \leqq x_1 \leqq \bar{k}_1, \quad x_2 \geqq k_{2\infty},$$

---

[21] Specifically, referring to the earlier construction, now let the subsequence of periods $\{t_s\}$ be such that

$$t_0 = 0$$

and

$$t_{s+1} = \min \left\{ t : t > t_s \text{ and} \left[h \left(\frac{(1-\alpha)\bar{k}_1 \alpha^s}{t - t_s}, \bar{k}_2 \right) h_1 \left(\frac{(1-\alpha)\bar{k}_1 \alpha^s}{t - t_s}, \bar{k}_2 \right)^{-1} \right. \right.$$
$$\left. \left. \times \left(\frac{(1-\alpha)\bar{k}_1 \alpha^s}{t - t_s} \right)^{-1} - 1 \right] (1-\alpha)\bar{k}_1 \alpha^s \geqq \beta \right\} \quad \text{for} \quad s \geqq 0$$

(which is legitimate since Case 2b is easily shown to be characterized by the property that

$$\lim_{x_1 \to 0^+} \frac{h_1(x_1, \bar{k}_2)x_1}{h(x_1, \bar{k}_2)} = 0 \quad \text{for} \quad \bar{k}_2 > 0).$$

Then, the rest of the argument is virtually unchanged from before since it simply involves calculating the lower bound

$$\sum_{t=0}^{t_{\sigma+1}-1} \left(\frac{1}{\alpha_t} - 1 \right) (k_{1t} - z_{1t}) \geqq \beta(\sigma + 1) \quad \text{for} \quad \sigma \geqq 0.$$

we see that

$$0 \leqq \sum_{s=0}^{t}\left(\frac{1}{\alpha_s} - 1\right)(k_{1s} - z_{1s}) \leqq \sum_{s=0}^{t}\left(\frac{1}{\alpha} - 1\right)(k_{1s} - z_{1s})$$
$$\leqq \left(\frac{1}{\alpha} - 1\right)\sum_{s=0}^{t}(k_{1s} - k_{1s} - k_{1s+1})$$
$$= \left(\frac{1}{\alpha} - 1\right)(\bar{k}_1 - k_{1t+1}) \leqq \left(\frac{1}{\alpha} - 1\right)\bar{k}_1 \quad \text{for} \quad t \geqq 0.$$

Hence, for every efficient growth such that $\lim_{t\to\infty} k_{2t} = k_{2\infty} > 0$, we can find an associated competitive price system with $q_{1,-1} = 1$. Moreover, by picking

$$q_2 - 1 = \sum_{s=0}^{\infty}\left(\frac{1}{\alpha_s} - 1\right)(k_{1s} - z_{1s}) < \infty,$$

so that

$$q_{2t} = \sum_{s=0}^{\infty}\left(\frac{1}{\alpha_s} - 1\right)(k_{1s} - z_{1s}) - \sum_{s=0}^{t}\left(\frac{1}{\alpha_s} - 1\right)(k_{1s} - z_{1s})$$
$$= \sum_{s=t+1}^{\infty}\left(\frac{1}{\alpha_s} - 1\right)(k_{1s} - z_{1s}),$$

we can also ensure that this competitive price system satisfies the requisite condition $\lim_{t\to\infty} q_{2t} = 0$ ■

(b) *Another anomalous feature of Case 2b* Consider the particular efficient growth path sketched in Footnote 21. If we pick consumption goods values

$$\bar{p}_t = (h_1(k_{1t} - z_{1t}, \bar{k}_2))^{-1}, \quad 0 \quad \text{for} \quad t \geqq 0, \tag{B.15}$$

then this path is "optimal" in the sense of 3 in the text

$$\theta \geqq \limsup_{t=\infty} \sum_{t=0}^{t} \bar{p}_t \, (c'_t - c_t) \tag{B.16}$$

for every (primed) solution to Equation (2), even though it has no associated competitive price system (Equation (4)) such that $p_t = \bar{p}_t$ for $t \geqq 0$.

Proof. Since we have already established the latter part of the assertion, all we need to establish is Equation (B.16). But this follows directly from the fact that an arbitrary feasible growth path satisfies (by monotonicity of h)

$$c'_{1t} = h(k'_{1t} - z'_{1t}, k'_{2t}) \leqq h(k'_{1t} - z'_{1t}, \bar{k}_2)$$

or (by differentiability and concavity of h)

$$\begin{aligned} c'_{1t} - c_{1t} &\leqq h(k'_{1t} - z'_{1t}, \bar{k}_2) - h(k_{1t} - z_{1t}, \bar{k}_2) \\ &\leqq h_1(k_{1t} - z_{1t}, \bar{k}_2)\left[(k'_{1t} - z'_{1t}) - (k_{1t} - z_{1t})\right] \end{aligned}$$

or (by reference to Equation (B.15))

$$\begin{aligned} \bar{p}_t \cdot (c'_t - c_t) = \bar{p}_{1t}(c'_{1t} - c_{1t}) &\leqq (k'_{1t} - z'_{1t}) - (k_{1t} - z_{1t}) \\ &= (k'_{1t} - k'_{1t+1}) - (k_{1t} - k_{1t+1}) \end{aligned}$$

or

$$\begin{aligned} \sum_{t=0}^{\ell} \bar{p}_t \cdot (c'_t - c_t) &\leqq \sum_{t=0}^{\ell} \left[(k'_{1t} - k'_{1t+1}) - (k_{1t} - k_{1t+1})\right] \\ &= k_{1\ell+1} - k'_{1\ell+1} \quad \text{for} \quad \ell \geqq 0. \end{aligned}$$

But the last inequality entails that

$$\begin{aligned} \limsup_{\ell\to\infty} \sum_{t=0}^{\ell} \bar{p}_t \cdot (c'_t - c_t) &\leqq \limsup_{\ell\to\infty} (k_{1\ell+1} - k'_{1\ell+1}) \\ &= \limsup_{\ell\to\infty} (k_{1\ell+1} - k'_{1\ell+1}) = -k'_{1\infty} \leqq 0. \end{aligned}$$ ■

References

Benveniste, L.M. (1976a). A complete characterization of efficiency for a general capital accumulation model. *Journal of Economic Theory* **12**, 325–337.

Benveniste, L.M. (1976b). Two notes on the Malinvaud condition for efficiency of infinite horizon programs. *Journal of Economic Theory* **12**, 338–346.

Benveniste, L.M. and Gale, D. (1975). An extension of Cass' characterization of infinite efficient programs. *Journal of Economic Theory* **10**, 229–238.

Block, W.R. (1970). On existence of weakly maximal programmes in a multisector economy. *The Review of Economic Studies* **37**, 275–280.

Cass, D. (1972). On capital overaccumulation in the aggregative neoclassical model of economic growth: A complete characterization. *Journal of Economic Theory* **4**, 224–240.

Cass, D. and Shell, K. (1976). The structure and stability of competitive dynamical systems. *Journal of Economic Theory* **12**, 31–70.

Cass, D. and Yaari, M.E. (1971). Present values playing the role of efficiency prices in the one-good growth model. *The Review of Economic Studies* **38**, 331–339.

Gale, D. (1967). On optimal development in a multi-sector economy. *The Review of Economic Studies* **34**, 1–18.

Kelley, J.L. and Namioka, I. (1963). *Linear topological spaces*. Princeton, NJ: Van Nostrand–Reinhold.

Kurz, M. (1969). Tightness and substitution in the theory of capital. *Journal of Economic Theory* **1**, 244–272.

Kurz, M. and Starrett, D.A. (1970). On the efficiency of competitive programmes in an infinite horizon model. *The Review of Economic Studies* **37**, 571–584.

Majumdar, M. (1974). Efficient programs in infinite dimensional spaces: A complete characterization. *Journal of Economic Theory* **7**, 355–369.

Majumdar, M., Mitra, I. and McFadden, D. (1976). On efficiency and Pareto optimally of competitive programs in closed multisector models. *Journal of Economic Theory* **13**, 26–46.

Malinvaud, E. (1953). Capital accumulation and efficient allocation of resources. *Econometrica* **21**, 233–268. A corrigendum, *Econometrica* **30**, 570–573.

McFadden, D. (1967). The evaluation of development programmes. *The Review of Economic Studies* **34**, 25–50.

McKenzie, L.W. (1976). Turnpike theory. *Econometrica* **44**, 841–865.

Mitra, T. (1978). Efficient growth with exhaustible resources in a neoclassical model. *Journal of Economic Theory* **17**, 114–129.

Mitra, T. (1979). Identifying inefficiency in smooth aggregative models of economic growth: A unifying criterion. *Journal of Mathematical Economics* **6**, 85–111.

Mitra, T. and Majumdar, M. (1976). A note on the role of the transversality condition in signalling capital overaccumulation. *Journal of Economic Theory* **13**, 47–57.

Nikaido, H. (1968). *Convex Structures and Economic Theory*. New York: Academic Press.

Peleg, B. (1970a). Efficiency prices for optimal consumption plans. *Journal of Mathematical Analysis and Applications* **29**, 83–90.

Peleg, B. (1970b). Efficiency prices for optimal consumption plans III. *Journal of Mathematical Analysis and Applications* **32**, 630–638.

Peleg, B. (1971). Efficiency prices for optimal consumption plans II. *Israel Journal of Mathematics* **9**, 222–234.

Peleg, B. (1972). Efficiency prices for optimal consumption plans IV. *SIAM Journal on Control and Optimization* **10**, 414–433.

Peleg, B. (1974). On competitive prices for optimal consumption plans. *SIAM Journal on Applied Mathematics* **26**, 239–253.

Peleg, B. and Ryder, H.E., Jr. (1972). On optimal consumption plans in a multisector economy. *The Review of Economic Studies* **39**, 159–169.

Peleg, B. and Yaari, M.E. (1970). Efficiency prices in an infinite-dimensional space. *Journal of Economic Theory* **2**, 41–85.

Peleg, B. and Zilcha, I. (1977). On competitive prices for optimal consumption plans II. *SIAM Journal on Applied Mathematics* **32**, 627–630.

Radner, R. (1967). Efficiency prices for infinite horizon production programmes. *The Review of Economic Studies* **34**, 51–66.

Rockafellar, R.T. (1970). *Convex Analysis*. Princeton, NJ: Princeton University Press.

von Weizsäcker, C.C. (1965). Existence of optimal programs of accumulation for an infinite time horizon. *The Review of Economic Studies* **32**, 85–104.

Weitzman, M.L. (1973). Duality theory for infinite horizon convex models. *Management Science* **19**, 783–789.

Chapter 3

Money in Consumption Loan Type Models: An Addendum☆, ☆☆

David Cass

1. The Cass–Okuno–Zilcha Conjecture

In the chapter by Cass, Okuno, and Zilcha in this volume, we presented several examples of consumption loan type models exhibiting the nonexistence of any competitive equilibrium that is Pareto optimal. One sort of example, involving nonmonotonicity in tastes, seemed very special (see Section 5.2). Evidently it depended on having just the right combination of some consumption satiation and some boundary endowments. We conjectured that such speciality wasn't essential to the intuitive proposition being advanced, that somewhat less than total satiation might unfavorably restrict potential intertemporal market transfers – even given the institution of money, in its role as a store of value, as a common means of facilitating trade between the present and the future. Rather, we proposed as a more likely reason for such speciality the particular analytic methodology being utilized, the limitation to considering only models for which competitive equilibria could be essentially characterized as the nonnegative solutions to a first-order difference equation (and thus completely represented in terms of a two-dimensional diagram).

It turns out that while our intuition was correct, our reasoning wasn't. In fact, it is now apparent that the only operative constraint was simply our lack of sufficient ingenuity.

In the next section I sketch a robust nonoptimality example; nonexistence of Pareto optimal equilibrium persists in the presence of small perturbations in both tastes and endowments. The peculiar nature of the satiation

☆This note was written during my visit as a Sherman Fairchild Distinguished Scholar at the California Institute of Technology.

☆☆Reprinted from David Cass. (1980). Money in consumption loan type models: An addendum. In Kareken, J.H. and Wallace, N. (Eds), *Models of Monetary Economies*, pp. 243–249, © Federal Reserve Bank of Minneapolis, 1980.

International Symposia in Economic Theory and Econometrics, Vol. 21B
S. Spear (Editor)

ISSN: 1571-0386/DOI: 10.1108/S1571-0386(2011)000021B006

phenomena introduced in this example entails other interesting anomalies as well. Two of these additional results are briefly discussed in the final section.

2. A Robust Nonoptimality Example

Consider the basic model described in Section 2 of Cass–Okuno–Zilcha (Chapter 1), and suppose once again that there are two consumers in every generation but the oldest, $G_0 = \{0\}$ and $G_t = \{2t-1, 2t\}$ for $t \geqq 1$, and that odd-numbered consumers, $h = 2t-1$ for $t \geqq 1$, are of α-type; even-numbered, $h = 2t$ for $t \geqq 1$, of β-type. Their respective tastes and endowments are assumed to be as specified in Figure 1a. The critical general features of this specification are that both α- and β-type consumers can become satiated in

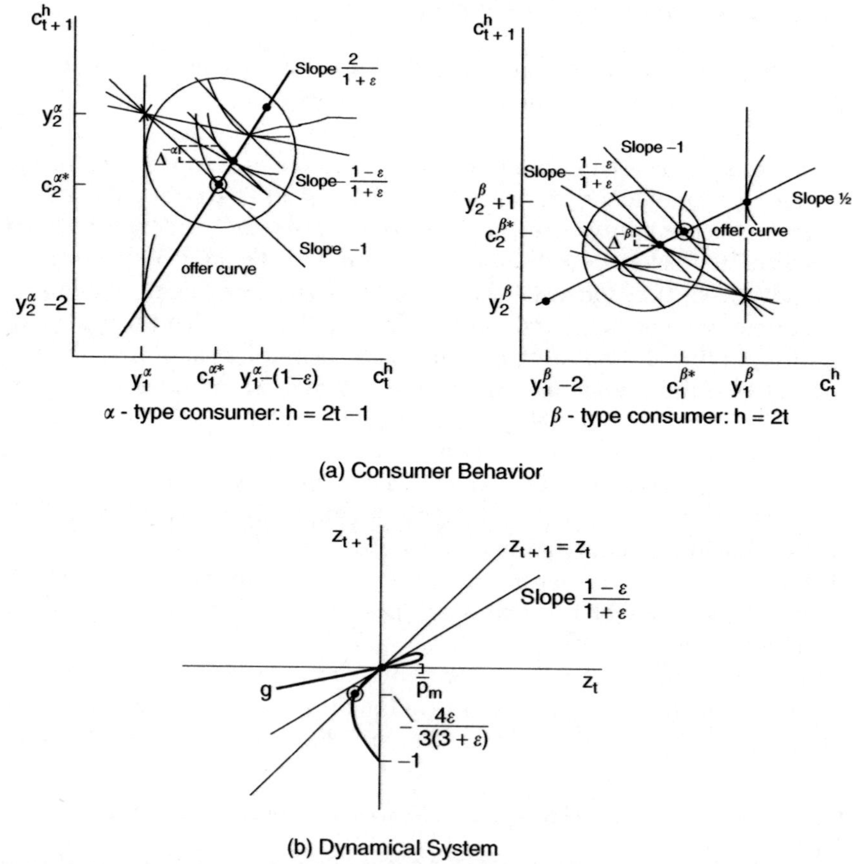

Figure 1: Nonoptimality due to Nonmonotonicity: An Example with Potential Satiation in Second-Period Consumption.

second-period consumption – though at least one type can never become satiated in first-period consumption – while the α- but not the β-type consumer is relatively overburdened with second-period income. Figure 1b exploits the more specific features introduced in order to simplify exposition, especially the particular linear structure of the offer curves of both types of consumers at all except very low real rates of return. The figure makes plain that, while there are a plethora of both barter and monetary equilibria in this example, nevertheless every competitive equilibrium must exhibit real rates of return that satisfy the uniform bound

$$\frac{\partial U^h(c^h)}{\partial c_t^h} \Big/ \frac{\partial U^h(c^h)}{\partial c_{t+1}^h} = p_t/p_{t+1} = z_{t+1}/z_t \leqq (1-\varepsilon)/(1+\varepsilon) < 1$$

for $h = 2t-1, 2t$, and $t \geqq 1$.

Hence, it is easily seen (referring to the encircled portions of Figure 1a and appealing to the specific characteristics of the geometric construction briefly remarked in the following paragraph) that every competitive allocation is dominated by a corresponding feasible allocation that is identical except for a sequence of sufficiently small one-for-one forward transfers between only α-type consumers

$$0 < -\Delta c_t^{2t-1} = \Delta c_{t+1}^{2t-1} = \Delta c^\alpha < \overline{\Delta}^\alpha \text{ for } \quad t \geqq 1$$

or alternatively, only β-type consumers

$$0 < -\Delta c_t^{2t} = \Delta c_{t+1}^{2t} = \Delta c^\beta < \overline{\Delta}^\beta \text{ for } \quad t \geqq 1.$$

That this example is legitimate and, more importantly, that its welfare significance is invariant to sufficiently small perturbations in both tastes and endowments should become self-evident from close examination of Figure 2. This figure contains directions for constructing a well-behaved utility function consistent with my specification of the α-type consumer; a similar procedure can be employed to justify my specification of the β-type consumer. Since both constructs are very closely patterned after that already analyzed at great length in Cass–Okuno–Zilcha (see Section A2 of Chapter 1), I omit further elaboration here.

3. Additional Difficulties Associated with Satiation Phenomena

3.1. Nonexistence of Competitive Equilibrium

Figure 3 displays a technically minor modification of the preceding example that entails a substantively major conclusion. By merely shifting portions of both consumers indifference maps so that the α-type (respectively, β-type)

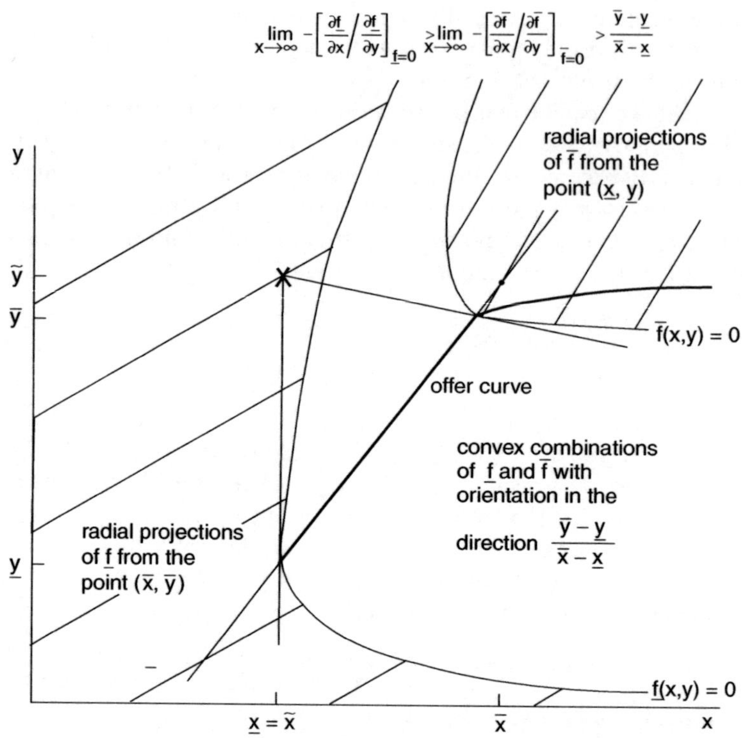

Figure 2: Construction of an Offer Curve Exhibiting Perverse Behavior at Extreme Relative Prices.

consumer's offer curve is considerably less (more) steeply sloped at negative real rates of return near zero, competitive equilibrium ceases to exist.

At first blush this result is somewhat surprising. All consumers' tastes and endowments continue to enjoy the same regularity properties as before upon closer inspection, however, the source of the difficulty is easily discovered. The peculiar second-period nature of satiation has now combined with the intrinsic one-directional nature of time in such a manner that there is simply not enough structural interrelationship between generations to admit trade – even trade only among members of each generation – through the market mechanism. Deficiency of this sort is well known to create difficulties for the existence of competitive equilibrium in the standard Arrow–Debreu model. (See, in particular, the illuminating seminal analysis of McKenzie, 1959[1].) This version of the example suggests that in the intertemporal context these

[1] Author names and years refer to the works listed at the end of this book.

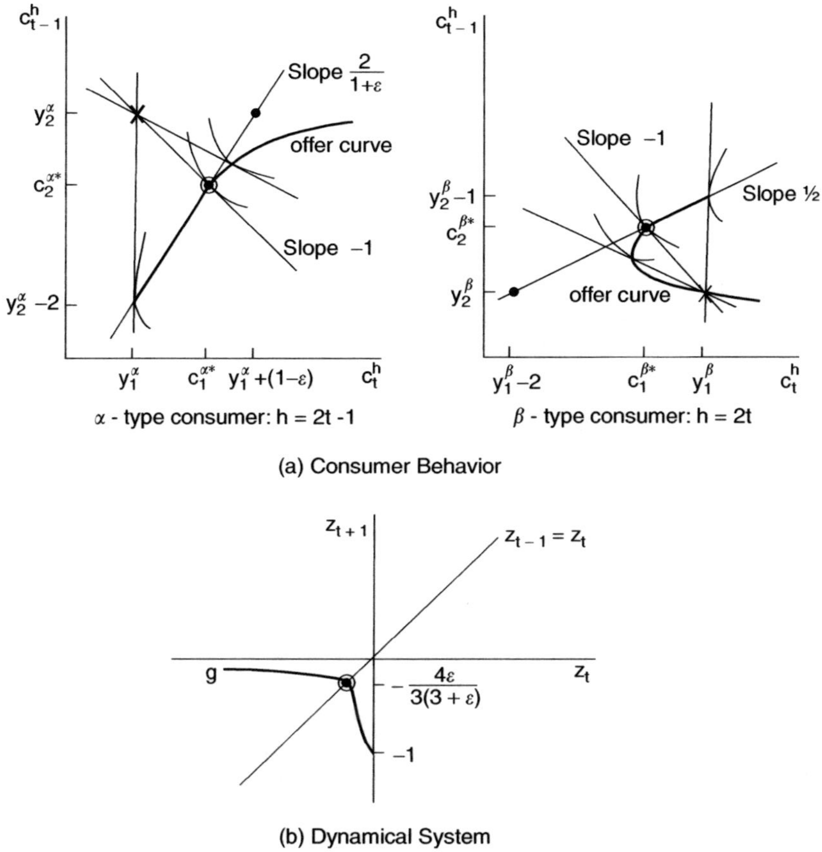

Figure 3: Version of the Example with No Competitive Equilibrium (Barter or Monetary).

difficulties should not be peremptorily dismissed as mere curiosities. It also hints at a commonality between the circumstances giving rise to nonoptimality and those giving rise to nonexistence, which should be thoroughly investigated.

3.2. Ineffectiveness of Social Security

Subject to well-known standard qualifications, the second basic theorem of welfare economics, that every Pareto optimal allocation is a competitive equilibrium (given an appropriate initial distribution of endowments), obtains in consumption loan type models (See, in particular, the even more comprehensive analysis of McFadden, Majumdar, and Mitra, forthcoming.). In the present example (in either its original or modified form), for instance, any redistribution of endowments according to the scheme

$$y^{h\delta} = \begin{cases} y^0 - \dfrac{4\varepsilon}{3(3+\varepsilon)} & \text{for} \quad h = 0 \\ c^{\alpha *} + (\delta, -\delta) & \text{for} \quad h = 2t-1, t \geqq 1 \\ c^{\beta *} + (-\delta, \delta) & \text{otherwise} \end{cases}.$$

permits attaining a barter equilibrium that is Pareto optimal (supported by prices $p_t = 1$ for $t \geqq 1$ and yielding the allocation)

$$c^h = \begin{cases} y^0 - \dfrac{4\varepsilon}{3(3+\varepsilon)} & \text{for} \quad h = 0 \\ c^{\alpha *} & \text{for} \quad h = 2t-1, t \geqq 1 \\ c^{\beta *} & \text{otherwise.} \end{cases}.$$

The central message of this example, of course, is that the historical advent of money as a store of value may not be an adequate proxy for such a redistribution of endowments. Thus, there remains at least partly unanswered an extremely interesting question: What are the simplest extra-market institutional arrangements – perhaps involving some direct redistribution of endowments – that will permit attaining Pareto optimality in a wide class of intertemporal market environments?

I hazard the opinion, based primarily on extensive analysis of consumption loan type models embodying both variety of commodities and diversity of consumers, that a minimal qualification for any such arrangement will be a large degree of flexibility in confronting heterogeneity across agents.

This view is suggestively supported (but by no means precisely or conclusively demonstrated) by considering, for instance, the scope of a perpetual per capita transfer τ from young to old – or a simple social security system – in the present example. It is a fairly straightforward matter to establish that whether or not such uniform social transfers are potent enough to permit attaining Pareto optimality through additional market transfers is problematic and ultimately depends on whether or not they conceivably admit barter equilibrium at some nonnegative real rate of return. Figure 4 presents a polar version of the example in which a simple social security system is necessarily ineffective. The figure is more or less self-explanatory once it is noted that any shift from first- to second-period income essentially results in some distorted rotation of the reflected generational offer curve (still defined relative to original endowments) around its intersection with the 45° line in the negative quadrant.

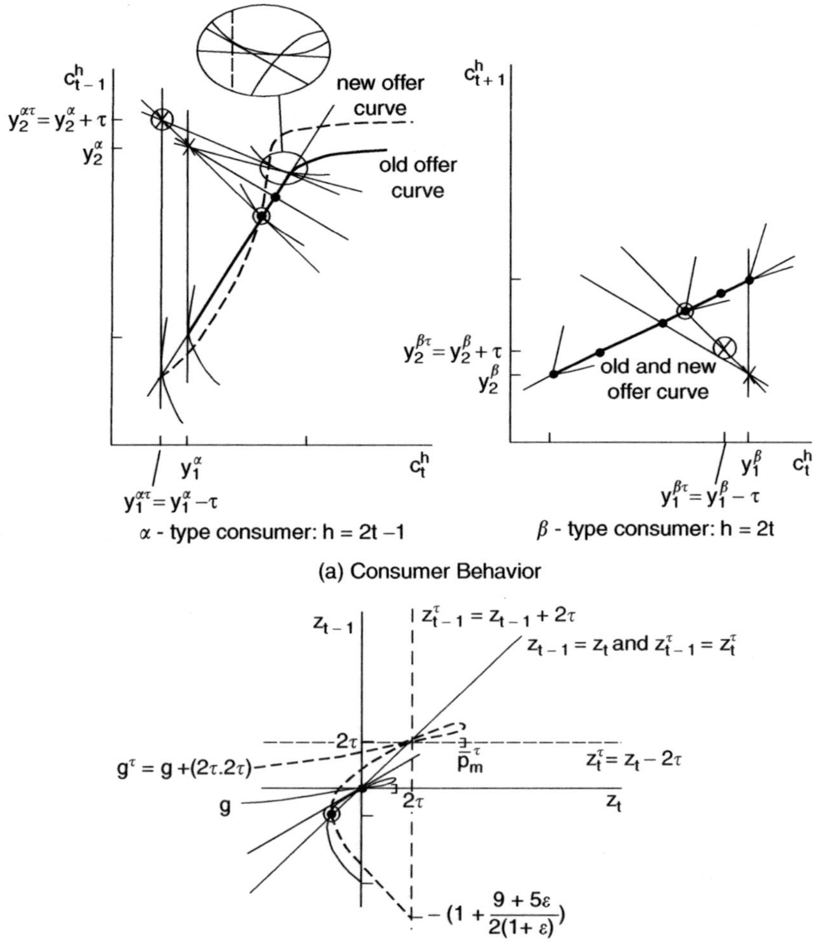

(a) Consumer Behavior

(b) Dynamical System

Figure 4: Version of the Example with a Simple Social Security System which will Not Permit Attaining Pareto Optimality.

Clearly, this counterexample depends on the particular structure of the distortion displayed in Figure 4b, which in turn depends on the particular character of the behavior displayed in Figure 4a – especially the relative sensitivity of the α-type consumer (and the absolute insensitivity of the β-type consumer) to shifts from first- to second-period income. The opposite polar version of the present example, reversing these sensitivities, yields a model in which a simple social security system is potentially effective.

Acknowledgment

I am very grateful to Caltech – and especially its fine group of social scientists – for providing me this excellent opportunity to conduct uninterrupted research in such a congenial environment.

Chapter 4
In Defense of a Basic Approach☆, ☆☆

David Cass and Karl Shell[a]

[a]*CARESS, Philadelphia, PA 19104, USA*

1. Fiat Money: Not Just Another Commodity

Macroeconomic control of contemporary private enterprise economies is exercised primarily through changes in the magnitude of the government's deficit (fiscal policy) and changes in the composition of the government's debt, that is, its cumulated deficits, between "fiat" money and "fiat" bonds (monetary policy). To understand macroeconomic policy, we must be able to explain how the private sector reacts to government expenditures, taxes and transfers, and money creation and extinction.

☆These reflections were set down several months after the Federal Reserve Bank of Minneapolis conference on "Models of Monetary Economies." Their proximate cause was the generally negative reaction by the conference participants to Neil Wallace's forthright assertion of the importance of consumption loan or overlapping-generations models for understanding monetary phenomena in a private, market economy. We support Wallace's basic position. Indeed, we have for some time believed (and preached) that these models offer an intellectually attractive framework for studying many aspects of decentralized intertemporal allocation – provided, of course, that some care is taken to distinguish between fundamental or inherent features and convenient or provisional simplifications. This opportunity to articulate our position is also a natural forum for us to air our misgivings about various currently fashionable prejudices in monetary and macroeconomic theory and to present our views about various more constructive alternatives for future development.

The collaboration underlying this paper has taken place over several years, encompassing both Shell's visit as a Guggenheim Fellow at CEPREMAP during 1977–1978 and Cass visit as a Sherman Fairchild Distinguished Scholar at Caltech during 1978–1979. The paper itself represents an effort to lay out the general methodological position motivating a series of specific analytical studies of overlapping-generations models. It thus constitutes part of a more extensive project being underwritten by a grant to the Center for Analytic Research in Economics and the Social Sciences (at Penn) from the National Science Foundation. We are grateful to all these institutions for their support and encouragement.

☆☆Reprinted from *Models of Monetary Economies*, J.H. Kareken and N. Wallace, eds., "In Defense of a Basic Approach", David Cass and Karl Shell, 251–260, © Federal Reserve Bank of Minneapolis, 1980

International Symposia in Economic Theory and Econometrics, Vol. 21B
S. Spear (Editor)

ISSN: 1571-0386/DOI: 10.1108/S1571-0386(2011)000021B007

Government debt (in its various forms) can serve in a host of roles for the private sector – as a store of value, as a convenient means for transactions, as an exclusive vehicle for tax payments, and so forth. These various roles are generally closely interdependent and strongly influenced by the particular conventional and institutional arrangements in an economy. One of them, however, is crucial to all the others: *If money and bonds do not serve as a value store, then they cannot serve any other useful function.* Our current research focuses on the role of money and bonds as a store of value – not because we are necessarily persuaded that this is the most interesting aspect of the paper assets created by the government, but rather because we are firmly convinced that this basic function must be well understood before we can begin to understand any of their more complicated functions.

Jim Tobin has taught us that, for most purposes of understanding decentralized allocation involving stores of value, there is no essential difference between paper currency, treasury bills, and any other government issue. So as a convenience, we will refer to all forms of government debt as simply *money*.

It is obvious (and well-known) that money cannot have a positive price – that is, cannot be a store of value – in the conventional finite-horizon model in which the "end of the world" is known with certainty. The reason is simple. At the end of the last period, money is worthless. Therefore, in the next-to-last period, all individuals desire to dispose of money holdings in order to avoid capital losses. This drives the price of money to zero at the end of the next-to-last period. And so on. Individuals with foresight, not wanting to be stuck with the monetary "hot-potato," thus drive the price of money to zero in each period.

Some students of money-macro may claim that it is easy to modify the classical Walrasian model to allow (even insure!) the price of money to be positive. Simply introduce money balances as arguments in utility functions or production functions, reflecting the reduced transaction costs in a monetary economy. (Never mind how we transform nominal to real when there are many commodities.) We reject this approach. Imbedding money in preferences or technologies does nothing to explain its role as a store of value. Moreover, such reduced forms are at best poor proxies for their structural counterparts. (We will have more to say about modeling transaction constraints below.) Worst of all, to the extent that this maneuver is successful, it is also likely to be misleading.

We know that money is not just another commodity. Tastes and endowments (including production possibilities) determine the relative price of apples in terms of oranges in the simple equilibrium model. But unlike ordinary Walrasian goods, the usefulness or "productivity" of money depends on its price. In particular, suppose that a barter equilibrium exists for a given market economy (with a given payments mechanism) without nominal money. Then it must be the case that, when such money is introduced into the economy, one of the new equilibria will be the old barter equilibrium with positive nominal money bearing a zero price. It could be that all households would be better off if the price of money were positive. But this does not imply that a zero price is a disequilibrium price. Trust in fiat money is only a recent development, and even today such faith is hardly universal.

2. Modeling Fiat Money: The Overlapping-Generations Approach

The natural way to avoid modeling "hot-potato" money is to avoid modeling a finite-horizon economy. Individuals surely know they won't be around forever. They likely don't even expect their influence to persist much beyond their own lifetimes; that would be silly. But they do believe – or, if you prefer, act as if they believe – that contemporary economic institutions are essentially immortal. An obvious model to build on, then, is Samuelson's model of overlapping generations: Economic agents come and go, disposing of their finite wealth over their finite lifetimes, while economic society is presumed to continue without known end.

It is unfortunate that this type of model has been almost exclusively associated with narrow issues in intertemporal welfare theory. (An outstanding exception, of course, is Bob Lucas' influential contribution to the money-macro field.) We, as much as anybody, must share the blame. Perhaps it would be useful to find a less connotative label for its basic structure; while *overlapping generations* is clearly better than *consumption loan*, it too carries overly restrictive associations. Be that as it may, this basic structure has two general features that we believe are indispensable to the development of macroeconomics as an intellectually convincing discipline. While both have already been mentioned, at least indirectly, both will bear repeating for emphasis.

First, it is genuinely dynamic. In this it significantly departs from the basically atemporal character of most received doctrine: There is explicit recognition of both the inherent mortality (as well as vitality) of the actors, together with the continual (as well as unceasing) evolution of their stage.

Second, it is fundamentally disaggregative. In this it is founded in perhaps the oldest theoretical tradition in economics: There is a clear distinction between economic agents' objectives and constraints – and hence the mainsprings of their individual behavior – and the economic system's coherent resolution of their joint interaction.

Isn't this, you ask, a pretentious basis on which to justify analysis of obviously rudimentary versions of the overlapping-generations model, for instance, that contained in several of the contributions to this volume? Not at all.

While it is important to distinguish the inherent underlying character of this model, it is also important to recognize the potential significance of its various provisional specializations. These would include such simplifying assumptions as that of homogeneous households (both within and across generations), two-period lifetimes, a single physical commodity, distribution without any production (or with, at most, very elementary production), complete and costless markets, and full and accurate information (concerning both the present and the future). Taken together they constitute reducing the model to its barest essential elements (within a conventional framework of maintained assumptions, to be sure). The parallel with the reduction of the classical Walrasian model to its leading special case of pure distribution of two commodities between two households is unmistakable. In both cases such reduction is perfectly acceptable for certain purposes, according to a fundamental precept: Skeletal models not only yield (or verify) definite counterexamples but also suggest (or illustrate) possible theorems. Perhaps most important, we are confident that, through the normal scientific process, tentative results derived from the simplest versions of the overlapping-generations model – and many other questions as well – will be investigated in much more general terms. Indeed, we know that some of these more extensive analyses are already well under way.

Following the cardinal rule that simple models can best be employed to produce counterexamples, variations of the overlapping generations parable have been insightfully utilized to teach us several valuable lessons. First and foremost, of course, are the optimality counterexamples contained in Paul Samuelson's seminal analysis itself: Purely by virtue of the one-directional, open-ended nature of time, *competitive allocation may fail to be Pareto optimal.* But there are other lessons to be learned as well, with both positive and normative implications. Especially instructive are the determinacy counterexamples stemming from the introduction of money into the basic story: Purely by virtue of the enormous latitude associated with the consistency criterion that aggregate outcomes accord with individual predictions, *there is typically a plethora of potential monetary equilibria.*

Vast multiplicity of potential competitive equilibria is an inherent property of the economy with money (or, for that matter, with any marketable asset that can serve as a temporary abode for purchasing power into perpetuity). This central feature turns out to be of crucial importance to the theory and practice of macroeconomic policy.

Consider first the solution concept normally employed in the standard general equilibrium model as applied to its overlapping-generations extension. Competitive equilibrium prices are consistent with market clearing and ultimately depend only on tastes, endowments, technology, the range of markets, and the actions of government (hereafter, exclusively limited to *monetary policy*[1]). But money is not desirable for its own sake, only for its market value (particularly by those individuals who are endowed with it). Hence, even in a nonstochastic environment, there are typically very many potential monetary equilibria associated with each perfectly anticipated monetary policy; within some limits, very many perceptions of the possible state of the economy (or predicted paths of market prices for commodities in terms of money) are consistent with realizations of the actual state of the economy (or observed paths of market prices for commodities in terms of money). And this remains so even if one prespecifies, for instance, some initial price, or equivalently, its reciprocal, the (present value) price of money.

A dual result to the last is that for each positive price of money there are typically very many potential monetary policies consistent with market clearing – each generally associated with a different set of competitive allocations. In short, monetary policy matters very much!

Even though the resulting competitive equilibrium is largely indeterminate, we still find this conventional solution concept too restrictive for the overlapping-generations model. For example, individuals might well believe that market prices follow a process (stochastic or nonstochastic) depending on some seemingly extraneous phenomenon, say, sunspot activity. Again within some limits, if individuals believe that the economy is affected by sunspot activity, then it might well be – even imposing the "rationality" requirement that expectations be fulfilled. In this sense, the future can be said to create its own uncertainty; because sunspot activity is held to be important, its level is a proper state variable, and its possible sequences of realizations must be fully accounted for in the appropriate solution concept.

The essential point is that in a truly dynamic context, even with perfect foresight and without intrinsic uncertainty, pure theory provides no obvious natural selection of the particular elements on which individuals condition their forecasts (a point made by Bob Shiller and others); the state variables of the system cannot be determined independent of individual beliefs. Furthermore, if in fact sunspot activity (or some less fanciful state variable, say, calendar time itself) induces undesirable fluctuations in the economy, it

[1] We adopt the convention employed in the overlapping generations (and related money-macro) literature of referring to a sequence of injections of money into the economy by means of lump-sum transfers (with either algebraic sign) as a *monetary policy*. However, we are aware of the confusion this might cause, since – especially given the rudimentary treatment of possible actions of government in this context – such means of control is much closer to what is traditionally recognized as fiscal policy. We ask to be excused for this convenient, if misleading usage.

may be altogether fitting for the government to announce and pursue a policy of counteracting the resultant market disruption. Economic agents – including both households and government, and no matter how sophisticated – must not only assess the "fundamentals" of the economy, but also may very well have to pay attention to the "psychology" of the market.

3. Working Toward General Theorems

What about more definite results? How do or will studies of such elementary models lead to general theorems concerning dynamic, disaggregative allocation processes? These questions are still largely, though not completely, unanswered.

The contrast between the central thrust of the first part of the Wallace paper and that of the major part of the Cass–Okuno–Zilcha chapter (together with its addendum) offers a nice illustration of this state of affairs. Both analyses deal with a plausible conjecture suggested by the simplest version of the overlapping-generations model, namely, that given the institution of fiat money, some competitive equilibrium (possibly non-monetary, likely monetary) must be Pareto optimal.

On the one hand, Wallace's work (as well as Brock and Scheinkman's parallel study) shows that this conjecture has a natural extension covering a particular class of active monetary policies. Specifically, Wallace considers the situation where the money supply is being increased (or decreased) at a constant rate by means of equal nominal transfers to (or taxes from) the households in each successive generation. Then, after insuring that his idealized economy is capable of attaining competitive equilibria that closely resemble steady states, he demonstrates that when the money supply is in fact not being strictly increased, some competitive equilibrium must be Pareto optimal. Throughout his analysis, Wallace maintains all of the various simplifying assumptions mentioned above.

On the other hand, Cass, Okuno, and Zilcha investigate the original conjecture itself and show that it is quite sensitive to relaxing just one of these standard provisional specializations. In particular, they demonstrate that the proposed result may not obtain when households display systematic diversity in tastes and endowments across succeeding generations – or even significant diversity within succeeding generations, provided households are also liable to substantial satiation in consumption over their life cycles.

Undoubtedly, this conjectured proposition (as well as its suggested extension) is valid in some more general contexts (at least when there is neither widespread household diversity nor excessive potential satiation). A precise statement and proof of this sort of general theorem, however, remains to be seen.

In fact, at this writing, there are virtually no well-established general theorems for the overlapping-generations model available in the literature. The prime reason for this paucity of substantial results is clear: Very little is known about the most basic properties of this model except in its rudest embodiments. Thus, for instance, only recently has serious work begun on uncovering the limiting conditions under which there necessarily exists *any* competitive equilibrium in the presence of many types of (finitely lived) households, many varieties of (exogenously given) commodities, and arbitrary (typically active) monetary policy. It is worthwhile to notice that this fundamental enterprise, which is currently being undertaken by Okuno, Zilcha, Balasko, and Shell, relies on obvious but critical insights gained from the simplest cases – for example, their common property that if there exists some competitive equilibrium (monetary or nonmonetary), then there exists a nonmonetary equilibrium. It is also important to realize that this work is relatively straightforward compared to that of formulating and analyzing the subtle issues involved in characterizing the intrinsic structure of the set of competitive equilibria (monetary as well as nonmonetary) in the same model or its even yet broader generalizations. Research into these more profound problems seems to us an essential next step in the further refinement of the overlapping-generations model. These crucial investigations are also presently being pursued by those mentioned above (as well as several others, e.g., McFadden, Mitra, and Majumdar).

The question of what constitutes a general result rather than a special case is at best nebulous. This is so even for our present purposes, where we have already explicitly focused on a particular class of economic models, those displaying the inherent structural features of the overlapping-generations parable. One basic reason is that the answer to this question ultimately depends on adopting and maintaining some limited reference framework, itself a specialized and idealized view of individual capacities and the context of social arrangements through which they range. Another is that, even within such a stylized purview, there is no absolute law distinguishing good from bad (or useful from useless or realistic from unrealistic or …) simplifications.

Here, as in our own work, we have already implicitly chosen a conventional neoclassical framework. This particular view, embracing a large part of modern economic theory, emphasizes individual rationality (an apt if much abused descriptive phrase) and concentrates on market exchange of private commodities by competitive agents. We are prepared to defend this position, even while conceding that there are many seemingly attractive modifications and extensions. We think it will be more rewarding, however, if instead we sketch our more eclectic views of what are, given the neoclassical orthodoxy, good and bad simplifications. The next section addresses this issue. These remarks can be taken as extended comments on each of the various simplifying assumptions listed in Section 2.

4. Good and Bad Simplifications

4.1. Diversity of Households and Commodities

Our synopsis of the state of current research into basic aspects of the overlapping-generations model suggested one of our most fundamental methodological biases. We firmly believe that a satisfactory general theory must, at a minimum, encompass some diversity among households as well as some variety among commodities. There is simply not much (except perhaps tractability) to recommend constructing an elaborate macroeconomic edifice on microeconomic foundations built without any reinforcement from the admixture of distributional effects. To put this point bluntly: A behavioral specification in terms of the first-order conditions describing rational choice by a representative household between consumption today and tomorrow is every bit as crude an approximation as one in terms of an aggregate consumption function.

We do, however, freely acknowledge that it also makes little sense to ignore the fact that there are recognizable patterns in the distribution of tastes and endowments across households; contemporary individuals are subject to many of the same formative influences, while by and large their social and economic environment itself evolves both slowly and smoothly. Our position necessarily embraces, and even positively encourages, introducing and analyzing (consistent and verifiable) regularities in aggregate behavior. Otherwise our proposed quest for a richer macroeconomics would be self-defeating.

In particular, this means that we certainly don't subscribe to the almost total agnosticism implicit in the excess demand characterizations pioneered by Hugo Sonnenschein. But then we also surely can't ignore the thrust of their central message: Diversity of households – together with what we have known for a long time, variety of commodities – will typically impose a significant constraint on our ability to derive substantial propositions concerning qualitative effects.

4.2. Reinterpreting Periods and Commodities

In contrast to the clearly limiting character of the postulate that representative households choose between just two (physical) commodities, it should be emphasized that certain of the simplifying assumptions that have been commonly adopted in the overlapping-generations literature are by themselves not at all restrictive. In particular, when markets are perfect, a completely general model with arbitrary but finite lifetimes is formally indistinguishable from a singularly special model with at most two-period lifetimes (but with many households in each generation and many commodities in each period) – given suitable reinterpretation of both *periods* and *commodities*. Such broad latitude in interpreting what are commodities (according to physical, spatial, temporal, eventual, ... characteristics) is so familiar from the Arrow–Debreu tradition that it needs no further elaboration here, except perhaps to underline an obvious but important caveat: Reinterpretation is severely circumscribed when, for instance, markets are incomplete or information is partial (say, especially, due to the intrinsic nature of time). In any case, it is simply inappropriate to complain that existing analyses based on the overlapping-generations parable necessarily involve incredibly low velocities of money, that is, holding periods of 25-year duration. (From this viewpoint, however, the existing analyses do typically involve incredibly uniform homogeneity in tastes.)

4.3. Capital Goods as Stores of Value

The competitive mechanism converts privately owned commodities into privately consumed goods. The standard general equilibrium literature makes clear that whether this is accomplished indirectly by production (treating technology as part of the household endowment) together with distribution or directly by distribution alone is an inessential detail. However, in models that treat time seriously, there is an important aspect of production that will need to be accounted for: Durable productive assets (land, machines, natural resources, and the like) also serve as stores of value. A first pass in understanding the role of government debt as a store of value allows us to ignore these capital goods, since the most important element common to all assets is the intrinsic difficulty in evaluating future terms of trade. Incorporation of many alternative assets into the model of overlapping generations must nonetheless be considered to have high priority on the research agenda. Imagine macroeconomics without a description of the choice between holding real assets and government debt (and other paper assets)!

4.4. The Costs of Trading

The fact that trading itself requires scarce resources cannot be avoided. One of money's principal functions is to reduce these transaction costs. While a fully satisfactory microeconomic theory of money and transactions has yet to be developed, it should be clear that the analysis must be dynamic. If trading somehow took place outside time, then the problems of matching buyers and sellers and settling their complicated sets of accounts would be of little consequence. In reality, however, all trades are dynamic, since the trading process itself requires time. Even so-called spot trades involve rather sophisticated institutional arrangements because actual contracts are not conveniently signed and executed on a perfectly synchronized basis.

When longer periods of time are involved, these difficulties are compounded. Futures trading requires more detailed monitoring procedures and more careful enforcement procedures to protect against the obvious hazards of contract nonperformance. As a result, the costs associated with borrowing are typically very high for the individual without tangible assets that can be used to guarantee her/his loan. In fact, the transaction costs on unsecured borrowing are so high that, as a good first approximation, it could be assumed that all spot and future purchases must be financed either from present money balances or from the money received from the sale of present commodity inventories.

This means that, in addition to their intertemporal (or solvency) constraints, individuals also face period-by-period (or liquidity) constraints that limit them to trades supportable by current holdings. Monetary policy, by controlling the amount, timing, and distribution of money holdings, has an effect on aggregate demand. The government's ability to influence individual liquidity constraints is an important source of the potency of its macroeconomic policies.

Liquidity constraints, representing imperfect borrowing markets, are readily incorporated into the overlapping-generations model; indeed, they have already been easily incorporated into fairly robust versions of the standard general equilibrium model (with, however, limited success since that model offers no satisfactory resolution of the "hot-potato" problem). Although a fuller understanding of the detailed structure of marketing activity is clearly desirable, we believe that straightforward modeling of constraints on individual liquidity may well capture many of the essential aspects of costly trading that are critical to macroeconomic policy.

4.5. Expectations

At the heart of macroeconomic theory is the determination of asset prices. But assets have value today in large measure because they have (or, more precisely, are believed to have) value tomorrow. Thus, asset prices must be largely based on individual expectations about the future. How are these beliefs formed, and what is the nature of the resulting competitive equilibrium?

The perfect-foresight (or, more fashionably, rational expectations) hypothesis provides a useful starting point for understanding this process. This is not because it is a realistic informational postulate; it is surely quite unrealistic. Rather, it is because the hypothesis is the exact analog of the familiar atemporal assumption of full information and because it is consonant with the ultimate outcome of many credible models of intelligent learning behavior. As such it provides a good benchmark (at least for some normative purposes) and accords with an inherent distaste for any theory of expectations formation that does not allow for consistent adaptation (at least in some limiting sense).

As we see it, then, the perfect-foresight hypothesis is at best a positive descriptive model only in terms of representing a plausible asymptotic structure for some very complicated process by which individuals discover how the state of the economy tomorrow will depend on the state of the world tomorrow. Modeling this process itself is, therefore, clearly of utmost importance. Unfortunately, like the rest of the professions, we have few specific suggestions to offer at this stage of our knowledge; idle conjecture without concrete analysis does not seem especially helpful. We can, however, foresee two obvious difficulties confronting such an enterprise.

We have argued earlier that, even given the perfect-foresight hypothesis, there is no obvious natural selection of the particular features of the world on which individuals focus in predicting the future of the economy. This must be doubly true when, in addition, individuals are groping toward enlightenment – particularly since individuals are assuredly mortal[2] (so that the learning process involves a continually changing progression of individuals) while, under the circumstances, their environment is apparently inconstant (so that there is absolutely no assurance that the world tomorrow will retain essential properties of the world today). Our parents' beliefs were greatly shaped by the advent of the New Deal; our children's will be by the advent of the OPEC cartel.

This observation suggests a related difficulty, namely, that there is no a priori justification for assuming (and therefore biasing research toward establishing) that a reasonable learning process necessarily converges to anything like perfect foresight. Even when the underlying economic "fundamentals" are agreed to be stationary, evolving market "psychology" may render perceptions of their import decidedly nonstationary. Furthermore, there is no obvious reason for assuming that an individual who holds "irrational" beliefs would be better off if converted to "rational" beliefs.

[2] Only gods are immortal – as well as omniscient. The assumption that households effectively live forever, not at all uncommon in the literature, is itself fairly unbelievable. But that infinitely lived households also accurately foretell eternity – even taken as an idealization – clearly defies common sense. Any fully evolved learning process necessarily requires frequently repeated individual performance, and this prerequisite is simply out of the question when a shaved die is only cast once (or, who knows, an unbalanced wheel is only spun once or ...).

Finally, we view attempts to avoid the deep problems associated with modeling expectations formation by arbitrarily restricting either the fundamental learning process or its presumed ultimate outcome – in particular, by concentrating on uniquely determined steady states – to be basically misleading, essentially investing pure technical simplification with the aura of hard economic law. In this regard, we should mention that such restriction plays a crucial part in the purported "rational expectations" proof of the quantity theory of money. Our rebuttal to this asserted claim has already been argued in Section 2.

5. Concluding Comments

There are now two main schools of thought dominating macroeconomics, the *rational expectations* (RE) school and the *Keynesian econometrics* (KE) school. The KE school tends to reject the results of the RE school on the grounds that the assumptions of competitive behavior, complete markets, and perfect foresight are unrealistic. According to the RE school, the KE approach is suspect because it is not derived from consistent individual maximizing behavior.

We do not join this debate; we have chosen instead to accumulate more intellectual capital. It is clear to us that more fundamental research is needed before these issues can be put in proper perspective. While each school rejects many of the assumptions as well as conclusions of the other school, from our present viewpoint it is not even necessarily evident that either group's policy recommendations follow given its philosophical and theoretical predilections.

We plan to play a part in developing a truly dynamic analysis of government debt and intertemporal allocation. To be useful, the analysis must also be fundamentally disaggregative. We have, therefore, no choice but to build our theories on the foundation of the overlapping-generations model. By definition, it is the only genuinely dynamic, basically disaggregate framework available.

Chapter 5

Existence of Competitive Equilibrium in a General Overlapping-Generations Model ☆

Yves Balasko[a,b], David Cass and Karl Shell[b]

[a]*Université Paris I and CEPREMAP, Paris, France*
[b]*CARESS, Philadelphia, PA 19104, USA*

1. Introduction

In the companion chapter, Balasko and Shell (1980) establish existence of competitive equilibrium for a pure-distribution, overlapping-generations economy without money (see, especially, Propositions (3.10) and (3.11) in Section 3). That argument is remarkably simple, but depends critically on some strong hypotheses concerning individual tastes and endowments. In particular, it is assumed that, in any given period, every living consumer has a utility function that is strictly increasing in every available commodity, as well as an endowment that is strictly positive in every available commodity.

These two assumptions are especially difficult to rationalize in an intergenerational context. How many teenagers do you know who are eager viewers of Lawrence Welk? How many "middle-agers" who are likely users of Clearasil? So much for increasing (much less strictly increasing) utility functions! Regarding strictly positive endowments, we invite the readers to dream up their own counterexamples. (Another hint: How do you respond to the commonly heard lament, "What I wouldn't give to be young again!"?)

In the present chapter, we do away with such unrealistically severe hypotheses. And we do more. Following the Arrow–Debreu tradition, we postulate fairly mild conditions on individual tastes and endowments. Of course, in line with the same tradition, we must then impose some further conditions on the potential economic interrelationships among consumers. This additional structure is an application to the overlapping-generations model of McKenzie's basic concept of irreducibility.

☆This article was originally published in *Journal of Economic Theory* 23, Yves Balasko, David Cass and Karl Shell, "Existence of Competitive Equilibrium in a General Overlapping-Generations Model", 307–322, © Elsevier, 1980.

International Symposia in Economic Theory and Econometrics, Vol. 21B
S. Spear (Editor)

ISSN: 1571-0386/DOI: 10.1108/S1571-0386(2011)000021B008

2. A General Overlapping-Generations Model

The details of our formal model are closely patterned after those elaborated in Balasko and Shell (1980) (see, especially, Section 2). The most significant differences in assumptions, terminology, and notation are the following:

1. In each period t ($t = 1, 2, \ldots$) there is an arbitrary, finite number of completely perishable physical commodities $1 \leq l^t < \infty$.
2. Each consumer h ($h = 0, 1, \ldots$) lives only two periods.[1] However, in each period t (including $t = 0$, the period just prior to the inception of economic activity) the newly born group of consumers, or generation t, $G^t \subset \{h : h \geq 0\}$ consists of an arbitrary, finite number of two-period lived members $1 \leq \#G^t < \infty$.
3. Consumption sets are simply the nonnegative orthants[2]

$$x_h = x_h^1 = (x_h^{1,1}, x_h^{1,2}, \ldots, x_h^{1,l^1}) \in \mathbb{R}_+^{l^1} \quad \text{for} \quad h \in G^0$$

and

$$x_h = (x_h^t, x_h^{t+1}) = (x_h^{t,1}, \ldots, x_h^{t,l^t}, x_h^{t+1,1}, \ldots, x_h^{t+1,l^{t+1}}) \in \mathbb{R}_+^{l^t + l^{t+1}}$$
$$\text{for} \quad h \in G^t, \; t \geq 1.$$

[1] Given our other maintained assumptions, this particular assumption is perfectly innocuous. The completely general economy with arbitrary, finite lifetimes is formally indistinguishable from the (apparently) singularly special one with (at most) two-period lifetimes – given suitable reinterpretation of both "periods" and "commodities." Because of its special relevance to our formulation, we present a detailed description of such reinterpretation in the concluding section.

This reinterpretation captures the essential feature of genuine generational overlap. More importantly, the assumption itself permits rather extensive simplification of the natural dynamical analysis associated with an overlapping-generations demographic structure.

[2] The introduction of consumption sets that are only required to be closed, convex, and bounded below – and, more broadly, production sets (as part of endowments), which are only required to exhibit standard regularity, convexity, and boundedness properties – is conceptually straightforward. Unfortunately, unlike our introduction of arbitrary numbers of coexisting commodities and contemporary consumers, this direction of generalization involves considerable additional notational and analytical complexity. This is reason enough to forego pursuing it. Another, perhaps more compelling, justification for generalizing in one but not the other direction is that multiplicity of commodities and consumers is, in a sense, necessary for consistency with our very convenient specialization to two-period lifetimes – as the discussion in the concluding section makes plain.

However, utility functions $u_h(\cdot)$ are only required to be continuous, quasiconcave, and without local maxima, while endowment vectors ω_h are only required to be nonnegative and nontrivial.

4. Allocation sequences are denoted by $x = (x_1, x_2, \ldots, x_h, \ldots)$, and price sequences by $\mathfrak{p} = (p^1, p^2, \ldots, p^t, \ldots)$. Also, the set of feasible allocation sequences is denoted by

$$\mathfrak{X} = \left\{ \mathfrak{x} : \mathfrak{x} \geq 0 \text{ and } \sum_{h \in G^{t-1} \cup G^t} x_h^t \leq \sum_{h \in G^{t-1} \cup G^t} \omega_h^t \text{ for } t \geq 1 \right\},$$

and the set of conceivable price sequences by[3]

$$\mathfrak{B} = \{\mathfrak{p} : \mathfrak{p} > 0\}.$$

5. As in Balasko and Shell (1980), $x_h(\mathfrak{p})$ represents the *ordinary* lifetime consumption profiles for consumer h given the price sequence $\mathfrak{p} \in \mathfrak{B}$, that is, the optimal solutions to the budget-constrained utility maximization problem[4]

$$\text{maximize } u_h(x_h) \text{ subject to } \mathfrak{p} \cdot x_h \leq \mathfrak{p} \cdot \omega_h \text{ and } x_h \geq 0. \tag{1}$$

We will also find it useful to have notation representing the *compensated* lifetime consumption profiles for consumer h given the price sequence $\mathfrak{p} \in \mathfrak{B}$ and the utility level $u_h \in \mathbb{R}$. So let $x_h(\mathfrak{p}, u_h)$ denote the optimal solutions to the utility-constrained budget minimization problem

$$\text{minimize } \mathfrak{p} \cdot x_h \text{ subject to } u_h(x_h) \geq u_h \text{ and } x_h \geq 0. \tag{2}$$

6. We assume that the economy is *intertemporaly irreducible* in the following precise sense (compare with McKenzie, 1959, pp. 58–59, 247): Let a *t-generation economy* $\mathscr{E}^t$ be specified by the tastes and endowments of the group of consumers born up through period t, that is, by $u_h(\cdot)$ and ω_h for $h \in H^t = \{h : h \in G^s \text{ for } 0 \leq s \leq t\}$. Then, we require that there be a subsequence of periods $\{t_v\}$ with the property that, given any t_v-generation economy $\mathscr{E}^{t_v}$ and any feasible allocation sequence $\mathfrak{x} \in \mathfrak{X}$, for every $H_1^{t_v}, H_2^{t_v} \subset H^{t_v}$ such that $H_1^{t_v}, H_2^{t_v} \neq \varnothing$, $H_1^{t_v} \cap H_2^{t_v} = \varnothing$ and

[3] We adopt the convention that, for any pair of vectors $\boldsymbol{x}$ and $\boldsymbol{y}$, (or, similarly, sequences $\mathfrak{x}$ and η), "$\boldsymbol{x} \geq \boldsymbol{y}$" means $x_i \geq y_i$ for every i, "$\boldsymbol{x} > \boldsymbol{y}$" means $x_i \geq y_i$ for every i and $x_i > y_i$ for some i, and "$\boldsymbol{x} \gg \boldsymbol{y}$" means $x_i > y_i$ for every i.

[4] It is also convenient to follow Balasko and Shell (1980) in letting x_h (or, similarly, ω_h) denote either the vector defined earlier (as in the expression $u_h(x_h)$) or the particular corresponding sequence $x_h = (x_h^1, 0, \ldots, 0, \ldots)$ for $h \in G^0$ and $x_h = (0, \ldots, 0, x_h^t, x_h^{t+1}, 0, \ldots)$ for $h \in G^t, t \geq 1$ (as in the expression $\mathfrak{p} \cdot x_h \leq \mathfrak{p} \cdot \omega_h$).

$H_1^{t_v} \cup H_2^{t_v} = H^{t_v}$, there exist $y_h \geq 0$ for $h \in H_1^{t_v}$ and $x'_h \geq 0$ for $h \in H_2^{t_v}$ such that

$$\sum_{h \in H_1^{t_v}} y_h^{t,i} = 0 \quad \text{whenever} \quad \sum_{h \in H_1^{t_v}} \omega_h^{t,i} = 0$$

$$\text{for} \quad 1 \leq i \leq l^t, \quad 1 \leq t \leq t_v + 1,$$

$$\sum_{h \in H_2^{t_v}} x_h^t \leq \sum_{h \in H^{t_v}} \omega_h + \sum_{h \in H_1^{t_v}} y_h = \sum_{h \in H_1^{t_v}} (\omega_h + y_h) + \sum_{h \in H_2^{t_v}} \omega_h$$

and

$$u_h(x'_h) \geq u_h(x_h) \quad \text{for every} \quad h \in H_2^{t_r}$$

and

$$u_h(x'_h) > u_h(x_h) \quad \text{for some} \quad h \in H_2^{t_r}.$$

In short, no matter how we split up the group of consumers born in period t_v, we can always augment just those commodities provided by the first subgroup in sufficient amount so that we can then redistribute the augmented total endowment of the whole group to improve the welfare of the second subgroup.[5]

3. The Existence of Competitive Equilibrium

3.1. Statement and Preliminary Discussion

We take the assumption that commodities are completely perishable to entail that they are also freely disposable. So, in accord with the basic precept that scare goods are necessarily related to positive prices, we define

[5] It is worth noting that our specific adaptation of McKenzie's ingenious condition is weaker than imposing the same restriction on every t-generation economy; it may simply be impossible to improve the welfare of some member of generation t without recourse to redistributions involving the endowment of some member of generation $t+1$. On the other hand, since such a circumstance can conceivably prevail for some member of all but a finite number of generations, it is equally clear that our condition is stronger than the requirement that the whole economy be irreducible (say, in the same precise sense we have prescribed for each t_v-generation economy). Whether our existence result can be extended to cover the broader situation remains to be seen.

A suggestive example of possible nonexistence when the economy is not intertemporaly irreducible is sketched in Cass (1979).

$(\mathfrak{x}, \mathfrak{p}) \in \mathfrak{X} \times \mathfrak{P}$ to be a *competitive equilibrium* if

$$x_h \in x_h(\mathfrak{p}) \quad \text{for} \quad h \geq 0$$

and

$$\sum_{h \in G^{t-1} \cup G^t} x_h^{t,i} = \sum_{h \in G^{t-1} \cup G^t} \omega_h^{t,i} \quad \text{whenever } p^{t,i} > 0 \text{ for } 1 \leq i \leq l^t, \quad t \geq 1.$$

Our central result is the following:

Existence Theorem. *Under the hypotheses stated above, there exists a competitive equilibrium.*

The proof of this Existence Theorem is similar in spirit to that presented in Balasko and Shell (1980), and revolves around the idea of taking limits of suitably truncated competitive equilibria. Specifically, we define $(\mathfrak{x}^t, \mathfrak{p}^t) \in \mathfrak{X} \times \mathfrak{P}$ to be a *t-period equilibrium* if

$$x_h \in x_h(\mathfrak{p}^t) \quad \text{for} \quad h \in H^t$$

and

$$\sum_{h \in G^{s-1} \cup G^s} x_h^{s,i} = \sum_{h \in G^{s-1} \cup G^s} \omega_h^{s,i} \quad \text{whenever } p^{s,i} > 0 \text{ for } 1 \leq i \leq l^s, \quad 1 \leq s \leq t.$$

In what follows we shall make frequent use of the obvious fact (and related observations) that if $t'' > t'$, then a t''-period equilibrium is also a t'-period equilibrium. Referring to the subsequence of periods $\{t_\nu\}$ singled out earlier, we shall demonstrate that (i) for every $\nu \geq 1$ there exists a t_ν-period equilibrium $(\mathfrak{x}^{t_\nu}, \mathfrak{p}^{t_\nu})$, and (ii) sequences of t_ν-period equilibria $\{(\mathfrak{x}^{t_\nu}, \mathfrak{p}^{t_\nu})\}$ essentially converge to some competitive equilibrium $(\mathfrak{x}^*, \mathfrak{p}^*)$ as ν approaches ∞.

The hard part of this argument involves establishing uniform bounds on the elements of the price sequence $\mathfrak{p}^{t_\nu}$. (The definition of $\mathfrak{X}$ already imposes uniform bounds on the elements of the feasible allocation sequence $\mathfrak{x}^{t_\nu}$.) The argument itself is somewhat easier to comprehend if we take it in gradual steps, considering first the polar special case where the generations $\{t_\nu\}$ always provide every commodity available in their second period of life,

$$\sum_{h \in G^{t_\nu}} \omega_h^{t_\nu+1} \gg 0 \quad \text{for } \nu \geq 1, \tag{3}$$

and then second, the general case where they may not,[6]

$$\sum_{h \in G^{t_\nu}} \omega_h^{t_\nu+1} > 0 \quad \text{for} \quad \nu \geq 1. \tag{4}$$

[6] Here and later on we appeal to the readily verified result that, for the economy to be intertemporaly irreducible, every generation must provide some commodity available in each of its periods of life, $\sum_{h \in G^0} \omega_h^1 > 0$ and $\sum_{h \in G^t} \omega_h^s > 0$ for $s = t, t+1, t \geq 1$.

The underlying reinterpretation discussed in the concluding section provides strong motivation for being especially interested in the general case (4). However, since the analysis is substantially less complicated (in detail, not in concept) for the special case (3) we will concentrate on it, and content ourselves with merely outlining the extension of the proof to cover the general case (4).

3.2. Proof for the Special Case (3)

Given arbitrary $\nu \geq 1$, it is easily verified that the corresponding t_ν-generation economy $\mathcal{E}^{t_\nu}$ exhibits all of the standard properties utilized in establishing the existence of competitive equilibrium. In particular, our assumption that the economy is intertemporaly irreducible guarantees that, for such a truncated economy, a compensated equilibrium is also a competitive equilibrium, the crucial part in all of the standard proofs (see, for instance, Arrow and Hahn, 1971, especially Chapter 5). Because this fundamental result also plays an essential role in our own subsequent analysis, we sketch a simple variant of McKenzie's original argument (drafted for our specific purposes) in Section 3.4.

Now, competitive equilibrium in the t_ν-generation economy necessarily yields t_ν-period equilibrium (by simply choosing arbitrary elements to fill out the feasible allocation sequence $\mathfrak{x}^{t_\nu}$ and related price sequence $\mathfrak{p}^{t_\nu}$). Thus, we know that, for every $\nu \geq 1$, there exists a t_ν-period equilibrium $(\mathfrak{x}^{t_\nu}, \mathfrak{p}^{t_\nu})$. But then, applying Cantor's diagonalization procedure, we also know that there exists a subsequence of periods $\{t_\xi\} \subset \{t_\nu\}$ with corresponding t_ξ-period equilibria $\{(\mathfrak{x}^{t_\xi}, \mathfrak{p}^{t_\xi})\}$ such that

$$\lim_{\xi \to \infty} \mathfrak{x}^{t_\xi} = \mathfrak{x}^* \in \mathfrak{X}.$$

Focus attention on this particular feasible allocation sequence $\mathfrak{x}^*$. *We claim that there exists* $\mathfrak{p}^* \in \mathfrak{P}$ *such that* $(\mathfrak{x}^*, \mathfrak{p}^*)$ *is a competitive equilibrium.*

This last assertion is established on the basis of the following pair of lemmas, whose role is to warrant applying Cantor's diagonalization procedure to derive the desired price sequence $\mathfrak{p}^*$ as well.

Lemma 1. *For every* $\nu \geq 1$ *there exists* $\mathfrak{p}^{t_\nu *} \in \mathfrak{P}$ *such that* $(\mathfrak{x}^*, \mathfrak{p}^{t_\nu *})$ *is a* t_ν*-period equilibrium.*

Proof of Lemma 1. Given arbitrary $\nu \geq 1$, consider a subsequence of periods $\{t_\xi\} \subset \{t_\nu\}$ with corresponding t_ξ-period equilibria $\{(\mathfrak{x}^{t_\xi}, \mathfrak{p}^{t_\xi})\}$ such that $\lim_{\xi \to \infty} \mathfrak{x}^{t_\xi} = \mathfrak{x}*$. Because every t_ξ-period equilibrium has the property that $x_h \in x_h(\mathfrak{p}^{t_\xi})$ for $h \in G^0$ and thus $p^1 > 0$, it follows that we can normalize $\mathfrak{p}^{t_\xi}$

so that

$$\|(p^1, p^2, \ldots, p^{t_v+1})\| = 1.$$

Hence, without any loss of generality we can assume that the first

$$\sum_{t=1}^{t_v+1} l^t$$

elements of $\mathfrak{p}^{t_\xi}$ converge to $(p^{1*}, p^{2*}, \ldots, p^{t_v+1*}) > 0$ as ξ approaches ∞. Finally, we can, therefore, employ a standard maneuver – which basically just involves switching back and forth between the budget-constrained utility maximization problem in Equation (1) and its utility-constrained budget minimization counterpart Equation (2) (where now $u_h = u_h(x_h)$ for $x_h \in x_h(\mathfrak{p}^{t_\xi})$) – in order to verify that every price sequence

$$\mathfrak{p}^{t_v*} = (p^{1*}, p^{2*}, \ldots, p^{t_v+1*}, p^{t_v+2}, \ldots) \in \mathfrak{B}$$

yields suitable equilibrium prices:[7] We know that, for every $t_\xi \geq t_v$, the t_ξ-period equilibrium $(\mathfrak{x}^{t_\xi}, \mathfrak{p}^{t_\xi})$ is also a t_v-period equilibrium, and that in a t_v-period equilibrium, for every $h \in G^t$, $0 \leq t \leq t_v$, ordinary lifetime consumption profiles are also compensated lifetime consumption profiles. Thus, introducing obvious terminology to emphasize the distinction, the t_ξ-period equilibrium $(\mathfrak{x}^{t_\xi}, \mathfrak{p}^{t_\xi})$ is also a t_v-period compensated equilibrium. Moreover, we know that compensated lifetime consumption profiles are upper hemicontinuous. Thus, going to the limit, $(\mathfrak{x}^*, \mathfrak{p}^{t_v*})$ is also a t_v-period compensated equilibrium. So, now invoking the assumption that the economy is intertemporaly irreducible, it is easily established that, at the price sequence $\mathfrak{p}^{t_v*}$, every consumer born in period t_v must have positive income

$$\mathfrak{p}^{t_v*} \cdot \omega_h > 0 \quad \text{for } h \in H^{t_v},$$

and hence that, by a well-known result, $(\mathfrak{x}^*, \mathfrak{p}^{t_v*})$ is a t_v-period equilibrium as well. ■

Lemma 2. *There exist nonnegative, finite constants $0 \leq K^t < \infty$ for $t \geq 1$ with the property that, if $(\mathfrak{x}^*, \mathfrak{p}^{t_v})$ is a t_v-period equilibrium, then $\mathfrak{p}^{t_v}$ can be normalized so that*

$$\|p^1\| = 1$$

and

$$\|p^{t+1}\| \leq K^t \quad \text{for} \quad 1 \leq t \leq t_v.$$

[7] As mentioned earlier, some details of this argument are more fully sketched in Section 3.4.

Proof of Lemma 2. Given arbitrary $v \geq 1$, consider a t_v-period equilibrium of the specific form $(\mathfrak{x}^*, \mathfrak{p}^{t_v})$. Since $x_h^* \in x_h(\mathfrak{p}^{t_v})$ for $h \in G^0$, we know that $p^1 > 0$, or that $\|p^1\| > 0$. Hence, we only need to establish that there exist bounds K^t such that, for every $1 \leq t \leq t_v$, the price sequence $\mathfrak{p}^{t_v}$ satisfies

$$\|p^{t+1}\|/\|p^1\| \leq K^t.$$

Suppose that this were not true, that is, that for some $1 \leq t \leq t_v$, there were a sequence of t_v-period equilibria $\{(\mathfrak{x}^*, \mathfrak{p}^\xi)\}$ ("$\mathfrak{p}^{t_v \xi}$" or "$(\mathfrak{p}^{t_v})^\xi$" would be more accurate, but more cumbersome notation) such that

$$\lim_{\xi \to \infty} \|p^{t+1\xi}\|/\|p^{1\xi}\| = \infty.$$

Since $p^{1\xi} > 0$, we can again normalize $\mathfrak{p}^\xi$ so that $\|(p^{1\xi}, p^{2\xi}, \ldots, p^{t_v+1\xi})\| = 1$, and, without loss of generality, assume that the first

$$\sum_{t=1}^{t_v+1} l^t$$

elements of $\mathfrak{p}^\xi$ converge to $(p^{1\infty}, p^{2\infty}, \ldots, p^{t_v+1\infty}) > 0$ as ξ approaches ∞. But this leads to the following inconsistency: On the one hand, by basically the same reasoning as in the proof of Lemma 1, we find that every price sequence

$$\mathfrak{p}^\infty = (p^{1\infty}, p^{2\infty}, \ldots, p^{t_v+1\infty}, p^{t_v+2}, \ldots) \in \mathfrak{B}$$

yields a t_v-period equilibrium $(\mathfrak{x}^*, \mathfrak{p}^\infty)$, so that $p^{1\infty} > 0$. On the other hand, given the particular character of the choice of $\{\mathfrak{p}^\xi\}$, we also find that for every $0 < K < \infty$ there exists $\xi_K < \infty$ such that

$$\|p^{1\xi}\| > 0, \|p^{t+1\xi}\| \leq 1 \quad \text{and} \quad \|p^{t+1\xi}\|/\|p^{1\xi}\| > K$$

or

$$1 > K\|p^{1\xi}\| > 0 \quad \text{for} \quad \xi > \xi_K,$$

so that $p^{1\infty} = 0$. Thus, we can conclude that the requisite bounds must in fact exist. ∎

The remainder of the argument (which depends on the provisional assumption (3) only insofar as it was used in establishing Lemmas 1 and 2) is now almost routine. Lemma 1 guarantees that, for every $v \geq 1$, there exists a t_v-period equilibrium of the specific form $(\mathfrak{x}^*, \mathfrak{p}^{t_v})$, while Lemma 2 justifies further restriction of the price sequence $\mathfrak{p}^{t_v}$ to the subset of conceivable price sequences

$$\mathfrak{B}^* = \{\mathfrak{p} : \mathfrak{p} \geq 0, \|p^1\| = 1 \text{ and } \|p^{t+1}\| \leq K^t \text{ for } t \geq 1\} \subset \mathfrak{B}.$$

Hence, once again applying Cantor's diagonalization procedure, we can choose a subsequence of periods $\{t_\xi\} \subset \{t_\nu\}$ with corresponding t_ξ-period equilibria $\{(\mathfrak{x}^*, \mathfrak{p}^{t_\xi})\}$ such that

$$\lim_{\xi \to \infty} \mathfrak{p}^{t_\xi} = \mathfrak{p}^* \subset \mathfrak{B}^*.$$

Finally, employing the same standard maneuver as in the proofs of Lemmas 1 and 2, it follows that, for every $\nu \geq 1$, $(\mathfrak{x}^*, \mathfrak{p}^*)$ is a t_ν-period equilibrium, and, therefore that, by definition, $(\mathfrak{x}^*, \mathfrak{p}^*)$ is also a competitive equilibrium. The proof of the Existence Theorem for the special case (3) is therefore complete.

3.3. Extension to the General Case (4)

In order to generalize the proof, we begin by observing that it is only necessary to consider the other polar special case where the generations $\{t_\nu\}$ *never* provide every commodity available in their second period of life,

$$\sum_{h \in G^{t_\nu}} \omega_h^{t_\nu+1} \not\gg 0 \quad \text{for} \quad \nu \geq 1 \tag{5}$$

(since we can always select the original subsequence of periods $\{t_\nu\}$ so that either assumption (3) or (5) obtains). Then, given the provisional assumption (5), the foregoing analysis requires two significant modifications.

3.3.1. Establishing Existence of t_ν-Period Equilibrium

Underlying our whole approach is the fundamental result that, for every $\nu \geq 1$, there exists a t_ν-period equilibrium $(\mathfrak{x}^{t_\nu}, \mathfrak{p}^{t_\nu})$. In the proof of this result, the only potential problem occurs in attempting to establish the existence of competitive equilibrium for the t_ν-generation economy $\mathscr{E}^{t_\nu}$ (or for any similar truncation of the whole economy). Among other things, generation t_ν's tastes may depend crucially on some commodities that are only provided in generation $(t_\nu + 1)$'s endowments. In order to circumvent this sort of possibility, we essentially introduce a proxy to represent the critical connections between generations t_ν and $t_\nu + 1$.

We noted previously that, for the economy to be intertemporaly irreducible, both generations must provide some commodity available during their common period of life,

$$\sum_{h \in G^t} \omega_h^{t_\nu+1} > 0 \quad \text{for} \quad t = t_\nu, t_\nu + 1.$$

Based on this commonality, we fabricate a consumer ν who has tastes for just the commodities available in period $t_\nu + 1$, tastes that are represented by a continuous, quasiconcave and strictly increasing utility function $u_v : \mathbb{R}_+^{l^{t_v+1}} \to \mathbb{R}$, and an endowment of just the commodities available in period $t_v + 1$, an endowment that is exactly the same as the total endowment of generation $t_v + 1$ during its first period of life,

$$\begin{aligned} \omega_v^t &= \sum_{h \in G^{t_v+1}} \omega_h^{t_v+1} > 0 \quad \text{for} \quad t = t_v + 1 \\ &= 0 \qquad\qquad\qquad\quad \text{otherwise.} \end{aligned}$$

Consider competitive equilibrium in the t_v-generation economy after the addition of this fictitious consumer v, say, the *augmented* t_v-generation economy $\mathscr{E}^v$.

For the purpose of establishing existence, the sole condition that needs to be explicitly verified is that $\mathscr{E}^v$ also satisfies the restriction imposed by the assumption that the economy is intertemporaly irreducible. But such verification follows directly from two observations. First, the feasible allocations for $\mathscr{E}^v$ are basically the same as the feasible allocation sequences up through period $t_v + 1$ for the whole economy – provided that we identify consumer v's consumption with generation $(t_v + 1)$'s total consumption during its first period of life,

$$x_v^{t_v+1} = \sum_{h \in G^{t_v+1}} x_h^{t_v+1}.$$

Second, now letting $H^v = H^{t_v} \cup \{v\}$, the restriction itself only requires checking in the extreme cases where either $H_1^v = \{v\}$ or $H_2^v = \{v\}$ – since in every other intermediate case, if it holds for the t_v-generation economy $\mathscr{E}^{t_v}$, then it holds for the augmented t_v-generation economy $\mathscr{E}^v$. And it is readily seen that the restriction holds in these extreme cases:

Case I. $H_1^v = \{v\}$. In this case $G^{t_v} \subset H_2^v$. But because the only direct connection between generation t_v and its successors is through generation $t_v + 1$, if the restriction doesn't hold for $\mathscr{E}^v$ with this particular partition, then it doesn't hold for $\mathscr{E}^{t_v+1}$ with the particular partition

$$H_1^{t_v+1} = \{h : h \in G^t \quad \text{for} \quad t_v + 1 \le t \le t_{v+1}\}.$$

Case II. $H_2^v = \{v\}$. In this case $G^{t_v} \subset H_1^v$. Hence, fictitious consumer v can be made better off by receiving the increases in total endowment of any amount such that

$$\sum_{h \in G^{t_v}} y_h^{t_v+1,i} > 0 \quad \text{whenever} \sum_{h \in G^{t_v}} \omega_h^{t_v+1,i} > 0 \quad \text{for} \quad 1 \le i \le l^{t_v+1}.$$

3.3.2. Converting t_v*-Period Compensated Equilibrium into* t_v*-Period Equilibrium*

In demonstrating both Lemmas 1 and 2, the only possible difficulty occurs in attempting to convert a t_v-period compensated equilibrium into a t_v-period equilibrium (along the lines more fully elaborated in the following section). For instance, in the last steps of the argument in the proof of Lemma 1, it may happen that, after going to the limit,

$$p^{t,i*} = 0 \quad \text{whenever} \sum_{h \in H^{t_v}} \omega_h^{t,i} > 0 \quad \text{for} \quad 1 \leq i \leq l^t, \ 1 \leq t \leq t_v + 1,$$

or that

$$\mathfrak{p}^{t_v*} \cdot \omega_h = 0 \quad \text{for} \quad h \in H^{t_v}.$$

To deal with this eventuality, we essentially just avoid those commodities that are neither provided nor consumed (in the particular feasible allocation sequence $\mathfrak{x}^*$) by generation t_v during its second period of life. In particular, we reorder the commodities available in period $t_v + 1$ so that

$$\begin{aligned} \sum_{h \in G^{t_v}} (\omega_h^{t_v+1,i} + x_h^{t_v+1,i*}) &> 0 \quad \text{for} \quad 1 \leq i \leq l^{t_v+1*} \leq l^{t_v+1} \\ &= 0 \quad \text{otherwise,} \end{aligned}$$

renormalize $\mathfrak{p}^{t_l}$ so that

$$\left\| (p^1, p^2, \ldots, p^{t_v+1,1}, \ldots, p^{t_v+1, l^{t_v+1*}}) \right\| = 1,$$

and repeat the same standard maneuver as before – except that now we find that, after going to the limit, $(\mathfrak{x}^*, \mathfrak{p}^{t_v*})$ only yields a t_v-period compensated equilibrium when we explicitly exclude the commodities presently labeled $t_v + 1, i$ for $l^{t_v+1*} < i \leq l^{t_v+1}$.[8] But this is enough to yield a similarly delimited t_v-period equilibrium and hence, provided $v > 1$, a t_{v-1}-period equilibrium.

For Lemma 2, the same amendment to the analysis is enough to yield uniform bounds on the price sequence $\mathfrak{p}^{t_v}$ up through period t_v, that is, provided $v > 1$, suitable restriction of a t_{v-1}-period equilibrium that is also a t_v-period equilibrium. But that is more than sufficient for the remainder of the argument.

---

[8] That is, when we explicitly require that $x_h^{t_v+1,i} = 0$ for $l^{t_v+1^*} < i \leq l^{t_v+1}$. It is perhaps worth remarking that we cannot resort to an analogous trick in the preceding extension of the proof (establishing existence of t_v-period equilibrium), basically because it runs afoul of Walrasian law.

3.4. Maneuvering Between Ordinary and Compensated Equilibria

A substantial part of our analysis has implicitly employed the following basic notion: Define $(\mathfrak{x}^t, \mathfrak{p}^t) \in \mathfrak{X} \times \mathfrak{P}$ to be a t-period compensated equilibrium if there exist $u_h \in \mathbb{R}$ for $h \in H^t$ such that

$$x_h \in x_h(\mathfrak{p}^t, u_h) \text{ and } \mathfrak{p}^t \cdot x_h = \mathfrak{p}^t \cdot \omega_h \text{ for } h \in H^t$$

and

$$\sum_{h \in G^{t-1} \cup G^t} x_h^{t,i} = \sum_{h \in G^{t-1} \cup G^t} \omega_h^{t,i} \quad \text{whenever } p^{t,i} > 0 \quad \text{for} \quad 1 \leq i \leq l^s, \ 1 \leq s \leq t.$$

Typically, we have focused on the specific situation where such a t-period compensated equilibrium is generated from a predetermined t-period equilibrium $(\mathfrak{x}^t, \mathfrak{p}^t)$ (so that, for instance, $u_h = u_h(x_h)$ for $x_h \in x_h(\mathfrak{p}^t)$). Under such circumstances, the various results we have appealed to are, on the whole, so well known that they require no detailed elaboration or documentation (as can be found, say, in Arrow and Hahn's treatise). One claim, however, perhaps merits further justification. This is our assertion (toward the end of the proof of Lemma 1) that, when the economy is intertemporaly irreducible, "it is easily established that … $\mathfrak{p}^{t_v*} \cdot \omega_h > 0$ for $h \in H^{t_v}$."

The proof is essentially the same as McKenzie's. Given the limiting t_v-period compensated equilibrium $(\mathfrak{x}^*, \mathfrak{p}^{t_v*})$, consider our specific condition applied to the t_v-generation economy $\mathscr{E}^{t_v}$ vis-à-vis the particular feasible allocation sequence $\mathfrak{x}^*$. Choose

$$H_2^{t_v} = \{h : h \in H^{t_v} \text{ and } \mathfrak{p}^{t_v*} \omega_h > 0\}.$$

Since, by derivation, $(p^{1^*}, p^{2^*}, \ldots, p^{t_v+1^*}) > 0$ and, by assumption (especially the provisional assumption (3)),

$$\sum_{h \in H^{t_v}} \omega_h^t \gg 0 \quad \text{for} \quad 1 \leq t \leq t_v + 1,$$

we know that $\mathfrak{p}^{t_v*} \cdot \omega_h > 0$ for some $h \in H^{t_v}$, or that $H_2^{t_v} \neq \varnothing$. Now suppose that $H_2^{t_v} \neq H^{t_v}$, or that $H_1^{t_v} = H^{t_v} - H_2^{t_v} \neq \varnothing$. We will show that this entails the contradiction

$$\mathfrak{p}^{t_v*} \cdot \omega_h > 0 \quad \text{for some} \quad h \in H_1^{t_v}. \tag{6}$$

Assume the postulated potential for redistribution denoted by $y_h \geq 0$ for $h \in H_1^{t_v}$ and $x_h' \geq 0$ for $h \in H_2^{t_v}$. By virtue of our particular choice of $H_2^{t_v}$ (as well as our particular derivation of $(\mathfrak{x}^*, \mathfrak{p}^{t_v*})$) we know that

$$\mathfrak{p}^{t_v*} x_h' \left\{ \begin{matrix} > \\ \geq \end{matrix} \right\} \mathfrak{p}^{t_v*} \cdot \omega_h \text{ according to } u_h(x_h') \left\{ \begin{matrix} > \\ = \end{matrix} \right\} u_h(x_h^*) \quad \text{for} \quad h \in H_2^{t_v}.$$

Thus, on the one hand, the properties that

$$u_h(x'_h) \geq u_h(x^*_h) \quad \text{for every} \quad h \in H_2^{t_v}$$

and

$$u_h(x'_h) > u_h(x^*_h) \quad \text{for some} \quad h \in H_2^{t_v}$$

yield the inequality

$$\mathfrak{p}^{t_v *} \cdot \sum_{h \in H_2^{t_v}} (x'_h - \omega_h) > 0. \tag{7}$$

On the other hand, the property that

$$\sum_{h \in H_2^{t_v}} x'_h \leq \sum_{h \in H_1^{t_v}} (\omega_h + y_h) + \sum_{h \in H_2^{t_v}} \omega_h$$

yields the inequality

$$\mathfrak{p}^{t_v *} \cdot \sum_{h \in H_2^{t_v}} (x'_h - \omega_h) \leq \mathfrak{p}^{t_v *} \sum_{h \in H_1^{t_v}} (\omega_h + y_h). \tag{8}$$

But Equations (7) and (8) together entail the inequality

$$\mathfrak{p}^{t_v *} \cdot \sum_{h \in H_1^{t_v}} (\omega_h - y_h) > 0,$$

which in turn entails the dichotomy that either Equation (6) (i) obtains or (ii) does not obtain, but $\mathfrak{p}^{t_v *} \cdot y_h > 0$ for some $h \in H_1^{t_v}$. In the first case we have already finished. In the second case we simply appeal to the remaining property of the postulated potential for redistribution that

$$\sum_{h \in H_1^{t_v}} y_h^{t,i} = 0 \quad \text{whenever} \quad \sum_{h \in H_1^{t_v}} \omega_h^{t,i} = 0$$
$$\text{for} \quad 1 \leq i \leq l^t, \quad 1 \leq t \leq t_r + 1.$$

It follows directly that this second case is impossible, that is, that the alleged contradiction in Equation (6) must in fact obtain.

4. The Inherent Demographic Structure of Overlapping Generations

Our purpose here is to outline an algorithm for converting a pure-distribution, overlapping-generations economy in which consumers have arbitrary but finite lifetimes into one in which they have at most two-period lifetimes. The essence of this algorithm consists in suitably redefining indices.

So now suppose that the time superscripts $\mathscr{t}(\mathscr{t} = \ldots 0, 1, \ldots)$ denote some conventional periods for describing economic behavior, say, for specificity, calendar dates. As before, market activity commences on calendar date 1. Continue to let the agent subscripts $h(h = 0, 1, \ldots)$ denote various individual consumers ordered in terms of their first periods of life, or their *birthdates* $-\infty < b_h < \infty$. This means, in particular, that if $h'' > h'$, then $b_{h''} \geq b_{h'}$. Now, however, since we no longer assume that consumers live just two periods, we also need to keep track of their last as well as their first periods of life, or their *deathdates* $b_h \leq d_h < \infty$. Moreover, because we are only concerned with market activity, we can presume that $1 \leq d_h$ for $h \geq 0$. Likewise, because we are only concerned with genuine overlap, we can presume that, for every $\mathscr{t} \geq 0$, there is some $h \geq 0$ such that $b_h = \mathscr{t} < d_h$. (There may also be some $h \geq 0$ such that $b_h < 0 < d_h$.)

All other notations retain their previous meanings. Thus, in particular, $H^{\mathscr{t}} = \{h : h \geq 0 \text{ and } b_h \leq \mathscr{t}\}$ denotes the group of consumers born in period $\mathscr{t}, 1 \leq l^{\mathscr{t}} < \infty$ denotes the number of commodities available in period $\mathscr{t}$, and $x_h^{\mathscr{t}} \in \mathbb{R}_+^{l^{\mathscr{t}}}$ denotes the quantity of commodities allocated to consumer h during period $\mathscr{t}$. Finally, note that the preceding specification entails that

$$\sup_{h \in H^{\mathscr{t}}} d_h = \max_{h \in H^{\mathscr{t}}} d_h > \mathscr{t} \quad \text{for} \quad \mathscr{t} \geq 0,$$

a result that is central to our procedure for converting from the present conventional periods $\mathscr{t}$ to the previous, say, telescoped periods t.

The basic idea behind this procedure is quite intuitive. At calendar date 0, the consumer with greatest future longevity must be at the end of the first half of his life. But this also means that his death date must occur just at the end of the second half of his life. Thus, we identify $t = 0$ with $\mathscr{t} \leq 0 = \mathscr{t}_0$ and $t = 1$ with $\mathscr{t}_0 < \mathscr{t} \leq \max_{h \in H^{\mathscr{t}_0}} d_h = \mathscr{t}_1$. Continuing in the same fashion, at calendar date $\mathscr{t}_1$, the consumer with the greatest future longevity – who must have been born during the interim $\mathscr{t}_0 < \mathscr{t} \leq \mathscr{t}_1$ – must be at the end of the first half of his life. So once again his death date must occur at the end of the second half of his life. Thus, we identify $t = 2$ with $\mathscr{t}_1 < \mathscr{t} \leq \max_{h \in H^1} d_h = \mathscr{t}_2$. And so on. Generally, then, we identify the telescoped periods t with the interims between terms $\mathscr{t}_{t-1} < \mathscr{t} \leq \mathscr{t}_t$ of the particular subsequence of conventional periods

$$\mathscr{t}_0 = 0 \quad \text{and} \quad \mathscr{t}_t = \max_{h \in H^{\mathscr{t}_{t-1}}} d_h \quad \text{for} \quad t \geq 1.$$

Figure 1 illustrates this correspondence for the leading special case where at least one consumer is born on each calendar date, and every consumer lives just three (conventional) periods.

All that remains is to account for generation composition and commodity classification in terms of the telescoped periods. But this amounts to a trivial

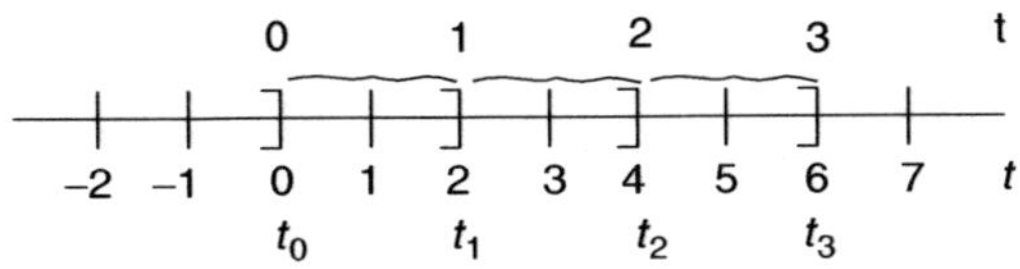

Figure 1.

exercise: Simply amalgamate indices over the corresponding interims of conventional periods. Thus, in particular, define

$$G^0 = \{h : h \geq 0 \text{ and } b_h \leq \mathscr{t}_0\} \quad \text{and}$$
$$G^t = \{h : h \geq 0 \text{ and } \mathscr{t}_{t-1} < b_n \leq \mathscr{t}_t\} \quad \text{for} \quad t \geq 1,$$
$$l^t = \sum_{\mathscr{t}_{t-1} < \mathscr{t} \leq \mathscr{t}_t} l^{\mathscr{t}} \quad \text{for} \quad t \geq 1$$

and

$$x_h^t = (x_h^{\mathscr{t}_{t-1}+1}, x_h^{\mathscr{t}_{t-1}+2}, \ldots, x_h^{t}) \in \underset{\mathscr{t}_{t-1} < \mathscr{t} \leq \mathscr{t}_l}{\times} \mathbb{R}_+^{l^{\mathscr{t}}} = \mathbb{R}_+^{l^t} \quad \text{for} \quad t \geq 1.$$

It is obvious from these definitions that generation t contains just those consumers born during period t, and that, even more importantly, members of generation t have tastes for and endowments of just the commodities that are available in periods t and $t+1$. In fact, typically – that is, when conventional lifetimes are lengthy or diverse – consumers will be directly concerned with a rather small subset of the potential goods available over their telescoped lifetimes. This observation, of course, provided an additional impetus – besides the economic motivation emphasized in the introductory section – for our undertaking this project to begin with.

Acknowledgment

Research support from the National Science Foundation under Grant SOC 78-06157 to the Center for Analytic Research in Economics and the Social Sciences at the University of Pennsylvania is gratefully acknowledged.

References

Arrow, K.J. and Hahn, F.H. (1971). *General Competitive Analysis*. San Francisco: Holden–Day.

Balasko, Y. and Shell, K. (1980). The overlapping-generations model, I: The case of pure exchange without money. *Journal of Economic Theory* **23**, 281–306.

Cass, D. (1979). Money in consumption-loan type models: An addendum. In Kareken, J. and Wallace, N. (Eds), *Models of Monetary Economies*. Minneapolis, MN: Federal Reserve Bank of Minneapolis.

McKenzie, L.W. (1959). On the existence of general equilibrium for a competitive market. *Econometrica* **27**, 54–71 and some corrections in *Econometrica* (1961), **29**, 247–248.

Chapter 6

Do Sunspots Matter?☆

David Cass and Karl Shell[a]

[a] *Department of Economics, Cornell University, Ithaca, NY, USA*

1. Introduction

What is the best strategy for playing the stock market? Should one concentrate on "fundamentals" or should one instead focus on the "psychology of the market"? These are interesting questions for those who would like to get rich on Wall Street. They are also interesting for macroeconomists.

For Keynes and many Keynesians, the volatility of investment is at least, in part, based on the volatility of market psychology or the animal spirits of capitalists, or, more generally, extrinsic uncertainty. This alleged unreliability of the intertemporal allocation of resources under laissez-faire capitalism is an important basis of the Keynesian claim for the desirability of active fiscal and monetary policies. On the other hand, devotees of the rational expectations school of macroeconomics hold that fundamentals play the determining role in the allocation of resources. Therefore, they claim that if the environment is stable (in particular, if the government does not behave capriciously), then private investment will also be appropriately stable.

In this chapter, we investigate whether or not rational expectations equilibria are immune to influence from extrinsic uncertainty. That is, can self-fulfilling prophecies have a real impact? Or, in short, do sunspots[1] matter?[2]

☆ This article was originally published in *Journal of Political Economy* 91, David Cass and Karl Shell, "Do Sunspots Matter?", 193–227, © University of Chicago Press, 1983.

[1] Throughout this chapter, "sunspots" is meant to represent extrinsic uncertainty, that is, random phenomena that do not affect tastes, endowments, or production possibilities. Of course, as Jevons noted, real-world sunspots may very well provide *intrinsic* uncertainty to the economy, affecting, for example, agricultural production possibilities. Here we are interested only in our highly stylized version of sunspot activity.

[2] We have been worrying about sunspots for some time. A theoretical example of a monetary overlapping-generations economy in which sunspots matter is reported in Shell (1977). Our colleague Costas Azariadis (1981) has presented similar results in a more familiar macroeconomic setting. These examples, however, are based on very complicated dynamic models that do not permit us to separate the respective roles of

International Symposia in Economic Theory and Econometrics, Vol. 21B
S. Spear (Editor)

ISSN: 1571-0386/DOI: 10.1108/S1571-0386(2011)000021B009

We consider a simple exchange economy with a finite time horizon, two commodities, two states of nature, and a finite number of consumers. In Section 2, consumers are introduced. They are assumed to have von Neumann–Morgenstern utility functions and commodity endowments that are independent of the state of nature. Since uncertainty does not then have any effect on the fundamentals of the economy, it is purely extrinsic uncertainty; we refer to it simply as sunspot activity. Throughout most of the chapters, we adopt a very strong version of the rational expectations hypothesis: Consumers share the same beliefs about sunspot activity. This allows the interpretation that subjective probabilities are equal to objective probabilities.

The usual extensions of general equilibrium theory fail to represent an essential and significant aspect of actual intertemporal economies: The trading process must take place in time. Individuals may be able to make complicated trades involving future deliveries contingent upon the revealed state of nature, but these trades must be struck when each of the parties is alive. Markets in all commodities may be complete, but consumers are restricted from participating in markets that meet (say) before they are born.

We assume that markets are complete. In Section 3, we describe the natural restrictions that must be imposed on market participation – namely, that consumers born after sunspot activity is observed cannot possibly trade on the securities market meant to provide the possibility of hedging against the effects of this uncertainty. Section 3 also provides a complete description of consumer behavior in the securities and commodities markets.

Section 4 defines and analyzes market equilibrium. This section might appear to be our mathematical ghetto. Indeed, there is a good deal of notation (which is the only way we know to make these ideas precise!), but the arguments themselves are not very complicated. Equilibrium in the economy with securities and commodities markets is shown to be equivalent to equilibrium in an economy with contingent-claims markets. (This equivalence is the one established by Arrow (1964).) The latter formulation of market equilibrium is the more tractable and is exclusively employed in the succeeding analysis. The traditional general equilibrium model yields "certainty equilibria" in which sunspots cannot matter. It is shown that, in principle, our market equilibrium concept is broader than that of the traditional model; certainty equilibrium is a special case of market equilibrium.

generational overlap, the infinite time horizon, and government debt. In this chapter, we focus on the implications of generational overlap in a very simple equilibrium model. In a companion chapter, Yves Balasko (forthcoming) investigates a more general formulation of the notion of extrinsic uncertainty. For an overview of the subject of rational expectations equilibria in which extrinsic uncertainty matters, see our propaganda piece, Cass and Shell (1980).

Section 5 is devoted to the degenerate – and contrafactual – case in which there are no restrictions on market participation. If consumers share the same probability beliefs, then sunspots do not matter; that is, sunspot activity does not affect the allocation of resources. In this case, market equilibrium is equivalent to certainty equilibrium. If, however, subjective probabilities differ across consumers, then sunspots are bound to matter. These ideas are presented in a series of three Edgeworth box diagrams in Section 5.

The reader should seek the return on his investment in Section 6, where the consequences of restricted market participation are analyzed. Attention is focused on the more difficult (not necessarily the more realistic) case of shared probability beliefs. There is always a market equilibrium in which sunspots do not matter, that is, a market equilibrium equivalent to a certainty equilibrium. But we also demonstrate that, in fact, our market equilibrium concept is broader than the traditional certainty equilibrium concept. In Section 6, we give simple examples in which sunspot equilibria are lotteries over certainty equilibria. Randomization over certainty equilibria is not, however, the only possible source of sunspot equilibria. A more subtle example presented in the appendix possesses a unique certainty equilibrium and (at least) one sunspot equilibrium.

Section 7 is devoted to the welfare analysis. Equilibrium allocations in which sunspots do not matter are Pareto optimal in the traditional sense. While equilibrium allocations in which sunspots do matter are not Pareto optimal in this sense, they are Pareto optimal in a natural, weaker sense, where each consumer is identified by his state of birth (as well as by the other usual parameters – namely, tastes and endowments).

The upshot of this analysis is that in a rational expectation, general equilibrium world, the presence of extrinsic uncertainty – sunspots, waves of pessimism/optimism, and so forth – may well have real effects. The lesson for macroeconomics is that, even if one assumes the most favorable informational and institutional conditions imaginable, there may be a role for the government to stabilize fluctuations arising from seemingly noneconomic disturbances.

2. Extrinsic Uncertainty

The basic parameters defining an economy – such as endowments, preferences, and production possibilities – are referred to as the fundamentals of that economy. We make a sharp distinction between those things that influence the fundamentals and those which do not. If a variable has an effect on the fundamentals, we say that it is *intrinsic* (to the economy); otherwise, the variable is said to be *extrinsic*. Our basic question is: What effect can an extrinsic variable, say, sunspot activity, have on the allocation of resources?

Before going further, we must introduce some elements of our model; even the concept of extrinsic variable remains vague until it is applied in a formal framework. The model we adopt in this chapter is the simplest possible for our purpose, but our results generalize quite readily. The more general arguments can be found in our working paper (Cass and Shell, 1981, especially Appendix 1, pp. 29–39).

We assume that there are two standard commodities, $i = 1, 2$, and two possible states of nature, $s = \alpha, \beta$. Let $x_h^i(s)$ denote consumption by consumer h of commodity i in state s, let $x_h(s)$ denote the vector of state-s consumptions, $(x_h^1(s), x_h^2(s))$, and let x_h denote the vector of prospective consumptions, $(x_h(\alpha), x_h(\beta)) = (x_h^1(\alpha), x_h^2(\alpha), x_h^1(\beta), x_h^2(\beta))$. Consumer h is endowed with prospective goods, denoted by the strictly positive vector $\omega_h = (\omega_h(\alpha), \omega_h(\beta)) = (\omega_h^1(\alpha), \omega_h^2(\alpha), \omega_h^1(\beta), \omega_h^2(\beta))$. The preferences of Mr. h are described by the utility function, $v_h(x_h)$, which is defined over his prospective consumption plans. There is no production in our simple economy; the fundamentals are endowments and preferences. We assume that uncertainty is purely extrinsic, allowing us to think of the random variable s as representing sunspot activity, identifying α with the state "sunspots" and β with the state "no sunspots."

Endowments are not affected by sunspot activity, that is,

$$\omega_h(\alpha) = \omega_h(\beta) \tag{1}$$

for each h. Conditions must also be imposed on preferences before we can say that uncertainty is extrinsic. We assume that consumer behavior is based on von Neumann–Morgenstern utilities. Consumer h believes that sunspots occur with probability $\pi_h(\alpha)$ and that no sunspots occur with probability $\pi_h(\beta) = 1 - \pi_h(\alpha)$. Preferences are then represented by the familiar expected utility criterion, that is,

$$v_h(x_h(\alpha), x_h(\beta)) = \pi_h(\alpha)u_h(x_h(\alpha)) + \pi_h(\beta)u_h(x_h(\beta)) \tag{2}$$

for each h. We assume that the functions u_h are smooth, strictly increasing, and strictly concave, implying that Mr. h exhibits strict risk aversion in his evaluation of lotteries. Underlying tastes – as described by the function u_h – are obviously independent of sunspot activity since the only effect of s on u_h is through its effect on the allocation $x_h(s)$; because of Equation (2), sunspot activity, unlike (say) rainfall, has no direct effect on the consumer's well-being. Since specifications (1) and (2) ensure that s is extrinsic, we are justified in referring to it as a measure of sunspot activity.

It is no surprise that underlying tastes are unaffected by uncertainty for von Neumann–Morgenstern consumers. In the axioms defining von Neumann–Morgenstern behavior, uncertainty is no more than the basis for constructing lotteries. We adopt the specification Equation (2) partly because the expected utility hypothesis is so familiar, but we have another reason.

Equations (1) and (2)imply that uncertainty is extrinsic, but taken together these conditions are more severe than is necessary. In particular, von Neumann–Morgenstern preferences are not the only ones that are unaffected by uncertainty. The more basic assumption would be that the consumer is indifferent between otherwise identical lotteries generated by different random variables. The utility function defined over prospective consumption plans is parameterized by subjective probabilities. If Mr. h is concerned only with lotteries and is not affected by sunspots per se, his preferences satisfy

$$v_h(x_h(\alpha), x_h(\beta);\ \ \pi_h(\alpha), \pi_h(\beta)) = v_h(x_h(\beta), x_h(\alpha);\ \ \pi_h(\beta), \pi_h(\alpha)). \qquad (3)$$

That is, Mr. h is interested only in payoffs and their respective probabilities – not in the "names" given to the states of nature.

Our assumption (Equation (2)) clearly entails Equation (3). And it entails more. The separability introduced in Equation (2) implies that Mr. h's consumption plan will be intertemporally consistent, that with perfect foresight he will not revise his plan after uncertainty has been revealed. (See Donaldson and Selden (1981) for further elaboration of this point.) Intertemporal consistency is essential to much of our analysis.

In most of the sequel – but the exceptions are significant – we assume that beliefs about sunspot activity are the same for each consumer, that is,

$$\pi_h(\alpha) = \pi(\alpha) \quad \text{so that } \pi_h(\beta) = \pi(\beta) \qquad (4)$$

for each h. The commonly held probabilities, $\pi(\alpha)$ and $\pi(\beta)$, can be thought of as objective probabilities, but that is not necessary. Equation (4) can also be taken as a strong version of the rational expectations hypothesis. A good case can be made against the realism of this assumption. In part, however, imposing Equation (4) is like tying one hand behind one's back. Without Equation (4) the point we shall make is easy to establish,[3] but even with Equation (4) we shall establish that sunspot activity can affect the allocation of resources.

We say that extrinsic uncertainty matters to the allocation of resources (or, simply, *sunspots matter*) if some consumer's allocation depends on the state of nature, that is,

$$x_h(\alpha) \neq x_h(\beta) \qquad (5)$$

for some h. If, on the other hand, all consumers' allocations are independent of the state of nature, that is,

$$x_h(\alpha) = x_h(\beta) \qquad (6)$$

[3] See the discussion based on Figure 3 in Section 5.

for each h, then we say that extrinsic uncertainty does not matter to the allocation of resources (or simply, *sunspots do not matter*). These definitions will be restated in terms of prices, instead of the quantities x_h, after market behavior has been introduced. The definitions could also be restated in terms of utilities. For example, sunspots would not matter if $u_h(x_h(\alpha)) = u_h(x_h(\beta))$ for each h. The utility-based definitions would be more appropriate in a general setting, but it turns out that these three ways of defining whether or not sunspots matter are equivalent under our simplifying assumptions of strict risk aversion and smooth utility functions.[4]

3. Market Participation

It is often argued that the Arrow–Debreu general equilibrium model is remarkably versatile. In particular, it is claimed that this model can be employed to analyze intertemporal market trading in the face of uncertainty; one needs only to define commodities appropriately to account for time and states of nature. There is, however, one fundamental and significant aspect of actual dynamic economies that is not reflected in the usual Arrow–Debreu framework. In the real world, the market trading process itself takes place in time. Trades can include promises to deliver commodities in the future under specific circumstances, but each of the parties to a trade must be alive on the trading date. Even if currently alive individuals can know today the prices that will prevail in the future, they simply cannot trade today with individuals whose birth dates are in the future.

Even in a world where birth dates and death dates vary across individuals, one can readily conceive of the existence of a complete array of markets. What cannot be imagined, however, is that there could be unrestricted participation in these markets. At any given time, some of the potential actors have already left the stage, while others have yet to come onstage. The distinction between the assumptions of complete markets and unrestricted market participation is important. Throughout this chapter, we assume that markets are complete. We show that the essential nature of the equilibrium allocation process is altered when the natural restrictions on market participation are incorporated into the analysis.

We now return to the formal model. Consumers were introduced in the previous section. Here, we place those consumers in time and then describe

[4] The utility-based definition does not include as sunspot equilibria trivial cases involving moving along flats in indifference curves (which would be included under the corresponding quantity-based definition) or rotating around kinks in indifference curves (which would be included under the corresponding price-based definition). The utility-based definition is given in the context of a general model in Cass and Shell (1981, Appendix 1, especially pp. 34–35).

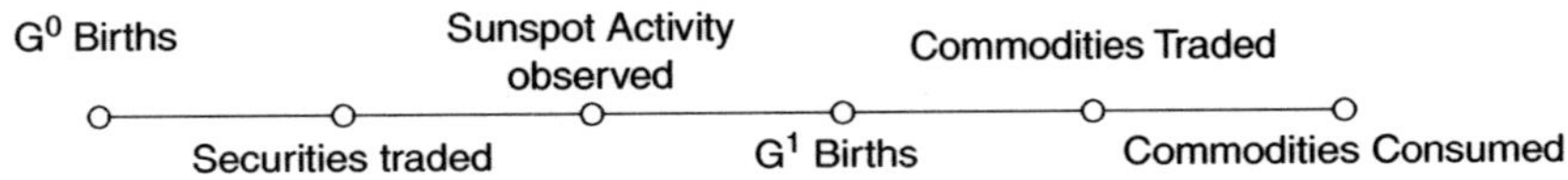

Figure 1: The Time Line.

the market structure for the abstract economy. The timing of trades is of critical importance. We urge the reader to rely heavily on Figure 1, our time line.

We assume that there are two generations. Consumers in generation 0 (G^0, for short) are born at the "beginning of time" and live to the "end of time." Consumers in generation 1 (G^1, for short) are born later than those in G^0 but, like those in G^0, live to the end of time. (This simple demography provides the basis for a finite-horizon overlapping-generations model.) The consumers in G^0 are born before sunspot activity is revealed. They can trade with each other on the market for securities that are contingent on the outcome of the extrinsic random variable, sunspot activity. They can also trade with each other and members of G^1 on the spot market for commodities, which meets after the observation of sunspot activity. On the other hand, consumers in G^1 are born after the degree of sunspot activity is known. They can trade with each other and consumers from G^0 on the spot commodities market, but, of course, they cannot trade on the securities market, which must convene before they are born. Thus, participation in the commodities market is unrestricted, while participation in the securities market is necessarily restricted.

Three assets can be traded on the securities market. Money, all of which is issued by consumers, is the unit of account. Without loss of generality, the nominal interest rate on money can be set equal to zero, so that a consumer who purchases a dollar on the securities market is able to exchange it on the spot market for one dollar's worth of commodities. A consumer who has issued a dollar of (inside) money on the securities market can pay off this debt by delivering a dollar's worth of commodities on the spot market. Let m_h be the purchases (or sales, if negative) of inside money by consumer h (in G^0) on the securities market.

A unit of money represents a promise that entitles the holder to a dollar's worth of commodities no matter what state of nature is observed. In our model, money is interesting only as a unit of account. There is no need for a pure store of value in this simple economy. Nor does money serve as a hedge against uncertainty. We next describe the mechanism by which consumers in G^0 can hedge against sunspot activity.

Consumers in G^0 are assumed to be able to buy and sell securities, the payoffs from which are contingent on sunspot activity. Consumer h is assumed to purchase $b_h(s)$ units of securities, each unit of which is worth one dollar on the spot market if state s has been observed but is worthless otherwise. The dollar price on the securities market of one unit of this security is $p_b(s)$, $s = \alpha$, β. Let b_h denote the vector of contingent securities purchased by consumer h, that is, $b_h = (b_h(\alpha), b_h(\beta))$, and let p_b denote the price vector $(p_b(\alpha), p_b(\beta))$.

Both generations trade on the spot market where the dollar price of commodity i, given that state s has been observed, is $p_c^i(s), s = \alpha, \beta$, and $i = 1, 2$. Let the commodity price vector $(p_c^1(s), p_c^2(s))$ be denoted by $p_c(s)$ and let p_c denote the price vector $(p_c(\alpha), p_c(\beta)) = (p_c^1(\alpha), p_c^2(\alpha), p_c^1(\beta), p_c^2(\beta))$.

We have by now accumulated sufficient notation to be able to describe formally the opportunities and the behavior of consumers. Opportunities, and thus behavior, are substantially different for consumers in different generations.

Consumer h in G^0 chooses a plan (x_h, m_h, b_h) that maximizes his expected utility subject to his market constraints, that is, which solves maximize

$$\pi(\alpha)u_h(x_h(\alpha)) + \pi(\beta)u_h(x_h(\beta))$$

subject to

$$\begin{aligned} & m_h + p_b \cdot b_h = 0, \\ & p_c(\alpha) \cdot x_h(\alpha) \leqq p_c(\alpha) \cdot \omega_h(\alpha) + m_h + b_h(\alpha), \\ & p_c(\beta) \cdot x_h(\beta) \leqq p_c(\beta) \cdot \omega_h(\beta) + m_h + b_h(\beta), \end{aligned} \tag{7'}$$

and

$$x_h \geqq 0$$

for h in G^0. The dot denotes inner product; thus, for example, $p_b \cdot b_h = p_b(\alpha)b_h(\alpha) + p_b(\beta)b_h(\beta)$ and $p_c(\alpha) \cdot x_h(\alpha) = p_c^1(\alpha)x_h^1(\alpha) + p_c^2(\alpha)x_h^2(\alpha)$.

Discussion of the constraints in Equation (7′) is in order. The first constraint tells us that consumers in G^0 must finance their purchases of securities from their sales of other securities. This seems to us to be a realistic assumption, but it is not essential. In the next section, we show that consumers in G^0 behave as if they were facing a complete array of Arrow–Debreu contingent-claims markets. The first constraint is written as an equality, which suggests nondisposability of securities. This is a technical maneuver made to simplify the analysis. The second and third constraints in Equation (7′) are based on an assumption of rational expectations: Sunspot activity is uncertain, but consumers in G^0 have perfect foresight about the prices that will prevail in each of the two states of nature. Then, in each state of nature, commodity purchases are financed by the sales of other commodities, net holdings of inside money, and net holdings of the security that pays off in that particular state.

Life is relatively simple for consumers in G^1. Before they are born, sunspot activity has been observed. These consumers do not have to make decisions under uncertainty, nor do they need to form expectations about prices. A consumer h in G^1 chooses a consumption vector $x_h(s)$ that maximizes his utility subject to his market constraints, that is, which solves

maximize

$$u_h(x_h(s))$$

subject to

$$p_c(s) \cdot x_h(s) \leqq p_c(s) \cdot \omega_h(s) \tag{8'}$$

and

$$x_h(s) \geqq 0$$

for $s = \alpha$, β, and h in G^1.

Whichever state of nature has occurred, the consumer in G^0 maximizes his utility. His consumption is financed from the market value of his endowments.

The market behavior of consumers is completely described by the system (Equations (7′) and (8′)). The next section treats market equilibrium.

4. Market Equilibrium

A market (or competitive) equilibrium can be defined by a system of prices for which consumer demands are consistent with constrained utility maximization and for which materials balance. Formally, then, a market equilibrium is a positive price vector $(p_b, p_c) = (p_b(\alpha), p_b(\beta), p_c(\alpha), p_c(\beta))$, which solves the system

$$\begin{aligned} \sum_{G^0} m_h &= 0, \\ \sum_{G^0} b_h(s) &= 0, \end{aligned} \tag{9'}$$

and

$$\sum_{H} x_h(s) \leqq \sum_{H} \omega_h(s),$$

where $(m_h, b_h(s), x_h(s))$, $s = \alpha, \beta$, is the solution to Equation (7) for h in G^0, $x_h(s)$ is the solution to Equation (8) for h in G^1, and H is the set of all consumers, that is, the union of G^0 and G^1, which implies, for example, that

$$\sum_{H} x_h(s) = \sum_{G^0} x_h(s) + \sum_{G^1} x_h(s).$$

The equations in (9′) require that for each of the three (nondisposable) securities (including money) demand is equated to supply. The sums in these equations are taken over G^0, reflecting two of our assumptions: (i) participation in these markets is not possible for consumers in G^1; and (ii) there is neither outside (i.e., government) money nor outside securities. Money taxes and transfers could have been included. However, since the time horizon is finite, unless the sum of taxes exactly equals the sum of transfers, the equilibrium price of money would necessarily be zero. This is the well-known problem of "hot-potato" money, which can be avoided in models with an unbounded time horizon (see, e.g., Cass and Shell, 1980).

The inequality in Equation (9) states that aggregate demand for each commodity in each state cannot exceed the corresponding aggregate supply. The sums are taken over H since there are no restrictions on commodity-market participation.

An immediate implication of equilibrium in the securities market can be drawn. Each consumer in G^0 must be indifferent between holding one unit of money and one unit of each of the two contingent securities. Hence, in equilibrium, the price of the composite commodity "one unit of sunspot security *and* one unit of nonsunspot security" must be equal to the price of money. This idea is formalized in the following proposition.

Proposition 1. *A market equilibrium price vector* $(p_b(\alpha), p_b(\beta), p_c(\alpha), p_c(\beta))$ *must satisfy* $p_b(\alpha)+p_b(\beta) = 1$.

Proof. Assume that $p_b(\alpha)+p_b(\beta)<1$. Each consumer in G^0 is then able to sell money and purchase more units of each of the contingent securities than the number of dollars that he sold. Consider, for instance, financial plans $(m_h, b_h(\alpha), b_h(\beta))$ with the property that $b_h(s) = (-m_h)/(p_b(\alpha)+p_b(\beta))$ for $s = \alpha, \beta$. Such plans clearly satisfy the equality constraint in Equation (7′). Furthermore, for each number N, there is a plan from this class that satisfies $m_h+b_h(s)>N$ for $s = \alpha, \beta$. Hence, the right-hand sides of the second and third constraints in Equation (7′) can be made arbitrarily large, so that consumers in G^0 can enjoy arbitrarily large consumption in each of the two states. This contradicts the inequality in Equation (9′); consumers in H can supply at most a finite amount of the commodities. Assuming $p_b(\alpha)+p_b(\beta)>1$ leads to a similar contradiction. In this case, consumers in G^0 are able to make arbitrarily large the right-hand sides of the second and third constraints in Equation (7′) by selling each of the two contingent securities in equal (but large) quantities while using the revenue to purchase money. The proof by contradiction is complete.

Proposition 1 is a consequence of the fact that, in equilibrium, there can be no pure arbitrage-profit opportunities on the securities market. The proof of Proposition 1 also establishes that, at equilibrium prices, a consumer in

G^0 can choose to buy or sell any quantity of money without constraining his consumption opportunities by this choice. Suppose that at equilibrium prices $(p_b(\alpha), p_b(\beta), p_c(\alpha), p_c(\beta))$, the vector $(x_h^*(\alpha), x_h^*(\beta), m_h^*, b_h^*(\alpha), b_h^*(\beta))$ is a particular solution to the constrained utility maximization problem (Equation (7′)). Consider another value of money purchases, m_h^{**}. Since $p_b(\alpha)+p_b(\beta)=1$, it follows from Equation (7′) that $(x_h^*(\alpha), x_h^*(\beta), m_h^{**}, b_h^{**}(\alpha), b_h^{**}(\beta))$ is also utility maximizing if $b_h^{**}(s)+m_h^{**}=b_h^*(s)+m_h^*$, $s=\alpha, \beta$. This allows us to think of the contingent securities as state-specific moneys.

An important assumption is implicit in the choice of (ordinary) money as the unit of account (cf. Equation (7′)). In any properly specified monetary economy, there is always an equilibrium in which the commodity price of money is zero (see Cass and Shell, 1980; Balasko and Shell, 1981). In order to simplify matters here, we have excluded this equilibrium. If the price of money is zero, then the prices of contingent securities must also be zero. This amounts to assuming that the securities market is closed, so that, in effect, all consumers are restricted from the securities market, which yields essentially the same equilibria as in the model where $H=G^1$.

Our contingent securities are exactly those studied by Arrow (1964). When perfect foresight and von Neumann–Morgenstern utilities are assumed, the traditional model with complete (Arrow) securities markets and complete spot markets is equivalent to the traditional model with complete (Arrow–Debreu) contingent-claims markets. This insight allows us to replace the equilibrium system Equations (7′)–(9′) with another that turns out to be easier to analyze. The analysis will be in terms of the new, more compact model, but the realism of our formulation is best judged by the extended model, Equations (7′)–(9′). We next formulate the reduced-form model and establish its equivalence to the extended model.

The price of a contract to deliver one unit of commodity $i=1, 2$ if state of nature $s=\alpha, \beta$ occurs is denoted by $p^i(s)$. We denote the vector of state-s prices $(p^1(s), p^2(s))$ by $p(s)$ and the full vector of contingent-claims prices $(p(\alpha), p(\beta))=(p^1(\alpha), p^2(\alpha), p^1(\beta), p^2(\beta))$ by p. Consumer h in G^0 chooses a prospective consumption plan $x_h=(x_h(\alpha), x_h(\beta))$ that maximizes his expected utility subject to his market constraints, that is, that solves

maximize

$$\pi(\alpha)u_h(x_h(\alpha))+\pi(\beta)u_h(x_h(\beta))$$

subject to

$$p\cdot x_h \leqq p\cdot\omega_h \tag{7}$$

and

$$x_h \geqq 0$$

for h in G^0. The value of his prospective consumption plan $p \cdot x_h = p(\alpha) \cdot x_h(\alpha) + p(\beta) \cdot x_h(\beta)$ must not exceed the value of his prospective endowments, $p \cdot \omega_h = p(\alpha) \cdot \omega_h(\alpha) + p(\beta) \cdot \omega_h(\beta)$. Consumers from G^0 are also able to trade on the market for spot commodities at prices $p_c(s)$ for $s = \alpha, \beta$. In the full-blown version of this model,[5] an equilibrium condition (in fact, a zero-arbitrage-profit condition analogous to that described in Proposition 1) is that the vectors $p(s)$ and $p_c(s)$ be proportional, so that without loss of generality we can set $p_c(s) = p(s)$ for $s = \alpha, \beta$. Thus, the consumption plan x_h that solves Equation (7) is the same as the one in which there is also a spot market but where prices are such that no profits can be made by arbitraging between the two markets. Setting the spot price $p_c^i(s)$ equal to the contingent-claims price $p^i(s)$, $i = 1, 2$ and $s = \alpha, \beta$, allows us to describe the behavior of consumers in G^1 in a fashion consistent with Equation (7).

Consumer h in G^1 trades only on the spot market. He chooses for each state of nature – after it has been revealed – a consumption bundle $x_h(s)$ that maximizes his utility subject to his market constraints, that is, that solves

maximize

$$u_h(x_h(s))$$

subject to

$$p(s) \cdot x_h(s) \leqq p(s) \cdot \omega_h(s) \tag{8}$$

and

$$x_h(s) \geqq 0$$

for $s = \alpha, \beta$, and h in G^1.

A market equilibrium for the reduced (contingent claims) economy is a positive price vector $p = (p(\alpha), p(\beta))$ that solves the system

$$\sum_H x_h \leqq \sum_H \omega_h, \tag{9}$$

where $x_h = (x_h(\alpha), x_h(\beta))$ is the solution to Equation (7) for h in G^0 and to Equation (8) for h in G^1. Inequality (9) is the materials balance condition.

The prices in the system (7′)–(9′) are dollar prices. There is no obvious unit of account for the reduced system (7)–(9). We have not chosen a normalization. If p solves Equations (7)–(9), then so does any nonnegative vector proportional to p. Thus, if p is unique up to a scalar multiple, then we say that the equilibrium is unique.

We establish in the following proposition that the economy described by Equations (7)–(9) is in all essentials equivalent to the one described by

[5] See Cass and Shell (1981, Section 3). The conditions of intermarket equilibrium are established in Lemma 1, pp. 16–17.

Equations (7′)–(9′) or, more accurately, that the former is a reduced-form version of the latter.

Proposition 2. (i) *If the price vector* $(p_b, p_c) = (p_b(\alpha), p_b(\beta), p_c(\alpha), p_c(\beta))$ *is a market equilibrium for the extended economy described by Equations* (7′)–(9′), *then any nonnegative price vector* $p = (p(\alpha), p(\beta))$ *that is proportional to the vector* $(p_b(\alpha)p_c(\alpha)\ p_b(\beta)p_c(\beta))$ *is a market equilibrium for the reduced economy described by Equations* (7)–(9). (ii) *If* $p = (p(\alpha), p(\beta))$ *is a market equilibrium for the reduced economy described by Equations* (7)–(9), *then there is a nonnegative price vector* $(p_b, p_c) = (p_b(\alpha), p_b(\beta), p_c(\alpha), p_c(\beta))$, *with* $(p_c(\alpha), p_c(\beta))$ proportional to $(p(\alpha)/p_b(\alpha), p(\beta)/p_b(\beta))$, *which is a market equilibrium for the economy described by Equations* (7′)–(9′).

Proof. (i) Assume that (p_b, p_c) is a solution to Equation (9′) and that the corresponding equilibrium allocation for consumer h in H is x_h. Set p equal to $\lambda(p_b(\alpha)p_c(\alpha), p_b(\beta)p_c(\beta))$, where λ is a positive scalar. Since $\lambda p_b(s)$ is a positive scalar for $s = \alpha, \beta, p$, and x_h for h in G^1 satisfy Equation (8). The clearing condition (9′) entails Equation (9), so it remains to show that p and x_h for h in G^0 satisfy Equation (7). The first three constraints in Equation (7′) reduce to

$$(p_b(\alpha)p_c(\alpha)) \cdot (x_h(\alpha) - \omega_h(\alpha)) - p_b(\alpha)m_h \leqq p_b(\alpha)b_h(\alpha)$$

and

$$(p_b(\beta)p_c(\beta)) \cdot (x_h(\beta) - \omega_h(\beta)) + (1 - p_b(\beta))m_h \leqq -p_b(\alpha)b_h(\alpha).$$

We can take $b_h(\alpha)$ to be an unconstrained slack variable for the system above. Therefore, after multiplying by λ and using Proposition 1, we can combine the two inequalities above to yield a more compact description of the constraints on the consumption plan of h in G^0, namely, $p \cdot x_h \leqq p \cdot \omega_h$. The proof of part (i) is complete. (ii) Assume that p is a solution to Equation (9) and that the corresponding equilibrium allocation for consumer h in H is x_h. Set p_c equal to $\lambda(p(\alpha)/p_b(\alpha), p(\beta)/p_b(\beta))$, where λ is a positive scalar, and $p_b(\alpha)$ and $p_b(\beta)$ are positive fractions satisfying $p_b(\alpha) + p_b(\beta) = 1$. Then for h in G^1, x_h obviously satisfies Equation (8′) at spot prices p_c. Next turn to Equation (7′). Set $m_h = 0$ for h in G^0 – which can be done without sacrificing any consumption opportunities for Mr. h – so that by construction the money market equilibrium condition in Equation (9′), $\sum_{G^0} m_h = 0$, is satisfied. Remember that the allocation x_h solves Equation (7) at prices p. Solve the equation

$$\lambda p(s) \cdot (x_h(s) - \omega_h(s)) = p_b(s)b_h(s) \tag{10}$$

for the sole unknown, $b_h(s)$, $s = \alpha, \beta$. From Equations (8) and (9), and nonsatiation, we have that

$$\sum_{G^0} p(s) \cdot (x_h(s) - \omega_h(s)) = 0$$

and therefore, from Equation (10), that the securities market equilibrium condition in Equation (9′), $\sum_{G^0} b_h(s) = 0$, is satisfied. It follows from Equation (7) and nonsatiation that, for h in G^0,

$$p(\alpha) \cdot (x_h(\alpha) - \omega_h(\alpha)) = -p(\beta) \cdot (x_h(\beta) - \omega_h(\beta)),$$

which, combined with Equation (10), yields $p_b(\alpha)b_h(\alpha) + p_b(\beta)b_h(\beta) = 0$, so that the first constraint in Equation (7′) is satisfied. Furthermore, that constraint and Equation (10) yield the system of equations

$$\begin{aligned} \lambda p(\alpha) \cdot (x_h(\alpha) - \omega_h(\alpha)) &= p_b(\alpha)b_h(\alpha) \\ \lambda p(\beta) \cdot (x_h(\beta) - \omega_h(\beta)) &= -p_b(\alpha)b_h(\alpha), \end{aligned} \tag{11}$$

where $b_h(\alpha)$ is a slack variable, which yields the result that, in the commodity space, the budget set implied by Equation (11) is the same as that implied by the (equality form of the) single budget constraint in Equation (7). Hence, if x_h is a solution to Equation (7) at prices p, then $(x_h, m_h = 0, b_h)$ is a solution to Equation (7′) at prices (p_b, p_c). Finally, it follows from Equation (9) that the materials balance condition, $\sum_H x_h \leqq \sum_H \omega_h$, is also satisfied. The proof of part (ii) is complete.

In the sequel, the (simpler) reduced form of the model, (7)–(9), replaces the (seemingly more realistic) extended form of the model (7′)–(9′).

In Section 2, we defined whether or not sunspots matter in terms of commodity allocations. An alternative definition, based on the equilibrium prices $p = (p(\alpha), p(\beta))$, can now be given. Because of the invariant endowment assumption (1), the von Neumann–Morgenstern utility hypothesis (2), the rational expectations postulate (4), and the strict risk-aversion assumption, we can say that sunspots matter if $(p(\alpha)/\pi(\alpha)) \neq (p(\beta)/\pi(\beta))$; otherwise, sunspots do not matter.

Prior to our fascination with sunspots (and other instances of extrinsic uncertainty), most general equilibrium economists and many commonsense economists had an instinct about what role should be assigned to sunspots in economic models: Ignore them! We refer to the parallel system in which sunspots are ignored as the certainty model; the corresponding equilibrium is, then, the certainty equilibrium. We next formally define certainty equilibrium, allowing a comparison to be made between this equilibrium concept and ours.

Consider the economy described in the preceding pages, but ignore (extrinsic) uncertainty. There are only two commodities. Mr. h in H consumes y_h^1 units of the first and y_h^2 units of the second. His corresponding endowments of the commodities are w_h^1 and w_h^2. The prices of the commodities are q^1 and q^2. Define the vectors y_h, w_h, and q by $y_h = (y_h^1, y_h^2)$, $w_h = (w_h^1, w_h^2) = \omega_h(s)$ for $s = \alpha,\ \beta$ from Equation (1), and

$q = (q^1, q^2)$. Mr. h chooses y_h in order to maximize his utility subject to his budget constraint, that is, to solve

maximize

$$u_h(y_h)$$

subject to

$$q \cdot y_h \leqq q \cdot w_h \tag{12}$$

and

$$y_h \geqq 0$$

for h in H. A *certainty equilibrium* is a positive price vector q satisfying materials balance, that is,

$$\sum_H y_h \leqq \sum_H w_h, \tag{13}$$

where y_h is the solution to Equation (12) for h in H.

Notice that each certainty equilibrium q is equivalent to the market equilibrium $p = (p(\alpha), p(\beta))$ defined by $p(s) = \pi(s)q$, $s = \alpha, \beta$. Furthermore, the corresponding allocations, y_h and $x_h = (x_h(\alpha), x_h(\beta))$, satisfy $y_h = x_h(s)$ for $s = \alpha, \beta$. Thus, every certainty equilibrium q corresponds to some market equilibrium p. Are there other equilibria that satisfy Equations (7)–(9)? This question is answered in the next two sections.

5. Unrestricted Market Participation

A basic theme of this chapter is that in a truly dynamic economy, in which generations overlap and in which there is (at least) potential uncertainty, market participation is necessarily restricted. Viewed from this perspective, the present section, in which we analyze an economy with unrestricted market participation, would seem to be a detour. This is not the case. Even with complete participation, our equilibrium concept (described formally by Equations (7)–(9)) is potentially different from the classical (certainty) equilibrium concept (described formally by Equations (12,13)). We establish in this section that sunspots do not matter in economies with strong rational expectations, complete markets, and unrestricted access to those markets. Under these strong assumptions, equilibrium in our model is thus essentially equivalent to equilibrium in the classical model. The strong assumptions are important. In particular, if consumers do not share the same beliefs about sunspot activity, then sunspots are bound to matter – even with perfect markets.

The assumption of unrestricted participation means that there are no consumers in G^1; G^1 is empty. Then, the set of all consumers H is identical with the set of unrestricted consumers G^0. Our formal model is then completely described by Equations (7) and (9). We next state our fundamental result on the structure of equilibrium with unrestricted market participation; assumption (4) is critical.

Proposition 3. *If market participation is unrestricted, then there is no equilibrium* $p = (p(\alpha), p(\beta))$ *in which sunspots matter.*

Proof. Suppose otherwise. That is, assume that there is an equilibrium in which $(p(\alpha)/\pi(\alpha)) \neq (p(\beta)/\pi(\beta))$, which implies that $x_h(\alpha) \neq x_h(\beta)$ for h in $G^0 = H$. Consider the alternative allocation $\overline{x}_h = (\overline{x}_h(\alpha), \overline{x}_h(\beta))$ defined by "averaging over states,"

$$\overline{x}_h(s) = \pi(\alpha)x_h(\alpha) + \pi(\beta)x_h(\beta),$$

for $s = \alpha, \beta, h$ in H. The allocation $\overline{x}_h$ is independent of sunspot activity and is feasible (i.e., Equation (9) is satisfied) since

$$\begin{aligned}\sum_H \overline{x}_h(s) &= \sum_H (\pi(\alpha)x_h(\alpha) + \pi(\beta)x_h(\beta))\\ &= \pi(\alpha)\sum_H x_h(\alpha) + \pi(\beta)\sum_H x_h(\beta)\\ &\leqq \pi(\alpha)\sum_H \omega_h(\alpha) + \pi(\beta)\sum_H \omega_h(\beta)\\ &= \sum_H \omega_h(s),\end{aligned}$$

for $s = \alpha, \beta$, by Equations (9) and (1). Because of the strict concavity of u_h, the alternative allocation $\overline{x}_h$ dominates the hypothesized equilibrium allocation x_h, that is,

$$\begin{aligned}v_h(\overline{x}_h(\alpha), \overline{x}_h(\beta)) &= \pi(\alpha)u_h(\overline{x}_h(\alpha)) + \pi(\beta)u_h(\overline{x}_h(\beta))\\ &= \pi(\alpha)u_h(\overline{x}_h(\alpha)) + (1 - \pi(\alpha))u_h(\overline{x}_h(\alpha))\\ &= u_h(\overline{x}_h(\alpha))\\ &= u_h(\pi(\alpha)x_h(\alpha) + \pi(\beta)x_h(\beta))\\ &> \pi(\alpha)u_h(x_h(\alpha)) + \pi(\beta)u_h(x_h(\beta))\\ &= v_h(x_h(\alpha), x_h(\beta))\end{aligned}$$

for h in H. The inequality is strict since $x_h(\alpha) \neq x_h(\beta)$. We have thus established that there is a feasible allocation that (strictly) Pareto dominates the proposed equilibrium allocation. This is a contradiction of the well-known result that an equilibrium allocation in an Arrow–Debreu economy (such as the one described in Equations (7) and (9)) is Pareto optimal.

A close reading of Proposition 3 and its proof reveals that it can be taken as a direct adaptation for our purposes of an important theorem of

Malinvaud (1972). Although condition (1) is extremely natural, it is stronger than is required for Proposition 3. As in Malinvaud's analysis, the assumption that $\omega_h(\alpha) = \omega_h(\beta)$ for each h could be weakened to $\Sigma_H \omega_h(\alpha) = \Sigma_H \omega_h(\beta)$. See also Balasko (forthcoming).

Proposition 3 and related phenomena in the model with unrestricted participation are illustrated in Figures 2–4. In drawing these box diagrams, we assume that there is only one commodity (rather than two) in each of the two states of nature. There are no consumers in G^1, and only two, Mr. A and Mr. B, in G^0.

Figure 2 is a diagrammatic illustration of Proposition 3. This example underscores the fact that Proposition 3 is based on the simple idea that rational, risk-averse individuals sharing the same beliefs will not take opposite sides of a bet, even if it is a fair bet. Allocations on the diagonal of the square yield tangency of indifference curves. Under the assumption of strict concavity, therefore, any allocation off the diagonal is Pareto dominated by some allocation on the diagonal. Consequently, since endowments lie on the diagonal, there are no mutually acceptable trades: Sunspots cannot matter.

Proposition 3 is critically dependent on the assumption that consumers share common beliefs about the probability of sunspots. Differing beliefs are a powerful motivation for trading in contingent claims. In Figure 3, once again endowments lie on the diagonal of the square. On the diagonal, the slope of Mr. h's indifference curve is given by the ratio of his subjective

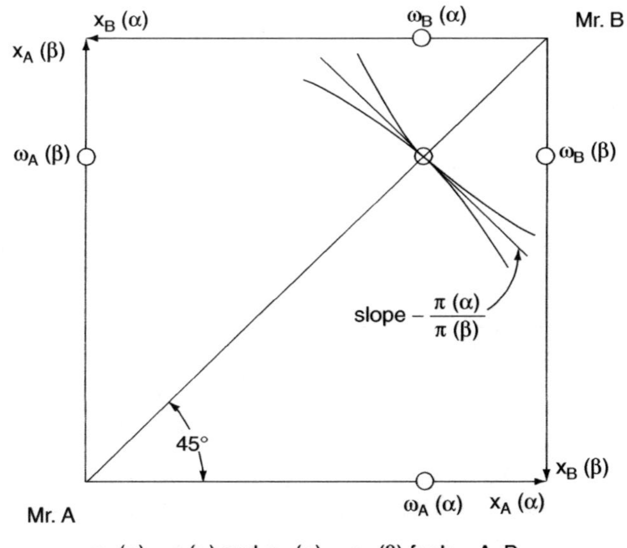

$\pi_h(\alpha) = \pi(\alpha)$ and $\omega_h(\alpha) = \omega_h(\beta)$ for h = A, B

Figure 2.

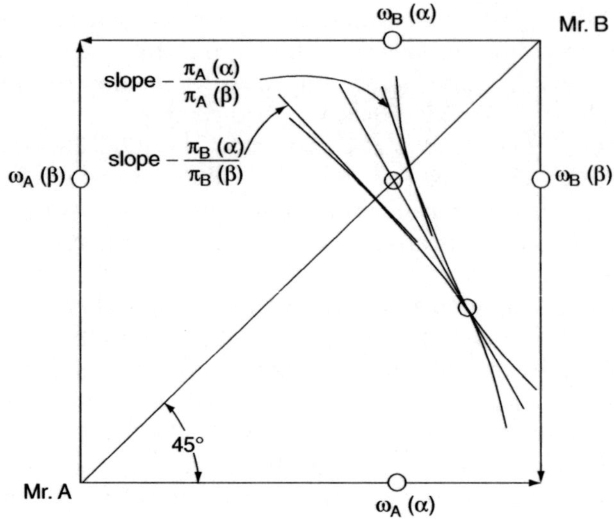

$\pi_A(\alpha) \neq \pi_B(\alpha)$, $\omega_h(\alpha) = \omega_h(\beta)$ for h = A, B

Figure 3.

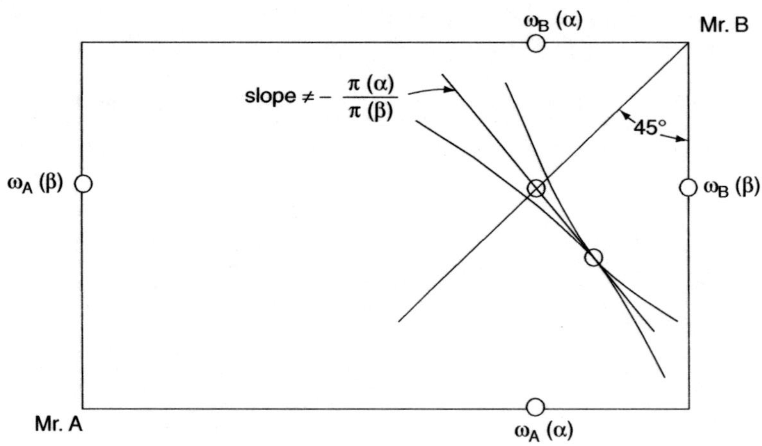

$\omega_A(\alpha) + \omega_B(\alpha) \neq \omega_A(\beta) + \omega_B(\beta)$

Figure 4.

probabilities, $(\pi_h(\alpha)/\pi_h(\beta))$. Hence, if Mr. A and Mr. B assess different likelihoods, that is, $(\pi_A(\alpha)/\pi_A(\beta)) \neq (\pi_B(\alpha)/\pi_B(\beta))$, then each allocation on the diagonal is Pareto dominated. All equilibrium allocations must be off diagonal: When beliefs differ across individuals, extrinsic uncertainty is bound to matter. In what follows, attention is restricted to the more intriguing case where beliefs are held in common – a very strong version of rational expectations. One should not, however, dismiss the practical importance of the consequences of the fact that rational individuals may have different forecasts because of different information. One of these consequences is that extrinsic uncertainty is likely to matter.

Of course, uncertainty also matters if it affects preferences or aggregate endowments. In Figure 4, Mr. A's endowments vary ceteris paribus with the state of nature. Since aggregate endowments then also vary with the state of nature, the box in Figure 4 is not a square. Individual welfare can be improved if Mr. A shares some risk with Mr. B. Equilibrium is not at the autarky point.

Proposition 3 can also be extended to apply to uncertainty that does not affect tastes or aggregate endowments but does affect individual endowments. The reader can supply the argument by using Figure 2. Mark an endowment that is off the diagonal. Then show that competitive equilibrium allocations must lie on the diagonal.

6. Restricted Market Participation

In this section, we show that – even when probability beliefs are held in common – the traditional (certainty) equilibrium concept is too narrow. We first establish an equivalence between traditional equilibria and equilibria in which sunspots do not matter. We then show that there can be other market equilibria – equilibria in which sunspots matter.

The following proposition assumes shared probability beliefs but is valid for either restricted or unrestricted market participation.

Proposition 4. *There is always some market equilibrium in which sunspots do not matter. Indeed, market equilibria in which sunspots do not matter are equivalent to the traditional (certainty) equilibria.*

Proof. We assume that H is nonempty, but either G^0 or G^1 could be empty. (i) Let q be a solution to Equation (13) with corresponding commodity allocations y_h. Then $p = (\pi(\alpha)q, \pi(\beta)q)$ is a solution to Equation (9) since, given p, $x_h = (y_h, y_h)$ is a solution to Equation (7) for h in G^0 and to Equation (8) for h in G^1, respectively if, given q, y_h is a solution to Equation (12) for h in H. (ii) Let p be a solution to Equation (9) such that sunspots do not matter, that is, such that $p(\alpha)/\pi(\alpha) = p(\beta)/\pi(\beta)$, with corresponding commodity allocations x_h, that is, so that $x_h(\alpha) = x_h(\beta)$. Then $q = p(\alpha)/\pi(\alpha)$ is a solution to Equation (13) since, given q, $y_h = x_h(\alpha)$ is a solution to Equation (12) for h in H if, given p, x_h is a solution to Equation (7) (and therefore also Equation (8)) for h in G^0 and to Equation (8) for h in G^1, respectively. (iii) The existence of a market equilibrium in which sunspots do not matter follows from (i) together with the existence of a certainty equilibrium, which can be established by the usual fixed-point argument (see, e.g., Debreu, 1959, chap. 5).

Thus, equilibrium allocations in which sunspots do not matter are unaltered as restrictions on securities market participation are introduced. What is altered is the set of potential market equilibrium allocations. The following observations demonstrate conclusively that, with restricted market participation, sunspots can matter.

Observation 1. Consider the case in which all consumers are excluded from participation in the securities market. Then there is an equilibrium in which sunspots matter if and only if there are at least two equilibria in which sunspots do not matter.

Proof. G^0 is empty and thus $H = G^1$. (i) Assume that there are (at least) two distinct equilibria in which sunspots do not matter, say, p_j for $j = 1, 2$. Then $q_j = p_j(\alpha)/\pi(\alpha) = p_j(\beta)/\pi(\beta)$ is a certainty equilibrium for $j = 1, 2$. Moreover, $p = (q_1, q_2)$ is a market equilibrium since it is a solution to Equation (9) when $H = G^1$. Furthermore, because q_1 and q_2 represent distinct equilibria, $p(\alpha)/\pi(\alpha) \neq p(\beta)/\pi(\beta)$; that is, p is a market equilibrium in which sunspots matter. (ii) Suppose p is a market equilibrium and that $p(\alpha)/\pi(\beta) \neq p(\beta)/\pi(\beta)$. Then, the two price vectors $p_1 = (\pi(\alpha)p(\alpha), \pi(\beta)p(\alpha))$ and $p_2 = (\pi(\alpha)p(\beta), \pi(\beta)p(\beta))$ represent distinct equilibria in which sunspots do not matter because p_j is a solution to Equation (9) when $H = G^1$ for $j = 1, 2$ while $\pi(\alpha)p(s)/\pi(\alpha) = \pi(\beta)p(s)/\pi(\beta)$ for $s = \alpha, \beta$.

In Observation 1, we give a method for constructing sunspot equilibria. Consider any economy in which all market participation is restricted and in which there are multiple certainty equilibria and thus multiple nonsunspot equilibria. A sunspot equilibrium is constructed as a lottery over certainty equilibria. For example, consider such an economy with two distinct certainty equilibria: q_1 and q_2. No one is able to trade in securities, but sunspot activity has been recorded (in, say, its effects on rocks). Consumers believe that if there had been sunspots, the price vector $p(\alpha) = q_1$ would prevail; otherwise $p(\beta) = q_2$ would prevail. Consumers' price-expectation formation is rational. These prices prevail simply because people believe they will. Sunspots matter.

Observation 1 is based on a completely degenerate case (included mostly for purposes of motivation): All consumers are excluded from the securities market. The next observation is based on an economy in which there is a single consumer able to participate in the securities market and another consumer who is unable to participate in the securities market. (In fact, the observation remains valid when we assume that there are many consumers in G^1.) As in the previous example, sunspots can matter and sunspot equilibria are (only) based on lotteries over certainty equilibria.

Observation 2. In the two-consumer example described above, there is an equilibrium in which sunspots matter if and only if there are at least two equilibria in which sunspots do not matter.

Proof. Let Mr. 0 be the consumer in G^0 and Mr. 1 be the consumer in G^1. (i) Assume there are (at least) two distinct nonsunspot equilibria, so there are two distinct certainty equilibria, q_1 and q_2. Let p be constructed as follows:

$$p = (\pi(\alpha)\lambda_1 q_1, \pi(\beta)\lambda_2 q_2), \tag{14}$$

where λ_j is the (optimal value of the Kuhn–Tucker–Lagrange) multiplier associated with the budget constraint in Equation (12) for $h = 0$ when the price vector q is set equal to q_j for $j = 1, 2$. Then, on the one hand, the concave programming problem (12) for $h = 0$ has the associated Lagrangian

$$L_j(y_0, \lambda_j) = u_0(y_0) + (\lambda_j q_j) \cdot (w_0 - y_0)$$

for $j = 1, 2$, where $w_0 = \omega_0(s)$ for $s = \alpha, \beta$. On the other hand, when p satisfies Equation (14), the concave programming problem (7) for $h = 0$ has the associated Lagrangian

$$\begin{aligned} L(x_0(\alpha), x_0(\beta), \mu) &= \pi(\alpha)\, u_0(x_0(\alpha)) + \pi(\beta)u_0(x_0(\beta)) \\ &\quad + \mu[\pi(\alpha)\lambda_1 q_1 \cdot (\omega_0(\alpha) - x_0(\alpha)) \\ &\quad + \pi(\beta)\lambda_2 q_2 \cdot (\omega_0(\beta) - x_0(\beta))] \\ &= \pi(\alpha)[u_0(x_0(\alpha)) + \mu\lambda_1 q_1 \cdot (\omega_0(\alpha) - x_0(\alpha))] \\ &\quad + \pi(\beta)[u_0(x_0(\beta)) + \mu\lambda_2 q_2 \cdot (\omega_0(\beta) - x_0(\beta))], \end{aligned}$$

where $w_0(s) = w_0$ for $s = \alpha, \beta$. We now appeal to the Kuhn–Tucker theorem for concave programming (see, e.g., Uzawa, 1958). Given $q = q_j$, let y_{0_j} the optimal solution to Equation (12) for $h = 0$, so that (y_{0_j}, λ_j) is a saddle point to the Lagrangian function L_j for $j = 1, 2$. A simple computation (based on the fact that L is essentially the average of L_1 and L_2.) verifies that at $(x_0(\alpha), x_0(\beta), \mu) = (y_{01}, y_{02}, 1)$ there is a saddle point to the Lagrangian function L. Hence, $(x_0(\alpha), x_0(\beta)) = (y_{01}, y_{02})$ must be the optimal solution to Equation (7) for $h = 0$. Finally, it is trivial to show that $(x_1(\alpha), x_1(\beta)) = (y_{11}, y_{12})$ is the optimal solution to Equation (8) for $h = 1$, so that p is a solution to Equation (9). We have constructed an equilibrium in which sunspots matter. (ii) The proof of the necessity part is essentially equivalent to that provided in step (ii) of the proof of Observation 1.

Observations 1 and 2 relate the existence of sunspot equilibria to the number of certainty equilibria (and, thus, to the number of nonsunspot equilibria). They are very particular to the specific assumptions employed (that there are no consumers in G^0 or only one consumer in G^0); they do not generalize in a meaningful way. The role of the two observations is simply to establish the existence of economic examples with perfect foresight and shared beliefs in which sunspots matter.

It should be remarked that, in rational expectations models of economies with outside money, we typically face a vast multiplicity of certainty equilibria (cf., e.g., Cass and Shell, 1980; Balasko and Shell, 1981). Whether or not this vast multiplicity has implications for the existence of monetary equilibria in which sunspots matter has yet to be investigated in a systematic way. While the results reported in Observations 1 and 2 might suggest that sunspot equilibria are likely to be important in monetary economies, there are good reasons to be cautious in making any such conjecture.

Indeed, focusing on Observations 1 and 2 could be misleading. In the specific models treated in this section, sunspot equilibria are in essence found by randomizing over (two) certainty equilibria. An example in the appendix shows that this is by no means the only source of sunspot equilibria. For the model with two consumers in G^0 and one consumer in G^1, we construct endowments, beliefs, and preferences for which there is a unique certainty equilibrium but there is also (at least) one sunspot equilibrium. Obviously, then, the sunspot equilibrium cannot be thought of as a lottery over certainty equilibria. Moreover, the example clearly establishes that multiplicity of certainty (or nonsunspot) equilibria is not required for the existence of a sunspot equilibrium.

We close this section with our principal result on the possibility of sunspot equilibria.

Proposition 5. *In the rational expectations economy with natural restrictions on market participation, there can be equilibria in which sunspots matter.*

Proof. It follows from Observation 1 or Observation 2 and the well-known possibility that traditional (certainty) equilibria can be nonunique. The proposition also follows directly from the appendix.

7. Sunspots and Welfare

Normative analysis in the dynamic setting is not merely a simple extension of normative analysis based on the atemporal economy. For example, in infinite horizon models with overlapping finite-lived consumers but no uncertainty, the two fundamental theorems of welfare economics must be cast, not in terms of efficient or Pareto-optimal allocations, but rather in terms of short-run (or weakly) efficient or Pareto-optimal allocations.[6] Our present concern is not with the effects of an infinite horizon but, instead, with the consequences of combining generational overlap with riskiness. The crucial element that distinguishes our welfare problem is that, for a given risk, some people must literally live with it, while for others – those born after the uncertainty is resolved – it is only a historical datum, albeit a possibly important one.

In this section, two welfare standards are defined: the traditional Pareto criterion and a (weaker) dynamic Pareto criterion. Connections between the two criteria and market equilibrium allocation are explored. One reason to introducing the dynamic Pareto optimality concept is that it is the correct concept for proving welfare theorems about sunspot equilibria. We also believe there is more to it than that.

Consider Mr. h from G^1. At the beginning of time, the economic planner must consider the two potential selves of Mr. h, Mr. h-if-sunspots, denoted by $h(\alpha)$, and Mr. h-if-no-sunspots, denoted by $h(\beta)$. Suppose α occurs and Mr. h is given a meager allocation. He objects on the grounds of inequity. He is told that had β occurred, he would have received an ample allocation. The planner assessed his utility in ex ante terms. In those terms, he was well treated.[7] Will Mr. h, now Mr. $h(\alpha)$, accept this argument? Probably not. The planner might imagine that he could have been Mr. $h(\beta)$ – or the Prince of Wales, for that matter – but, as far as he is concerned, he came into the world as Mr. $h(\alpha)$, and nothing can alter that fact. Furthermore, he points out (to gain allies and to heat up the debate) that, given the planner's ex ante point of view, there would be no pure equity argument in favor of the Equal Rights Amendment. Before conception, were not each of us potentially male and potentially female?

Mr. $h(\alpha)$'s (ex post) point of view, that he is separate from Mr. $h(\beta)$, motivates our definition of dynamic Pareto optimality. The (ex ante) point of view of our (straw man) planner motivates our definition of Pareto optimality (in the traditional sense).

An allocation $x = (\ldots, x_h, \ldots)$, where $x_h = (x_h(\alpha), x_h(\beta))$, is said to be *dynamically Pareto optimal* if there is no other allocation $x' = (\ldots, x'_h, \ldots)$ with the properties:

$$v_h(x'_h) \geqq v_h(x_h) \quad \text{for } h \text{ in } G^0$$

and

$$u_h(x'_h(s)) \geqq u_h(x_h(s)) \quad \text{for } h \text{ in } G^1 \text{ and } s = \alpha, \beta, \tag{i}$$

[6] See Cass (1972, especially Section 3) and Balasko and Shell (1980, especially Section 4).
[7] Our focus here is on equity, not efficiency. In fact, in the model treated in this chapter, if ex post utilities differ, $u_{h(\alpha)} \neq u_{h(\beta)}$, then the allocation is ex ante inoptimal (in the traditional sense).

with at least one strict inequality, and

$$\sum_H x'_h \leqq \sum_H x_h. \tag{ii}$$

Compare our definition of dynamic Pareto optimality with the concept of conditional Pareto optimality introduced by Muench (1977). Also see Peled (forthcoming). Of course, an allocation is said to be Pareto optimal (in the traditional sense) if, in the definition above, the two conditions in (i) are replaced by the single condition

$$v_h(x'_h) \geqq v_h(x_h) \quad \text{for } h \text{ in } H. \tag{i$'$}$$

Thus, every Pareto-optimal allocation is dynamically Pareto optimal, but the converse is not true.

The next two propositions are our formal welfare results. Market equilibria are identified with dynamically Pareto-optimal allocations. Nonsunspot equilibria are identified with Pareto-optimal allocations.

Proposition 6. *Every market equilibrium allocation is dynamically Pareto optimal. Every dynamically Pareto-optimal allocation can be achieved as a market equilibrium allocation under some assignment of endowments that may depend on sunspot activity (or, equivalently, under some lump-sum tax-subsidy scheme that may depend on sunspot activity).*

Proof. It follows directly from Equations (7)–(9) and the traditional theorems of welfare economics (see, e.g., Arrow and Hahn, 1971, chap. 4), when Mr. $h(\alpha)$ and Mr. $h(\beta)$ are treated as separate individuals if h is in G^1. If $h(\alpha)$ and $h(\beta)$ are to be treated separately, then obviously for the second part of the proposition, "their" endowments, $\omega_h(\alpha)$ and $\omega_h(\beta)$, will not in general be equal.

Proposition 7. *Every market equilibrium allocation in which sunspots do not matter is Pareto optimal. Every Pareto-optimal allocation can be achieved as a market equilibrium allocation (in which sunspots do not matter) under some assignment of endowments that is independent of sunspot activity (or, equivalently, under some lump-sum tax-subsidy scheme that is independent of sunspot activity).*

Proof. It follows from the equivalence of (traditional) certainty equilibria and nonsunspot equilibria – see Proposition 4 – together with the traditional theorems of welfare economics.

The Pareto-optimal allocations form a subset of the dynamically Pareto-optimal allocations. The Pareto-optimal allocations are, in fact, those dynamically Pareto-optimal allocations for which the planner has fixed the relative welfare weights between Mr. $h(\alpha)$ and Mr. $h(\beta)$ (for h in G^1) equal to the relative likelihoods of birth state α and birth state β. This may or may not be a socially desirable procedure.[8] If it is deemed worthy, though, it provides a justification for government intervention to offset the real effects of sunspots. Put another way, those who hold briefs for the traditional Pareto criterion as an ethical norm should tend to be especially sympathetic to government stabilization policies designed to counteract the effects of sunspots.

8. Concluding Remarks

In truly dynamic economies, there are inescapable restrictions on market participation. We have shown that the traditional notion of equilibrium in dynamic models is too narrow. Sunspots can matter.

How much do sunspots matter? Are sunspot equilibria "likely" relative to nonsunspot equilibria? Are they stable to shocks, including variations in government policies? We expect to be able to analyze these issues in the model developed in this chapter. The model must be extended, however, in order to be able to analyze the macro-oriented questions raised by sunspot activity. We could then ask: Are sunspot equilibria more "likely" in monetary than in nonmonetary economies? What policies should the government pursue in the face of sunspot activity?[9]

Acknowledgments

We gratefully acknowledge the research support under NSF grant 80-07012 to the Center for Analytic Research in Economics and the Social Sciences at the University of Pennsylvania. We also thank the members of the GNRS Seminaire d'Econométrie, especially Jean-Michel Grandmont, for helpful criticism. We have also benefited from interaction with our colleagues Costas Azariadis and Yves Balasko.

Appendix

The special demographic structure underlying Observations 1 and 2 allowed us to provide simple examples of market equilibria in which sunspots

[8] We tend to believe that this approach is not compelling.

[9] We have been discussing the "micro" questions with Yves Balasko. We expect the recent advances in overlapping-generations theory to be of use for the "macro" problems. We should record here that "sunspot activity" has also been observed to be emanating from Costas Azariadis, Roger Guesnerie, and Steve Spear.

matter. In those particular examples, all sunspot equilibria are merely lotteries over certainty equilibria. Here we substantiate our claim that this result does not generalize.

For this purpose, we construct an economy in which there is a unique certainty equilibrium – and thus, by Proposition 4, a unique nonsunspot equilibrium – yet in which there is at least one sunspot equilibrium. In other words, we establish that, in general, multiplicity of certainty equilibria is not required for there to be an equilibrium in which sunspots matter.[10] Our example, therefore, also illustrates the basic point that an equilibrium in which sunspots matter need not be based on a lottery over certainty equilibria.

Consider the general formulation that is the centerpiece of Section 6. If we are to go beyond Observations 1 and 2, there must be at least two consumers in G^0. Hence, assume now that there are two consumers, Mr. 0_A and Mr. 0_B, born before sunspot activity is observed, and one consumer, Mr. 1, born afterward. These consumers will turn out to be very nicely behaved. As in the main body of the chapter, utility functions satisfy standard assumptions (e.g., monotonicity and smoothness). Furthermore, demand functions are of the textbook variety (e.g., both commodities are normal goods for each consumer, and the first commodity is a gross substitute for the second). The reason for presenting the example here – rather than in Section 6 – is that its construction is, of necessity, somewhat intricate.

In constructing this example, we adopt the following strategy: First, we specify an endowment vector that is independent of sunspot activity – that is, so that $\omega_h(s) = \omega_h$ for $h = 0_A$, 0_B, 1 and $s = \alpha$, β. Then we choose a contingent-claims price vector so that sunspots will matter – that is, so that $p(\alpha)$ is not proportional to $p(\beta)$ – and a commodity allocation vector that is affordable (by each consumer) and feasible (for the economy), which satisfy the additional properties

$$x_{0_A}(\alpha) \not\leq x_{0_A}(\beta), x_{0_B}(\alpha) > x_{0_B}(\beta) \text{ and } x_1(\alpha) < x_1(\beta) \tag{A.1}$$

and

$$p(s) \cdot x_h(s) \neq p(s) \cdot w_h \tag{A.2}$$

[10] In our current research with Yves Balasko, we have completed the circle by demonstrating the converse result as well, namely, that the existence of sunspot equilibria is not necessary for there to be multiplicity of certainty equilibria. It is also noteworthy that the same analysis establishes that, generically, the sort of example we present here will have an even number of sunspot equilibria.

for $h = 0_A, 0_B$ and $s = \alpha, \beta$. Because of Equation (A.1), it is then possible to find common probabilities $\pi(s)$ and additively separable utility functions

$$u_h(x^1, x^2) = \phi_h[f_h(x^1) + g_h(x^2)] \tag{A.3}$$

such that the price vector is an equilibrium supporting the allocation vector. Thus, this is an equilibrium in which sunspots matter, while from Equation (A.2), prices q proportional to either $p(\alpha)$ or $p(\beta)$ will generally not be certainty equilibria.[11] Finally, when we limit the component functions g_h so that the derivative elasticity condition

$$-\frac{g_h''(x^2)x^2}{g_h'(x^2)} < \frac{x^2}{x_h^2 - w^2} \quad \text{for } x^2 \geqq w_h^2 \tag{A.4}$$

is satisfied, it is further established that the construction is compatible with uniqueness of certainty equilibrium.

This program will be carried out in two steps. First, using the utility specification (A.3), we exhibit an equilibrium p in which sunspots matter (and which will not generally reduce to a lottery over certainty equilibria). Second, using (for the first time) the elasticity condition (A.4), we establish that this sort of equilibrium is consistent with there being only one certainty equilibrium q.

Step 1: We begin by specifying endowments and designing prices and allocations that admit sufficient degrees of freedom to enable us then to select suitable probabilities and utility functions. The reader is urged to consult Figure A1, which provides a geometric illustration of the method for designing the price-allocation pair. (i) Let $w_h = (1, 1)$ for $h = 0_A, 0_B$, and $w_1 = (2, 2)$, where $\omega_h(s) = w_h$, for $h = 0_A, 0_B, 1$ and $s = \alpha, \beta$. (ii) Choose prices $p = (p(\alpha), p(\beta)) = (p^\alpha, 1, p^\beta, 1)$ satisfying the further restriction $0 < p^\beta < p^\alpha < 1$. (iii) Then choose a scalar γ satisfying the restriction $0 < \gamma < (p^\alpha - p^\beta)/2$, so that the pair of equations

$$(p^\alpha, 1) \cdot (x^1, x^2) = (p^\alpha, 1) \cdot (1, 1) - \gamma$$

and

$$(p^\beta, 1) \cdot (x^1, x^2) = (p^\beta, 1) \cdot (1, 1) + \gamma$$

has a positive solution (x^1, x^2).

[11] That is, to put it another way, the sunspot equilibrium p will generally not be a lottery over certainty equilibria $q^\alpha = p(\alpha)/\pi(\alpha)$ and $q^\beta = p(\beta)/\pi(\beta)$. This interesting result by itself can be guaranteed by imposing additional, mild restrictions on, say, the component functions g_{0_A} and g_{0_B}. But such restrictions are superfluous in view of the much stronger result that we state next.

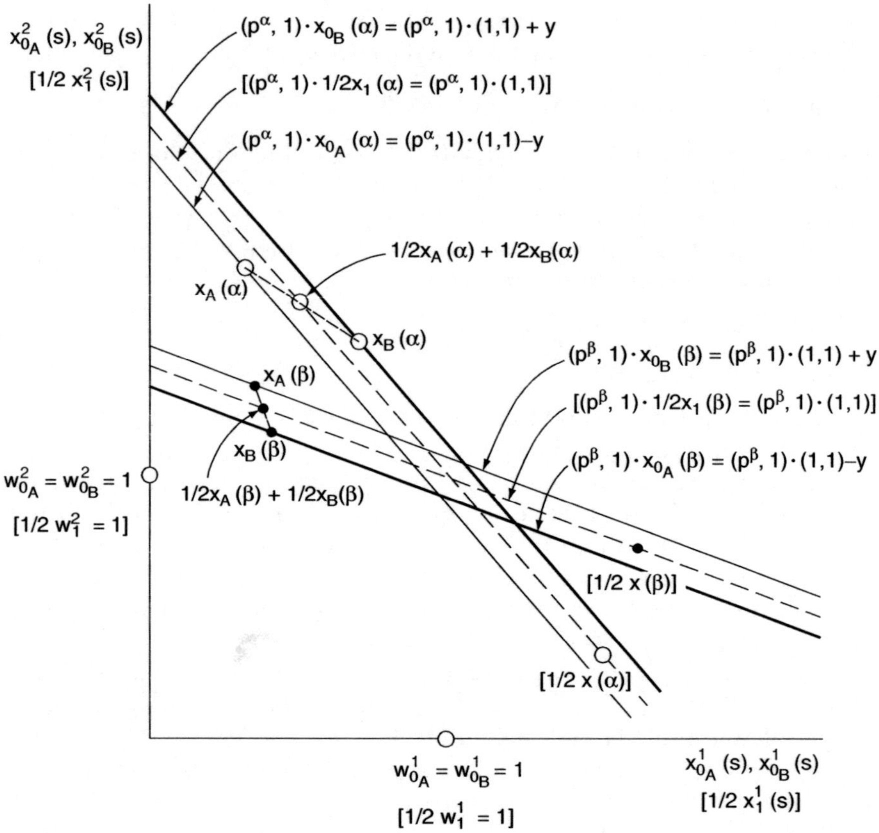

Figure A1.

Consider $x_{0_A} = x_A = (x_A(\alpha), x_A(\beta)) = (\xi_A, \theta_A\xi_A, p^\alpha(1-\xi_A) + (1-\gamma), p^\beta(1-\theta_A\xi_A) + (1+\gamma))$ such that $0 < \xi_A < 1$, $1 < \theta_A < 1/\xi_A$, and $p^\alpha(1-\xi_A) + (1-\gamma) > p^\beta(1-\theta_A\xi_A) + (1+\gamma)$. In other words, consider choosing $x_{0_A} = x_A$ so that

$$(p^\alpha, 1) \cdot x_A(\alpha) = (p^\alpha, 1) \cdot (1,1) - \gamma$$

and

$$(p^\beta, 1) \cdot x_A(\beta) = (p^\beta, 1) \cdot (1,1) + \gamma,$$

which implies that $(p^\alpha, 1) \cdot x_A(\alpha) + (p^\beta, 1) \cdot x_A(\beta) = (p^\alpha, 1) \cdot (1, 1) + (p^\beta, 1) \cdot (1, 1)$, and

$$0 < x^1_A(\alpha) < x^1_A(\beta) < 1$$

and

$$2 < x_A^2(\alpha) < x_A^2(\beta) < 1.$$

Similarly, consider $x_{0_B} = x_B = (x_B(\alpha), x_B(\beta)) = (\xi_B, \theta_B\xi_B, p^\alpha(1-\xi_B) + (1-\gamma), p^\beta(1-\theta_B\xi_B) + (1+\gamma))$ such that $0 < \xi_B < 1$, $0 < \theta_B < 1$, and $p^\alpha(1-\xi_B) + (1+\gamma) > p^\beta(1-\theta_B\xi_B) + (1-\gamma)$ – or choosing $x_{0_B} = x_B$ so that

$$(p^\alpha, 1) \cdot x_B(\alpha) = (p^\alpha, 1) \cdot (1, 1) + \gamma$$

and

$$(p^\beta, 1) \cdot x_B(\beta) = (p^\beta, 1) \cdot (1, 1) - \gamma,$$

which implies that $(p^\alpha, 1) \cdot x_B(\alpha) + (p^\beta, 1) \cdot x_B(\beta) = (p^\alpha, 1) \cdot (1, 1) + (p^\beta, 1) \cdot (1, 1)$, and

$$1 > x_B^1(\alpha) > x_B^1(\beta) > 0$$

and

$$2 > x_B^2(\alpha) > x_B^2(\beta) > 1.$$

(The representation of x_h in terms of the parameters ξ_h and θ_h turns out to be useful in subsequent calculations. Also, note that a whole subscript, for example, 0_A, is used in denoting a variable, while a partial subscript, for example, A, is used in denoting a particular value of that variable. Thus, x_A is a particular value of the variable x_{0_A}, x is a particular value of the variable x_1, and so forth.)

(iv) Choose ξ_A, θ_A, ξ_B, and θ_B so that, in addition, $\gamma \leqq (1-\theta_A\xi_A)(p^\alpha - p^\beta)/2$ and $\xi_A(\theta_A - 1) < \xi_B(\theta_B - 1)$. In particular, the second of these restrictions implies that $[1 - x_A^1(\alpha)] + [1 - x_B^1(\alpha)] < [1 - x_A^1(\beta)] + [1 - x_B^1(\beta)]$, while the previous restrictions, $x_A^2(\alpha) > x_A^2(\beta)$ and $x_B^2(\alpha) > x_B^2(\beta)$ imply that $[1 - x_A^2(\alpha)] + [1 - x_B^2(\alpha)] < [1 - x_A^2(\beta)] + [1 - x_B^2(\beta)]$. The role of the first restriction will be explained later.

It is easily verified that all the various restrictions on ξ_h and θ_h (or, equivalently, x_A and x_B) will obtain, for instance, if $\xi_A \sim 0$, $\xi_B = 1/2$, and $\theta_A - 1 = 1 - \theta_B \sim 0$.

(v) Finally, choose $x_1 = x = (x(\alpha), x(\beta))$ so that $x^i(s) = [1 - x_A^i(s)] + [1 - x_B^i(s)] + 2$ for $i = 1, 2$; $s = \alpha, \beta$, which, from the foregoing, implies that $(p^s, 1) \cdot x(s) = (p^s, 1) \cdot (2, 2)$ for $s = \alpha, \beta$, $0 < x(\alpha) < x(\beta)$, and $x_A^i(s) + x_B^i(s) + x_B^i(s) = 1 + 1 + 2$ for $i = 1, 2$; $s = \alpha, \beta$.

When one refers to Figure A1, it should be clear that, given the price vector $(p^\alpha, 1, p^\beta, 1)$, the allocation vector $(x_A(\alpha), x_A(\beta), x_B(\alpha), x_B(\beta), x(\alpha), x(\beta))$ satisfies the budget and nonnegativity constraints in Equations (7) and (8), as well as the materials balance condition (9). Thus, for the first step of our program, all that remains is to verify that with judicious choices of probabilities and utility functions, the allocation vector also yields optimal solutions to the programming problems (7) and (8).

Consider u_h having the additively separable form (A.3) with $\phi_h : \mathbb{R} \to \mathbb{R}$, $f_h : \mathbb{R}_+ \to \mathbb{R}$ and $g_h : \mathbb{R}_+ \to \mathbb{R}$ (at least) twice continuously differentiable, strictly increasing, and (at least for one of the functions, strictly) concave. Our argument will rely heavily on the elementary result that, given constants $0<\xi_1<\xi_2$ (respectively, $\xi_1<\xi_2$) and $0<\lambda<1$ (respectively, $0<\lambda\leqq 1$), one can always find a function $\Psi : \mathbb{R}_+ \to \mathbb{R}$ (respectively, $\Psi : \mathbb{R} \to \mathbb{R}$) that is smooth, strictly increasing, and strictly concave (respectively, concave) and that satisfies the conditions

$$\lim_{\xi\to 0^+} \Psi'(\xi) = \infty \text{ and } \frac{\Psi'(\xi_2)}{\Psi'(\xi_1)} = \lambda, \text{respectively} \frac{\Psi'(\xi_2)}{\Psi'(\xi_1)} = \lambda.$$

In particular, Ψ can always be chosen from the class of functions having constant derivative elasticity, so that $\Psi'(\xi) = M\xi^{-\mu}$ for $\xi\geqq 0$ with $M>0$ and $\mu>0$. In using this simple observation to construct utility functions, we begin with Mr. 1, proceed to Mr. 0_B, and finish with Mr. 0_A since their respective consumption bundles are increasingly more complicated to reconcile with optimizing behavior.

So consider Mr. 1, and suppose that $u_1(x^1, x^2) = \phi_1[f_1(x^1) + g_1(x^2)]$. Then direct application of the Kuhn–Tucker theorem for concave programming (together with some straightforward manipulation) yields the result that x solves the problem

maximize

$$\phi_1\{f_1[x_1^1(s)] + g_1[x_1^2(s)]\}$$

subject to

$$(p^s, 1) \cdot x_1(s) = (p^s, 1) \cdot (2, 2)$$

and

$$x_1(s) \geqq 0$$

for $s = \alpha$, β if and only if x satisfies the first-order conditions

$$\frac{f_1'[x^1(\alpha)]}{g_1'[x^2(\alpha)]} = p^\alpha$$

and

$$\frac{f_1'[x^1(\alpha)]}{f_1'[x^2(\beta)]} = \frac{p^\alpha g_1'[x^2(\alpha)]}{p^\beta g_1'[x^2(\beta)]}. \tag{A.5}$$

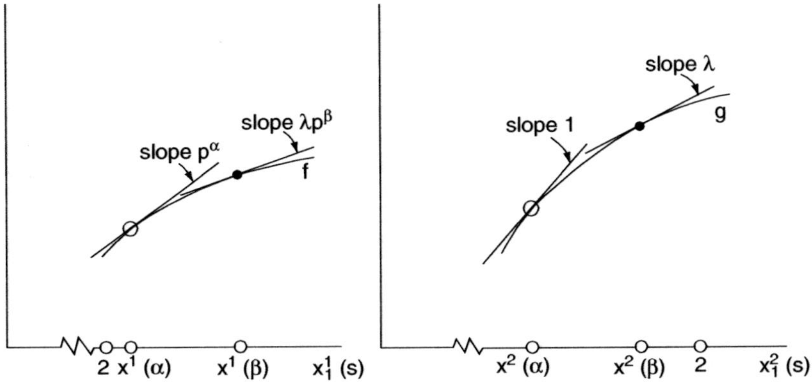

Figure A2.

But since, by construction, $p^\alpha/p^\beta > 1$ while $x(\alpha) < x(\beta)$, these conditions will obtain if we choose $\phi_1' = c > 0$, and $f_1 = f$ and $g_1 = g$, so that

$$\frac{f'[x^1(\alpha)]}{g'[x^2(\alpha)]} = p^\alpha, \frac{g'[x^2(\alpha)]}{g'[x^2(\beta)]} = \frac{1}{\lambda} > 1, \text{and } \frac{f'[x^1(\alpha)]}{f'[x^1(\beta)]} = \frac{p^\alpha}{p^\beta}\frac{1}{\lambda} > 1. \tag{A.6}$$

An example of such functions is depicted in Figure A2.

For Mr. 0_B, similar reasoning yields the result that x_B solves the problem

maximize

$$\pi(\alpha)\phi_{0_B}\{f_{0_B}[x^1_{0_B}(\alpha)] + g_{0_B}[x^2_{0_B}(\alpha)]\} + \pi(\beta)\phi_{0_B}\{f_{0_B}[x^1_{0_B}(\beta)] + g_{0_B}[x^2_{0_B}(\beta)]\}$$

subject to

$$(p^\alpha, 1) \cdot x_{0_B}(\alpha) + (p^\beta, 1) \cdot x_{0_B}(\beta) \leqq (p^\alpha, 1) \cdot (1, 1) + (p^\beta, 1) \cdot (1, 1)$$

and

$$x_{0_B} \geqq 0$$

if and only if x_B satisfies the first-order conditions

$$\frac{f'_{0_B}[x^1_B(\alpha)]}{g'_{0_B}[x^2_B(\alpha)]} = p^\alpha,$$

$$\frac{f'_{0_B}[x^1_B(\alpha)]}{f'_{0_B}[x^1_B(\beta)]} = \frac{p^\alpha g'_{0_B}[x^2_B(\alpha)]}{p^\beta g'_{0_B}[x^2_B(\beta)]}, \tag{A.7}$$

and

$$\frac{\phi'_{0_B}\{f_{0_B}[x^1_B(\alpha)]+g_{0_B}[x^2_B(\alpha)]\}}{\phi'_{0_B}\{f_{0_B}[x^1_B(\beta)]+g_{0_B}[x^2_B(\beta)]\}}\frac{g'_{0_B}[x^2_B(\alpha)]}{g'_{0_B}[x^2_B(\beta)]}=\frac{\pi(\beta)}{\pi(\alpha)}.$$

In this case, since by construction $x_B(\alpha) > x_B(\beta)$, these conditions will obtain if we choose $\pi(\beta)/\pi(\alpha) = [1-\pi(\alpha)]/\pi(\alpha) < p^\beta/p^\alpha$ and $\phi'_{0_B} = c_B > 0$ and $f_{0_B} = f_B$ and $g_{0_B} = g_0$, so that

$$\frac{f'_B[x^1_B(\alpha)]}{g'_B[x^2_B(\alpha)]}=p^\alpha,$$

$$\frac{g'_B[x^2_B(\alpha)]}{g'_B[x^2_B(\beta)]}=\frac{\pi(\beta)}{\pi(\alpha)}<\frac{p^\beta}{p^\alpha}, \tag{A.8}$$

and

$$\frac{f'_B[x^1_B(\alpha)]}{f'_B[x^1_B(\beta)]}=\frac{p^\alpha}{p^\beta}\frac{\pi(\beta)}{\pi(\alpha)}<1.$$

Finally, consider Mr. 0_A. From an argument parallel with that for Mr. 0_B, we know that x_A must satisfy first-order conditions like Equation (A.7),

$$\frac{f'_{0_A}[x^1_A(\alpha)]}{g'_{0_A}[x^2_A(\alpha)]}=p^\alpha,$$

$$\frac{f'_{0_A}[x^1_A(\alpha)]}{f'_{0_A}[x^1_A(\beta)]}=\frac{p^\alpha g'_{0_A}[x^2_A(\alpha)]}{p^\beta g'_{0_A}[x^2_A(\beta)]}, \tag{A.9}$$

and

$$\frac{\phi'_{0_A}\{f_{0_A}[x^1_A(\alpha)]+g_{0_A}[x^2_A(\alpha)]\}}{\phi'_{0_A}\{f_{0_A}[x^1_A(\beta)]+g_{0_A}[x^2_A(\beta)]\}}\frac{g'_{0_A}[x^2_A(\alpha)]}{g'_{0_A}[x^2_A(\beta)]}=\frac{\pi(\beta)}{\pi(\alpha)}.$$

The difficulty here is that we have just chosen $\pi(\beta)/\pi(\alpha) < p^\beta/p^\alpha$, while, by earlier construction, $x^1_A(\alpha) < x^1_A(\beta)$ and $x^2_A(\alpha) > x^2_A(\beta)$. However, this is where we can employ the extra degree of freedom afforded by cleverly selecting the transforming function ϕ_{0_A} (representing "overall" risk aversion). For, if we knew that

$$f_{0_A}[x^1_A(\alpha)]+g_{0_A}[x^2_A(\alpha)]>f_{0_A}[x^1_A(\beta)]+g_{0_A}[x^2_A(\beta)], \tag{A.10}$$

then we could choose $\phi_{0_A} = \phi_A, f_{0_A}$, and $g_{0_A} = g_A$ so that

$$\frac{f'_A[x^1_A(\alpha)]}{g'_A[x^2_A(\alpha)]}=p^\alpha, \frac{p^\beta}{p^\alpha}<\frac{g'_A[x^2_A(\alpha)]}{g'_A[x^2_A(\beta)]}=\lambda<1,$$

$$\frac{f'_A[x_A^1(\alpha)]}{f'_A[x_A^1(\beta)]} = \frac{p^\alpha}{p^\beta}\lambda > 1, \tag{A.11}$$

and

$$\frac{\phi'_A\{f_A[x_A^1(\alpha)] + g_A[x_A^2(\alpha)]\}}{\phi'_A\{f_A[x_A^2(\beta)] + g_A[x_A^2(\beta)]\}}\lambda = \frac{\pi(\beta)}{\pi(\alpha)}.$$

And our earlier limitation on the choice of x_A that $\gamma \leqq (1-\theta_A\xi_A)(p^\alpha - p^\beta)/2$ was designed precisely to ensure Equation (A.10): To begin with, notice that the first listed condition in Equation (A.9) is essentially a normalization of f'_{0_A}, in terms of $p^\alpha g'_{0_A}[x_A^2(\alpha)]$, and is therefore only tangentially related to the other two conditions. If we utilize this observation together with the representation of x_A in terms of ξ_A and θ_A, it follows that Equation (A.10) holds (for smooth and strictly concave functions f_{0_A} and g_{0_A} restricted only by the first listed condition in Equation (A.9)) if

$$\begin{aligned} f_{0_A}[x_A^1(\beta)] - f_{0_A}[x_A^1(\alpha)] &< f'_{0_A}[x_A^1(\alpha)](x_A^1(\beta) - x_A^1(\alpha)) \\ &\leqq g'_{0_A}[x_A^2(\alpha)](x_A^2(\alpha) - x_A^2(\beta)) < g_{0_A}[x_A^2(\alpha)] - g_{0_A}[x_A^2(\beta)] \end{aligned}$$

if

$$p^\alpha(x_A^1(\beta) - x_A^1(\alpha)) \leqq x_A^2(\alpha) - x_A^2(\beta)$$

if

$$p^\alpha(\theta_A\xi_A - \xi_A) \leqq [p^\alpha(1 - \xi_A) + (1 - \gamma)] - [p^\beta(1 - \theta_A\xi_A) + (1 + \gamma)]$$

if

$$\gamma \leqq (1 - \theta_A\xi_A)(p^\alpha - p^\beta)/2.$$

This completes the first step of our program.

Step 2: It remains only to demonstrate that the procedure of step 1 can also be carried out under the additional restriction that the component functions g_h satisfy the elasticity condition (A.4) and that, for such an economy, there is a unique certainty equilibrium. It turns out that we have enough flexibility even after further limiting attention to component functions exhibiting constant elasticity, that is, g_h satisfying

$$g'_h(x^2) = N(x^2)^{-\nu} \text{ for } x^2 \geqq 0 \text{ with } N > 0 \text{ and } 0 < \nu \leqq 1. \tag{A.4'}$$

The essential point is to ensure that this strengthened condition, (A.4′), is consistent with Equations (A.6), (A.8), and (A.11) since, given the original condition, (A.4), a routine argument (which we outline below for the sake of completeness) establishes uniqueness of certainty equilibrium.

So, once more, consider the optimizing behavior of Mr. 1, Mr. 0_B, and Mr. 0_A, in turn, as described in Equations (A.6), (A.8), and (A.11), respectively.

It is immediately obvious that there is no problem with Mr. 1 since

$$\frac{g'[x^2(\alpha)]}{g'[x^2(\beta)]} = \frac{N[x^2(\alpha)]^{-v}}{N[x^2(\beta)]^{-v}} = \left[\frac{x^2(\beta)}{x^2(\alpha)}\right]^v > 1$$

for every ($N > 0$ and) $0 < v \leqq 1$. For Mr. 0_B and Mr. 0_A, the argument is only slightly more complicated; we merely need to verify that, given all previous restrictions on x_B and x_A, we can still choose these consumption bundles so that

$$\frac{g'_B[x^2_B(\alpha)]}{g'_B[x^2(\beta)]} = \left[\frac{x^2_B(\beta)}{x^2_B(\alpha)}\right]^{v_B} < \frac{p^\beta}{p^\alpha} < \frac{g'_A[x^2_A(\alpha)]}{g'_A[x^2(\beta)]} = \left[\frac{x^2_A(\beta)}{x^2_A(\alpha)}\right]^{v_A} < 1 \quad \text{(A.12)}$$

for some $0 < v_B \leqq 1$ and $0 < v_A \leqq 1$. In fact, it is easily demonstrated that $v_B = v_A = 1$ will do: again, if we explicitly use the representation of x_h in terms of ξ_h and θ_h, then Equation (A.12) becomes

$$\frac{p^\beta(1 - \theta_B\xi_B) + (1 - \gamma)}{p^\alpha(1 - \xi_B) + (1 + \gamma)} < \frac{p^\beta}{p^\alpha} < \frac{p^\beta(1 - \theta_A\xi_A) + (1 - \gamma)}{p^\alpha(1 - \xi_A) + (1 - \gamma)} < 1. \quad \text{(A.13)}$$

But, just as before, Equation (A.13) will obtain, for instance, if $\xi_B = 1/2$, $\xi_A \sim 0$ and $1 - \theta_B = \theta_A - 1 \sim 0$.

In order to show that for this sort of economy there can be only a single certainty equilibrium, it suffices to show that aggregate excess demand for commodity 1 is strictly decreasing in the relative price of commodity 1 (when all consumers ignore sunspot activity). For this purpose, it is unnecessary to distinguish between the three consumers since each has the same type of utility function and, hence, the same structure of excess demand. Thus, following the lead from the last part of Section 4, we now let prices of commodities be (q^1, q^2), the representative consumer's demand for commodities be (y^1, y^2), his endowment be (w^1, w^2), his excess demand be $(z^1, z^2) = (y^1 - w^1, -y^2 - w^2)$ and – when needed later – his income be $w = q^1w^1 + q^1w^2$. Also, suppose that commodity 2 is the numeraire, so that $q^2 = 1$ and $q^1/q^2 = q^1$. Then it is straightforward to derive the following excess demand function for commodity 1 given that the representative consumer's utility function is additively separable, $u(y^1, y^2) = \phi[f(y^1) + g(y^2)]$:[12]

[12] The calculation assumes that

$$\lim_{y^1 \to 0^+} f'(y^1) = \lim_{y^2 \to 0^+} g'(y^2) = \infty,$$

which is consistent with our preceding construction. Notice also that the transforming function ϕ plays no role here (though it clearly did before); if there is no risk, then overall aversion to risk has absolutely no effect on individual behavior. This result is of critical importance to the approach we have taken in this appendix since it introduces a significant wedge between the economy with and the economy without extrinsic uncertainty.

$$f'(w^1 + z^1) - g'(w^2 - q^1z^1)q^1 = 0 \text{ for } q^1 > 0. \tag{A.14}$$

Implicit differentiation of Equation (A.14) yields, after some simplification (in particular, when the budget constraint $-q^1z^1 = z^2$ is used),

$$\begin{aligned}\frac{dz^1}{dq^1} &= \frac{g'(w^2 - q^1z^1) - g''(w^2 - q^1z^1)q^1z^1}{f''(w^1 + z^1) + g''(w^2 - q^1z^1)(q^1)^2} \\ &= \frac{g'(w^2 + z^2)}{f''(w^1 + z^1) + g''(w^2 + z^2)(q^1)^2}\left[1 + \frac{g''(w^2 + z^2)\,z^2}{g'(w^2 + z^2)}\right] \\ &< 0\end{aligned}$$

if and only if

$$1 + \frac{g''(w^2 + z^2)z^2}{g'(w^2 + z^2)} > 0$$

or

$$-\frac{g''(y^2)y^2}{g'(y^2)} < \frac{y^2}{y^2 - w^2} \text{ for } y^2 \geqq w^2.$$

That is, under the elasticity condition (A.4), each consumer's excess demand (and hence the economy's aggregate excess demand) for commodity 1 must be strictly decreasing in that commodity's relative price.

This completes the second and final step of our program. We have constructed an economy with only one certainty equilibrium and at least one sunspot equilibrium.

Our final calculation is intended to underline the fact that there is nothing unusual about the specifications (A.3)–(A.4). Essentially repeating the immediately preceding analysis, but now in terms of the ordinary demand function for commodity 1 (depending on the relative price q^1 and correspondingly measured income w), reveals the following property of the Engle curves for the representative consumer:

$$\frac{\partial y^1}{\partial w} = \frac{g''(y^2)q^1}{f''(y^1) + g''(y^2)(q^1)^2} > 0$$

and

$$\frac{\partial y^2}{\partial w} = 1 - q^1\frac{\partial y^1}{\partial w} = 1 - \frac{g''(y^2)(q^1)^2}{f''(y^1) + g''(y^2)(q^1)^2} > 0.$$

That is, both commodities are normal goods for each consumer.

References

Arrow, K.J. (1964). The role of securities in the optimal allocation of risk-bearing. *Review of Economic Studies* **31** (April), 91–96.

Arrow, K.J. and Hahn, F.H. (1971). *General Competitive Analysis*. San Francisco, CA: Holden-Day.

Azariadis, C. (1981). Self-fulfilling prophecies. *Journal of Economic Theory* **25** (December), 380–396.

Balasko, Y. (1983). Extrinsic uncertainty revisited. *Journal of Economic Theory* **31**, 203–210.

Balasko, Y. and Shell, K. (1980). The overlapping-generations model. I: The case of pure exchange without money. *Journal of Economic Theory* **23** (December), 281–306.

Balasko, Y. and Shell, K. (1981). The overlapping-generations model. II: The case of pure exchange with Money. *Journal of Economic Theory* **24** (February), 112–142.

Cass, D. (1972). Distinguishing inefficient competitive growth paths. *Journal of Economic Theory* **4** (April), 224–240.

Cass, D. and Shell, K. (1980). In defense of a basic approach. In Kareken, J.H. and Wallace, N. (Eds), *Models of Monetary Economies*. Minneapolis, MN: Federal Reserve Bank of Minneapolis.

Cass, D., and Shell, K. (1981)."Do Sunspots Matter?" Center Analytic Res. Econ. Soc. Sci. (CARESS) Working Paper No. 81-09R. Philadelphia, PA: University of Pennsylvania, May. (Also appearing in French translation as "Les Tâches solaires ont-elles de l'importance?" *Cahiers du Séminaire d'Econométrie* 24 [1982]: 93–127).

Debreu, G. (1959). *Theory of Value: An Axiomatic Analysis of Economic Equilibrium*. New York: Wiley.

Donaldson, J.B. and Selden, L. (1981). Arrow-Debreu preferences and the reopening of contingent claims markets. *Economic Letters* **8** (3), 209–216.

Malinvaud, E. (1972). The allocation of individual risks in large markets. *Journal of Economic Theory* **4** (April), 312–328.

Muench, T.J. (1977). Optimality, the interaction of spot and futures markets, and the nonneutrality of money in the Lucas model. *Journal of Economic Theory* **15** (August), 325–344.

Peled, D. (1983). Informational diversity over time and the optimality of monetary equilibrium. *Journal of Economic Theory* **31**, 203–210.

Shell, K. (1977). Monnaie et allocation intertemporelle. CNRS Séminaire d'Econométrie de M. Edmond Malinvaud. Paris, November.

Uzawa, H. (1958). The Kuhn–Tucker theorem in concave programming. In Arrow, K.J., Hurwicz, L. and Uzawa, H. (Eds), *Studies in Linear and Non-Linear Programming*. Stanford: Stanford University Press.

Chapter 7

Optimality with Unbounded Numbers of Households: I. Overlapping (or Overlapping Generations) Structure and the First Basic Theorem of Welfare☆

David Cass

1. Introduction

Modern welfare economics is founded on the two basic theorems characterizing the optimality properties of competitive equilibrium. (See, for instance, the deservedly famous general formulation by Arrow, 1951.) However, dating from the seminal contribution of Samuelson (1958) (and even earlier, Malinvaud, 1953), it has been well known that in models of economies that capture the one-directional, open-ended structure of time, the first of these fundamental results simply may not hold; competitive allocation may not be Pareto optimal (or even efficient).

Much has been written trying to "explain" this particular sort of market "failure". It is now generally understood that the potential nonoptimality of intertemporal equilibrium has nothing at all to do with such conventional problems as absence of markets or restraints on behavior. Rather, it has to do with the nature of time itself, and in particular, with the fact that a serious treatment of dynamic allocation processes necessarily involves introducing an infinity of both scarce objects and active agents into the traditional Wahasian framework (see, for instance, the nice exposition by Shell, 1971). What seems to me not yet clearly articulated is precisely why this "double-infinity" (to use Shell's apt phrase) makes a difference. For example, the model generated by a countable collection of standard (finite-dimensional) pure-exchange models also involves unbounded numbers of commodities and households, and yet obviously both basic theorems of welfare still apply.

☆This article was originally published in *Optimalité et Structures: Mélanges en Hommage à Edouard Roussier*, Edited by G. Ritschard and D. Royer, 17–42, © Economica, 1985.

International Symposia in Economic Theory and Econometrics, Vol. 21B
S. Spear (Editor)

ISSN: 1571-0386/DOI: 10.1108/S1571-0386(2011)000021B010

Thus, the primary purpose of this note is to try and formalize the intrinsic properties of a general (possibly infinite-dimensional) pure-exchange model that may lead to falsification of the first basic theorem. This goal is achieved – at least insofar as it can be without more detailed specification of preferences – by the first theorem (together with two entirely different kinds of examples) presented in Section 3. Roughly speaking, this result establishes that the critical issue is simply whether or not there are unbounded (amounts or) numbers of commodities for which arbitrarily selected subsets of households have shared tastes.

The leading case of a model exhibiting such unlimited overlap is, of course, the familiar overlapping-generations model. My basic approach therefore motivates asking a further question, namely, what actually distinguishes this particular model? A satisfactory answer requires pinpointing the special features of generational structure, a task accomplished by the two propositions presented in Section 4. This analysis demonstrates that the characteristic properties of the overlapping-generations model are just two: First, each household has tastes for only a finite subset of commodities (say, households are *mortal*). Second, only a finite subset of households has tastes for each commodity (say, households are *evolutionary*).

Finally, I should underline that my investigation is conducted in terms of a very unrestricted specification of an economy's opportunities for pure distribution, one admitting the possibility of unbounded amounts of resources, as well as the possibility of unbounded numbers of commodities or households. This general model is presented in the following section. Given such broad possibilities, the notion of competitive behavior itself may not be well defined; budget constraints – represented in what I consider their only plausible form, as inequalities between sums of market values – may yield unlimited individual opportunities. For this reason, one might justifiably wonder whether concern with competitive allocation makes any sense, even from a purely normative viewpoint. To complete the investigation begun here, I plan on addressing this issue in a subsequent note, proposing, defending, and analyzing what I also consider the only plausible case in which households are mortal.

2. A General Model

The economy is represented by the standard Arrow—Debreu model of pure distribution with free disposal, but suitably elaborated to incorporate the possibility that there may be unbounded amounts of resources, as well as unbounded numbers of commodities or households. It can therefore be described, briefly, in the following terms.

2.1. Commodities

Commodities are labeled by the superscript $c \in C$, where C is a subset (possibly the whole set) of the integers. Quantities of commodities are nonnegative, and are denoted by the scalar $x^c \geqq 0$ or vector $\boldsymbol{x} = (\ldots, x^c, \ldots) \geqq 0$.[1] I assume throughout that there are positive amounts of commodities (possibly unbounded) available to the economy. These are called simply *resources*, and are denoted $r^c > 0$ or $r = (\ldots, r^c, \ldots) \gg 0$. Finally, the market prices of commodities, called simply *prices*, are denoted p^c or $p = (\ldots, p^c, \ldots)$.

2.2. Households

Households are labeled by the subscript $h \in H$, where H is a subset (again possibly the whole set) of the integers. I assume throughout that households have *preferences* over consumption of commodities. These are represented by utility functions $u_h : \mathbb{R}_+^{\#C} \to \mathbb{R}$ that are weakly monotone.[2]

For each household $h \in H$, let $C_h \subset C$ be the subset of commodities, which are (potentially) goods, that is, the smallest among all sets $C'_h \subset C$ with the property that if $x'_h \geqq 0$, $x''_h \geqq 0$, and $x^{c'}_h = x^{c''}_h$ for $c \in C'_h$, then $u_h(x'_h) = u_h(x''_h)$ (possibly the set C itself). Obviously, by virtue of weak monotonicity, $C_h \neq \emptyset$ for $h \in H$.

Hence, there is no significant loss in analytic generality (and considerable gain in notational simplicity) in assuming each commodity is a good for some household,

$$C = \bigcup_{h \in H} C_h,$$

and then restricting each household to consuming just its own goods,

$$x_h \in X_h = \{x_h : x_h \geqq 0 \text{ and } x^c_h = 0 \quad \text{for } c \notin C_h\}.$$

---

[1] I adopt the generally accepted convention that, for any pair of vectors $\boldsymbol{x}'$ and $\boldsymbol{x}''$, $\boldsymbol{x}' \geqq \boldsymbol{x}''$ means $x^{c'} \geqq x^{c''}$ for every $c \in C$, $\boldsymbol{x}' > \boldsymbol{x}''$ means $x^{c'} \geqq x^c$ for every $c \in C$, with strict inequality for some c, while $\boldsymbol{x}' \gg \boldsymbol{x}''$ means $x^{c'} > x^c$ for every $c \in C$.

[2] Since I will not be concerned with questions of existence, I need neither regularity nor convexity. This monotonicity assumption, namely, that if $x'_h \geqq 0$, $x''_h \geqq 0$ and $x'_h \geqq [\text{resp.} \gg] \, x''_h$, then $u_h(x'_h) \geqq [\text{resp.} >] \, u_h(x''_h)$, is ultimately based on two more primitive assumptions, that households are never locally satiated in consumption of commodities, and that they can freely dispose of unwanted commodities. It permits me to specify both that for feasible allocations) materials balance and that (in competitive equilibrium) prices are nonnegative as well as nontrivial.

Properties of the subsets C_h themselves (e.g., how much they intersect, or whether they are finite) play a central role in my analysis. For this reason it will be convenient to let

$$C_{H'} = \bigcup_{h \in H'} C_h \quad \text{for} \quad H' \subset H$$

denote the subset of commodities which are goods for an arbitrary subset of households.

Finally, I assume throughout that households own given amounts of the various resources available to the economy. Such *endowments* are denoted by $e_h^c \geqq 0$ or $e_h = (\ldots, e_h^c, \ldots) \geqq 0$. By definition, endowments must satisfy materials balance,

$$\sum_{h \in H} e_h^c = r^c \quad \text{for} \quad c \in C.$$

But any other special properties (for instance, whether they are goods, $e_h \in X_h$ for $h \in H$) are immaterial for my present purposes – again because I will not be concerned with questions of existence.

2.3. Allocations

An allocation of commodities to each household is denoted as $a = (\ldots, x_h, \ldots)$. It is *feasible* if (i) households receive just their own goods,

$$x_h \in x_h \quad \text{for} \quad h \in H, \tag{1}$$

and (ii) materials balance,

$$\sum_{h \in H} x_h^c = r^c \quad \text{for} \quad c \in C. \tag{2}$$

Following Balasko and Shell (1980), whose terminology is especially appropriate for this general model, I distinguish two types of optimality. On the one hand, a feasible allocation a is *weakly Pareto optimal* if there is no other feasible allocation a' that (i) replicates a except for a finite number of commodities, that is, has the property that there is a $C' \subset C$ such that $\#C' \leqq \infty$ and

$$x_h^{c'} = x_h^c \quad \text{for} \quad h \in H,\ c \notin C',$$

and (ii) dominates a in terms of utility, that is, has the property that $u_h(x_h') \geqq u_h(x_h)$ for $h \in H$, with strict inequality for some h.

On the other hand, a feasible allocation a is simply *Pareto optimal* if there is no other feasible allocation a' that dominates a in terms of utility.

It is self-evident that Pareto optimal allocations are weakly Pareto optimal. However, weakly Pareto optimal allocations are necessarily Pareto optimal only when there are bounded numbers of commodities. Thus (as is well-known), when the number of commodities is unbounded, this distinction plays a crucial role in describing the optimality (or efficiency) properties of competitive equilibrium.

2.4. Equilibrium

Given preferences and endowments, a price-allocation pair (p, a) is a competitive equilibrium if (i) prices are nonnegative and nontrivial, $p > 0$, (ii) households optimize, for each $h \in H$, x_h is an optimal solution to the problem

$$\begin{aligned} &\text{maximize} && u_h(x'_h) \\ &\text{subject to} && \sum_{c \in C} p^c x_h^{c'} \leqq \sum_{c \in C} p^c e_h^c \\ &\text{and} && x'_h \in X_h \end{aligned} \tag{3}$$

and (iii) markets clear, for each $c \in C$,

$$\sum_{h \in H} x_h^c = \sum_{h \in H} e_h^c = r^c. \tag{4}$$

I will sometimes refer to such a feasible allocation as being *competitive.*

2.5. Overlap

In order to study the optimality of competitive equilibrium (when $\#C = \infty$ or $\#H = \infty$), it is necessary to categorize various ways in which households' preferences may overlap. In this regard, the simplest, useful distinction is whether or not the economy actually consists of a number of essentially unrelated subeconomies.

I will say that the economy has *indecomposable structure* if there is no partition of households into a pair of nonempty subsets H^α and H^β such that $C_{H^\alpha} \cap C_{H^\beta} = \emptyset$; otherwise it has *decomposable structure.* Since the second case can always effectively be reduced to the first, I will assume throughout (sometimes, for emphasis, explicitly) that the economy has indecomposable structure.

A second simple, but extremely useful taxonomy involves merely counting the possible numbers of overlap in terms of the sets C_h. Unfortunately, even such an elementary classification entails introducing substantial additional notation.

Consider exhaustive collections of nonempty, finite, and disjoint subsets of households, denoted by $H = [H^\nu]$, together with their corresponding subsets of goods, denoted symmetrically by $C^\nu = C_{H^\nu}$ for $\nu \in N$. Here the index set N is some subset of the positive integers, which can be taken to be the whole set when there are unbounded numbers of households (motivating my choice of notation). Now, associate with each collection H the set of goods for which there is some overlap in preferences,

$$C(H) = \{c : c \in C^{v'} \cap C^{v} \quad \text{for some } v' \in N,\ v'' \in N,\ v' \neq v''\}.$$

I will say that the economy has *trivial overlapping structure* if there is some H such that $\#C(H) = 0$. Otherwise, I will say that it has *finite overlapping structure* if there is some H such that $\#C(H) < \infty$, and *overlapping struture* if there is no H such that $\#C(H) < \infty$.

For future reference, note especially that if $\#C < \infty$, then the economy *cannot* have overlapping structure. Further, if $\#H < \infty$, then the economy *must* have trivial overlapping structure, and conversely (since it is presumed to have indecomposable structure).

The foregoing is based on a very unsophisticated notion of the way in which households may be interrelated. Nonetheless, it turns out to provide a complete framework for describing situations where the first basic theorem may fail.

3. The First Basic Theorem Reconsidered

It is now firmly established that, for the overlapping-generations specialization of the model just outlined (see the following section for a precise description), the usual statement of the first basic theorem of welfare must be modified by replacing the property of Pareto optimality with that of weak Pareto optimality.[3] This is also true here. It is most instructive, though, proceeding to this final conclusion by beginning with a general sufficient condition for Pareto optimality of competitive allocation, formulated in terms of finite resource value. My particular formulation has the important additional virtue of yielding a catalog of the several circumstances under which, because of size alone, market failure is possible.

Lemma. *If (p, a) is a competitive equilibrium, and there is some partition of households $H = [H^{v}]$ with associated overlap of goods $C(H)$ such that*

$$\sum_{c \in C(H)} p^{c} r^{c} < \infty, \tag{5}$$

then the competitive allocation a is Pareto optimal.

[3] See, for instance, Balasko and Shell (1980), Benveniste (1983), or Okuno and Zilcha (1980). In this literature, the notion of weak Pareto optimality is often referred to as *short-run* Pareto optimality (because the latter term has an intertemporal flavor). I should note in passing that both this type of result as well as the more general proposition from which it derives (the analogue of the Lemma introduced below) were originally established by Malinvaud (1953) in the closely related context of characterizing efficient growth paths.

Proof of Lemma. To start with, notice that, for any feasible allocation a', materials balance Equation (2) together with the second hypothesis of the lemma imply that

$$\sum_{c\in C(H)} p^c\left(\sum_{v\in N}\sum_{h\in H^v} x_h^{c'}\right) = \sum_{c\in C(H)} p^c \sum_{h\in H} x_h^{c'} = \sum_{c\in C(H)} p^c r^c < \infty. \tag{6}$$

Thus, following the usual pattern for proofs of this sort, my strategy consists simply of showing that if the conclusion of the lemma were false, then Equation (6) would be contradicted. This argument is based on two easily demonstrated (and generally well-known) results, whose proofs are sketched in an appendix merely for the sake of completeness.

Claim 1. If x_h is an optimal solution to Equation (3), then

$$\sum_{c\in C} p^c x_h^c = \sum_{c\in C} p^c e_h^c < \infty,$$

while $x_h' \in X_h$ and $u_h(x_h') =$ [resp. $>$] $u_h(x_h)$ imply

$$\sum_{c\in C} p^c x_h^{c'} \geqq [\text{resp.} >] \sum_{c\in C} p^c x_h^c.$$

Claim 2. If $(p, a) \geqq 0$, then

$$\sum_{c\in C'} p^c \sum_{h\in H'} x_h^c = \sum_{h\in H'}\sum_{c\in C'} p^c x_h^c \quad \text{for } C' \subset C,\ H' \subset H. \tag{7}$$

Given the validity of these two claims, the rest of the proof then proceeds as follows.

Assume that the conclusion of the lemma is false, that is, there is some feasible allocation a' that dominates a in terms of utility. Then, from the first hypothesis of the lemma (in particular, from household optimization Equation (3)) and Claim 1, it follows that

$$\sum_{c\in C} p^c x_h^{c'} \geqq \sum_{c\in C} p^c x_h^c \quad \text{for } h \in H,$$

with strict inequality for some h.

Hence, given any H with associated $C(H)$, it also follows that (since $\#H^v < \infty$ for $v \in N$)

$$\sum_{h\in H^v}\sum_{c\in C} p^c x_h^{c'} \geqq \sum_{h\in H^v}\sum_{c\in C} p^c x_h^c \quad \text{for } v \in N,$$

with strict inequality for some v

or

$$\sum_{h\in H^v}\left(\sum_{c\in C(H)} p^c x_h^{c'} + \sum_{c\in C-C(H)} p^c x_h^{c'}\right)$$
$$\geqq \sum_{h\in H^v}\left(\sum_{c\in C(H)} p^c x_h^c + \sum_{c\in C-C(H)} p^c x_h^c\right) \quad \text{for} \quad v \in N, \tag{8}$$

with strict inequality for some v.

Now suppose that Equation (8) would enable us to deduce that

$$\sum_{h\in H^v}\sum_{c\in C(H)} p^c x_h^{c'} \geqq \sum_{h\in H^v}\sum_{c\in C(H)} p^c x_h^c \tag{9}$$

with strict inequality for some v.

Then from Equation (6) (applied to both a' and a) and Claim 2 we would immediately get the contradiction

$$\sum_{c\in C(H)} p^c r^c = \sum_{c\in C(H)} p^c\left(\sum_{v\in N}\sum_{h\in H^v} x_h^{c'}\right) = \sum_{v\in N}\sum_{h\in H^v}\sum_{c\in C(H)} p^c x_h^{c'}$$
$$> \sum_{v\in N}\sum_{h\in H^v}\sum_{c\in C(H)} p^c x_h^c = \sum_{c\in C(H)} p^c\left(\sum_{v\in N}\sum_{h\in H^v} x_h^c\right) = \sum_{c\in C(H)} p^c r^c.$$

So all that remains to be shown is that, by virtue of the distinction between C and $C(H)$, Equation (9) is in fact a consequence of Equation (8).

To see that this is the case, focus on an arbitrary subset of households H^v. Since a is hypothesized, and a' is assumed to be feasible, we know (from Equation (1)) that

$$x_h^{c'} = x_h^c = 0 \quad \text{for } c \in C-C(H)$$

and either $c \in C^v$, $h \notin H^v$ or $c \notin C^v$, $h \in H^v$, while (from Equation (2)) that

$$\sum_{v\in N}\sum_{h\in H^v} x_h^{c'} = \sum_{h\in H} x_h^{c'} = r^c = \sum_{h\in H} x_h^c = \sum_{v\in N}\sum_{h\in H^v} x_h^c \quad \text{for } c \in C-C(H).$$

Hence, we also know that

$$\sum_{h\in H^v} x_h^{c'} = \sum_{h\in H^v} x_h^c = \begin{cases} 0 & \text{for} \quad c \in C-C(H),\ c \notin C^v \\ r^c & \text{for} \quad c \in C-C(H),\ c \notin C^v \end{cases}$$

or

$$p^c \sum_{h\in H^v} x_h^{c'} = p^c \sum_{h\in H^v} x_h^c \quad \text{for} \quad c \in C-C(H). \tag{10}$$

Once more employing Claim 2, it then follows from Equation (10) that

$$\sum_{h\in H^v}\sum_{c\in C-C(H)} p^c x_h^{c'} = \sum_{c\in C-C(H)} p^c \sum_{h\in H^v} x_h^{c'}$$
$$= \sum_{c\in C-C(H)} p^c \sum_{h\in H^v} x_h^c = \sum_{h\in H^v}\sum_{c\in C-C(H)} p^c x_h^c. \quad (11)$$

But using Equation (11) to cancel common terms on both sides of the inequality (8) yields the desired inequality (9), and the proof is complete. □

A direct consequence of Lemma is two distinct conditions under which competitive allocation is always Pareto optimal.

Theorem 1. *If (i) the economy has trivial overlapping structure or (ii) the economy has finite overlapping structure, but there are bounded resources of every common good, then every competitive allocation is Pareto optimal.*

Proof of Theorem 1. (i) Obviously, if there is some H such that $\#C(H) = 0$, then

$$\sum_{c\in C(H)} p^c r^c = 0 < \infty$$

for every $p > 0$, and the Lemma applies to every competitive equilibrium (ii). Similarly, if there is some H such that $\#C(H) < \infty$ and $r^c < \infty$ for $c \in C(H)$, then

$$\sum_{c\in C(H)} p^c r^c \leqq \#C(H) \max_{c\in C(H)} p^c r^c < \infty$$

for every $p > 0$, and once again the Lemma applies to every competitive equilibrium. □

The primary interest of Theorem 1 is that denial of both alternatives thus yields two distinct sets of circumstances in which problems may arise. Recalling that, when the economy has indecomposable structure, it also has trivial overlapping structure if and only if there are bounded numbers of households; these two cases are:

Case I. Unbounded resources. $\#H = \infty$, $\#C(H) < \infty$ for some H and if $\#C(H) < \infty$, then $r^c = \infty$ for some $c \in C(H)$, that is, the economy has finite overlapping structure but there are unbounded resources of some common good.

Case II. Overlapping structure. $\#H = \infty$ and $\#C(H) = \infty$ for every H, that is, the economy has overlapping structure (so that there are necessarily unbounded numbers of commodities).

For both cases there are economies in which competitive allocation may or may not be Pareto optimal. Uncovering the precise circumstances under which markets fail on account of size, and in particular, because of overlapping structure, requires looking at more specific properties of preferences. This problem has been intensively studied for the overlapping-generations specialization of my model (again, refer to the papers cited earlier); further detailed analysis here for the general version of the model would take me too far afield. Rather, I will simply content myself with presenting examples in which the competitive mechanism breaks down for each of the two possible cases.

Example 1. Self-defeating property rights.

In this example there are just two commodities, say, $c = \{1, 2\}$, with the first but not the second available in unlimited amount, say, $r^1 = \infty$ and $r^2 = 1/\alpha$ with $0 < \alpha < 1$. There are, however, unbounded numbers of households, say, $H = \{0, 1, 2, \ldots\}$, and for each household both commodities are goods, $C_h = C$ for $h \in H$. Preferences and endowments are described by

$$u_h(x_h) = f^1(x_h^1) + \alpha^{-h} f^2(\alpha^h x_h^2),$$

where $f^i : \mathbb{R}_+ \to \mathbb{R}$ is differentiable, strictly increasing and concave for $i = 1, 2$, and

$$e_h = (1, \alpha^{-h}),$$

respectively.

It is easily verified that, for this example, there is a unique competitive allocation, $x_h = (1, \alpha^{-h})$ for $h \in H$, supported, say, by the prices $p = (f^{1'}(1), f^{2'}(1))$. However, this allocation is not Pareto optimal: Since no household is satiated in the first commodity, any alternative allocation a' such that $x_h^{1'} > 1$ and $x_h^{2'} = \alpha^{-h}$ for $h \in H$ is both feasible and (strictly) dominates the allocation a in terms of utility. (Notice that, for this competitive equilibrium,

$$\sum_{c \in C(H)} p^c r^c = p^1 r^1 + p^2 r^2 = f^{1'}(1)\,\infty + f^{2'}(1)/\alpha = \infty$$

for every H, so that Lemma is inapplicable). □

Example 2. Ineffective consumption loans

In this example there are unbounded numbers of both commodities and households, say, $C = H = \{\pm 1, \pm 2, \pm 3, \ldots\}$, but all commodities are available in only limited amounts. Each household values just two commodities as goods,

$$C_h = \begin{cases} \{-h, h\} & \text{for } h = 1, 2, 3, \ldots \\ \{h, -h+1\} & \text{otherwise,} \end{cases}$$

and is endowed with one unit of both its goods,

$$e_h = \begin{cases} (e_h^{-h}, e_h^h) = (1,1) & \text{for} \quad h = 1,2,3,\ldots \\ (e_h^h, e_h^{-h+1}) = (1,1) & \text{otherwise.} \end{cases}$$

This special pattern is displayed by the asterisks in Figure 1.

Finally, preferences are described by $u_h : \mathbb{R}_2^+ \to \mathbb{R}$, where u_h is differentiable, strictly increasing and strictly quasi-concave.

With a bit of effort, it can be verified that, for this example, there is again a unique competitive allocation, the autarchic allocation $x_h = e_h$ for $h \in H$, and that, furthermore, this allocation will not be Pareto optimal, for instance, when

$$u_h(x^1, x^2) = u_{-h}(x^2, x^1) = f(x^1, x^2),$$

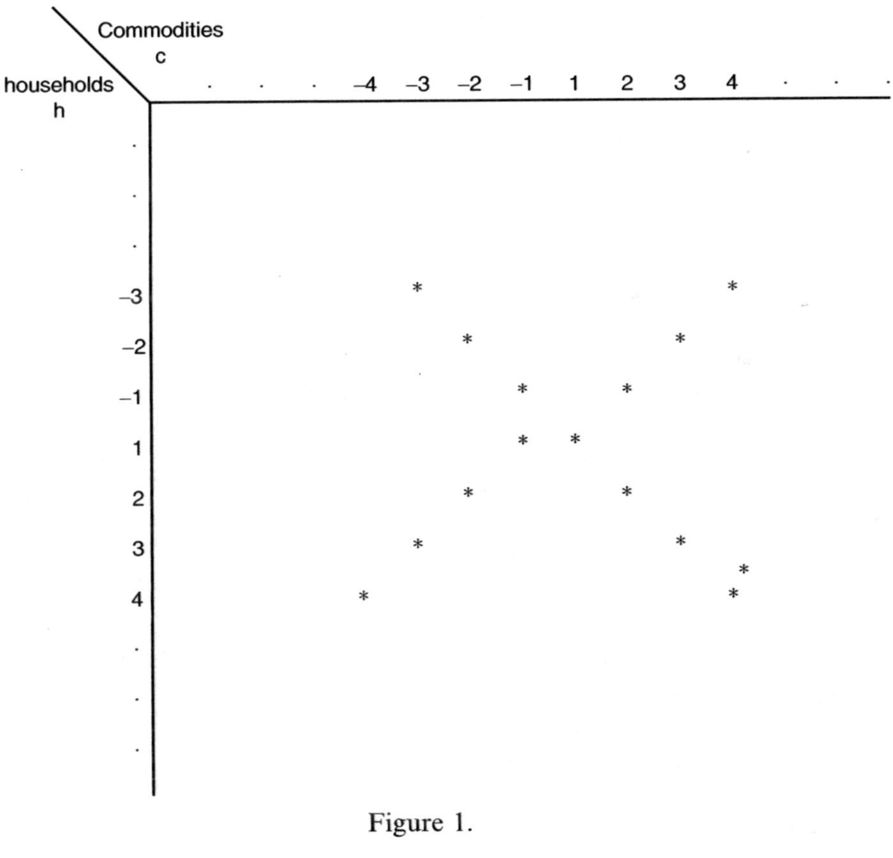

Figure 1.

where

$$f_1(1,1)/f_2(1,1)<1$$

for $h = 1, 2, 3, \ldots$. □

The reason for my being so sketchy in elaborating the potential difficulty raised by this last example is that, as one might suspect from scrutinizing Figure 1 closely, it is really nothing more than a disguised version of Samuelson's original example. I have clothed it in this particular garb because I also want to use it to illustrate the central result of the following section, an algorithm for converting any model that has the basic elements of overlapping-generations structure into the canonical two-period lifetime, overlapping-generations model itself. And once given such reformulation, establishing the claims made for Example 2 is a routine exercise (left to the interested reader).

Before turning to the issue of when my general model will reduce to an overlapping-generations model, however, I first want to complete my discussion of optimality by presenting the promised restatement of the first basic theorem.

Theorem 2. *Suppose resources are bounded. Then every competitive allocation is weakly Pareto optimal.*

Remark. Of course, the stronger conclusion of Theorem 1 takes precedence under suitable conditions, and especially, when there are bounded numbers of commodities or households.

Proof of Theorem 2. Given a particular competitive equilibrium, say, (p', a'), focus on an arbitrary, finite subset of commodities, say, $C^f \subset C$ such that $\#C^f < \infty$. Then consider the derived economy involving just the commodities C^f and households $H^f = \{h{:}h \in H \text{ and } C_h \cap C_f \neq \emptyset\}$, where quantities are denoted x^f, utility functions are defined by

$$u_h^f(x_h^f) = u_h(x_h) \quad \text{with } x_h = \begin{cases} x_h^{fc} & \text{for } c \in C^f \\ x_h^{c'} & \text{otherwise,} \end{cases}$$

and so on. It is clear that, for such a derived economy, (i) resources are bounded (since $r^{fc} = r^c < \infty$ for $c \in C^f$) while (ii) the economy itself has (at most) finite overlapping structure (since $\#C^f < \infty$), and that, moreover, $(p^{f'}, a^{f'})$ is a competitive equilibrium. Hence, by Theorem 1, $a^{f'}$ is Pareto optimal. A fortiori, a' is weakly Pareto optimal (since C^f was arbitrarily chosen). □

4. The Inherent Structure of Overlapping Generations

As I have suggested several times already, my one remaining objective is to relate the general model presented in Section 2 to its well-known overlapping-generations incarnation. Bear in mind that, throughout this discussion, I am assuming that there are unbounded numbers of both commodities and households, $\#C = \#H = \infty$.

4.1. Canonical Representation

Let the superscript $t \in T$ denote time periods, where $T = \{0, 1, 2, \ldots\}$. Then the standard overlapping-generations formulation is the special case where my general model can be represented in the following manner:[4]

(i) Commodity indices are denoted

$$C = \bigcup_{t \in T} I^{t+1}$$

with $I^1 = \{1, 2, \ldots, \ell^1\}$ and

$$I^{t+1} = \left\{ \sum_{s=1}^{t} \ell^s + 1, \sum_{s=1}^{t} \ell^s + 2, \ldots, \sum_{s=1}^{t+1} \ell^s \right\},$$

where $0 < \ell^{t+1} < \infty$, for $t \geqq 0$;

(ii) Household indices are denoted

$$H = \bigcup_{t \in T} G^t$$

with $G^\circ = \{1, 2, \ldots, m^\circ\}$ and

$$G^{t+1} = \left\{ \sum_{s=0}^{t} m^s + 1, \sum_{s=0}^{t} m^s + 2, \ldots, \sum_{s=0}^{t+1} m^s \right\},$$

where $0 < m^t < \infty$, for $t \geqq 0$; and (most) important of all;

(iii) Consumption sets satisfy $C_h \subset I^1$ for $h \in G^\circ$ and

$$C_h \subset I^t \cup I^{t+1} \quad \text{for } h \in G^t,\ t \geqq 1.$$

---

[4] See, in particular, Balasko et al. (1980), especially Section 4 (pp. 319–321). My presentation of this model is intentionally abbreviated because more complete descriptions, including ample, detailed interpretation, abound in the literature (once again, refer, for instance, to the papers cited earlier).

Put succinctly, successive *generations* G^t for $t \geqq 0$ consist of two-period lived households who have (potentially) shared tastes with both their immediate predecessors $C_{G^t} \cup C_{G^{t-1}} \subset I^t$ and their immediate successors $C_{G^t} \cup C_{G^{t+1}} \subset I^{t+1}$.

4.2. Generational Structure

I have made (and will continue to make) extensive use of the notation C_h and $C_{H'}$ denoting the subsets of commodities that are goods. Here and in the remaining subsections of this note it will also be convenient to have at hand the parallel notation

$$H^c = \{h : h \in H \text{ and } c \in C_h\} \quad \text{for} \quad c \in C$$

and

$$H^{C'} = \bigcup_{c \in C'} H^c \quad \text{for} \quad C' \subset C$$

denoting the subsets of households that are consumers. I will say that the economy has *generational structure* if households exhibit the following pair of properties.

Households are mortal: Each household has tastes for only a bounded number of commodities,

$$\#C_h < \infty \quad \text{for} \quad h \in H. \tag{12}$$

Households are evolutionary: Only bounded numbers of households have tastes for each commodity,

$$\#H^c < \infty \quad \text{for} \quad c \in C. \tag{13}$$

Obviously, if the economy has an overlapping-generations representation, then it has generational structure. Much more interesting is that the converse proposition is also valid.

Proposition 1. *Maintain the assumption that the economy has indecomposable structure. If the economy has generational structure, then there is a relabeling of commodities and households such that it has an overlapping-generations representation.*

Proof of Proposition 1. While the argument is conceptually simple, it is (as far as I can see, unavoidably) notationally complex.

For any pair of equal-sized sets of integers A and B, let the symbol $A \xrightarrow{r} B$ denote the operation of replacing A with B, that is, of relabeling the indices in A with those in B. Now consider the following relabeling algorithm.

Begin by picking a nonempty, finite subset of households, say, $\underline{H}(0)$. Then continue recursively according to the rules:

For $t = 0$ (given $\underline{H}(0)$). Define

$$C(0) = C_{\underline{H}(0)}$$

and

$$H(0) = \underline{H}(0) \cup \{h : h \in H, h \notin \underline{H}(0)$$

but

$$C_h \subset C(0)\}.$$

Now relabel

$$C(0) \xrightarrow{r} I^1 \text{ with } \ell^1 = \#C(0)$$

and

$$H(0) \xrightarrow{r} G^o \text{ with } m^o = \#H(0).$$

For $t+1>0$ (given $\underline{H}(t)$, $C(t)$, and $H(t)$). Define

$$\underline{H}(t+1) = \underline{H}(t) \cup \{h : h \in H, h \notin \underline{H}(t) \quad \text{but} \quad C_h \cap C(t) \neq \emptyset\}, C(t+1) = C_{\underline{H}(t+1)}$$

and

$$H(t+1) = \underline{H}(t+1) \cup \{h : h \in H, h \notin \underline{H}(t+1) \quad \text{but} \quad C_h \subset C(t+1)\}.$$

Now relabel

$$C(t+1) - C(t) \xrightarrow{r} I^{t+2} \text{ with } \sum_{s=1}^{t+1} \ell^s = \#C(t) \text{ and } \ell^{t+2} = \#(C(t+1) - C(t))$$

and

$$H(t+1) - H(t) \xrightarrow{r} G^{t+1} \text{ with } \sum_{s=0}^{t} m^s = \#H(t) \text{ and}$$

$$m^{t+1} = \#(H(t+1) - (H(t)).$$

Note especially that, at each step in this algorithm, the definition of $\underline{H}(t+1)$ picks up the succeeding households that overlap with generation t, while the definition of $H(t+1)$ picks up, in addition, the succeeding households that don't overlap with generation t but must be included in generation $t+1$ anyway (because their consumption is concentrated in period $t+1$).

In order to establish that the foregoing procedure actually works, I only need to verify that (i) $0 < \ell^1 < \infty, 0 < m^\circ < \infty$, and $C_h \subset I^1$ for $h \in G^\circ$, (ii) $0 < \ell^{t+2} < \infty, 0 < m^{t+1} < \infty$, and $C_h \subset I^{t+1} \cup I^{t+2}$ for $h \in G^{t+1}, t \geqq 0$, and

(iii) for every $h \in H$ there is some $t \in T$ such that $h \in H(t)$. This verification relies heavily on the facts that, for every nonempty, finite subset of households H', Equation (12) entails

$$0 < \#C_{H'} \leqq \sum_{h \in H'} \#C_h \leqq \#H' \max_{h \in H'} \#C_h < \infty, \tag{12'}$$

and that, for every nonempty, finite subset of commodities C', Equation (13) entails

$$0 < \#H^{C'} \leqq \sum_{c \in C'} \#H^c \leqq \#C' \max_{c \in C'} \#H^c < \infty. \tag{13'}$$

Very briefly, it goes as follows

(i) On the one hand, the initial choice of $\underline{H}(0)$ plus the definition of $C(0)$ plus Equation (12′) yield $0 < \ell^1 < \infty$. On the other hand, the additional definition of $H(0)$ plus Equation (13′) yield both $1 < m^\circ < \infty$ and (upon relabeling) $C_h \subset I^1$ for $h \in G^\circ$.

(ii) (This is essentially an expanded repetition of the argument in (i)). Notice first that the definition of $\underline{H}(t+1)$ plus the maintained assumption that the economy has indecomposable structure plus Equation (13′) yield $0 < \#(\underline{H}(t+1) - \underline{H}(t)) < \infty$. Hence, on the one hand, the definition of $C(t+1)$ plus Equation (12′) yield $0 < \ell^{t+2} < \infty$. On the other hand, the additional definition of $H(t+1)$ plus Equation (13′) yield both $0 < m^{t+1} < \infty$ and (upon relabeling) $C_h \subset I^{t+1} \cup I^{t+2}$ for $h \in G^{t+1}$.

(iii) Finally, the definition of the whole sequence $\{H(t)\}$ implies that if $h \in H$ and $C_h \cap C_{H(t)} \neq \emptyset$, then $h \in H(t+1)$. Hence, if $h \in H$ but there is no $t \in T$ such that $h \in H(t)$, then $C_h \cap C_{H(t)} = \emptyset$ for $t \in I$. But this means that the assumption that the economy has indecomposable structure would be violated by choosing $H^\alpha = \cup\ H(t)$ and $H^\beta = H - H^\alpha$, $t \in I$.

4.3. Samuelson Revisited

A concrete application is undoubtedly helpful. So once again consider the example whose structure is illustrated in Figure 1. Since both the rows (indicating the order of $\#C_h$) and the columns (indicating the order of $\#H^c$) in this table have only a finite number of entries, the example clearly fulfills the requirements for having an overlapping-generations representation. From further study of this figure (showing that there are no $h' \neq h''$ such that $C_{h'} \subset C''_h$, and that for all but $h = 1$, there are h', $h'' \neq h$ with $h' \neq h''$ such that $C_{h'} \cap C_h \neq \emptyset$ and $C_{h''} \cap C_h \neq \emptyset$) it becomes evident that, in applying the relabeling algorithm, $H(t) = \underline{H}(t)$ for every choice of $\underline{H}(0)$, and that the choice of $\underline{H}(0) = \{1\}$ will greatly simplify matters. (Deriving the more complicated representations corresponding to other choices is left to the industrious reader.) Thus, in the initial step we find that, for $t = 0$,

$$C(0) = \{1, -1\} \xrightarrow{r} I^1 = \{1, 2\}$$

and $H(0) = \{1\} = G^\circ$.

Proceeding to the next two steps (and summarizing the resulting calculations), we find that, for $t = 1$,

$$C(1) - C(0) = \{2\} \xrightarrow{r} I^2 = \{3\}$$

and $H(1) - H(0) = \{-1\} \xrightarrow{r} G^1 = \{2\}$,
and that, for $t = 2$,

$$C(2) - C(1) = \{-2\} \xrightarrow{r} I^3 = \{4\}$$

and $H(2) - H(1) = \{2\} \xrightarrow{r} G^2 = \{3\}$.

This alternating rhythm (moving from $h > 0$ to $-h$ to $h+1$ in the original labeling) continues, and is easily seen to yield the simple pattern displayed by the asterisks in Figure 2. But this is just Samuelson's original example, as I had claimed earlier.

4.4. Overlapping Structure

It is fairly straightforward to verify the intuition that the overlapping-generations model provides the most convenient – if not also the most plausible – framework for generating examples exhibiting overlapping structure (in the general sense that I have been using this term). In fact, this result only depends on one of the two characteristic properties of this model, that households are evolutionary.

Proposition 2. *Maintain the assumption that the economy has indecomposable structure. If households are evolutionary, then the economy has overlapping structure.*

Proof of Proposition 2. Suppose that the conclusion is false, that is, there is some partition of households H such that $0 < \#C(H) < \infty$. Then focus attention on the particular collections of subsets in this partition $H(c) \subset H$ for $c \in C(H)$ defined by the condition that $H^v \in H(c)$ if $c \in C_{H^v}$, and denote the whole subset of households derived from each such collection of subsets by

$$H(c) = \bigcup_{H^v \in \mathbf{H}(c)} H^v. \tag{14}$$

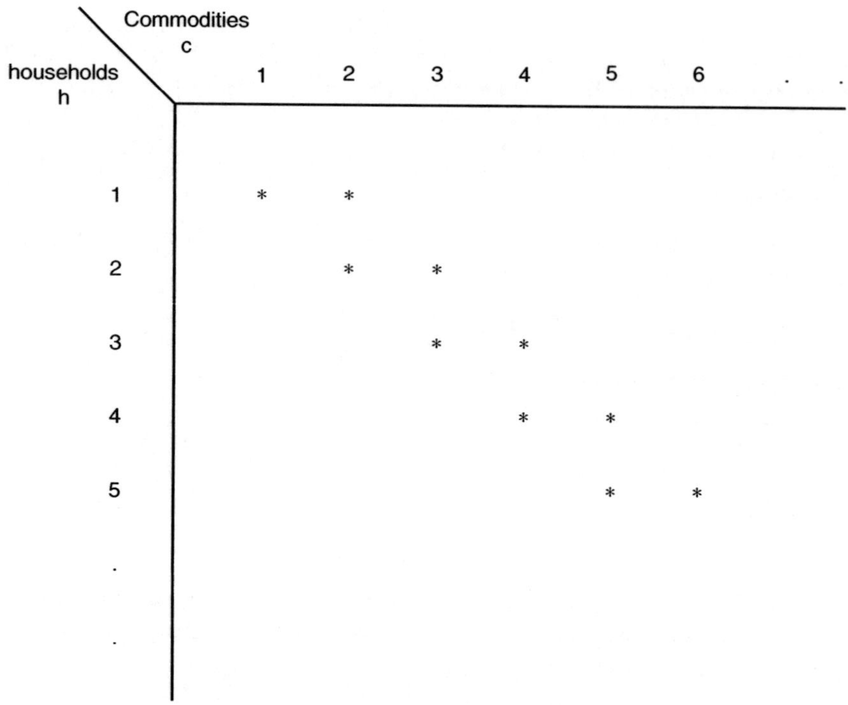

Figure 2.

The assumption that households are evolutionary and the definition of a partition of households H imply that

$$\#H(c) \leqq \#H^c < \infty \quad \text{for } c \in C(H)$$

and

$$\#H^v < \infty \quad \text{for } H^v \in H(c), c \in C(H),$$

respectively, so that

$$\#H(c) \leqq \#H(c) \max_{H^v \in \mathbf{H}(c)} \#H^v < \infty \quad \text{for } c \in C(H). \tag{15}$$

Also, the specification Equation (14) implies that

$$\text{if } h \in H \text{ and } c \in C_h, \text{ then } h \in H(c) \quad \text{for } c \in C(H). \tag{16}$$

So finally, consider the partition of H into the pair of subsets $H^\alpha = \cup H(c)$ and $H^\beta = H - H^\alpha$. Then my original supposition that c∈C(H).

$0 < \#C(H) < \infty$ together with Equation (15) entail that

$$0 < \#H^\alpha \leqq \#C(H) \max_{c \in C(H)} \#H(c) < \infty,$$

while the definition of the overlap of goods $C(H)$ together with Equation (16) entail that

$$C_{H^\alpha} \cap C_{H^\beta} = \emptyset,$$

so that the maintained assumption that the economy has indecomposable structure has been violated, and the proof is complete. □

Acknowledgments

My contribution to this volume was written while I was visiting CEPREMAP and Geneva during a sabbatical leave from Pennsylvania. I would like to thank all three institutions for their generous support. Financial assistance from the NSF under grant S0C83-09049 is also gratefully acknowledged.

Appendix

The sole purpose of this appendix is to provide proofs for the two claims utilized in establishing the fundamental Lemma of Section 3.

Proof of Claim 1.

(i) $\sum_{c \in C} p^c e^c_h < \infty$. Suppose otherwise. Then the consumption bundle

$$x^{c'}_h = \begin{cases} x^c_h + \varepsilon & \text{for } c \in C_h \\ 0 & \text{otherwise,} \end{cases}$$

where $\varepsilon > 0$, satisfies the constraints in Equation (3) but yields, by weak monotonicity, $u_h(x'_h) > u_h(x_h)$, in contradiction to the hypothesis of the claim

(ii) $\sum_{c \in C} p x^c_h = \sum_{c \in C} p e^c_h$. Suppose otherwise. Then, since $\sum_{c \in C} p x^c_h = \sum_{c \in C} p e^c_h < \infty$, the consumption bundle

$$x^{c'}_h = \begin{cases} x^c_h + (\lambda / p^c)\varepsilon^c & \text{for } c \in C_h \text{ such that } p^c > 0 \\ x^c_h + \lambda \varepsilon^c & \text{for } c \in C_h \text{ such that } p^c > 0 \\ 0 & \text{otherwise,} \end{cases}$$

where $\lambda > 0, \varepsilon^c > 0$ for $c \in C_h$ and

$$\lambda < \frac{\sum_{c \in C} p^c e_h^c - \sum_{c \in C} p^c x_h^c}{\sum_{c \in C_h} \varepsilon^c},$$

again satisfies the constraints in Equation (3) but yields $u_h(x_h') > u_h(x_h)$, a contradiction.

(iii) $x_h' \in X_h$ and $u_h(x_h') \geqq$ [resp. $>$] $u_h(x_h)$ imply $\sum_{c \in C} p^c x_h^{c'} \geqq$ [resp. $>$] $\sum_{c \in C} p^c x_h^c$. Here, the consumption bundle constructed from x_h' as in (ii) [resp. x_h' itself] yields a contradiction to the hypothesis of the claim. □

Proof of Claim 2. This argument is based on elementary results concerning the properties of sum $\sum_{\nu \in N'} \alpha^\nu$ for $N' \subset N$ of nonnegative numbers $\alpha^\nu \geqq 0$ for $\nu \in N$, for example, if

$$\sum_{\nu \in N'} \alpha^\nu \leqq b < \infty \quad \text{for} \quad N' \subset N \text{ such that } \#N' < \infty,$$

then

$$\sum_{\nu \in N} \alpha^\nu = b' \leqq b.$$

Consider the two possible cases, where the right-hand sum in Equation (7) is unbounded, and bounded, respectively, and for simplicity take $C' = C$ and $H' = H$.

Case 1.

$$\sum_{h \in H} \sum_{c \in C} p^c x_h^c = \infty.$$

Suppose that the conclusion of the claim is false, that is,

$$\sum_{c \in C} p^c \sum_{h \in H} x_h^c = k < \infty.$$

Then by the hypothesis of the claim (and always assuming that $\#C' < \infty$ for $C' \subset C$ or $\#H' < \infty$ for $H' \subset H$)

$$\sum_{c \in C'} p^c \sum_{h \in H} x_h^c \leqq k \quad \text{for} \quad C' \subset C$$

so that

$$\sum_{c \in C'} p^c \sum_{h \in H'} x_h^c \leqq k \quad \text{for} \quad H' \subset H, C' \subset C$$

or, by interchanging the order of summation,

$$\sum_{h\in H'}\sum_{c\in C'} p^c x_h^c \leqq k \quad \text{for} \quad C' \subset C, H' \subset H$$

so that

$$\sum_{h\in H'}\sum_{c\in C'} p^c x_h^c \leqq k \quad \text{for} \quad H' \subset H$$

and hence

$$\sum_{h\in H}\sum_{c\in C} p^c x_h^c \leqq k' \leqq k,$$

contrary to the supposition of the case being considered.

Case 2.

$$\sum_{h\in H}\sum_{c\in C} p^c x_h^c = k' < \infty.$$

By similar reasoning as in the previous case, it follows that

$$\sum_{c\in C} p^c \sum_{h\in H} x_h^c = k \leqq k',$$

and hence, by precisely the same reasoning, that

$$k' \leqq k,$$

which again yields the desired conclusion. □

References

Arrow, K.J. (1951). An extension of the basic theorems of classical welfare economics. In Neyman, J. (Ed.), *Proceedings of the Second Berkeley Symposium on Mathematical Statistics and Probability*. Berkeley, CA: University of California Press.

Balasko, Y. and Shell, K. (1980). The overlapping-generations model, I: The case of pure exchange without money. *Journal of Economic Theory* **23**, 281–306.

Balasko, Y., Cass, D. and Shell, K. (1980). Existence of competitive equilibrium in a general overlapping-generations model. *Journal of Economic Theory* **23**, 307–322.

Benveniste, L. (1983). Dynamic models of capital accumulation and generational distribution: A unified structure. CARESS Working Paper, University of Pennsylvania, PA, USA.

Malinvaud, E. (1953). Capital accumulation and efficient allocation of resources. *Econometrica* **21**, 233–268. and a corrigendum. *Econometrica* (1962) **30**, 570–573.

Okuno, M. and Zilcha, I. (1980). On the efficiency of a competitive equilibrium in infinite horizon monetary economies. *The Review of Economic Studies* **47**, 797–807.

Samuelson, P.A. (1958). An exact consumption-loan model of interest with or without the social contrivance of money. *The Journal of Political Economy* **66**, 467–482.

Shell, K. (1971). Notes on the economics of infinity. *The Journal of Political Economy* **79**, 1002–1011.

Chapter 8

On the Existence of Optimal Stationary Equilibria with a Fixed Supply of Fiat Money: I. The Case of a Single Consumer☆

Lawrence M. Benveniste[a] and David Cass

[a]*Federal Reserve Board of Governors, Washington, DC*

1. Introduction and Summary

Is there an optimal quantity of money? This seems a deep and important question. In one form or another it has seduced and preoccupied some of the finest minds in our profession. It is also absolutely ill defined.

We believe that the basic issues suggested by the question can be adequately framed only within a model where money has an explicit, definite role, and can be usefully analyzed only by employing the sharp, powerful tools supplied by the modern theory of welfare economics.

In this chapter, we consider a basic version of the overlapping-generations model. In our model, money provides the sole means for executing intertemporal exchange. So we can legitimately focus on a single critical question: Does this device permit attaining an intertemporal distribution of goods that is Pareto optimal? The polemics by Cass and Shell (1980), Kareken and Wallace (1980), and Wallace (1980) alone argue cogently for such an undertaking. But our chief justification is really quite obvious. In this setting, without money (inside or outside), certain Pareto-improving exchanges may simply not be possible. On the other hand, with money they may become so.

Malinvaud (1953) was the first to recognize explicitly that there is a serious, potential difficulty with competitive allocation in a truly dynamic economy. But it was Samuelson (1958) who had the additional insight that the institution of money might provide an effective remedy. Subsequently,

☆This article was originally published in *Journal of Political Economy* 94, Lawrence M. Benveniste and David Cass, "On the Existence of Optimal Stationary Equilibria with a Fixed Supply of Fiat Money: I. The Case of a Single Consumer", 402–417, © University of Chicago Press, 1986.

International Symposia in Economic Theory and Econometrics, Vol. 21B
S. Spear (Editor)

ISSN: 1571-0386/DOI: 10.1108/S1571-0386(2011)000021B011

many others have refined and extended the main themes of these two extraordinary, seminal papers.

Samuelson's principal result was that a (properly priced) fixed supply of fiat money is sufficient to engineer the efficient operation of markets over time. However, this result appeared to depend crucially on certain special assumptions, particularly the hypotheses of essentially identical individuals and of a single consumption good. Much of the later analysis by such authors as Diamond (1965), Cass and Yaari (1966), Shell (1971), and Gale (1973) dealt with this same limited specification.

Cass et al. (1979) and Cass (1980) expressly raised doubts about the efficacy of a purely passive monetary policy. They constructed a series of examples contradicting several of the conclusions deriving from Samuelson's original model. The most disturbing counterexamples show that, even with a fixed supply of money, there might be no competitive distributions that are Pareto optimal.

Since they worked with the same single-commodity model as Samuelson did, Cass, Okuno, and Zilcha based their analysis on denying Samuelson's assumptions of homogeneous individuals' (both within and across generations) having "nice" preferences (and endowments). At the time they wrote that paper, the authors, including the second author of this chapter, understood that their examples themselves were somewhat special. But they also believed that this speciality had mainly to do with their self-imposed restriction to a single-commodity world. So they conjectured that merely enlarging the commodity space would strike an even more telling blow to Samuelson's central result.

This conjecture was wrong. In fact, this chapter together with its sequel (Benveniste and Cass, forthcoming) will establish that Samuelson's insight is far more robust than we, anyway, originally believed. We demonstrate conclusively that the restorative power of a fixed supply of money does not depend on the homogeneity of individuals – within generations – or the number of commodities.[1]

The precise theorem we establish is that, if there is a fixed supply of fiat or outside money, and individuals are also permitted to issue bonds or inside money (and required to redeem it), then there is always at least one

[1] It remains to be seen how well this result withstands introducing heterogeneity of individuals between generations. Along this line, and building on the formulation of Balasko and Shell (1981), Millan (1982) has shown that there will always exist a Pareto-optimal equilibrium with a fixed supply of fiat money (for the case of a single good but many consumers) provided, for example, that endowments and preferences converge asymptotically to those of a well-behaved static economy. Of course, without some element of stationarity in the underlying structure of technology and tastes, one can seriously question the relevance of postulating perfect foresight.

Pareto-optimal stationary equilibrium. There may also be other stationary equilibria, and these may or may not be Pareto optimal.

Here we work with the simplest possible generalization of Samuelson's model: We maintain his very elementary demographic structure and merely expand the list of commodities. In each period a single, typical individual is born, and he lives 2 periods. Although our main result is true for any finite number of commodities, we will tell the story in terms of only two. This allows us to illustrate its important points graphically. The proof for many commodities is identical, with 2 replaced by n. We also greatly simplify our task by adopting unnecessarily strong hypotheses about preferences and endowments. These too can be greatly relaxed without substantially altering the argument.

A compelling reason for concentrating on this special case is that by doing so we lay bare the central idea that underlies our argument. Our more general proof is merely an adaptation of the same basic approach, albeit a much more elaborate one.

The most general (pure distribution) model in which our main result holds is one in which each generation contains an arbitrary, finite number of individuals having a variety of preferences, endowments, and lifetimes, but generations are essentially replicated period after period. In particular, this means that there is the same arbitrary, finite number of commodities available in each period. Besides the usual continuity and convexity of preferences, a very weak form of monotonicity is also required (as suggested by Cass, Okuno, and Zilcha's previous work).

Our analysis can also be extended to include the possibility that final goods are produced from (stationary) capital stocks and (exogenous) primary factors.

As we noted at the outset, these claims will be justified in a subsequent chapter. The plan of this chapter is as follows. Our model is presented in Section 2. In Section 3, we introduce the notion of a Pareto-optimal stationary equilibrium, while in Section 4 we detour to present a special case whose simple graphical representation can be exploited to illustrate (and qualify the import of) our main result. Finally, this fundamental theorem itself is stated and proved in Section 5.

2. The Economy

2.1. Consumers and Time

We suppose that time is discrete and has neither beginning nor end. Time periods are labeled by the subscript $t = 0, \pm 1, \pm 2, \ldots$. In each period only one new individual is born, and he lives only during that period (his youth) and the next period (his prime). The individual born in period t will be referred to variously as Mr. t, the consumer (born in period t), and so on. There is no production in the economy. Instead, each consumer is endowed with positive amounts of two perishable commodities in both periods of his life. He also has preferences over consumption of the same commodities. All consumers are, but for date of birth, identical in endowments and preferences. We will sometimes allude to this essential similarity by referring to the representative consumer.

We will let (y_1, y_2) denote the representative consumer's endowment. So Mr. t receives amounts of commodities described by the two-dimensional vector $\boldsymbol{y}_1$ at the beginning of his youth, period t, and those described by y_2 at the beginning of his prime, period $t+1$. His consumption of the two commodities during periods t and $t+1$ will be denoted by the four-dimensional vector $\boldsymbol{c}^t = (\boldsymbol{c}^t_t, \boldsymbol{c}^t_{t+1})$.

Consumers will be trading in commodities, money, and bonds. Money here is fiat (or outside) money. The supply of fiat money remains fixed over time and will be denoted m. In particular, this means that the government or policy maker plays a purely passive role (in terms of creating or extinguishing government debt) in the economy. Bonds are consumption loans (or inside money) created by consumers themselves as a means of exchanging credit. Mr. t's financial portfolio, that is, his money balances and bond holdings at the end of his youth, will be denoted (m^t, b^t).[2]

The representative consumer's preferences are described by a utility function $u : \mathrm{R}^4_+ \to \mathrm{R}$. This function is assumed to be differentiable, strictly quasi-concave, and (differentiably) strictly monotone; that is, the marginal utility of each commodity consumed is always positive. So commodities will always be goods.

2.2. Markets and Demand

Market transactions during period t are reckoned in terms of an invariant unit of account (say, "dollars"). Goods and money prices are denoted p_t and p_{tm} (dollars per unit in period t), respectively. A bond issued in period t sells at the price p_{tb} and is a contract obligating its issuer to repay \$1 at the beginning of period $t+1$.

[2] In principle, Mr. t could also hold a portfolio at the end of his prime. However, as he must exit the scene solvent (and has no bequest motive), this further option offers him no possible advantage (when the economy is in equilibrium), and we therefore ignore it.

Consumers behave competitively on the goods, money, and bond markets and have full information or perfect foresight concerning all the market prices they will face.

When market prices are $\langle p_t \rangle$, $\langle p_{tm} \rangle$, and $\langle p_{tb} \rangle$,[3] Mr. t can afford the nonnegative consumption bundle $c^t \geqq 0$[4] if he can finance it through some transactions on the money and bond markets, that is, if there is a financial portfolio (m^t, b^t) that satisfies the two accounting constraints

$$\begin{aligned} &p_t c_t^t + p_{tm} m^t + p_{tb} b^t \leqq p_t y_1, \\ &p_{t+1} c_{t+1}^t \leqq p_{t+1} y_2 + p_{t+1m} m^{t'} + b^t, \end{aligned} \tag{1}$$

with $0 \leqq m^{t'} \leqq m^t$.

These are ordinary spot market budget constraints. Notice especially that Mr. t is expressly permitted to dispose of money freely and issue (i.e., short sell) bonds (but not money). Both are important aspects of the distinction between inside and outside moneys.

Among all the market opportunities (1), Mr. t chooses the consumption bundle $\bar{c}^t$ and an associated financial portfolio $(\bar{m}^t, \bar{b}^t)$ that yield him maximum utility.

Looking ahead, we will be interested only in situations where (i) the fixed supply of fiat money is actually transferred from consumer to consumer (though perhaps to no real effect, i.e., when the price of money is zero) and (ii) each consumer is actually constrained in his demand for goods. These requirements impose a number of qualitative restrictions on (equilibrium) market prices.

1. Obviously, goods prices must always be positive, that is, $p_t \gg 0$ for all t.
2. The price of money must always be nonnegative, that is, $p_{tm} \geqq 0$ for all t, and must be identically zero if it is ever zero, that is, either $p_{tm} = 0$ for all t or $p_{tm} > 0$ for all t.

   For the first, if Mr. t has chosen to hold the fixed supply of fiat money, $m^t = m > 0$, then he will also choose to sell it (rather than throw it away) only if $p_{t+1m} \geqq 0$. For the second, if $p_{tm} > 0$ but $p_{t+1m} = 0$, then Mr. t will clearly choose not to hold any money, while if $p_{tm} = 0$ but $p_{t+1m} > 0$, then he would clearly like to hold unlimited money balances (and thereby finance unlimited consumption during his prime).

---

[3] We use the notation $\langle x_t \rangle$ to represent the (double-infinite) sequence $(\ldots, x_{-1}, x_0, x_1, \ldots)$.

[4] We adopt one of the more common conventions for denoting n-dimensional vector inequalities, namely, $x \geqq y$ when $x_i \geqq y_i$ for all i, $x > y$ when $x_i \geqq y_i$ for all i and $x \neq y$, and $x \gg y$ when $x_i > y_i$ for all i.

3. The bond price must always be positive, that is, $p_{tb} > 0$ for all t. Otherwise (as in the preceding argument) Mr. t would clearly like to float unlimited consumption loans.
4. Finally, when the price of money is always positive, the (gross) nominal returns on money and bonds must always be the same, that is,[5]

$$\frac{p_{t+1m}}{p_{tm}} = \frac{1}{p_{tb}} \quad \text{for all } t. \tag{2}$$

Here, for instance, if $p_{t+1m}/p_{tm} < 1/p_{tb}$, then Mr. t will choose not to hold any money (since he would do better to hold an equivalent amount in bonds), while if $p_{t+1m}/p_{tm} < 1/p_{tb}$, then he would like to arbitrage from bonds to money in unlimited amounts (and again thereby finance unlimited consumption during his prime).

Two important facts emerge from these considerations. In the first place, we can assume without any loss of generality that the nominal return in the economy is identically one, that is, that $p_{tb} = 1$ for all t.[6] Then second, it follows (particularly from Equation (2)) that the price of money is a nonnegative constant, that is, that $p_{tm} = p_m \geqq 0$ for all t. For this reason, we can also assume without any loss of generality (and will find it convenient to do so) that the fixed supply of fiat money is simply one unit, that is, that $m = 1$.

Given this convention that the nominal return in the economy is one, Mr. t can be viewed as solving his demand problem by first choosing $\bar{c}^t$ as the solution to

$$\begin{aligned} &\text{maximize} \quad u(c^t) \\ &\text{subject to} \quad p_t c_t^t + p_{t+1} c_{t+1}^t \leqq p_t y_1 + p_{t+1} y_2 \text{ and } c^t \geqq 0 \end{aligned} \tag{3}$$

[5] In fact, when the price of money is identically zero, Equation (2) can be viewed as the appropriate definition of the nominal return on money (i.e., 0/0).

[6] This amounts to identifying the unit of account with bonds or inside money (rather than, as conventionally, with outside money) since now a bond both costs and returns \$1. Formally, such identification is accomplished by the following "monetary reform"

$$f_t = \begin{cases} \prod_{s=t}^{-1} \frac{1}{p_{sb}} & \text{for } t \leqq -1 \\ 1 & \text{for } t = 0 \\ \prod_{s=0}^{t-1} p_{sb} & t \geqq 1 \end{cases}$$

(given a system of market prices for which $p_{tb} > 0$ for all t): One old dollar in period t becomes, for example, new dollars (and, correspondingly, each old bond in period t becomes $p_{tb} f_t$ new bonds).

and then picking $(\bar{m}^t, \bar{b}^t)$ to support the requisite credit position at the end of his youth,

$$p_m\bar{m}^t + \bar{b}^t = p_t(y_1 - \bar{c}_t^t). \tag{4}$$

2.3. Distributions and Equilibrium

In each period there are only two consumers alive, one in his youth and the other in his prime. These consumers are endowed with y_1 and y_2, respectively, so that the total resources available for their consumption during that period are, say, $y = y_1 + y_2$. For the most part we will take the endowment (y_1, y_2) (and hence also the resources y) as given. Occasionally, however, it will be useful to treat them as parameters.

A conceivable *distribution* of consumption to all consumers $\langle c^t \geqq 0 \rangle$ will be said to be *feasible* if materials balance in each period, that is, $c_t^{t-1} + c_t^t = y$ for all t, and to be *stationary* if each consumer receives the same consumption bundle, that is, $c^t = (c_1, c_2)$ for all t.

A (market or competitive) *equilibrium* is a sequence of prices of goods and a price of money $(\langle p_t \rangle, p_m)$ such that each market clears, that is,

$$\bar{c}_t^{t-1} + \bar{c}_t^t = y, \; \bar{m}^t = 1, \; \bar{b}^t = 0 \quad \text{for all } t, \tag{5}$$

when each consumer optimizes and can support his choice with the appropriate financial portfolio, that is, when $\bar{c}_t^t$ solves Equation (3) and $(\bar{m}^t, \bar{b}^t) = (1, 0)$ satisfies Equation (4).

We will sometimes refer to the feasible distribution $\langle \bar{c}^t \rangle$ associated with an equilibrium $(\langle p_t \rangle, p_m)$ as an *equilibrium distribution* and, when $\bar{c}^t = (\bar{c}_1, \bar{c}_2)$ for all t, to the equilibrium itself as a *stationary equilibrium*. This latter reference is legitimate for the following reason: Under these circumstances, without any loss of generality we can assume that there exist, say, current value (in contrast to present value) goods prices $p \gg 0$ and an interest rate $-1 < r < \infty$ such that $p_t = (1 + r)^{-t}p$ for all t.[7]

Now observe that, in such a stationary equilibrium, substituting from Equation (5) into Equation (4) yields

$$p_m = (1 + r)^{-1}p(y_1 - \bar{c}_1) \quad \text{for all } t.$$

Hence if $p_m > 0$, then $r = 0$. This very basic result – that in a stationary equilibrium with a positive price of money the interest rate must be zero – motivates

[7] This kind of result is well known in the folklore (and is analogous to Malinvaud's (1953) characterization of stationary competitive growth paths). However, it does require proof, which we forgo presenting (in the interests of conserving space).

the following definition. We will say that a stationary equilibrium is *monetary* (respectively *barter*) if $p_m > 0$ or $p_m = 0$ but $r = 0$ ($p_m = 0$ and $r \neq 0$). In other words, it turns out to be extremely useful (even with a slight abuse of terminology) to distinguish all the stationary equilibria that display a zero interest rate from those that do not.

3. Pareto-Optimal Stationary Equilibria

In the setting, we have just described the existence of some (e.g., barter) stationary equilibrium is not very difficult to verify. However, we cannot be sure that the resulting stationary distribution is at all desirable.

The irreversibility of time dictates a natural concept of optimality. A feasible distribution $\langle c^t \rangle$ is *Pareto optimal* if there does not exist another feasible distribution $\langle \tilde{c}^t \rangle$ such that, starting only with some historical period $-\infty < \tilde{t} < \infty$, the second differs from the first *and* dominates it in terms of utility, that is,

$$\tilde{c}^t = c^t \quad \text{for all } t \leqq \tilde{t} - 2 \text{ and } \tilde{c}^{\tilde{t}-1}_{\tilde{t}-1} = c^{\tilde{t}-1}_{\tilde{t}-1}$$

and

$$u(\tilde{c}^t) \geqq u(c^t) \quad \text{for all } t \geqq \tilde{t} - 1,$$

with strict inequality for some t. Notice, in particular, that such potential redistributions may affect Mr. $\tilde{t} - 1$ in his prime.

Starrett (1972) has demonstrated that a stationary equilibrium distribution – or, for short, a stationary equilibrium – is Pareto optimal (in this sense) if and only if the interest rate is nonnegative. So the task of establishing the potential efficacy of the market mechanism when there is a fixed supply of fiat money requires just exhibiting a stationary equilibrium with this property. For this purpose, we will rely heavily on an important fact about stationary monetary equilibria.

Fact. The distribution associated with any stationary monetary equilibrium is described by the solution to the problem

$$\begin{aligned} &\text{maximize} \quad u(c_1, c_2) \\ &\text{subject to} \quad c_1 + c_2 \leqq y \text{ and } (c_1, c_2) \geqq 0. \end{aligned} \tag{6}$$

Proof of the Fact. Since u is strictly quasi-concave and y is strictly positive, the argument simply involves showing that the Kuhn–Tucker conditions for Equation (3) when $p_t = p_{t+1} = p \gg 0$ are the same as those for Equation (6) at $\bar{c}^t = (\bar{c}_1, \bar{c}_2)$. We leave this routine exercise for the interested reader. Q.E.D.

The solution to Equation (6), of course, yields precisely the *golden rule distribution*, that is, the unique stationary distribution that, from the representative consumer's viewpoint, is best among all feasible stationary distributions. Since it is also the equilibrium distribution in any stationary monetary equilibrium (so that the interest rate is zero), it must be Pareto optimal.

It will be convenient to denote the golden rule consumption bundle by (c_1^*, c_2^*) and the corresponding support prices (i.e., the Lagrange multipliers associated with the feasibility constraints in Equation (6)) by[8]

$$p^* = (p_1^*, p_2^*) = \left(\max_j \{u_{j1}(c_1^*, c_2^*)\}, \max_j \{u_{j2}(c_1^*, c_2^*)\} \right).$$

Also note that, if $(\langle p_t = p \rangle, p_m)$ is a stationary monetary equilibrium, then we can assume without any loss of generality that $p = p^*$ and $p_m = p_m^* = p^*(y_1 - c_1^*)$.

We are now in position to motivate and describe the main result of this chapter. Take the endowment (y_1, y_2) (and thus the resources $y = y_1 + y_2$) as given. Then, on the one hand, if $p^*(y_1 - c_1^*) \geqq 0$, the economy can achieve the golden rule distribution $\langle c^t = (c_1^*, c_2^*) \rangle$ corresponding to the stationary monetary equilibrium $(\langle p^t = p^* \rangle, p_m^*)$, that is, a Pareto-optimal equilibrium. On the other hand, when $p^*(y_1 - c_1^*) < 0$, matters are not so open and shut. For all we know at this point, there then may be no equilibrium distribution – stationary or otherwise – that is Pareto optimal. We will show, however, that even in this second case the market can sustain a stationary barter equilibrium with a positive interest rate and, hence, a stationary equilibrium that is Pareto optimal.

Before we turn to a precise statement and proof of this fundamental theorem, we first detour in order to illustrate it graphically for a particular version of the model and at the same time suggest that actually engineering Pareto optimality (in either case) may not be such a simple undertaking (see the related discussion in Cass et al. (1979)).

4. Multiple Stationary Equilibria

Since from here on we will focus attention exclusively on stationary equilibria, we will drop the superfluous adjective (but caution the reader to keep it in mind). In this section, we introduce a simplifying expository assumption and utilize it to exemplify (i) our main result and (ii) the possibility, by virtue of our main result, that barter equilibria with both

[8] In this expression $u_{ji}(c_1^*, c_2^*)$ (and later on such shorthand as u_{ji}^*) refers to the partial derivative of u with respect to the ith coordinate of c_j evaluated at (c_1^*, c_2^*).

positive and negative interest rates may coexist even when there is no monetary equilibrium. This annoying possibility emphasizes a fundamental difference between the single- and many-commodity cases; in the simpler case there is *either* a monetary equilibrium *or* a no-barter equilibrium with a negative interest rate (again see Cass et al. (1979), especially pp. 49–57).

When the utility function exhibits additive separability between youth and prime, that is, when $u(c_1, c_2) = f(c_1) + g(c_2)$, the set of potential equilibria has a very nice graphical representation in terms of the Edgeworth–Bowley box diagram. So we will adopt this convenient specialization to construct and explain examples illustrating our main result and its implications. We will also take the liberty of arguing rather informally. However, everything we say can be established quite precisely.

Let f, g: $\mathbb{R}^2_+ \to \mathbb{R}$ be differentiable, (differentiably) strictly monotone, and strictly concave. Then the utility function $u(c_1, c_2) = f(c_1) + g(c_2)$ satisfies our maintained assumptions. Moreover, if $(\langle p_t = (1+r)^{-t}p\rangle, p_m = 0)$ supports the distribution $(\bar{c}_1, \bar{c}_2)$, then, by virtue of this additive separability, $\bar{c}_1$ is the optimal solution to the problem

$$\begin{aligned} &\text{maximize} \quad f(c_1) \\ &\text{subject to} \quad pc_1 \leqq py_1 \text{ and } c_1 \geqq 0, \end{aligned} \tag{7}$$

while $\bar{c}_2$ is the optimal solution to the problem

$$\begin{aligned} &\text{maximize} \quad f(c_2) \\ &\text{subject to} \quad pc_2 \leqq py_2 \text{ and } c_2 \geqq 0^{\cdot} \end{aligned} \tag{8}$$

In other words, p is simply an equilibrium for the standard two-person, two-good pure exchange model where, say, Mr. 1 has endowment y_1, and preferences represented by f and Mr. 2 has endowment y_2 and preferences represented by g. This permits us to use the classroom box diagram to describe the set of potential equilibria, as we do in Figure 1.

In Figure 1, Mr. 1's endowment and consumption are measured from the southwest corner, Mr. 2's from the northeast. The dimensions of the box represent the total resources available, while any point in the box represents a feasible allocation. In particular, the curve labeled C is the ordinary contract curve, the point labeled (y_1, y_2) an endowment allocation, and the point labeled $(\bar{c}_1, \bar{c}_2)$ an equilibrium allocation supported by prices p.

Points lying on C are characterized by the fact that, for some positive number λ,

$$f_i(c_1) = \lambda g_i(c_2), \quad i = 1, 2. \tag{9}$$

Indeed, λ is just the ratio of Mr. 1's marginal utility of income to Mr. 2's, if, for instance, the endowment allocation were $(c_1, c_2) \in C$. Hence each point lying on C represents a potential equilibrium distribution (reverting to our

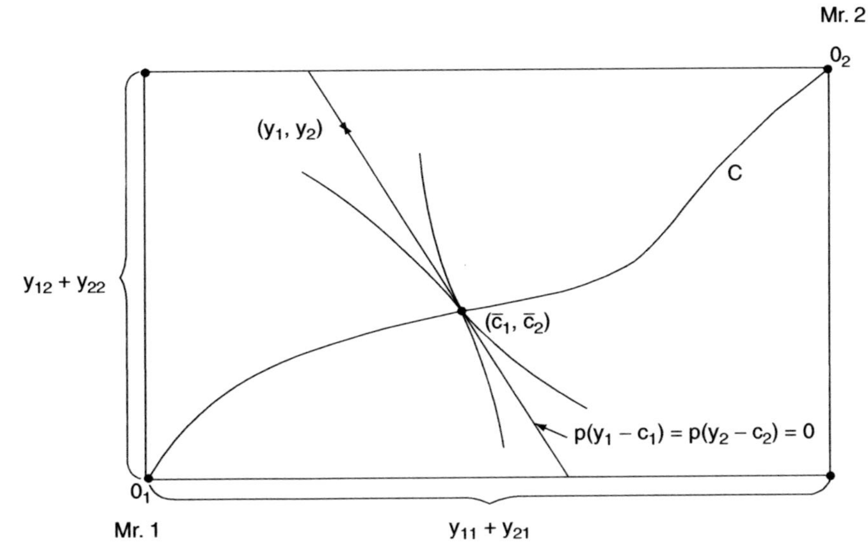

Figure 1.

original interpretation of this model) supported by goods prices $p_i = g_i(c_2)$, $i = 1, 2$, and the interest rate $r = \lambda - 1$. These become actual equilibrium distributions when, as depicted, the standard endowment (y_1, y_2) satisfies $p(y_1 - c_1) = p(y_2 - c_2) = 0$. Moreover, the particular point lying on C that satisfies Equation (9) with $\lambda = 1$ represents the golden rule distribution, that is, is simply (c_1^*, c_2^*).

It is well known that, in the simplest pure exchange model, there exist endowment allocations (y_1, y_2) and utility functions (f, g) (even "nice" concave utility functions) for which there are multiple equilibria. (Typically there is an odd number of equilibria.) Figure 2 illustrates the least complicated situation where there are just three equilibria. In this example, say, f has been normalized so that the middle allocation represents the monetary equilibrium distribution (c_1^*, c_2^*). It then follows directly from monotonicity and strict concavity that the interest rate associated with the southwest distribution (c_1^+, c_2^+) (the northeast distribution $[c_1^-, c_2^-]$) must be positive (negative). The difficulty raised by this example is obvious: Can a policy maker guarantee that, even with stationary, perfect-foresight expectations, the economy will end up at a "+" or a "*" rather than a "−"? And this difficulty can be compounded further.

In order to see this, we first look more closely at the possibilities for achieving monetary equilibrium in this particular model. This also makes clear how our main result fits into the picture.

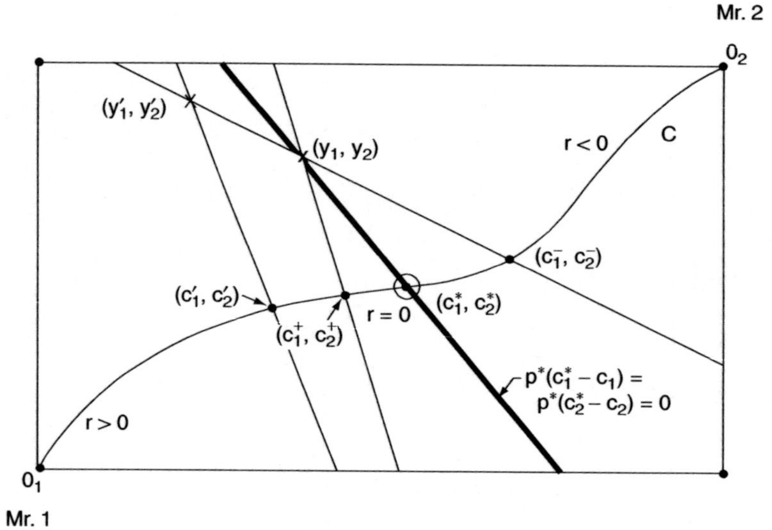

Figure 2.

Figure 2 shows that monetary equilibrium is achievable only when Mr. 1's and Mr. 2's endowments lie on or above the line described by $p^*(c_1^* - c_1) = p^*(c_2^* - c_2) = 0$, that is, when $p^*(y_1 - c_1^*) \geqq 0$. In the next section, we demonstrate that all other endowments, that is, all points lying below this line, have an important property: Each yields some barter equilibrium with a positive interest rate.[9] This fundamental conclusion is illustrated in Figure 2 by the particular endowment (y_1', y_2'), which has associated the barter equilibrium distribution (c_1', c_2').

But now notice that (y_1', y_2') also yields the barter equilibrium distribution (c_1^-, c_2^-), which exhibits a negative interest rate, but not the monetary equilibrium distribution (c_1^*, c_2^*). (It will generally yield some other barter equilibrium distribution as well; this may exhibit a positive or negative interest rate.) In any case, this potential additional complication in attaining "good" equilibria (when monetary equilibrium is not achievable) renders the policy maker's job even more difficult (especially, one might imagine, if he or she has been infected by monetarism).

[9] For the particular version of our model under discussion, essentially the same result (applied differently) was discovered earlier by Postlewaite (1978).

5. Existence of a Pareto-Optimal Stationary Equilibrium

Our main result is that, for every positive endowment, either there is an achievable monetary equilibrium or there must be at least one barter equilibrium with a positive interest rate. Thus, we can legitimately claim that *there always exists some Pareto-optimal stationary equilibrium.*

A precise restatement of the strong assumptions about preferences we employ here to establish this fundamental theorem is as follows:

Assumption 1. *u: $\mathbb{R}^4_+ \to \mathbb{R}$ is differentiable.*

Assumption 2. *u is (differentiably) strictly monotone; that is, $u_{ji} > 0, j, i = 1, 2$.*

Assumption 3. *u is strictly quasi-concave.*

Since our purpose here is primarily pedagogical, we will omit details of various standard or routine arguments.

Theorem 1. *Suppose $(y_1, y_2) \gg 0$, Assumptions 1–3 are satisfied, and $p^*(y_1 - c_1^*) < 0$. Then there exist $p \gg 0$ and $r > 0$ such that $(\langle p_t = (1 + r)^{-t} p\rangle, p_m = 0)$ is an equilibrium.*

Remark. The hypothesis that $p^*(y_1 - c_1^*) < 0$ is equivalent to denying that $p^*(y_1 - c_1^*) \geqq 0$, that is, denying that monetary equilibrium is achievable.

Proof of Theorem 1. We begin by introducing some useful notation. Let $P = \{p : p \geqq 0 \text{ and } p_1 + p_2 = 1\}$ be the set of normalized goods prices, $c = (c_1, c_2)$ be the representative bundle, and $C = \{c : 0 \leqq c_j \leqq 2y, j = 1, 2\}$ be the set of representative bundles for which each period's component does not exceed twice the resources available, $y = y_1 + y_2 \gg 0$.

For $p \in P$, define $c(p) = (c_1(p), c_2(p))$ to be the solution to the problem

$$\begin{aligned} &\text{maximize} \quad u(c_1, c_2) \\ &\text{subject to} \quad p(c_1 + c_2) \leqq py, pc_1 \leqq py_1, c \in C. \end{aligned} \tag{10}$$

Because u is continuous (in fact, differentiable) and strictly quasi-concave and the constraint set in Equation (10) is nonempty, compact, and convex, $c(p)$ is a well-defined, single-valued function. Moreover, since $(y_1, y_2) \gg 0$, the correspondence from P to C that determines the constraint set in Equation (10) is continuous. Hence $c(p)$ is also continuous. (Establishing this last assertion is a standard argument, and we therefore omit it.)

Again for $p \in P$, define $z(p)$ to be the total excess demand function, $z(p) = (c_1(p) + c_2(p)) - y$. Since $c(p)$ is continuous, $z(p)$ is continuous. Also, since strict monotonicity guarantees that the first constraint in Equation (10) is binding, $z(p)$ satisfies (the appropriate version of) Walras' law

$$pz(p) = 0. \tag{11}$$

Finally, for the purpose of establishing existence, define a correspondence from P to P by

$$\psi(p') = \{p'' : p'' \text{ is an optimal solution to the problem } \max_{p \in P} pz(p')\}$$

for $p' \in P$. It follows from well-known results that if $z(p)$ is a continuous function, then $\psi(p)$ is a nonempty, convex-valued, and upper hemicontinuous correspondence. (We also omit this standard argument.) So applying the Kakutani fixed point theorem, we know there exists a fixed point $p \in \psi(p)$.

Let $(c_1(p), c_2(p)) = (\bar{c}_1, \bar{c}_2)$ at the fixed point p. It follows directly from strict monotonicity and Walras' law (11) that $p \gg 0$ and that

$$\bar{c}_1 + \bar{c}_2 = y. \tag{12}$$

But Equation (12) together with Equation (10) implies that, in fact, $(\bar{c}_1, \bar{c}_2)$ is also the solution to Equation (10) when the constraint $c \in C$ is replaced by nonnegativity alone, $(c_1, c_2) \geqq 0$. We use this fact to show that there exists $r > 0$ such that $\langle \bar{c}^t = (\bar{c}_1, \bar{c}_2) \rangle$ is an equilibrium distribution given $(\langle p_t = (1+r)^{-t} p \rangle, p_m = 0)$.

Necessary conditions that $(\bar{c}_1, \bar{c}_2)$ be such a solution to Equation (10)[10] are that there exist nonnegative multipliers, say $\bar{\lambda}_j, j - 1, 2$, such that

$$\begin{aligned} \bar{u}_{1i} &\leqq (\bar{\lambda}_1 + \bar{\lambda}_2) p_i, \quad = \text{if } \bar{c}_{1i} > 0, \quad i = 1, 2, \\ \bar{u}_{2i} &\leqq \bar{\lambda}_1 p_i, \quad = \text{if } \bar{c}_{2i} > 0, \quad i = 1, 2, \\ p(\bar{c}_1 + \bar{c}_2) &\leqq py, \quad = \text{if } \bar{\lambda}_1 > 0, \\ p\bar{c}_1 &\leqq py_1, \quad = \text{if } \bar{\lambda}_2 > 0. \end{aligned} \tag{13}$$

Now notice that it must be the case that $\bar{\lambda}_1 > 0$ and $\bar{\lambda}_2 > 0$ in Equation (13): On the one hand, if $\bar{\lambda}_1 = 0$, then (by the assumption $\bar{u}_{2i} > 0$, $i = 1, 2$) the second condition in Equation (13) would be violated. On the other hand, if $\bar{\lambda}_1 > 0$ but $\bar{\lambda}_2 = 0$, then the first three conditions entail both $(\bar{c}_1, \bar{c}_2) = (c_1^*, c_1^*)$ and $p = p^*/\bar{\lambda}_1$ or, by the hypothesis $p^*(y_1 - c_1^*) < 0$, the last condition in Equation (13) would be violated.

So finally, define $r = \bar{\lambda}_2/\bar{\lambda}_1$. It is then easily verified that when the second budget constraint in Equation (13) is multiplied by r and added to the first, Equation (13) also provides sufficient conditions for $(\bar{c}_1, \bar{c}_2)$ to be the solution to Equation (3) when $p_t = (1+r)p_{t+1} = (1+r)^{-t}p$. Moreover, since $\bar{\lambda}_2 > 0$, the last condition in Equation (13) yields $p(y_1 - \bar{c}_1) = 0$, so that the money and bond market-clearing conditions in Equation (5) are consistent

[10] In this context, strict quasi-concavity of u together with strict positivity of (y_1, y_2) ensures that the Kuhn–Tucker conditions are both necessary and sufficient for a solution.

with Equation (4) when $p_m = 0$. To complete the argument, observe that Equation (12) is itself the necessary goods market-clearing condition in Equation (5). Q.E.D.

We have one concluding comment. For those endowments for which $p^*(y_1 - c_1^*) > 0$, both monetary and barter equilibria are achievable. An interesting conclusion that can be drawn from essentially the same argument as the foregoing is that, in this situation, there must be at least one barter equilibrium with a negative interest rate. That is, except in the borderline case for which $p^*(y_1 - c_1^*) = 0$, monetary equilibrium always coexists with some Pareto-dominated barter equilibrium – as in Samuelson's original model.

Theorem 2. *Suppose* $(y_1, y_2) \gg 0$, *Assumptions 1–3 are satisfied, and* $p^*(y_1 - c_1^*) > 0$. *Then there exist* $p \gg 0$ *and* $-1 < r'0$ *such that* $(\langle p_t = (1 + r)^{-t}p\rangle, p_m = 0)$ *is an equilibrium.*

The proof of this mirror-image result is almost identical to that of Theorem 1 after making the following modification: Reverse the inequality in the second constraint in Equation (10); that is, replace $pc_1 \leqq py_1$ with $pc_1 \geqq py_1$.

Acknowledgments

Research support under NSF grants SES-8007012 and SES-8309049 is gratefully acknowledged. The final version of the chapter also benefited from thoughtful comments by the referees of *the Journal of Political Economy*. We, of course, bear ultimate responsibility.

References

Balasko, Y. and Shell, K. (1981). The overlapping-generations model. II: The case of pure exchange with money. *Journal of Economic Theory* **24** (February), 112–142.

Benveniste, L. M. and Cass, D. (forthcoming). On the existence of optimal stationary equilibria with a fixed supply of fiat money: II. The case of many consumers with arbitrary lifetimes. Mimeographed. Philadelphia, PA: University of Pennsylvania.

Cass, D. (1980). Money in consumption loan type models: An addendum. In Kareken, J.H. and Wallace, N. (Eds), *Models of Monetary Economies*. Minneapolis, MN: Federal Reserve Bank of Minneapolis.

Cass, D., Okuno, M. and Zilcha, I. (1979). The role of money in supporting the Pareto optimality of competitive equilibrium in consumption-loan type models. *Journal of Economic Theory* **20** (February), 41–80.

Cass, D. and Shell, K. (1980). In defense of a basic approach. In Kareken, J.H. and Wallace, N. (Eds), *Models of Monetary Economies*. Minneapolis, MN: Federal Reserve Bank of Minneapolis.

Cass, D. and Yaari, M.E. (1966). A re-examination of the pure consumption loans model. *Journal of Political Economy* **74** (August), 353–367.

Diamond, P.A. (1965). National debt in a neoclassical growth model. *The American Economic Review* **55** (December), 1126–1150.

Gale, D. (1973). Pure exchange equilibrium of dynamic economic models. *Journal of Economic Theory* **6** (February), 12–36.

Kareken, J.H. and Wallace, N. (1980). Introduction. In Kareken, J.H. and Wallace, N. (Eds), *Models of Monetary Economies*. Minneapolis, MN: Federal Reserve Bank of Minneapolis.

Malinvaud, E. (1953). Capital accumulation and efficient allocation of resources. *Econometrica* **21** (April), 233–268.

Millan, T. (1982). Existence of optimal competitive equilibria in the over-lapping-generations model. Mimeographed. Barcelona: University of Aútonoma Barcelona.

Postlewaite, A. (1978). A short note on values of Pareto efficient allocations. Mimeographed. Champaign-Urbana, IL: University of Illinois.

Samuelson, P.A. (1958). An exact consumption-loan model of interest with or without the social contrivance of money. *Journal of Political Economy* **66** (December), 467–482.

Shell, K. (1971). Notes on the economics of infinity. *Journal of Political Economy* **79** (September/October), 1002–1011.

Starrett, D.A. (1972). On golden rules, the 'Biological Theory of Interest,' and competitive inefficiency. *Journal of Political Economy* **80** (March/April), 276–291.

Wallace, N. (1980). The overlapping generations model of fiat money. In Kareken, J.H. and Wallace, N. (Eds), *Models of Monetary Economies*. Minneapolis, MN: Federal Reserve Bank of Minneapolis.

FURTHER READING

Grandmont, J.-M. (1983). *Money and Value: A Reconsideration of Classical and Neoclassical Monetary Theories*. Cambridge: Cambridge University Press.

Okuno, M. and Zilcha, I. (1983). Optimal steady-state in stationary consumption-loan type models. *Journal of Economic Theory* **31** (December), 355–363.

Chapter 9
Sunspots and Incomplete Financial Markets: The Leading Example ☆

David Cass

1. Introduction

To even the most casual reader of the daily business pages, it must be fairly obvious that financial markets react (or overreact) to much news which clearly (or, at least, arguably) has little or no direct bearing on "fundamentals." Some prominent current items are: the threats issuing from various Middle Eastern factions; the Fed's weekly announcement of previous changes in the money supply; the outcome of this fall's Congressional elections; and the great deficit debate. Contrary to one's instinctive reaction as a trained economist, several recent studies have convincingly demonstrated that such market behavior is not necessarily "noneconomic" or "irrational." Prices and returns – and hence market allocation itself – may very well consistently depend on purely expectational phenomena. Moreover, self-fulfilling beliefs about market forces may have significant consequences for individual welfare. In short, "sunspots" may matter, and they may matter very much.[1]

The purpose of this chapter is to advance a further important reason for sunspot effects, namely, that the inherent nature of sunspot beliefs (or, more generally, of uncertainty about the future) militates against ever having a complete array of Arrow–Debreu markets. The logic buttressing this position is simple, but compelling: suppose that, as of today, the range of future

☆This article was originally published in Ed. G. Feiwel, *The Economics of Imperfect Competition and Employment: Joan Robinson and Beyond*, 1989, Macmillan Publishers Limited. Reproduced with permission of Palgrave Macmillan.

[1] I refer, especially, to my previous papers with Karl Shell (1980) – for an introduction to this basic idea – and (1983) – for an elaboration in terms of a specific model. The effective paper by Shiller (1978) develops a similar general theme, but in the macroeconometric rather than microequilibrium tradition. The second Cass–Shell paper also contains references to other work based on our original conception, which, of course, ultimately stems from Keynes (1936).

International Symposia in Economic Theory and Econometrics, Vol. 21B
S. Spear (Editor)

ISSN: 1571-0386/DOI: 10.1108/S1571-0386(2011)000021B012

markets was complete. (By this I mean that there is common agreement as to what will "count" tomorrow, and also full opportunity to hedge against all mutually foreseen events.) Then what prevents some agency from successfully instilling an updated, expanded view of the world? Say, for instance, the "psychology" of the market, attending to the Ayatullah Khomeini, Paul Volcker, Ronald Reagen or, even, Beryl Sprinkel (the present Chairman of the CEA), decides that what will really count tomorrow is some heretofore unrecognized or unimagined aspect of "reality." And, honestly, don't we see such revisions being made all the time?

My analysis of the resulting situation, where all conceived market risk cannot be fully covered, is carried out for the simplest possible case; I want to avoid, as much as possible, obscuring the central message with unnecessary technical detail. This intendedly unadorned model is described and investigated in the two following sections. In Section 1, I introduce the conventional formulation where there are no sunspot beliefs (and markets are complete), while in Section 2 I extend the model to the more plausible and interesting situation where there are sunspot beliefs (but markets are incomplete). Some of my results exactly duplicate those reported earlier in Cass and Shell (1983). In particular, the set of equilibrium allocations when there are no sunspot beliefs is (after a suitable transformation) contained within the set when there are, while equilibrium allocation itself is (in the traditional sense) Pareto optimal if and only if sunspots don't matter. But there are striking differences as well. Thus, except in the unlikely circumstance where there are no incentives to trade, *there always exists a continuum of distinct equilibria in which sunspots matter*, while, for example, *such an equilibrium may be unequivocally Pareto dominated by an equilibrium in which they don't.*

Admittedly, the simple case considered here is just the leading example of a single rationale for sunspot effects I plan, in a series of subsequent chapters, first, to present the general version of these particular results (entailing an extensive analysis of general equilibrium with incomplete or, equivalently, restricted financial markets), and second, to provide a general framework for understanding why sunspots should matter (encompassing my present story, Shell's and my earlier story, and many others as well).

2. The Standard Pure-Exchange Model

My basic framework involves pure distribution through competitive markets in a 2×2 economy. This textbook example is so familiar that I only need to outline my particular representation.

There are two periods, today and tomorrow, labeled by the superscripts $t = 0,1$. In each period there is a single physical commodity, say, the *good*, denoted y^t for $t = 0,1$ or $y = (y^0, y^1)$. Today, a single financial instrument, say, *money*, denoted as m, is also available. There are spot markets for both goods and money. The spot prices for goods are denoted q^t for $t = 0,1$ or $\mathbf{q} = (q^0, q^1)$, while, by convention, money costs, say, one "dollar" in today's spot market and returns one "dollar" in tomorrow's. Finally, there are also just two households in the economy, Mr. 1 and Mr. 2, labeled by the subscripts $h = 1,2$.

Mr. h is endowed with positive amounts of both goods $e_h = (e_h^0, e_h^1) \gg 0$ and has preferences over nonnegative consumption of both goods $v_h : \mathbb{R}_+^2 \to \mathbb{R}$. For simplicity, I will assume throughout that utility functions are differentiable, strictly increasing and strictly concave (on the positive orthant), and that zero consumption of either good is infinitely undesirable, that is

$$\text{if } y_h^0 = 0 \quad \text{or} \quad y_h^1 = 0, \quad \text{then } v_h(y_h) = -\infty \quad \text{for } h = 1, 2. \tag{1}$$

Let $\mathbf{y} = (y_1, y_2)$ denote a commodity allocation and $\boldsymbol{m} = (m_1, m_2)$ denote money balances (after today's trading) I will say that an allocation $\boldsymbol{y}$ is (i) *feasible* if it is nonnegative, $\mathbf{y} \geqq 0$, and materials balance,

$$\sum_h y_h^t = \sum_h e_h^t \quad \text{for} \quad t = 0, 1; \tag{2}$$

(ii) *Pareto optimal* if there is no other feasible allocation $\mathbf{y}'$ that dominates $\mathbf{y}$ in terms of utility,

$$v_h(y_h') \geqq v_h(y_h) \quad \text{for } h = 1, 2, \text{ with strict inequality for some } h; \tag{3}$$

and (iii) *competitive* if there are some positive spot prices $\boldsymbol{q} \gg 0$ and associated money balances $\boldsymbol{m}$ (which can be of either sign) such that each household optimizes, (y_h, m_h) is the solution to the problem

$$\begin{aligned} &\text{maximize} && v_h(y_h') \\ &\text{subject to} && q^0 y_h^{0'} + m_h' \leqq q^0 e_h^0, \\ &&& q^1 y_h^{1'} \leqq q^1 e_h^1 + m_h' \\ &\text{and} && y_h' \geqq 0 \end{aligned} \tag{4}$$

for $h = 1,2$, and each market clears,

$$\sum_h y_h^t = \sum_h e_h^t \quad \text{for} \quad t = 0, 1 \tag{5}$$

and

$$\sum_h m_h = 0.$$

It will often be convenient to refer to an equilibrium price–allocation–balance triplet $(\boldsymbol{q},\boldsymbol{y},\boldsymbol{m})$ as a *monetary equilibrium.*

A skeptical reader might reasonably question my emphasis on money. After all, m represents pure inside money, indicating nothing more than borrowing and lending between households. Moreover, it is well known that the "extended" forms of Equations (4) and (5) are essentially equivalent to the "reduced" form obtained by replacing the pair of spot market budget constraints in Equation (4) with the overall contingent market budget constraint

$$\boldsymbol{q}y_h \leqq \boldsymbol{q}e_h,$$

and then dropping the money (or loan) market clearing in Equation (5) to leave just materials balance (Equation (2)).

The sole reason for my being so explicit – in effect adopting Arrow's (1964) rather than Debreu's (1959) viewpoint about complete markets – is that my formulation permits the most natural introduction of the sunspot beliefs that lead to incomplete markets. However, I should emphasize that I will appeal to this essential equivalence to claim without proof various well-established results, for example, that there always exists at least one monetary equilibrium, and that every competitive allocation generated by a monetary equilibrium is Pareto optimal. In particular, in the sequel I will make generous use of the fact that there is a monetary equilibrium in which households borrow and lend among themselves, that is, $m_h \neq 0$ for $h = 1,2$, if and only if there are positive incentives to trade, or households' marginal rates of time preference differ at their endowments, that is

$$\frac{\partial v_1(e_1)}{\partial y^0} \Big/ \frac{\partial v_1(e_1)}{\partial y^1} \neq \frac{\partial v_2(e_2)}{\partial y^0} \Big/ \frac{\partial v_2(e_2)}{\partial y^1}. \qquad (6)$$

3. How Sunspots Can Affect Allocation

The basic idea here is very simple; I want to elaborate the standard pure-exchange model to encompass Mr. 1's and Mr. 2's common belief that some purely extrinsic event, say, *sunspots*, will affect the level of the spot market prices (or, symmetrically, financial market returns) they face tomorrow.

3.1. Sunspots

So suppose now that each household expects tomorrow's spot prices to depend on the observed value of the two possible random events, sunspots or no sunspots, labeled by the superscripts $s = \alpha,\beta$, and having positive probabilities $0<\pi^{\alpha}<1$ and $\pi^{\beta}=1-\pi^{\alpha}$, respectively. In general, this new situation requires two changes in the description of the underlying market opportunities: on the one hand, surely, spot prices for tomorrow's physical commodities may actually depend on the event s. On the other hand, perhaps, nominal returns on the financial instrument may also depend on the event s. Let the notation $x=(x^{0},x^{1\alpha},x^{1\beta})$ (with corresponding prices $\boldsymbol{p}=(p^{0},p^{1\alpha},p^{1\beta})$) represent goods, and the notation b (with corresponding nontrivial returns $(r^{\alpha},r^{\beta})>0$) represent, now say, *bonds*, when there are sunspot beliefs. Also, note that, with such altered market opportunities, Mr. h's endowments and preferences will become, say, $\omega_h=(\omega_h^{0},\omega_h^{1\alpha},\omega_h^{1\beta})\equiv(e_h^{0},e_h^{1},e_h^{1})$ (independent of the sunspot lottery) and $u_h(x_h)=u_h(x_h^{0},x_h^{1\alpha},x_h^{1\beta})\equiv\pi^{\alpha}v_h(x_h^{0},x_h^{1\alpha})+\pi^{\beta}v_h(x_h^{0},x_h^{1\beta})$ (expected over the sunspot lottery), respectively.

Parallel with the previous formulation, let $\boldsymbol{x}=(x_1,x_2)$ denote a commodity allocation and $\boldsymbol{b}=(b_1,b_2)$ denote bond holdings (after today's trading), and say that an allocation $\boldsymbol{x}$ is (i) *feasible* if it is nonnegative, $\mathbf{x}\geqq 0$, and materials balance,

$$\sum_h x_h^{0}=\sum_h \omega_h^{0} \tag{2^s}$$

and

$$\sum_h x_h^{1s}=\sum_h \omega_h^{1s} \quad \text{for} \quad s=\alpha,\beta;$$

(ii) *Pareto optimal* if there is no other feasible allocation $\boldsymbol{x}'$ that dominates $\boldsymbol{x}$ in terms of utility,

$$u_h(x_h')\geqq u_h(x_h) \quad \text{for} \quad h=1,2, \text{ with strict inequality for some } h: \tag{3^s}$$

and (iii) *competitive* if there are some positive spot prices $\boldsymbol{p}\gg 0$ and associated bond holdings $\boldsymbol{b}$ (which can again be of either sign) such that each household optimizes, (x_h,b_h) is the solution to the problem

$$\begin{aligned} &\text{maximize} && u_h(x_h') \\ &\text{subject to} && p^{0}x_h^{0'}+b_h'\leqq p^{0}\omega_h^{0}, \\ & && p^{1s}x_h^{1s'}\leqq p^{1s}\omega_h^{1s}+r^{s}b_h' \quad \text{for} \quad s=\alpha,\beta \\ &\text{and} && x_h'\geqq 0 \end{aligned} \tag{4^s}$$

for $h=1,2$, and each market clears,

$$\begin{aligned} &\sum_h x_h^{0}=\sum_h \omega_h^{0}, \\ &\sum_h b_h=0 \end{aligned} \tag{5^s}$$

and

$$\sum_h x_h^{1s} = \sum_h \omega_h^{1s} \quad \text{for} \quad s = \alpha, \beta.$$

To distinguish this reformulation, I will refer to an equilibrium price–allocation–holding triplet $(\boldsymbol{p},\boldsymbol{x},\boldsymbol{b})$ as *a financial equilibrium.*

The main issue in this setting is whether such a different view of the world has any real effect on the outcome of market allocation. Following the lead of my earlier joint work, I will say that, for a feasible allocation x, *sunspots matter* (resp. *don't matter*) if

$$x_h^{1\alpha} \neq x_h^{1\beta} (\text{resp. } x_h^{1\alpha} = x_h^{1\beta}) \text{ for } h = 1, 2.$$

The remainder of the chapter then focuses on showing that, though sunspots may not matter, there is strong reason to believe that they invariably will, and even stronger reason, when they do, for active market intervention.[2]

3.2. Equilibrium

It is self-evident that in the presence (or with the advent) of sunspot beliefs, markets are incomplete; there are two possible future states of the world, but only one available financial instrument that can serve to hedge. Putting too much weight on this fact would be, in one important sense, misleading. The first existence result of this section, together with the brief optimality analysis of the next, supports the conclusion that, even when there are sunspot beliefs, the market mechanism is capable of achieving every Pareto optimal allocation (given appropriate endowments). The only problem is that, as the second existence result, also together with the following optimality analysis demonstrates, under these circumstances it will typically do much, much worse (given arbitrary endowments).

Proposition 1. (i) If $(\boldsymbol{q},\boldsymbol{y},\boldsymbol{m})$ is a monetary equilibrium, $r^s > 0$ for $s = \alpha, \beta$ or Equation (6) doesn't obtain, and $(x_h^0, x_h^{1s}) = (y_h^0, y_h^1)$ for $s = \alpha, \beta$, $h = 1, 2$, then there are $\boldsymbol{p}$ and $\boldsymbol{b}$ such that $(\boldsymbol{p},\boldsymbol{x},\boldsymbol{b})$ is a financial equilibrium (in which, by definition, sunspots don't matter). (ii) If $(\boldsymbol{p},\boldsymbol{x},\boldsymbol{b})$ is a financial equilibrium in which sunspots don't matter and $(y_h^0, y_h^1) = (x_h^0, x_h^{1s})$ for $s = \alpha, \beta$, $h = 1, 2$, then there are $\boldsymbol{q}$ and $\boldsymbol{m}$ such that $(\boldsymbol{q},\boldsymbol{y},\boldsymbol{m})$ is a monetary equilibrium.

[2] The first of these conclusions requires only minor, additional technical qualification, and the second none at all, even in the most general model of the effects of extrinsic uncertainty when financial markets are incomplete. As I mentioned before, I will justify these claims in forthcoming work.

Proof of Proposition 1. The argument simply involves comparing first-order conditions for the two problems given in Equations (4) and (4^s). On the one hand, associating the multipliers μ_h^0 and μ_h^1 with the two budget constraints in Equation (4), and then applying the Kuhn–Tucker theorem for concave programming (given the maintained assumptions on endowments and preferences together with Equation (1)) yields the following necessary and sufficient conditions for household maximization when there are no sunspot beliefs:

$$\begin{aligned} &\frac{\partial v_h(y_h)}{\partial y^0} = \mu_h^0 q^0, \\ &\frac{\partial v_h(y_h)}{\partial y^1} = \mu_h^1 q^1, \\ &\mu_h^0 = \mu_h^1, \\ &-q^0(y_h^0 - e_h^0) = m_h \end{aligned} \tag{7}$$

and

$$q^1(y_h^1 - e_h^1) = m_h$$

for $h = 1, 2$. On the other hand, associating the multipliers λ_h^0 and λ_h^{1s} for $s = \alpha,\beta$, with the three budget constraints in Equation (4^s), and then repeating the process (assuming that sunspots don't matter) yields:

$$\begin{aligned} &\frac{\partial v_h(y_h)}{\partial y^0} = \lambda_h^0 p^0, \\ &\frac{\partial v_h(y_h)}{\partial y^1} = \lambda_h^{1s}(p^{1s}/\pi^s) \quad \text{for} \quad s = \alpha, \beta, \\ &\lambda_h^{1\alpha} r^\alpha + \lambda_h^{1\beta} r^\beta = \lambda_h^0, \\ &-p^0(y_h^0 - e_h^0) = b_h \end{aligned} \tag{7^s}$$

and

$$p^{1s}(y_h^1 - e_h^1) = r^s b_h \quad \text{for} \quad s = \alpha, \beta$$

for $h = 1, 2$. Now consider each of the asserted implications in turn.

(i) If $r^s > 0$ for $s = \alpha$, β, then choose

$$p^0 = q^0, \lambda_h^0 = \mu_h^0, p^{1s} = r^s q^1 \quad \text{for} \quad s = \alpha, \beta, \lambda_h^{1s} = (\pi^s/r^s)\mu_h^0 \quad \text{for}$$
$$s = \alpha, \beta, \quad \text{and} \quad b_h = m_h,$$

while if, for example, $m^h = 0$, $r^\alpha > 0$, and $r^\beta = 0$, then choose

$$p^0 = q^0, \lambda_h^0 = \mu_h^0, \lambda_h^{1\alpha} = (\mu_h^0/r^\alpha), p^{1\alpha} = \pi^\alpha r^\alpha q^1, \lambda_h^{1\beta} = \mu_h^0, p^{1\beta} = \pi^\beta q^1,$$
$$\text{and} \quad b_h = m_h.$$

In both cases, direct substitution immediately reveals that Equation (7^s) follows from Equation (7).

(ii) Here, a straightforward calculation (ultimately based on the hypothesis that sunspots don't matter) shows that Equation (7^s) implies that

$$\left(\lambda_h^{1s}/\lambda_h^0\right) = \psi^s \quad \text{for} \quad s = \alpha, \beta, \; h = 1, 2,$$

where

$$\psi^\alpha = 1/\left(r^\alpha + \left[(p^{1\alpha}/\pi^\alpha)/(p^{1\beta}/\pi^\beta)\right] r^\beta\right) \tag{8}$$

and

$$\psi^\beta = [(p^{1\alpha}/\pi^\alpha)/(p^{1\beta}/\dot{\pi}^\beta)]\psi^\alpha.$$

So now choose

$$q^0 = p^0, q^1 = \psi^\alpha(p^{1\alpha}/\pi^\alpha) = \psi^\beta(p^{1\beta}/\pi^\beta), \mu_h^0 = \lambda_h^0, \quad \text{and} \quad m_h = b_h, \tag{9}$$

noting, in particular, that then Equations (7^s), (8), and (9) imply that

$$\begin{aligned}
q^1(y_h^1 - e_h^1) &= \pi^\alpha q^1(y_h^1 - e_h^1) + \pi^\beta q^1(y_h^1 - e_h^1) \\
&= \psi^\alpha p^{1\alpha}(y_h^1 - e_h^1) + \psi^\beta p^{1\beta}(y_h^1 - e_h^1) \\
&= \psi^\alpha r^\alpha b_h + \psi^\beta r^\beta b_h \\
&= [(\lambda_h^{1\alpha} r^\alpha + \lambda_h^{1\beta} r^\beta)/\lambda_h^0] b_h \\
&= m_h.
\end{aligned}$$

Thus, once again, direct substitution immediately reveals that Equation (7) follows from Equation (7^s). ■

In other words, this proposition establishes that there is essentially an equivalence between the competitive allocations generated by monetary equilibria and those generated by just the financial equilibria in which sunspots don't matter. Indeed, the only case in which this relation fails is when there are positive incentives to trade, that is, Equation (6) obtains, but some return is zero, that is (without loss of generality, since the labeling of states is perfectly arbitrary), $r^\alpha > 0$ and $r^\beta = 0$. And, for the polar case, it turns out that *sunspots always matter*. This special result is worth recording explicitly; among other things, it provides a heuristic rationale for my subsequent analysis: think of the economy as being characterized by returns (as well as preferences and endowments). Then, assuming that the set (or some selected subset) of financial equilibria varies "regularly" with respect to these particular parameters, there must be – at the very least – many ordinary cases (corresponding to $r^\alpha > 0$, $r^\beta > 0$ but $r^\beta / r^\alpha \sim 0$) in which sunspots matter.[3]

Corollary. Suppose that $r^\alpha > 0$ but $r^\beta = 0$. If Equation (6) obtains, then sunspots always matter in financial equilibrium.[4]

Proof of the Corollary. Suppose that the conclusion is false, that is, there is some financial equilibrium $(\boldsymbol{p},\boldsymbol{x},\boldsymbol{b})$ in which $x_h^{1s} = y_h^1$ for $s = \alpha, \beta$, $h = 1, 2$. Then from the first-order conditions (7^s) it follows that $p^{1\beta}(y_h^1 - e_h^1) = r^\beta b_h = 0$ or $y_h^1 = e_h^1$ for $h = 1, 2$. But then from the second implication in Proposition 1, it also follows that there is a monetary equilibrium $(\boldsymbol{q},\boldsymbol{y},\boldsymbol{m})$ in which $y_h^1 = e_h^1$ or $q^1(y_h^1 - e_h^1) = m_h = 0$ for $h = 1,2$, which contradicts the hypothesis that Equation (6) obtains. □

The essence of this corollary (and its converse) is that, in the polar case when only a single return is positive, financial equilibria in which sunspots don't matter are extremely rare (corresponding to the situations where there are no incentives to trade). Shortly, I will embroider on this basic theme and establish, for the ordinary case where both returns are positive, what is undoubtedly the most fascinating property of this leading example, its superabundance of sunspot equilibria. But first I would like to comment on one feature of my model that has probably not escaped the attention of a perceptive reader, namely, that when $r^\alpha > 0$ and $r^\beta > 0$, I could just as well specify $r^\alpha = r^\beta = I$, that is, bonds are money. (The validity of this claim hinges on the fact that the constraint set in Equation (4^s) is unaffected when each of tomorrow's spot market budget constraints is multiplied by the reciprocal of its corresponding return.) There is, however, purely in terms of interpretation, a good reason for introducing the more general parameterization: the underlying motivation for studying this particular model is probably best reflected by thinking of p^{1s} as (more or less) fixed but r^s as

---

[3] In the original version of this paper, I pursued precisely such a line of reasoning in order to display a host of financial equilibria in which sunspots matter. The specific argument involved demonstrating that a particular subset of financial equilibria (namely, the subset labeled $E_1(r)$ in the proof of Proposition 2 below) varies upper hemicontinuously with respect to returns (when they are restricted, e.g., to sum to one).

[4] In fact, for this leading example, the opposite statement is also true: If Equation (6) doesn't obtain, then sunspots never matter in financial equilibrium.

This result follows directly from the easily verified observation that, in the polar case, whether or not there is any competitive allocation for which sunspots matter depends only on whether or not

$$\frac{\partial u_1(\omega_1)}{\partial x^0} \bigg/ \frac{\partial u_1(\omega_1)}{\partial x^{1\alpha}} \neq \frac{\partial u_2(\omega_2)}{\partial x^0} \bigg/ \frac{\partial u_2(\omega_2)}{\partial x^{1\alpha}},$$

which is equivalent to Equation (6).

(more or less) variable. Thus, for instance, $r^\alpha < r^\beta$ because the report of an "unexpectedly" large previous increase in the money supply entails a decrease in the current market value of outstanding long-term bonds (and thus their current nominal return), because it signals that "obviously" future interest rates are going to increase.

Of course, my real reason for introducing such seemingly superfluous generality is somewhat more practical, as we shall now see.

For this purpose it is useful to restrict attention to present value prices

$$P = \{p \gg 0 : p^0 = 1\}$$

and unit sum returns

$$R = \{r = (r^\alpha, r^\beta) \gg 0 : r^\alpha + r^\beta = 1\}.$$

Proposition 2. Suppose that $r \in R$ and that Equation (6) obtains. Then there is a one-parameter family of financial equilibria yielding distinct competitive allocations for which sunspots matter.

Proof of Proposition 2. The argument is based on a fairly subtle analysis of the structure of the set of financial equilibria, whose details I defer to the appendix. The central idea of my approach is that competitive allocations can be parameterized by relating financial equilibria in the original model to those in another model where tomorrow's units of account have been adjusted so that Mr. 1 acts as if he faces a complete set of Arrow securities, that is, where x_1 is the solution to the standard problem.

$$\begin{array}{ll} \text{maximize} & u_1(x_1') \\ \text{subject to} & \boldsymbol{p}x_1' \leqq \boldsymbol{p}\omega_1 \\ \text{and} & x_1' \geqq 0. \end{array} \tag{10}$$

In order to implement this approach, define

$$E(r) = \{(\boldsymbol{p}, \boldsymbol{x}, \boldsymbol{b}) : (\boldsymbol{p}, \boldsymbol{x}, \boldsymbol{b}) \text{ is a financial equilibrium with } \boldsymbol{p} \in P\},$$
$$E_1(r) = \{(\boldsymbol{p}, \boldsymbol{x}, \boldsymbol{b}) \in E(r) : x_1 \text{ is the solution to (10)}\}$$

and

$$\psi(r) = \{\psi = (\psi^\alpha, \psi^\beta) \gg 0 : \psi^\alpha r^\alpha + \psi^\beta r^\beta = 1\}$$

for $r \in R$.

Claim. $E_1(r) \neq \phi$ and

$$E(r) = \bigcup_{\psi \in \psi(r)} \{((1, p^{1\alpha}/\psi^\alpha, p^{1\beta}/\psi^\beta), \boldsymbol{x}, \boldsymbol{b}) : (\boldsymbol{p}, \boldsymbol{x}, \boldsymbol{b}) \in E_1(\psi^\alpha r^\alpha, \psi^\beta r^\beta)\}$$

for $r \in R$.

Since exploiting this structure involves varying the returns r by varying the parameters ψ, it will be convenient to denote $r^{\psi} = (\psi^{\alpha}r^{\alpha}, \psi^{\beta}r^{\beta})$. Notice especially that the set of parameters $\psi(r)$ is diffeomorphic to the interval $\{\psi^{\alpha} : 0<\psi^{\alpha}<1/r^{\alpha}\}$, and that $r^{\psi} \in R$ for $\psi \in \psi(r)$. So, in short, the claim simply asserts that, given $r \in R$, the set of financial equilibria, and thus the set of competitive allocations can be parameterized by Mr. 1's valuation of his wealth tomorrow in state α relative to his wealth today ψ^{α} (see the concluding argument in the appendix).

Assuming its validity, the balance of the proof is straightforward, and consists of showing that, for given $r \in R$, (i) if $\psi' \in \psi(r)$, $(\boldsymbol{p}', \boldsymbol{x}', \boldsymbol{b}) \in E_1(r^{\psi'})$, $\psi'' \in \psi(r)$, $(\boldsymbol{p}'', \boldsymbol{x}'', \boldsymbol{b}'') \in E_1(r^{\psi''})$, and $\boldsymbol{x}' = \boldsymbol{x}''$, then $\psi' = \psi''$ (and, in fact, $(\boldsymbol{p}', \boldsymbol{x}', \boldsymbol{b}') = (\boldsymbol{p}'', \boldsymbol{x}'', \boldsymbol{b}'')$), that is, the competitive allocations are uniquely related to the parameter ψ^{α}, while (ii) if $\psi \in \psi(r)$, $(\boldsymbol{p}, \boldsymbol{x}, \boldsymbol{b}) \in E_1(r^{\psi})$ and $x_h^{1\alpha} = x_h^{1\beta} = y_h^1$ for $h = 1, 2$, then $\psi^{\alpha} = \pi^{\alpha}/r^{\alpha}$, that is, there is a single value of the parameter ψ^{α} at which sunspots may not matter.

As in the Proof of Proposition 1, my argument here simply involves manipulating the first-order conditions for two different problems, now Equation (10) describing Mr. 1's behavior and Equation (4^s) (with r^{ψ} replacing r) describing Mr. 2's behavior. Thus, on the one hand, associating the multiplier λ_1 with the single budget constraint in Equation (10), we have for $h = 1$

$$\begin{aligned}
&\pi^{\alpha}\frac{\partial v_1(x_1^0, x_1^{1\alpha})}{\partial x^0} + \pi^{\beta}\frac{\partial v_1(x_1^0, x_1^{1\beta})}{\partial x^0} = \lambda_1, \\
&\pi^{s}\frac{\partial v_1(x_1^0, x_1^{1s})}{\partial x^{1s}} = \lambda_1 p^{1s} \quad \text{for} \quad s = \alpha, \beta
\end{aligned} \tag{11}$$

and

$$\boldsymbol{p}x_1 = \boldsymbol{p}\omega_1.$$

On the other hand, again associating the multipliers λ_h^0 and λ_h^{1s} for $s = \alpha$, β with the three budget constraints in Equation (4^s), we have for $h = 2$

$$\begin{aligned}
&\pi^{\alpha}\frac{\partial v_2(x_2^0, x_2^{1\alpha})}{\partial x^0} + \pi^{\beta}\frac{\partial v_2(x_2^0, x_2^{1\beta})}{\partial x^0} = \lambda_2^0, \\
&\pi^{s}\frac{\partial v_2(x_2^0, x_2^{1s})}{\partial x^{1s}} = \lambda_2^{1s} p^{1s} \quad \text{for} \ s = \alpha, \beta, \\
&\qquad \lambda_2^{1\alpha}(\psi^{\alpha}r^{\alpha}) + \lambda_2^{1\beta}(\psi^{\beta}r^{\beta}) = \lambda_2^0, \\
&\qquad\qquad -(x_2^0 - e_2^0) = b_2
\end{aligned} \tag{12}$$

and

$$p^{1s}(x_2^{1s} - e_2^1) = (\psi^s r^s)b_2 \quad \text{for} \ s = \alpha, \beta$$

(i) From the supposition that Equation (6) obtains together with Proposition 1, we know that if $\psi \in \psi(r)$ and $(\boldsymbol{p}, \boldsymbol{x}, \boldsymbol{b}) \in E_1(r^{\psi})$, so $((1, p^{1\alpha}/\psi^{\alpha}, p^{1\beta}/\psi^{\beta}), \boldsymbol{x}, \boldsymbol{b}) \in E(r)$, then $x_h \neq \omega_h$ for $h = 1,2$. Moreover, if $x' = x''$, then Equation (11) immediately yields $\boldsymbol{p} = \boldsymbol{p}$, so that the last two expressions in Equation (12) yield $\psi' = \psi''$.

(ii) The second part of Equation (11) immediately yields $\pi^{\beta}/\pi^{\alpha} = p^{1\beta}/p^{1\alpha}$. But here again from the supposition that Equation (6) obtains together with Proposition 1 we know that $y_h^1 \neq e_h^1$ for $h = 1, 2$. So the last part of Equation (12) also yields $p^{1\beta}/p^{1\alpha} = \psi^{\beta} r^{\beta}/\psi^{\alpha} r^{\alpha}$. Then an obvious calculation (using $\psi \in \psi(r)$) yields the desired conclusion.[5] □

It appears that, by employing techniques from differential topology (along the basic lines I have just elaborated), this result can be considerably generalized. Be that as it may, the proposition itself in conjunction with Proposition 1 seems to me to establish an overwhelming presumption that, with incomplete financial markets, the raw likelihood of attaining financial equilibria in which sunspots don't matter is practically nil.

3.3. Optimality

Risk-averse households will always refuse a lottery in favor of its expected value. For this simple reason, in this world of sunspot beliefs, the criterion of Pareto optimality always rejects financial equilibria in which sunspots matter.

[5] Ailsa Röell has suggested a clever alternative to the specific parameterization I have used here. Her central idea – which renders the argument for this leading case (but not for its most interesting generalizations) somewhat more transparent – is the following: let the bond be simply money, so that $\boldsymbol{r} = (1, \boldsymbol{I})$. Then the budget set in Equation (4^s) is essentially the same as that described by

$$p^0(x_h^0 - e_h^0) + p^{1\alpha}(x_h^{1\alpha} - e_h^1) \leqq 0,$$
$$p^{1\alpha}(x_h^{1\alpha} - e_h^1) = p^{1\beta}(x_h^{1\beta} - e_h^1)$$

and $x_h \geqq 0$.

But this means, in particular, that by parameterizing, for instance, $p^{1\alpha} = \theta p^{1\beta}$ with $\theta \in (0, 1]$ a subset of the financial equilibria are essentially the same as the ordinary Walrasian equilibria generated by the 2×2 economies for which the two commodities are identified with goods 0 and $(1,\alpha)$, and the two households have preferences and endowments described by

$$u_h^0(y_h^0, y_h^1) = \pi^{\alpha} v_h(y_h^0, y_h^1) + \pi^{\beta} v_h(y_h^0, e_h^1 + \theta(y_h^1 - e_h^1))$$

and e_h, respectively. With this reformulation it is easily shown that, if Equation (6) obtains, then (i) there is (at least) one distinct Walrasian equilibrium associated with each value of the parameter θ while (ii) $y_h^1 = e_h^1 + \theta(y_h^1 - e_h^1)$ for $h = 1,2$, that is, sunspots don't matter, if and only if $\theta = 1$.

Proposition 3. The competitive allocation generated by a financial equilibrium is Pareto optimal if and only if sunspots don't matter.

Proof of Proposition 3. (i) (necessity) Suppose $\boldsymbol{x}$ is a competitive allocation in which sunspots matter. Then the average allocation $\boldsymbol{x}'$ defined by

$$x'_h = (x_h^0, \pi^\alpha x_h^{1\alpha} + \pi^\beta x_h^{1\beta}, \pi^\alpha x_h^{1\alpha} + \pi^\beta x_h^{1\beta}) \quad \text{for } h = 1,2 \tag{13}$$

is feasible (since $\omega_h^{1\alpha} = \omega_h^{1\beta} \equiv e_h^1$ for $h = 1{,}2$) and Pareto dominates $\boldsymbol{x}$ in terms of utility (since v_h is strictly concave for $h = 1$, 2). That is, $\boldsymbol{x}$ is not Pareto optimal. (ii) (sufficiency) Suppose $\boldsymbol{x}$ is a competitive allocation in which sunspots don't matter. Then, if it isn't Pareto optimal, by the preceding argument it can be dominated by another feasible allocation for which sunspots don't matter. But, in light of the second implication in Proposition 1, this contradicts the first basic theorem of welfare (which applies to the standard pure-exchange model described in Section 2). □

I almost needn't emphasize that this proposition in conjunction with Proposition 2 tells us that, when perceived market influences outrun available financial instruments, there is very likely to be ample justification for the government to interfere (directly or indirectly) in the operation of financial markets. Perhaps even more interesting is that Propositions 1 and 3 together with Hart's (1975) remarkable analysis of optimality with incomplete markets strongly suggest that a competitive allocation in which sunspots matter might even be Pareto dominated by one in which they don't (for given arbitrary endowments). This intriguing possibility can be readily verified in terms of examples built from additively separable utility functions,

$$v_h(y_h) = f_h^0(y_h^0) + f_h^1(y_h^1) \quad \text{for } h = 1,2.$$

I forgo presenting a specific example (since its construction is clear-cut but tedious).[6]

---

[6] The specific procedure I have in mind consists of the following steps:

(i) Pick a positive feasible allocation $x \gg 0$ for which sunspots matter;

(ii) Pick positive values of the derivatives $f_h^{0'}(x_h^0) > 0$ and $f_h^1(x_h^{1s}) > 0$ for $s = \alpha$, β, $h = 1{,}2$ (together with probabilities, returns, prices, and multipliers) so that the first-order conditions for Equation (4^s) are satisfied at the chosen allocation x, and these values are consistent with strict concavity; and finally

(iii) Pick positive values of the derivatives $f_h^{1'}(\pi^\alpha x_h^{1\alpha} + \pi^\beta X_h^{1\beta}) > 0$ for $h = 1{,}2$ (now together with just prices and multipliers) so that the first-order conditions for Equation (4^s) are satisfied at the average allocation x' defined by Equation (13) (which are simply (7^s) with $(y_h^1, y_h^1) = (x_h^{0'}, x_h^{1s'})$ for $s = \alpha, \beta$, $h = 1{,}2$), and again these values are consistent with strict concavity.

This construction works because of the fact that, for $f: \mathbb{R}_+ \to \mathbb{R}$ differentiable, strictly increasing and strictly concave, specifying $f'(x')$ and $f'(x'')$ for $x' \neq x''$ leaves great latitude in also specifying $f'(\lambda x' + (1-\lambda)x'')$ for $0<\lambda<1$.

Acknowledgment

This research was undertaken while I was visiting at CEPREMAP and Geneva during a sabbatical leave from Pennsylvania. I would like to thank all three institutions for their generous support. Financial assistance from the NSF under grant SOC83-09049 is also gratefully acknowledged.

The final version of the chapter has benefited substantially from several people's comments and reactions. In particular, an astute observation by Martin Hellwig significantly strengthened the most striking of my results (Proposition 2 below). Of course, I am solely responsible for the ultimate outcome.

Appendix

My only purpose in this appendix is to establish the Claim used in proving Proposition 2. Since I justify a more general statement of the essence of this basic result elsewhere (1984)], I permit myself to be somewhat sketchy here (especially regarding the details of various routine "ε–δ" arguments).

Proof of the Claim. Define the set

$$P^{\varepsilon} = \{\boldsymbol{p} \in \boldsymbol{P} : \varepsilon \leqq p^{1s} \leqq 1/\varepsilon \quad \text{for } s = \alpha, \beta\}$$

for $\varepsilon > 0$, and pick a bound

$$\overline{x} \gg \omega_1 + \omega_2.$$

Now consider the equilibrium model obtained when the solution to Equation (4^s) is replaced by the solution to

$$\begin{aligned} &\text{maximize} && u_1(x_1') \\ &\text{subject to} && \boldsymbol{p}x_1' \leq \boldsymbol{p}\omega_1 \\ &\text{and} && 0 \leqq x_1' \leqq \overline{x} \end{aligned} \tag{A.1}$$

and $b_1 = -b_2$ for $h = 1$, and by the solution to

$$\begin{aligned} &\text{maximize} && u_2(x_2') \\ &\text{subject to} && p^0 x_2^{0'} + b_2' \leqq p^0 \omega_2^0, \\ & && p^{1s} x_2^{1s'} \leqq p^{1s} \omega_2^{1s} + r^s b_2' \quad \text{for } s = \alpha, \beta \\ &\text{and} && 0 \leqq x_2' \leqq \overline{x} \end{aligned} \tag{A.2}$$

for $h = 2$. Then the argument proceeds by establishing the following series of results, for given $r \in R$.

(i) If $(\boldsymbol{p},\boldsymbol{x},\boldsymbol{b})$ is a financial equilibrium in this new model, then it is also a financial equilibrium in the original model.
Market clearing Equation (5^s) implies that $x_h \leqq \omega_1 + \omega_2 \ll \overline{x}$ for $h = 1$, 2. So all that needs to be shown is that if x_1 is the solution to Equation (10) and $b_1 = -b_2$, then (x_1,b_1) is the solution to Equation (4^s) for $h = 1$. Since $r \in R$, $r^\alpha + r^\beta = 1$, so that adding up the constraints in Equation (4^s) for $h = 1$ yields the constraint in Equation (10). Hence, feasible solutions to Equation (4^s) for $h = 1$ also yield feasible solutions to Equation (10). Moreover, since u_2 is monotone (recall that v_2 is monotone and π^s is positive for $s = \alpha$, β), the solution to Equation (4^s) for $h = 2$ together with market clearing Equation (5^s) yields

$$p^0(x_1^0 - \omega_1^0) = -p^0(x_2^0 - \omega_2^0) = b_2 = -b_1$$

and

$$p^{1s}(x_1^{1s} - \omega_1^{1s}) = -p^{1s}(x_2^{1s} - \omega_2^{1s}) = -r^s b_2 = r^s b_1 \quad \text{for } s = \alpha, \beta.$$

Hence, (x_1,b_1) is a feasible solution, and thus necessarily also the solution to Equation (4^s) for $h = 1$.

(ii) The solution to problem (A.1) [resp. (A.2)], say, $x_1(\boldsymbol{p})$ [resp. $(x_2(\boldsymbol{p}),b_2(\boldsymbol{p}))$], is well defined and continuous for $\boldsymbol{p} \in P$ [resp. $\boldsymbol{p} \in P^\varepsilon$ for every $\epsilon > 0$], and these satisfy the appropriate (weak) form of Walras's Law,

$$\boldsymbol{p}x_h(\boldsymbol{p}) \leqq \boldsymbol{p}\omega_h, \quad \text{with equality if } x_h(\boldsymbol{p}) \ll \overline{x},$$

for $h = 1$, 2.
Given my strong assumptions on u_h and ω_h, these results are well known for the problem (A.1). For the problem (A.2), they follow from exactly the same sort of reasoning once it is noted that, when $r \in R$, the feasible solutions to problem (A.2) are uniformly bounded

(iii) The mapping $\varphi^\varepsilon : P^\varepsilon \to P^\varepsilon$ defined by

$$\boldsymbol{p} \to \{\boldsymbol{p}' : \boldsymbol{p}' \text{ is an optimal solution to the problem}$$

$$\max_{p'' \in P^\varepsilon} \boldsymbol{p}(x_1(\boldsymbol{p}) + x_2(p) - \omega_1 - \omega_2)\}$$

has a fixed point $\boldsymbol{p}^\varepsilon \in \varphi^\varepsilon(\boldsymbol{p}^\varepsilon)$.
This follows from a standard argument based on the regularity properties asserted in (ii).

(iv) If ε is sufficiently small, then a fixed point $\boldsymbol{p}^\varepsilon \in \varphi^\varepsilon(\boldsymbol{p}^\varepsilon)$ yields a financial equilibrium $(\boldsymbol{p},\boldsymbol{x},\boldsymbol{b}) = (\boldsymbol{p}^\varepsilon,(x_1(\boldsymbol{p}^\varepsilon),x_2(\boldsymbol{p}^\varepsilon)),(-b_2(\boldsymbol{p}^\varepsilon),b_2(\boldsymbol{p}^\varepsilon)))$.

This too follows from a standard argument, but now based on Walras's Law and the monotonicity assumption on u_1.

From the equivalence property asserted in (i) together with the existence property asserted in (iv) it follows immediately that, in fact, $E_1(r) \neq \phi$ for $r \in R$. So all that remains to be established is that, again for given $r \in R$,

(v) $$E(r) = \bigcup_{\psi \in \psi(r)} \{((1, p^{1\alpha}/\psi^\alpha, p^{1\beta}/\psi^\beta), \boldsymbol{x}, \boldsymbol{b}) : \ (\boldsymbol{p}, \boldsymbol{x}, \boldsymbol{b}) \in E_1(r^\psi)\}.$$

Consider once again the first-order conditions for Equation (4^s) (given $(\tilde{\boldsymbol{p}}, \tilde{\boldsymbol{x}}, \tilde{\boldsymbol{b}},) \in E(r)$)

$$\begin{aligned} \pi^\alpha \frac{\partial v_h(\tilde{x}_h^0, \tilde{x}_h^{1\alpha})}{\partial x^0} + \pi^\beta \frac{\partial v_h(\tilde{x}_h^0, \tilde{x}_h^{1\beta})}{\partial x^0} &= \tilde{\lambda}_h^0, \\ \pi^s \frac{\partial v_h(\tilde{x}_h^1, \tilde{x}_h^{1s})}{\partial x^{1s}} &= \tilde{\lambda}_h^{1s} \tilde{p}^{1s} \quad \text{for } s = \alpha, \beta, \\ \tilde{\lambda}_h^{1\alpha} r^\alpha + \tilde{\lambda}_h^{1\beta} r^\beta &= \tilde{\lambda}_h^0, \\ -(\tilde{x}_h^0 - e_h^0) &= \tilde{b}_h \end{aligned} \tag{A3}$$

and

$$\tilde{p}^{1s}(\tilde{x}_h^{1s} - e_h^1) = r^s \tilde{b}_h \quad \text{for } s = \alpha, \beta$$

for $h = 1, 2$. Now simply identify ψ^s with $\tilde{\lambda}_1^{1s}/\tilde{\lambda}_1^0$ for $s = \alpha, \beta$. From the equivalence property asserted in (i) it follows that Equation (11) together with $b_1 = -b_2$ is equivalent to problem (A.3) for $h = 1$ when $\tilde{\boldsymbol{p}} = (1, p^{1\alpha}/\psi^\alpha, p^{1\beta}/\psi^\beta)$, $(\tilde{x}_1, \tilde{b}_1) = (x_1, b_1)$ and $(\tilde{\lambda}_1^0, \tilde{\lambda}_1^{1\alpha}, \tilde{\lambda}_1^{1\beta}) = \lambda_1(1, \psi^\alpha, \psi^\beta)$ (given $(\boldsymbol{p}, \boldsymbol{x}, \boldsymbol{b}) \in E_1(r^\psi)$). Similarly, Equation (12) is equivalent to problem (A.3) when $\tilde{\boldsymbol{p}} = (1, p^{1\alpha}/\psi^\alpha, p^{1\beta}/\psi^\beta)$, $(\tilde{x}_2, \tilde{b}_2) = (x_2, b_2)$ and $(\tilde{\lambda}_2^0, \tilde{\lambda}_2^{1\alpha}, \tilde{\lambda}_2^{1\beta}) = (\lambda_2^0, \lambda_2^{1\alpha}\psi^\alpha, \lambda_2^{1\beta}\psi^\beta)$. In other words, $(\boldsymbol{p}, \boldsymbol{x}, \boldsymbol{b}) \in E_1(r^\psi)$ is equivalent to $(\tilde{\boldsymbol{p}}, \tilde{\boldsymbol{x}}, \tilde{\boldsymbol{b}}) = ((1, p^{1\alpha}/\psi^\alpha, p^{1\beta}/\psi^\beta), \boldsymbol{x}, \boldsymbol{b}) \in E(r)$ for $\psi \in \Psi(r)$, and the proof is complete. □

References

Arrow, K.J. (1964). The role of securities in the optimal allocation of risk-bearing. *Review of Economic Studies* **31**, 91–96.

Cass, D. (1984). Competitive equilibrium with incomplete financial markets. CARESS Working Paper, University of Pennsylvania.

Cass, D. and Shell, K. (1980). In defense of a basic approach. In Kareken, J.N. and Wallace, N. (Eds), *Models of Monetary Economies*. Minneapolis, MN: Federal Reserve Bank of Minneapolis.

Cass, D. and Shell, K. (1983). Do sunspots matter? *Journal of Political Economy* **91**, 193–227.

Debreu, G. (1959). *Theory of Value*. New York: Wiley, chapter 7.
Hart, O.D. (1975). On the optimality of equilibrium when the market structure is incomplete. *Journal of Economic Theory* **11**, 418–443.
Keynes, J.M. (1936). *The General Theory of Employment, Interest and Money*. London: Macmillan, chapter 12.
Shiller, R.J. (1978). Rational expectations and the dynamic structure of macroeconomic models: A critical view. *Journal of Monetary Economics* **4**, 1–44.

Chapter 10

The Structure of Financial Equilibrium with Exogenous Yields: The Case of Incomplete Markets☆

Yves Balasko[a] and David Cass

[a]*Département d'économetrie, Université de Genève, 2, rue Dancet, 1211 Genève 4, Suisse*

1. Introduction

THE PAST SEVERAL YEARS have witnessed rapidly growing interest in models of competitive equilibrium with incomplete (or potentially incomplete) financial markets. There are alternative ways of describing this general development. However, two distinct – and polar – approaches to modeling the financial structure of a market economy clearly stand out. The first, and older, basically follows Debreu's (1959) vision of the operation of (complete) markets under uncertainty; in this approach, nominal yields from financial instruments are assumed to depend, usually in linear fashion, on spot market prices for commodities. Thus, the prototype instrument is essentially a commodity futures contract. The second, and newer, approach follows Arrow's (1964) vision; nominal yields are viewed as being set or determined independently of spot prices. Here the prototype is a fixed coupon bond.

Both approaches have taken similar routes. While early work focused on the classical problems of existence and optimality (e.g., the seminal papers by Radner (1972) and Hart (1975)), later contributions have been more concerned with investigating the underlying structure of the equilibrium set itself (in part, to overcome intrinsic difficulties with existence in the Radner–Hart tradition; see, especially, Magill and Shafer (1985), Duffie and Shafer (1985, 1986), and Younès (1986)).

In this chapter, we pursue the newer approach, and study the properties of equilibrium in an exchange economy in which financial markets are inherently incomplete. At the outset we stress that in our formulation the

☆This article was originally published in *Econometrica* 57, Yves Balasko and David Cass, "The Structure of Financial Equilibrium with Exogenous Yields: The Case of Incomplete Markets", 135–162, ©The Econometric Society, 1989.

International Symposia in Economic Theory and Econometrics, Vol. 21B
S. Spear (Editor)

ISSN: 1571-0386/DOI: 10.1108/S1571-0386(2011)000021B013

payoffs or yields from each financial instrument are fixed or predetermined; they do not depend on either its own price or any other endogenous variable. While our conception of a financial instrument is fairly broad, the simplest example is an ordinary bond or debenture (which pays a fixed interest rate on the par value at which it will be amortized at the end of a given term). For this reason, we refer to the financial instruments themselves as *bonds*, and to their yields as being – from the perspective of the market forces that we examine – *exogenous*. It is important to bear in mind that these are merely handy labels.

There are two reasonable arguments for concentrating on this seemingly special model of financial markets:

(i) The yields from many financial instruments are, in fact, best conceived as being determined in their own right. This is obvious, for example, in the case of debentures and certain forms of insurance. We think it is also a plausible view in the case of common stocks and other assets whose yields depend largely on beliefs about their future values (in particular, beyond the horizon being explicitly considered). In any case, for the purposes of choosing a single, canonical model for representing financial markets in general equilibrium theory, we find Arrow's vision equally as compelling as Debreu's.

(ii) Our position is reinforced by contrasting this model to its polar opposite, where all yields depend linearly on spot prices. In the first place, with exogenous yields one encounters no difficulty whatsoever in establishing existence of what we refer to as *financial equilibrium* (see, especially, Cass (1984), Werner (1985), and Duffie (1987)). More important, this model captures an aspect of financial equilibrium, which, in general, *only* the most common version of its polar opposite doesn't. Namely, provided that spot market budget constraints are *not* linear homogeneous in prices, incompleteness of financial markets very likely results in severe indeterminacy of equilibrium allocation.

This last assertion is the central message of the chapter. More precisely, we establish the following fundamental proposition: Suppose that there are $N+1$ spot markets, but only $0<M<N$ distinct bonds, so that the, say, *deficiency* in financial markets is $n=N-M$. Then (subject to some relatively innocuous technical qualifications) *the set of equilibrium allocations will contain a smooth, n-dimensional submanifold.* In other words, we show that market incompleteness almost invariably leads to (at least) a comparable degree of allocation indeterminateness.

To be sure, we conduct our investigation within an especially hospitable – and therefore naturally suspect – setting. This is an analytic convenience, permitting derivation of precise results, and not a logical necessity. Incorporating some yields which depend, say, on spot market prices for commodities introduces the possibility that there may be no financial equilibrium (for some patterns of endowments), but does not alter the fact that, when there is, allocation may be extremely indeterminate. We illustrate this important point by means of a leading example, and show that it is absence of homogeneous budget constraints, not presence of exogenous bond yields per se, which is the essential basis for generating a substantial degree of real indeterminacy. (Geanakoplos and Mas-Colell (1989) provide additional, persuasive support for this contention.)

The specific plan and content of this chapter are as follows.

In Section 2, we describe our basic model and underline its most important features. The key feature of the model is that because bond yields are exogenous (and because all households have unrestricted access to bond markets), we can also take bond prices as exogenous; flexible spot prices alone suffice to clear all markets (again, see Cass (1984) and Duffie (1987)). For simplicity, we refer to the combination of exogenous bond prices and yields as bond *returns*. Having returns given as a primitive of the model provides two substantial benefits:

(i) It permits very broad latitude in interpreting the spot market structure of the economy. In particular, it enables us to encompass such diverse markets as those for resale of long-term debentures, or for futures in foreign exchange.
(ii) It introduces very effective means for studying properties of financial equilibrium. In particular, it enables us to convert the extensive form of the model, involving $N+1$ spot market budget constraints in both goods and bonds, into a reduced form involving only $n+1$, say, *real* market budget constraints in just goods.

The latter maneuver, of course, explains why n, the deficiency in financial markets, becomes a critical number in our formulation. This conversion amounts to introducing an especially convenient parameterization of the overall influence of incomplete financial markets on households' real exchange opportunities.

Relying heavily on the reduced form of the model, in Section 3 we elaborate the leading example of incomplete financial markets. There are two households, one commodity (in each of three states) and three spot markets, but only one bond. This allows us to picture financial equilibrium in a three-dimensional Edgeworth-Bowley box diagram. It also allows us to illustrate the central message of this chapter. Here there is one too few bonds to permit complete risk sharing. So there are likewise one too many degrees of freedom to determine (locally) unique market allocation: Generally, the set of equilibrium allocations contains a smooth curve.

We exploit the leading example to make two further, crucial points. First, we temporarily adopt the assumption that the single financial instrument, rather than being a bond, has yields which depend on spot prices. We then demonstrate that the indeterminacy property is quite robust. Except in the extreme circumstance where this dependence is linear homogeneous, the same logic which applied before still applies now, and leads to the same kind of conclusion (though with some complication). Second, we describe how – even taking returns as exogenous – there may be no indeterminacy of equilibrium allocation under certain other extreme circumstances. This serves to explain why our main result is only generic, and to motivate additional assumptions utilized in its proof.

In order to go beyond the leading example we need to know a great deal about the structure of the equilibrium set for our specific model. This problem is investigated, in some depth, at the beginning of Section 4 (essentially following the program laid out in Balasko (1988)). The most important implication of this analysis is that, except on a nongeneric subset of endowments, the set of equilibrium spot prices contains a smooth, n-dimensional submanifold. In other words, generally the economy exhibits n degrees of price or *nominal* indeterminacy.

The reader who is uninterested in mathematical detail should skip ahead to the second part of Section 4. There we present our main result that nominal indeterminacy generally leads to the same degree of allocation or *real* indeterminacy. This result requires, as noted earlier, additional assumptions designed to rule out borderline cases. These concern first, the number (and, implicitly, diversity) of households in the economy, and second, the nature of the bond returns they face. In Section 4, we introduce these assumptions as merely technical prerequisites.

In Section 5, we focus on the second kind of technical prerequisite, and verify an economic (rather than purely mathematic) alternative. This condition amounts to postulating the general analogue of inside money – that households have the opportunity to transfer wealth from some particular spot to every other spot. In that same section, we also relax the assumption that bond prices and their yields are fixed or predetermined; we show that, if returns are treated as variables rather than parameters, then (not surprisingly) the degree of real indeterminacy increases dramatically, from n to nM. (This last number represents the dimension of the smooth manifold of all M-dimensional, no-arbitrage portfolio wealth subspaces in $\mathbb{R}^{N+1}$.) Thus, ultimately, we provide a *maximal* (as well as a minimal) measure of the effect that incomplete markets might have on the determinacy of equilibrium allocation.

All our proofs are collected in the Appendix.

In independent work, Geanakoplos and Mas-Colell (1989) have contributed a very neat complement to our own results. They concentrate on what we refer to as the *leading case*, where there are just two periods, with uncertainty in the second. However, in contrast to our main approach, they take today's bond prices (but not tomorrow's yields) as variables rather than parameters; in short, all prices become endogenous (while bond yields remain exogenous). They then show that the degree of real indeterminacy increases from n to $N-1$, independent of M, the number of bonds.

These various results can be easily related, also concentrating on the leading case (and ignoring all other subtleties). Take bond returns as fixed. The deficiency in financial markets alone induces n degrees of real indeterminacy. Now consider, on the one hand, freeing up today's bond prices, that is, treating them as variables rather than parameters. Roughly speaking, since these prices can be arbitrarily normalized, this increase in nominal indeterminacy will only contribute an additional $M-1$ degrees of real indeterminacy. (Note that $N-1=n+(M-1)$.) Consider, on the other hand, also freeing up bond yields. Again roughly speaking, since different bond return matrices can represent identical portfolio wealth subspaces, this will only add yet another $(n-1)(M-1)$ degrees of real indeterminacy. (Note that $nM=n+(M-1)+(n-1)(M-1)$). So, finally, except when $n=1$ or $M=1$, we see the following picture:

	minimal (fixed returns)	intermediate (variable prices)	maximal (variable returns)
degree of indeterminacy	n	$<N-1$	$<nM$

In general, for instance, when there are more than two periods, and bonds are marketed at other than today's spot, or when bond yields are viewed as being generated by other underlying variables (e.g., interest rates), matters are more complicated: There will be many further intermediate cases, depending on what are taken as variables (for particular interpretive purposes).

We also mention some other closely related work. Cass (1988) provided a specific example of real indeterminacy, and then more general analysis (1985), which we have refined here. Werner (1986) synthesizes our main result with that of Geanakoplos and Mas-Colell (for the leading case). And Balasko et al. (1987) extend both main results (again for the leading case) to the situation where financial market imperfection stems from the stylized fact that households' participation on these markets – whether complete or otherwise – is never virtually unrestricted.

2. The Basic Model

2.1. Extensive Form

There are L types of physical commodities (labeled by superscript $c=1, 2, \dots, L$, and referred to as *goods*), and M types of financial instruments (labeled by superscript $i=1, 2, \dots, M$, and referred to as *bonds*). Both goods and (in general, some subset of) bonds are traded on each of $N+1$ spot markets (labeled by superscript $s = 0, 1, \ldots, N$, and referred to as *spots*). Altogether, then, there are $l = L(N+1)$ goods being traded. Their quantities and spot prices will be represented by the vectors $\boldsymbol{x} = (x^0, \ldots, x^s, \ldots, x^N)$ (with $\boldsymbol{x}^s = (x^{sTimes1}, \ldots, x^{sTimesc}, \ldots, x^{sTimesL})$) and $\boldsymbol{p} = (p^0, \ldots, p^s, \ldots, p^N)$ (with $\boldsymbol{p}^s = (p^{s,1}, \ldots, p^{s,c}, \ldots, p^{s,L})$), respectively. (Note: All prices are positive, and are measured in units of account, referred to as *dollars*. It will be convenient, for example, in representing dollar values of spot market transactions to treat price vectors as rows. Otherwise, we maintain the standard convention.) Quantities of bonds will be represented by the vector $\boldsymbol{b} = (b^1, \ldots, b^i, \ldots, b^M)$. Finally, there are m households (labeled by the subscript $h = 1,2, \ldots, m$), who are described by utility functions $u_h : \mathbb{R}^l \to \mathbb{R}$ and goods endowments $\omega_h \in \mathbb{R}^l$. We make the following assumption throughout, for $h = 1,2, \ldots, m$:

Assumption A1. *u_h is C^2, differentiably strictly increasing (i.e., $Du_h(x_h) \gg 0$) and differentiably strictly quasi-concave (i.e., $Du_h(x_h)^T \Delta x = 0$ and $\Delta x \neq 0 \Rightarrow \Delta x^T D^2 u_h(x_h) \Delta x < 0$), and has indifference surfaces bounded below.*

The basic financial structure of the economy is, in essence, quite simple. However, since it constitutes such an important element of our model, we describe it fairly (perhaps overly) carefully.

Ownership of one unit of bond i entitles a household to receive returns, possibly nonpositive, of $r^{s,i}$ dollars at each spot s. Bonds are issued and redeemed by households, but their returns are taken as a primitive aspect of the economy. It is helpful (but unduly restrictive, as Example 3 below illustrates) to think of returns as being generated in the following way. Bond i has a price, say $\pi^i = -r^{s,i} > 0$ set or determined at some particular spot $s = s^i$, and by convention or fiat promises a yield, say, $\rho^{s,i} = r^{s,i} \geq 0$ at the other spots $s \neq s^i$ (with $\rho^{s,i} > 0$ at some spot). In other words, credit obligations prescribed by the yields of bond i are traded between households at spot s^i (so that the subset of bonds $\{i: s^i = s\}$ is traded at spot s). A classic example will illuminate the general picture. Let

$$\mathbf{R} = \begin{bmatrix} r^{0,1} & \cdots & r^{0,i} & \cdots & r^{0,M} \\ \vdots & \ddots & & & \\ r^{s,1} & & r^{s,i} & & \\ \vdots & & & \ddots & \\ r^{N,1} & & & & r^{N,M} \end{bmatrix} = \begin{bmatrix} r^0 \\ \vdots \\ r^s \\ \vdots \\ r^N \end{bmatrix}$$

$= ((N+1) \times M)$-demensional matrix of bond returns.

Example 1. (a single resale market): $M = 2$ and $N = 2$; the three spots represent today, tomorrow, and the day after tomorrow; the first bond represents a two-period debenture (with par value 1 and interest rate $r>0$), the second the possibility of its resale tomorrow. If the debenture originally sells for q^0, and will resell for q^1, then the economy's bond returns take the form

$$\mathbf{R} = \begin{bmatrix} -\pi^1 & \rho^{0,2} \\ \rho^{1,1} & -\pi^2 \\ \rho^{2,1} & \rho^{2,2} \end{bmatrix} = \begin{bmatrix} -q^0 & 0 \\ r & -q^1 \\ 1+r & 1+r \end{bmatrix}.$$

In fact, this example is too simple for our primary objective; since $\mathrm{M} = \mathrm{N}$, financial markets are complete, and the economy reduces to the standard Walrasian model (following Arrow). It can be expanded to be made consistent with the assumption, adopted throughout the rest of this chapter, that markets are inherently incomplete:

Assumption A2. $0<M<N$.

Example 2. (multiple potential resale markets): $M = 3$ and $N = 6$; now there are two possible events tomorrow, say, α and, β, and two further possible events the day after tomorrow, say, a and b. Thus, for instance, spot 0 represents today, but spot 1 represents tomorrow in the event α while spot 6 represents the day after tomorrow in the chain of events (β, b). Here, after obvious modification of notation, returns take the form

$$\mathbf{R} = \cdots = \begin{bmatrix} -q^0 & 0 & 0 \\ r & -q^\alpha & 0 \\ r & 0 & -q^\beta \\ 1+r & 1+r & 0 \\ 1+r & 1+r & 0 \\ 1+r & 0 & 1+r \\ 1+r & 0 & 1+r \end{bmatrix}. \qquad (1)$$

Taking the new issue and resale prices positive, Equation (1) satisfies two additional assumptions which we also maintain hereafter:

Assumption A3. *Rank* $R = M$.

Assumption A4. *There is no* $b \in \mathbb{R}^M$ *such that* $Rb>0$.

Assumption A3 simply states that there are no redundant bonds, and Assumption A4 states that there are no arbitrage possibilities on bond markets. (Positive spot prices already ensure that there are no arbitrage possibilities on goods markets.) On the one hand, we lose no generality by adopting the first assumption; otherwise – when rank $R = M' < M$ – households would be indifferent between the financial opportunities represented by R and those represented by R', an $((N+1) \times M')$-dimensional, full-rank submatrix of R. On the other hand, the second is required for existence of financial equilibrium; otherwise – when there is some portfolio providing nonnegative, nontrivial returns – households would have unlimited consumption opportunities at some spot (and hence couldn't be optimizing while both goods and bond markets are clearing).

A third example is useful for illustrating how these assumptions come into play, as well as the potential for variety of interpretation implicit in our formulation of the basic financial structure. The idea of the example (which we utilize for other purposes in Section 5) was suggested by unpublished work of Herakles Polemarchakis.

Example 3. (foreign exchange markets): $M = 4$ and $N = 5$; the even (respectively, odd) numbered spots represent seriatim, today, tomorrow in event α, and tomorrow in event β, all in New York (respectively, Paris); the first three bonds represent (at different date-events) current exchange of \$US in New York for ff in Paris, and the fourth a futures exchange of the same kind. If current exchange rates are d^0, d^α, and d^β, and the futures contract specifies d (all in terms of \$US/ff, then

$$\mathbf{R} = \begin{bmatrix} -d^0 & 0 & 0 & 0 \\ 1 & 0 & 0 & 0 \\ 0 & -d^\alpha & 0 & -d \\ 0 & 1 & 0 & 1 \\ 0 & 0 & -d^\beta & -d \\ 0 & 0 & 1 & 1 \end{bmatrix}. \tag{2}$$

Observe that Assumption A3 simply means that $d^\alpha \neq d$ or $d^\beta \neq d$, and Assumption A4 means that (in addition to having positive exchange rates) $\min\{d^\alpha, d^\beta\} < d < \max\{d^\alpha, d^\beta\}$. Furthermore, notice that both conditions are robust to small perturbations of the parameters (a fact which, for instance, enables us to analyze variability of bond returns later on, in Section 5).

Finally, we should emphasize (and reemphasize) that, for our purposes, it is only the pattern, and not the genesis of the bond returns on the left-hand sides of Equations (1) and (2), which matters.

Now let

$$P = \{p \in \mathbb{R}^l_{++}\}$$
$$= \text{set of possible spot prices}$$

and

$$\Omega = \{\omega = (\omega_1, \ldots, \omega_h, \ldots, \omega_m) \in (\mathbb{R}^l)^m\}$$
$$= \text{set of possible goods endowments (and allocations).}$$

Then, given $\omega \in \Omega$, $p \in P$ is a *financial equilibrium* if, when households optimize, that is, given p (and R), (x_h, b_h) solves the problem:

$$\begin{array}{l} \text{maximize } u_h(x_h) \\ \text{subject to } p^s(x^s_h - \omega^s_h) = r^s b_h \quad (s = 1, 2, \ldots, N;\ h = 1, 2, \ldots, m), \end{array} \tag{3}$$

both goods and bond markets clear, that is,

$$\sum_h (x^{s,c}_h - \omega^{s,c}_h) = 0, (s, c) = (0, 1), (0, 2), \ldots, (N, L), \tag{4}$$

and

$$\sum_h b^i_h = 0 \quad (i = 1, 2, \ldots M). \tag{5}$$

2.2. Reduced Form

The system described by Equations (3)–(5) has a number of special features which permit simplification and facilitate analysis.

(i) When the units of all prices and bonds are changed by a common factor, the spot market budget constraints in Equation (3) are unaffected. This implies that nothing is lost by normalizing all prices. A convenient normalization singles out the first good at the first spot as the numeraire. So, hereafter, we further restrict the set of possible spot prices so that $p^{0,1} = 1$,

$$P = \{p \in \mathbb{R}^l_{++} : p^{0,1} = 1\}.$$

(ii) Summing each of the spot market budget constraints in Equation (3) over all households, and then interchanging the order of summation yields the equations

$$\sum_c p^{s,c} \sum_h (x^{s,c}_h - \omega^{s,c}_h) = \sum_i r^{s,i} \left(\sum_h b^i_h \right) \quad (s = 0, 1, \ldots, N). \tag{6}$$

The system (6) implies, by virtue of Assumption A3, that if Equation (4) is satisfied, then Equation (5) is also satisfied. In other words, the bond market clearing equations are actually superfluous, and can be ignored.

(iii) Knowing that we needn't keep track of bond market clearing, there is no reason to keep track of the households' portfolio holdings either. Fortunately, again by virtue of Assumption A3, the spot market budget constraints in Equation (3) can be reduced to eliminate portfolio holdings. This can be seen as follows. Without loss of generality (by relabeling spots appropriately), we can partition

$$\mathbf{R} = \begin{bmatrix} R' \\ - \quad -- \quad - \\ R'' \end{bmatrix},$$

where R'' is an $(M \times M)$-dimensional, full-rank matrix. Now consider the $N+1$ budget constraints in Equation (3). Use the last M of these constraints to solve for b_h, substitute the resulting expression into the first $n+1 = (N+1) - M$, and rewrite these remaining, say, *reduced form budget constraints* in more compact form. This yields (by introducing suitable notation)

$$\psi(p)(x_h - \omega_h) = 0, \tag{7}$$

where

$$\psi(p) = \begin{bmatrix} p^0 & & & 0 & & \\ & \ddots & & & \ddots & \\ & & p^j & & a^{j,k}p^{n+k} & \\ & & & \ddots & & \ddots \\ & 0 & & & p^n & \end{bmatrix}$$

with $A = -R'R''^{-1}$, an $((n+1) \times M)$-dimensional matrix of, say, *reduced form bond returns*.

The *price function* ψ (which depends parametrically on bond returns R through their reduced form A) plays the same role in our incomplete markets model that the price vector $\boldsymbol{p}$ itself does in the standard Walrasian model. Notice, especially, that ψ, and hence Equation (7) is still linear in spot market prices. By utilizing these reduced form budget constraints, the optimization problem in Equation (3) can be converted into the convenient, concise form

$$\begin{aligned} &\text{Maximize } u_h(x_h) \\ &\text{subject to } \psi(p)(x_h - \omega_h) = 0. \end{aligned} \tag{8}$$

(Note: After this conversion, the implications of requiring that there be no arbitrage possibilities are not immediately apparent. Thus, it is worth remarking that Assumption A4 is, by virtue of one version of the Theorem of the Alternative (see, e.g., Corollary 2 to Theorem 2.9 in Gale (1960)), equivalent to the condition that

$$\text{there is some } v \in \mathbb{R}^{N+1}_{++} \text{such that } vR = 0. \tag{9}$$

In terms of A, it is easily verified that Equation (9) itself is equivalent to the condition that

$$\text{there is some } \lambda \in \mathbb{R}^{n+1}_{++} \text{such that } \lambda \mathrm{A} \gg 0; \tag{10}$$

simply partition $v = (v', v'')$ conformably with R, and identify $\lambda = v'$. Here the row vectors $\boldsymbol{v}$ and $\boldsymbol{\lambda}$ are implicit values or prices). Let the row vector $\boldsymbol{\lambda}_h = (\lambda_h^0, \ldots, \lambda_h^j, \ldots, \lambda_h^n)$ represent the Lagrange multipliers associated with the $n+1$ budget constraints in Equation (8). Then, the optimal solution to Equation (8) is characterized by Equation (7) together with the first-order conditions

$$Du_h(x_h)^T = \lambda_h \psi(p). \tag{11}$$

We denote the smooth demand functions generated from Equations (7) and (11) by $f_n : P \times \mathbb{R}^l \to \mathbb{R}^l$.

For future reference, it will be necessary to have an analogous description of standard Walrasian behavior, when Equations (7), (8), and (11) are replaced by

$$p(x_h - \omega_h) = 0, \tag{7'}$$

$$\begin{array}{c} \text{maximize } u_h(x_h) \\ \text{subject to } p(x_h - \omega_h) = 0, \end{array} \tag{8'}$$

and, say,

$$Du_h(x_h)^T = \mu_h p, \tag{11'}$$

respectively. We denote these smooth demand functions by $g_h : P \times \mathbb{R}^l \to \mathbb{R}^l$.

We conclude this subsection by explicitly noting that, after the foregoing reformulation, a financial equilibrium simply becomes a solution to the system of equations

$$\sum_h (f_n(p, \omega_h) - \omega_h) = 0. \tag{12}$$

The balance of this chapter is devoted to studying the structure of these solutions, a task accomplished through intensive analysis of the *equilibrium set*

$$E = \left\{ (p,\omega) \in P \times \Omega : \sum_h (f_h(p,\omega_h) - \omega_h) = 0 \right\}.$$

It will be convenient, in this analysis, to let

$$\begin{aligned} P_\omega &= (p \in P : (p,\omega) \in E) \quad \text{for } \omega \in \Omega \\ &= \text{set of financial equilibria} \\ &\quad \text{(corresponding to given goods endowments),} \\ &\quad f(p,\omega) = (f_1(p,\omega_1),\ldots,f_h(p,\omega_h),\ldots,f_m(p,\omega_m)), \end{aligned}$$

and

$$\begin{aligned} X_\omega &= \{x \in \Omega : \text{there is } p \in P_\omega \text{ such that } x = f(p,\omega)\} \quad \text{for } \omega \in \Omega \\ &= \text{set of equilibrium allocations} \\ &\quad \text{(corresponding to given goods endowments).} \end{aligned}$$

As we emphasized in the introduction, we are especially interested in the dimension of P_ω, or the degree of nominal indeterminacy, and how it translates into the dimension of X_ω, or the degree of real indeterminacy. It is very revealing to begin by looking closely at the simplest possible example, where $m = 2$, $L = 1$, $M = 1$, but $N = 2$.

3. The Leading Example: Geometric Intuition

In picturing this example, it is easiest to describe allocation, within the Edgeworth–Bowley box diagram, in terms of excess demands $z_1 = x_1 - \omega_1$ and $z_2 = x_2 - \omega_2$ (so that the origin for both our figures corresponds to ω_1 from Mr. 1's perspective, and ω_2 from Mr. 2's). Then, as background, recall the geometry involved in depicting equilibrium for the standard Walrasian model when there are only two households and three goods. Mr. *h's offer surface* is defined by the solutions to Equations (7′) and (11′), which (dropping superfluous superscripts and converting to excess demand) can be rewritten explicitly as

$$z_h^0 + p^1 z_h^1 + p^2 z_h^2 = 0 \tag{13'}$$

and

$$Du_h(z_h + \omega_h)^T = \mu_h(1, p^1, p^2).$$

In Equation (13′), z_h (together with μ_h) is parameterized by p, or, equivalently, by the *budget plane* generated by p. Equilibrium allocations in this model then correspond to just those points of intersection between

Mr. 1's and Mr. 2's offer surfaces which can be supported by a *common* budget plane, or, equivalently, at which the associated gradients of the two households' utility functions are colinear. Generally, such points of intersection will be isolated, and finite and odd in number.

Now consider the financial equilibrium model in the same context. Here, Mr. h's offer surface is defined by the solutions to Equations (7) and (11), which can be rewritten explicitly as

$$\begin{aligned} z_h^0 + a^0 p^2 z_h^2 &= 0, \\ p^1 z_h^1 + a^1 p^2 z_h^2 &= 0, \end{aligned} \tag{13}$$

and

$$Du_h(z_h + \omega_h)^T = (\lambda_h^0, \lambda_h^1 p^1, (\lambda_h^0 a^0 + \lambda_h^1 a^1) p^2).$$

So, by way of contrast with Equation (13′), in Equation (13) z_h (together with λ_h) is parameterized by p *given*

$$A = \begin{bmatrix} a^0 \\ a^1 \end{bmatrix},$$

or, equivalently, by the *budget line* generated by p given A.

Notice, in particular, that the orientation of these budget lines is determined solely by the sign pattern of A, and that, generally, they intersect opposite orthants (excluding – by virtue of the no-arbitrage condition (10) – both the positive and negative orthants). A typical point on Mr. 1's offer surface is illustrated in Figure 1 for the situation where $a^0 > 0$ and $a^1 < 0$

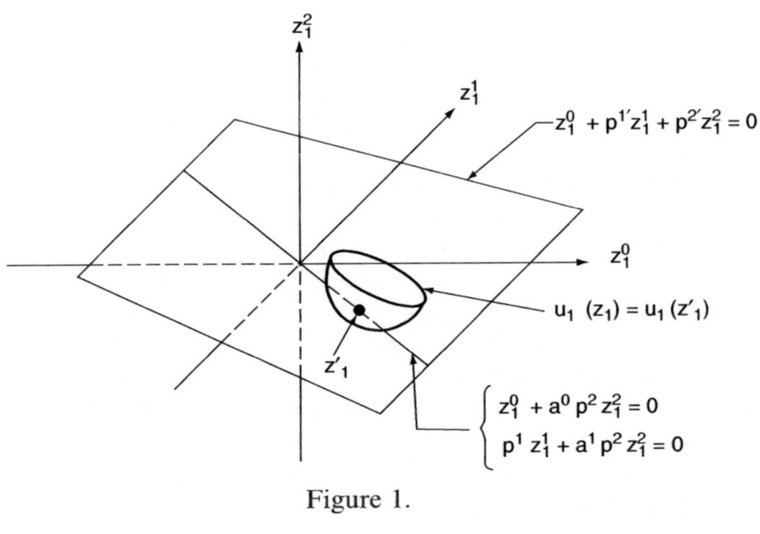

Figure 1.

(e.g., where

$$\begin{bmatrix} a^0 \\ a^1 \end{bmatrix} = \begin{bmatrix} \pi/\rho^1 \\ -\rho^2/\rho^1 \end{bmatrix}$$

corresponds to a bond with price $\pi > 0$ at spot 0, and yields $\rho^1 > 0$ and $\rho^2 > 0$ at spots 1 and 2, respectively).

In fact, it is obvious geometrically, and easily verified analytically that – restricting attention to the appropriate pair of opposite orthants – the solutions to Equation (13) are identical to those for Equation (13′): For specificity, again suppose that $a^0 > 0$ and $a^1 < 0$ (so that, typically, $z_h^s \neq 0$ and sign $z_h^0 = -\text{sign } z_h^1 = -\text{sign } z_h^2$). Then, on the one hand, if (z_h, λ_h) satisfies Equation (13) for some p given A, $(z_h, \mu_h = \lambda_h^0)$ satisfies Equation (13′) when p is replaced by

$$p' = \left(1, [\lambda_h^1/\lambda_h^0]p^1, [a^0 + (\lambda_h^1/\lambda_h^0)a^1]p^2\right).$$

On the other hand, if (z_h, μ_h) satisfies Equation (13′) for some, say, $p = p'$, then $(z_h, \lambda_h = \mu_h(1, [a^0 z_h^1/a^1 z_h^0]p^{1'}))$ satisfies Equation (13) for

$$p = \left(1, \left[\frac{a^1 z_h^0}{a^0 z_h^1}\right], \left[\frac{-z_h^0}{a^0 z_h^2}\right]\right)$$

given A. In other words, for all practical purposes, the offer surfaces generated by spot-cum-bond markets are the same as those generated by Walrasian markets. So, taking license, we can simply refer to "the" offer surfaces. This fact is also depicted in Figure 1.

What is the significant difference between these two models then? Just this: In the financial equilibrium model, equilibrium allocations correspond to *all* points of intersection between Mr. 1's and Mr. 2's offer surfaces (still restricting attention to the appropriate pair of opposite orthants); each such point is "supported" by a common budget line. Generally, this set of equilibrium allocations will contain a smooth curve. (Note: This absolutely fundamental result does not follow immediately from geometric considerations alone. The differential analysis in the following section – when applied to this leading example – reveals that, except for a nongeneric subset of endowments, the offer surfaces will intersect in a curve in *each* permissible pair of opposite orthants.) In Figure 2, we display the situation where $Du_1(\omega_1)$ and $Du_2(\omega_2)$ are not colinear, and a^0 and a^1 are signed in such a way that budget lines "support" a curve including the endowment point. (The reader is free to attempt visualizing the alternative situation where the set of equilibrium allocations does not contain (ω_1, ω_2)).

Notice too that the case depicted in Figure 2 also illustrates Hart's striking observation, namely, that with an incomplete market structure,

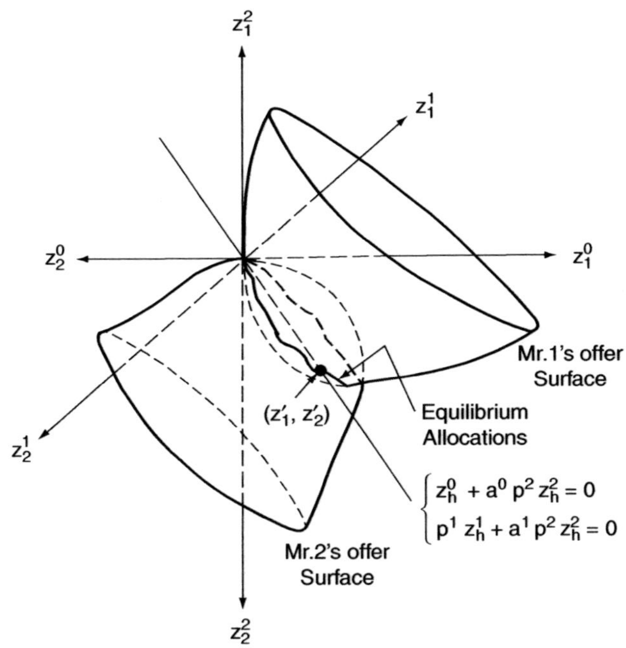

Figure 2.

it may be possible to Pareto rank some of the equilibrium allocations. Here, the endowment point is Pareto dominated by *every* other equilibrium allocation.

A moment's reflection should make it clear that this line of argument is not limited to our polar specification of financial markets. Budget lines – rather than budget planes – result from incomplete markets – not from exogenous yields. Thus, in particular, even when yields depend on spot prices, budget lines may "support" an enormous number of the points of intersection between offer surfaces. The pertinent issue is simply whether or not the induced return structure still admits enough perturbation of these budget lines (through, for instance, perturbation of spot prices).

To be concrete, suppose that, instead of a bond, the single financial instrument is an installment contract to buy the good at both spots 1 and 2. (Here, the spots are best interpreted as today, tomorrow in event α, and tomorrow in event β.) The down payment is π, at spot 0; the only installment payment is q, at both spots 1 and 2. In short, the "price" of the financial instrument is π, and it promises yields of $\rho^s = p^s - q$ at $s = 1, 2$. Under this specification, the analogue of the budget line described by the first two equations in Equation (13) is

$$z_h^0 + \left[\frac{\pi}{p^2 - q}\right] p^2 z_h^2 = 0$$

and

$$p^1 z_h^1 - \left[\frac{p^1 - q}{p^2 - q}\right] p^2 z_h^2 = 0$$

or, better,

$$z_h^0 + \left[\frac{\pi}{(p^2 - q)/p^2}\right] z_h^2 = 0 \tag{14}$$

and

$$z_h^1 - \left[\frac{(p^1 - q)/p^1}{(p^2 - q)/p^2}\right] z_h^2 = 0.$$

By comparing the two budget lines, it is easily seen that, for instance, treating π as a variable and q as a parameter, each budget set in our model corresponds to some budget set in this model, whatever the sign pattern of A. So, the set of equilibrium allocations now *contains* the set generated by our model. (Indeed, even treating both π and q as parameters, the set of equilibrium allocations will still generally contain a smooth curve.)

This particular respecification is especially favorable for conveying our central message. Less dramatically, we can conceive of the yields depending on spot prices (and other variables or parameters) in more restricted fashion, say,

$$\rho^s = \phi^s(p^s), \quad s = 1, 2,$$

where $\phi^s(p^s)/p^s$ has bounded range. Then, typically, the extent of real indeterminacy will be more circumscribed. However, it is only in the extreme case

$$\phi^s(p^s) = \delta^s p^s, \quad \delta^s \neq 0 \text{ given}, \ s = 1, 2,$$

where $\phi^s(p^s)/p^s = \delta^s$ is constant, that we would be assured of generic local uniqueness: Under this specification, the budget line now becomes

$$z_h^0 + \left[\frac{\pi}{\delta^2}\right] z_h^2 = 0 \tag{15}$$

and

$$z_h^1 + \left[\frac{\delta^1}{\delta^2}\right] z_h^1 = 0.$$

Generally, even treating π as a variable (which is necessary to ensure existence of financial equilibrium), such budget lines simply cannot "support" more than a limited number of the points of intersection between offer surfaces.

We must stress explicitly that, even under our own specification, there are also several extreme circumstances in which there will be no real indeterminacy.

To begin with, the leading example itself requires $m = 2$; with a single household, the only equilibrium allocation is the household's endowment. Moreover, even with two households, when $Du_1(\omega_1)$ and $Du_2(\omega_2)$ are colinear, so that the endowments already constitute a Pareto optimal allocation, again the only equilibrium allocation is the households' endowments. (In this case, the sole point of intersection between offer surfaces is a tangency at the endowment point.)

Broadly speaking, this pair of borderline cases indicates that – in order for nominal to translate into real indeterminacy – there must be sufficiently disparate incentives for exchange of goods (in terms of both number and, implicitly, diversity of households).

Finally, we notice that, even given exogenous yields, we may encounter the same sort of difficulty which is inherent in the budget line (15). This would occur, however, only in the borderline cases where $a^0 = 0$ or $a^1 = 0$, where the budget line (13) must lie in the plane $z_h^0 = 0$ or the plane $z_h^1 = 0$, respectively. Again broadly speaking, this indicates that there must be sufficiently flexible opportunities for exchange of credit (within the confines of incomplete bond markets).

In the next section, where we present our main result, we adopt two additional assumptions (and employ the differential approach) just so as to avoid these various kinds of borderline cases.

4. The General Structure: Analytic Results

4.1. Properties of Financial Equilibrium

Since this subsection (as well as the end of the following subsection) is likely to be read only by specialists, we will be fairly terse.

Essentially, here we formalize the following observation. The system (12) consists of l equations in the $(l-1)+ml$ variables p and ω (bear in mind that $p^{0,1} = 1$ is not treated as a variable). However, by virtue of the $n+1$ budget constraints in Equation (8), $n+1$ of these equations are redundant. So we would expect, generally, to have $[(l-1)+ml]-[1-(n+1)] = n+ml$ degrees of freedom in solving the remaining equations, or, equivalently, treating the ml endowments as parameters, we would expect, generally, to have n degrees of freedom in choosing equilibrium spot prices.

Our first basic theorem is the precise parallel, in our specific setting, of fundamental results for the standard Walrasian model which are recapitulated (from earlier work) in Theorems 3.1.2 and 3.2.2 in Balasko (1988).

For the typical household h, identify $\mathbb{R}^{n+1}$ with the set of possible reduced form wealths, and $\mathbb{R}^{l-(n+1)}$ with, say, the set of possible goods endowments exclusive of the first good at spots $s = 0,1, \dots , n$.

Theorem 1. *E is a smooth, $(n+ml)$-dimensional manifold. Moreover, E is diffeomorphic to*

$$P \times (\mathbb{R}^{n+1})^m \times (\mathbb{R}^{l-(n+1)})^{m-1}.$$

In order to proceed with our program, we need to introduce additional parameters into the description of the equilibrium manifold (so that it can be suitably projected into a smooth, equal-dimensional, connected manifold encompassing the set of possible goods endowments). This is accomplished by utilizing a variant of the parameterization originally employed by Cass (1984, 1985, 1988). This simple but very useful trick – which involves singling out the behavior of Mr. 1 for special treatment – basically enables us to fully exploit the common linear structure of the reduced form budget constraints Equation (7).

Let

$$\Lambda = \{\lambda \in \mathbb{R}^{n+1}_{++} : \lambda^0 = 1 \text{ and } \lambda A \gg 0\}$$

represent the set of possible (normalized) Lagrange multipliers in the first-order condition (11), noting that it is an open, n-dimensional and convex (hence connected) set. Also let

$$E_1 = \left\{(p,\lambda,\omega) \in P \times \Lambda \times \Omega : (g_1(\lambda\psi(p),\omega_1) - \omega_1) + \sum_{h>1}(f_h(p,\omega_h) - \omega_h) = 0\right\}$$

represent the set generated by the Equation (12) after replacing Mr. 1's demand with his standard Walrasian demand at "individualized" prices composed by multiplying (normalized) Lagrange multipliers together with the price function ψ.

Theorem 2. *E is diffeomorphic to E_1.*

Eventually we use this smooth relationship between E and E_1 to establish that, generically, the set of equilibrium allocations X_ω has smooth, n-dimensional submanifold structure largely because, generically, the set of financial equilibria P_ω has the same nice structure. In order to verify this latter result, we require, as suggested above, analogues of important properties enjoyed by the natural projection of the equilibrium manifold for the standard Walrasian model (see, especially, Chapter 4 in Balasko (1988)).

Let π_{E_1} denote the restriction to E_1 of the projection of $P \times \Lambda \times \Omega$ onto $\Lambda \times \Omega$, and V the set of its regular values in $\Lambda \times \Omega$.

Theorem 3. π_{E_1} *is proper and subjective. Hence, in particular,* $\Lambda \times \Omega \backslash V$ *is a closed set of Lebesque measure zero, so that* V *is an open, dense subset of* $\Lambda \times \Omega$.

We mention in passing that this theorem provides a direct proof of existence for the most general smooth formulation of this type of financial equilibrium model (the problem previously studied by Cass (1984), Werner (1985), and Duffie (1987) for particular – but not necessarily smooth – formulations of such models). Evidently, our result could be applied, by using suitable approximation techniques, to establish existence for a larger class of models in which utility functions are merely required to be continuous.

4.2. Indeterminacy of Equilibrium Allocation

The main result of this chapter, stated in the following theorem, requires two additional assumptions (besides the maintained Assumptions A1–A4). First, there must be enough participants in the market relative to its deficiency of bonds:

Assumption A5. $m > n$.

Second, there must be enough variety of nonzero elements in the matrix of reduced form bond returns, as, for instance, given in Assumption A6:

Assumption A6. $a^{0,k} \neq 0,\ k = 1, 2, \ldots, M,$ *and* $a^{j,1} \neq 0,\ j = 1, 2, \ldots, n.$

Although there are alternatives (particularly for Assumption A6) some version of each assumption is indispensable (as our discussion of the leading example surely made plain). We return to this issue at the beginning of the following section.

Theorem 4. *If* Assumptions A5 and A6 *are satisfied, then there is an open, dense subset of* Ω, *say,* $\tilde{\Omega}$, *such that, for every* $\omega \in \tilde{\Omega}, X_\omega$ *contains a smooth, n-dimensional submanifold, say,* $\tilde{X}_\omega$.

Thus, repeating for emphasis (and suppressing all technicalities), *market incompleteness typically leads to (at least) a comparable degree of allocation indeterminateness.*

This fundamental theorem follows from a series of three related lemmas. Referring back to the leading example, the argument essentially generalizes the fact that a typical point of intersection between offer surfaces will not be supported by a common plane (and must therefore lie on a curve of intersections between offer surfaces which are only "supported" by common budget lines).

In order to develop this insight, we unfortunately (but unavoidably) require more notation. Given Assumption A5, let the subscript 0 denote the first $n+1$ households, so that, for example, $x_0 = (x_1, \ldots, x_h, \ldots, x_{n+1})$. Also let

$$\mathbf{D}_0^{\bullet 1}(x_0) = \begin{bmatrix} D_{x^{0,1}} u_1(x_1) & \ldots & D_{x^{j,1}} u_1(x_1) & \ldots & D_{x^{n,1}} u_1(x_1) \\ \vdots & \ddots & & & \\ D_{x^{0,1}} u_h(x_h) & \ldots & D_{x^{j,1}} u_h(x_h) & & \\ \vdots & & & \ddots & \\ D_{x^{0,1}} u_{n+1}(x_{n+1}) & & & & D_{x^{n,1}} u_{n+1}(x_{n+1}) \end{bmatrix}$$

an $(n+1)^2$-dimensional matrix,

$$\tilde{V} = \{(\lambda, \omega) \in V : \text{there is } (p, \lambda, \omega) \in \pi_{E_1}^{-1}(\lambda, \omega)$$
$$\text{such that rank } D_0^{\bullet 1}(f_0(p, \omega_0)) = n + 1\}$$

and

$$\tilde{\Omega} = \{\omega \in \Omega : \text{there is } \lambda \in \Lambda \text{ such that } (\lambda, \omega) \in \tilde{V}\}.$$

Lemma 1. *$\tilde{V}$ is an open, dense subset of V (and hence of $\Lambda \times \Omega$).*

Lemma 2. *$\tilde{\Omega}$ is an open, dense subset of Ω. Furthermore, for every $\omega \in \tilde{\Omega}$, there is a smooth, n-dimensional submanifold of P_ω, say $\tilde{P}_\omega$, such that, for every $p \in \tilde{P}_\omega$,*

$$\text{rank } D_0^{\bullet 1}(f_0(p, \omega_0)) = n + 1.$$

Lemma 3. *For every $\omega \in \tilde{\Omega}$, f restricted to $\tilde{P}_\omega \times \{\omega\}$ is a diffeormophism. Hence, in particular, for every $\omega \in \tilde{\Omega}$,*

$$\tilde{X}_\omega = f(\tilde{P}_\omega, \omega)$$

is a smooth, n-dimensional submanifold of X_ω.

5. Refinement and Extension

In this section, we indicate how the purely mathematic requirement A6 can be replaced by a more meaningful economic assumption, and how Theorem 4 extends to encompass variability in bond returns (e.g., because of variability in some prices or yields). This analysis presupposes familiarity with the basic logic of the proof for Theorem 4, in particular, some appreciation of the important part played by the construct (25) in its last step.

5.1. Availability of Positive Credit

The role of Assumption A6 is to guarantee that the right-hand side of Equation (25) describes a diffeomorphism. This assumption, just as would any wholly algebraic alternative, suffers from two serious defects: First, it is couched in terms of the reduced form matrix A rather than the bond return matrix R itself. Second, even translated from A to R, it would be difficult to interpret and justify when additional institutional structure is employed to specify a detailed pattern of bond returns. For this reason, we believe that it is important to try to provide substantive alternatives. Here we provide one such assumption, which has the virtues of being both intelligible and plausible.

So now assume, without any loss of generality (by relabeling spot 0), that it is possible to transfer wealth from spot 0 to all other spots $s>0$:

Assumption A6′. *There is* $b^+ \in \mathbb{R}^M$ *such that* $r^0 b^+ < 0$ *and* $r^s b^+ > 0$, $s = 1,2, \ldots, N$.

Assumption A6′ would be satisfied, for instance, in the leading case when the bond market potentially supplies inside money, that is, when there is a bond which has price 1 as well as identical yields 1.

Parallel with the reduction in Assumption A4 to condition (10), Assumption A6′ can be reduced to the equivalent condition

$$\text{there is } \mu \in \mathbb{R}^M_{++} \text{ such that } a^0\mu > 0 \text{ and } a^j\mu < 0,\ j = 1, 2, \ldots, n; \qquad (16)$$

simply identify $\mu = R''b^+$ We present a pair of results which establish that conditions (10) and (16) suffice to guarantee that the right-hand side of Equation (25) describes a diffeomorphism.

Careful scrutiny of this key matrix expansion shows that its critical elements are those involving the spot price ratios for the first type of good. Identify $\boldsymbol{q}^s$ with $p^{s,1}$ for $s \neq 0$ (so that $\boldsymbol{q}$ is a positive, N-dimensional vector) and $b^{j,k}$ with $a^{j,k}(p^{n+k,1}/p^{j,1})$ (so that, basically, B is an arbitrary,

($(n+1) \times M$)-dimensional matrix). Now consider the mapping such that $q \to B$ according to the system of equations

$$a^{0,k}q^{n+k} = b^{0,k} \quad (k = 1, 2, \ldots, M), \tag{17}$$

and

$$-b^{j,k}q^j + a^{j,k}q^{n+k} = 0 \quad (j = 1, 2, \ldots, n; \; k = 1, 2, \ldots, M).$$

It is easily checked that the right-hand side of Equation (25) describes a diffeomorphism provided that, taking both A and B as given, if $q \gg 0$ is a solution to Equation (17), then it is the unique positive solution.

In order to characterize when this is the case, and thus, on these grounds justify Assumption A6′, let

$$J = \{0, 1, \ldots, n\},$$
$$K = \{1, 2, \ldots, M\},$$

and

$$K^0 = \{k \in K : a^{0,k} \neq 0\}.$$

Lemma 4. If $q \gg 0$ *is a solution to Equation* (17)*, then it is the unique positive solution if and only if A satisfies the two conditions*

(i) $K^0 \neq \emptyset$, *and*

(ii) *there are no subsets* $J' \subset J$ and $K' \subset K$ *such that*

$$0 \in J' \quad \text{and} \quad K^0 \subset K',$$
$$J' \neq J \quad \text{or} \quad K' \neq K,$$

while $j \notin J',\ k \in K' \Rightarrow a^{j,k} = 0$ *and* $j \in J',\ k \notin K' \Rightarrow a^{j,k} = 0$.

Theorem 5. *If A satisfies conditions* (10) and (16), *then it also satisfies conditions (i) and (ii) in* Lemma 4.

Note that Example 2 satisfies Assumption A6′, but that Example 3 doesn't. However, more realistic embedding of foreign exchange markets in a broader institutional context, including domestic financial markets, would clearly remedy this deficiency.

5.2. Variability of Bond Returns

Refer again to Examples 2 and 3. In both instances it would make sense to consider some of the nonzero elements of the bond returns R as variables rather than as parameters. Moreover, one can calculate (for particular choices of a square, full-rank submatrix) the effect of varying these elements on the reduced form A, and thus, presumably, on the degree of real indeterminacy. But – even for these fairly trivial examples – what a tangle! (Try your hand in the simplest possible setting involving Equation (2), where $m = 2$ and $L = 1$.) In order to cut through this thicket, we think it is reasonable instead to abstract even further, and to study the more general problem: Granted sufficient variability of bond returns, what might be the maximal degree of real indeterminacy in our model?

So consider varying A within

$$\begin{aligned} A &= \{A \in (\mathbb{R}^M)^{n+1} : \text{there is } \lambda \in \mathbb{R}^{n+1}_{++} \text{ such that } \lambda A \gg 0\} \\ &= \text{the set of all reduced form bond return matrices that entail no} \\ &\quad\ \text{arbitrage possibilities.} \end{aligned}$$

Correspondingly, redefine the domains of the functions ψ and f_h to include A explicitly, and the ambient space of the equilibrium set $E \subset P \times A \times \Omega$ to be $\mathbb{R}^l \times (\mathbb{R}^M)^{n+1} \times \mathbb{R}^l$. (Here we use the symbol $(\mathbb{R}^M)^{n+1}$ to denote the space of all $((n+1) \times M)$-dimensional matrices.) Also, now let

$$\begin{aligned} E_1 = \{(p, A, \lambda, \omega) \in p \times \Gamma \times \Omega : (g_1(\lambda\psi(p, A), \omega_1) - \omega_1) \\ + \sum_{h>1} (f_h(p, A, \omega_h) - \omega_h) = 0\}, \end{aligned}$$

where

$$\Gamma = \{(A, \lambda) \in A \times \mathbb{R}^{n+1}_{++} : \lambda^0 = 1 \text{ and } \lambda A \gg 0\},$$

an open, $((n+1)\ M + n)$-dimensional, connected set, and let

$$\pi_{E_1} = \text{restriction to } E_1 \text{ of the projection of } P \times \Gamma \times \Omega \text{ onto } \Gamma \times \Omega.$$

It is easily checked that, mutatis mutandis, Theorems 1–3 remain valid. Note especially that, with variable bond returns,

$$\dim E = \dim(\Gamma \times \Omega) = (n+1)M + n + ml.$$

However, not all this potential nominal variability contributes to increasing the degree of real indeterminacy since different reduced forms A may represent identical financial opportunities. In particular, it turns out that the maximal degree of real indeterminacy is nM; this is the dimension of the Grassmanian manifold of all M-dimensional linear subspaces in N-dimensional Eucidean space.

The intuition behind this last observation (and the reason for this particular degree of indeterminacy) is the following. Go back to the extensive form of our model (3)–(5). The budget set, that is, the set of consumption demands x_h, which can be financed by some portfolio holdings b_h, is unaffected if each budget constraint in Equation (3) is multiplied by an arbitrary positive constant. Picking such constants to accord with the no-arbitrage condition (9), this means that nothing is lost by restricting attention to bond return matrices **R** such that

$$\mathbf{1}\mathbb{R} = 0.$$

But these generate portfolio wealth subspaces

$$W = \{w \in \mathbb{R}^{N+1} : \text{there is } b \in \mathbb{R}^{M} \text{such that } w = Rb\}$$

such that

$$\dim W = M$$

and $W \subset \{w \in \mathbb{R}^{N+1} : \mathbf{1}w = 0\}$ (which is isomorphic to $\mathbb{R}^N$), while different financial opportunities simply correspond to different portfolio wealth subspaces.

Theorem 6. *If* Assumption A5 *is satisfied, then there is an open, dense subset of* Ω, *say* $\tilde{\tilde{\Omega}}$, *such that, for every* $\omega \in \tilde{\tilde{\Omega}}$, X_ω *contains a smooth, nM-dimensional submanifold, say,* $\tilde{\tilde{X}}_\omega$.

Acknowledgments

This is a substantially revised version of CARESS Working Paper #85-23. Comments by a number of colleagues, as well as criticism by the referees of this journal, have been extremely helpful, we believe, in improving our presentation. We also gratefully acknowledge research support from the Swiss and U.S. National Science Foundations (under Grants #1.118.0.85 and SES-8509957, respectively).

Appendix

Proof of Theorem 1. Since this argument basically mimics those in the proofs of Theorems 3.1.2 and 3.2.2 in Balasko (1988), there is no need to repeat them entirely. Rather, we content ourselves with presenting an independent demonstration of the first property.

Because

$$\operatorname{rank} \psi(p) = n + 1 \quad \text{for } p \in P$$

while, from the budget constraints in Equation (8),

$$\psi(p) \sum_h (f_h(p, \omega_h) - \omega_h)^T = 0,$$

we know that the Jacobian of Equation (12) has, at most, rank equal to $l-(n+1)$. To see that, in fact, it always has maximal rank – and that, therefore, E can be parameterized locally – simply observe that, for example,

$$\text{rank}\frac{\partial \sum_h (f_h(p,\omega_h)-\omega_h)}{\partial \omega_1} = \text{rank}\frac{\partial (f_1(p,\omega_1)-\omega_1)}{\partial \omega_1} = l-(n+1)$$

(see Proposition 2 in Balasko and Cass (1985)). The claimed dimensionality of E then follows directly from the standard calculation

$$\begin{aligned}\dim E &= \dim(p \times \Omega) - \text{codim } E \\ &= [(l-1)+ml] - [l-(n+1)] = n+ml.\end{aligned}$$

Proof of Theorem 2. Consider the mappings α: $E \to P \times \Lambda \times \Omega$ such that

$$(p,\omega) \mapsto (p, ([D_{x^{s,1}} u_1(f_1(p,\omega_1))]/[p^{s,1} D_{x^{0,1}} u_1(f_1(p,\omega_1))], s=0,1,\ldots,n), \omega)$$

and

$$\beta : E_1 \to P \times \Omega \quad \text{such that} \quad (p,\lambda,\omega) \mapsto (p,\omega).$$

On the one hand, if $(p,\ \omega) \in E$, then – comparing the Lagrangean conditions (7′) and (11′) (with p replaced by $\lambda\psi(p)$) to Equations (7) and (11) for $h=1$ – it follows that $g_1(\lambda\psi(p),\omega_1) = f_1(p,\omega_1)$ when $\lambda = \lambda_1/\lambda_1^0$, or that $\alpha(p,\ \omega) \in E_1$. On the other hand, if $(p,\ \lambda,\ \omega) \in E_1$, then

$$g_1(\lambda\psi(p),\omega_1) - \omega_1 = -\sum_{h>1}(f_h(p,\omega_h) - \omega_h),$$

and – utilizing the budget constraints (7) for $h>1$ – it follows that

$$\psi(p)(g_1(\lambda\psi(p),\omega_1) - \omega_1) = 0.$$

Hence, since $(x_1,\mu_1) = (g_1(\lambda\psi(p),\omega_1), D_{x^{0,1}} u_1(g_1(\lambda\psi(p),\omega_1)))$ also satisfies the first-order condition (7′) (with p replaced by $\lambda\psi(p)$), $(x_1,\mu_1\lambda)$ satisfies the Lagrangean conditions (7) and (11), or $f_1(p,\omega_1) = g_1(\lambda\psi(p),\omega_1)$, or $\beta(p,\lambda,\omega) \in E$. So $\alpha(E) = E_1$.

Finally, it is obvious that $\beta \circ \alpha$ is the identity on E, and that both α and β are smooth.

Proof of Theorem 3. (Properness): We need to show that, if $K \subset \Lambda \times \Omega$ is compact, then $\pi_{E_1}^{-1}(K)$ is also compact. So consider a sequence $(p^\nu,\lambda^\nu,\omega^\nu)$, $\nu = 1,2,\ldots,$ such that

$$(p^\nu,\lambda^\nu,\omega^\nu) \in \pi_{E_1}^{-1}(K). \tag{18}$$

Since K is compact, the sequence $(\lambda^\nu,\omega^\nu), \nu = 1,2,\ldots,$ has a convergent subsequence, without any loss of generality, the original sequence itself, such that

$$\lim_{\nu\to\infty}(\lambda^\nu,\omega^\nu)=(\lambda,\omega)\in K. \tag{19}$$

What is required, then, is to demonstrate that a sequence satisfying Equations (18) and (19) has a convergent subsequence, again without any loss of generality, the original sequence itself, such that

$$\lim_{\nu\to\infty}(p^\nu,\lambda^\nu,\omega^\nu)=(p,\lambda,\omega)\in \pi_{E^1}^{-1}(\lambda,\omega).$$

Now Equation (19) implies that there are bounds $\underline{\omega},\bar{\omega}\in\Omega$ such that $\underline{\omega}\le\omega^\nu\le\bar{\omega}$. Using the lower bound $\underline{\omega}$, monotonicity of u_h implies that $u_h(\underline{\omega}_h)\le u_h(\omega_h^\nu)\le u_h(x_h^\nu)$ (where $x_1^\nu=g_1(\lambda^\nu\psi(p^\nu),\omega_1^\nu)$ and $x_h^\nu=f_h(p^\nu,\omega_h^\nu)$, $h=2,3,\ldots,m$), so that the lower boundedness of indifference surfaces themselves implies that there is also a lower bound $\underline{x}\in\Omega$ such that $\underline{x}\le x^\nu$. Thus, now using this lower bound $\underline{x}$ together with the upper bound $\bar{\omega}$, goods market clearing $\sum_h(x_h^\nu-\omega_h^\nu)=0$ implies that

$$x_1^\nu=\sum_h\omega_h^\nu-\sum_{h>1}x_h^\nu\le\sum_h\bar{\omega}_h-\sum_{h>1}\underline{x}_h.$$

Hence, we can assume, without any loss of generality, that

$$\lim_{\nu\to\infty}x_1^\nu=x_1\in\mathbb{R}^l. \tag{20}$$

Consider the corresponding sequence of first-order condition (11′) (with $p=\lambda^\nu\psi(p^\nu)$) for $h=1$. By smoothness and monotonicity of u_1 it follows from $D_{h^{0,1}}u_1(x_1^\nu)=\mu_1^\nu$ and Equation (20) that

$$\lim_{\nu\to\infty}\mu_1^\nu=\mu_1\in\mathbb{R}_+,$$

and therefore from

$$D_{x^s}u_1(x_1^\nu)^T=\mu_1^\nu\lambda^{s\nu}p^{s\nu}\qquad(s=0,1,\ldots,n)$$
$$=\mu_1^\nu\left(\sum_j\lambda^{j\nu}a^{j,s-n}\right)p^{s\nu}\qquad(s=n+1,n+2,\ldots,N),$$

Equations (19) and (20) that

$$\lim_{\nu\to\infty}p^\nu=p\in P.$$

Moreover, since g_1 and f_h, $h=2,3,\ldots,m$, are all continuous, $(p,\lambda,\omega)\in\pi_{E_1}^{-1}(\lambda,\omega)$, and the argument is complete.

(Subjectivity): Consider a Pareto optimal allocation $\omega^*\in\Omega$ supported by prices $p'\in P$. Pick $\lambda^*\in\Lambda$, and let

$$p^* = \left(p^{0'}, p^{1'}/\lambda^{1*}, \ldots, p^{n'}/\lambda^{n*}, p^{n+1'} \Big/ \sum_j \lambda^{j*} a^{j1}, \ldots, p^{N'} \Big/ \sum_j \lambda^{j*} a^{jM}\right),$$

$$\mu_1 = D_{x^{0,1}} u_1(\omega_1^*),$$

and

$$\lambda_h = D_{x^{0,1}} u_h(\omega_h^*)\lambda^* \quad (h = 2, 3, \ldots, m).$$

It is easily checked (using the Lagrangean conditions (7′) and (11′) for $h = 1$, and conditions (7) and (11) otherwise) that

$$\omega_1^* = g_1(\lambda^* \psi(p^*), \omega_1^*)$$

and

$$\omega_h^* - f_h(p^*, \omega_h^*) \quad (h = 2, 3, \ldots, m),$$

and (using the Pareto optimality of ω^*) that, in fact,

$$\pi_{E_1}^{-1}(\lambda^*, \omega^*) = \{(p^*, \lambda^*, \omega^*)\}.$$

It is also easily checked that $(\lambda^*, \omega^*) \in V$: Direct calculation reveals that

$$\frac{\partial\left((g_1^{s,c}(\lambda^*\psi(p^*), \omega_1^*) - \omega_1^{s,c^*}) + \sum_{h>1}(f_h^{s,c}(p^*, \omega_h^*) - \omega_h^{s,c^*}), (s,c) \neq (0,1)\right)}{\partial(p^{s,c}, (s,c) \neq (0,1))}$$

$$= \left[B_1 + \sum_{h>1} B_h\right] \begin{bmatrix} I_{L-1} & & & & & & 0 \\ & \lambda^{1*} I_L & & & & & \\ & & \ddots & & & & \\ & & & \lambda^{n*} I_L & & & \\ & & & & \left(\sum_j \lambda^{j*} a^{j,1}\right) I_L & & \\ & & & & & \ddots & \\ & 0 & & & & & \left(\sum_j \lambda^{j*} a^{j,M}\right) I_L \end{bmatrix}, \tag{21}$$

where the $(l-1)^2$-dimensional matrix B_1 is negative definite, the $(l-1)^2$-dimensional matrix B_h is negative semi-definite, h=2,3, … , m, and, for example, I_L is the L^2-dimensional identity (see, especially, Theorem 2 in Balasko and Cass (1985)). Hence, Equation (21) has maximal rank $l-1$, so that, by definition, (λ^*, ω^*) is a regular value of π_{E_1}.

Thus, we have a regular value whose inverse image contains an odd number of elements. Moreover, π_{E_1} is a smooth, proper mapping from a smooth, boundaryless manifold into a smooth, connected manifold of the same dimension. It follows from the Theorem on page 24 of Milnor (1965) that the mod 2 degree of π_{E_1}, that is, $\#\pi_{E_1}^{-1}(\lambda, \omega)$ (modulo 2), is the same for all regular values. So, on the one hand, $\pi_{E_1}^{-1}(\lambda, \omega) \neq \varnothing$ for $(\lambda, \omega) \in V$. On the other hand, by definition, $\pi_{E_1}^{-1}(\lambda, \omega) \neq \varnothing$ for $(\lambda, \omega) \in (\Lambda \times \Omega) \backslash V$. So $\pi_{E_1}(E_1) = \Lambda \times \Omega$.

(Genericity): Given properness and subjectivity, this follows immediately from Sard's Theorem (see, e.g., Milnor (1965, p. 25)).

Proof of Theorem 4. Note that, in the course of proving Theorem 2, we likewise established that if $(p, \lambda, \omega) \in E_1$, then $g_1(\lambda\psi(p), \omega_1) = f_1(p, \omega_1)$. So, while ostensibly analyzing in terms of E_1, we are permitted, for example, expressly calculating in terms of the first-order condition (11). These play a major role in the argument, and it is useful to transform them slightly at the outset. So let

$$\bar{\lambda}_h = (\lambda_h^0 p^{0,1}, \ldots, \lambda_h^j p^{j,1}, \ldots, \lambda_h^n p^{n,1}),$$

and

$$\underline{p}^s = (p^{s,2}/p^{s,1}, \ldots, p^{s,c}/p^{s,1}, \ldots, p^{s,L}/p^{s,1}) \quad (s = 0, 1, \ldots, N).$$

Then rewrite Equation (11) substituting $\bar{\lambda}_h$ and $(1, \underline{p}^s)$ for λ_h and p^s,

$$Du_h(x_h)^T = \lambda_h \psi(p)$$

$$= \lambda_h \begin{bmatrix} p^0 & & & & \\ & \ddots & 0 & \ddots & \\ & & p^j & & a^{j,k}\ p^{n+k} \\ & 0 & & \ddots & \ddots \\ & & & p^n & \end{bmatrix}$$

$$= \bar{\lambda}_h \begin{bmatrix} (1, \underline{p}^0) & & & & \\ & \ddots & 0 & & \ddots \\ & & (1, \underline{p}^j) & & a^{j,k}\ (p^{n+k,1}/p^{j,1})\ (1, \underline{p}^{n+k}) \\ & 0 & & \ddots & \ddots \\ & & & (1, \underline{p}^n) & \end{bmatrix} \tag{22}$$

Proof of Lemma 1. For convenience, let

$$P_{(\lambda,\omega)} = \{p \in P : (p, \lambda, \omega) \in \pi_{E_1}^{-1}(\lambda, \omega)\} \text{ for } (\lambda, \omega) \in \Lambda \times \Omega.$$

Then, to begin with, take $(\lambda', \omega') \in$ V.

(Openness): If $(\lambda', \omega') \in \tilde{V}$, then, since V is open, while D_0^{-1} and f_0 are continuous, there is a neighborhood of (λ', ω'), say, $\tilde{V}'$, such that $\tilde{V}' \subset \tilde{V}$.

(Denseness): Now suppose $(\lambda', \omega') \notin \tilde{V}$ (since otherwise there's nothing left to prove). Consider an arbitrary neighborhood of (λ', ω') in V, say, V'. Then we can construct $(\lambda', \omega) \in V'$ and $p \in P_{(\lambda,\omega)}$ such that

$$\text{rank } D_0^{\bullet 1}(f_0(p, \omega_0)) = n + 1 \tag{23}$$

as follows: (i) Pick $p \in P_{(\lambda',\omega')}$ and (ii) Take $x' = f(p, \omega')$. Recall the fact that R^l (the commodity space) is diffeomorphic to $P \times W$ (the standard Walrasian price–wealth space) through each of the mappings

$$x_h \mapsto (p, w) = (Du_h(x_h)^T, Du_h(x_h)^T x_h)/D_{x^{0,1}} u_h(x_h)$$

(see, e.g., Theorem 2.4.1 in Balasko (1988)). This entails that, given p, the first-order condition (22) transforms sufficiently small perturbations of $\bar{\lambda}_h/\bar{\lambda}_h^0$ into arbitrarily small perturbations of $(x_h, \bar{\lambda}_h)$. So we can pick $\bar{\lambda}_h/\bar{\lambda}_h^0 \in \mathbb{R}^{n+1}_{++}$, $h = 1, 2, \ldots, n+1$, such that

$$\begin{aligned} \text{rank}[\bar{\lambda}_h, h = 1, 2, \ldots, n+1] = \quad & \text{rank}[\bar{\lambda}_h \big/ \bar{\lambda}_h^0, h = 1, 2, \ldots, n+1] = n+1, \\ (x_h, \bar{\lambda}_h) \text{ solves (22)} \quad & (h = 1, 2, \ldots, n+1), \\ x_h = x'_h \quad & (h = n+2, n+3, \ldots, m), \end{aligned}$$

and

$$(\bar{\lambda}_1/\bar{\lambda}_1^0, \omega' + (x - x')) \in V'.$$

(iii) Pick $(\lambda, \omega) = (\bar{\lambda}_1/.\bar{\lambda}_1^0, \omega' + (x - x'))$. It is then easily checked that $p \in P_{(\lambda,\omega)}$ with $x = f(p, \omega)$, so that

$$\text{rank } D_0^{\bullet 1}(f_0(p, \omega_0)) = \text{rank } D_0^{\bullet 1}(x_0) = \text{rank}[\bar{\lambda}_h, h = 1, 2, \ldots, n+1] = n+1.$$

Proof of Lemma 2. The first assertion follows immediately from the preceding lemma. The second also follows from that lemma after observing that, for $\omega \in \tilde{\Omega}$, if we take $(\lambda, \omega) \in \tilde{V}$ and $(p, \lambda, \omega) \in \pi_{E_1}^{-1}(\lambda, \omega)$ satisfying property (23), then – utilizing the diffeomorphism exhibited in the proof of Theorem 2 – we can map some neighborhood of λ into a neighborhood of $p \in P_\omega$ while at the same time preserving property (23).

Proof of Lemma 3. Take $\omega \in \tilde{\Omega}$, and consider f restricted to $\tilde{P}_\omega \times \{\omega\}$, say, $\tilde{f}_\omega : \tilde{P}_\omega \to \tilde{X}_\omega$. Then $\tilde{f}_\omega$ maps p smoothly into $x = f(p, \omega)$ such that rank $D_0^{\bullet 1}(x_0) = n+1$, that is, such that $D_0^{\bullet 1}(x_0)^{-1}$ is well defined. So we can display a system of equations from which it is easily inferred that $\tilde{f}_\omega$ is one-to-one and $\tilde{f}_\omega^{-1}$ is smooth, as follows:

(i) Utilize the equations given by the first-order condition (22) for $h = 1,2, \ldots, n+1$ to identify

$$[\bar{\lambda}_h, h = 1,2,\ldots,n+1] = D_0^{\bullet 1}(x_0). \tag{24}$$

(ii) Given Equation (24), rearrange these same equations to eliminate $\bar{\lambda}_h$, which yields equations relating $\underline{p}^s$ and $p^{s,1}$, $s = 1,2, \ldots, N$, to x_0,

$$D_0^{\bullet 1}(x_0)^{-1} D_0^{\setminus 1}(x_0) = \begin{bmatrix} \underline{p}^0 & & & & & \\ & \ddots & 0 & & \ddots & \\ & & \underline{p}^j & a^{j,k} & (p^{n+k,1}/p^{j,1}) & (1,\underline{p}^{n+k}) \\ & 0 & & \ddots & & \\ & & & \underline{p}^n & & \ddots \end{bmatrix} \tag{25}$$

where $D_0^{\setminus 1}(x_0)$ is the matrix formed from $[Du_h(x_h)^T, h = 1,2, \ldots, n+1]$ after deleting the elements of $D_0^{\bullet 1}(x_0)$.

(iii) Append the equations relating p^s to $p^{s,1}$ and $\underline{p}^s$,

$$\begin{aligned} p^s &= (1, \underline{p}^s), \\ &= p^{s,1}(1, \underline{p}^s), \text{ otherwise.} \end{aligned} \tag{26}$$

The desired result ultimately follows from the fact that Assumption A6 implies that the right-hand side of Equation (25) is diffeomorphism, so that Equations (25)–(26) provide the formula for $\tilde{f}_\omega^{-1}$. (Filling in the details is a straightforward, though laborious exercise.)

Proof of Lemma 4. Throughout this argument we use the fact that, if $q \gg 0$ is a solution to Equation (17), then sign $b^{j,k}$ = sign $a^{j,k}$.

(Necessity): Equation (17) can be displayed in matrix form as

$$Cq = d,$$

where C is a $((n+1)M \times N)$-dimensional matrix, and d is a conformable $(n+1)M$-dimensional vector. When the solution to Equation (17) is unique, rank $C = N = n + M \leq (n+1)M$. So, on the one hand, if condition (i) were not true, then

$$Cq = 0 \text{ for } q \gg 0,$$

a contradiction. On the other hand, if condition (ii) were not true, then

$$\begin{aligned} C\tilde{q} = 0 \text{ for } \tilde{q}^s &= 0, \ s = j, j \in J', \text{ and } s = n + k, k \in K', \\ &= q^s > 0, \text{ otherwise,} \end{aligned}$$

also leading to a contradiction. (Note: The construction $\tilde{q}$ actually establishes a stronger condition than (ii), namely that the restriction $0 \in J'$ and $K^0 \subset K'$ can be replaced by the restriction $J' \neq \emptyset$ or $K' \neq \emptyset$. However, conditions (i) and (ii) suffice, as we now demonstrate.)

(Sufficiency): Here we simply sketch an algorithm for computing the unique positive solution in a finite number of steps.

Step 0: Consider $J^0 = (0\}$ and, without loss of generality (by appropriately relabeling, say, columns of C), $K^0 = (1,2, \ldots , M^0\}$, where $K^0 \neq \emptyset$ by condition (i). Then the equations

$$a^{0,k} q^{n+k} = b^{0,k}, k \in K^0,$$

uniquely determine

$$q^{n+k} = b^{0,k} / a^{0,k}, \ k \in K^0.$$

Step 1: Consider, without loss of generality (by appropriately relabeling rows of C),

$$J^1 = \{0, 1, \ldots, n^1\} = J^0 \cup \{j \in J : j \notin J^0 \text{ and } a^{j,k} \neq 0 \text{ for some } k \in K^0\}$$

and $K^1 = K^0$, where $J^1 \backslash J^0 \neq \emptyset$ by condition (ii). For each $j \in J^1 \backslash J^0$ pick $k(j) \in K^1$ such that $a^{j,k(j)} \neq 0$. Then the equations

$$-b^{j,k(j)} q^j + a^{j,k(j)} q^{n+k(j)} = 0, \quad j \in J^1 \backslash J^0,$$

uniquely determine

$$q^j = (a^{j,k(j)} / b^{j,k(j)}) q^{n+k(j)}, \quad j \in J^1 \backslash J^0.$$

Step 2: Consider $J^2 = J^1$ and, without loss of generality,

$$\begin{aligned} K^2 &= \{0, \ldots, M^0, M^0 + 1, \ldots, M^2\} \\ &= K^1 \cup \{k \in K : k \notin K^0 \text{ and } a^{j,k} \neq 0 \text{ for some } j \in J^1\}, \end{aligned}$$

where $K^2\backslash K^1 \neq \emptyset$ by condition (ii). For each $k \in K^2\backslash K^1$ pick $j(k) \in J^2$ such that $a^{j(k),k} \neq 0$. Then the equations

$$-b^{j(k),k}q^{j(k)} + a^{j(k),k}q^{n+k} = 0, \quad k \in K^2\backslash K^1,$$

uniquely determine

$$q^{n+k} = (b^{j(k),k}/a^{j(k),k})q^{j(k)}, \quad k \in K^2\backslash K^1.$$

$$\vdots$$

Proceed in similar fashion, alternating between expanding the subsets of J and then K, until the finite step $t < N$ at which $n^t = n$ and $M^t = M$, and hence $J^t = J$ and $K^t = K$.

Proof of Theorem 5. Equation (16) implies condition (i). So suppose condition (ii) isn't satisfied. Now, Equation (10) implies that it can't be the case that $J' = J$ and $K' \neq K$ (since, if it were, then $\lambda a^k = 0$ for $k \in K\backslash K' \neq \emptyset$), while Equation (16) implies that it can't be the case that $J' \neq J$ and $K' = K$ (since, if it were, then $a^j\mu = 0$ for $j \in J\backslash J' \neq \emptyset$). So also take $J' \neq J$ and $K' \neq K$. Then, Equation (10) implies

$$\lambda a^k = \sum_{j \in J\backslash J'} \lambda^j a^{j,k} > 0, \quad k \in K\backslash K'$$

or

$$\sum_{k \in K\backslash K'} \left(\sum_{j \in J\backslash J'} \lambda^j a^{j,k} \right) \mu^k > 0,$$

while Equation (16) implies (recalling that $0 \in J'$)

$$a^j \mu = \sum_{k \in K\backslash K'} a^{j,k}\mu^k < 0, \quad j \in J\backslash J',$$

or

$$\sum_{j \in J\backslash J'} \lambda^j \left(\sum_{k \in K\backslash K'} a^{j,k}\mu^k \right) = \sum_{k \in K\backslash K'} \left(\sum_{j \in J\backslash J'} \lambda^j a^{j,k} \right) \mu^k < 0,$$

a contradiction.

Proof of Theorem 6. This amounts, mutatis mutandis, to repeating the steps leading to Theorem 4, and is therefore omitted. (Note: For such purpose, the analogue of Assumption A6 is a perturbation of A taking, for example, $a^{0,k} \neq 0$, $k = 1,2, \ldots, M$, and $a^{j,1} \neq 0$, $j = 1,2, \ldots, n$, as given.)

References

Arrow, K.J. (1964). The role of securities in the optimal allocation of risk-bearing. *Review of Economic Studies* **31**, 91–96.

Balasko, Y. (1988). *Foundations of the Theory of General Equilibrium*. Orlando, FL: Academic Press.

Balasko, Y. and Cass, D. (1985). Regular demand with several, general budget constraints. CARESS Working Paper, University of Pennsylvania.

Balasko, Y., Cass, D. and Sinconolfi, P. (1987). The structure of financial equilibrium with exogenous yields: II. Restricted participation. CARESS Working Paper, University of Pennsylvania.

Cass, D. (1984). Equilibrium with incomplete financial markets. CARESS Working Paper, University of Pennsylvania.

Cass, D. (1985). On the 'number' of equilibrium allocations with incomplete financial markets. CARESS Working Paper, University of Pennsylvania.

Cass, D. (1988). Sunspots and incomplete financial markets: The leading example. In Feiwel, G. (Ed.), *Joan Robinson and Modern Economic Theory*. London: Macmillan.

Debreu, G. (1959). *Theory of Value*. Chapter 7New York: Wiley.

Duffie, D. (1987). Stochastic equilibria with incomplete financial markets. *Journal of Economic Theory* **41**, 405–416.

Duffie, D. and Shafer, W. (1985). Equilibrium in incomplete markets: I. A basic model of generic existence. *Journal of Mathematical Economics* **14**, 285–300.

Duffie, D. and Shafer, W. (1986). Equilibrium in incomplete markets: II. Generic existence in stochastic economies. *Journal of Mathematical Economics* **15**, 199–216.

Gale, D. (1960). *The Theory of Linear Economic Models*. Chapter 2New York: McGraw-Hill.

Geanakoplos, J. and Mas-Colell, A. (1989). Real indeterminacy with financial assets. *Journal of Economic Theory* **47** (1), 22–38.

Hart, O.D. (1975). On the optimality of equilibrium when the market structure is incomplete. *Journal of Economic Theory* **11**, 418–443.

Magill, M.J.P. and Shafer, W.J. (1985). Equilibrium and efficiency in a canonical asset trading model. MRG Working Paper, University of Southern California.

Milnor, J.W. (1965). *Topology from the Differentiable Viewpoint*. Charlottesville, VA: University Press of Virginia.

Radner, R. (1972). Existence of equilibrium plans, prices and price expectations in a sequence of markets. *Econometrica* **40**, 289–303.

Werner, J. (1985). Equilibrium in economies with incomplete financial markets. *Journal of Economic Theory* **36**, 110–119.

Werner, J. (1986). Asset prices and real indeterminacy in equilibrium with financial markets. Working Paper, University of Bonn.

Younés, Y. (1986). Competitive equilibrium for incomplete market structures. CARESS Working Paper, University of Pennsylvania.

FURTHER READING

Chae, S. (1988). Existence of competitive equilibrium with incomplete markets. *Journal of Economic Theory* **44**, 179–188.

Geanakoplos, J. and Polemarchakis, H. (1986). Existence, regularity and constrained suboptimality of competitive allocations when the asset market is incomplete. In Heller, W.P., Starr, R.M. and Starrett, D.A. (Eds), *Uncertainty, Information and Communication, Essays in Honor of Kenneth J. Arrow* (Vol. III). Cambridge, England: Cambridge University Press.

Husseini, S., Lasry, J.-M. and Magill, M. (1986). Existence of equilibrium with incomplete markets. MRG Working Paper, CEREMADE.

McManus, D. (1986). Regular options equilibria. CARESS Working Paper, University of Pennsylvania.

Repullo, R. (1983). Equilibrium and efficiency in economies with a sequence of markets. Chapter 6, Ph.D. Dissertation, London School of Economics, London, England.

Chapter 11

Sunspot Equilibrium in an Overlapping-Generations Economy with an Idealized Contingent-Commodities Market[☆]

David Cass and Karl Shell[a]

[a] *Department of Economics, University of Pennsylvania, Philadelphia, PA, USA*

1. Introduction and Summary

1.1. Economic Complexity

The subject of this volume is economic complexity, which can be taken to be the analysis of *complicated solutions to relatively simple economic models.* Consider, for example, the chapters devoted to economic dynamics. A focus of these contributions is on the nonstationary paths that arise in economies with stationary environments. We know that business cycles (periodic solutions) and even "chaotic" fluctuations (aperiodic solutions) can occur even though all the economic fundamentals are nonfluctuating (stationary). In some of the other chapters, including ours, the focus is on stochastic outcomes in nonstochastic economic environments. We know that economic outcomes can be random even though all the economic fundamentals (such as preferences, endowments, and technology) are nonrandom. In particular, "sunspots" can affect the allocation of resources even though the economic fundamentals are unaffected by sunspots.

1.2. Stochastic Outcomes in Nonstochastic Economies

The current chapter is on *sunspot equilibrium*; we analyze the stochastic outcomes to a rational-expectations model of a competitive economy in which the fundamentals are nonstochastic. The fact that economies generate

[☆] This article was originally published as: Cass, D. and K. Shell, Sunspot Equilibrium in an Overlapping-Generations Economy with an Idealized Contingent-Commodities Market. *Economic Complexity: Chaos, Sunspots, Bubbles and Nonlinearity*, Edited by W. A. Barnett, J. Geweke and K. Shell, 3–20, © Cambridge University Press, 1989. Reproduced with the permission of the publisher, co-author and author's estate.

International Symposia in Economic Theory and Econometrics, Vol. 21B
S. Spear (Editor)

ISSN: 1571-0386/DOI: 10.1108/S1571-0386(2011)000021B014

uncertainty, as well as transmitting uncertainty arising from outside the economy, should come as no surprise. An economy is a social system in which the individual participants cannot be certain of the behavior of the others. In seeking to optimize his own actions, an economic actor must attempt to predict the moves of all other economic actors. Because he is uncertain about the moves of others, he is also uncertain about economic outcomes (such as prices), even if he is completely certain about the economic fundamentals. Nor should the existence of sunspot equilibria come as a surprise to the economist conversant with game theory. Pure-strategy equilibrium is not the only type of solution to nonstochastic games. Mixed-strategy equilibrium and, more generally, correlated equilibrium are staples of noncooperative game theory. There is no obvious reason that the stochastic equilibria that arise in game-theoretic models of imperfect competition must vanish in the limit as the economy becomes competitive.

Thinking of an economy as a social system composed of strategic decision makers should lead one to accept as natural the idea that the market economy itself creates uncertainty. The reader of business and financial news is well aware of the important role of market uncertainty. Businessmen face uncertainties that are not based on their uncertainty about economic fundamentals; they are, for example, uncertain about the overall level of consumer confidence, the confidence and financial plans of their customers, the production and marketing plans of their rivals, and the tax and regulatory plans of government agencies. For these reasons, we should expect sunspot equilibria to be the rule rather than the exception.

1.3. The Overlapping-Generations Model and Sunspot Equilibrium

The histories of the overlapping-generations (OG) model and sunspot equilibrium are intertwined.[1] It is our ambition to persuade the reader that, although sunspot equilibrium is an essential aspect in the analysis of OG economies, sunspot phenomena are far more general. However, we first return to the original source of sunspots: the OG model.

The OG model began with Samuelson (1958)[2] who provided an example of perfect-foresight nonmonetary, competitive equilibrium that is not Pareto

[1] A major reason for this is, of course, that the earliest research on sunspot equilibrium was based on either the overlapping-generations model or closely related models. Perhaps another reason has to do with proximity. At the time of our discovery of sunspots, CARESS was a leading center of research on the overlapping-generations model. Even at the time we discovered sunspots, both of us were listing as our prime research interest "OG models."

[2] For a detailed and very enthusiastic account of the many virtues of the OG model for macro- and monetary analysis, see our propaganda piece, Cass and Shell (1980).

optimal. For his example, there is also a very simple monetary competitive equilibrium that is Pareto optimal.[3] His example also establishes that the public debt need not be retired in perfect-foresight economies.[4]

What is the source of possible inoptimality in Samuelson's model? The OG model differs from the Arrow–Debreu model in two ways:

1. The time horizon is unbounded and the generations overlap. Hence, in the discrete model, there is both a countable infinity of dated commodities and a countable infinity of traders.
2. Trades are restricted by the natural vitality and mortality of the economic actors.

Property 1, the so-called double-infinity property (including the stipulation of the overlapping structure of the generations), is *the* source of the possible failure of Pareto optimality of perfect-foresight (i.e., nonsunspot), competitive equilibrium. See Shell (1971) and Cass (1985). Property 2, the restricted-participation property, has been incorrectly cited in the literature as causing the failure of optimality in perfect-foresight, OG economies. Shell (1971) establishes that this property is not binding for perfect-foresight (i.e., nonsunspot) equilibria: The set of perfect-foresight equilibria derived on the assumption that traders are constrained by property 2 is identical to the set of perfect-foresight equilibria derived on the assumption that market participation is unrestricted.

Although property 2 plays no role in the analysis of nonsunspot equilibrium, it is important in the analysis of sunspot equilibrium. In Cass and Shell (1983), we showed how such restrictions on market participation are a source of sunspot equilibrium. Here we show how the double infinity (property 1) of the OG model is yet another source of sunspot equilibrium.

The first work on sunspot equilibrium was reported in Shell (1977), which is based on our joint research efforts on the infinite-horizon, OG economy. In this unpublished paper, it was assumed that there is no intrinsic uncertainty. The only randomness is in the level of sunspot activity, which has no effect on the economic fundamentals. We showed that there is an equilibrium in which rational individuals believe that the general price level is affected by the level of sunspot activity and that these beliefs are self-justifying. It was assumed that the economy is "shocked" by sunspots in each period. In this first example of sunspot equilibrium, economic fluctuations are generated within the private sector, and the stabilizing

[3] For an up-to-date welfare analysis of the OG model, see Balasko and Shell (1980, Section 2, 4, and 5).

[4] For an analysis of fiscal policy, equilibrium, and welfare in the perfect-foresight OG model, see Balasko and Shell (1981). For an analysis of debt retirement and equilibrium in the OG model, see Balasko and Shell (1986).

(contrasunspot) fiscal policy must be perpetually active. This is contrary to the notion that erratic behavior in rational-expectations economies is solely the fault of the erratic behavior of the government.

Azariadis (1981) effectively translated our pure-exchange OG model into the simple production–consumption model popular with macroeconomists. Azariadis and Guesnerie (1982, 1986) and Spear (1984) provided sufficient conditions for the existence of *stationary* sunspot equilibria. Peck (1988) showed how nonstationary sunspot equilibria can be constructed for a very wide class of one-good OG models. His method of construction would seem to extend beyond the one-good case. His result suggests that sunspot equilibria are not flukes in the OG model.

1.4. The Sources of Sunspot Equilibria

We previously argued (Section 1.2) that since an economy is a social system in which individuals must attempt to predict the moves of others, it should not be surprising that the economy generates uncertainty. Because extrinsic uncertainty is so likely to affect economic outcomes, it is natural to ask: Which economies, if any, are immunized against the effects of extrinsic uncertainty?

We answer this question in Cass and Shell (1983, Section VII, pp. 215–218). In an economy with convex preferences and convex technologies, a sunspot-equilibrium allocation is never Pareto optimal. Hence, in a convex environment, if the preconditions of Pareto optimality are met, we know that extrinsic uncertainty cannot matter.

Such is the hold on economists of the basic Arrow–Debreu model that we are frequently asked for "the cause" of or "the reason" for sunspot equilibria. (These questions have the same roots as the idea that failures in Pareto optimality and other nice properties of Arrow–Debreu equilibrium must necessarily be identified with some particular "market failures.") In attempting to respond to these questions, we have pursued the following program: Relax the usual preconditions for Pareto optimality of equilibrium allocations, one at a time, and provide, for each weakening of the assumptions, an example of sunspot equilibrium.[5] In what follows, we list some of these sources of sunspot equilibrium.

[5] Our joint program is referred to as the Philadelphia Pholk Theorem by Shell (1987) in his *Palgrave* entry on sunspots. The PPT is the assertion: "In each 'class' of models in which Pareto-optimal allocations are not guaranteed, one can find an example of sunspot equilibrium." The "proof" is based on several examples constructed by us and our coauthors. Of course, time does not stand still. The pholk theorem is now also identified with Ithaca, Geneva, Evanston, New Brunswick, Paris, New York, Pittsburgh, ...

1.4.1. Restrictions on Market Participation

In Cass and Shell (1983), we relaxed the perfect market assumption in a way that is motivated by intertemporal economic theory. All markets are assumed to be open and competitive, but participation in these markets is restricted to economic actors who are alive when the market convenes. In particular, the members of the "young" generation cannot participate in a market for securities based on a state of nature that is revealed before their birth. It was shown that sunspot equilibria can be generated in an economy that is Arrow–Debreu except for restrictions on market participation. If there is no intrinsic uncertainty, then the Walrasian equilibria are unaffected by the restrictions on market participation. They are thought of as the nonsunspot equilibria. We showed that there can also be new equilibria, the sunspot equilibria, in which the allocation of resources is affected by extrinsic uncertainty. Balasko et al. (1988) provided some comparative statics for the Cass and Shell (1983) economy. In the effect on the existence of sunspot equilibrium, varying the proportion of market-restricted consumers is similar to varying the endowments of the economy.

Natural restrictions on market participation obviously arise in the OG model. Hence, in that model, restricted participation is *a* source of sunspot equilibria. There is one other source of sunspot equilibria in OG models – the double infinity of consumers and dated commodities (along with the structure of generational overlap), which is analyzed in Sections 2 and 3.

1.4.2. Incomplete Markets

Cass (1986) showed that, in an example with securities markets that are not complete, there is a continuum of sunspot competitive equilibria if the endowments are not Pareto optimal (see also Siconolfi, 1987). Cass's securities are purely financial, but subsequent work has indicated that missing markets in general, whether for financial or real commodities, can cause sunspot equilibria to exist.

One is free to interpret an economy with externalities as nothing more than an economy with incomplete markets. Hence, by showing that incomplete markets can be a source of sunspot equilibria, one also establishes that externalities can be sources of sunspot equilibria. Spear (1988) worked out an interesting dynamic model with an externality in the private investment process. He showed that sunspots can affect the equilibrium outcome, and he generated equilibria that seem to be in agreement with some features of actual economic time series.

1.4.3. Imperfect Competition

Peck and Shell (1985) analyzed the role for extrinsic uncertainty in a general-equilibrium model of imperfect competition. The model is like the

Arrow–Debreu model except that the price-taking assumption is replaced by the assumption of strategic behavior. For this model, there is a sunspot Nash equilibrium if and only if endowments are not Pareto optimal. Allowing for asymmetric information even further broadens the class of sunspot Nash equilibria. The work of Peck and Shell provided the first formal link between the relatively well-established tradition of extrinsic uncertainty in game theory and the relatively recent tradition of extrinsic uncertainty in formal economic equilibrium models. They showed that, in the market-game environment, every correlated equilibrium is a sunspot equilibrium but that some sunspot equilibria are not correlated equilibria.

1.4.4. Nonconvexities

Guesnerie and Laffont (1987) provided examples of sunspot equilibria in economies with nonconvex preferences. In contrast, Cass and Polemarchakis (1988) proved that sunspots cannot matter in competitive equilibrium if preferences are strictly convex, even if there are nonconvexities in production.

1.5. Sunspot Equilibria in the Idealized Overlapping-Generations Economy: Overview and Summary of Sections 2 and 3

We first found sunspot equilibria during the course of our joint research on Samuelson's model of overlapping generations. Two features distinguish the OG model from the standard Walrasian model:

1. Participation in markets in the OG economy is naturally restricted by the lifetimes of the individual traders (see Cass and Shell, 1983 and Section 1.4.1). In the standard Walrasian model, market participation is unrestricted.
2. In the OG economy, there is the double infinity of traders and dated commodities (see Shell, 1971) along with the overlapping structure of generations (see Cass, 1985). The standard Walrasian model is based on a finite number of commodities and a finite number of consumers.

We know that the first feature, restricted market participation, is a source of sunspot equilibrium (see Cass and Shell, 1983). To isolate the sources of sunspot equilibria, we construct in Section 3 a highly idealized OG economy in which the first feature, restricted market participation, is assumed away. We postulate in the spirit of Shell (1971) that the market for contingent commodities meets before the beginning of economic time and that each consumer can purchase a full spectrum of contingent claims, even those based on states of nature that were revealed before the consumer's birth date.

A special case of the model developed in Section 2 is further specified in Section 3. For this example, we find three rational-expectations competitive equilibria:

1. a nonsunspot, nonmonetary competitive equilibrium (which is autarky);
2. a nonsunspot, monetary competitive equilibrium; and
3. a sunspot, nonmonetary competitive equilibrium.

In our example, the nonsunspot, monetary competitive-equilibrium allocation is Pareto optimal. It also Pareto dominates the sunspot, nonmonetary competitive-equilibrium allocation, which in turn Pareto dominates the nonsunspot, nonmonetary competitive-equilibrium allocation. The two nonmonetary equilibria are not Pareto optimal, but they are weakly Pareto optimal. Even though the sunspot equilibrium allocation is weakly Pareto optimal, the planner could not convert it to full Pareto optimality without intervening in the first period.

We conclude that *a* source of sunspot equilibria in the OG economy is the second distinguishing feature of the model, the double-infinity property.

Our example also suggests that sunspots might conceivably be useful as a coordinating device to attenuate a tendency toward oversaving. Lump-sum transfers of outside money to the private sector attenuate any tendency to oversaving and do so costlessly because these transfers do not distort economic decisions. Wagers on sunspots might, under some circumstances, serve to attenuate oversaving, but they are always costly in strictly convex economies because they introduce individual risks into situations in which there is no aggregate risk.

In Samuelsonian prose: The "social contrivance of sunspots" may serve as an imperfect substitute for the "social contrivance of money."

2. An Idealized Overlapping-Generations Model with Sunspots

In each generation there is only one consumer, labeled by his birth date $t = 0, 1, \ldots$ and referred to as Mr. t. Mr. 0 is active only during period 1, while Mr. $t > 0$ is alive and active during both periods t and $t+1$. In each period $t = 1, 2, \ldots$ there is only one standard commodity. The economy's level of sunspot activity s is a random variable, realized at the beginning of period 1 and taking on the values α or β. All consumers share the same probability beliefs about the occurrence of sunspots, and these common probabilities $\pi(\alpha)$ and $\pi(\beta)$ satisfy $0 < \pi(\alpha) < 1$ and $\pi(\beta) = 1 - \pi(\alpha)$.

Let $x_t^\tau(s) \in \mathbb{R}_+$ denote consumption by Mr. t in period τ and state s, and

$$x_0 = [x_0^1(\alpha), x_0^1(\beta)] \quad \text{and} \quad x_t = [x_t^t(\alpha), x_t^{t+1}(\alpha), x_t^t(\beta), x_t^{t+1}(\beta)],$$
$$\text{for} \quad t = 1, 2, \ldots .$$

Assume that Mr. 0 has a utility function $v_0 : \mathbb{R}_+^2 \to \mathbb{R}$ with the von Neumann–Morgenstern representation

$$\begin{aligned} v_0(x_0) &= v_0[x_0^1(\alpha), x_0^1(\beta)] \\ &= \pi(\alpha)\phi[x_0^1(\alpha)] + \pi(\beta)\phi[x_0^1(\beta)], \end{aligned}$$

where $\phi : \mathbb{R}_+ \to \mathbb{R}$ is smooth, strictly increasing, and strictly concave. Similarly, assume that Mr. $t>0$ also has a von Neumann–Morgenstern utility function $v_t : \mathbb{R}_+^4 \to \mathbb{R}$, but with the special form

$$\begin{aligned} v_t(x_t) &= v_t[x_t^t(\alpha), x_t^{t+1}(\alpha), x_t^t(\beta), x_t^{t+1}(\beta)] \\ &= \pi(\alpha)\psi[ax_t^t(a) + bx_t^{t+1}(\alpha)] + \pi(\beta)\psi[ax_t^t(\beta) + bx_t^{t+1}(\beta)], \end{aligned}$$

where $0<a<b$ and $\psi : \mathbb{R}_+ \to \mathbb{R}$ is smooth, strictly increasing, and strictly concave. So, in particular, Mr. t's certainty utility function ψ exhibits a constant marginal rate of substitution that is less than one,

$$\frac{\partial\psi(ax^1 + bx^2)/\partial x^1}{\partial\psi(ax^1 + bx^2)/\partial x^2} = \frac{a}{b} < 1.$$

Let $\omega_t^\tau(s) \in \mathbb{R}_+$ denote the endowment of Mr. t in period τ and state s, and

$$\omega_0 = [\omega_0^1(\alpha), \omega_0^1(\beta)] \quad \text{and} \quad \omega_t = [\omega_t^t(\alpha), \omega_t^{t+1}(\alpha), \omega_t^t(\beta), \omega_t^{t+1}(\beta)]$$
$$\text{for} \quad t = 1, 2, \ldots .$$

Specify that sunspots do not affect endowments and assume that endowments are stationary so that, independent of state and birth date, Mr. t's endowment is, say, $\omega^1>0$ when young and $\omega^2>0$ when old. Then we have

$$\omega_0 = (\omega^2, \omega^2) \text{ and } \omega_t = (\omega^1, \omega^1, \omega^2, \omega^2) \quad \text{for} \quad t = 1, 2, \ldots .$$

Assume for the moment that there is no outside money in the economy, but that there is a complete set of Arrow securities markets or, what amounts to the same thing, a complete set of contingent-claims markets, and that all consumers can participate on all these markets. Let $p^t(s)$ denote the price (before sunspot activity is observed) of a claim for one unit of commodity in period t if state s is realized. Given these contingent-claims prices and the fundamentals (i.e., preferences and endowments) described earlier, we can proceed to characterize consumer behavior.

Mr. 0's optimal consumption bundle x_0 solves the problem:

$$\begin{aligned} &\text{maximize} && \pi(\alpha)\phi[x_0^1(\alpha)] + \pi(\beta)\phi[x_0^1(\beta)] \\ &\text{subject to} && p^1(\alpha)x_0^1(\alpha) + p^1(\beta)x_0^1(\beta) \leq p^1(\alpha)\omega^2 + p^1(\beta)\omega^2 \\ &\text{and} && x_0 \geq 0, \end{aligned} \tag{1}$$

whereas Mr. t's optimal consumption bundle x_t solves the problem:

$$\begin{aligned} &\text{maximize} && \pi(\alpha)\psi[ax_t^t(\alpha) + bx_t^{t+1}(\alpha)] + \pi(\beta)\psi[ax_t^t(\beta) + bx_t^{t+1}(\beta)] \\ &\text{subject to} && p^t(\alpha)x_t^t(\alpha) + p^{t+1}(\alpha)x_t^{t+1}(\alpha) + p^t(\beta)x_t^t(\beta) + p^{t+1}(\beta)x_t^{t+1}(\beta) \\ &&& \leq p^t(\alpha)\omega^1 + p^{t+1}(\alpha)\omega^2 + p^t(\beta)\omega^1 + p^{t+1}(\beta)\omega^2 \\ &\text{and} && x_t \geq 0. \end{aligned} \tag{2}$$

Interior solutions to these problems are characterized by the Lagrangean conditions, which, after some simplification, can be written as

$$p^1(\alpha)[x_0^1(\alpha) - \omega^2] + p^1(\beta)[x_0^1(\beta) - \omega^2] = 0 \tag{3}$$

and

$$\frac{\phi'[x_0^1(\alpha)]}{\phi'[x_0^1(\beta)]} = \frac{p^1(\alpha)/\pi(\alpha)}{p^1(\beta)/\pi(\beta)} \tag{4}$$

for Equation (1), and

$$\begin{aligned} p^t(\alpha)[x_t^t(\alpha) - \omega^1] + p^{t+1}(\alpha)[x_t^{t+1}(\alpha) - \omega^2] \\ + p^t(\beta)[x_t^t(\beta) - \omega^1] + p^{t+1}(\beta)[x_t^{t-1}(\beta) - \omega^2] = 0, \end{aligned} \tag{5}$$

$$\frac{p^t(\alpha)}{p^{t+1}(\alpha)} = \frac{p^t(\beta)}{p^{t+1}(\beta)} = \frac{a}{b}, \tag{6}$$

and

$$\frac{\psi'[ax_t^t(\alpha) + bx_t^{t+1}(\alpha)]}{\psi'[ax_t^t(\beta) + bx_t^{t+1}(\beta)]} = \frac{p^t(\alpha)/\pi(\alpha)}{p^t(\beta)/\pi(\beta)} \tag{7}$$

for Equation (2).

Definition. The contingent-claims price sequence

$$p^1(\alpha), p^1(\beta), p^2(\alpha), p^2(\beta), \ldots, p^t(\alpha), p^t(\beta), \ldots \tag{8}$$

is said to be a *nonmonetary competitive equilibrium* if we have

$$x_{t-1}^t(s) - \omega^2 = -[x_t^t(s) - \omega^1] \quad \text{for} \quad t = 1, 2, \ldots \tag{9}$$

where x_0 is the optimal solution to Equation (1), and x_t is the optimal solution to Equation (2) for $t = 1,2,\ldots$. The sequence of these optimal consumption bundles

$$x_0, x_1, \ldots, x_t, \ldots$$

is the associated *nonmonetary competitive equilibrium allocation.*

Equation (9) is the materials balance condition; and when consumers optimize, it is the (contingent-claims) market-clearing condition.

Next we provide the corresponding nonsunspot and sunspot concepts.

Definition. A nonmonetary competitive equilibrium is said to be nonsunspot if, in addition, the associated allocation sequence satisfies

$$x_0^1(\alpha) = x_0^1(\beta) \quad \text{and} \quad [x_t^t(\alpha), x_t^{t+1}(\alpha)] = [x_t^t(\beta), x_t^{t+1}(\beta)] \quad \text{for} \quad t = 1, 2, \ldots. \tag{10}$$

Otherwise, it is said to be a *sunspot, nonmonetary competitive equilibrium.*

We shall also need the concept of a monetary competitive equilibrium. Suppose that the economy is as described previously with the sole exception that the government transfers one unit of paper money independent of the state of nature to Mr. 0 in period 1. Let $p^m(s)$ be the money price in state s. Then Mr. 0's problem becomes finding the optimal consumption bundle x_0 that solves

$$\begin{array}{ll} \text{maximize} & \pi(\alpha)\phi[x_0^1(\alpha)] + \pi(\beta)\phi[x_0^1(\beta)] \\ \text{subject to} & p^1(\alpha)x_0^1(\alpha) + p^1(\beta)x_0^1(\beta) \\ & \quad \leq p^1(\alpha)\omega^2 + p^1(\beta)\omega^2 + p^m(\alpha) + p^m(\beta) \\ \text{and} & x_0 \geq 0. \end{array} \tag{1^{m}}$$

Interior solutions to Equation (1^{m}) are characterized by the simplified Lagrangean conditions

$$p^1(\alpha)[x_0^1(\alpha) - \omega^2] + p^1(\beta)[x_0^1(\beta) - \omega^2] - [p^m(\alpha) + p^m(\beta)] = 0 \tag{3^{m}}$$

and Equation (4).

Definition. A monetary competitive equilibrium is a money price vector $[p^m(\alpha), p^m(\beta)]$ and a contingent-claims price sequence Equation (8) with the property that both the contingent-commodities market-clearing Equation (9) and the money-market-clearing conditions $-p^1(s)[x_1^1(s) - \omega_1^1(s)] = p^m(s)$, for $s = \alpha, \beta$, hold when x_0 is the optimal solution to Equation (1^{m}), and x_t is the optimal solution to Equation (2) for $t = 1, 2, \ldots$. If, in addition, property (10) is satisfied, then we have a nonsunspot, monetary competitive equilibrium.

In the following section we present three (stationary) competitive equilibria for this example. The nonsunspot nonmonetary and the nonsunspot monetary equilibria are simple and straightforward to display. The sunspot nonmonetary equilibrium, however, requires further specification of the parameters in the example.

3. Three Competitive Equilibria and Their Properties

3.1. A Nonsunspot Nonmonetary Competitive Equilibrium

Using the simplified Lagrangean conditions (3), (4), (5), and (7), it is easily verified that the autarkic (and thus stationary) allocation described as

$$x_0^1(s) = \omega^2 \quad \text{for} \quad s = \alpha, \beta$$

and

$$[x_t^t(s), x_t^{t+1}(s)] = (\omega^1, \omega^2) \quad \text{for} \quad t = 1, 2, \ldots \text{ and } \quad s = \alpha, \beta \tag{11}$$

is a nonsunspot, nonmonetary competitive equilibrium allocation when supporting prices are defined (up to some normalization) by

$$\frac{p^1(\alpha)}{\pi(\alpha)} = \frac{p^1(\beta)}{\pi(\beta)} > 0$$

and

$$p^{t+1}(s) = \left(\frac{b}{a}\right) p^t(s) \quad \text{for} \quad t = 1, 2, \ldots \text{ and } \quad s = \alpha, \beta. \tag{12}$$

Because, by hypothesis, we have $b/a > 1$, the second condition in Equation (12) implies that "present-value" contingent-claims prices explode, that is,

$$\lim_{t-\infty} \frac{p^t(s)}{p^1(s)} = \infty \quad \text{for} \quad s = \alpha, \beta. \tag{13}$$

Now, because it is a competitive equilibrium allocation, we know that the sequence defined by Equation (11) is weakly (or, equivalently, short-run) Pareto optimal. Equation (13), however, suggests that this autarkic allocation is not (fully) Pareto optimal. This conjecture is in fact established by the next equilibrium we display.

3.2. A Nonsunspot Monetary Competitive Equilibrium

Consider the stationary allocation described by

$$x_0^1(s) = \omega^1 + \omega^2 \quad \text{for} \quad s = \alpha, \beta$$

and

$$[x_t^t(s), x_t^{t+1}(s)] = (0, \omega^1 + \omega^2) \quad \text{for} \quad t = 1, 2, \ldots \quad \text{and} \quad s = \alpha, \beta. \tag{14}$$

Because, again by hypothesis, we have

$$\left.\frac{\partial\psi(ax^1 + bx^2)/\partial x^1}{\partial\psi(ax^1 + bx^2)/\partial x^2}\right|_{(x^1,x^2)=(0.\omega^1+\omega^2)} = \frac{a}{b} < 1,$$

it is easily verified (e.g., by attempting to improve on Mr. 0's welfare by perturbing the sequence (14)) that this particular stationary allocation is Pareto optimal. Moreover, because of the strict monotonicity of ϕ and ψ, we have

$$\phi(\omega^1 + \omega^2) > \phi(\omega^2) \quad \text{and} \quad \psi[b(\omega^1 + \omega^2)] > \psi(a\omega^1 + b\omega^2),$$

so that allocation (14) clearly Pareto dominates the autarkic allocation (11); this demonstrates directly that the autarkic allocation is not Pareto optimal. Finally, the sequence (14) is also a nonsunspot, monetary competitive equilibrium allocation when supporting prices are defined by

$$\frac{p^m(\alpha)}{\pi(\alpha)} = \frac{p^m(\beta)}{\pi(\beta)} > 0 \quad \text{and} \quad p^m(\alpha) + p^m(\beta) = p^1(\alpha)\omega^1 + p^1(\beta)\omega^1 \tag{15}$$

and

$$\frac{p^1(\alpha)}{\pi(\alpha)} = \frac{p^1(\beta)}{\pi(\beta)} > 0$$

and

$$p^{t+1}(s) = p^t(s) \quad \text{for} \quad t = 1, 2, \ldots \quad \text{and} \quad s = \alpha, \beta. \tag{16}$$

The last claim is now easily verified by using the simplified Lagrangean conditions (3^{m}) and (4) together with conditions (5),

$$\frac{p^t(s)}{p^{t+1}(s)} > \frac{a}{b} \quad \text{for} \quad s = \alpha, \beta,$$

and (7), because the latter constitutes the (simplified) Kuhn–Tucker conditions characterizing an optimal solution to Equation (2), for which $x_t^t(s) = 0$ and $x_t^{t+1}(s) > 0$ for $s = \alpha$, β.

3.3. A Sunspot Nonmonetary Competitive Equilibrium

The aim in this section is to specify in more detail the parameters of our example in order to construct a sunspot nonmonetary competitive equilibrium. In such an equilibrium, at least one consumer chooses (and thus strictly prefers) an optimal consumption bundle different from his endowment. Hence, this construction guarantees that the associated allocation Pareto dominates the (autarkic) nonsunspot nonmonetary equilibrium allocation (11).

Our strategy is to restrict attention to allocations that are stationary after the level of sunspot activity is revealed. (So, in this sense, all three of our displayed equilibria are "stationary.") Consider an allocation of the form

$$x_0^1(s) = x^{2,s} \quad \text{for} \quad s = \alpha, \beta$$

and

$$[x_t^t(s), x_t^{t+1}(s)] = (x^{1,s}, x^{2,s}) \quad \text{for} \quad t = 1, 2, \ldots \quad \text{and} \quad s = \alpha, \beta. \tag{17}$$

Choose the parameters in Equation (17) so that Mr. $t>0$ will be better off in state α than in autarky, but better off in autarky than in state β. In particular, consider $(x^{1,s}, x^{2,s})$ for $s = \alpha$, β that satisfies the following conditions:

$$\begin{aligned} &0 < x^{1,\alpha} < \omega^1 < x^{1,\beta}, 0 < x^{2,\beta} < \omega^2 < x^{2,\alpha}; \\ &x^{i,\alpha} - \omega^i = -(x^{i,\beta} - \omega^i) \quad \text{for} \quad i = 1, 2; \\ &x^{2,s} - \omega^2 = -(x^{1,s} - \omega^1) \quad \text{for} \quad s = \alpha, \beta. \end{aligned} \tag{18}$$

The properties described by Equation (18) are illustrated in Figure 1, together with the relationship between the stationary allocations (17) and (18) and the nonsunspot monetary and nonsunspot nonmonctary allocations. Note, especially, that the last condition of Equation (18) implies that the market-clearing conditions in Equation (8) are satisfied and (together with the first inequalities in Equation (18)) that we have

$$x^{2,\alpha} - x^{2,\beta} = -(x^{1,\alpha} - x^{1,\beta}) > 0. \tag{19}$$

If an allocation satisfying conditions (17) and (18) is to be supported as a competitive-equilibrium allocation, then from Mr. t's first-order condition (6), the real rate of interest after sunspot activity is revealed must equal his constant marginal rate of substitution a/b, so that

$$p^{t+1}(s) = \left(\frac{b}{a}\right) p^t(s) \quad \text{for} \quad t = 1, 2, \ldots \quad \text{and} \quad s = \alpha, \beta. \tag{20}$$

Make further specification that

$$p^1(\alpha) = p^1(\beta) > 0, \tag{21}$$

which in conjunction with Equation (20) yields

$$p^t(\alpha) = p^t(\beta) > 0 \quad \text{for} \quad t = 1, 2, \ldots \tag{22}$$

at contingent-claims prices satisfying Equation (22). The middle condition in Equation (18) implies that both budget constraints (3) and (5) are satisfied.

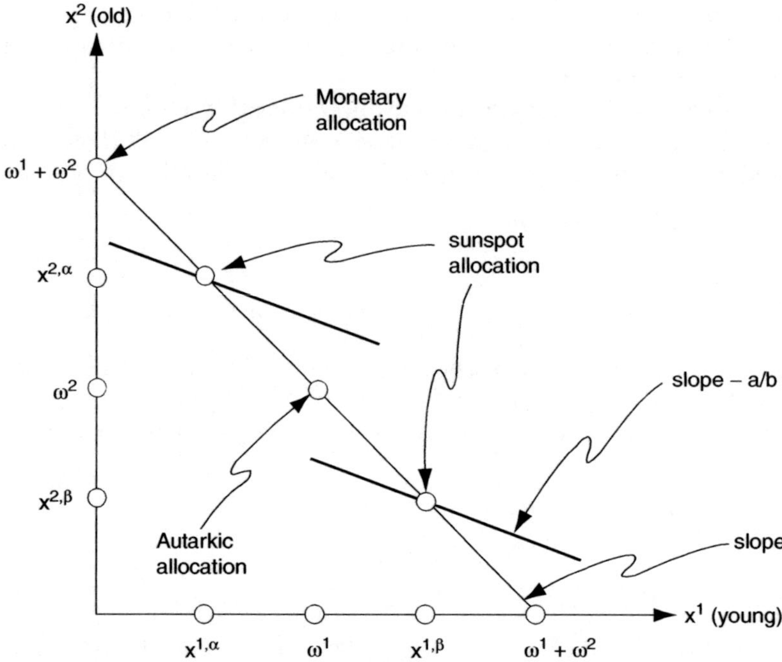

Figure 1.

Now substitute from Equation (17) and (22) into Mr. *t*'s other first-order condition, Equation (7), which after simplification yields

$$\frac{\psi'(ax^{1,\alpha}+bx^{2,\alpha})}{\psi'(ax^{1,\beta}+bx^{2,\beta})}=\frac{1-\pi(\alpha)}{\pi(\alpha)}. \tag{23}$$

Condition (19), together with the assumption that $0<a<b$, implies that

$$ax^{1,\alpha}+bx^{2,\alpha}=ax^{1,\beta}+bx^{2,\beta}+(-a+b)(x^{2,\alpha}-x^{2,\beta})>ax^{1,\beta}+bx^{2,\beta},$$

or that, by strict concavity of ψ, the left-hand side of Equation (23) must be less than one. So we can solve Equation (23) for $0<\pi(\alpha)<1$, in which case both of Mr. *t*'s first-order conditions (6) and (7), will be satisfied.

Given the foregoing specification of consumption (in Equations (17) and (18)), prices (in Equations (20) and (21)), and probabilities (in Equation (23)), all that remains is to guarantee that Mr. 0's first-order condition (4) is also satisfied. This is accomplished by further restricting ϕ to exhibit the property

$$\frac{\phi'(x^{2,\alpha})}{\phi'(x^{2,\beta})} = \frac{1-\pi(\alpha)}{\pi(\alpha)} < 1,$$

which is possible because ϕ is strictly concave whereas, from the first inequalities in Equation (18), we have $x^{2,\alpha} > x^{2,\beta}$.

We have displayed a sunspot nonmonetary competitive equilibrium.

Remark 1. Constructing this sunspot equilibrium required balancing various considerations (e.g., Mr. t's risk aversion against his relative welfare improvement in state α over state β). This balancing does not seem to be so delicate as to lead us to believe that we are dealing with a razor's edge situation. In particular, the simplifying assumption of linear indifference curves is not essential even for our specific example. From Figure 1, one can see that we basically need only the property that the marginal rate of substitution along some line $x^1 + x^2 = k > 0$ be equal and less than unity (for at least two distinct points). Thus, for instance, a more general specification that would justify our specific construction is

$$\psi(x^1, x^2) = f[ax^1 + bx^2 + cg(x^1 + x^2)],$$

where $0 < a < b$, $c > 0$, and both f and g are smooth, strictly increasing, and strictly concave.

Remark 2. As we mentioned at the beginning of this subsection, the sunspot allocations (17) and (18). Pareto dominates the nonsunspot, nonmonetary competitive-equilibrium allocation (11). However, although weakly Pareto optimal, it in turn is itself not Pareto optimal; it also is Pareto dominated by the nonsunspot, monetary competitive-equilibrium allocation (14). This fact is easily deduced by employing the relationships displayed in Figure 1, together with the strict monotonicity of ϕ and ψ, which yield

$$\phi(\omega^1 + \omega^2) > \max_s \phi(x^{2,s}) > \pi(\alpha)\phi(x^{2,\alpha}) + \pi(\beta)\phi(x^{2,\beta})$$

and

$$\begin{aligned}\psi[b(\omega^1 + \omega^2)] &> \max_s \psi(ax^{1,s} + bx^{2,s}) \\ &> \pi(\alpha)\psi(ax^{1,\alpha} + bx^{2,\alpha}) + \pi(\beta)\psi(ax^{1,\beta} + bx^{2,\beta}).\end{aligned}$$

3.4. Sunspots, Money, and Welfare

We reemphasize the following welfare considerations:

1. The nonsunspot monetary competitive-equilibrium allocation (14) is Pareto optimal; it also (strictly) Pareto dominates both the nonsunspot

nonmonetary competitive-equilibrium allocation (11) and the sunspot nonmonetary competitive-equilibrium allocations (17) and (18).
2. Both nonmonetary allocations are weakly Pareto optimal. Although sunspot allocations cannot be Pareto optimal, the sunspot allocation from our example Pareto dominates the nonsunspot, nonmonetary competitive-equilibrium allocation from our example. In other words, our example suggests that, in an OG setting, sunspots might be employed as a coordinating device to attenuate a tendency toward oversaving; that is, *sunspots can serve as imperfect substitutes for the social contrivance of money*.

The sunspot allocation has another striking welfare property. Even though it is weakly Pareto optimal, a planner seeking to restore Pareto optimality would have to intervene in the first period.[6] This distinguishes this more complicated OG model from the one-good, one-state OG model. In the latter case the planner could wait any finite number of periods before intervening and still convert a weakly Pareto optimal allocation to Pareto optimality.

To paraphrase Samuelson (1967), one might question the importance of distinguishing between weakly Pareto-optimal allocations and fully Pareto-optimal allocations on the grounds that *based solely on a finite history* that one cannot observe a difference between weak Pareto optima and full Pareto optima. The importance of Samuelson's point aside, it is accurate for the one-good, one-state model. Samuleson's point is, however, not accurate for one sunspot-equilibrium allocation. This weakly Pareto optimal allocation can be detected (or *observed*) to be not Pareto optimal immediately after the first-period contingent allocation has been assigned.[7] Once the allocation has been contaminated by sunspots, it cannot be extended to be Pareto optimal.

Perhaps, in future work, one can move from constructing examples to establishing theorems for economies with many commodities per period, many consumers per generation, more general demographic structure, and naturally restricted market participation. Can the existence of sunspot, nonmonetary competitive equilibria in the general case be related as in our

[6] The sunspot allocation is not *observationally Pareto optimal* (see Burke, 1987) because we need only observe a *finite* history to determine that it is not (fully) Pareto optimal. Clearly, in the finite history, the complete contingent allocation (*not* merely the realized allocation) must be observed.

[7] Our example need not necessarily be interpreted as a sunspot equilibrium. It is, of course, also an example of equilibrium for a two-good, one-state OG model. The equilibrium is weakly Pareto optimal; and after the first-period allocation is made, it is revealed that the intertemporal allocation could not be fully Pareto optimal. If symmetry breaking occurs in the first period, it can never be repaired.

special example to the structure of the set of nonsunspot (monetary and nonmonetary) competitive equilibria? If so, the idea that sunspots may partly fill the same role as money would be strengthened.

Acknowledgments

Research support from National Science Foundation grants SES-8509957 and SES-8606944 is gratefully acknowledged. The chapter is based on notes dated 10/16/81, which were prepared for a CARESS workshop. We thank Roger Guesnerie for his stimulating discussion in Austin, Texas and Walt Heller, Jim Peck, Steve Spear, and Raghu Sundaram for their comments. We take this opportunity to record our debt to Paul Samuelson, whose overlapping-generations model serves as a foundation for intelligent macroeconomics and provides two sources of sunspot equilibria.

References

Azariadis, C. (1981). Self-fulfilling prophecies. *Journal of Economic Theory* **25** (3), 380–396.

Azariadis, C. and Guesnerie, R. (1982). Prophéties créatice et persistance des théories. *Revue Economique* **33**, 787–806.

Azariadis, C. and Guesnerie, R. (1986). Sunspots and cycles. *Review of Economic Studies* **53** (5), 725–738.

Balasko, Y., Cass, D. and Shell, K. (1988). Market participation and sunspot equilibria. CAE Working Paper No. 88-11, March 1988, Cornell University and CARESS Working Paper No. 88-08, March 1988, University of Pennsylvania, Pennsylvania, PA.

Balasko, Y. and Shell, K. (1980). The overlapping-generations model, I: The case of pure exchange without money. *Journal of Economic Theory* **23** (3), 281–306.

Balasko, Y. and Shell, K. (1981). The overlapping-generations model, II: The case of pure exchange with money. *Journal of Economic Theory* **24** (1), 112–142.

Balasko, Y. and Shell, K. (1986). Lump-sum taxes and transfers: Public debt in the overlapping-generations model. In Heller, W.P., Starr, R.M. and Starrett, D.A. (Eds), *Essays in Honor of Kenneth J. Arrow, Volume II: Equilibrium Analysis*. New York: Cambridge University Press, pp. 121–153.

Burke, J. (1987). Bounded foresight, efficiency, and the core of overlapping-generations economies. Mimeo, November, Texas A & M University.

Cass, D. (1985). Optimality with unbounded numbers of households: I. Overlapping (or overlapping-generations) structure and the first basic theorem of welfare. In Ritschard, G. and Royer, D. (Eds), *Optimalité et Structures: Mélanges en Hommage à Edouard Rossier*. Paris: Economica, pp. 17–42.

Cass, D. (1986). Sunspots and incomplete financial markets: The leading example. CARESS Working Paper No. 84-06 RR, University of Pennsylvania, March (forthcoming in *Joan Robinson and Modern Economics*, edited by G. Feiwel).

Cass, D. and Polemarchakis, N.M. (1988). Convexity and sunspots: A comment. CARESS Working Paper No. 88-06, January, University of Pennsylvania.

Cass, D. and Shell, K. (1980). In defense of a basic approach. In Kareken, J. and Wallace, N. (Eds), *Models of Monetary Economies*. Minneapolis, MN: Federal Reserve Bank of Minneapolis, pp. 251–260.

Cass, D. and Shell, K. (1983). Do sunspots matter? *Journal of Political Economy* **91** (2), 193–227.

Guesnerie, R., Laffont, J.-J. (1987). Tâches solaires en horizon fini. Preliminary Mimeo, October, EHESS, Paris.

Peck, J. (1988). On the existence of sunspot equilibria in an overlapping-generations model. *Journal of Economic Theory* **44** (1), 19–42.

Peck, J., and Shell, K. (1985). Market uncertainty: Sunspot equilibria in imperfectly competitive economies. CARESS Working Paper No. 85-21, University of Pennsylvania, July. Revised version appears as "Market uncertainty: Correlated equilibrium and sunspot equilibrium in imperfectly competitive economies," Center for Analytic Economics Working Paper No. 88-22, May, Cornell University.

Samuelson, P.A. (1958). An exact consumption-loan model of interest with or without the social contrivance of money. *Journal of Political Economy* **66** (6), 467–482.

Samuelson, P.A. (1967). A turnpike refutation of the golden rule in a welfare-maximizing many-year plan. In Shell, K. (Ed.), *Essays on the Theory of Optimal Economic Growth*. Cambridge: MIT Press, pp. 269–280.

Shell, K. (1971). Notes on the economics of infinity. *Journal of Political Economy* **79** (5), 1002–1011.

Shell, K. (1977). Monnaie et allocation intertemporelle. Mimeo, November 21, CNRS séminaire d'econométrie de M. Edmond Malinvaud, Paris (Title and abstract in French; text in English).

Shell, K. (1987). Sunspot equilibrium. In Eatwell, J., Milgate, M. and Newman, P. (Eds), *The New Palgrave: A Dictionary of Economics*, Vol. 4. New York: The Stockton Press, pp. 549–551.

Siconolfi, P. (1987). Sunspot equilibria and incomplete financial markets. CARESS Working Paper No. 87-20, August, University of Pennsylvania.

Spear, S.E. (1984). Sufficient conditions for the existence of sunspot equilibria. *Journal of Economic Theory* **34** (2), 360–370.

Spear, S. E. (1988). Growth, externalities, and sunspots. Mimeo, Carnegie-Mellon University.

Further Reading

Benveniste, L. and Cass, D. (1984). Segregated commodity markets and sunspots. CARESS Working Paper No. 84-22, October, University of Pennsylvania, Pennsylvania, PA.

Chapter 12

The Structure of Financial Equilibrium with Exogenous Yields: The Case of Restricted Participation☆, ☆☆

Yves Balasko[a], David Cass and Paolo Siconolfi[b]

[a]*University of Geneva, 1211 Geneva 4, Switzerland*
[b]*Columbia University, New York, NY 10027, USA*

1. Introduction

Most of the papers we reference concern various aspects of pure exchange of goods and credit when financial markets are (at least potentially) incomplete. A large part of this rapidly growing literature has focused on two basic kinds of problems: First, those raised by the fact that, when the yields from financial instruments depend on spot prices for commodities, competitive equilibrium may not even exist. And second, those related to the fact that, *except* when all the yields depend in linear homogeneous fashion on spot prices, equilibrium allocation may be quite indeterminate.

This chapter is intended to be an initial contribution to understanding how similar problems arise as a consequence of a different sort of "friction" on financial markets, namely, that households' participation on these markets is usually subject to a wide range of diverse restrictions.

We do not explain at all where these restrictions come from, they are a primitive in our formulation. We also consider only the simplest, tractable form of restrictions, linear homogeneous constraints on portfolio holdings. And, finally, we concentrate on what we believe to be a leading polar case, where, in particular, the typical financial instrument i ($i = 1, 2, \ldots, M$) costs q^i dollars today and promises to return a yield – independent of its price and every other endogenous variable – of $r^{s,i}$ dollars in state s tomorrow ($s = 1, 2, \ldots, N$).

☆This article was originally published in *Journal of Mathematical Economics* 19, Yves Balasko, David Cass and Paolo Siconolfi, "The Structure of Financial Equilibrium with Exogenous Yields: The Case of Restricted Participation", 195–216, © Elsevier, 1990.

☆☆This is a revised version of CARESS Working Paper No. 87–16, benefiting from comments by a referee and an Associate Editor of this journal.

International Symposia in Economic Theory and Econometrics, Vol. 21B
S. Spear (Editor)

ISSN: 1571-0386/DOI: 10.1108/S1571-0386(2011)000021B015

Concentrating on this very specific model with just two periods (the *leading* case) and completely exogenous yields (a *polar* case) enables us to (i) postulate arbitrary portfolio constraints (and yield structure) and yet (ii) derive definite measures of the degree of indeterminacy – while avoiding any difficulties with existence. At the end of this chapter, we comment briefly on how robust our analysis seems to introducing more subtle portfolio restrictions, to complicating the genesis of yields, or to increasing the number of periods.

Being precise about our results requires having at hand a detailed description of our model (provided in Sections 2 and 4). Consequently now stating them only very broadly, we demonstrate three main conclusions.

- *There is no loss of generality in assuming that each household's portfolio choice subspace has the same dimension as the wealth space it generates.* In other words, a situation in which some households are indifferent between alternative portfolio choices can always be converted into one in which they are not (Theorems 1 and 2 of Section 3).
- Suppose that, when households are classified according to the portfolio restrictions they face, some particular type of household is both abundantly represented and actually restricted (so that the dimension of its wealth space is, say, M_0, with $0<M_0<N$). Suppose further that the wealth space of this particular type permits maximum wealth insurance (alternatively, positive wealth accumulation). *Then, generically in endowments, the set of equilibrium allocations contains a smooth, $(N-1)$-dimensional (alternatively, $(N-M_0)$-dimensional) submanifold.* In other words, restricted participation basically leads to the same degree of real indeterminacy as do incomplete markets, following Geanakoplos and Mas-Colell (1989) (alternatively, Balasko and Cass (1989)) (Theorem 4 of Section 5).
- Suppose that there are at least three periods, and that some financial instruments are traded tomorrow (as well as today). *Then, the set of their no-arbitrage prices may not be rich enough to clear the financial markets.* In other words, even after excluding the well-known difficulty associated with changes in the dimension of wealth spaces (Hart, 1973), financial equilibrium may fail to exist when restrictions on participation involve future as well as present market transactions (Example 2 of Section 6).

The only directly related work we know about is that of Benveniste (1985, 1986) (who characterizes when financial markets are essentially complete despite restricted participation), Siconolfi (1986a, 1986b) (who establishes existence under increasingly general specification of the portfolio choice set, including that investigated here), and Younès (1987) (who, utilizing his own imaginative reformulation of exchange opportunities (Younès, 1986), also investigates properties of competitive equilibrium when households face different, linear homogeneous constraints on their market transactions).

We should emphasize that our results and Younès' are complementary, since he provides sufficient conditions for existence and (generic, local) uniqueness in the opposite leading polar case, where all yields depend in linear homogeneous fashion on spot prices. Finally, we might also mention that Balasko et al. (1988) study sunspot equilibria in an extreme version of our present model, where there is a complete array of financial instruments, but each household is either absolutely restricted or absolutely unrestricted.

2. A Leading Polar Case

There are L types of physical commodities (labeled by superscript $c = 1, 2, \ldots, L$, and referred to as *goods*) and M types of credit or financial instruments (labeled by superscript $i = 1, 2, \ldots, M$, and referred to as *bonds*). Both goods and bonds are traded on a spot market today, while only goods will be traded on a spot market in one of N possible states of the world tomorrow (these markets are labeled by superscript $s = 0, 1, \ldots, N$, and are referred to as *spots*). So, altogether there are $l = L(N+1)$ goods, whose quantities and (spot) prices are represented by the vectors

$$\boldsymbol{x} = (x^0, \ldots, x^s, \ldots, x^N) \quad [\text{with } x^s = (x^{s,1}, \ldots, x^{s,c}, \ldots, x^{s,L})]$$

and

$$\boldsymbol{p} = (p^0, \ldots, p^s, \ldots, p^N) \quad [\text{with } p^s = (p^{s,1}, \ldots, p^{s,c}, \ldots, p^{s,L})],$$

respectively. The quantities and prices of bonds are represented by the vectors

$$\boldsymbol{b} = (b^1, \ldots, b^i, \ldots, b^M) \quad \text{and} \quad \boldsymbol{q} = (q^1, \ldots, q^i, \ldots, q^M),$$

respectively. (Note: All prices are measured in units of account, referred to as *dollars*. It will be convenient, for example, in representing dollar values of spot market transactions to treat every price vector as a row. Otherwise we maintain the standard convention.) As already mentioned in the introduction, the typical bond, which costs q^i dollars at spot $s = 0$, promises to return a yield of $r^{s,i}$ dollars at spot $s > 0$. Finally, there are m households (labeled by subscript $h = 1, 2, \ldots, m$), who are described by (i) utility functions $u_h : \Re^l \to \Re$, (ii) goods endowments $\omega_h \in \Re^l$, and (iii) portfolio constraints $B_h \subset \Re^M$. We assume throughout that, for $h = 1, 2, \ldots, m$.

A.1. u_h *is* C^2, *differentiably strictly increasing* (i.e., $Du_h(x_h) \gg 0$) and *differentiably strictly quasi-concave* (i.e., $Du_h(x_u)^{\mathrm{T}}\Delta x = 0$ and

$\Delta x \neq 0 \Rightarrow \Delta x^{\mathrm{T}} D^2 u_h(x_h) \Delta x < 0$), *and has indifference surfaces bounded below*; and

A.2. *B_h is an M_h-dimensional linear subspace of* $\Re^M$ with $0 \leqq M_h \leqq M$.

Let

$$P = \{p \in \Re^l_{++}\},$$
= set of (no-arbitrage) spot goods prices,

$$Q = \left\{ q \in \Re^M : \text{there is no } h \text{ with } b_h \in B_h \text{ s.t.} \begin{bmatrix} -q \\ R \end{bmatrix} b_h > 0 \right\},$$
= set of no-arbitrage bond prices,

$$R = \begin{bmatrix} r^{1,1} & \ldots & r^{1,i} & \ldots & r^{1,M} \\ \vdots & \ddots & & & \\ r^{s,1} & & r^{s,i} & & \\ \vdots & & & \ddots & \\ r^{N,1} & & & & r^{N,M} \end{bmatrix} = \begin{bmatrix} r^1 \\ \vdots \\ r^s \\ \vdots \\ r^N \end{bmatrix},$$
= $(N \times M)$ – dimensional matrix of bond yields

and

$$\Omega = \{\omega = (\omega_1, \ldots, \omega_h, \ldots, \omega_m) \in (\Re^l)^m\},$$
= set of possible goods endowments (and allocations).

Then, given $\omega \in \Omega$, $(p, q) \in P \times Q$ is a *financial equilibrium* (sometimes, to break the monotony, abbreviated fe) if, when households optimize, that is,

given $(p, q), (x_h, b_h)$ solves the problem (1)

$$\begin{aligned} &\text{maximize} \quad u_h(x_h) \\ &\text{subject to} \quad p^0(x_h^0 - \omega_h^0) = -q b_h, \end{aligned}$$

$$p^s(x_h^s - \omega_h^s) = r^s b_h \quad \text{for all } s > 0$$

and

$$b_h \in B_h, \quad h = 1, 2, \ldots, m,$$

both goods and bond markets clear, that is,

$$\sum_h (x_h^{s,c} - \omega_h^{s,c}) = 0, \quad (s, c) = (0, 1), (0, 2), \ldots, (N, L) \tag{2}$$

and

$$\sum_h b_h^i = 0, \quad i = 1, 2, \ldots, M. \tag{3}$$

Remark. This model of *restricted participation* reduces to the more familiar model of *incomplete markets* when $M < N$ and $B_h = \Re^M$, $h = 1, 2, \ldots, m$. The principal differences between these two models are that, for the special case,

- there is, a priori, no loss of generality in assuming that

$$\text{rank } R = M, \tag{4}$$

  that is, that there are no redundant bonds, and
- given Equation (4), Equation (2) implies Equation (3), so that (as first established in Cass (1984), and then exploited in Balasko and Cass (1989))

$$\text{for every } q \in Q, \text{ there exists a financial equilibrium,} \tag{5}$$

  that is, provided there are no-arbitrage opportunities on the bond market, flexible spot goods prices alone suffice to clear both goods and bond markets.

For the general case, however, matters are much more complicated. Even though (as we demonstrate in the following section) there is justification for an analogue of property (4), there is no simplification corresponding to property (5). In other words, with restricted participation it is necessary to keep track of both Equations (2) and (3), and therefore, roughly speaking, fully flexible prices are required in order to clear both goods and bond markets.

3. Transformation of Financial Opportunities

For $h = 1, 2, \ldots, m$, let

$$W_h(q) = \left\{ w_h \in \Re^{N+1} : \text{there is } b_h \in B_h \text{ s.t. } w_h = \begin{bmatrix} -q \\ R \end{bmatrix} b_h \right\} \quad \text{for} \quad q \in Q$$
$$= \text{subspace of portfolio wealth possibilities.}$$

Consider the situation where, for some h,

$$\dim W_h(q) < \dim B_h \quad \text{for} \quad q \in Q \tag{6}$$

(which implies that rank $R < M$). Then the differential approach for analyzing the structure of financial equilibrium faces a basic obstacle: The household's optimal portfolio choice is a correspondence, not a function. And there is no satisfactory justification for ruling out this situation on a priori grounds. Indeed, one significant source of restricted participation is financial intermediation (in our stylized setting, by some particular household), which typically involves redundancy.

In this section, we show how this obstacle can be overcome by transforming the economy's financial opportunities. The essential idea is very intuitive, and can be seen by example.

Example 1. Suppose

$$M = 3, \quad N = 2, \quad R = \begin{bmatrix} 1 & 0 & 1 \\ 0 & 1 & 1 \end{bmatrix}, \quad m = 3 \quad \text{and}$$

$$B_1 = \Re^3, \quad B_2 = \{b_2 \in \Re^3 : b_2^1 = b_2^2 \& b_2^3 = 0\} \quad \text{and}$$

$$B_3 = \{b_3 \in \Re^3 : b_3^1 = b_3^2 = 0\}.$$

Then, clearly, $Q = \{q \in \Re^3_{++} : q^3 = q^1 + q^2\}$ while dim $W_1(q) = 2 < 3 =$ dim B_1 for $q \in Q$. But precisely because Mr. 1 can, for instance, reproduce bond 3 by combining equal amounts of bonds 1 and 2 (and thereby provide intermediation between Mr. 2 and Mr. 3), it is obvious that – in terms of equilibrium allocation – these financial opportunities are equivalent to those where

$$M' = 2, \quad R' = \begin{bmatrix} 1 & 0 \\ 0 & 1 \end{bmatrix} \quad \text{and}$$

$$B_1' = \Re^2 \quad \text{and} \quad B_2' = B_3' = \{b' \in \Re^2 : b^{1'} = b^{2'}\}.$$

Now clearly, $Q' = \{q' \in \Re^2_{++}\}$ while, for all three households,

$$\dim W_h'(q') = \dim B_h' \quad \text{for} \quad q' \in Q'. \qquad \square$$

In general, such conversion of the, say, *original* economy with financial opportunities $\{R, B_h, h = 1, 2, \ldots, m\}$ exhibiting the property (6) into an equivalent, say, *transformed* economy with financial opportunities $\{R', B_h', h = 1, 2, \ldots, m\}$ satisfying the condition

$$\dim W_h'(q') = \dim B_h' \quad \text{for} \quad q' \in Q', \quad h = 1, 2, \ldots, m, \tag{7}$$

involves more elaborate calculation. We outline the logic of this algebra, relegating proofs to the appendix in order to avoid overly diverting the flow of our development.

For $h = 1, 2, \ldots, m$, let $B_h^0 = \{b_h \in B_h : Rb_h = 0\}$, and consider the subspace generated by these sets of zero wealth portfolios, $B^0 = \sum_h B_h^0$. If Equation (6) obtains, then $B_h^0 \neq \{0\}$, and B^0 is k-dimensional, where

$0<k\leqq M$–rank R. Without loss of generality (by relabeling and transforming appropriately) we can pick a basis for B^0, say, A^0, such that

$$A^0 = \begin{bmatrix} A' \\ -I_k \end{bmatrix},$$

where A' is an $((M-k)\times k)$-dimensional matrix, and I_k is the k^2-dimensional identity. Then, partitioning R and q conformably with A^0, we have

$$RA^0 = [R' \quad R''] \begin{bmatrix} A' \\ -I_k \end{bmatrix} = R'A' - R'' = 0$$

or

$$R'' = R'A' \tag{8}$$

and, for $q\in Q$ (for which it must be the case that $qb_h = 0$ for $b_h \in B_h^0$, $h = 1,2, \ldots , m$ or $qb = 0$ for $b\in B^0$),

$$qA^0 = (q', q'') \begin{bmatrix} A' \\ -I_k \end{bmatrix} = q'A' - q'' = 0$$

or

$$q'' = q'A', \tag{9}$$

where R' and q' represent the yields and (no-arbitrage) prices associated with the first $M' = M$–k original bonds. Finally, define for $h = 1, 2, \ldots , m$,

$$B'_h = \{b'_h \in \Re^{M'} : \text{there is } b_h = (t'_h, t''_h) \in B_h \text{ s.t. } b'_h = t'_h + A't''_h\}.$$

We now simply relate, ceteris paribus, financial equilibria in the original economy to those in the transformed economy (distinguishing the latter from the former by means of the symbol "prime"). Our specific objective calls for bringing quantities as well as prices explicitly into the picture (representing goods allocations by $x = (x_1, \ldots , x_h, \ldots , x_m)$ and portfolio holdings by $b = (b_1, \ldots , b_h, \ldots , b_m)$).

Theorem 1. *If (p, q, x, b) represents an fe in the original economy, then there are q' and b' such that $(p', q', x', b',) = (p, q', x, b')$ represents a fe in the transformed economy. Conversely, if (p', q', x', b') represents a fe in the transformed economy, then there are q and b such that $(p, q, x, b) = (p', q, x', b)$ represents a fe in the original economy.*

Proof of Theorem 1. See the appendix.

Of course, this equivalence would be of no avail if condition (7) was not satisfied.

Theorem 2. *Condition* (7) *is satisfied.*

Proof of Theorem 2. See the appendix.

The foregoing argument permits us to assert that there is no loss of generality if we assume hereafter that, for $h = 1, 2, \ldots, m$.

A.3. $\dim W_h(q) = \dim B_h$ for $q \in Q$.

4. Properties of Financial Equilibrium

In order to trace the effects of restricted participation on equilibrium allocation, we will need a thorough understanding of the structure of the solutions to the equations generated by Equations (1)–(3). This analysis follows the program laid out in Balasko (1988), and parallels our earlier investigations concerning financial equilibrium with incomplete markets (reported in Balasko and Cass (1985, 1989)). In both this and the following section, we draw freely from the results contained in that work.

Here we begin by discussing properties of no-arbitrage bond prices, then turn to characterizing optimal household behavior, and conclude by describing the structure of the equilibrium set itself. Unfortunately (but unavoidably) our presentation is quite notation intensive. For instance, throughout the sequel we will find it very useful to treat prices for and quantities of the first type of commodity asymmetrically. So, at the outset, let

$$\begin{aligned} p^{\backslash 1} &= (p^{0,1}, \ldots, p^{s,1}, \ldots, p^{N,1}) \\ &= \text{vector of spot goods prices for } \textit{just} \text{ the first type of commodity} \end{aligned}$$

and

$$\begin{aligned} p^{\backslash 1} &= ((p^{0,2}, \ldots, p^{0,c}, \ldots, p^{0,L}), \ldots, (p^{s,2}, \ldots, p^{s,c}, \ldots, p^{s,L}), \ldots, \\ &\quad (p^{N,2}, \ldots, p^{N,c}, \ldots, p^{N,L})) \\ &= \text{vector of spot goods price for } \textit{all but} \text{ the first type of commodity,} \end{aligned}$$

with a parallel convention regarding $x^{\cdot 1}$ and $x^{\backslash 1}$.

4.1. No-Arbitrage Bond Prices

For $h = 1, 2, \ldots, m$, let

$$Q_h^M = \left\{ q \in \Re^M : \text{there is no } b_h \in B_h \text{ s.t.} \begin{bmatrix} -q \\ R \end{bmatrix} b_h > 0 \right\},$$

so that

$$Q = \bigcap_h Q_h^M.$$

Lemma 1. *Q (and hence Q_h^M) is nonempty and open.*

Proof of Lemma 1. *Nonemptiness.* Consider the set

$$Q^M = \left\{ q \in \Re^M : \text{there is no } b \in \Re^M \text{ s.t.} \begin{bmatrix} -q \\ R \end{bmatrix} b > 0 \right\} \subset Q_h^M, \quad h = 1, 2, \ldots, m.$$

Take $q = \sum_s r^s$. Then clearly $q \in Q^M$ (since otherwise we would have the contradiction that, for some $b \in \Re^M$, $(-qb, r^1 b, \ldots, r^s b, \ldots, r^N b) > 0$ but $-qb + \sum_s r^s b = 0$), so $q \in Q$.

Openness. Take $q \in Q$, and suppose that, for some h, there is a sequence q^ν, $\nu = 1, 2, \ldots$, such that $q^\nu \notin Q_h^M$ but $\lim_{\nu\to\infty} q^\nu = q$. Picking $b_h^\nu \in B_h$, such that

$$||b_h^\nu|| = 1 \quad \text{and} \quad \begin{bmatrix} -q^\nu \\ R \end{bmatrix} b_h^\nu > 0,$$

it follows that for some subsequence of indices, say, ν^j, $j = 1, 2, \ldots$,

$$\lim_{j\to\infty} b_h^{\nu j} = b_h \in B_h, \quad b_h \neq 0 \quad \text{and} \quad \begin{bmatrix} -q \\ R \end{bmatrix} b_h = 0,$$

which contradicts Assumption A.3. □

4.2. Optimal Household Behavior

The analysis of household demand is greatly facilitated by introducing "individualized" bond prices, bond yields, and budget constraints.

Consider the typical household h. Pick a basis for B_h, say, A_h, an $(M \times M_h)$-dimensional, full-rank matrix, and let $y_h \in \Re^{M_h}$ represent portfolio activities relative to this basis, that is, interpret

$$b_h = A_h y_h.$$

Transform q and R accordingly, that is, interpret

$$q_h = qA_h \quad \text{and} \quad R_h = RA_h.$$

Here, however, we will only require that

$$q_h \in Q_h = \{q_h \in \Re_h^{M_h} : \text{there is } q \in Q_h^M \text{ s.t. } q_h = qA_h\}$$
$$= \left\{ q_h \in \Re_h^{M_h} : \text{there is no } y_h \in \Re^{M_h} \text{ s.t. } \begin{bmatrix} -q_h \\ R_h \end{bmatrix} y_h > 0 \right\};$$

obviously, our analysis remains valid with Q substituted for Q_h^M in the definition of Q_h. We should also emphasize that, under Assumption A.3,

$$\text{rank } R_h = M_h.$$

Finally, let

$$\phi_h(p, q_h) = \begin{bmatrix} p^0 & & & & q_h \\ & \ddots & & 0 & \\ & & p^s & & \\ 0 & & & \ddots & \\ & & & p^N & -R_h \end{bmatrix}.$$

After introducing these constructs, the problem in Equation (1) is transformed into the concise (and tractable) form

$$\text{maximize} \quad u_h(x_h) \tag{10}$$

$$\text{subject to} \quad \phi_h(p, q_h) \begin{pmatrix} x_h - \omega_h \\ y_h \end{pmatrix} = 0,$$

where the $((N+1) \times (l+M))$-dimensional price–yield matrix $\phi_h(p,q_h)$ plays much the same role as does the l-dimensional price vector $\boldsymbol{p}$ in the standard Walrasian model.

Let the row vector $\boldsymbol{\mu}_h = (\mu_h^0, \ldots, \mu_h^s, \ldots, \mu_h^N)$ represent the Lagrange multipliers associated with the $N+1$ budget constraints in Equation (10). Then the solution to Equation (10) is characterized by the Lagrangean conditions

$$(Du_h(x_h)^{\mathrm{T}}, 0) = \mu_h \phi_h(p, q_h) \tag{11}$$

and

$$\phi_h(p, q_h) \begin{pmatrix} x_h - \omega_h \\ y_h \end{pmatrix} = 0.$$

Treating x_h and y_h as variables (thereby suppressing μ_h), and p, q_h, and ω_h as parameters, let the functions

$$(f_h, g_h) : P \times Q_h \times \Re^l \to \Re^l \times \Re^{M_h}$$

represent the solutions to Equation (11). (Note: Hereafter we use (f_h, g_h) and (x_h, y_h) interchangeably.)

Lemma 2. *(f_h, g_h) is well defined and continuously differentiable. Furthermore,*

$$\text{if} \quad Du_h(x_h) \sim p \quad \text{and} \quad (x_h - \omega_h, y_h) = 0, \tag{12}$$

$$\text{then} \quad \frac{\partial(x_h^{\backslash 1}, y_h)}{\partial(p^{\backslash 1}, q_h)} \quad \text{is negative definite}$$

and

$$\text{rank} \; \frac{\partial(x_h^{\backslash 1} - \omega_h^{\backslash 1}, y_h)}{\partial \omega_h} = l + M_h - (N+1). \tag{13}$$

Proof of Lemma 2. Given Assumptions A.1–A.3, this amounts to routine (and tedious) adaptation of the central development in Balasko and Cass (1985), and is therefore omitted. □

4.3. The Equilibrium Manifold

Utilizing the preceding reformulation, the market clearing Equations (2)–(3) can be rewritten

$$\sum_h (x_h^{s,c} - \omega_h^{s,c}) = \sum_h (f_h^{s,c}(p, qA_h, \omega_h) - \omega_h^{s,c}) = 0,$$
$$(s, c) = (0,1), (0,2), \ldots, (N, L) \tag{14}$$

and

$$\sum_h b_h^i = \sum_h a_h^i y_h = \sum_h a_h^i g_h(p, qA_h, \omega_h) = 0, \quad i = 1, 2, \ldots, M, \tag{15}$$

where a_h^i is the ith row of A_h. This system consists of $l + M$ equations in the $l + M + ml$ variables p, q, and ω. However, by virtue of the $N+1$ budget constraints in Equation (10), at least $N+1$ equations are redundant; in particular, it is easily verified that the goods market clearing equations for the first type of commodity are redundant. Further, let $A = (A_1, \ldots, A_h, \ldots, A_m)$, an $(M \times \sum_h M_h)$-dimensional matrix and suppose that rank $A = M' < M$. Then, in addition, M–M' of the bond market clearing equations is also redundant. This last is merely a nuisance (it can be handled directly by dropping the offending equations, and then redefining the no-arbitrage bond prices accordingly). Thus, for simplicity, we assume hereafter that

A.4. rank $A = M$.

Now let

$$E = \{(p, q, \omega) \in P \times Q \times \Omega : (p, q, \omega) \text{ solves } (14) - (15)\}$$
$$= \text{the equilibrium set,}$$
$$P^{\cdot 1} = \{p^{\cdot 1} \in \Re^{N+1}_{++}\},$$
$$\pi_E = \text{restriction to } E \text{ of the projection of } P \times Q \times \Omega \text{ onto } P^{\cdot 1} \times \Omega$$

and

$$V = \{(p^{\cdot 1}, \omega) \in P^{\cdot 1} \times \Omega : (p^{\cdot 1}, \omega) \text{ is a regular value of } \pi_E\}.$$

Theorem 3. *E is a smooth, $((N+1)+ml)$-dimensional manifold. Furthermore, π_E is proper and subjective, so that V is an open, dense subset of $P^{\cdot 1} \times \Omega$.*

Proof of Theorem 3. This argument basically amounts to elaborating the proofs for similar results in the Walrasian (or, better, the incomplete markets) model.

Smoothness and dimension. From the discussion at the beginning of this subsection, we know that the Jacobian of Equations (14)–(15) can have, at most, rank equal $l + M - (N+1)$. To see that, in fact, it has maximal rank, consider

$$\frac{\partial \sum_h (x_h^{\backslash 1} - \omega_h^{\backslash 1}, b_h)}{\partial \omega} = \frac{\partial \sum_h (x_h^{\backslash 1} - \omega_h^{\backslash 1}, A_h y_h)}{\partial \omega}$$
$$= \begin{bmatrix} \dfrac{\partial (x_1^{\backslash 1} - \omega_1^{\backslash 1})}{\partial \omega_1} & \cdots & \dfrac{\partial (x_m^{\backslash 1} - \omega_m^{\backslash 1})}{\partial \omega_m} \\ A_1 \dfrac{\partial y_1}{\partial \omega_1} & & A_m \dfrac{\partial y_m}{\partial \omega_m} \end{bmatrix}$$

an $((l + M - (N+1)) \times ml)$-dimensional matrix, and suppose that, for $(\Delta x^{\backslash 1}, \Delta b) \in \Re^{l+M-(N+1)}$,

$$0 = (\Delta x^{\backslash 1 \mathrm{T}}, \Delta b^{\mathrm{T}}) \frac{\partial \sum_h (x_h^{\backslash 1} - \omega_h^{\backslash 1}, b_h)}{\partial \omega}$$
$$= \left[\Delta x^{\backslash 1 \mathrm{T}} \frac{\partial (x_1^{\backslash 1} - \omega_1^{\backslash 1})}{\partial \omega_1} + \Delta b^{\mathrm{T}} A_1 \frac{\partial y_1}{\partial \omega_1} \ldots \Delta x^{\backslash 1 \mathrm{T}} \frac{\partial (x_m^{\backslash 1} - \omega_m^{\backslash 1})}{\partial \omega_m} + \Delta b^{\mathrm{T}} A_m \frac{\partial y_m}{\partial \omega_m} \right].$$

Then property (13) implies that $\Delta x^{\backslash 1} = 0$ and $\Delta b^{T} A_h = 0$, $h = 1, 2, \dots, m$, while Assumption A.4 implies that $\Delta b = 0$. So we can conclude that

$$\text{rank}\frac{\partial \sum_h (x_h^{\backslash 1} - \omega_h^{\backslash 1}, b_h)}{\partial \omega} = l + M - (N+1),$$

or that E can be parametrized locally in terms of p, q, and $ml - (l + M - (N+1))$ elements of ω. It also follows directly that

$$\begin{aligned} \dim E &= \dim(P \times Q \times \Omega) - \operatorname{codim} E \\ &= (l + M + ml) - (l + M - (N+1)) = (N+1) + ml. \end{aligned}$$

Properness. Take $K \subset P^{\cdot 1} \times \Omega$ compact. We need to show that $\pi_E^{-1}(K)$ is also compact. Consider a sequence $(p^{\nu}, q^{\nu}, \omega^{\nu}) \in \pi_E^{-1}(K)$, $\nu = 1, 2, \dots$, and let $q_h^{\nu} = q^{\nu} A_h \in Q_h$, $h = 1, 2, \dots, m$. Then, pursuing the same line of reasoning as in the proof of Theorem 4.3 in Balasko and Cass (1989), it can be readily verified that there is a subsequence of indices, say, ν^j, $j = 1, 2, \dots$, such that

$$\lim_{j \to \infty} (p^{\cdot 1 \nu j}, \omega^{\nu j}) = (p^{\cdot 1}, \omega) \in K \tag{16}$$

and

$$\lim_{j \to \infty} (p^{\nu j}, q_h^{\nu j}) = (p, q_h) \in P \times Q_h, \quad h = 1, 2, \dots, m.$$

Moreover, since $q_h^{\nu^j} = q^{\nu^j} A_h$ with $q^{\nu^j} \in Q$, $h = 1, 2, \dots, m$, Assumption A.4 implies that

$$\lim_{j \to \infty} q^{\nu j} = q \in Q.$$

Hence, we have established that

$$\lim_{j \to \infty} (p^{\nu^j}, q^{\nu^j}, \omega^{\nu^j}) = (p, q, \omega) \in P \times Q \times \Omega. \tag{17}$$

Finally, since (f_h, g_h), $h = 1, 2, \dots, m$, are continuous, Equations (16) and (17) imply that $(p, q, \omega) \in \pi_E^{-1}(p^{\cdot 1}, \omega) \subset \pi_E^{-1}(K)$.

Subjectivity. Take $\omega^* \in \Omega$ a Pareto optimal allocation supported by $p^* \in P$, and let $q^* = \sum_s r^s \in Q$. It is easily checked (using the Lagrangean conditions (11) with $\mu_h \sim 1$) that

$$(\omega_h^*, 0) = (f_h(p^*, q^* A_h, \omega_h^*), g_h(p^*, q^* A_h, \omega_h^*)), \quad h = 1, 2, \dots, m,$$

and (using the Pareto optimality of ω^*) that

$$\pi_E^{-1}(p^{\cdot 1 *}, \omega^*) = \{(p^*, q^*, \omega^*)\}.$$

It can also be shown that $(p^{\cdot 1*}, \omega^*) \in V$. Consider

$$\left.\frac{\partial \sum_h (x_h^{\setminus 1} - \omega_h^{\setminus 1}, b_h)}{\partial (p^{\setminus 1}, q)}\right|_{(p^*,q^*,\omega^*)} = \left.\frac{\partial \sum_h (x_h^{\setminus 1} - A_h y_h)}{\partial (p^{\setminus 1}, q)}\right|_{(p^*,q^*,\omega^*)}$$

$$= \sum_h \begin{bmatrix} \dfrac{\partial x_h^{\setminus 1}}{\partial p^{\setminus 1}} & \dfrac{\partial x_h^{\setminus 1}}{\partial q_h} A_h^{\mathrm{T}} \\ A_h \dfrac{\partial y_h}{\partial p^{\setminus 1}} & \dfrac{\partial y_h}{\partial q_h} A_h^{\mathrm{T}} \end{bmatrix}_{(p^*,q^*,\omega^*)}$$

an $(l + M - (N+1))^2$-dimensional matrix, and suppose that, for $(\Delta p^{\setminus 1}, \Delta q) \in \Re^{l+M-(N+1)}$,

$$0 = (\Delta p^{\setminus 1\mathrm{T}}, \Delta q^{\mathrm{T}}) \left.\frac{\partial \sum_h (x_h^{\setminus 1} - \omega_h^{\setminus 1}, b_h)}{\partial (p^{\setminus 1}, q)}\right|_{(p^*,q^*,\omega^*)}$$

so that

$$0 = (\Delta p^{\setminus 1\mathrm{T}}, \Delta q^{\mathrm{T}}) \left.\frac{\partial \sum_h (x_h^{\setminus 1} - \omega_h^{\setminus 1}, b_h)}{\partial (p^{\setminus 1}, q)}\right|_{(p^*,q^*,\omega^*)} \begin{pmatrix} \Delta p^{\setminus 1} \\ \Delta q \end{pmatrix}$$

(after some simplification)

$$= \sum_h (\Delta p^{\setminus 1\mathrm{T}}, \Delta q^{\mathrm{T}} A_h) \left.\frac{\partial \sum_h (x_h^{\setminus 1} - y_h)}{\partial (p^{\setminus 1}, q_h)}\right|_{(p^*,q^*,\omega^*)} \begin{pmatrix} \Delta p^{\setminus 1} \\ \Delta q \end{pmatrix}.$$

Now property (12) implies that $\Delta p^{/1} = 0$ and $\Delta q^{\mathrm{T}} A_h = 0$, $h = 1, 2, \ldots, m$, while Assumption A.4 implies that $\Delta q^{\mathrm{T}} = 0$. So we can conclude that

$$\operatorname{rank} \left.\frac{\partial \sum_h (x_h^{\setminus 1} - \omega_h^{\setminus 1}, b_h)}{\partial (p^{\setminus 1}, q)}\right|_{(p^*,q^*,\omega^*)} = l + M - (N+1),$$

or that $(p^{\cdot 1^*}, \omega^*)$ is a regular value of π_E.

Thus, we have a regular value whose inverse image contains an odd number of elements. Moreover, π_E is a smooth, proper mapping from a smooth, boundaryless manifold into a smooth, connected manifold of equal dimension. It follows from a theorem of Milnor (1965, p. 24) that the mod 2 degree of π_E is the same for all regular values. So, on the one hand, $\pi_E^{-1}(p^{\cdot 1}, \omega) \neq \phi$ for $(p^{\cdot 1}, \omega) \in V$. On the other hand, by definition, $\pi_E^{-1}(p^{\cdot 1}, \omega) \neq \phi$ for $(p^{\cdot 1}, \omega) \in (p^{\cdot 1} \times \Omega) \setminus V$. So $\pi_E(E) = R^{\cdot 1} \times \Omega$.

Genericity. Given properness and subjectivity, this is an immediate implication of Sard's Theorem (see, e.g., Milnor (1965, p. 16)). □

5. Indeterminacy of Equilibrium Allocation

Let

$$E_\omega = \{(p,q) \in P \times Q : (p,q,\omega) \in E\} \quad \text{for} \quad \omega \in \Omega$$
$$= \text{set of financial equilibria (corresponding to given good endowments).}$$

An immediate consequence of Theorem 3 is that, for generic ω, E_ω contains a smooth, $(N+1)$-dimensional submanifold; in short, there will generally be $N+1$ degrees of equilibrium price or *nominal* indeterminacy. In this section, we address the more interesting question: To what extent does this nominal indeterminacy translate into equilibrium allocation or *real* indeterminacy?

The first obvious response is that at least two degrees of nominal indeterminacy are always superfluous. Homogeneity of the budget constraints together with homogeneity of the portfolio constraints in Equation (1) permits adopting two spot market price normalizations. (Note: In particular, the first budget constraint is homogeneous in spot good prices and bond prices, while each budget constraint is homogeneous in spot good prices and portfolio holdings. Thus, for example, we could have taken

$$P = \{p \in \Re^l_{++} : p^{0,1} = p^{N,1} = 1\} \tag{18}$$

at the outset. The only significant change in the preceding results would be that dim $E = (N-1) + ml$, rather $(N+1) + ml$.) Two other pertinent observations motivate introducing additional assumptions to ensure that the remaining $N-1$ degrees of nominal indeterminacy translate into (some degree of) real indeterminacy:

- Without sufficiently disparate incentives for exchange of goods, there may be no real indeterminacy. For extreme examples, consider the case where $m = 1$ or where ω is a Pareto optimal allocation.
- Without sufficiently flexible (but still limited) opportunities for exchange of credit, there may be no real indeterminacy. For extreme examples, consider the case where $B_h = \{0\}$, $h = 1, 2, \ldots, m$, or where $M < N$ and

$$R = \begin{bmatrix} I_M \\ 0 \end{bmatrix}.$$

(Note: For the latter, "no real indeterminacy" translates formally into "generic, local uniqueness.") The following specification is designed to avoid these kinds of borderline cases.

Suppose that some group of households, say, the first m_0 households, faces common portfolio constraints, say,

$$B_h = B_0, h = 1, 2, \ldots, m_0.$$

Denote, for $h = 1, 2, \ldots, m_0$, $M_h = M_0$, $A_h = A_0$, $R_h = R_0$, and so on (e.g., $x_0 = (x_1, \ldots, x_h, \ldots, x_{m0})$). Also let $n_0 = N{-}M_0$, a measure of this group's deficiency in access to the bond market. Assume that

A.5. $m_0 > n_0$;

A.6. $0 < n_0 < N$; and

A.7. R_0 is in general position (alternatively, there is $y_0 \in \Re^{M_0}$ such that $R_0 y_0 \gg 0$).

Roughly speaking, Assumptions A.5–A.7 mean that this group is *numerous*, is *restricted*, but not completely, and is *flexible*, in the sense that, relative to its deficiency in access to the bond market, it can achieve maximum wealth insurance (alternatively, positive wealth accumulation). (For more complete discussion and analysis of this last kind of assumption and its variants, see Balasko and Cass (1989), Geanakoplos and Mas-Colell (1989), and Werner (1986)).

Under Assumptions A.5–A.7 (and given the maintained Assumptions A.1–A.4), nominal indeterminacy translates into a precise degree of real indeterminacy.

Let

$$f(p, q, \omega) = (f_1(p, qA_1, \omega_1), \ldots, f_h(p, qA_h, \omega_h), \ldots, f_m(p, qA_m, \omega_m))$$

and

$$\begin{aligned} X_\omega &= \{x \in \Omega : \text{ there is } (p, q) \in E_\omega \text{ s.t. } x = f(p, q, \omega)\} \quad \text{for} \quad \omega \in \Omega \\ &= \text{set of equilibrium allocations} \\ &\quad \text{(corresponding to given good endowments).} \end{aligned}$$

Theorem 4. *If Assumptions A.5–A.7 are satisfied, then there is an open, dense subset of* Ω*, say,* $\tilde{\Omega}$*, such that, for every* $\omega \in \tilde{\Omega}$*,* X_ω *contains a smooth, (N–1)-dimensional (alternatively,* n_0*-dimensional) submanifold, say,* $\tilde{X}_\omega$.

Aside from the fact that we must account for the diversity of portfolio constraints, our proof of this fundamental result essentially mimics the proof of Theorem 4.4 in Balasko and Cass (1989). (We could almost as well have mimicked the proof of Theorem 1 in Geanakoplos and Mas-Colell (1989).) For this reason, we will merely restate the essential steps in the proof for the simplified situation where (in terms of nominal indeterminacy) P is described by Equation (18) and where (in terms of financial opportunities) $m_0 = n_0 + 1$; the interested reader can refer to the working paper from which this article has been distilled for details.

Let (by slightly abusing our previous usage)

$$D_0^{\cdot 1}(x_0) = \begin{bmatrix} D_{x^{0,1}}u_1(x_1) & \dots & D_{x^{s,1}}u_1(x_1) & \dots & D_{x^{n_0,1}}u_1(x_1) \\ \vdots & \ddots & & & \\ D_{x^{0,1}}u_h(x_h) & \dots & D_{x^{s,1}}u_h(x_h) & & \\ \vdots & & & \ddots & \\ D_{x^{0,1}}u_{m0}(x_{m0}) & & & & D_{x^{n_0,1}}u_{m0}(x_{m0}) \end{bmatrix}$$

an $(n_0 + 1)^2$-dimensional matrix,

$$\begin{aligned} \tilde{V} = \{(p^{\cdot 1}, \omega) \in V &: \text{there is } (p, q, \omega) \in \pi_E^{-1}(p^{\cdot 1}, \omega) \\ &\text{s.t. rank } D_0^{\cdot 1}(f_0(p, q, \omega_0)) = n_0 + 1\} \end{aligned}$$

and

$$\tilde{\Omega} = \{\omega \in \Omega : \text{there is } p^{\cdot 1} \in P^{\cdot 1} \text{ s.t. } (p^{\cdot 1}, \omega) \in \tilde{V}\}.$$

Lemma 3. *$\tilde{V}$ is an open, dense subset of V (and hence of $P^{\cdot 1} \times \Omega$).*

Lemma 4. *$\tilde{\Omega}$ is an open, dense subset of Ω. Furthermore, for every $\omega \in \tilde{\Omega}$, there is a smooth, (N–1)-dimensional (alternatively, n_0-dimensional) submanifold of E_ω, say $\tilde{E}_\omega$, such that, for every $(p, q) \in \tilde{E}_\omega$,*

$$\text{rank } D_0^{\cdot 1}(f_0(p, q, \omega_0)) = n_0 + 1.$$

Lemma 5. *For every $\omega \in \tilde{\Omega}$, f restricted to $\tilde{E}_\omega \times \{\omega\}$ is a diffeomorphism. Hence, in particular, for every $\omega \in \tilde{\Omega}$,*

$$\tilde{X}_\omega = f(\tilde{E}_\omega, \omega)$$

is a smooth, (N–1)-dimensional (alternatively, n_0-dimensional) submanifold of X_ω.

6. Extensions

Our main conclusion, that restricted participation (as does market incompleteness) typically leads to significant real indeterminacy, most likely survives substantial generalization beyond our very specific model. This remains to be seen. However, the main obstacles appear to be technical, not conceptual.

Some of these obstacles can clearly be bypassed in ways that are already well understood. For instance, consider introducing some (but not all) inequalities in the description of portfolio constraints. This should be amenable to the "exceptional case" approach employed by, say, McManus (1986) and Magill and Shafer (1990) (in establishing generic optimality when (i) all yields depend on spot prices and (ii) financial markets are potentially complete). The basic idea we have in mind here is simple: The financial equilibria in which small perturbations of endowments would shift equality to inequality constraints cannot be, in general, very significant. Similarly, introducing some (but not full) dependence of yields on spot prices should, at least to some extent (see our concluding qualification), be amenable to the "pseudo-equilibrium" approach pioneered by Duffie and Shafer (1985, 1986) (in establishing generic existence when (i) the dependence is linear but (ii) financial markets are actually incomplete).

Other obstacles will clearly require breaking new ground. For instance, consider introducing three or more periods, one obviously desirable extension of our analysis. This raises an interesting, unforeseen variant of the nonexistence problem, which can best be illustrated by example.

For this purpose, assume that there are just three spots, now interpreted as time periods, and two bonds, now providing overall returns of the form

$$R(q) = \begin{bmatrix} -q^1 & 0 \\ r^{1,1} & -q^2 \\ r^{2,1} & r^{2,2} \end{bmatrix}. \tag{19}$$

Example 2. $L = 1$, $r^{s,i} > 0$, $m = 2$ and $B_h = \{b_h \in \Re^2 : b_h^2 = \theta_h b_h^1\}$ with $\theta_h > 0$, $h = 1, 2$, and

$$\theta_1 \neq \theta_2. \tag{20}$$

In this case, we can easily exhibit preferences and endowments for which there is no financial equilibrium. In particular, take

$$u_h(x_h) = \sum_s v_h(x_h^s) \tag{21}$$

and $\omega_h \in \Re^3$ such that

$$v_1'(\omega_1^s)/v_2'(\omega_2^s) = \begin{cases} 1 & \text{for} \quad s = 0 \\ \theta_2/\theta_1 & \text{for} \quad s = 1 \\ (r^{2,1} + \theta_2 r^{2,2})/(r^{2,1} + \theta_1 r^{2,2}) & \text{for} \quad s = 2. \end{cases} \tag{22}$$

Then, modifying our previous notation to be consistent with Equation (19), we can make the following assertions.

- The only candidate for an equilibrium allocation is $x = \omega$.

Since here $A_h\begin{bmatrix}1\\ \theta_h\end{bmatrix}$, Equation (20) entails that $b_1+b_2=A_1y_1+A_2y_2=0$ if and only if $y_1=y_2=0$. But then the budget constraints in Equation (11) entail that $x_h=\omega_h$, $h=1, 2$.

– For every $(p, q)\in P\times Q$, $(x_h, y_h)=(\omega_h, 0)$ cannot satisfy the first-order conditions in Equation (11) for both Mr. 1 and Mr. 2.

On the one hand, from Equation (21),

$$Du_h(\omega_h)^{\mathrm{T}}=(\mu_h^0p^0,\mu_h^1p^1,\mu_h^2p^2)$$

entails

$$\mu_1^s/\mu_2^s=v_1'(\omega_1^s)/v_2'(\omega_2^s),\quad s=0,1,2. \tag{23}$$

On the other hand, from $R_h(q)=R(q)A_h$,

$$\mu_hR_h(q)=0$$

entails

$$\mu_h^0q^1=[(\mu_h^1r^{1,1})+\mu_h^2(r^{2,1}+\theta_hr^{2,2})]+[-\mu_h^1\theta_h]q^2,\quad h=1,2. \tag{24}$$

But then Equations (20), (22), and (23) entail that Equation (24) has no solution. □

This example is, of course, nongeneric; small perturbations of u_h or ω would permit solutions to Equation (24). So it seems that the underlying structural defect that the example displays can probably be patched up – though this needs further study. In any event, notice that nonexistence occurs despite the fact that condition (7) is satisfied (since dim $W_h(q)=1$ for $q\in Q$, $h=1, 2$); it is simply not a problem associated with change in the dimension (or some other irregular behavior) of wealth spaces.

Finally, we should emphasize that, for most generalizations of our model, there doesn't appear to be any natural way of avoiding the fundamental obstacle represented by property (6) – except by willing it away.

Acknowledgment

Research support from the Swiss and U.S. National Science Foundations (under grants nos. 1.118.0.85 and SES-8509957, respectively) is also gratefully acknowledged.

Appendix

Our sole purpose here is to provide proofs for Theorems 1 and 2.

Proof of Theorem 1. To begin with, take (p, q, x, b) to represent a fe in the original economy. Then $q \in Q$, and from Equations (8)–(9) it is easily seen that $W'_h(q') = W_h(q)$, $h = 1, 2, \dots, m$: Using the definition of B'_h, correspond

$$w'_h = \begin{bmatrix} -q' \\ R' \end{bmatrix} b'_h = \begin{bmatrix} -q' \\ R' \end{bmatrix} (t'_h + A' t''_h)$$

to

$$w_h = \begin{bmatrix} -q \\ R \end{bmatrix} b_h = \begin{bmatrix} -(q', q'') \\ R' R'' \end{bmatrix} \begin{pmatrix} t'_h \\ t''_h \end{pmatrix}$$

$$= \begin{bmatrix} -(q', q' A') \\ R' R' A' \end{bmatrix} \begin{pmatrix} t'_h \\ t''_h \end{pmatrix} = \begin{bmatrix} -q \\ R \end{bmatrix} (t'_h + A' t''_h).$$

So, when $p' = p$, the constraints in (1′) and (1) describe exactly the same consumption possibilities. Finally, given $b_h = (t'_h, t''_h) \in B_h$, pick

$$b'_h = t'_h + A' t''_h, \quad h = 1, 2, \dots, m.$$

Obviously, for this choice,

$$w'_h = w_h, \quad h = 1, 2, \dots, m,$$

so that, taking $(p', q') = (p, q'), (x'_h, b'_h) = (x_h, b'_h)$ solves (1′) while

$$\sum_h b'_h = \sum_h (t'_h + A' t''_h) = \sum_h t'_h + A' \sum_h t''_h = 0$$

so that $(x', b') = (x, b')$ solves (2′)–(3′).

Now take (p', q', x', b') to represent a fe in the transformed economy. Pick $q = (q', q' A')$. Here again it is easily seen that $W_h(q) = W'_h(q')$, $h = 1, 2, \dots, m$. So proceeding as before, given $b'_h = t'_h + A' t''_h \in B'_h$, pick

$$b_h = \tilde{b}_h + \approx{b}_h, \tilde{b}_h = (t'_h, t''_h) \quad \text{and} \quad \approx{b}_h \in B^0_h \cap B^0, \quad h = 1, 2, \dots, m,$$

where

$$\sum_h \approx{b}_h = \begin{bmatrix} A' \\ -I_k \end{bmatrix} \left(\sum_h t''_h \right) = \begin{bmatrix} A' \sum_h t''_h \\ -\sum_h t''_h \end{bmatrix} \in B^0.$$

Obviously, here again for this choice

$$w_h = w'_h, \quad h = 1, 2, \dots, m$$

so that, taking $(p, q) = (p', q), (x_h, b_h) = (x'_h, b_h)$ solves (1) while

$$\sum_h b_h = \sum_h (\tilde{b}_h + \overset{\approx}{b}_h) = \sum_h (t'_h, t''_h) + \left(A' \sum_h t''_h, - \sum_h t''_h \right)$$
$$= \sum_h (t'_h + A' t''_h, 0) = 0$$

so that $(x, b) = (x', b)$ solves (2)–(3). □

Proof of Theorem 2. Suppose, to the contrary, that, for some h and $q' \in Q'$, $\dim W'_h(q') < \dim B'_h$. Then there is some $b'_h = t'_h + A' t''_h \in B'_h$ such that, first, $b'_h \neq 0$, and second

$$R' b'_h = R'(t'_h + A' t''_h) = R' t'_h + R' A' t''_h$$
$$= R' t'_h + R'' t''_h = [R' R''] \begin{pmatrix} t'_h \\ t''_h \end{pmatrix} = R b_h = 0.$$

The second property means that $b_h \in B^0_h = B_h \cap B^0$, that is, that there is $y \in \Re^k$ such that

$$b_h = \begin{pmatrix} t'_h \\ t''_h \end{pmatrix} = \begin{bmatrix} A' \\ -I_k \end{bmatrix} y = \begin{pmatrix} A' y \\ -y \end{pmatrix}.$$

However, this contradicts the first property, since it entails that

$$b'_h = t'_h + A' t''_h = A' y - A' y = 0. \qquad \square$$

References

Balasko, Y. (1988). *Foundations of the theory of general equilibrium*. Orlando, FL: Academic Press.

Balasko, Y. and Cass, D. (1985). Regular demand with several, general budget constraints. CARESS Working Paper No. 85-20. University of Pennsylvania, Philadelphia, PA, August.

Balasko, Y. and Cass, D. (1989). The structure of financial equilibrium with exogenous yields: The case of incomplete markets. *Econometrica* **57**, 135–162.

Balasko, Y., Cass, D. and Shell, K. (1988). Market participation and sunspot equilibria. CARESS Working Paper No. 88-08. University of Pennsylvania, Philadelphia, PA, March.

Benveniste, L.M. (1985). Local credit markets: How financial intermediaries coordinate the flow of credit. CARESS Working Paper No. 85-22. University of Pennsylvania, Philadelphia, PA, August.

Benveniste, L.M. (1986). Decentralized credit markets with intermediaries: The relationship between complete and efficient markets, preliminary paper, Board of Governors of the Federal Reserve System, Washington, DC, December.

Cass, D. (1984). Competitive equilibrium with incomplete financial markets. CARESS Working Paper No. 84-09. University of Pennsylvania, Philadelphia, PA, April.

Duffie, D. and Shafer, W. (1985). Equilibrium in incomplete markets: I. A basic model of generic existence. *Journal of Mathematical Economics* **14**, 285–300.

Duffie, D. and Shafer, W. (1986). Equilibrium in incomplete markets: II. Generic existence in stochastic economies. *Journal of Mathematical Economics* **15**, 199–216.

Geanakoplos, J. and Mas-Colell, A. (1989). Real indeterminacy with financial assets. *Journal of Economic Theory* **47**, 22–28.

Hart, O.D. (1973). On the optimality of equilibrium when the market structure is incomplete. *Journal of Economic Theory* **11**, 427–431.

Magill, M.J.P. and Shafer, W.J. (1990). Characterisation of generically complete real asset structures. *Journal of Mathematical Economics* **19**, 167–194.

McManus, D. (1986). Regular options equilibria. CARESS Working Paper No. 86-13. University of Pennsylvania, Philadelphia, PA, December.

Milnor, J.W. (1965). *Topology from the Differentiable Viewpoint*. Charlottesville, VA: University Press of Virginia.

Siconolfi, P. (1986a). Equilibrium with restricted participation on incomplete financial markets. CARESS Working Paper No. 86-03. University of Pennsylvania, Philadelphia, PA, August.

Siconolfi, P. (1986b). Equilibrium with asymmetric constraints on portfolio holdings and incomplete financial markets. CARESS Working Paper No. 86-21. University of Pennsylvania, Philadelphia, PA, November.

Werner, J. (1986). Asset prices and real indeterminacy in equilibrium with financial markets, preliminary paper, University of Bonn, Bonn, October.

Younès, Y. (1986). Competitive equilibrium for incomplete market structures. CARESS Working Papers Nos 86-7 and 86-18. University of Pennsylvania, Philadelphia, PA, October.

Younès, Y. (1987) Access asymétrique des agents économiques a des marchés incomplets, Working Paper. CEPREMAP, Paris, February.

Chapter 13

Convexity and Sunspots: A Remark ☆

David Cass and Herakles M. Polemarchakis[a,b]

[a]*Graduate School of Business, Columbia University, New York, New York 10027, USA*
[b]*C.O.R.E., Louvain la Neuve, Belgium*

Economies in which competitive equilibrium allocations are optimal and individual preferences are strictly convex are immune to sunspots; this is so even in the presence of non-convexities in production. Journal of Economic Literature *Classification Numbers: 021, 026.* © *1990 Academic Press, Inc.*

We want to know which economies are immune to sunspots, that is, do not allow extrinsic variables to have a nontrivial effect on the allocation of resources at a competitive equilibrium.

Cass and Shell (1983) characterize one such class of economies: Finite, convex economies with complete markets in contingent commodities. In particular, their argument makes use of the convexity assumption and thus leaves open the question of whether nonconvexities in the production technologies of firms or in the preferences of households may allow sunspots to play a role.

Guesnerie and Laffont (1988) give examples of economies with non-convexities in preferences that possess nontrivial sunspot equilibria.

Here we maintain the assumptions that preferences are strictly convex and, in addition, that competitive equilibrium allocations are optimal, whenever they exist. We allow for nonconvexities, in particular for increasing returns to scale, in production. We show that nevertheless sunspot equilibria do not exist. This, in a way, completes the characterization.

The intuition behind our result is twofold. Technically, our argument is based on the observation that a competitive equilibrium for an economy is also a competitive equilibrium for its convexification; thus, it extends the characterization of Cass and Shell (1983). More fundamentally, however, our argument is based on the observation that strictly risk-averse individuals never agree to gamble, as long as the odds are known.

☆ This article was originally published in *Journal of Economic Theory* 52, David Cass and H.M. Polemarchakis, "Convexity and Sunspots: A Remark", 433–439, © Elsevier, 1990.

International Symposia in Economic Theory and Econometrics, Vol. 21B
S. Spear (Editor)

ISSN: 1571-0386/DOI: 10.1108/S1571-0386(2011)000021B016

Commodities are indexed by $n = 1, \ldots, N$ and $s = 1, \ldots, S$; commodity bundles are thus $c = (\ldots, c(s), \ldots)$, where $c(s) = (\ldots, c_n(s), \ldots)$. The index s captures extrinsic variables that do not affect the fundamental structure of the economy.

A private ownership economy is

$$E = \{Y^f, f = 1, \ldots, F; (X^h, R^h, e^h, \theta^h), h = 1, \ldots, H);$$

a firm, f, is characterized by its production set Y^f, a subset of the commodity space; a household, h, is characterized by its preference relation R^h defined on the consumption set X^h, a subset of the commodity space, by its initial endowment of commodities $e^h = (\ldots, e^h(s), \ldots)$, a commodity bundle, and by its ownership shares of firms $\theta^h = (\ldots, \theta^{h,f}, \ldots)$. The strong preference and indifference relations derived from R^h are P^h and I^h, respectively; the complement of the indifference relation is $\sim I^h$.

The particular commodity bundles associated with firm f and household h are $y^f = (\ldots, y^f(s), \ldots)$ and $x^h = (\ldots, x^h(s), \ldots)$, respectively, while relevant aggregates are $y = \sum_f y^f$ and, similarly, $Y = \sum_f Y^f, x = \sum_h x^h$, and $e = \sum_h e^h$. An allocation for the economy E is $(y, x) = (\ldots, y^f, \ldots x^h, \ldots)$ such that $y^f \in Y^f$, for all f, $x^h \in X^h$, for all h, and $x = y + e$.

Prices for the economy E are $p = (\ldots, p(s), \ldots)$, where $p(s) = (\ldots, p_n(s), \ldots)$.

At prices p, firm f maximizes its profits $\pi^f = p \cdot y^f$ over its production set; household h maximizes its preference relation over its consumption set subject to the budget constraint $p \cdot x^h \leq p \cdot e^h + \sum_f \theta^{h,f} \pi^f$.

A competitive equilibrium for the economy E is a pair $[\hat{p}, (\hat{y}, \hat{x})]$ of prices and an allocation such that, at $\hat{p}, \hat{y}^f$ is maximal for firm f and $\hat{x}^h$ is maximal for household h.

Let σ be a permutation of the set $(1, \ldots, S\}$; let c be a commodity bundle. We define the commodity bundle $c_\sigma = (\ldots, c_\sigma(s), \ldots)$ by setting $c_\sigma(s) = c(\sigma(s))$.

That the index s captures extrinsic variables, sunspots, which do not affect the fundamental structure of the economy we can now make precise:

(i) $y \in Y$ if and only if $y_\sigma \in Y$, for all σ;

(ii) $e = e_\sigma$, for all σ; and

(iii) for all h, $x \in X^h$ if and only if $x_\sigma \in X^h$, for all σ; also, $x \, R^h x'$ if and only if $x_\sigma R^h x_{\sigma'}$, for all σ, σ'. (1)

Remark. This formulation basically follows Balasko (1983, Section 2). It would be stronger than (1-i) to assume that individual firms' production sets exhibit the same symmetry property, and even stronger to assume that they are products of sunspot-independent production sets. Similarly, it would be stronger than (1-ii) to assume that individual households' endowments are sunspot-independent. Finally, (1-iii) is weaker than the assumption of sunspot-independent von Neumann–Morgenstern preferences. While, in a stochastic setting, (1-iii) only allows for sunspots which occur with the same probability, this is merely a very convenient simplification; as Balasko's argument illustrates, what is essential is that preferences over lotteries only depend on the total probability associated with each distinct consumption outcome. It is of course important that households agree on the probability law that governs sunspot activity.

We say that an economy E is *immune to sunspots in the weak sense* if and only if, whenever $(\hat{y}, \hat{x})$ is a competitive equilibrium allocation, there exists another allocation $(\bar{y}, \bar{x})$ with the properties that, for all h, $x^{-h} I^h \hat{x}^h$ and

$$x^{-h} = x_{\sigma}^{-h}, \quad \text{for all } \sigma. \tag{2}$$

When the two consumption allocations necessarily coincide, that is, when every such allocation $(\bar{y}, \bar{x})$ also has the property that

$$\bar{x} = \hat{x}, \tag{3}$$

we say that the economy is *immune to sunspots in the strong sense*.

Remark. Note that Equation (2) and (1-ii) imply, from the market clearing equation $\bar{x} = \bar{y} + e$, that $\bar{y} = \bar{y}_{\sigma}$, for all σ, while Equation (3) implies that, in fact, we can take $(\bar{y}, \bar{x}) = (\hat{y}, \hat{x})$. The distinction between weak and strong immunity is required to account for the possibility that, because of perfect substitutability between commodities, sunspots may affect a competitive equilibrium consumption allocation, but only trivially so.

We say that the economy E satisfies the *competitive optimality property* if and only if, whenever $[\hat{p}, (\hat{y}, \hat{x})]$ is a competitive equilibrium, the allocation $(\hat{y}, \hat{x})$ is optimal in the sense of Pareto.

Remark. The requirement that an economy satisfies the competitive optimality property is very weak, at least for finite economies. In particular, it allows for nonconvexities in production, which may jeopardize the existence but not the optimality of competitive equilibria, as in Debreu (1959, Section 6.2).

We first consider convex economies in which the production sector as well as the consumption sector is convex: For all f, Y^f is a convex set, and for all h, X^h is a convex set and R^h is a convex preference relation. This is the case considered by Cass and Shell (1983, Section V); we basically reformulate their argument here because it considerably simplifies presenting our main result.

Lemma. (essentially Cass and Shell, 1983, Proposition 3). *A convex economy E that satisfies the competitive optimality property is immune to sunspots in the weak sense.*

Proof. Let $[\hat{p}, (\hat{y}, \hat{x})]$ be a competitive equilibrium for the economy E. Consider the allocation $(\bar{y}, \bar{x})$ defined by $\bar{y}^f \in Y^f$ such that $\bar{y}^f(s) = (1/S)\sum_{s'} y^f(s')$, for all s, and $\bar{x}^h \in X^h$ such that $\bar{x}^h(s) = (1/S)\sum_{s'} x^h(s')$, for all s. From Equation (1) and convexity, the allocation is well defined. If, for all h, $\bar{x}^h I^h \hat{x}^h$, then from Equation (2) the argument is complete. So suppose not: In particular, for some $h', \bar{x}^{h'} \sim I^{h'} \hat{x}^{h'}$. But from (1-iii) and the convexity of R^h, $\bar{x}^h R^h \hat{x}^h$ for all h. It follows that $\bar{x}^{h'} P^{h'} \hat{x}^{h'}$, which contradicts the Pareto optimality of the allocation $(\hat{y}, \hat{x})$, and hence the competitive optimality property for the economy E. ∎

Corollary. A convex economy E that satisfies the competitive optimality property is immune to sunspots in the strong sense, as long as individual preferences are strictly convex.

Proof. It suffices to observe that if $\bar{x} \neq \hat{x}$, then an allocation of the form $(y, x) = \lambda(\bar{y}, \bar{x}) + (1 - \lambda)(\hat{y}, \hat{x})$, with $0 < \lambda < 1$, Pareto dominates the competitive allocation $(\hat{y}, \hat{x})$, which contradicts the competitive optimality property for the economy E.

Given an economy E in which only the consumption sector is convex, we obtain its convexification, the economy $E_k = \{Y^f_k, f = 1, 2, \ldots,; (X^h, R^h, e^h, \theta^h), h = 1, 2, \ldots,\}$, by replacing every production set Y^f by its convex hull Y^f_k.

We can now state and prove the result that is the focus of our remark.

Proposition. *An economy E whose consumption sector is convex and whose convexification E_k satisfies the competitive optimality property is immune to sunspots in the strong sense, as long as individual preferences are strictly convex.*

Proof. Let E be economy with a convex consumption sector and strictly convex individual preferences, and E_k be its convexification. Let $[\hat{p}, (\hat{y}, \hat{x})]$ be a competitive equilibrium for the economy E. We will show that the allocation $(\bar{y}, \bar{x}) = (\hat{y}, \hat{x})$ satisfies Equation (2) (as well as Equation (3)). It is straightforward that the pair $[\hat{p}, (\hat{y}, \hat{x})]$ is also a competitive equilibrium for the convexified economy E_k. It suffices to observe that by profit maximization in the economy E at prices $\hat{p}$, the production set Y^f is contained in the half-plane $H^f(\hat{p}) = \{y : \hat{p} \cdot y \leq \hat{p} \cdot \hat{y}^f\}$; hence, its convex hull Y^f_k is contained in $H^f(\hat{p}) : \hat{y}^f$ is also profit maximizing at $\hat{p}$ in the economy E_k. Since E_k satisfies the competitive optimality property, exactly the same argument that earlier established the lemma and its corollary now establishes that the consumption allocation $\bar{x} = \hat{x}$ satisfies Equation (2), as desired. ∎

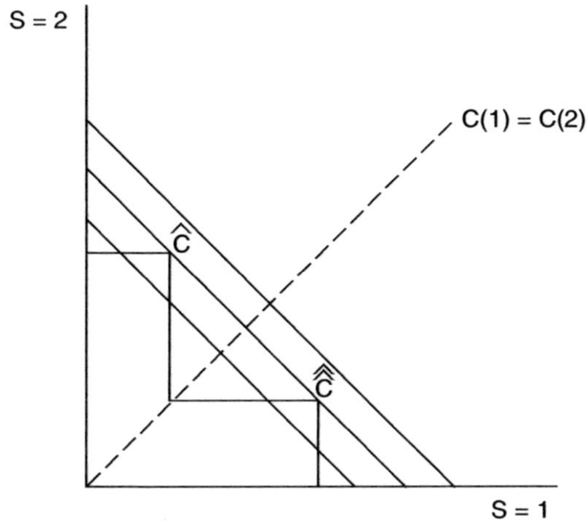

Figure 1.

Remark. Economies in which technologies fail to be convex while preferences are convex but not strictly so may allow for sunspot equilibria. Consider the economy in Figure 1. Endowments and the technology jointly yield a nonconvex production possibility set; consumption bundles at different sunspot values are perfect substitutes. The allocation described by the bundle $\hat{c}$ (or $\hat{\hat{c}}$) is a competitive equilibrium allocation with sunspots; no sunspot-independent allocation exists, which is preference equivalent. The strong convexity assumption on preferences is akin to risk aversion, as noted by Yaari (1969). Note that the technology in Figure 1 satisfies the symmetry conditions (1-i) and (1-ii) with respect to the sunspot index *s*, but it is not a product technology. Whether a similar example with a product technology is possible we do not know.

Remark. Economies in which technologies are convex but preferences fail to be so may allow for sunspot equilibria. This was pointed out by Guesnerie and Laffont (1988) and we mention it only for completeness. Consider the economy in Figure 2. Endowments and the technology jointly allow a one-to-one transformation of consumption bundles across states of nature; the preference relation is nonconvex. The allocation described by the bundle $\hat{c}$ (or $\hat{\hat{c}}$) is a competitive equilibrium allocation with sunpots; no sunspot-independent allocation exists, which is preference equivalent.

Starting with Cass and Shell's original example (reported in Shell, 1977), sunspot equilibria have been extensively studied in the recent literature, largely (perhaps overly) in the context of overlapping-generations models,

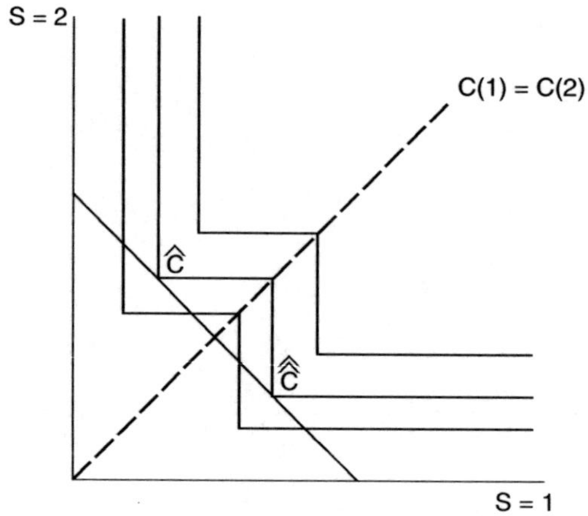

Figure 2.

for instance, by Azariadis (1982). That economies with such demographic structure are not immune to sunspots is hardly surprising, as our characterization (and, previously, the analysis by Cass and Shell, 1983, 1989) emphasizes. These economies fail to satisfy the competitive optimality property for two basic reasons: First, there is the particular (overlapping) double-infinity structure of commodities and households originally recognized by Samuelson (1958), and then elaborated and underlined by Shell (1971) and Cass (1985). Second, there are the specific restrictions on market participation imposed by the fact that households cannot hedge against events occurring before their births. And – as the Cass and Shell papers clearly demonstrate – either reason is, by itself, sufficient for the existence of nontrivial sunspot equilibria.

Acknowledgment

This work was supported in part by National Science Foundation Grants SES 85-09957 and SES 87-06670. Discussions with R. Guesnerie were illuminating.

References

Azariadis, C. (1982). Self-fulfilling prophecies. *Journal of Economic Theory* **25**, 380–396.

Balasko, Y. (1983). Extrinsic uncertainty revisited. *Journal of Economic Theory* **31**, 203–210.

Cass, D. (1985). Optimality with unbounded numbers of households: I. Overlapping (or overlapping-generations) structure and the first basic theorem of welfare. In Ritschard, G. and Royer, D. (Eds), *Optimalité et structures: Mélanges en hommage à Edouard Rossier*. Paris: Economica.

Cass, D. and Shell, K. (1983). Do sunspots matter? *Journal of Political Economy* **91**, 193–227.

Cass, D. and Shell, K. (1989). Sunspot equilibrium in an overlapping-generations economy with an idealized contingent-commodities market. In Barnett, W.A., Geweke, J. and Shell, K. (Eds), *Economic Complexity: Chaos, Sunspots, Bubbles and Nonlinearity*. London: Cambridge University Press.

Debreu, G. (1959). *Theory of Value*. New York: Wiley.

Guesnerie, R. and Laffont, J.-J. (1988). Notes sur les equilibres à taches soiaires en horizon fini. In *Mélanges economiques: Essais en l'honneur de Edmond Malinvaud*. Paris: Economica.

Samuelson, P.A. (1958). An exact consumption-loan model of interest with or without the social contrivance of money. *Journal of Political Economy* **66**, 467–482.

Shell, K. (1971). Notes on the economics of infinity. *Journal of Political Economy* **79**, 1002–1011.

Shell, K. (1977). Monnaie et allocation intertemporelle, mimeo, November 21, 1977, CNRS Séminaire d'econométrie de M. Edmond Malinvaud.

Yaari, M. (1969). Some remarks on measures of risk aversion and on their uses. *Journal of Economic Theory* **1**, 315–329.

Chapter 14

Perfect Equilibrium with Incomplete Financial Markets: An Elementary Exposition☆

David Cass

1. Introduction

Value and capital is a real masterpiece, clearly and forcefully demonstrating the importance of treating time explicitly, and thus recognizing that economic plans made today unavoidably depend on beliefs about potential opportunities available tomorrow. Hicks focused his analysis on price uncertainty, starting from the position that, even in the absence of more fundamental sources of uncertainty, there is no convincing rationale for assuming either that individuals' future price expectations will be identical, or if they were, that individuals' future plans (based on these expectations) will be coordinated. In other words, self-fulfilling expectations, or perfect foresight, or – in Hicks's own term – perfect equilibrium is unlikely even under the best of circumstances. But then why not a full range of current markets for trading forward, obviating the need for individuals to guess the potential course of future prices? Because in fact there is also fundamental uncertainty in the economic environment. In Hicks's own words:

> *Thirdly, even if price expectations are consistent, still people may foresee their own wants incorrectly, or make wrong estimates of the results of the technical processes of production. ... Generally, then, it is uncertainty of the future, and the desire to keep one's hands free to meet that uncertainty, which limit the extent of forward trading under capitalism; the ultimate cause why the first two kinds of disequilibrium cannot be met more efficiently reduces itself to the unavoidable presence of the third and fourth kinds. (Hicks, 1946, pp. 134 and 136)*[1]

☆This article was originally published in McKenzie, L.W. and Zamagni, S. (Eds) (1991). *Value and Capital: Fifty Years Later*. Macmillan Publishers Limited. Reproduced with permission of Palgrave Macmillan.

[1] Given his focus on price uncertainty, Hicks was necessarily led to the consideration that even point expectations would ordinarily represent a summary statistic, and thus

International Symposia in Economic Theory and Econometrics, Vol. 21B
S. Spear (Editor)

ISSN: 1571-0386/DOI: 10.1108/S1571-0386(2011)000021B017

Thus, for Hicks, uncertainty about such fundamentals as preferences, endowments, and technology is the basic explanation for incompleteness of markets, and therefore also imperfections in equilibrium.

The post-war development of equilibrium theory introduced an ingenious framework for dealing with such fundamental uncertainty, the Arrow–Debreu conceptualization of states of the world (with claims marketed contingent on them), and hence at least a partial justification for reconsidering the fiction of perfect equilibrium. I do not propose to defend such methodology here. Rather, my aim is much more modest: I simply want to describe a further recent development in this tradition that – moving back toward considering Hicks's basic conclusion directly – concentrates on the possibility that trading forward is restricted by incompleteness of financial markets.

2. The Model: A Representative Example

Most of the major results concerning "incomplete markets" are only generic, that is, they are true except for an insignificant subset of possible parameter configurations. My goal here is to illustrate these results in terms of a simple but representative example, one which permits relatively elementary analysis. For this purpose, when discussing a result that is (within a well-specified conventional context) true without qualification, I will use the term "general" or "generally." On the other hand, when a result is only true generically, I will use the term "typical" or "typically" (in contrast to "exceptional" or "exceptionally"). At the very end of the chapter I provide a short, concise guide to the literature.

There are two periods, today and tomorrow, with two possible states of the world tomorrow. Let $s = 0$ denote today, and $s = \alpha, \beta$ the two states tomorrow. The economy involves one type of physical commodity or good, one type of (inside) financial instrument or asset and two households. There is no production. The two households exchange the good and the asset on a spot market today, and then – depending on which state has been realized – fulfill their financial commitments and again exchange the good on a spot market tomorrow. The financial market is incomplete, since there is only one instrument that can be used to hedge against the two possible future outcomes, namely, a spot market opening when state α occurs, or one opening when state β occurs. Let $h = 1, 2$ denote the two households, and $x^h = (x^h(0), x^h(\alpha), x^h(\beta))$ represent consumption of the good and a^h holding of the asset or portfolio. Spot prices for the good are, in terms of unit of

in principle could not be self-fulfilling. This is the "fourth kind" of "disequilibrium" alluded to.

account or dollars, $p = (p(0), p(\alpha), p(\beta))$, while the asset costs q dollars today and promises (potential) yields $y = (y(\alpha), y(\beta))$ dollars tomorrow. Both households have identical preferences of the special form

$$u^h(x^h) = \sum_s \log x^h(s)$$

but different, though symmetric endowments of the form

$$\omega^h = \begin{cases} (1/2, \varepsilon, 1-\varepsilon), & \text{for} \quad h = 1 \\ (1/2, 1-\varepsilon, \varepsilon), & \text{for} \quad h = 2 \end{cases}$$

where $0 \leq \varepsilon \leq 1/2$.

I will eventually compare results under two polar specifications of the asset. For the first, the asset can be thought of as a bond, whose underlying yields are denned in terms of a par value 1 together with a nominal rate i. For simplicity (and without any loss of generality) I take $i = 0$, so that yields themselves are $y = (1, 1)$. For the second, the asset can be thought of as a type of future, whose underlying yields are defined in terms of a single unit of the good, so that yields themselves are $y = (p(\alpha), p(\beta))$.

In this setting, equilibrium can be described by prices (p, q) such that if both households optimize, that is, (x^h, a^h) solves

$$\begin{array}{ll} \text{maximize} & u^h(x^h) \\ \text{subject to} & p(0)x^h(0) = p(0)\omega^h(0) - qa^h \\ & p(\alpha)x^h(\alpha) = p(\alpha)\omega^h(\alpha) + y(\alpha)a^h \\ & p(\beta)x^h(\beta) = p(\beta)\omega^h(\beta) + y(\beta)a^h \\ \text{and} & x^h \geq 0 \end{array} \tag{1}$$

for $h = 1, 2$, then both spot goods and asset markets clear, that is,

$$x^1 + x^2 = 1 \tag{2}$$

and

$$a^1 + a^2 = 0 \tag{3}$$

Remarks.

1. Adopting the natural convention that p is nonnegative, and noting that u^h is strictly increasing, examination of Equations (1)–(3) immediately reveals that if (p, q) is an equilibrium, then all prices must be strictly positive. But if this is the case, then any single market-clearing condition suffices for all four (this follows from adding up the two households' budget constraints from Equation (1), and is analogous to Walras's law). The first implication reflects the

requirement that there be no free lunch, and, in particular, that there be no arbitrage possibility on the asset market,[2] the second, the assumption that the market structure is incomplete, and, in particular, that a choice of portfolio completely determines the consumption of goods.
2. Clearly, given the symmetry of (u^1, ω^1) and (u^2, ω^2), there are incentives for trade when $\varepsilon < 1/2$. However, in the situation where these are evidently strongest (when $\varepsilon = 0$), there can be no equilibrium (since then, for every $(p, q) \gg 0$, the solution to Equation (1) must satisfy $a^h > 0$). Moreover, even where there is an equilibrium (which, as I will demonstrate shortly, is the case when $\varepsilon > 0$), it is not Pareto optimal when $\varepsilon < 1/2$ (since then, as I will also demonstrate later on, $Du^1(x^1)$ and $Du^2(x^2)$ cannot be colinear). In contrast to well-known properties of the standard Arrow–Debreu model – in which there are complete contingent claims, or equivalently, spot goods and financial markets – the former result (i.e., nonexistence given irreducibility) is in fact exceptional, while the latter result (i.e., nonoptimality given existence) is in fact typical.

Building on the first remark, I find it most convenient to formulate the analysis of equilibrium in terms of the absence of an arbitrage possibility (as reflected in the households' first-order conditions) together with the asset market-clearing condition. The logic of this procedure is as follows: I begin by concentrating on the case where the asset is a bond, for reasons that will become clear later on.

1. Consider first the particular linear structure of the budget constraints in Equation (1). Since all the budget constraints together are linear homogeneous in spot goods prices and bond units, we can normalize, say, $p(\alpha) = 1$. But since the first is also linear homogeneous in spot 0 prices (of both the good and the asset), we can also normalize, say, $p(0) = 1$. So, adopting the normalization $p(0) = p(\alpha) = 1$, we need only concern ourselves with $(p(\beta), q) \gg 0$ for which Equations (1) and (3) are satisfied.

[2] Let $r = (-q, y(\alpha), y(\beta))$ represent the overall returns to holding one unit of the asset. In general, the requirement that there be no arbitrage possibility means that there is *no* portfolio a^+ that provides nonnegative, nontrivial overall returns (or wealth across all spots) $w = ra^+ > 0$. When $p \gg 0$, $y \gg 0$ whether the asset is a bond or a future, and this requirement is satisfied iff $q > 0$, which is equivalent to the condition that there be *some* positive values of wealth across all spots $\lambda = (\lambda(0), \lambda(\alpha), \lambda(\beta)) \gg 0$ at which holding one unit of the asset provides zero profit $\lambda \cdot r = 0$. (The generalization of this fact is one version of Farkas lemma.) For some purposes, analytic and interpretative, this latter characterization is more useful.

2. Now viewing the budget constraints in Equation (1) as parameterizing x^h in terms of a^h,

$$x^h = \omega^h + (-q, 1, 1/p(\beta))a^h, \tag{4}$$

and thus defining $U^h(a^h) = u^h(x^h)$, this problem can be compactly rewritten as

$$\text{maximize } U^h(a^h) \tag{5}$$

The unique solution to Equation (5) is characterized by the first-order condition

$$DU^h(a^h) = Du^h(x^h) \cdot Dx^h = Du^h(x^h) \cdot (-q, 1, 1/p(\beta)) = 0 \tag{6}$$

or, utilizing the particular log-linear structure of u^h,

$$\begin{aligned} &- \left[1/(\omega^h(0) - qa^h)\right]q + \left\{1/[\omega^h(\alpha) + a^h]\right\} \\ &+ \left\{1/[\omega^h(\beta) + a^h/p(\beta)]\right\}/p(\beta) = 0 \end{aligned} \tag{7}$$

Notice especially that Equation (6) or Equation (7) is equivalent to the statement that the household's own values of wealth across all spots

$$\lambda^h(s) = D_{x(s)}u^h(x^h)/p(s), \quad \text{for} \quad s = 0, \alpha, \beta$$

themselves reflect no arbitrage possibilities,

$$\lambda^h \cdot [-q, y(\alpha), y(\beta)] = \lambda^h \cdot (-q, 1, 1) = 0. \tag{8}$$

- Finally, bring Equation (3) into the picture by defining $a = -a^1 = a^2$. Then substituting into Equation (7), utilizing the particular symmetric structure of ω^h and simplifying a bit yields an implicit description of equilibrium:

$$-1/\left[(1/2q) + a\right] + 1/(\varepsilon - a) + 1/[p(\beta)(1 - \varepsilon) - a] = 0 \tag{9}$$

and

$$-1/\left[(1/2q) - a\right] + 1/[(1 - \varepsilon) + a] + 1/[p(\beta)\varepsilon + a] = 0$$

where it is understood that we are only interested in solutions for which $(p(\beta), q) \gg 0$ and – in order that $(x^1, x^2) \gg 0$ –

$$-\min\left[1/2q, (1 - \varepsilon), p(\beta)\varepsilon\right] < a < \min\left[1/2q, \varepsilon, p(\beta)(1 - \varepsilon)\right] \tag{10}$$

I now turn to the problem of studying the possible acceptable solutions to Equation (9), and their implications for Equation (4).

3. Existence and Determinacy

Here and in the sequel I assume that $\varepsilon > 0$, so that $\omega^h \gg 0$, for $h = 1, 2$. This ensures that my specification of preferences and endowments now satisfies the usual assumptions that have been maintained in the differential analysis of perfect equilibrium with incomplete financial markets.

3.1. Underlying Yields Specified in Dollars: Bonds

In this subsection I illustrate two fundamental results. First, there is generally an equilibrium. Second, even after having ruled out obviously inconsequential price or nominal indeterminacy, there remains a large, further degree of indeterminacy that typically results in a comparable degree of allocation or real indeterminacy.

3.1.1. Existence

By solving both the parts in Equation (9) for $1/2q$, we can transform this system into the more manageable form

$$1/2q = \frac{(\varepsilon - a)[p(\beta)(1-\varepsilon) - a]}{(\varepsilon - a) + [p(\beta)(1-\varepsilon) - a]} - a = \phi[a, p(\beta)]$$

$$\text{and} \quad 1/2q = \frac{[(1-\varepsilon) + a][p(\beta)\varepsilon + a]}{[(1-\varepsilon) + a] + [p(\beta)\varepsilon + a]} + a = \psi[a, p(\beta)] \tag{11}$$

The Typical Case. $\varepsilon < 1/2$.

Straightforward calculations reveal that

$$\phi(0, p(\beta))\{\gtreqless\}\psi(0, p(\beta)) \quad \text{according as } p(\beta)\{\lesseqgtr\}1, \tag{12}$$

while

$$D_a\phi(a, p(\beta)) = -\frac{(\varepsilon - a)^2 + [p(\beta)(1-\varepsilon) - a]^2}{\{(\varepsilon - a) + [p(\beta)(1-\varepsilon) - a]\}^2} - 1 < 0 \tag{13}$$

and

$$D_a\psi(a, p(\beta)) = \frac{[(1-\varepsilon) + a]^2 + [p(\beta)\varepsilon + a)]^2}{\{[(1-\varepsilon) + a] + [p(\beta)\varepsilon + a)]\}^2} + 1 > 0$$

for $\underline{a}(p(\beta)) = -\min[(1-\varepsilon), p(\beta)\varepsilon] < a < \min[\varepsilon, p(\beta)(1-\varepsilon)] = \bar{a}(p(\beta))$. Equations (11)–(13) imply that, for every $p(\beta) > 0$, there is a unique solution to Equation (9) that satisfies $q > 0$ and Equation (10), as depicted in Figure 1. In other words, in this case, for every $p(\beta) > 0$ there is a unique equilibrium such that

$$a\{\gtreqless\}0 \text{ according as } p(\beta)\{\lesseqgtr\}1 \tag{14}$$

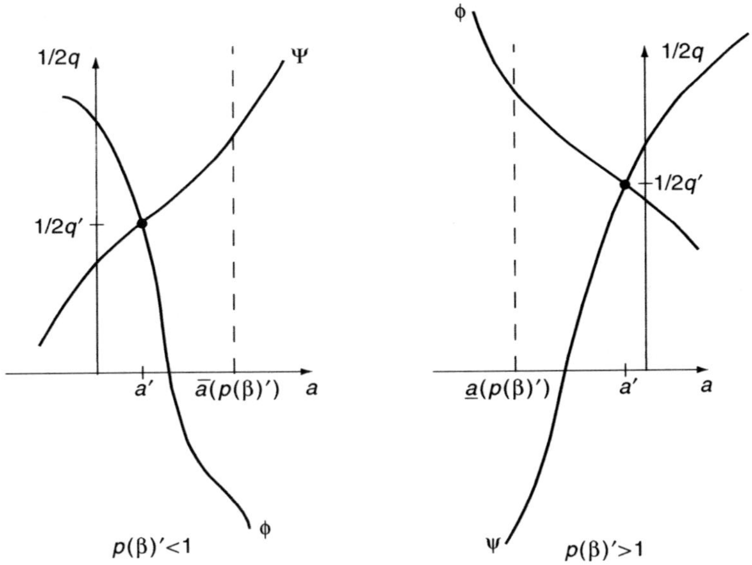

Figure 1.

The Exceptional Case. $\varepsilon = 1/2$.
In contrast, though here Equation (13) still obtains,

$$\phi[0, p(\beta)] = p(\beta)/2[1 + p(\beta)] = \psi[0, p(\beta)] \quad \text{for} \quad p(\beta) > 0$$

In other words, in this case, for every $p(\beta) > 0$ there is a unique equilibrium such that

$$a = 0 \tag{15}$$

3.1.2. Indeterminacy

In view of Equation (4), Equation (14) entails that

$$p(\beta)' \neq p(\beta)'' \geq x^{h'} \neq x^{h''}, \quad \text{for} \quad h = 1, 2,$$

while Equation (15) entails that

$$x^h = \omega^h, \text{ for } \quad h = 1, 2, \qquad \text{for} \quad p(\beta) > 0$$

In other words, in the typical case, one dimension of nominal indeterminacy creates the same dimension of real indeterminacy, while in the exceptional case, it creates none at all. (The latter result should not be surprising; when

$\varepsilon = 1/2$, the two households are identical in all respects, so $Du^1(\omega^1) = Du^2(\omega^2)$ and the endowment allocation is itself Pareto optimal.)

Remark. Suppose that, instead of being a bond, the asset promises yields of the form $y = (p(\alpha), 1)$ (i.e., underlying yields of one unit of good in state α or one dollar in state β.) Then, again appealing to the linear structure of the budget constraints in Equation (1), it is clear that we can still normalize prices so that $p(0) = p(\alpha) = 1$, and so that the preceding argument remains valid. This observation underscores the fact that real indeterminacy ultimately stems from having some asset yields that are not linearly homogeneous in their corresponding spot goods prices – rather than from simply having all underlying asset yields specified in dollars.

3.2. Underlying Yields Specified in Goods: Futures

In this subsection I illustrate three fundamental results. First, again there is generally an equilibrium. Second, now after having ruled out inconsequential nominal indeterminacy, equilibrium is typically (locally) unique. (In fact, I give the generic qualification in this second result rather short shrift, since it also applies to the standard Arrow–Debreu model.) Third – a technically significant amendment to the first result – when the model is generalized to include more than one type of good, and more than one type of asset, whose underlying yields do not depend on the same good, existence may fail (but only exceptionally).

3.2.1. The Representative Example

Consider the situation where the asset is a future instead of a bond. Since each of the budget constraints in Equation (1) is then linear homogeneous in its corresponding spot prices, we can now normalize prices so that, say, $p(0) = p(\alpha) = p(\beta) = 1$. But by retracing the earlier argument, it is easily seen that this means that now equilibrium is described by the system Equations (9) and (10) with the additional restriction $p(\beta) = 1$. And from Equations (14) and (15) we have already seen that this in turn means that now equilibrium is unique, and yields the autarchic allocation. (This result too is not surprising; when $p = 1$, the two households are basically identically situated – in the sense that by merely switching labels for the two states, Mr. 1 becomes Mr. 2, and vice versa – so there can be no trade on the asset market.)[3]

[3] Similar computations establish that existence and uniqueness persist even upon permitting arbitrary log-linear utility functions and broader specification of endowments. For existence this is not a fluke, but for uniqueness it surely depends on log-linearity; more typically there will be an odd, finite number of equilibria.

3.2.2. An Expanded Version

In order to introduce more subtle considerations, but still keep the analysis as simple as possible, suppose now that there are two types of goods in state β, denoted $c = 1, 2$, and also two types of assets, denoted $i = 1, 2$. Elaborate the notation we have been using in the natural way, for instance, let $x_c^h(\beta)$ represent household h's consumption of good c in state β, and y_i the yields associated with asset i. Assume that asset i promises yields $y_i = (p(\alpha), p_i(\beta))$ (i.e., underlying yields of one unit of good in state α or one unit of good $c = i$ in state β). Finally, so that we can utilize the analysis of the original model for this expanded version, take preferences to have the form

$$u^h(x^h) = \log x^h(0) + \log x^h(\alpha) + (\delta^h \log x_1^h(\beta) + (1 - \delta^h)\log x_2^h(\beta))$$

with $0 < \delta^h < 1$, and endowments to have the form

$$\omega^h = \begin{cases} (1/2, \varepsilon, (1/2)(1 - \varepsilon, 1 - \varepsilon)), & \text{for } h = 1 \\ (1/2, 1 - \varepsilon, (1/2)(\varepsilon, \varepsilon)), & \text{for } h = 2 \end{cases}$$

In this model an equilibrium is described by prices $(p, q) = (p(0), p(\alpha), (p_1(\beta), (p_2(\beta)), (q_1, q_2))$ such that if households optimize, that is, (x^h, a^h) solves

$$\begin{aligned} \text{maximize} \quad & u^h(x^h) \\ \text{subject to} \quad & p(0)x^h(0) = p(0)\omega^h(0) - q_1 a_1^h - q_2 a_2^h, \\ & p(\alpha)x^h(\alpha) = p(\alpha)\omega^h(\alpha) + y_1(\alpha)a_1^h + y_2(\alpha)a_2^h, \\ & p_1(\beta)x_1^h(\beta) + p_2(\beta)x_2^h(\beta) = p_1(\beta)\omega_1^h(\beta) + p_2(\beta)\omega_2^h(\beta) \\ & +y_1(\beta)a_1^h + y_2(\beta)a_2^h \\ \text{and} \quad & x^h\{\geq 0 \end{aligned} \tag{16}$$

for $h = 1, 2$, then both spot goods and asset markets clear, that is,

$$x^1(0) + x^2(0) = 1$$
$$x^1(\alpha) + x^2(\alpha) = 1$$
$$x_1^1(\beta) + x_1^2(\beta) = 1/2$$

and

$$x_2^1(\beta) + x_2^2(\beta) = 1/2 \tag{17}$$

and

$$a_1^1 + a_1^2 = 0$$

and

$$a_2^1 + a_2^2 = 0 \tag{18}$$

Reiterating earlier reasoning, we can still normalize prices spot-by-spot, say, $p(0) = p(\alpha) = p_1(\beta) = 1$. However, now the financial market is potentially complete, since y_1 and y_2 are not colinear when $p_2(\beta) \neq 1$.[4] So there are two possible sorts of equilibrium, that in which $p_2(\beta) \neq 1$, and that in which $p_2(\beta) = 1$. For our purposes here, we will consider an exceptional case where the utility weights satisfy the restriction

$$\delta^1 = (1 - \delta^2) = \delta \neq 1/2 \tag{19}$$

Independent Yields: $p_2(\beta) \neq 1$

In this case the financial market is actually complete. This means that the resulting allocation must be the same as that in the standard Arrow–Debreu model with the same preferences and endowments. But it easily verified that this allocation (which must be Pareto optimal) is described by:

$$x^h = \begin{cases} (1/2, 1/2, 1/2\ (\delta, 1-\delta)), & \text{for} \quad h = 1 \\ (1/2, 1/2, 1/2\ (1-\delta, \delta)), & \text{for} \quad h = 2 \end{cases}$$

with supporting prices $p = 1$, and hence $p_2(\beta) = 1$, a contradiction. So there can be no equilibrium of this kind when Equation (19) obtains.

Dependent Yields: $p_2(\beta) = 1$

In this case one of the assets, say, $i = 2$, is redundant (when there is no arbitrage possibility), so that, for convenience dropping the asset subscript

[4] I should emphasize that the critical feature of this example is that, in contrast, y_1 and y_2 are colinear when $p_2(\beta) = 1$, which entails that demand is discontinuous at prices (p, q) such that (i) there is no arbitrage possibility and (ii) $p = 1$. (Formally, such discontinuity occurs because the dimension of the wealth space generated by the two assets collapses from 2, when $p_1(\beta) \neq 1$, to 1, when $p_1(\beta) = 1$.) To put it another way, "potentially" not "complete" best conveys the significance of the example. This can be clearly seen from the fact that the subsequent analysis applies equally well upon modifying the example in the following way. Replace state α with two states α' and α'', described (e.g., in terms of endowments) exactly as before for state α except for the utility weights, which become $\delta^h(\alpha') = \delta^h(\alpha'') = 1/2$. Then the financial market is inherently incomplete, though equilibria in the two versions of the example are practically the same (identifying $p(\alpha) = 1$ with $p(\alpha') = p(\alpha'') = 1$).

and letting $p_2(\beta)/p_1(\beta) = \tilde{p}(\beta)$, Equation (16) can be rewritten

$$\begin{aligned} &\text{maximize} && u^h(x^h) \\ &\text{subject to} && p(0)x^h(0) = p(0)\omega^h(0) - qa^h \\ &&& p(\alpha)x^h(\alpha) = p(\alpha)\omega^h(\alpha) + ya^h \\ &&& p_1(\beta)[x_1^h(\beta) + \tilde{p}(\beta)x_2^h(\beta)] = p_1(\beta)[\omega_1^h(\beta) \\ &&& +\tilde{p}(\beta)\omega_2^h(\beta)] + ya^h \\ &\text{and} && x^h \geq 0 \end{aligned} \tag{16'}$$

while Equation (18) becomes simply

$$a^1 + a^2 = 0 \tag{18'}$$

The analysis of an equilibrium in which $\tilde{p}(\beta) = 1$ (and, more generally, in this model with a single future) is facilitated by utilizing a trick closely related to Hicks's celebrated observation (e.g., Hicks, 1946, p. 33) that when relative prices are fixed, commodities can be lumped together as a sort of composite. (It is now important to bear in mind that, whenever I discuss an equilibrium described by Equations (16′), (17), and (18′), the single future has promised yields $y = (p(\alpha), p_1(\beta))$ and prices are normalized so that $p(0) = p(\alpha) = p_1(\beta) = 1$.)

For the moment ignore the fact that we are interested in the special case $p_2(\beta) = 1$ or $\tilde{p}(\beta) = 1$, and the parameter configuration Equation (19). Then, in any equilibrium, household h will choose consumption in state β by solving a subproblem of the form

$$\begin{aligned} &\text{maximize} && \delta^h \log x_1^h(\beta) + (1 - \delta^h) \log x_2^h(\beta) \\ &\text{subject to} && x_1^h(\beta) + \tilde{p}(\beta)x_2^h(\beta) = w^h(\beta) \\ &\text{and} && (x_1^h(\beta), x_2^h(\beta)) \geq 0 \end{aligned} \tag{20}$$

where

$$w^h(\beta) = \tilde{\omega}^h(\beta) + ya^h \quad \text{for} \quad \tilde{\omega}^h(\beta) = \omega_1^h(\beta) + \tilde{p}(\beta)\omega_2^h(\beta) \tag{21}$$

Equation (20) yields spot goods submarket demands

$$x_c^h(\beta) = \begin{cases} \delta^h w^h(\beta), & \text{for} \quad c = 1 \\ (1 - \delta^h)w^h(\beta)/\tilde{p}(\beta), & \text{for} \quad c = 2 \end{cases} \tag{22}$$

whose utility is

$$\begin{aligned} (\delta^h \log \delta^h &+ (1 - \delta^h) \log ((1 - \delta^h)/\tilde{p}(\beta)) \\ &+ \log w^h(\beta) \sim \log w^h(\beta) \end{aligned} \tag{23}$$

Equations (21)–(23) permit identifying the equilibria described by Equations (16′), (17), and (18′) with those described by Equations (1)–(3) – where, when

$\tilde{p}(\beta) = 1$, the asset is a future, and prices are normalized $p(0) = p(\alpha) = p(\beta) = 1$, while, when $\tilde{p}(\beta) \neq 1$, the asset is a bond, and prices are normalized $p(0) = p(\alpha) = 1$. (We shall utilize the latter fact in the following section.)

In the present case, this can be seen as follows: first, take $\tilde{p}(\beta) = 1$. Then $\tilde{\omega}^h(\beta) = \omega_1^h(\beta) + \omega_2^h(\beta) = \omega^h(\beta)$, for $h = 1,2$. Second, identify $w^h(\beta)$ with $x^h(\beta)$. Then – referring especially to Equation (23) – (16′) can be replaced by Equation (1) provided – referring especially to Equation (22) – the β spot goods market-clearing conditions in Equation (17) are also replaced by

$$\delta^1 x^1(\beta) + \delta^2 x^2(\beta) = 1/2 \tag{24}$$

and

$$(1 - \delta^1)x^1(\beta) = (1 - \delta^2)x^2(\beta) = 1/2,$$

which imply the β spot goods market-clearing condition in Equation (2),

$$x^1(\beta) + x^2(\beta) = 1 \tag{25}$$

In other words, in order to have an equilibrium in which $p_2(\beta) = 1$, the autarchic equilibrium we found earlier must satisfy Equation (24) given Equation (19). But it is easily verified that Equation (24) then reduces to $\delta(1-\varepsilon) + (1-\delta)\,\varepsilon = 1/2$, which requires $\varepsilon = 1/2$ (since $\delta \neq 1/2$). So now, in the typical case where $\varepsilon < 1/2$, there can be no equilibrium of this kind when Equation (19) obtains.

Remarks.

1. That this result is exceptional (say, in terms of endowments) is revealed by the fact that it requires a very special configuration of equilibrium prices for the standard Arrow–Debreu model. For similar reasons, it would also be exceptional to have both an equilibrium in which y_1 and y_2 are not colinear (i.e., in which financial markets are complete) and one in which they are (i.e., in which financial markets are incomplete).
2. Suppose that, instead of being futures, asset i promises yields of the form $y_i = (1, p_i(\beta))$ (i.e., underlying yields of one dollar in state α or one unit of good $c = i$ in state β). Then a considerably more elaborate variation of the preceding argument demonstrates that there will still be no equilibrium when Equation (19) obtains and $\varepsilon < 1/2$. This observation underscores the fact that existence problems ultimately stem from having some, but not necessarily all, underlying yields specified in terms of goods.

4. Optimality

Earlier I claimed that an equilibrium allocation will not be Pareto optimal when $\varepsilon < 1/2$. We are now in a position to verify this claim, whether the asset is a bond or a future.

For an interior feasible allocation, Pareto optimality is equivalent to the condition that $Du^1(x^1)$ and $Du^2(x^2)$ be colinear, since this is the only situation in which there is no solution to the inequality

$$(Du^1(x^1) \cdot (-\mathrm{d}x), Du^2(x^2) \cdot \mathrm{d}x) \gg 0$$

where $\mathrm{d}x = (\mathrm{d}x(0), \ \mathrm{d}x(\alpha), \ \mathrm{d}x(\beta))$.[5] Now, from Equation (4) and the particular log-linear structure of u^h, it follows that in equilibrium (again with $a = -a^1 = a^2$)

$$x^1 = (1/2 + qa, \varepsilon - a, \ 1 - [\varepsilon + a/p(\beta)]) \gg 0$$

and

$$x^2 = (1/2 - qa, 1 - (\varepsilon - a), \varepsilon + a/p(\beta)) \gg 0$$

and so

$$Du^1(x^1) = \{1/(1/2 + qa), 1/(\varepsilon - a), 1/)1 - [\varepsilon + a/p(\beta)])\}$$

and

$$Du^2(x^2) = \{1/(1/2 - qa), 1/[1 - (\varepsilon - a)], 1/[\varepsilon + a/p(\beta)]\} \tag{26}$$

But, when $\varepsilon < 1/2$, from Equation (14) it also follows that in equilibrium

$$1/(1/2 + qa) > 1/(1/2 - qa) \tag{27}$$

while

$$1/\{1 - [\varepsilon + a/p(\beta)]\} < 1/[\varepsilon + a/p(\beta)], \quad \text{for } p(\beta) > 1,$$
$$1/\{1 - [\varepsilon + a/p(\beta)]\} < 1/[\varepsilon + a/p(\beta)]$$

---

[5] Suppose $x^h \gg 0$. Because u^h is differentiable, for sufficiently small perturbations $\mathrm{d}x^h$, $x^h + \mathrm{d}x^h > 0$ and

$$Du^h(x^h) \cdot \mathrm{d}x^h > 0 \Rightarrow u^h(x^h + \mathrm{d}x^h) > u^h(x^h)$$

while because u^h is also strictly concave, for arbitrary perturbations $\mathrm{d}x^h$ satisfying $x^h + \mathrm{d}x^h > 0$ and $\lambda > 0$,

$$u^h(x^h + \mathrm{d}x^h) \geqq u^h(x^h) \Rightarrow Du^h(x^h) \cdot (\lambda \mathrm{d}x^h) > 0$$

This permits me to conduct the analysis of Pareto improvements in terms of "infinitesimal" perturbations $\mathrm{d}x^h$. Also note that feasible reallocations require such perturbations satisfying $\mathrm{d}x = -\mathrm{d}x^1 = \mathrm{d}x^2$.

while

$$1/(\varepsilon - a) > 1/(1 - (\varepsilon - a)), \quad \text{for } p(\beta) = 1$$

and

$$1/(1/2 + qa) < 1/(1/2 - qa)$$

while

$$1/(\varepsilon - a) > 1/[1 - (\varepsilon - a)], \quad \text{for } p(\beta) < 1$$

Utilizing the inequalities in Equation (27) to compare the expressions in Equation (26) immediately shows that $Du^1(x^1)$ and $Du^2(x^2)$ cannot be colinear when $\varepsilon < 1/2$; for instance, the first inequality in Equation (27) translates into $D_{x(0)}u^1(x^1) > D_{x(0)}u^2(x^2)$ while $D_{x(\beta)}u^1(x^1) < D_{x(\beta)}u^2(x^2)$, and so on.

Another interesting (if perhaps now unremarkable) conclusion also follows from Equation (14). In this typical case, when $p(\beta) = 1$, allocation is autarchic, while when $p(\beta) \neq 1$, it is not. In other words, when the asset is a bond, every equilibrium in which $p(\beta) \neq 1$ strictly Pareto dominates that in which $p(\beta) = 1$ (since, in the former, both households choose to trade). This illustrates the fact that, with incomplete financial markets, one may even be able to rank (some) equilibria according to the Pareto criterion.

A plausible criticism against using the Pareto criterion in this context is that it implicitly permits the "planner" much greater latitude in reallocating goods than does the market structure itself. This has led to exploration of the idea that if the "planner" were also appropriately constrained by the market structure, then equilibrium allocation might – in this sense – be constrained Pareto optimal. I will discuss two different ways in which the "planner" might be considered so constrained.

For this purpose we will rely heavily on the households' "no arbitrage" condition (8). So it is more convenient to argue in terms of the households' own values of wealth, $\lambda^h = (\lambda^h(0), \lambda^h(\alpha), \lambda^h(\beta))$, and perturbations converted into dollars (given appropriate normalization of prices), $\mathrm{d}w = -\mathrm{d}w^1 = \mathrm{d}w^2 = (\mathrm{d}x(0), \mathrm{d}x(\alpha), p(\beta)\mathrm{d}x(\beta))$. Note that $Du^h(x)\mathrm{d}x = \lambda^h \mathrm{d}w$ by definition. Also, hereafter I consider only the typical case $\varepsilon < 1/2$.

4.1. Constrained Optimality at Original Equilibrium Prices

The essential idea here is that, after an equilibrium has been "achieved," the planner can reallocate spot 0 goods and assets freely, but spot $s \neq 0$ goods only in so far as is consistent with tie original spot $s \neq 0$ budget constraints (these having been adjusted according to the reallocation of assets). It is straightforward to show that such reallocation cannot lead to a Pareto improvement.

With such reallocation, at equilibrium spot goods prices for $s \neq 0$,

$$\mathrm{d}w = (\mathrm{d}x(0), y(\alpha)\mathrm{d}a, y(\beta)\mathrm{d}a) = (\mathrm{d}x(0), (1,1)\mathrm{d}a) \tag{28}$$

(Notice that for a bond, $\mathrm{d}x(\beta) = [1/p(\beta)]\mathrm{d}a$, so that $\mathrm{d}w(\beta) = p(\beta)\mathrm{d}x(\beta) = \mathrm{d}a$, while for a future, $p(\beta) = 1$, so that once again $\mathrm{d}w(\beta) = \mathrm{d}x(\beta) = \mathrm{d}a$.) But from Equation (8) we know that

$$\lambda^h(0)q = (\lambda^h(\alpha), \lambda^h(\beta)) \cdot (1,1) \tag{29}$$

Hence Equations (28) and (29) entail that

$$\begin{aligned}\lambda^1(-\mathrm{d}w) &= -\lambda^1(0)\mathrm{d}x(0) - [\lambda^1(\alpha), \lambda^2(\beta)] \cdot (1,1)\mathrm{d}a \\ &= -\lambda^1(0)[\mathrm{d}x(0) + q\mathrm{d}a]\end{aligned}$$

and

$$\begin{aligned}\lambda^2 \cdot \mathrm{d}w &= \lambda^2(0)\mathrm{d}x(0) + [\lambda^2(\alpha), \lambda^2(\beta)] \cdot (1,1)\mathrm{d}a \\ &= \lambda^2(0)[\mathrm{d}x(0) + q\mathrm{d}a]\end{aligned}$$

so that sign $\lambda^1 \cdot (-\mathrm{d}w) = -$sign $\lambda^2 \cdot \mathrm{d}w$. But this is nothing more than the statement that if one household gains, then the other necessarily loses.

It is worth emphasizing that this is a quite general result, and, in particular, does not depend on there being a single type of good.

4.2. Constrained Suboptimality at Adjusted Equilibrium Prices

In the simple example I have mainly considered, where there is only a single type of good, reallocation according to Equation (28) is consistent with equilibrium in the spot $s \neq 0$ markets at the original equilibrium prices but new portfolios of assets $a' = -a^{1\prime} = a^{2\prime} = a + \mathrm{d}a$. When there are more types of goods such is typically not the case. From this viewpoint it is hard to understand why – even if he can only reallocate spot 0 goods and assets (say, after spot 0 trading has taken place but before some state has been realized, and therefore before some spot $s \neq 0$ market has been opened) – the "planner" should not be allowed to try and take advantage or, perhaps better, be required to take account of this additional complication. In order to investigate the ramifications of this observation, I return to the expanded version of the example introduced in the preceding section. My analysis is somewhat casual (since a rigorous argument simply requires more powerful techniques), and therefore I do not provide many details for the calculations (which are straightforward in principle, but tedious in practice); it is only intended to suggest why, typically, the "planner" is now capable of engineering a Pareto improvement.

So again consider the model where there are two types of goods in state β, but just a single future with promised yields $y = (p(\alpha), p_1(\beta))$, and where we do not restrict $p_2(\beta) = 1$.[6] From reasoning similar to that employed earlier, we can identify equilibrium in this model with equilibrium in the original model, but where there is now a bond rather than a future. Simply identify $(1 + \tilde{p}(\beta))/2$ with $p(\beta)$ (so that the relative price $\tilde{p}(\beta) = 2p(\beta) - 1$ and $w^h(\beta)/[(1 + \tilde{p}(\beta)/2]$ with $x(\beta)$ (so that wealth $w^h(\beta) = p(\beta)x^h(\beta)$), and then replace the β spot market-clearing conditions in Equation (17) by

$$\begin{aligned} &\delta^1 w^1(\beta) + \delta^2 w^2(\beta) = p(\beta)[\delta^1 x^1(\beta) + \delta^2 x^2(\beta)] = 1/2 \\ \text{and } &[(1 - \delta^1)w^1(\beta) + (1 - \delta^2)w^2(\beta)]/\tilde{p}(\beta) = p(\beta)[(1 - \delta^1)x^1(\beta) \\ &\quad + (1 - \delta^2)x^2(\beta)]/(2p(\beta) - 1) = 1/2, \end{aligned} \tag{30}$$

which once again imply Equation (25).[7]

In an equilibrium, in addition to the system of Equations (11) and (30) provides a second, explicit relationship between $p(\beta)$ and a, since

$$x^1(\beta) = (1 - \varepsilon) - a/p(\beta) \quad \text{and} \quad x^2(\beta) = \varepsilon + a/p(\beta) \tag{31}$$

Substituting from Equation (31) into the first part of Equation (30), and assuming that

$$\delta^1 \neq \delta^2 \tag{32}$$

this relationship can be expressed as the linear function

$$p(\beta) = \mu + \nu a \tag{33}$$

where $\mu = (1/2)/(\delta^1(1 - \varepsilon) + \delta^2\varepsilon)$ and $\nu = (\delta^1 - \delta^2)/(\delta^1(1 - \varepsilon) + \delta^2\varepsilon) \neq 0$.

It is not hard to show that Equations (11) and (33) have a solution with $p(\beta) > 1/2$ – typically (locally) unique – as illustrated in Figure 2.

Now suppose we allow the "planner" to reallocate while taking account of the change in $p(\beta)$ required to satisfy Equation (33). It is also not hard

[6] I should mention explicitly that this sort of analysis only seems to make sense when financial instruments have underlying yields specified in terms of goods. Otherwise, there is no natural price normalization, equilibrium in spot $s \neq 0$ markets will typically not be (locally) unique, and the "planner" has no hope of predicting the future effect of reallocating assets.

[7] The explanation for the particular form of this correspondence is not complicated. Since $\omega_c^h(\beta) = (1/2)\omega^h(\beta)$, for $c = 1, 2$, in Equation (21)

$$w^h(\beta) = \{[1 + \tilde{p}(\beta)]/2\}\omega^h(\beta) + ya^h = p(\beta)\omega^h(\beta) + ya^h$$

so that in Equation (23)

$$\begin{aligned} \log w^h(\beta) &= \log([1 + \tilde{p}(\beta)]/2) + \log\omega^h(\beta) + (y/\{[1 + \tilde{p}(\beta)]/2\}a^h) \\ &\sim \log(\omega^h(\beta) + [y/p(\beta)]a^h) \end{aligned}$$

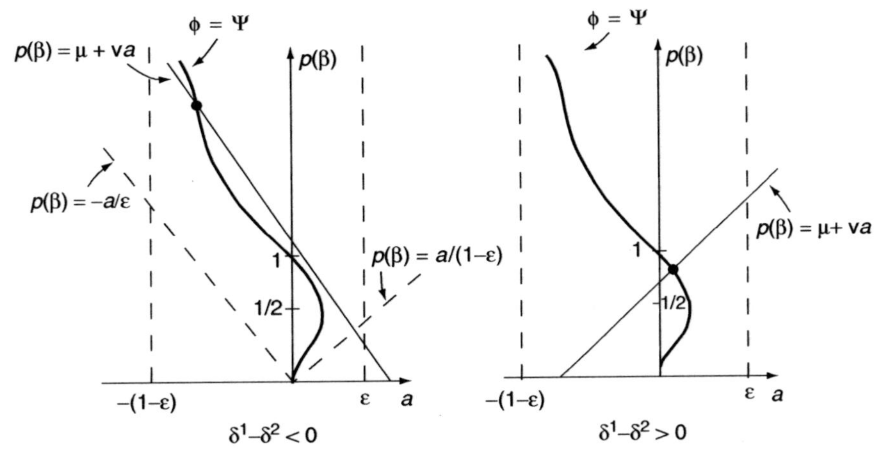

Figure 2.

to show that, in terms of the original model, such reallocations must take the form

$$\mathrm{d}w = (\mathrm{d}x(0), \mathrm{d}a, (1 + \chi[a, p(\beta)])\mathrm{d}a)$$

where

$$\begin{aligned} \chi[a, p(\beta)] &= \left[\varepsilon - 2x_2^2(\beta)\right]v \\ &= \left(\varepsilon - \left\{(1 - \delta^2)[(2p(\beta)/(2p(\beta) - 1)][\varepsilon + a/p(\beta)]\right\}\right)v \end{aligned} \tag{34}$$

So, again utilizing Equation (29),

$$\begin{aligned} \lambda^1 \cdot (-\mathrm{d}w) &= -\lambda^1(0)(\mathrm{d}x(0) + q\mathrm{d}a) - \lambda^1(\beta)\chi[a, p(\beta)]\mathrm{d}a \\ \text{and } \lambda^2 \cdot (\mathrm{d}w) &= \lambda^2(0)(\mathrm{d}x(0) + q\mathrm{d}a) + \lambda^2(\beta)\chi(a, p(\beta))\mathrm{d}a \end{aligned} \tag{35}$$

The upshot is that, provided (i) $(\lambda^1(0),\ \lambda^1(\beta))$ and $(\lambda^2(0),\ \lambda^2(\beta))$ are not colinear and (ii) $\chi[a,\ p(\beta)] \neq 0$, there is a reallocation (represented by $(\mathrm{d}x(0),\ \mathrm{d}a)$) such that both expressions in Equation (35) are positive, that is, in which both households gain. And it is certainly plausible that these are typical cases. For instance, $\chi[a,\ p(\beta)] = 0$ means that, in the β spot market, each household chooses to consume his own endowment of good 2.

Remark. It is at this last step where a more subtle genericity argument – indeed, one involving utility as well as endowment perturbations – is indispensable. Notice, however, that it is possible to perturb δ^2 so as to insure $\chi[a,\ p(\beta)] \neq 0$ (since the second utility parameter δ^1 can be adjusted to maintain the original equilibrium through Equation (33)). Notice too that the specification Equation (32) is required; otherwise, when $\delta^1 = \delta^2 = \delta$, $p(\beta) = (1/2)/(\delta^1(1-\varepsilon)+\delta^2\varepsilon) = (1/2)/\delta > 1/2$ is invariant.

5. A Short, Concise Guide to the Literature

It is fair to say that the seminal papers in this literature are Diamond (1967), Radner (1972), and Hart (1975): Diamond was the first to recognize that, despite incompleteness, financial markets may yield a systematic form of constrained optimality; Radner provided the earliest analysis of a general model of incomplete financial markets with asset yields specified in units of commodities (ensuring existence by imposing a priori bounds on asset trading); Hart sharpened the focus on both questions of optimality (e.g., he constructed the first example of Pareto ranking of equilibria) and existence (he also constructed the first example of nonexistence of equilibrium).

As in the body of the chapter, I will present the subsequent developments in what I view as logical rather than chronological order, and will refer to assets whose yields are specified in units of account as bonds, to those whose yields are specified in units of commodities as futures. I make no pretence of being either comprehensive,[8] or even – from various authors' viewpoints – balanced.

5.1. Existence

Not surprisingly this problem (when there are no constraints on asset trading) has attracted the most attention. The first solutions proposed avoided difficulty by simply switching attention from futures to bonds, in effect following Arrow (1964) rather than, as did Radner, Debreu (1959), Cass (1984), Werner (1985), and Duffie (1987). At about the same time several authors established that:

(i) existence would typically occur with potentially complete markets in futures: McManus (1986), Repullo (1986), and Magill and Shafer (1990);

[8] In particular, I deliberately avoid presenting many details of model specification, for example, whether there are just two or more than two periods, and – except where necessary – whether futures take the simple form of paying off in terms of units of a specific commodity or some more general pattern (and perhaps structure, as with options). Similarly, I am purposely vague about the precise sense in which results are typical (rather than general) since this tends to vary depending on the model (as well as the goal). The interested reader should look at the papers themselves to fill in these gaps.

(ii) existence would generally occur when futures are specified in terms of a single numéraire (e.g., gold): Geanakoplos and Polemarchakis (1986) and Chae (1988).

On the technically more difficult level, the first general argument (covering both inherent incompleteness and arbitrary futures) that existence would typically occur was devised by Duffie and Shafer (1985, 1986). Several alternative approaches yielding the same result have since been elaborated: Younès, (1986), Geanakoplos and Shafer (1990), Hirsch et al. (1990), and Husseini, et al. (1990). Polemarchakis and Ku (1990) constructed an example suggesting some nebulousness in defining what sensibly constitutes "typical."

5.2. Determinacy or (Local) Uniqueness

Cass (1989) constructed an example showing that "solving" the existence problem by focusing on bonds typically introduces the additional complication of extensive real indeterminacy. General analysis of this disturbing side effect has yielded several sharper results: Werner (1986), Polemarchakis (1988), Balasko and Cass (1989), Geanakoplos and Mas-Colell (1989), and Werner (1990). Typical (local) uniqueness with futures rather than bonds is more or less a direct consequence of the various existence arguments (a point especially emphasized by Geanakoplos and Polemarchakis).

It is perhaps worth reiterating, as was mentioned earlier, that both problems with existence and lack of (local) uniqueness occur in models featuring aspects of both bonds and futures.

5.3. Optimality

Grossman (1977) developed the general characterization of constrained optimality. Following Stiglitz (1982) and others, Geanakoplos and Polemarchakis (1986) demonstrated – within the context of their specific formulation – that accounting for future spot market price adjustments typically reverses this conclusion. Their analysis has recently been extended to a model including productive firms (and thus stocks, or futures whose yields are determined endogenously) (Geanakoplos et al., 1990).

Including Diamond's seminal paper, there have been other attempts to include productive firms: generic existence (Duffie and Shafer, 1987) and constrained optimality (Grossman and Hart, 1979). This task faces a daunting prospect right at the outset, namely, prescribing the firm's objective in an environment with incomplete financial markets. I note without comment that there is no hint of agreement in the papers just cited.

Acknowledgment

Research support from the NSF under grant #SES 88-08524 is gratefully acknowledged.

References

Arrow, K.J. (1964). The role of securities in the optimal allocation of risk-bearing. *Review of Economic Studies* **31**, 91–96.

Balasko, Y. and Cass, D. (1989). The structure of financial equilibrium with exogenous yields: The case of incomplete markets. *Econometrica* **57**, 135–162.

Cass, D. (1984). Competitive equilibrium with incomplete financial markets. CARESS Working Paper, University of Pennsylvania, Pennsylvania, PA.

Cass, D. (1989). Sunspots and incomplete financial markets: The leading example. In Feiwel, G. (Ed.), *The Economics of Imperfect Competition: Joan Robinson and Beyond*. London: Macmillan.

Chae, S. (1988). Existence of competitive equilibrium with incomplete markets. *Journal of Economic Theory* **44**, 179–188.

Debreu, G. (1959). *Theory of Value*. New York: Wiley, 1959. Chapter 7.

Diamond, P. (1967). The role of a stock market in a general equilibrium model with technological uncertainty. *American Economic Review* **57**, 759–776.

Duffie, D. (1987). Stochastic equilibria with incomplete financial markets. *Journal of Economic Theory* **41**, 405–416.

Duffie, D. and Shafer, W. (1985). Equilibrium in incomplete markets: I. A basic model of generic existence. *Journal of Mathematical Economics* **14**, 285–300.

Duffie, D. and Shafer, W. (1986). Equilibrium in incomplete markets: II. Generic existence in stochastic economies. *Journal of Mathematical Economics* **15**, 199–216.

Duffie, D. and Shafer, W. (1987). Equilibrium and the role of the firm in incomplete markets. Working paper, Graduate School of Business, Stanford University, USA.

Geanakoplos, J., Magill, M., Quinzii, M. and Drèze, J. (1990). Generic inefficiency of stock market equilibrium when markets are incomplete. *Journal of Mathematical Economics* **19**, 113–151.

Geanakoplos, J. and Mas-Colell, A. (1989). Real indeterminacy with financial assets. *Journal of Economic Theory* **47**, 22–38.

Geanakoplos, J. and Polemarchakis, H. (1986). Existence, regularity and constrained suboptimality of competitive allocations when the asset market is incomplete. In Heller, W.P., Starr, R.M. and Starrett, D.A. (Eds), *Uncertainty, Information and Communication, Essays in Honor of Kenneth J. Arrow* (Vol. III). Cambridge: Cambridge University Press.

Geanakoplos, J. and Shafer, W. (1990). Solving systems of simultaneous equations in economies. *Journal of Mathematical Economics* **19**, 69–93.

Grossman, S.J. (1977). A characterization of the optimality of equilibrium in incomplete markets. *Journal of Economic Theory* **15**, 1–15.

Grossman, S.J. and Hart, O. (1979). A theory of competitive equilibrium in stock market economies. *Econometrica* **47**, 293–330.

Hart, O.D. (1975). On the optimality of equilibrium when the market structure is incomplete. *Journal of Economic Theory* **11**, 418–443.

Hicks, J.R. (1946). *Value and Capital*, (2nd edition). Oxford: Clarendon Press.

Hirsch, M.D., Magill, M. and Mas-Colell, A. (1990). A geometric approach to a class of existence problems. *Journal of Mathematical Economics* **19**, 95–106.

Husseini, S., Lasry, J.-M. and Magill, M. (1990). Existence of equilibrium with incomplete markets. *Journal of Mathematical Economics* **19**, 39–67.

Magill, M.J.P. and Shafer, W.J. (1990). Characterization of generically complete real asset structures. *Journal of Mathematical Economics* **19**, 167–194.

McManus, D. (1986). Regular options equilibria. CARESS Working Paper, University of Pennsylvania, Pennsylvania, PA.

Polemarchakis, H.M. and Ku, B.-I. (1990). Options and equilibrium. *Journal of Mathematical Economics* **19**, 107–112.

Polemarchakis, H.M. (1988). Portfolio choice, exchange rates and indeterminacy. *Journal of Economic Theory* **46**, 414–421.

Radner, R. (1972). Existence of equilibrium plans, prices and price expectations in a sequence of markets. *Econometrica* **40**, 289–303.

Repullo, R. (1986). On the generic existence of Radner equilibria when there are as many securities as states of nature. *Economic Letters* **21**, 101–105.

Stiglitz, J.E. (1982). The inefficiency of stock market equilibrium. *Review of Economic Studies* **49**, 241–261.

Werner, J. (1985). Equilibrium in economies with incomplete financial markets. *Journal of Economic Theory* **36**, 110–119.

Werner, J. (1986). Asset prices and real indeterminacy in equilibrium with financial markets. Working paper, University of Bonn, Germany.

Werner, J. (1990). Structure of financial markets and real indeterminacy of equilibria. *Journal of Mathematical Economics* **19**, 217–232.

Younès, Y. (1986) Competitive equilibrium for incomplete market structures. CARESS Working Paper, University of Pennsylvania, USA.

Chapter 15

Indefinitely Sustained Consumption Despite Exhaustible Natural Resources ☆

David Cass and Tapan Mitra

Department of Economics, Cornell University, Ithaca, NY 14853, USA

1. Introduction

Ultimately, the only conceivable limit to continued economic progress is lack of human imagination and ingenuity. Timely accumulation of capital goods, including, in particular, stores of technical knowledge (concerning social as well as natural phenomena), can surely offset any foreseeable depletion of natural resources, no matter how shortsightedly or inflexibly specified. *But is such propitious growth even within the realm of possibility?*

In order to lay a solid basis for providing precise answers to this critical question, we pose the following fundamental problem: Assuming a fairly unrestricted specification of technology – that is, a reasonably general description of an economy's feasible growth paths given initial stocks of both capital goods and exhaustible resources – what additional technological conditions governing capital–resource substitution determine whether the economy is capable of sustaining consumption – that is, of providing uniformly positive welfare – forever?

Our solution to this problem yields – under quite generally maintained assumptions on technology – a single, simple substitution condition that is both necessary and sufficient for indefinitely sustained consumption. This substitution condition is tantamount to an easily understood growth requirement: *The economy must be capable, starting from arbitrary, positive stocks and growing with pure, arithmetic accumulation, of either, at best, achieving resource independence or, at worst, avoiding resource exhaustion.*

Our general characterization captures the essential feature of a leading special case previously reported by both Solow (1974) and Stiglitz (1974, 1979): When technology is specifically represented in terms of an aggregative

☆This article was originally published in *Economic Theory* 1, David Cass and Tapan Mitra, "Indefinitely sustained consumption despite exhaustible natural resources", 119–146, © Springer, 1991.

International Symposia in Economic Theory and Econometrics, Vol. 21B
S. Spear (Editor)

ISSN: 1571-0386/DOI: 10.1108/S1571-0386(2011)000021B018

neoclassical production function with constant elasticity of substitution, our characterization is equivalent to their condition that the elasticity of substitution be greater than one, or equal to one, provided, in addition, that the capital stock exponent exceed that of the resource flow. But our analysis also reaches far beyond this very explicit example; even within the confines of an aggregative specification of technology we permit substantial discontinuity (e.g., by admitting scale indivisibilities for capital stocks) as well as other significant nonconvexity (e.g., by admitting increasing returns to resource flows at low levels of capacity utilization). Moreover, our basic result can be readily modified to address the deeper problem of characterizing the technological possibilities for continually increasing and asymptotically unbounded consumption, and can be easily extended to include the broader situation where the specification of technology involves many different commodities, both natural (e.g., specific mineral compounds) and produced (e.g., detailed extraction techniques).

Our analysis focuses on a particularly suitable reformulation of the usual neoclassical parable. The core of the paper consists of presentation of that canonical model together with description of the fundamental problem (Section 2), and statement and proof of our general characterization (Section 3). A concluding discussion (Section 4) outlines some possible approaches for elaborating our analysis in order to encompass the potential for increasing and unbounded consumption as well as the presence of many different types of commodities. Finally, we also investigate the robustness of our central results to further relaxation of crucial maintained assumptions (appendix).

2. Specification of Technology

2.1. A Conventional Neoclassical Model

Economic activity begins in period 0, and continues unendingly over periods $t = 0,1,2, \ldots$. In each period a (net) flow of final goods output y is produced from a flow of exhaustible resources d (for "*d*epletion") and a previously accumulated stock of capital goods k (for "*k*apital") according to a (net) *output production* function $f : \mathbb{R}^2_+ \rightarrow \mathbb{R}$. This output is then allocated between consumption goods c and (net) investment goods i. Thus, the stock of exhaustible resources available next period is simply those not utilized this period, while the stock of capital goods available next period consists of those utilized this period plus investment goods produced this period (possibly a negative quantity). The economy's intertemporal production possibilities are further constrained by its historically given initial stocks of both exhaustible resources $\tilde{r}$ and capital goods $\tilde{k}$.

These possibilities can be concisely represented by defining the economy's *feasible growth paths* as the solutions to the dynamical system:

$$\begin{cases} (c_t, d_t, k_t) \geqq 0, \quad c_t + i_t \leqq y_t = f(d_t, k_t) \quad \text{and} \quad k_{t+1} = k_t + i_t \quad \text{for} \quad t \geqq 0 \\ \text{and} \\ \sum_{t=0}^{\infty} d_t \leqq \tilde{r} \quad \text{and} \quad k_0 \leqq \tilde{k}. \end{cases} \tag{1}$$

Note that Equation (1) presumes the availability of free disposal for both output and initial stocks. Standard specifications of the economy's static technology require that $f \in C$ be everywhere increasing in d, initially increasing in k (at least when $d > 0$), and jointly concave (and perhaps linear homogeneous) in d and k, and that it satisfies $f(0,0) = 0$ and $f(d, k) \geqq -k$. For our particular purposes, such neoclassical assumptions lead to three essentially different cases. These are exemplified in Figure 1, and will be distinguished more precisely in the following subsection.

The model detailed below, the formulation we will actually concentrate attention on, is substantially more general than the sort of conventional parable just sketched. However, both models share several basic features that are well worth remarking at the outset:

1. *Time is treated as a discrete variable*. While such treatment facilitates the use of elementary analytic techniques, it also necessitates the imposition of a potentially objectionable restriction on the applicability of our central characterization. The role of this additional restriction, which essentially amounts to the technological assumption that isoquants are downward sloping, is explored in some detail in appendix. In particular, there we will indicate how our general theorem can be simplified conceptually – though, in terms of the mathematical foundations required, not analytically – by switching to a continuous time framework, and thereby avoiding any such monotonicity requirement altogether.
2. *Technology is specified in terms of net rather than gross outputs*. In principle, such general specification is merely a matter of notation. Thus, for instance, in describing the conventional neoclassical formulation, we could have equally well defined f in terms of a (gross) output production function $g : \mathbb{R}_+^2 \rightarrow \mathbb{R}_+$ together with a (real) capital depreciation schedule $\delta : \mathbb{R}_+^2 \rightarrow \mathbb{R}_+$ by the identity $f \equiv g - \delta$ (requiring, in particular, that $\delta(d, k) \leqq k$).

   In practice, however, our particular specification is possibly a matter of substance, since it ostensibly permits direct conversion of undepreciated capital goods (represented by the difference $k - \delta(d, k)$) into consumption goods. Thus, for instance, in Equation (1) (net) investment goods output

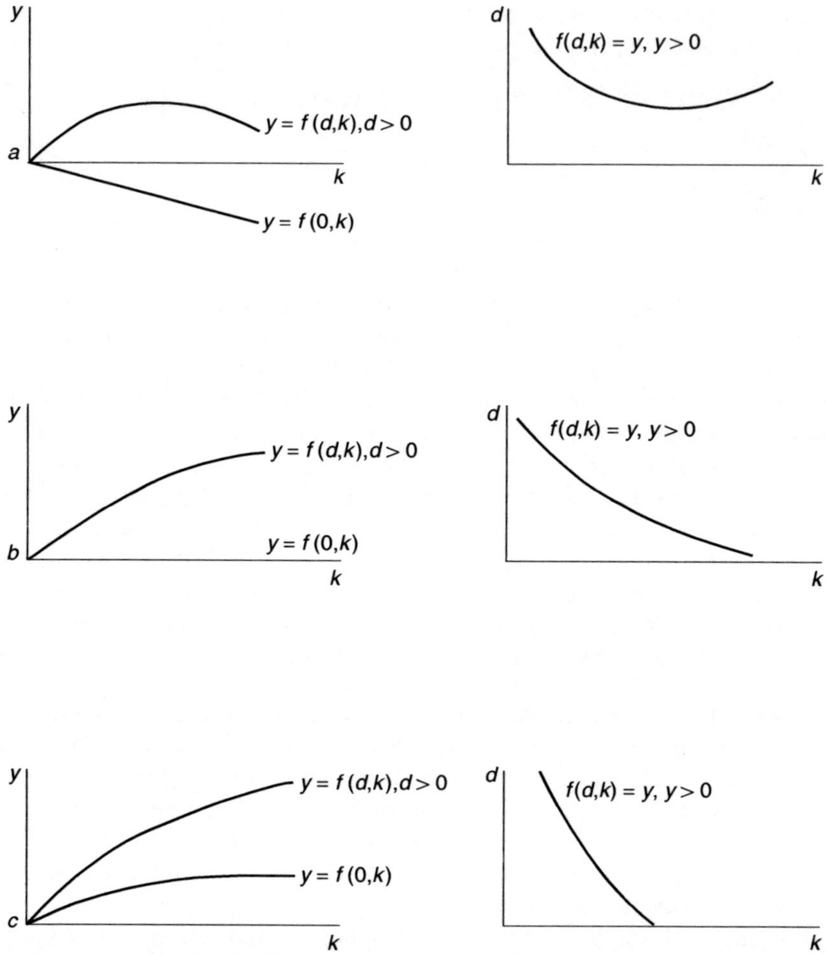

Figure 1: Typical Examples of the Standard (Net) Output Production Function. (a) $f(0, k) < 0$ for $k > 0$ (and $\lim_{k\to\infty} f(d,k) < 0$ for $d > 0$). (b) $f(0, k) = 0$ for $k > 0$ (and $\lim_{k\to\infty} f(d,k) = \infty$ for $d > 0$). (c) $f(0, k) > 0$ for $k > 0$ (and $\lim_{k\to\infty} f(0,k) = \infty$).

need only satisfy the constraint $-k_t \leqq i_t \geqq y_t$, and hence consumption goods output the constraint

$$0 \leqq c_t \leqq y_t - i_t \leqq y_t + k_t = \overbrace{[y_t + \delta(d_t, k_t)]}^{\text{(gross) final goods}} + \overbrace{[k_t - \delta(d_t, k_t)]}^{\text{undepreciated capital goods}}$$

for $t \geqq 0$. A broad justification for this amorphous specification will be implicit in our suggested methodology for treating many different types of commodities. A more narrow justification is inherent in our present analysis itself. It turns out that, but for some exceptionally irregular technologies, all the growth paths we will consider either exhibit, or can be easily modified to exhibit the property that (net) investment goods output is always nonnegative, so that consumption goods output is always less than (net) final goods output. In other words, what on first appearance seems a substantial limitation, upon further inspection becomes just an expositional convenience.

3. *Exhaustible resources (e.g., fossil fuel stocks) are the only primary factors explicitly recognized.* As with the net–gross distinction, here again the initial impression is somewhat deceiving. For, suppose that we were equally concerned with the constraining influence of other primary factors, short-lived (e.g., labor service flows) or long-lived (e.g., land space stocks). Then, to the extent that their availability over time is constant, their restrictive properties could be incorporated directly into the description of the economy's static technology (for instance, the specification of f). Moreover, to the extent that variation in their availability over time is endogenous, their feasible (net) output flows and input stocks could be included along with those of any other produced factors in our ultimate generalization involving many different types of commodities.
4. *Allocation choices are highly aggregative.* Regarding this feature, it is important to bear in mind a point we have already stressed: The central result for our canonical aggregative model largely carries over to a general disaggregative model. Such extension is more than simply generalization for its own sake. Indeed, it permits explicitly recognizing a number of basic technological considerations inherently related to questions concerning "the limits of growth." Specifically, by introducing heterogeneity of capital – beyond the present crude division between exhaustible resources (i.e., necessarily depletable stocks) and capital goods (i.e., potentially augmentable stocks) – we can expressly model such diverse phenomena (regarding just exhaustible resources) as (i) variability in quality, (ii) stock–flow interdependence, and (iii) recovery and recycling. Perhaps more critically, our general disaggregative model can capture significant aspects of the most fundamental long-run substitution possibility of all, the offset to resource exhaustion provided by technical progress – at least insofar as research and development can be accurately portrayed as an activity involving the accumulation and utilization of stocks of knowledge. (Incidentally, our underlying concern with just this sort of generality in large part motivates our repeated emphasis on weakening the technological assumptions required for our analysis. Why should a growth process involving, say, the invention and utilization of fusion-electric power be subject to any of the conventionally presumed regularities, for instance, generalized diminishing returns?)

2.2. Reformulation into Canonical Form

Because we are primarily interested in the question of the perpetual sustainability of consumption, and because its resolution ultimately depends on properties of the asymptotic substitutability of capital for resources, it is especially convenient to reformulate the representation of feasible growth paths in terms of a *resource requirement* function $h : H \to \mathbb{R}_+$ with $H \subset \mathbb{R} \times \mathbb{R}_+$. h describes the minimum resource depletion required to yield a given output level from a given capital stock (together with fixed primary factors), while H circumscribes the conceivable pairs of output level and capital stock. For instance, starting with the output production function f, we would have, formally,

$$h(y,k) = \text{minimum } d \quad \text{subject to } y \leqq f(d,k) \quad \text{and} \quad d \geqq 0 \quad \text{for} \quad (y,k) \in H$$

with

$$H = \{(y,k) : k \geqq 0 \text{ and there exists } d \geqq 0 \text{ such that } y \leqq f(d,k)\}.$$

Roughly speaking, then, h is simply a "partial inverse" of f, while H is its corresponding domain. (Of course, h as well as f could be derived directly from the primitive set of all feasible combinations of outputs and inputs, or the *technology set*, the more basic approach we actually adopt in treating many different types of commodities.)

Utilizing the definitions of these two fundamental constructs (and also suppressing superfluous notation for intermediate flows), it is easily verified that the dynamical system Equation (1) is equivalent (but for permitting outright wastage of consumption goods) to the dynamical system

$$\begin{cases} c_t \geqq 0 \quad \text{and} \quad (c_t + k_{t+1} - k_t, k_t) \in H \quad \text{for} \quad t \geqq 0 \\ \text{and} \\ \sum_{t=0}^{\infty} h(c_t + k_{t+1} - k_t, k_t) \leqq \tilde{r} \quad \text{and} \quad k_0 \leqq \tilde{k}. \end{cases} \tag{2}$$

This particular representation of feasible growth paths will be the focus of our investigation. Before we can proceed, however, we first need to impose some structure on both H and h (now listed in the natural order for detailing their specification). One obvious way of accomplishing this task is simply to deduce the properties that they inherit from standard specifications of f. It turns out that such structure is considerably more restrictive than absolutely necessary for our purposes. Thus, while we have drawn some inspiration from examples like those shown in Figure 1, we have found it more appropriate to introduce our maintained assumptions, as it were, *ab initio*.

In stating these minimal assumptions, it is convenient to have at hand specific notation for cross-sections of H, as well as for certain bounds related to the possible behavior of h. So, to begin with, we define

$$H(y) = \{k : (y,k) \in H\} \quad \text{for} \quad y \in R,$$
$$H(k) = \{y : (y,k) \in H\} \quad \text{for} \quad k \in R_+,$$
$$\bar{y} = \sup\left\{ y : y \geqq 0 \text{ and } \inf_{k' \in H(y)} h(y,k') = 0 \right\},$$

and

$$\underline{k}(y) = \inf\left\{ k : k \in H(y) \text{ and } \inf_{k' \in H(y),\ k' \leqq k} h(y,k') = 0 \right\} \quad \text{for} \quad y \in \mathbb{R}_+$$

with

$$\underline{k} = \inf_{y>0} \underline{k}(y),$$

where, by convention, $\inf \phi = -\sup \phi = \infty$. To interpret these various bounds, we ignore the (economically) implausible but (mathematically) tractable irregularity where, for some $0<y<\bar{y}$, $\underline{k}(y)<\infty$ but either $(y, \underline{k}(y)) \notin H$ or $(y, \underline{k}(y)) \in H$ and $h(y, \underline{k}(y))>0$. Then, $\bar{y}$ represents the upper bound (possibly zero) on *sustainable* output levels, that is, output levels that can be produced – perhaps only from unlimited capital stocks – without any resource depletion, while $\underline{k}$ represents the lower bound (possibly infinity) on *sustaining* capital stocks, that is, minimum capital stocks from which positive output levels can be produced without any resource depletion, themselves denoted $\underline{k}(y)$ for $y>0$. Figure 2, which replicates the examples of Figure 1, but now labeled in terms of h rather than f, suggests the intuitive basis for these definitions. On the one hand, when $\bar{y} = 0$ (i.e., as displayed in Figure 2a, when every isoquant lies uniformly above the k-axis) sustained consumption appears a very unlikely prospect. On the other hand, when $\underline{k} < \infty$ (i.e., as displayed in Figure 2c, when some isoquant intersects the k-axis) it appears a very likely one. (Both conjectures are in fact correct under the neoclassical assumptions listed earlier.) While our analysis is, therefore, primarily directed toward the less obvious, more important intermediate case in which $\bar{y}>0$ and $\underline{k} = \infty$ (displayed in Figure 2b), our results also cover these two polar cases.

Regarding the domain and properties of the resource requirement function itself, we assume, for H, that

H1. For every $0<k<\underline{k}$, there exists $y>0$ such that $(y, k) \in H$; and

H2. If $(y, k) \in H$, $0<y' \leqq y$ and $k' \geqq k$, then $(y', k') \in H$;

and, for h, that

h1. For every $k \geqq 0$, h is increasing in y on $\{y: y \in H(k) \text{ and } y>0\}$;

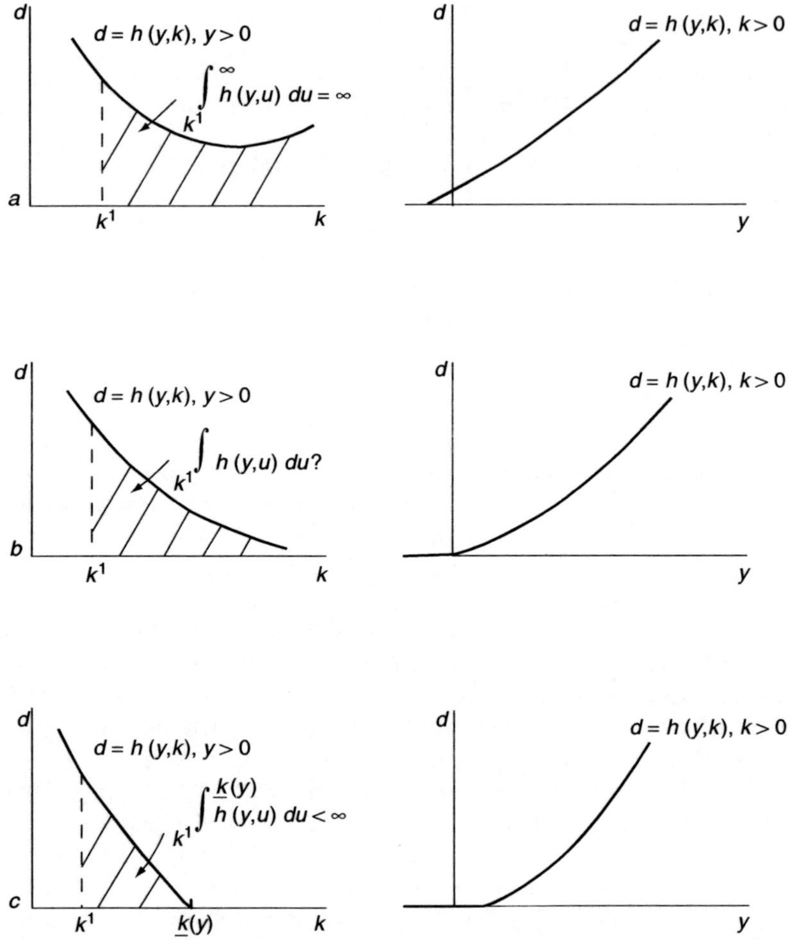

Figure 2: Corresponding Examples of our Canonical Resource Requirement Function. (a) $\bar{y}=0$ and $\underline{k}=\underline{k}(y)=\infty$. (b) $\bar{y}>0$ and $\underline{k}=\underline{k}(y)=\infty$. (c) $\bar{y}=\infty$ and $0=\underline{k}\leqq k(y)<\infty$.

h2. If $\bar{y}>0$, then, for every $0<y<\bar{y}$, h is decreasing – and hence integrable (in the sense of Riemann) – in k on (k: $k\in H(y)$ and $k<\underline{k}(y)\}$; and

h3. If $\bar{y}>0$, then there is a positive constant $v>0$ with the property that, for every $k\geqq 0$,

$$y'\in H(k) \quad \text{and} \quad 0<y''\leqq y' \Rightarrow \frac{h(y',k)}{y'}\geqq v\frac{h(y'',k)}{y''}.$$

Note for future reference that H2 and h1 entail that $\underline{k}(y)$ is increasing in y, so that, in particular,

$$\underline{k}(0) \leqq \lim_{y \to 0^+} \underline{k}(y) = \inf_{y>0} \underline{k}(y) = \underline{k} \leqq \underline{k}(y) \quad \text{for} \quad y > 0.$$

We reemphasize the fact that these maintained assumptions, though consistent with conventional neoclassical assumptions (the "leading case" referred to below), are very much weaker. Indeed, as should become apparent from the subsequent analysis, they are so unrestrictive as to be almost, but not quite completely, unobjectionable. With this assertion clearly in mind, then, consider the following interpretive comments. (i) Both H1 and H2 are innocuous, as well as transparent, since they simply state, respectively, that some positive output level can be produced from every positive, nonsustaining capital stock, and that both output and capital can be disposed of – provided, in the background, there is sufficient accompanying depletion. (ii) h1 and h2 then sharpen the terms on which (given a feasible production point) either less output can be produced or more capital employed, since, at a minimum, they amount, respectively, to free disposal of output and (within the limits specified) free disposal of capital. (iii) Of course, h1 also embodies the obvious natural productivity hypothesis concerning increased resource utilization (and, to a somewhat lesser degree, presuming h1 obtains, h2 one obvious possible productivity hypothesis concerning increased capital intensity). That is, h1 entails that additional depletion can typically yield additional output, everything else the same (and h2, again within the limits specified, that capital goods can typically replace exhaustible resources, everything else the same). (iv) In particular, h1 and h2 would both be true in the leading case where, for every $k \geqq 0$, h is increasing in y on $H(k)$, that is, where the labeling of isoquants is increasing in the northeast direction, and where, for every $y > 0$, h is decreasing in k on $H(y)$, that is, where isoquants are downward sloping, respectively. Recall, however, that the isoquants in question represent constant *net* final goods output, so that even as it stands, h2 is not indisputable; with capital deepening, greater depletion may be required simply to offset higher depreciation, everything else the same. (v) Finally, h3 is a very mild version of the classical law of diminishing returns to a single factor. As we shall demonstrate later on, its basic purpose is to rule out the extremely implausible possibility that average returns to exhaustible resources are asymptotically unbounded. In particular, h3 would be true in the leading case where, for every $k \geqq 0$, $h(0, k) = 0$ and h is convex in y on $H(k)$, that is, where capital can be costlessly stored and depletion is in fact subject to universal diminishing returns.

Much of our lengthy analysis revolves around the two assumptions h2 and h3. Thus, it is worth emphasizing again that h2 can be replaced by a much weaker regularity requirement in continuous time (see h2′ in appendix), and stressing explicitly that h3 can be replaced by an even weaker curvature condition upon deeper investigation (see h3′ in appendix).

The basic nature of our maintained assumptions has already been exhibited by Figures 1 and 2; various aspects of their generality are now highlighted by Figure 3. Notice especially that no continuity restrictions (beyond those implicit in the monotonicity assumptions) are imposed on either resource utilization or capital intensity, and that, as previously remarked, only the mildest convexity restriction is imposed on resource utilization.

2.3. The Fundamental Existence Problem

Given the description of all feasible growth paths together with the specification of the resource requirement function, our goal is to characterize the static technologies (represented by H and h) that admit the possibility of indefinitely sustained consumption. *Specifically, we seek substitution conditions on h (additional to the maintained assumptions h1, h2, and h3), which are both necessary and sufficient to guarantee that, for every positive pair of initial stocks* $(\tilde{r}, \tilde{k}) \gg 0$, *there exists a feasible growth path (i.e., a solution to Equation* (2)) $\{(c_t, k_t)\}$ *along which consumption goods output is uniformly positive* $\inf_{t \geqq 0} c_t = c > 0$. Utilizing H2 and h1 in simplifying Equation (2), this fundamental existence problem can be succinctly stated as follows: Find substitution conditions, say SC, with the property that

$$\begin{cases} \text{for every } (\tilde{r}, \tilde{k}) > 0 \text{ there exists } (c, \{k_t\}) \text{ such that} \\ (c + k_{t+1} - k_t, k_t) \in H \quad \text{for} \quad t \geqq 0 \\ \text{and} \\ c > 0, \ \sum_{t=0}^{\infty} h(c + k_{t+1} - k_t, k_t) \leqq \tilde{r} \quad \text{and} \quad k_0 \leqq \tilde{k} \end{cases} \tag{3}$$

if and only if

h satisfies SC.

A word of caution: Our concern is with the existence *not* the magnitude of indefinitely sustained consumption. It is obvious to us – as well as to many others who have commented on our analysis – that an economy may well be viable in our narrow technological sense (i.e., $\inf_{t \geqq 0} c_t$ may be positive) and yet not in some broad "socio-biological" sense (e.g., $\{c_t\}$ may be insufficient to forestall humanity's extinction). (All this, of course, presumes that one can conceivably define suitable units for prejudging the effects of alternative streams of consumption goods output, a point we shall return to in

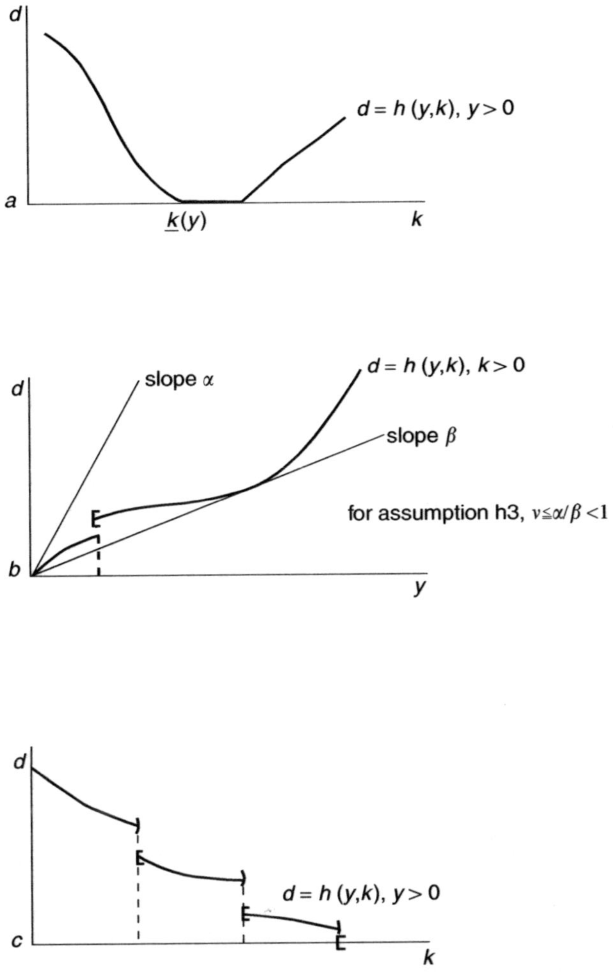

Figure 3: Various Productivity Phenomena Encompassed by the Technological Assumptions. (a) Substantial Depletion Required to Offset Depreciation with Large Stocks of Capital Goods. (b) Increasing Returns to Resources at Low Levels of Capacity Utilization. (c) Significant Indivisibilities in Substituting Capital for Resources.

Section 4.) Nonetheless, we do not apologize for this seemingly damaging inadequacy in our approach. Rather, we argue that our tack is the only sensible course to pursue. We simply cannot begin to address (possibly) more germane questions without already having solved this fundamental existence problem. (See too the closely related remarks in Solow Stiglitz [1974, especially p. 37].)

3. A Complete Characterization

Our basic theorem is a complete characterization of the circumstances under which it is feasible to sustain uniformly positive consumption forever, stated in terms of just a single capital-resource substitution condition.

Substitution condition. For every $0<k<\underline{k}$,

$$\lim_{y\to 0^+} 1/y \int_k^{\underline{k}(y)} h(y,u)\mathrm{d}u = 0. \tag{SC}$$

That is, formally, we will establish the following simple sustainability equivalence.

Sustainability Theorem. *Suppose H satisfies* H1–H2 *and h satisfies* h1–h3. *Then Equation* (3) *obtains if and only if substitution condition* (SC) *obtains.*

Before detailing the proof of this fundamental result, it is worthwhile digressing a bit to interpret (and, indirectly, to motivate) the crucial substitution condition (SC) itself. This can be usefully accomplished on at least two distinct levels:

1. *The technical interpretation.* Note first that if $\underline{k}=0$, then substitution condition (SC) is vacuously true. So we need only be concerned with the situation in which $\underline{k}>0$. Now, the integral in substitution condition (SC) is nothing more than the area, relative to the k-axes, under the y-level isoquant from arbitrary $k<\underline{k}$ such that $k\in H(y)$, say k', to $\underline{k}(y)$. (Refer back to Figure 2.) Hence, the limit in substitution condition (SC) is nothing more than the requirement that this area be finite for small positive y, and that it approach zero faster than y does.
   The geometry of this interpretation is especially clear when h is linear homogeneous, that is, when there are constant returns to scale, since then we can convert substitution condition (SC) into a substitution condition involving only the unit-level isoquant. Briefly, this can be seen as follows: h linear homogeneous implies $\underline{k}(y)$ linear homogeneous implies (i) $\underline{k}>0$ if and only if $\underline{k}=k(y)=\infty$ for $y>0$, while (ii) $\underline{k}=0$ if an only if $\underline{k}\leqq\underline{k}(y)<\infty$ for $y>0$. Thus, when $\underline{k}>0$, the integral in substitution condition (SC) can be rewritten (using the change of variable $v=u/y$)

$$\begin{aligned}\int_k^{\underline{k}(y)} h(y,u)\mathrm{d}u &= y^2\int_k^{\infty} h(1,u/y)\mathrm{d}u/y\\ &= y^2\int_{k/y}^{\infty} h(1,\upsilon)\mathrm{d}\upsilon = y^2\int_{k/y}^{\underline{k}(1)} h(1,\upsilon)\mathrm{d}\upsilon\end{aligned}\tag{4}$$

   and substitution condition (SC) will be verified (substituting from

Equation (4) into substitution condition (SC)) if and only if

for every $0<k<\underline{k}(1)$ such that $k \in H(1)$,

$$\int_k^{\underline{k}(1)} h(1,u)\mathrm{d}u<\infty, \tag{5}$$

while, when $\underline{k}=0$ (Equation (5)) is immediately verified. In short, under this additional homogeneity property, substitution condition (SC) is equivalent to Equation (5), which is nothing more than the requirement that the area "under" the unit-level isoquant be finite. (See also the companion discussion in Mitra Solow (1974, especially pp. 15–16).)

2. *The economic interpretation.* For this interpretation we again ignore the implausible irregularity where $\underline{k}(y)<\infty$ but either $(y,\underline{k}(y))\notin H$ or $(y,\underline{k}(y))\in H$ and $h(y,\underline{k}(y))>0$. (It is, nonetheless, covered by the Sustainability Theorem.) So, consider only situations in which either $\underline{k}(y)<\infty, (y,\underline{k}(y))\in H$ and $h(y,\underline{k}(y))=0$ or $\underline{k}(y)=\infty$. Also, consider only growth paths exhibiting *pure, arithmetic accumulation*, which is satisfying the two additional properties

$$c_t=0 \quad \text{for} \quad t\geqq 0 \tag{6}$$

and, for some $y>0$,

$$k_0\leqq \underline{k}(y) \quad \text{and} \quad k_{t+1}=\begin{cases} k_t+y & \text{for} \quad 0\leqq t<t_y \\ \underline{k}(y) & \text{otherwise,}\end{cases} \tag{7}$$

where $t_y=\sup\{t\colon\ t\geqq 0 \text{ and } t\leqq(\underline{k}(y)-k_0)/y\}$. (The descriptive label is slightly inappropriate when $\underline{k}(y)<\infty$ and therefore $t_y<\infty$.) *Then it can be shown that, for every positive pair of initial stocks* $(\tilde{r},\tilde{k})\gg 0$, *there exists a feasible growth path exhibiting pure, arithmetic accumulation (i.e., a solution to Equation* (2) *satisfying Equations* (6)–(7)) $\{k_t\}$ *if and only if h satisfies substitution condition* (SC). In other words, basically repeating ourselves from Section 1, substitution condition (SC) essentially amounts to the requirement that the economy must be capable, starting from arbitrary, positive stocks and growing with pure, arithmetic accumulation, of either, at best, achieving resource independence (when $\underline{k}<\infty$ and thus, typically, $t_y<\infty$) or, at worst, avoiding resource exhaustion (when $\underline{k}=\infty$ and thus, necessarily, $t_y=\infty$).

The proof of this interesting interpretive equivalence is a somewhat simplified (but nonetheless complicated) version of the proof of our main result. For this reason we will content ourselves with merely sketching the argument for the intermediate case in which we have $\bar{y}>0$ as well as $\bar{k}=\infty$ (and hence the hypothesis in both h2 and h3 as well as $\underline{k}(y)=\infty$ in substitution condition (SC)).

Sufficiency. We want to show that if h satisfies substitution condition (SC), then there exists a solution to Equation (2) satisfying (6)–(7). Toward this end, pick $k_0 = \tilde{k}$, and $0 < y < \bar{y}$ such that $(y, \tilde{k} - y) \in H$ (using H1 and H2) and

$$1/y \int_{\tilde{k}-y}^{\infty} h(y,u)\mathrm{d}u \leqq \tilde{r} \tag{8}$$

(using H2 and substitution condition (SC)). Then, given these particular values of k_0 and y, Equations (6) and (7) themselves yield a solution to Equation (2), since $(y, \tilde{k} - y) \in H$ implies $(c_t + k_{t+1} - k_t, k_t) = (y, \tilde{k} + yt) \in H$ for $t \geqq 0$ (using H2), while

$$\begin{aligned}
\sum_{t=0}^{\infty} h(c_t + k_{t+1} - k_t, k_t) &= \sum_{t=0}^{\infty} h(y, \tilde{k} + yt) \\
&= 1/y \sum_{t=0}^{\infty} h(y, \tilde{k} + yt)y \\
&\leqq 1/y \textstyle\int_{\tilde{k}-y}^{\infty} h(y,u)\mathrm{d}u && \text{(using h2)} \\
&\leqq \tilde{r}. && \text{(using Equation (8))}
\end{aligned}$$

Necessity. We want to show that if, for every $(\tilde{r}, \tilde{k}) \gg 0$, there exists a solution to Equation (2) satisfying Equations (6) and (7), then h satisfies substitution condition (SC). Toward this end, given arbitrary $(\tilde{r}, \tilde{k}) \gg 0$, suppose we have a solution to Equation (2) satisfying Equations (6) and (7). Then, the resource bound in Equation (2) yields the following chain of inequalities:

$$\begin{aligned}
\tilde{r} &\geqq \sum_{t=0}^{\infty} h(c_t + k_{t+1} - k_t, k_t) \\
&= \sum_{t=0}^{\infty} h(y, k_0 + yt) \\
&= \sum_{t=0}^{\infty} \frac{h(y,\, k_0 + yt)}{y} y \\
&\geqq v/y' \sum_{t=0}^{\infty} h(y', k_0 + yt)y \quad \text{for} \quad 0 < y' < \min\{y, \bar{y}\} && \text{[using h3]} \\
&\geqq v/y' \textstyle\int_{k_0}^{\infty} h(y', u)du && \text{[using h2]} \\
&\geqq v/y' \textstyle\int_{\tilde{k}}^{\infty} h(y', u)du && \text{[since } k_0 \leqq \tilde{k}] \\
&> 0,
\end{aligned}$$

or, ignoring intermediate steps (and rearranging constant terms), the following inequality:

$$\text{for every } 0 < y' < \min\{y, \bar{y}\},$$
$$0 < 1/y' \int_{\tilde{k}}^{\infty} h(y', u)\mathrm{d}u \leqq \tilde{r}/v. \tag{9}$$

But, because we started with arbitrary $(\tilde{r}, \tilde{k}) \gg 0$, Equation (9) is simply one equivalent restatement of substitution condition (SC) in "ε–δ" form. ■

One crucial step in both sides of the foregoing argument merits explicit comment. In order to go from sums to integrals we used the elementary result for monotone functions that, under the conclusion of h2,

$$\text{for every } k^i \in H(y) \text{ such that } k^i < \underline{k}(y), i = 1, 2,$$
$$h(y, k^2)(k^2 - k^1) \leqq \int_{k^1}^{k^2} h(y, u)du \leqq h(y, k^1)(k^2 - k^1).$$

This is the characteristic role that such restriction plays in our analysis, explaining why it can be dispensed within continuous time, where sums are naturally replaced by integrals at the outset. (The sufficiency argument for the Sustainability Theorem together with the necessity counterexamples in appendix will delimit the extent to which h2 can be dispensed with in discrete time.)

A final aside: It is straightforward but tedious to show that, when h corresponds to f with constant elasticity of substitution $\sigma \geqq 0$, say, given arbitrary $0 < \delta < 1$ and $\rho \geqq -1$,

$$f(d, k) - [(1 - \delta)d^{-\rho} + \delta k^{-\rho}]^{-1/\rho}$$

with

$$\sigma = 1/(1 + \rho),$$

h satisfies substitution condition (SC) if and only if $\sigma > 1$ or $\sigma = 1$ and $\delta > 1/2$. The details of verifying this relationship (between our theorem and the Solow–Stiglitz example) are left as an exercise for the reader.

We are now ready to proceed with the

Proof of the Sustainability Theorem. *Sufficiency*. We will show that, under the maintained assumptions, the substitution condition substitution condition (SC) can be used to construct a solution to Equation (2) satisfying

$c_t = c > 0$ for $t \geqq 0$, that is, a solution to the dynamical system

$$\begin{cases} (c + k_{t+1} - k_t, k_t) \in H \quad \text{for} \quad t \geqq 0 \\ \text{and} \\ c > 0, \sum_{t=0}^{\infty} h(c + k_{t+1} - k_t, k_t) \leqq \tilde{r} \quad \text{and} \quad k_0 \leqq \tilde{k}. \end{cases} \tag{10}$$

In fact, we will show that this construction can be completed without any reference to either h2 or h3.

There are two cases to consider, one ($\underline{k} = 0$) trivial, the other ($\underline{k} > 0$) not. In both cases the argument is slightly complicated by the possibility mentioned twice earlier, that $\underline{k}(y) < \infty$ but either $(y, \underline{k}(y)) \in H$ or $(y, \underline{k}(y)) \in H$ and $h(y, \underline{k}(y)) > 0$. Examples of resource requirement functions exhibiting these sorts of irregularity are illustrated in Figure 4.

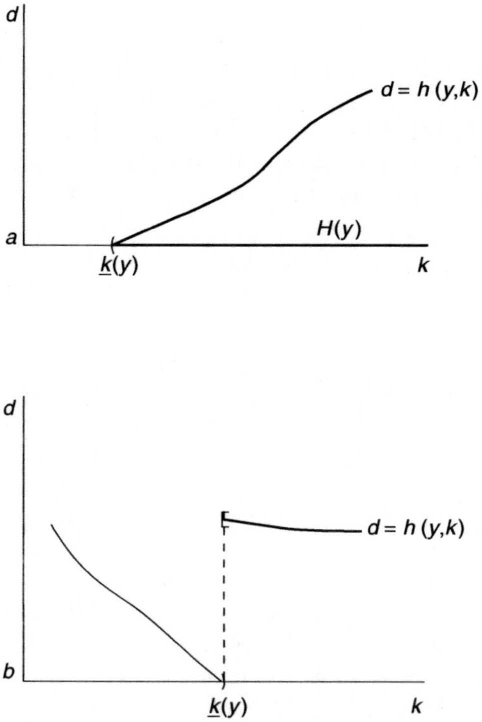

Figure 4: Illustration of the Irregularity Involved in the Proof of Sufficiency. (a) $\underline{k}(y) < \infty$ but $(y, \underline{k}(y)) \notin H$. (b) $\underline{k}(y) < \infty$ but $(y, \underline{k}(y)) \notin H$ and $h(y, \underline{k}(y)) > 0$.

Case 1. $\underline{k} = 0$.

Pick $\{\alpha_t\}$ such that $\alpha_t > 0$ for $t \geqq 0$ and $\sum_{t=0}^{\infty} \alpha_t \leqq \tilde{r}$ (e.g., $\alpha_t = ab^t$ with $0 < b < 1$ and $0 < a \leqq (1-b)\tilde{r}$), and using the supposition of this case, $y > 0$ such that $\underline{k}(y) \leqq \tilde{k} - y/4$. Then, appealing to the definition of $\underline{k}(y)$, define $\{k_t\}$ such that

$$(y, k_t) \in H, \quad \underline{k}(y) - y/4 \leqq k_t \leqq \underline{k}(y) + y/4 \quad \text{and} \quad h(y, k_t) \leqq \alpha_t \quad \text{for} \quad t \geqq 0$$

with corresponding

$$c_t = y - (k_{t+1} - k_t) \quad \text{for} \quad t \geqq 0.$$

It follows that $c_t \geqq y/2 > 0$ and $(c_t + k_{t+1} - k_t, k_t) = (y, k_t) \in H$ for $t \geqq 0$, while

$$\sum_{t=0}^{\infty} h(y, k_t) \leqq \sum_{t=0}^{\infty} \alpha_t \leqq \tilde{r}$$

and $k_0 \leqq \tilde{k}$, that is, $\{(c_t, k_t)\}$ is a solution to Equation (2). Hence $(c, \{k_t\})$ with $c = y/2 \leqq c_t$ for $t \geqq 0$ is a solution to Equation (10) (using H2 and h1).

Case 2. $\underline{k} > 0$.

Pick $\{\alpha_t\}$ such that $\alpha_t > 0$ for $t \geqq 0$ and $\sum_{t=0}^{\infty} \alpha_t \leqq \tilde{r}/2, 0 < k \leqq \tilde{k}$ such that $k < \underline{k}$ (without loss of generality, $k = \tilde{k}$), and $0 < \lambda < 1/2$ and $y > 0$ such that $(y, \tilde{k} - \lambda y) \in H$ (using H1 and H2) and

$$1/\lambda y \int_{\tilde{k}-\lambda y}^{\underline{k}(y)} h(y, u) \mathrm{d}u \leqq \tilde{r}/2$$

(using H2 and substitution condition (SC)). Then, proceed to define $\{k_t\}$ inductively as follows: First, for $t = 0$, pick k_0 such that $\tilde{k} - \lambda y \leqq k_0 < \tilde{k}$ and

$$h(y, k_0) - \alpha_0 \leqq \inf_{\tilde{k}-\lambda y \leqq k < \tilde{k}} h(y, k),$$

so that

$$[h(y, k_0) - \alpha_0]\lambda y \leqq \int_{\tilde{k}-\lambda y}^{\tilde{k}} \left[\inf_{\tilde{k}-\lambda y \leqq k < \tilde{k}} h(y, k) \right] \mathrm{d}u \leqq \int_{\tilde{k}-\lambda y}^{\tilde{k}} h(y, u) \mathrm{d}u.$$

or

$$h(y, k_0) \leqq 1/\lambda y \int_{\tilde{k}-\lambda y}^{\tilde{k}} h(y, u) \mathrm{d}u + \alpha_0. \tag{11}$$

Then, for $t+1 > 0$, given k_t such that $k_t + 2\lambda y \leqq \underline{k}(y)$ (e.g., when $\underline{k}(y) = \infty$), pick k_{t+1} such that $k_t + \lambda y \leqq k_{t+1} < k_t + 2\lambda y$ and

$$h(y, k_{t+1}) - \alpha_{t+1} \leqq \inf_{k_t + \lambda y \leqq k < k_t + 2\lambda y} h(y, k),$$

so that

$$\lambda y \leqq k_{t+1} - k_t < 2\lambda y < y \tag{12}$$

and

$$[h(y,k_{t+1}) - \alpha_{t+1}]\lambda y \leqq \int_{k_t+\lambda y}^{k_t+2\lambda y} \left[\inf_{k_t+\lambda y \leqq k < k_t+2\lambda y} h(y,k)\right] \mathrm{d}u \leqq \int_{k_t+\lambda y}^{k_t+2\lambda y} h(y,u)\mathrm{d}u$$

or

$$h(y,k_{t+1}) \leqq 1/\lambda y \int_{k_t+\lambda y}^{k_t+2\lambda y} h(y,u)\mathrm{d}u + \alpha_{t+1}. \tag{13}$$

Finally, for $t+1>0$, given k_t such that $k_t < k_{t-1} + 2\lambda y \leqq \underline{k}(y) < k_t + 2\lambda y$ (for convenience, defining $k_{-1} = \tilde{k} - 2\lambda y$), pick k_s for $s \geqq t+1$ such that $k_t \leqq k_s < k_t + 2\lambda$y, so that

$$k_s - k_{s-1} \leqq |k_s - k_{s-1}| < 2\lambda y < y, \tag{14}$$

and

$$h(y,k_s) \leqq \alpha_s. \tag{15}$$

Examples of such sequences $\{k_t\}$ in the two possible cases ($\underline{k}(y) = \infty$ and $\underline{k}(y) = \infty$) are illustrated in Figure 5.

Given our initial specifications of $\{\alpha_t\}$, λ, and y, it follows from the particulars of this construction (especially those represented by the inequalities (11)–(15)) that $\{(c_t,\ k_t)\}$ with $c_t = y-(k_{t+1}-k_t)$ for $t \geqq 0$ is a solution to Equation (2), since $c_t = y-(k_{t+1}-k_t) > (1-2\lambda)y > 0$ and $(c_t+k_{t+1}-k_t,\ k_t) = (y,\ k_t) \in H$ for $t \geqq 0$, while

$$\begin{aligned}
\sum_{t=0}^{\infty} h(c_t + k_{t+1} - k_t, k_t) &= \sum_{t=0}^{\infty} h(y,k_t) \\
&\leqq \sum_{\{t:t\geqq 0 \text{ and } k_{t-1}+2\lambda y \leqq \underline{k}(y)\}} \left[1/\lambda y \int_{k_{t-1}+\lambda y}^{k_{t-1}+2\lambda y} h(y,u)\mathrm{d}u + \alpha_t\right] \\
&\quad + \sum_{\{t:t\geqq 0 \text{ and } k_{t-1}+2\lambda y > \underline{k}(y)\}} [\alpha_t] \\
&\leqq 1/\lambda y \int_{\tilde{k}-\lambda y}^{\underline{k}(y)} h(y,u)\mathrm{d}u + \sum_{t=0}^{\infty} \alpha_t \\
&\leqq \tilde{r}
\end{aligned}$$

and $k_0 \leqq \tilde{k}$. Hence, $(c,\{k_t\})$ with $c = (1-2\lambda)y < c_t$ for $t \geqq 0$ is a solution to Equation (10) (using H2 and h1).

Remarks. We have already noted that neither h2 nor h3 plays any part whatsoever in the preceding proof. Moreover, since h1 only appears in the

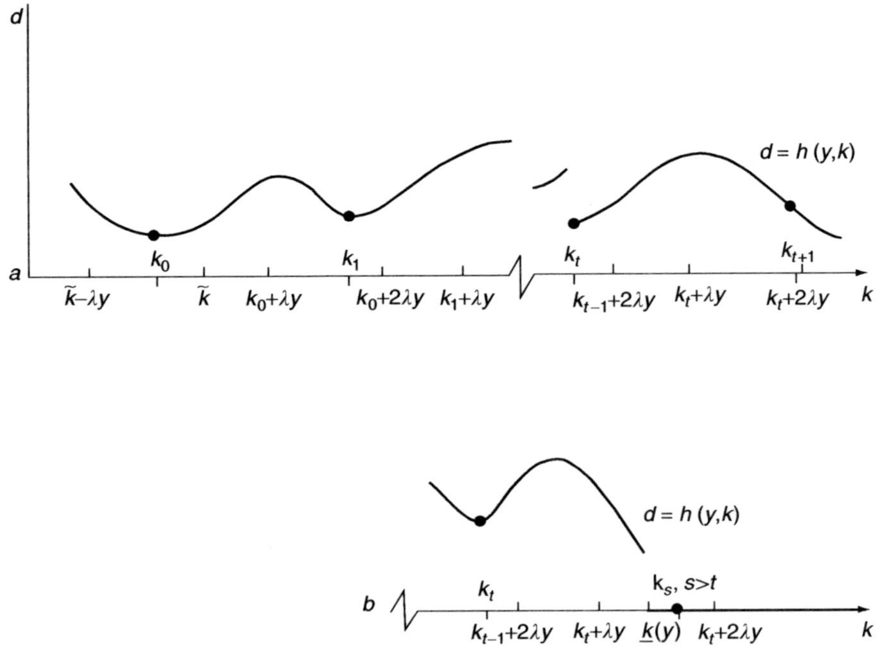

Figure 5: Illustration of the Construction Employed in the Proof of Sufficiency. (a) $\underline{k}(y) = \infty$ and (b) $\underline{k}(y) < \infty$.

final scene of that argument, it is clear that even this assumption, innocuous as it is, can be retired from the stage – provided that the constancy requirement $c_t = c > 0$ for $t \geqq 0$ is replaced by the less restrictive (but equally meaningful) uniformity requirement $\inf_{t \geqq 0} c_t = c > 0$. Furthermore, in somewhat the same spirit, it turns out that the substitution condition (SC) itself can be weakened, by replacing "lim" with "lim inf" (for necessity as well as sufficiency), a development we will discuss further in appendix.

It is also worth noting that the foregoing construction can be easily simplified to yield a solution to Equation (2) satisfying Equations (6) and (7) when h does in fact exhibit the monotonicity property h2 (without the openness irregularity illustrated in Figure 4). This generalization of the interpretive sufficiency argument presented earlier is based on the readily verified observation that substitution condition (SC) entails $\bar{y} > 0$, so that in defining $\{k_t\}$ above we can choose $0 < y < \bar{y}$, $\lambda = 1/2$ and – given that h satisfies h2 – $k_t = \min\{k_{t+1} + y, \underline{k}(y)\}$ (with $k_{-1} = \tilde{k} - y$) for $t \geqq 0$.

Necessity. This proof naturally decomposes into two steps, the first relying on neither h2 nor h3, and the second relying, in a fundamental way, on both assumptions. To underline this distinction (which is also convenient in developing the parallel argument for continuous time) we present the first as a separate result.

Lemma. *Suppose H satisfies* H2 *and h satisfies* h1. *Given arbitrary* $(\tilde{r}, \tilde{k}) \gg 0$, if $(c, \{k_t\})$ *is a solution to the dynamical system*

$$\begin{cases} (c + k_{t+1} - k_t, k_t) \in H \quad \text{for} \quad t \geqq 0 \\ \text{and} \\ c > 0, \sum_{t=0}^{\infty} h(c + k_{t+1} - k_t, k_t) \leqq \tilde{r} \quad \text{and} \quad k_0 \leqq \tilde{k}, \end{cases} \tag{10}$$

then $c \leqq \bar{y}$ *and, for every* $0 < y < c$, $\underline{k}(y) \leqq \sup_{t \geqq 0} k_t$.

Proof of the Lemma. Suppose $(c, \{k_t\})$ is a solution to Equation (10). Let

$$t^+(y, \tau) = \{t : 0 \leqq t \leqq \tau \text{ and } c + k_{t+1} - k_t \geqq y\}$$

and

$$\begin{aligned} t^-(y, \tau) &= \{0, 1, \ldots, \tau\} - t^+(y, \tau)\} \\ &= \{t : 0 \leqq t \leqq \tau \text{ and } c + k_{t+1} - k_t < y\} \end{aligned}$$

for $y \in \mathbb{R}, \tau \geqq 0$. In particular, the former definition reduces to

$$t^+(c, \tau) = \{t : 0 \leqq t \leqq \tau \text{ and } k_{t+1} - k_t \geqq 0\}$$

for $y = c$. Also let

$$n[A] = \text{number of elements in } A$$

for $A \subset \{0,1,2 \ldots\}$. Then, there are two cases to consider.

Case 1. $\lim_{\tau \to \infty} n[t^+(c, \tau)] = \infty$.

To analyze this case, we use the fact that the resource bound in Equation (10) yields the following chain of inequalities:

$$\begin{aligned}
\tilde{r} &\geqq \sum_{t=0}^{\infty} h(c+k_{t+1}-k_t, k_t) \\
&\geqq \sum_{t=0}^{\tau} h(c+k_{t+1}-k_t, k_t) \quad \text{for} \quad \tau \geqq 0 \\
&\geqq \sum_{t\in t^+(c,\tau)} h(c+k_{t+1}-k_t, k_t) \\
&\geqq \sum_{t\in t^+(c,\tau)} h(y,k_t) \quad \text{for} \quad 0<y<c \quad (\text{using H2 and h1}) \\
&\geqq \sum_{t\in t^+(c,\tau)} \inf_{k\in H(y),\ k\leqq \sup_{t\geqq 0} k_t} h(y,k) \\
&= n[t^+(c,\tau)] \inf_{k\in H(y),\ k\leqq \sup_{t\geqq 0} k_t} h(y,k).
\end{aligned}$$

By the supposition of this case, however, the final inequality can be true if and only if

$$\text{for every } 0<y<c, \inf_{k\in H(y),\, k\leqq \sup_{t\geqq 0} k_t} h(y,k) = 0. \tag{16}$$

But Equation (16) implies $c \leqq \bar{y}$ – since otherwise, that is, if $\bar{y}<c$, then by virtue of the definition of $\bar{y}$ there exists $\bar{y}<y'<c$ such that

$$0< \inf_{k\in H(y')} h(y',k) \leqq \inf_{k\in H(y'),\, k\leqq \sup_{t\geqq 0} k_t} h(y',k),$$

contradicting Equation (16) – as well as, for every $0<y<c$, $\underline{k}(y) \leqq \sup_{t\geqq 0} k_t$ – since otherwise, that is, if there exists $0<y'<c$ such that $\sup_{t\geqq 0} k_t < \underline{k}(y')$, then by virtue of the definition of $\underline{k}(y')$

$$0< \inf_{k\in H(y'),\, k\leqq \sup_{t\geqq 0} k_t} h(y',k),$$

again contradicting Equation (16).

Case 2. $\lim_{\tau\to\infty} n[t^+(c,\tau)]<\infty$, that is, there exists $\tau'>0$ such that

$$t^+(c,\tau) = t^+(c,\tau') \quad \text{for} \quad \tau \geqq \tau'.$$

By the supposition of this case, we know that

$$\sum_{t\in t^+(c,\tau)} (k_{t+1}-k_t) \leqq \sum_{t\in t^+(c,\tau')} (k_{t+1}-k_t) = K<\infty \quad \text{for} \quad \tau \geqq 0.$$

Hence, we also know that

$$0 \leqq k_{\tau+1} = k_0 + \sum_{t=0}^{\tau}(k_{t+1} - k_t) = k_0 + \sum_{t\in t^+(c,\tau)}(k_{t+1} - k_t) + \sum_{t\in t^-(c,\tau)}(k_{t+1} - k_t)$$
$$\leqq k_0 + K + \sum_{t\in t^-(c,\tau)}(k_{t+1} - k_t)$$

or that (since $t \in t^-(c,\tau)$ implies $c + k_{t+1} - k_t < c$ implies $-(k_{t+1} - k_t) > 0$

$$0 \leqq -\sum_{t\in t^-(c,\tau)}(k_{t+1} - k_t) \leqq k_0 + K \quad \text{for} \quad \tau \geqq 0.$$

It then follows that

$$0 \leqq -n[t^-(y,\tau)](y-c) \leqq -\sum_{t\in t^-(y,\tau)}(k_{t+1} - k_t) \leqq -\sum_{t\in t^-(c,\tau)}(k_{t+1} - k_t) \leqq k_0 + K$$

or that

$$0 \leqq n[t^-(y,\tau)] \leqq (k_0 + K)/-(y-c) \quad \text{for} \quad y<c, \tau \geqq 0.$$

Thus, in this case, the resource bound in Equation (10) yields the following chain of inequalities:

$$\begin{aligned}
\tilde{r} &\geqq \sum_{t=0}^{\infty} h(c + k_{t+1} - k_t, k_t) \\
&\geqq \sum_{t=0}^{\tau} h(c + k_{t+1} - k_t, k_t) \quad \text{for} \quad \tau \geqq 0 \\
&\geqq \sum_{t\in t^+(y,\tau)} h(c + k_{t+1} - k_t, k_t) \quad \text{for} \quad 0<y<c \\
&\geqq \sum_{t\in t^+(y,\tau)} h(y, k_t) \quad \text{(using H2 and h1)} \\
&\geqq \sum_{t\in t^+(y,\tau)} \inf_{k\in H(y),\, k \leqq \sup_{t\geqq 0} k_t} h(y,k) \\
&= n[t^+(y,\tau)] \inf_{k\in H(y),\, k \leqq \sup_{t\geqq 0} k_t} h(y,k) \\
&= [(\tau+1) - n[t^-(y,\tau)]] \inf_{k\in H(y),\, k \leqq \sup_{t\geqq 0} k_t} h(y,k) \\
&\geqq [(\tau+1) - (k_0 + K)/-(y-c)] \inf_{k\in H(y),\, k \leqq \sup_{t\geqq 0} k_t} h(y,k).
\end{aligned}$$

As before, the final inequality entails the desired conclusion. ■

In order to complete the proof of necessity, now suppose that $\underline{k} > 0$ and that, given arbitrary $\tilde{r} > 0$ and $0 < \tilde{k} < \underline{k}$, $(c, \{k_t\})$ is a solution to

Equation (10). Utilizing the Lemma, we will show that the existence of such a feasible growth path yields the inequality

$$\text{for every } 0<y<c, \quad 0<1/y\int_{\tilde{k}}^{\underline{k}(y)} h(y,u)du \leqq \tilde{r}/v \tag{17}$$

(recalling the introduction of the constant $v>0$ in h3). But, as in the interpretive necessity argument presented earlier, Equation (17) is simply one equivalent restatement of substitution condition (SC) in "$\varepsilon - \delta$" form.

So, given arbitrary $0<y<c$, consider the two possible cases.

Case 1. $k_t \geqq \underline{k}(y)$ for some $t>0$, that is, there exists $t_y>0$ such that

$$k_t \begin{Bmatrix} < \\ \geqq \end{Bmatrix} \underline{k}(y) \text{ according to } t \begin{Bmatrix} < \\ = \end{Bmatrix} t_y \tag{18}$$

and

Case 2. $k_t < \underline{k}(y)$ for every $t \geqq 0$, that is, by virtue of the second property asserted in the Lemma,

$$k_t < \underline{k}(y) \text{ for } t \geqq 0 \text{ but } \sup_{t \geqq 0} k_t = \underline{k}(y). \tag{19}$$

Bear in mind that in both cases y is fixed for the purposes of this analysis, and that, by virtue of the first property asserted in the Lemma, in both cases the triggering hypothesis of both h2 and h3 is satisfied.

Focus first on the possibility described by Equation (18), and let

$$t^+(t_y) = \{t : 0 \leqq t < t_y \text{ and } k_{t+1} - k_t \geqq 0\}$$

(noticing that, by the nature of this case, $t_y - 1 \in t^+(t_y)$) and

$$\tilde{h}(y,k) = \begin{Bmatrix} h(y,\tilde{k}) & \text{for} & 0 \leqq k \leqq \tilde{k} \\ h(y,k) & \text{for} & k \geqq \tilde{k} \end{Bmatrix}$$

(noticing that, again by the nature of this case, there must exist $0 \leqq t' < t_y$ such that $k_{t'} \leqq \tilde{k}$, $k_{t'+1} - k_{t'} \geqq 0$ and, since we have $0<y<c$, $(y+k_{t'+1}-k_{t'}, k_{t'}) \in H$ (using H2), which implies that $(y, \tilde{k}) \in H$ (using H2), which implies that h is well defined and decreasing in k on $(0, \underline{k}(y))$ (using H2 and h2). Then, in this case the resource bound in Equation (10) yields the following

chain of inequalities:

$$
\begin{aligned}
\tilde{r} &\geqq \sum_{t=0}^{\infty} h(c + k_{t+1} - k_t, k_t) \\
&\geqq \sum_{t \in t^+(t_y)} h(c + k_{t+1} - k_t, k_t) \\
&\geqq \sum_{t \in t^+(t_y)} h(y + k_{t+1} - k_t, k_t) \quad \text{(using H2 and h1)} \\
&\geqq \sum_{t \in t^+(t_y)} \frac{h(y + k_{t+1} - k_t, k_t)}{(y + k_{t+1} - k_t)} (k_{t+1} - k_t) \\
&\geqq \sum_{t \in t^+(t_y)} v \frac{h(y, k_t)}{(y)} (k_{t+1} - k_t) \quad \text{(using h3)} \\
&\geqq v/y \sum_{t \in t^+(t_y)} \tilde{h}(y, k_t)(k_{t+1} - k_t) \quad \text{(using h2)} \\
&\geqq v/y \sum_{t=0}^{t_y - 1} \tilde{h}(y, k_t)(k_{t+1} - k_t) \\
&\qquad\qquad [\text{since } 0 \leqq t < t_y \text{ but } t \notin t^+(t_y) \Rightarrow k_{t+1} - k_t < 0] \\
&\geqq v/y \left[\sum_{t=0}^{t_y - 2} \tilde{h}(y, k_t)(k_{t+1} - k_t) + \tilde{h}(y, k_{t_y - 1})(\underline{k}(y) - k_{t_y - 1}) \right] \\
&\qquad\qquad [\text{since } k_{t_y - 1} < \underline{k}(y) \leqq k_{t_y}] \\
&\geqq v/y \int_{\min\limits_{0 \leqq t < t_y} k_t}^{\underline{k}(y)} \left[\text{since } 0 \leqq k', k'' < \underline{k}(y) \Rightarrow \tilde{h}(y, k')(k'' - k') \geqq \int_{k'}^{k''} \tilde{h}(y, u) du \right] \\
&\geqq v/y \int_{\tilde{k}}^{\underline{k}(y)} h(y, u) du \quad \left[\text{since } \min_{0 \leqq t < t_y} k_t \leqq \tilde{k} \right] \\
&> 0.
\end{aligned}
$$

These in turn immediately yield the desired conclusion in Equation (17).

For the possibility described by Equation (19), the argument is essentially the same, but formulated in terms of the subsets of periods

$$t^+(\tau) = \{t : 0 \leqq t < \tau \text{ and } k_{t+1} - k_t \geqq 0\} \quad \text{for} \quad \tau \geqq 0,$$

and completed by going from the chain of inequalities

$$\tilde{r} \geqq \sum_{t=0}^{\infty} h(c + k_{t+1} - k_t, k_t) \geqq \cdots \geqq v/y \int_{\tilde{k}}^{\max\limits_{0 \leqq t \leqq \tau} k_t} \tilde{h}(y, u) du \quad \text{for} \quad \tau \geqq 0$$

to the desired conclusion in Equation (17) by means of Equation (19)

$$\tilde{r} \geqq v/y \int_{\tilde{k}}^{\sup_{t \geqq 0} k_t} \tilde{h}(y, u)\mathrm{d}u = v/y \int_{\tilde{k}}^{\underline{k}(y)} h(y, u)\mathrm{d}u > 0. \quad \blacksquare$$

Remarks. The essential idea in the preceding proof is to go from the resource bound in Equation (10) (or, more accurately, Equation (3)) to the integral limit in substitution condition (SC). The crucial steps in this logical progression involve replacing "$h(c + k_{t+1} - k_t, k_t)$" by "$h(y, k_t)(k_{t+1} - k_t)/y$" and "$\sum$" by "$\int$", utilizing, respectively, h3 and h2. Shortly we will demonstrate that this particular procedure is not accidental, that these pivotal assumptions are in fact fundamental to the result. Less apparent is the role of h1. However, it too provides indispensable support, as we shall also soon demonstrate. Finally, while H1 plays no part whatsoever in the necessity deduction, quite obviously it was essential in the sufficiency construction, since without it, so as to speak, the economy may never leave – or, for that matter, even reach – the starting gate. For this reason alone, we have little more to say about this assumption – just as, for an equally compelling reason (namely, that it is basically unimpeachable), we will also have little more to say about H2.

4. Two Possible Generalizations

Our purpose in this final section is to outline two of the more interesting generalizations of our analysis. These involve first, the potential for increasing and unbounded consumption, and second, the presence of many different commodities. Our treatment is only intended to be suggestive, not exhaustive.

4.1. Increasing and Unbounded Consumption

The essential idea here is to tie consumption to the level of the capital stock, and then to characterize the growth paths exhibiting increasing and unbounded growth. For simplicity we again focus on the intermediate case in which $\bar{y} > 0$ as well as $\underline{k} = \infty$.

So now think of $c_t = \text{constant} \cdot \phi(k_t)$, where $\phi : \mathbb{R}_+ \to \mathbb{R}$ is strictly increasing and satisfies, say, $\phi(0) = 1$ and also $\phi(\infty) = \infty$. Then, in effect strengthening H1 and h2 to encompass ϕ as well as h, suppose that

for every $k > 0$ there is a positive constant $c > 0$ such that

$$(c'\phi(k'), k') \in H \quad \text{for} \quad k' \geqq k, \quad 0 < c' \leqq c \tag{20}$$

and

$$h(c'\phi(k'),k')/c'\phi(k') \text{ is decreasing in } k' \text{ for } k' \geqq k, \quad 0 < c' \leqq c. \tag{21}$$

Finally, consider feasible growth paths of the specific form

$$\begin{cases} k_{t+1} - k_t \geqq 0 \quad \text{and} \quad (c\phi(k_t) + k_{t+1} - k_t, k_t) \in H \quad \text{for} \quad t \geqq 0, \\ \lim_{t\to\infty} k_t = \infty \\ \text{and} \\ c > 0, \sum_{t=0}^{\infty} h(c\phi(k_t) + k_{t+1} - k_t, k_t) \leqq \tilde{r} \quad \text{and} \quad k_0 \leqq \tilde{k}. \end{cases} \tag{22}$$

The analogue of our Sustainability Theorem obviously also requires a stronger SC, namely, for every $k > 0$,

$$\lim_{y\to 0^+} \int_k^{\infty} \frac{h(y\phi(u),u)}{y\phi(u)} \mathrm{d}u = 0. \tag{SC^s}$$

In these terms the following result is easily demonstrated.

"Growth" Theorem. *For every* $(\tilde{r}, \tilde{k}) \gg 0$ *there exists* $(c, \{k_t\})$ *satisfying Equation* (22) *if and only if Equation* (SC^s) *obtains.*

Proof of "Growth" Theorem. *Sufficiency*. Pick $y > 0$ such that $0 < y\phi(\tilde{k}) < \tilde{k}$, $(y\phi(k), k) \in H$ for $k \geqq \tilde{k}/2$ (using Equation (20)) and

$$\int_{\tilde{k}/2}^{\infty} \frac{h(y\phi(u),u)}{y\phi(u)} \mathrm{d}u \leqq \tilde{r}/2 \tag{23}$$

(using Equations (20) and (SC^s)), and consider the particular growth path defined by

$$\begin{cases} k_0 = \tilde{k} \\ \text{and} \\ k_{t+1} = k_t + y\phi(k_t)/2 \quad \text{and} \quad c_t = y\phi(k_t)/2 \quad \text{for} \quad t \geqq 0. \end{cases} \tag{24}$$

Then

$$\begin{aligned}\sum_{t=0}^{\infty} h(c_t + k_{t+1} - k_t, k_t) &= \sum_{t=0}^{\infty} h(y\phi(k_t), k_t) \\ &= \sum_{t=0}^{\infty} \frac{h(y\phi(k_t), k_t)}{y\phi(k_t)/2}(y\phi(k_t)/2) \\ &\leqq 2\int_{\tilde{k}-y\phi(\tilde{k})/2}^{\infty} \frac{h(y\phi(u), u)}{y\phi(u)}\mathrm{d}u \quad \text{(using Equation (21))} \\ &\leqq 2\int_{\tilde{k}/2}^{\infty} \frac{h(y\phi(u), u)}{y\phi(u)}\mathrm{d}u \\ &\leqq \tilde{r} \quad \text{[using Equation (23)]}\end{aligned}$$

Thus, Equation (24) yields a solution to Equation (22) with $c = y/2$.

Necessity. Suppose that Equation (22) has a solution for arbitrary $(\tilde{r}, \tilde{k}) \gg 0$. It is straightforward to show that this implies that

$$\text{for every } 0<y<c, \quad \int_{\tilde{k}}^{\infty} \frac{h(y\phi(u), u)}{y\phi(u)}\mathrm{d}u \leqq \tilde{r}/v$$

$$\begin{aligned}\tilde{r} &\geqq \sum_{t=0}^{\infty} h(c\phi(k_t) + k_{t+1} - k_t, k_t) \\ &\geqq \sum_{t=0}^{\infty} h(y\phi(k_t) + k_{t+1} - k_t, k_t) \quad \text{for} \quad 0<y<c \quad \text{(using H2 and h1)} \\ &\geqq \sum_{t=0}^{\infty} \frac{h(y\phi(k_t) + k_{t+1} - k_t, k_t)}{y\phi(k_t) + k_{t+1} - k_t}(k_{t+1} - k_t) \\ &\geqq v\sum_{t=0}^{\infty} \frac{h(y\phi(k_t), k_t)}{y\phi(k_t)}(k_{t+1} - k_t) \quad \text{(using h3)} \\ &\geqq v\sum_{\tilde{k}}^{\infty} \frac{h(y\phi(u), u)}{y\phi(u)}\mathrm{d}u. \quad \text{(using Equation (21))}\end{aligned}$$

■

It is worth noting – concerning the requirement that the capital stock be increasing and unbounded – that when, say, ϕ is uniformly Lipschitzian (i.e., there is a positive constant $\lambda>0$ such that $|\phi(k') - \phi(k'')| < \lambda|k' - k''|$ for k', $k'' \geqq 0$ and $k' \neq k''$), Equation (22) has a solution if and only if

$$\begin{cases} (c\phi(k_t) + k_{t+1} - k_t, k_t) \in H \quad \text{for} \quad t \geqq 0 \\ \text{and} \\ c>0, \sum_{t=0}^{\infty} h(c\phi(k_t) + k_{t+1} - k_t, k_t) \leqq \tilde{r} \quad \text{and} \quad k_0 \leqq \tilde{k} \end{cases}$$

have a solution. In other words, when natural resources are actually indispensable (in the sense that $\underline{k} = \infty$), unlimited growth is equally indispensable. This result (whose proof we will not detail) also means that the preceding argument provides a simpler demonstration of our Sustainability Theorem for this intermediate case (by simply taking $\phi(k) = 1$ for $k \geqq 0$).

4.2. Many Types of Commodities

For this kind of generalization, the crucial problem is to guarantee that the "natural" aggregation procedure provides suitable approximation. Without any pretense of presenting the most delicate analysis possible, we consider the following basic set-up.

There are $\ell \geqq 1$ types of consumption goods with flows denoted $C = (c^1, c^2, \ldots, c^\ell) \in \mathbb{R}^\ell_+, m \geqq 1$ types of exhaustible resources with (input) flows denoted $D = (d^1, d^2, \ldots, d^m) \in \mathbb{R}^m_+$ and stocks denoted $R = (r^1, r^2, \ldots, r^m) \in \mathbb{R}^m_+$ and $n \geqq 1$ types of capital goods with (net output) flows denoted $Z = (z^1, z^2, \ldots, z^n) \in \mathbb{R}^n$ and (input) stocks denoted $K = (k^1, k^2, \ldots, k^n) \in \mathbb{R}^n_+$. The (final) output of economic welfare is measured by a *consumption index* $c = \psi(C)$, where $\psi : \mathbb{R}^\ell_+ \to \mathbb{R}_+$ is a nondecreasing function initialized so that $\psi(0) = 0$, while the possibilities for converting inputs into (final) outputs are summarized by a technology set

$$T \subset \{(c, Z, D, K) \in \mathbb{R}_+ \times \mathbb{R}^n \times \mathbb{R}^m_+ \times \mathbb{R}^n_+ : Z + K \geqq 0\}.$$

Finally, given initial stocks of exhaustible resources $\tilde{R} \gg 0$ and capital goods $\tilde{K} > 0$, in such a setting feasible growth paths are described by

$$\begin{cases} (c_t, K_{t+1} - K_t, D_t, K_t) \in T \quad \text{for} \quad t \geqq 0 \\ \text{and} \\ \sum\limits_{t=0}^{\infty} D_t \leqq \tilde{R} \quad \text{and} \quad K_0 \leqq K. \end{cases} \tag{25}$$

To relate this model to the aggregative model, we simply identify d with $D \cdot \mathbf{1}$, z with $Z \cdot \mathbf{1}$ and k with $K \cdot \mathbf{1}$, where "$\mathbf{1}$" always denotes a conformable vector of ones, and then define

$$\begin{aligned} H = \{&(y, k) \in \mathbb{R} \times \mathbb{R}_+ : \text{there exists } (c, Z, D, K) \in T \\ &\text{such that } c + Z \cdot \mathbf{1} \geqq y \text{ and } K \cdot \mathbf{1} = k\} \end{aligned}$$

and

$$h(y,k) = \text{infimum } D \cdot \mathbf{1} \quad \text{on} \quad \{D \in \mathbb{R}^m_+ : (c, Z, D, K) \in T, c + Z \cdot \mathbf{1} \geqq y \text{ and } K \cdot \mathbf{1} = k\}$$
$$\text{for } (y,k) \in H.$$

One set of assumptions about T that both entail our previously maintained assumptions and enable us to adapt our previous analysis – and which are surely much stronger than necessary for either purpose – are as follows:

T0. (Inactivity) $0 \in T$;

T1. (Productivity) (a) If $K > 0$, then there exists $(c, Z, D) \in \mathbb{R}_+ \times \mathbb{R}^n \times \mathbb{R}^m_+$ such that $(c, Z, D, K) \in T, (c + Z \cdot \mathbf{1}) \gg 0$ and $K{+}Z > 0$; (b) If $(c, Z, D, K) \in T, (c + Z \cdot \mathbf{1}) \gg 0$ and $K{+}Z > 0$, then there exists $(c', Z', D') \in \mathbb{R}_+ \times \mathbb{R}^n \times \mathbb{R}^m_+$ such that $(c', D', Z', K + Z) \in T$, $(c', Z' \cdot \mathbf{1}) \geqq (c, Z \cdot \mathbf{1})$ and $K{+}Z{+}Z' > 0$;

T2. (Disposability) There is a partition of capital goods, say, $K = (K^1, K^2) = ((k^1, k^2, \ldots, k^{n'}), (k^{n'+1}, k^{n'+2}, \ldots, k^n))$, such that if $(c, Z, D, K) \in T, 0 \leqq c' \leqq c, Z' \leqq Z, K^{1'} \geqq K^1$ and $(K^{1'}, K^2) + Z' \geqq 0$ (resp., $K^{2'} \geqq K^2$ and $(K^1, K^{2'}) + Z' \geqq 0$), then $(c', Z', D, (K^{1'}, K^2)) \in T$) (resp., there exists $D' \geqq D$ such that $(c', D', Z', (K^1, K^{2'})) \in T$);

T3. (Substitutability) There are constants $0 < M < \infty$ and $1 \leqq N < \infty$ such that for every $K > 0$ and associated

$$(c, z, k) \in \{(c, z, k) \in \mathbb{R}_+ \times \mathbb{R} \times \mathbb{R}_+ : \text{there exists } (c', D', Z') \in \mathbb{R}_+ \times \mathbb{R}^h \times \mathbb{R}^m_+$$
$$\text{such that } (c', Z', D', K) \in T,\ c' \geqq c,\ Z' \cdot \mathbf{1} \geqq z,\ K + Z' > 0 \text{ and } K \cdot \mathbf{1} = k\},$$
$$Mh(c + z, k/N) \geqq \text{infimum } D' \cdot \mathbf{1} \quad \text{on} \quad \{D' \in \mathbb{R}^m_+ : (c', Z', D', K) \in T, c' \geqq c,$$
$$Z' \cdot \mathbf{1} \geqq z \quad \text{and} \quad K + Z' > 0\};$$

and

T4. (Convexity) T is convex.

Some brief remarks about this formulation:

1. As we have already stressed, when $n > 1$, the notion of capital goods is very broad. Thus, for example, these could in principle include such diverse commodities as exhaustible resources themselves (double-counted so as to permit indirect as well as direct stock–flow interaction) or cumulated technical knowledge.
2. The consumption index ψ is fairly arbitrary; it could very well, for example, incorporate subsistence level consumption requirements.

More generally, there is great leeway in the choice of units for measuring the variety of commodities this model encompasses, though obviously the specification of T may be rendered more or less plausible depending on such choice. Thus, in particular, aggregation employing constant weights that are identically same is not really, in itself, especially restrictive.

3. There is no loss of generality in assuming that $\tilde{R} \gg 0$; an exhaustible resource is only relevant if it is actually available at some point.
4. In order to allow the possibility that all capital goods – unlike consumption or investment goods – are not freely disposable, we require the equality constraint $K \cdot \mathbf{1} = k$ (rather than the inequality $K \cdot \mathbf{1} \geqq k$) in relating aggregates to disaggregates, for instance, in defining H and h, or in using h to provide an upper bound on minimal exhaustible resource requirements, as in T3.
5. Two simple observations clearly underscore the fact that T0–T4 provide overkill, namely, that T2 implies a strong form of h2,

h2^s. For every y, h is decreasing in k on $H(y)$,
while T0, T2, and T4 imply an extremely strong form of h3.

h3^s. For every k, $h(0, k) = 0$ and h is convex in y on $H(k)$.
We leave as an exercise for the reader to verify these results, as well as the two remaining requisites, that T1a implies H1, while T2 also implies H2 and h1.

Now, once again, consider feasible growth paths of the specific form

$$\begin{cases} (c, K_{t+1} - K_t, D_t, K_t) \in T \quad \text{for} \quad t \geqq 0 \\ \text{and} \\ c > 0, \sum_{t=0}^{\infty} D_t \leqq \tilde{R} \quad \text{and} \quad K_0 \leqq \tilde{K}. \end{cases} \tag{26}$$

Generalized Sustainability Theorem. *Suppose T satisfies* T0–T4. *Then, for every $\tilde{R} \gg 0$ and $\tilde{K} > 0$ there exists* $(c, \{(D_t, K_t)\})$ *satisfying Equation* (26) *if and only if substitution condition* (SC) *obtains.*

Proof of the Generalized Sustainability Theorem. Note that, by virtue of h2^s, $h(y, k) = 0$ for $k > \underline{k}(y)$, so that substitution condition (SC) becomes simply, for every $k > 0$,

$$\lim_{y \to 0^+} 1/y \int_k^{\infty} h(y, u) \mathrm{d}u = 0 \tag{27}$$

Sufficiency. Let $\tilde{r} = \min \tilde{R}^i$ and $\tilde{k} = \tilde{K} \cdot \mathbf{1}/N$. Then pick $\{\alpha_t\}$ such that $\alpha_t > 0$ and $\sum_{t=0}^{\infty} \alpha_t \leqq \tilde{r}/2$, and $y' > 0$ such that, for every $0 < y < y', (y, \tilde{k} - y/2N) \in H$ and

$$1/y \int_{\tilde{k}-y/2N}^{\infty} h(y,u)\mathrm{d}u \leqq \tilde{r}(N/4M) \tag{28}$$

(using H1, H2, and (27)). Consider, first, $\{k_t\}$ such that

$$k_t = \tilde{k} + y/2N \quad \text{for} \quad t \geqq 0.$$

It follows from Equation (28) that for every $0 < y < y'$

$$\begin{aligned}\sum_{t=0}^{\infty} h(y,k_t) &= (2N/y)\sum_{t=0}^{\infty} h(y, \tilde{k} + (y/2N)t)(y/2N)\\ &\leqq (2N/y)\int_{\tilde{k}-y/2N}^{\infty} h(y,u)\mathrm{d}u \quad \text{(using h2}^{\mathrm{s}}\text{)}\\ &\leqq \tilde{r}/2M.\end{aligned} \tag{29}$$

Now define

$$\mathrm{d}(c,z,K) = \text{infimum } D' \cdot \mathbf{1} \quad \text{on} \quad \{D' \in \mathbb{R}_+^m : (c', Z', D', K) \in T, c' \geqq c, Z' \cdot \mathbf{1} \geqq z \text{ and } K + Z' > 0\}$$

for $(c,z,K) \in \mathbb{R}_+ \times \mathbb{R} \times \mathbb{R}_+^n$, and consider, second, $\{(c_t, Z_t, D_t, K_t)\}$ such that for some $0 < y < y'$

$$\text{for} \quad t = 0, \quad K_0 = \tilde{K}, \quad (c_0, Z_0, D_0, K_0) \in T, \quad c_0 = Z_0 \cdot \mathbf{1} = y/2, \\ K_0 + Z_0 > 0 \text{ and } D_0 \cdot \mathbf{1} - \alpha_0 \leqq d(y/2, y/2, K) \quad \text{(using T1a and T2)} \tag{30}$$

and

$$\text{for} \quad t > 0, \quad K_t = K_{t-1} + Z_{t-1}, \quad (c_t, Z_t, D_t, K_t) \in T, \\ c_t = Z_t \cdot \mathbf{1} = y/2, \quad K_t + Z_t > 0 \\ \text{and} \quad D_t \cdot \mathbf{1} - \alpha_t \leqq d(y/2, y/2, K_t) \quad \text{[using T1b and T2].} \tag{31}$$

Since $\{k_t\}$ and $\{K_t\}$ have been specified such that $k_t = K_t \cdot \mathbf{1}/N$ for $t \geqq 0$, it follows from Equations (30) and (31) that, for $i = 1,2, \ldots, m$,

$$\begin{aligned}\sum_{t=0}^{\infty} D_t^i &\leqq \sum_{t=0}^{\infty} D_t \cdot \mathbf{1} \\ &\leqq \sum_{t=0}^{\infty} [\mathrm{d}(y/2, y/2, K_t) + \alpha_t] \\ &\leqq \sum_{t=0}^{\infty} [Mh(y, k_t) + \alpha_t] \quad \text{(using T3)} \\ &\leqq \tilde{r} \quad \text{(using (29))} \\ &\leqq \tilde{R}^i.\end{aligned}$$

Thus, Equations (30) and (31) yield a solution to Equation (26) with $c = y/2$.

Necessity. This follows directly upon noticing that every solution to Equation (26) yields a solution to Equation (10) with the same c, and $k_t = K_t \cdot \mathbf{1}$ for $t \geqq 0$ as well as $(\tilde{r}, \tilde{k}) = (\tilde{R} \cdot \mathbf{1}, \tilde{K} \cdot \mathbf{1})$. And since, given our maintained assumptions, the original proof of necessity only depended on the existence of a solution to Equation (10) for arbitrary $(\tilde{r}, \tilde{k}) \gg 0$, it obviously applies here too, and we are finished. ■

Acknowledgments

This is a revised version of CARESS Working Paper #79–27. An even earlier preliminary paper by Mitra (1978) contained the seminal idea developed more thoroughly here. Both of our research efforts were supported by the NSF, while much of Cass's participation took place during his tenure as a Sherman Fairchild Distinguished Scholar at Caltech. We thank both institutions for their support and encouragement.

Appendix

We have clearly demonstrated that sufficiency of the substitution condition (SC) basically rests on just H1 and H2. In contrast, we have merely asserted that necessity critically depends on h1, h2, and h3 (as well as H2). The purpose of this appendix is to substantiate this latter claim. We will demonstrate by example that, without any one of these three assumptions, Equation (3) may be satisfied even when condition (SC) is not. Along the way we will also establish that h2 can be replaced by a weaker regularity requirement when time is modeled as being continuous rather than discrete, and that h3 can be replaced by a weaker curvature condition provided that (SC) itself is reformulated in terms of "lim inf" rather than "lim".

A.1. Counterexample to Dropping Assumption h1

Suppose that

$$h(y,k) = \begin{cases} g(k) - y & \text{for } y \leqq g(k) \\ a & \text{otherwise} \end{cases} \tag{A.1}$$

with $H = \mathbb{R} \times \mathbb{R}_+$, where $g: \mathbb{R}_+ \to \mathbb{R}_+$ is decreasing and satisfies $g(0) > g(\infty) = \lim_{k\to\infty} g(k) > 0$, and $a > 0$. Such a resource requirement function effectively embodies the antithesis of h1, since, up to some limit (determined solely by the capital stock), more output always requires less depletion. The salient features of condition (A.1) are depicted in Figure A1. For an economy enjoying this peculiar static technology, it is fairly obvious that Equation (3) is satisfied, since, for instance, given arbitrary $(\tilde{r}, \tilde{k}) \gg 0$, the

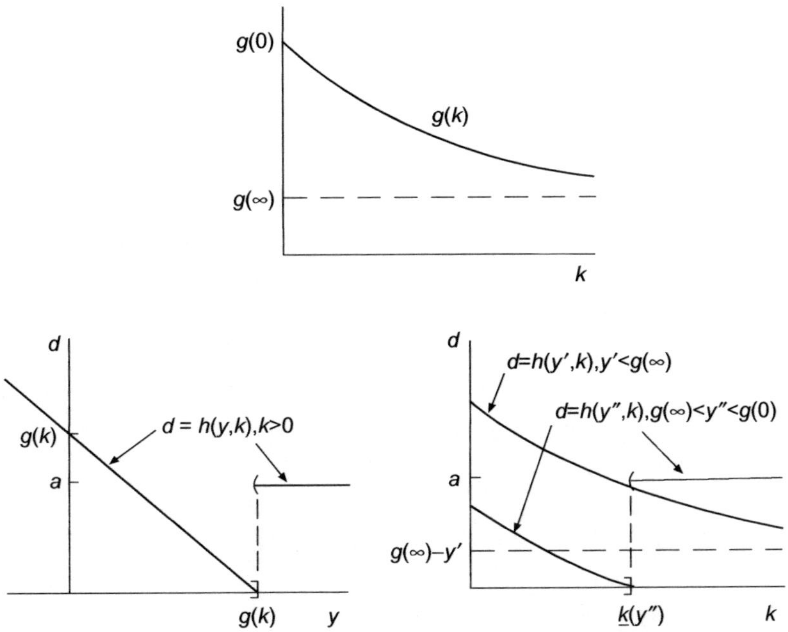

$h(y,k) = \begin{cases} g(k)-y & \text{for } y \leq g(k) \text{ with } H=\mathbb{R}\times\mathbb{R}_+, \text{ where } g: \mathbb{R}_+ \to \mathbb{R} \\ a & \text{otherwise} \end{cases}$

is decreasing and satisfies $g(0) > g(\infty) > 0$, and $a > 0$

Figure A1: Critical Features of the Example Showing that without Assumption h1, Condition (SC) is Not Necessary.

growth path described by

$$c_t = g(\infty) \quad \text{for} \quad t \geqq 0$$

and

$$k_0 = \tilde{k} \quad \text{and} \quad k_{t+1} = k_t + [g(k_t) - g(\infty)] \quad \text{for} \quad t \geqq 0$$

is a solution to Equation (10). Equally obvious is the fact that condition (SC) is not satisfied, since $\underline{k}(y) = \underline{k} = \infty$ for $0 < y \leqq g(\infty)]$ but, for every $0 < k < \underline{k}$,

$$\begin{aligned}\lim_{y\to 0^+} 1/y \int_k^{\underline{k}(y)} [g(u) - y]\,\mathrm{d}u &= \left[1/y \int_k^{\infty} [g(u) - y]\,\mathrm{d}u\right]_{0<y<g(\infty)} \\ &= \left[1/y \int_k^{\infty} [g(\infty) - y]\,\mathrm{d}u\right]_{0<y<g(\infty)} \\ &= \infty.\end{aligned}$$

Two further points about this particular example are worth making explicitly. (i) The argument is very direct. Though much more complicated in detail, the basic logic for each of the succeeding examples in this appendix is absolutely identical: First, describe a particular resource requirement function. Second, exhibit a solution to Equation (10) (given arbitrary $(\tilde{r}, \tilde{k}) \gg 0$). Third, and finally, verify violation of condition (SC). (ii) Equation (A.1) fails to satisfy h3 as well as h1. This follows immediately from the observation that

$$\frac{h(y,k)}{y} = \frac{g(k)}{y} - 1 \begin{Bmatrix} > \\ = \end{Bmatrix} 0 \text{ according as } y \begin{Bmatrix} < \\ = \end{Bmatrix} g(k),$$

so that, though $\bar{y} = g(0)$, for every $v > 0$ and every $k \geqq 0$, if $y' = g(k)$ and $0 < y'' < y'$, then

$$0 = \frac{g(k)}{y'} - 1 = \frac{h(y',k)}{y'} < v\frac{h(y'',k)}{y''} = v\left[\frac{g(k)}{y''} - 1\right].$$

Thus, one could legitimately puzzle over the appropriate interpretation of the example. However, because Equation (A.1) does satisfy the still weaker version of diminishing returns presented below, it seems quite properly viewed as basically a counterexample to dropping h1 rather than to dropping h3.

A.2. Counterexamples to Dropping Assumption h2

These two examples exhibit quite distinct kinds of nonmonotonicity. Though either one by itself would suffice for our present purpose, we include both in order to emphasize the wide variety of situations that can be covered in continuous, but not discrete time. (Refer to the analysis in the following Section A.3.) Our elaboration of each example is intentionally abbreviated, since, as noted above, it is logically straightforward. In particular, among other more minor details, we leave to the readers' explicit verification that, in both examples, h1 and h3 are satisfied.

Example A2a. Suppose that

$$h(y,k) = f(y)g(k) \tag{A.2}$$

with $H = \mathbb{R} \times \mathbb{R}_+$, where $f : \mathbb{R} \to \mathbb{R}_+$ is increasing and convex, and satisfies $f(y)\begin{Bmatrix} > \\ = \end{Bmatrix}0$ according to $y\begin{Bmatrix} > \\ = \end{Bmatrix}0$ and $\lim_{y\to 0^+} f(y)/y = 0$, while if (i) $g_1 : [0,1] \to \mathbb{R}_+$ is continuous and satisfies $g_1(x)\begin{Bmatrix} > \\ = \end{Bmatrix}0$ according to $x(1-x)\begin{Bmatrix} > \\ = \end{Bmatrix}0$, and (ii) $g_2 : \mathbb{R}_+ \to \mathbb{R}_+$ is decreasing and satisfies $0 < \int_0^\infty g_2(u)\, du < \infty$, then

$$g(k) = \begin{cases} g_1(k-n) + g_2(k) & \text{for} \quad n \leqq k \leqq n+1,\ n = 0, 2, 4, \ldots \\ g_2(k) & \text{otherwise.} \end{cases}$$

In a manner of speaking, the isoquants suffer chronic (as well as uniform) "bumpiness," as exhibited in Figure A2.

To see that Equation (10) has a solution, let

$$y_{nm} = (n - \tilde{k})/m \quad \text{for} \quad n \geqq \tilde{k} \text{ and } m \geqq 2(n - \tilde{k})$$

both integral, and consider the growth paths described by

$$c_t = y_{nm} \quad \text{for} \quad t \geqq 0$$

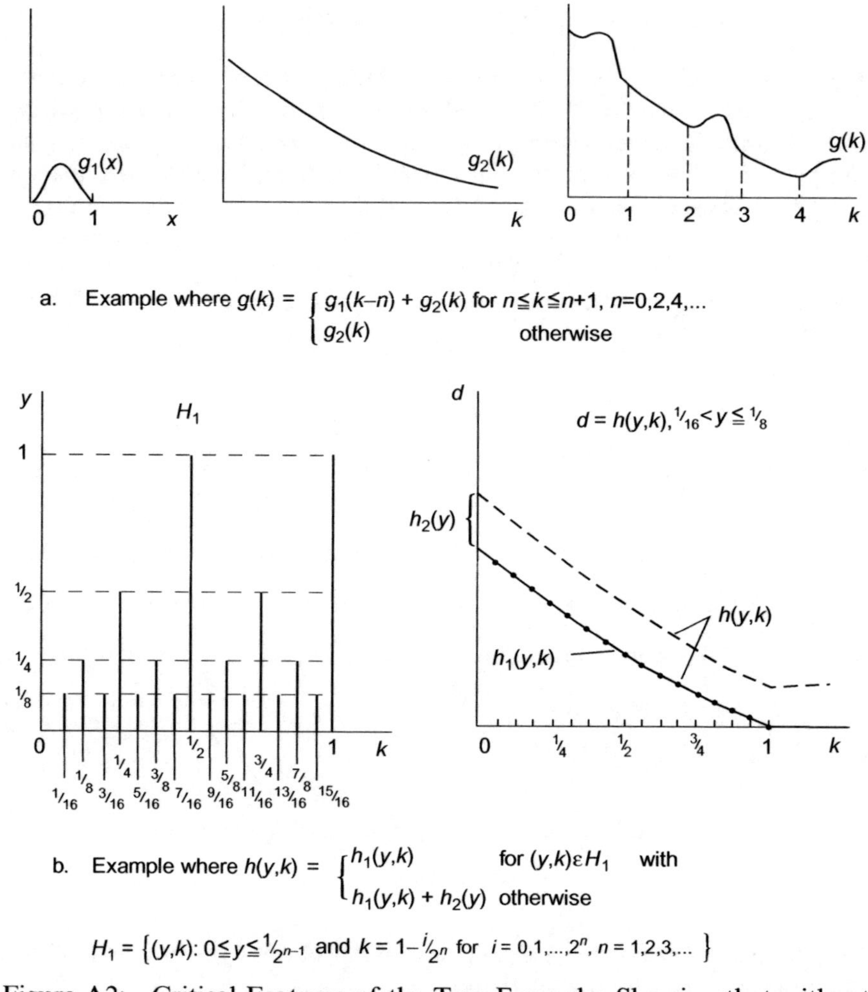

Figure A2: Critical Features of the Two Examples Showing that without Assumption h2, Condition (SC) is Not Necessary.

and

$$k_0 = \tilde{k} \text{ and } k_{t+1} = \begin{cases} k_t + y_{nm} & \text{for} \quad 0 \leqq t \leqq m-1 \\ k_t + 1 & \text{otherwise.} \end{cases}$$

Then all that needs checking is that, for some n and m, the resource bound will be satisfied. Direct calculation yields

$$\begin{aligned}
\sum_{t=0}^{\infty} h(c_t + k_{t+1} - k_t, k_t) &= \sum_{t=0}^{m-1} h(2y_{nm}, \tilde{k} + y_{nm}t) \\
&\quad + \sum_{t=m}^{\infty} h(y_{nm} + 1, \tilde{k} + y_{nm}m + (t - m)) \\
&= (f(2y_{nm})/y_{nm}) \sum_{t=0}^{m-1} g(\tilde{k} + y_{nm}t)y_{nm} \\
&\quad + f(y_{nm} + 1) \sum_{t=m}^{\infty} g_2(n + (t - m)) \\
&\leqq (f(2y_{nm})/y_{nm}) \sum_{t=0}^{m-1} g(\tilde{k} + y_{nm}t)y_{nm} \\
&\quad + f(y_{nm} + 1) \int_{n-1}^{\infty} g_2(u)\, du.
\end{aligned} \tag{A.3}$$

So just pick n large enough so that

$$f(y_{nm} + 1) \int_{n-1}^{\infty} g_2(u)\, \mathrm{d}u \leqq f(2) \int_{n-1}^{\infty} g_2(u)\, \mathrm{d}u \leqq \bar{r}/2. \tag{A.4}$$

and m large enough (with corresponding y_{nm} small enough) so that

$$\begin{cases} \sum_{t=0}^{m-1} g(\tilde{k} + y_{nm}t)y_{nm} \leqq 2 \int_{\tilde{k}}^{n} g(u)\, \mathrm{d}u \\ \text{and} \\ 4(f(2y_{nm})/2y_{nm}) \int_{\tilde{k}}^{n} g(u)\, \mathrm{d}u \leqq \tilde{r}/2, \end{cases} \tag{A.5}$$

and the desired conclusion follows immediately upon using Equations (A.4) and (A.5) to extend the chain of inequalities in Equation (A.3).

Finally, to see formally that (SC) is not satisfied (informally, this is obvious from Figure (A2a), let

$$n(k) = \min \{n : n \text{ is even and } n \geqq k) \quad \text{for} \quad k \geqq 0.$$

Then, because $\underline{k} = \infty$, for every $0 < k < \tilde{k}$,

$$\int_{k}^{\underline{k}(y)} h(y, u)\, \mathrm{d}u = f(y) \left(\sum_{i=0}^{\infty} \int_{n(k)+2i}^{n(k)+2i+1} g_1(u - (n(k) + 2i))\, \mathrm{d}u + \int_{k}^{\infty} g_2(u)\, \mathrm{d}u \right)$$

or

$$\lim_{y\to 0^+} 1/y \int_k^{\underline{k}(y)} h(y,u)\,\mathrm{d}u$$
$$= \left[(f(y)/y)\left(\sum_{i=0}^{\infty} \int_{n(k)+2i}^{n(k)+2i+1} g_1(u-(n(k)+2i))\,\mathrm{d}u + \int_k^{\infty} g_2(u)\,\mathrm{d}u \right) \right]_{y>0} = \infty.$$

Example A2b. Suppose that

$$h(y,\ k) = \begin{cases} h_1(y,\ k) & \text{for} \quad (y,\ k) \in H_1 \\ h_1(y,\ k) + h_2(y) & \text{otherwise} \end{cases} \tag{A.6}$$

with $H = \mathbb{R} \times \mathbb{R}_+$ and

$$H_1 = \{(y,k) : 0 \leqq y \leqq 1/2^{n-1} \quad \text{and} \quad k = 1 - i/2^n \text{ for } i = 0,\ 1, \ldots, 2^n,\ \ n = 1,2,3\ldots\},$$

where $h_1 : [0,1]^2 \to \mathbb{R}_+$ is increasing in y, decreasing in k, and convex in y, and satisfies $\lim_{y\to 0^+} h_1(y,k)/y = 0$ and $h_1(y,k)\left\{\begin{matrix} > \\ = \end{matrix}\right\}0$ according to $k\left\{\begin{matrix} < \\ = \end{matrix}\right\}1$ for $0 < y \leqq 1$, while $h_2 : \mathbb{R} \to \mathbb{R}_+$ is increasing and convex, and satisfies $h_2(0) = 0$ and $\lim_{y\to 0^+} h_2(y)/y > 0$. This example is hard to describe in words, but not in pictures, as Figure A2b attests.

Now let n be a positive integer such that $1/2^n \leqq \tilde{k}$, and consider the growth paths described by

$$c_t = 1/2^n \quad \text{for} \quad t \geqq 0$$

and

$$k_0 = 1/2^n \text{ and } k_{t+1} = \begin{cases} k_t + 1/2^n & \text{for} \quad 0 \leqq t \leqq 2^n - 2 \\ 1 & \text{otherwise.} \end{cases}$$

Then, in this instance direct calculation yields

$$\begin{aligned}\sum_{t=m}^{\infty} h(c_t + k_{t+1} - k_t, k_t) &= \sum_{t=0}^{2^n-2} h(1/2^{n-1}), (t+1)/2^n) \\ &= \sum_{t=0}^{2^n-2} h_1(1/2^{n-1}), (t+1)2^n) \\ &= 1/(1/2^n) \sum_{t=0}^{2^n-2} h_1(1/2^{n-1}, (t+1/2^n)(1/2^n) \\ &\leqq 2/(1/2^{n-1}) \int_0^{1-1/2^n} h_1(1/2^{n-1}, u)\, du \\ &\leqq 2/(1/2^{n-1}) \int_0^1 h_1(1/2^{n-1}, u)\, du \\ &\leqq \tilde{r}\end{aligned}$$

for n large enough.

Finally, observe that, for every $0 < y \leqq 1$, h is integrable in k on [0, 1], and has closed form, for every $0 \leqq k^1 \leqq k^2 \leqq 1$,

$$\int_{k^1}^{k^2} h(y, u)\, du = \int_{k^1}^{k^2} h_2(y)\, du = h_2(y)(k^2 - k^1)$$

(since, if $1/2^n < y \leqq 1/2^{n-1}$, then there are only a finite number of points $k_i = 1 - i/2^n$ for $i = 0, 1, \ldots, 2^n$). Hence, because $\underline{k}(y) = \underline{k} = 1$ for $0 < y \leqq 1$, for every $0 < k < \underline{k}$,

$$\lim_{y\to 0^+} 1/y \int_k^{\underline{k}(y)} h(y, u) = \lim_{y\to 0^+} 1/y \int_k^1 h_2(y)\, du = \left(\lim_{y\to 0^+} h_2(y)/y\right)(1 - k) > 0.$$

A.3. Modeling with Continuous Time: Weakening Assumption h2

For simplicity we again illustrate the main point by focusing on the intermediate case in which $\bar{y} > 0$ as well as $\underline{k} = \infty$. A similar modification of the analysis (but with additional – and purely technical – complication) applies in the general case.

In this setting a feasible growth path is a solution to the dynamical system

$$\begin{cases} c(t) \geqq 0 \text{ and } (c(t) + (\dot{k}(t), k(t)) \in H \text{ for } t \geqq 0 \\ \text{and} \\ \int_0^\infty h(c(s) + \dot{k}(s), k(s))\, ds \leqq \tilde{r} \quad \text{and} \quad k(0) \leqq \tilde{k}, \end{cases} \tag{A.7}$$

where $t \in [0, \infty]$ and $k(t) = k(0) + \int_0^t \dot{k}(s)\,\mathrm{d}s$ (so it is understood that, by hypothesis, all requisite integrals are well-defined, say, in the sense of Riemann). Now replace h2 by the weaker regularity requirement

h2′. If $\bar{y} > 0$, then, for every $0 < y < \bar{y}$, h is integrable in k on $\{k : k \in H(y) \text{ and } k < \underline{k}(y)\}$,

and consider feasible growth paths of the specific form

$$\begin{cases} \dot{k}(t) \geqq 0 \text{ and } (c + \dot{k}(t), k(t)) \in H \text{ for } t \geqq 0. \\ \lim_{t \to \infty} k(t) = \infty \\ \text{and} \\ c > 0, \int_0^\infty h(c + \dot{k}(s), k(s))\, ds \leqq \tilde{r} \text{ and } k(0) \leqq \tilde{k}. \end{cases} \tag{A.8}$$

In the same spirit as the argument underlying the "Growth" Theorem in Section 4.1, the following result is also easily demonstrated.

Sustainability Theorem in Continuous Time. *For every* $(\tilde{r}, \tilde{k}) \gg 0$ *there exists* $(c, \{k(t)\})$ *satisfying Equation* (A.8) *if and only if* (SC) *obtains.*

Proof of the Sustainability Theorem in Continuous Time. *Sufficiency*. Pick $y > 0$ such that $(y, \tilde{k}) \in H$ (using H1) and

$$1/y \int_{\tilde{k}}^{\infty} h(y, u)\,\mathrm{d}u \leqq \tilde{r}/2 \tag{A.9}$$

(using substitution condition (SC)), and consider the particular growth path defined by

$$\begin{cases} k(0) = \tilde{k} \\ \text{and} \\ c(t) = y/2 \text{ and } \dot{k}(t) = y/2 \text{ for } t \geqq 0. \end{cases} \tag{A.10}$$

Then

$$\begin{aligned} \int_0^\infty h(c(s) + \dot{k}(s), k(s))\,\mathrm{d}s &= \int_0^\infty h(y, k(0) + (y/2)s)\,\mathrm{d}s \\ &= 2/y \int_{\tilde{k}}^{\infty} (y, u)\,\mathrm{d}u \quad \text{[changing variables} \\ &\qquad \text{from } s \text{ to } u = k(s)] \\ &\leqq \tilde{r} \quad \text{(using (A.9)).} \end{aligned}$$

Thus, Equation (A.10) yields a solution to Equation (A.8) with $c = y/2$.

Necessity. Suppose that Equation (A.8) has a solution for arbitrary $(\tilde{r}, \tilde{k}) \gg 0$. Again it is straightforward to show that this implies that

$$\begin{aligned}
&\text{for every } 0<y<c,\\
&1/y \int_{\tilde{k}}^{\infty} h(y,u)\,\mathrm{d}u \leqq \tilde{r}/v;\\
&\tilde{r} \geqq \int_0^{\infty} h(c+\dot{k}(s), k(s))\,\mathrm{d}s\\
&\quad \geqq \int_0^{\infty} h(y+\dot{k}(s), k(s))\,\mathrm{d}s \quad \text{for} \quad 0<y<c \quad \text{(using H1 and h1)}\\
&\quad \geqq \int_0^{\infty} \frac{h(y)+\dot{k}(s), k(s))}{y+\dot{k}(s)}\dot{k}(s)\,\mathrm{d}s\\
&\quad \geqq v \int_0^{\infty} \frac{h(y), k(s))}{y}\dot{k}(s)\,\mathrm{d}s \quad \text{(using h3)}\\
&\quad \geqq v/y \int_{\tilde{k}}^{\infty} h(y,u)\,\mathrm{d}u \quad \text{(changing variables from ``}s\text{'' to ``}u=k(s)\text{'']}.
\end{aligned}$$

A.4. Counterexamples to Dropping Assumption h3

As in the examples concerning the necessity of h2, these two examples differ markedly from one another. However, unlike there, here the difference has substantial significance. On the one hand, the first example – involving average returns to exhaustible resources that become "too large" at high levels of output – represents situations where a substitution condition like substitution condition (SC) is simply inappropriate; sustained consumption typically requires geometric accumulation. (These are, in our view, extremely implausible situations anyway). On the other hand, the second example – involving average returns to exhaustible resources that behave "too erratically" at low levels of output – represents situations where, with suitable relaxation of h3, a parallel relaxation of substitution condition (SC) will still apply, as we demonstrate in the Section A.5. (These are, in our view, distinctly plausible situations, especially when translated into the disaggregative terms we proposed in Section 4.2.) Once again, our argument is purposely terse.

Example A3a. Suppose, as earlier, that

$$h(y,k) = f(y)g(k) \tag{A.2}$$

with $H = \mathbb{R} \times \mathbb{R}_+$, where now $f : \mathbb{R} \to \mathbb{R}_+$ is increasing (and strictly increasing for $y \geqq 0$) and satisfies $\lim_{y\to 0^+} f(y)/y = 0$ and $0 < f(\infty) = \lim_{y\to 0} f(y) < \infty$ (so that $\lim_{y \to \infty^+} f(y)/y = 0$), while $g : \mathbb{R}_+ \to \mathbb{R}_+$ is decreasing and satisfies, for every $k > 0$,

$$\int_k^\infty g(u)\,\mathrm{d}u = \infty \quad \text{and} \quad \int_k^\infty \frac{g(u)}{u}\,\mathrm{d}u < \infty$$

(for instance, $g(k) = k^{-1/2}$). As Figure A3a suggests, h3 isn't satisfied, since obviously $\bar{y} = \infty$ (noting that $\lim_{k \to \infty} g(k) = 0$), but for every $v > 0$ and every $k \geqq 0$, if $0 < y'' < y'$, then

$$\frac{h(y',k)}{y'} = \frac{f(y')}{y'} g(k) < v \frac{f(y'')}{y''} g(k) = v \frac{h(y'',k)}{y''}$$

for y' large enough (noting that $g(k) > 0$).

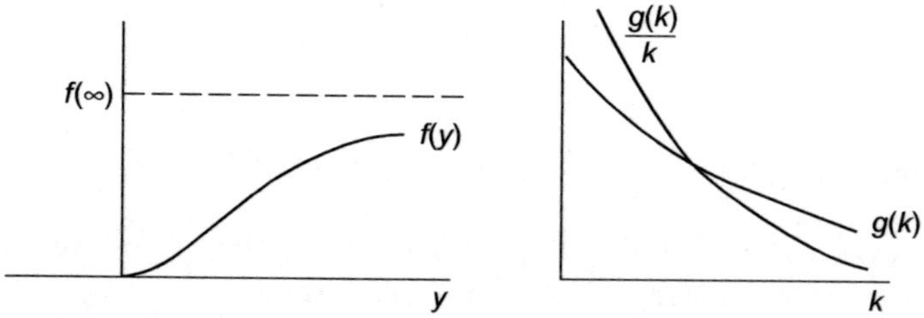

a. Examine where $\lim_{y \to \infty} f(y) = f(\infty) < \infty$ (so that $\lim_{y \to \infty} \frac{f(y)}{y} = 0$), while $\int_k^\infty g(u)\mathrm{d}u = \infty$ but $\int_k^\infty \frac{g(u)}{u}\mathrm{d}u < \infty$ for $k > 0$

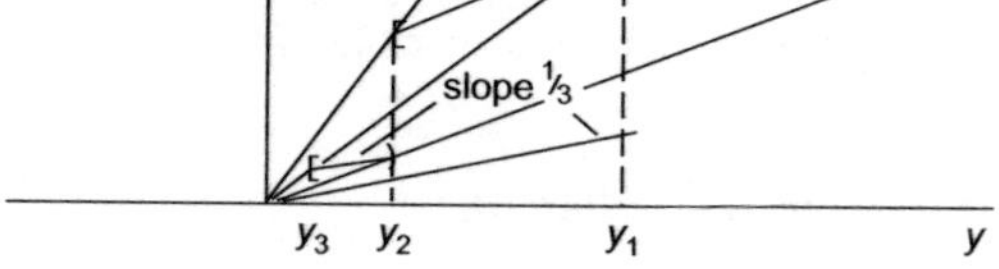

b. Example where $\liminf_{y \to 0^+} \frac{f(y)}{y} = 0 < \limsup_{y \to 0^+} \frac{f(y)}{y}$

Figure A3: Critical Features of the Two examples Showing that without Assumption h3, Condition (SC) is Not Necessary.

Let $0<y\leqq\tilde{k}/2$, $0<\lambda<1$ and n be a positive integer, and consider the growth paths described by

$$c_t = y \quad \text{for} \quad t\geqq 0$$

and

$$k_0 = \tilde{k} \text{ and } k_{t+1} = \begin{cases} k_t + y & \text{for} \quad 0\leqq t\leqq n-1 \\ (1+\lambda)k_t & \text{otherwise.} \end{cases}$$

Then direct calculation yields

$$\begin{aligned}\sum_{t=0}^{\infty} h(c_t + k_{t+1} - k_t, k_t) &= \sum_{t=0}^{n-1} f(2y)g(\tilde{k}+yt) + \sum_{t=0}^{\infty} f(y+\lambda k_t)g(k_t) \\ &\leqq (f(2y)/y)\sum_{t=0}^{n-1} g(\tilde{k}+yt)y + f(\infty)\sum_{t=n}^{\infty}\frac{g(k_t)}{\lambda k_t}(k_{t+1}-k_t) \\ &\leqq 2(f(2y)/2y)\int_{\tilde{k}-y}^{\tilde{k}+(n-1)y} g(u)\mathrm{d}u \\ &\quad + (f(\infty)/\lambda)\int_{(1-\lambda)(\tilde{k}+ny)}^{\infty}\frac{g(u)}{u}\,\mathrm{d}u. \end{aligned} \tag{A.11}$$

So just pick ny large enough so that

$$(f(\infty)/\lambda)\int_{(1-\lambda)(\tilde{k}+ny)}^{\infty}\frac{g(u)}{u}\mathrm{d}u \leqq \tilde{r}/2, \tag{A.12}$$

and (fixing ny) y small enough so that

$$2(f(2y)/2y)\int_{\tilde{k}-y}^{\tilde{k}+(n-1)y} g(u)\,\mathrm{d}u \leqq 2(f(2y)/2y)\int_{\tilde{k}/2}^{\tilde{k}+ny} g(u)\,\mathrm{d}u \leqq \tilde{r}/2, \tag{A.13}$$

and, as before, the desired conclusion follows immediately upon using Equations (A.12) and (A.13) to extend the chain of inequalities in Equation (A.11).

Finally, because $\underline{k}=\infty$, for every $0<k<\underline{k}$,

$$\begin{aligned}\lim_{y\to 0^+} 1/y\int_{k}^{\underline{k}(y)} h(y,u)\,\mathrm{d}u &= \left[1/y\int_{k}^{\infty} f(y)g(u)\,\mathrm{d}u\right]_{y>0} \\ &= \left[(f)(y)/y\int_{k}^{\infty} g(u)\,\mathrm{d}u\right]_{y>0} = \infty.\end{aligned}$$

Example A3b. Suppose, once more, that

$$h(y,k) = f(y)g(k) \tag{A.2}$$

with $H=\mathbb{R}\times\mathbb{R}_+$, where now $f:\mathbb{R}\to\mathbb{R}_+$ is as depicted in Figure A3b, while $g : \mathbb{R}_+ \to \mathbb{R}_+$ is decreasing and satisfies, for every $k>0$, $0<\int_k^\infty g(u)\,du<\infty$.

Explicitly, f is defined by the formula

$$f(y) = \begin{cases} (1+\alpha)y_1 + (y - y_1) & \text{for} \quad y \geqq y_1 \\ y_i/i + (y - y_i)/(i+1) & \text{for} \quad y_{i+1} \leqq y < y_i, i = 2, 3, \ldots \\ 0 & \text{for} \quad y \leqq 0, \end{cases}$$

where $\alpha>0$, $y_1>0$, and $y_{i+1} = \min\{y : y_i/i + (y - y_i)/(i+1) \leqq (1+\alpha)y\}$ for $i>1$. For this example, h3 isn't satisfied since again $\bar{y} = \infty$, but now, for every $v>0$ and every $k \geqq 0$, if $0<y'' = y_{i+1}<y'<y_i$, then

$$\lim_{y' \to y_1} \frac{h(y', k)}{y'} = \frac{1}{i} g(k) < v(1+\alpha)g(k) = v\frac{h(y'', k)}{y''}$$

for i large enough.

In fact, the critical feature of this example is precisely that

$$\liminf_{y \to 0^+} \frac{f(y)}{y} = \lim_{i \to \infty} \left[\lim_{y \to y_i^-} \frac{f(y)}{y} \right] = \lim_{i \to \infty} \frac{1}{i} = 0 <$$

$$(1+\alpha) = \lim_{i \to \infty} \frac{f(y_i)}{y_i} = \lim_{i \to \infty} \left[\lim_{y \to y_i^+} \frac{f(y)}{y} \right] = \limsup_{y \to 0^+} \frac{f(y)}{y}.$$

Hence, on the one side, the demonstration that Equation (10) has a solution follows from the observations that $\underline{k} = \infty$ and that, for every $0<k<\underline{k}$,

$$\liminf_{y \to 0^+} 1/y \int_k^{\underline{k}(y)} h(y, u)\,du = \left[\liminf_{y \to 0^+} \frac{f(y)}{y} \right] \int_k^\infty g(u)\,du = 0. \tag{A.14}$$

(As we show in the Section A.5, Equation (A.14) completely captures the only implication of substitution condition (SC) we actually needed for the sufficiency argument in the proof of the Sustainability Theorem.) On the other side, the verification that substitution condition (SC) itself is not satisfied follows from the observations that $\underline{k} = \infty$ and that, for every $0<k<\underline{k}$,

$$\limsup_{y \to 0^+} 1/y \int_k^{\underline{k}(y)} h(y, u)\,du = \left[\limsup_{y \to 0^+} \frac{f(y)}{y} \right] \int_k^\infty g(u)\,du$$

$$= (1+\alpha) \int_k^\infty g(u)\,du > 0.$$

A.5. Erratically Behaved Average Returns: Weakening Assumption h3

Consider replacing h3 by the weaker assumption

h3′. If $\bar{y}>0, \underline{k}=\infty$ and, for every $k \geqq 0$,

$$\liminf_{y \to 0^+} \frac{h(y,k)}{y} = 0,$$

then there exists a positive constant $v>0$ and, for every $c>0$, a smaller, positive output level $0<y<c$ and $v>0$ with the property that, for every $k \geqq 0$,

$$y' \in H(k), y'' = y \quad \text{and} \quad y'' \leqq y' \Rightarrow \frac{h(y',k)}{y'} \geqq v \frac{h(y'',k)}{y''},$$

and sustainability condition (SC) by the weaker condition

$$\text{for every } 0<k<\underline{k},$$
$$\liminf_{y \to 0^+} 1/y \int_0^{\underline{k}(y)} h(y,u)\, du = 0. \tag{SC′}$$

Condition h3′ is a significant relaxation in the sense that it permits including the additional cases shown in Figure A4.

These changes require some minor adjustments in the previous proof of the Sustainability Theorem.

Sufficiency. Clearly (SC′) suffices for our earlier construction, since it too permits picking $0<\lambda<1/2$ and $y>0$ such that $(y, \tilde{k}-\lambda y) \in H$ and

$$1/\lambda y \int_{\tilde{k}-\lambda y}^{\underline{k}(y)} h(y,u)\, du \leqq \tilde{r}/2$$

(cf. top p. 22).

Necessity. We introduce an additional lemma, and then suitable corresponding modification of the concluding argument (currently on pp. 30–33), as follows:

Lemma′. (given the Lemma on p. 25). If Equation (10) has a solution for every $(\tilde{r}, \tilde{k}) \gg 0$, then

$$\text{for every } 0<k<\underline{k},$$
$$\liminf_{y \to 0^+} \frac{h(y,k)}{y} = 0. \tag{A.15}$$

Proof of the Lemma′. Given $\tilde{r}>0$ and $0<\tilde{k}<\underline{k}$, suppose that $(c,\{k_t\})$ is a solution to Equation (10). Then, by virtue of the Lemma, $0<c \leqq \bar{y}$ – so that the conclusion of h2 obtains – while, for every $0<y<c$, $\underline{k}(y) \leqq \sup_{t \geqq 0} k_t$ – so that (recalling that $k_0 \leqq \tilde{k} < \underline{k} \leqq k(y)$ for $y \geqq 0$), for every $\tilde{k}<k'<\tilde{k}$, there exists $0<t'<\infty$ such that

$$k_t\left\{\begin{matrix} < \\ \geqq \end{matrix}\right\}k' \text{ according as } 0\leqq t\left\{\begin{matrix} < \\ = \end{matrix}\right\}t'.$$

So let

$$t^+(t')=\{t:0\leqq t<t' \quad \text{and} \quad k_{t+1}-k_t>0\}$$

(noting that $t'-1\in t^+(t')$) and

$$k'_{t+1}=\min\{k',k_{t+1}\} \quad \text{for} \quad t\in t^+(t')$$

(noting that $k'_{t+1}=k'$, for $t=t'-1$, $=k_{t+1}$, for $t\in t^+(t')$, $t<t'-1$). Then the resource bound in Equation (10) yields the following chain of inequalities:

$$\begin{aligned}
\tilde{r} &\geqq \sum_{t=0}^{\infty} h(c+k_{t+1}-k_t,k_t) \\
&= \sum_{t\in t^+(t')} h(c+k_{t+1}-k_t,k_t) \\
&\geqq \sum_{t\in t^+(t')} h(c+k'_{t+1}-k_t,k_t) \quad \text{(using H2 and h1)} \\
&\geqq \sum_{t\in t^+(t')} h(k'_{t+1}-k_t,k') \quad \text{(using H2, h1, and h2)} \\
&= \sum_{t\in t^+(t')} \frac{h(k'_{t+1}-k_t,k')}{k'_{t+1}-k_t}(k'_{t+1}-k_t) \\
&\geqq \sum_{t\in t^+(t')} \left[\overset{\text{inf}}{y\in\{y:y\in H(k')} \text{ and } y\leqq k'\}\frac{h(y,k')}{y}\right](k'_{t+1}-k_t) \\
&\geqq \left[\overset{\text{inf}}{y\in\{y:y\in H(k')} \text{ and } y\leqq k'\}\frac{h(y,k')}{y}\right](k'-\tilde{k})
\end{aligned}$$

But since $\tilde{r}>0$ and $0<\tilde{k}<k'<\underline{k}$ are arbitrary, the last inequality obtains only if

for every $0<k<\underline{k}$,

$$\overset{\text{inf}}{y\in\{y:y\in H(k)} \quad \text{and} \quad y\leqq k\}\frac{h(y,k)}{y}=0$$

a property that itself obtains only if Equation (A.15) does.

The balance of the proof distinguishes the two cases $\underline{k}<\infty$ and $\underline{k}=\infty$.

Case 1. $\underline{k} < \infty$.

Take $0 < k < \underline{k}$. Then, by virtue of H1 and h2, there is y' such that for every $0 < y < y'$,

$$(y, k) \in H \text{ and } 0 < 1/y \int_k^{\underline{k}(y)} h(y, u)\, du \leqq \frac{h(y, k)}{y}(\underline{k}(y) - k).$$

Hence, by virtue of the Lemma′ together with $\lim_{y \to 0^+} \underline{k}(y) = \underline{k} > k$,

$$\liminf_{y \to 0^+} 1/y \int_k^{\underline{k}(y)} h(y, u)\, du = 0.$$

Case 2. $\underline{k} = \infty$.

Now, by virtue of the Lemma′, all the triggering hypotheses of h3′ are satisfied, so that our previous argument is virtually unchanged (by picking suitable $0 < y < c$). ■

References

Mitra, T. (1978). On maintainable consumption levels and exhaustible resources. Working paper 198. SUNY at Stony Brook.

Solow, R.M. (1974). Intergenerational equity and exhaustible resources. *The Review of Economic Studies* **41**, 22–49.

Stiglitz, J.E. (1974). Growth with exhaustible natural resources: Efficient and optimal growth paths. *The Review of Economic Studies* **41**, 123–138.

Stiglitz, J.E. (1979). A Neoclassical analysis of the economics of natural resources. In Smith, V.K. (Ed.), *Scarcity and Growth Reconsidered.* Baltimore, MD: Johns Hopkins University Press.